Mastering the Olympus OM

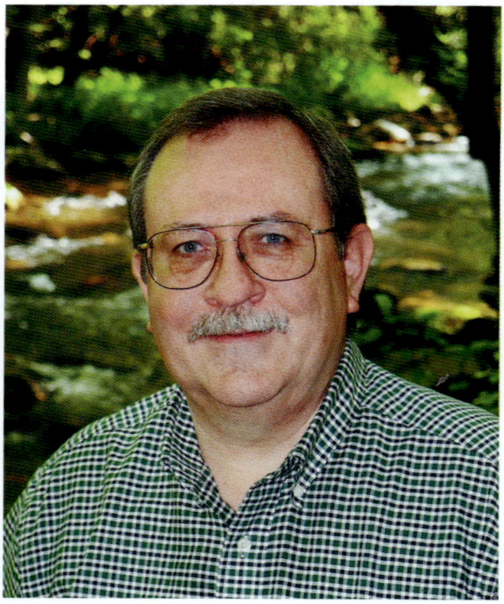

Darrell Young (DigitalDarrell) is a professional nature and event photographer and an active member of Professional Photographers of America, North American Nature Photography Association, and Nikon Professional Services. He's been an avid photographer since 1968 when his mother gave him a Brownie Hawkeye camera.

Darrell is a full-time professional photographer with 35 years of experience in event shooting. He also produces commercial and editorial images for two major stock agencies. When Darrell writes a book on a particular camera, it is based on real-life experience with the camera in a production environment.

Living in the foothills of Great Smoky Mountains National Park has given Darrell a real concern for environmental issues and a deep interest in nature photography. You will often find him on the trails and byways of the Appalachian Mountains, standing behind a tripod with a beautiful landscape in view.

Darrell Young

Mastering the Olympus OM-D E-M1 Mark II

rockynook

Mastering the Olympus OM-D E-M1 Mark II
Darrell Young
www.PictureAndPen.com

Project editor: Jocelyn Howell
Content editor: Alan Hess
Project manager: Lisa Brazieal
Marketing coordinator: Mercedes Murray
Layout and type: Petra Strauch
Cover design: Helmut Kraus, www.exclam.de
Back cover image: © Alan Hess

ISBN: 978-1-68198-254-0
1st Edition (2nd printing, August 2018)

Rocky Nook Inc.
1010 B Street, Suite 350
San Rafael, CA 94901
USA

www.rockynook.com

Distributed in the U.S. by Ingram Publisher Services
Distributed in the UK and Europe by Publishers Group UK

Library of Congress Control Number: 2016960857

This book is printed on acid-free paper.
Printed in Korea

This book is dedicated to:

My wife of many years, Brenda; the love of my life and best friend…

My children, Autumn, David, Emily, Hannah, and Ethan,
five priceless gifts…

My mother and father, Barbara and Vaughn, who brought me into this world and guided my early life, teaching me sound principles to live by…

The wonderful staff of Rocky Nook, including:
Scott Cowlin, Ted Waitt, Joan Dixon, Jocelyn Howell,
Lisa Brazieal, and Mercedes Murray…

And, finally, to Olympus, who makes the world's best mirrorless cameras and lenses.

Special Thanks to:

Brad Berger of **www.Berger-Bros.com** (800-542-8811) for helping me obtain an Olympus OM-D E-M1 Mark II early in its production cycle so that I could write this book. I personally buy from and recommend Berger-Bros.com for Olympus cameras, lenses, and accessories. They offer old-time service and classes for your photographic educational needs!

Table of Contents

Control Location Reference

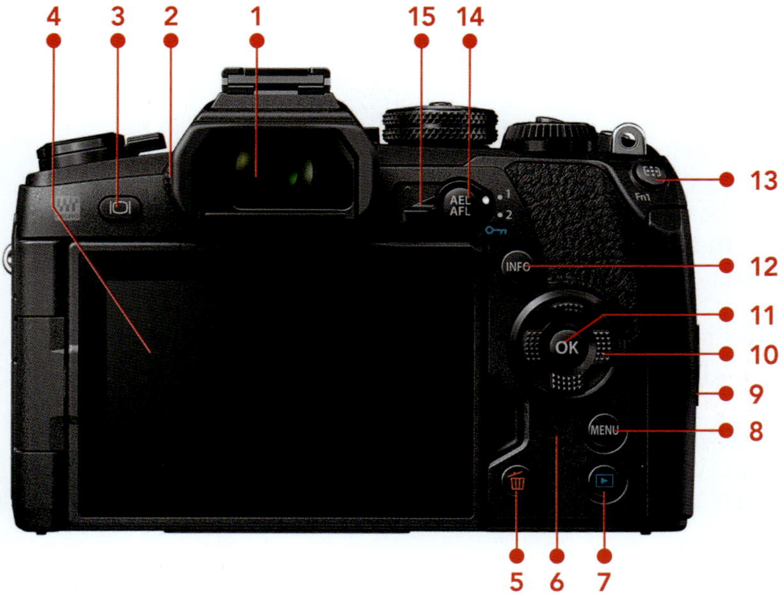

Figure 1: Back of camera body

1. Viewfinder (EVF)
2. Diopter adjustment dial
3. LV button
4. Monitor (Live view touch screen)
5. Erase button (Delete)
6. Speaker
7. Playback button
8. Menu button
9. Card slot cover (memory card)
10. Arrow Pad buttons
11. OK button
12. Info button
13. Fn1 button
14. AEL/AFL button
15. Lever

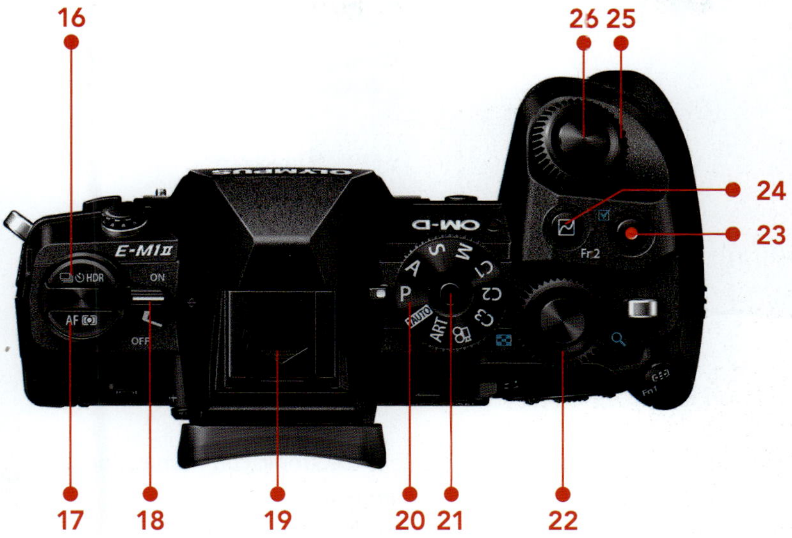

Figure 2: Top of camera body

16. Sequential shooting/Self-timer/HDR button
17. AF/Metering mode button
18. On/Off lever
19. Hot shoe
20. Mode Dial
21. Mode Dial lock button
22. Rear Dial
23. Movie button
24. Fn2 button
25. Front Dial
26. Shutter button

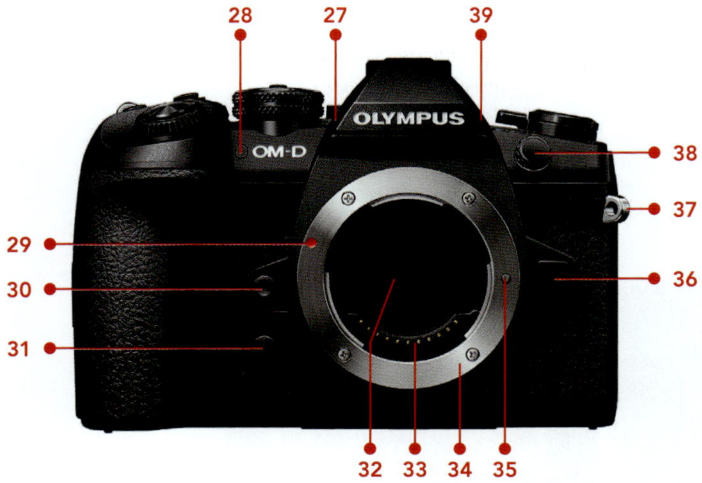

Figure 3: Front of camera body

27. Stereo microphone (right channel)
28. Self-timer lamp/AF illuminator
29. Lens attachment mark
30. One-Touch White Balance button
31. Preview button
32. Micro Four Thirds (4:3) Imaging Sensor (20 MP)
33. Lens electronic communication connectors
34. Lens bayonet mount
35. Lens lock pin
36. Lens release button
37. Strap eyelet
38. External flash connector (wired)
39. Stereo microphone (left channel)

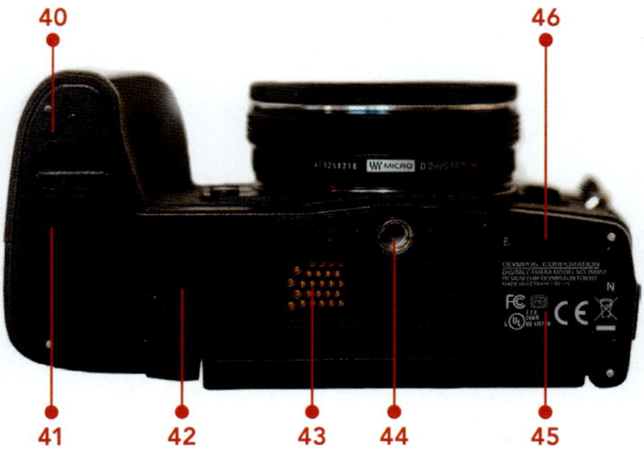

Figure 4: Bottom of camera body

40. Power battery holder (PBH) pin hole
41. Battery compartment cover
42. Battery compartment lock lever
43. Power battery holder electronic connectors (rubber cover removed)
44. Tripod socket
45. Camera ID plate
46. Serial number

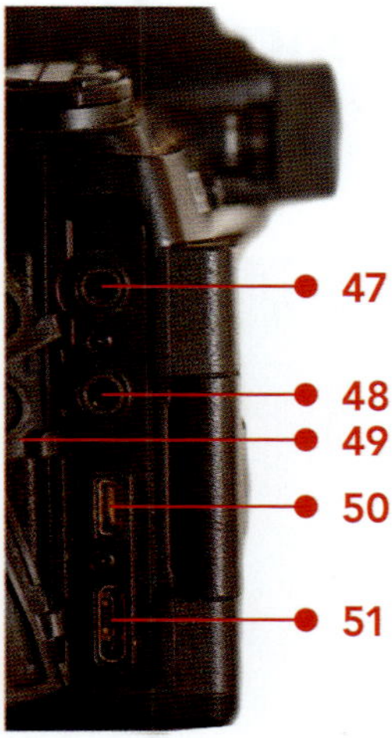

Figure 5: Bottom of camera body

47. Microphone connector
48. Headphone connector
49. Rubber covers (held open)
50. HDMI connector (Type D)
51. USB connector (Type C)

Colors and Wording Legend

Throughout this book, you'll notice in the step-by-step instructions that there are colored terms as well as terms that are displayed in italic or bold font.

1. Blue is used to refer to the camera's physical features.
2. Green is for functions and settings displayed on the camera's screens.
3. *Italic* is for textual prompts seen on the camera's LCD screens.
4. *Italic* or **bold** type is also used on select occasions for special emphasis.

Here is a sample paragraph with the colors and italic font in use:

Press the MENU button to open Shooting Menu 1, and then scroll to the Card Setup option by pressing the right Arrow pad button. Select Format and choose Yes from the menu. *All images on Memory card will be deleted.* Press the OK button to format the memory card. See page 131 in the **Shooting Menu 1** chapter, under the **Card Setup** heading for deeper information.

With Card Setup highlighted, you can press the Info button to use the camera's menu help system. The help system will inform you of the purpose of the Card Setup function, with the following explanation: *Delete all pictures in the memory card or format the memory card.*

01 Camera Setup and Control Reference

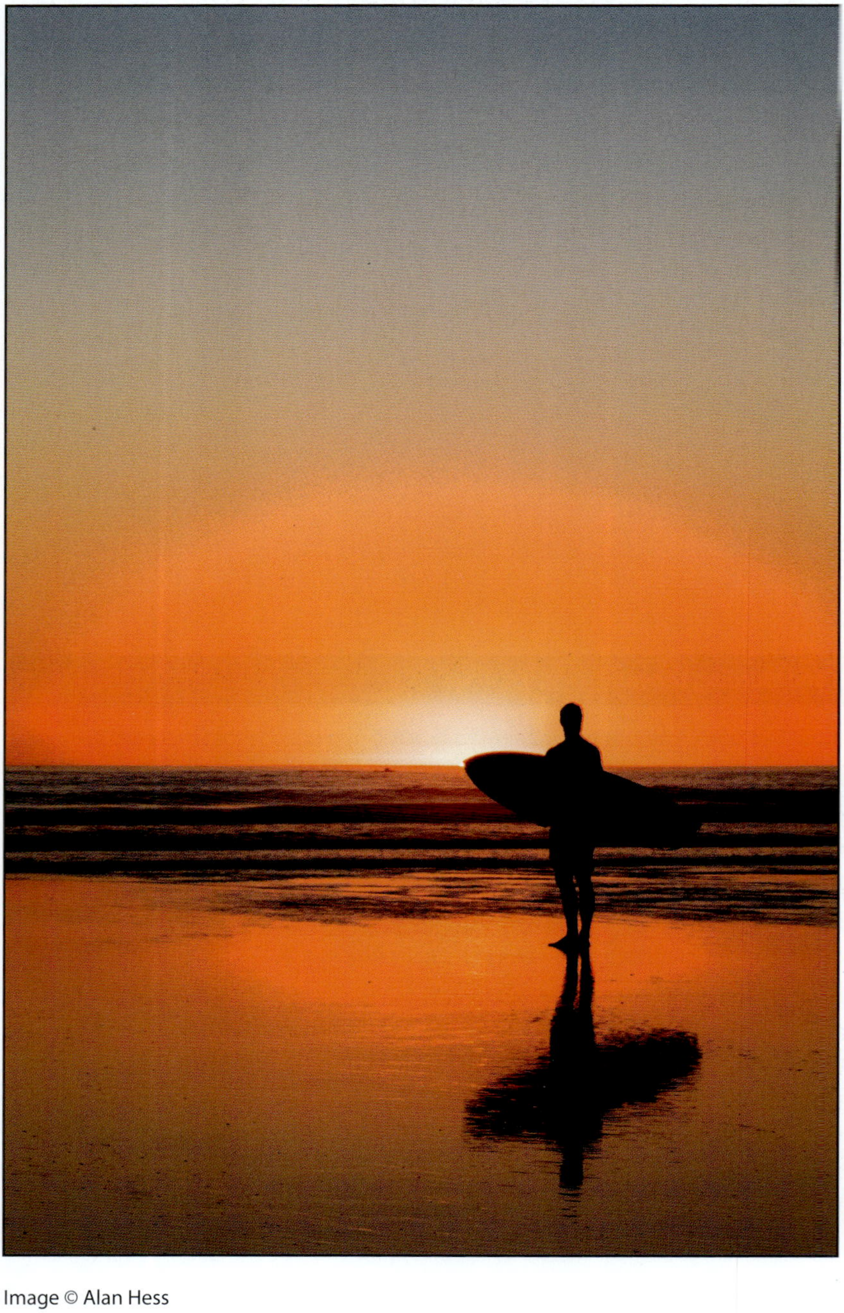

Image © Alan Hess

Congratulations! You've purchased, or are about to purchase, Olympus's professional-level, mirrorless, interchangeable lens, Micro Four Thirds format camera: the OM-D E-M1 Mark II (a.k.a., E-M1II).

While no professional digital camera is inexpensive, the E-M1 I provides passionate photographers with a camera that has excellent resolution, an interactive electronic viewfinder, easy-to-use physical controls, and deep custom menu configurability with many programmable controls.

The E-M1II's strong, magnesium-alloy and aluminum body is weather sealed, dust sealed, and freeze proof. Therefore, it should remain a reliable camera for years of faithful service.

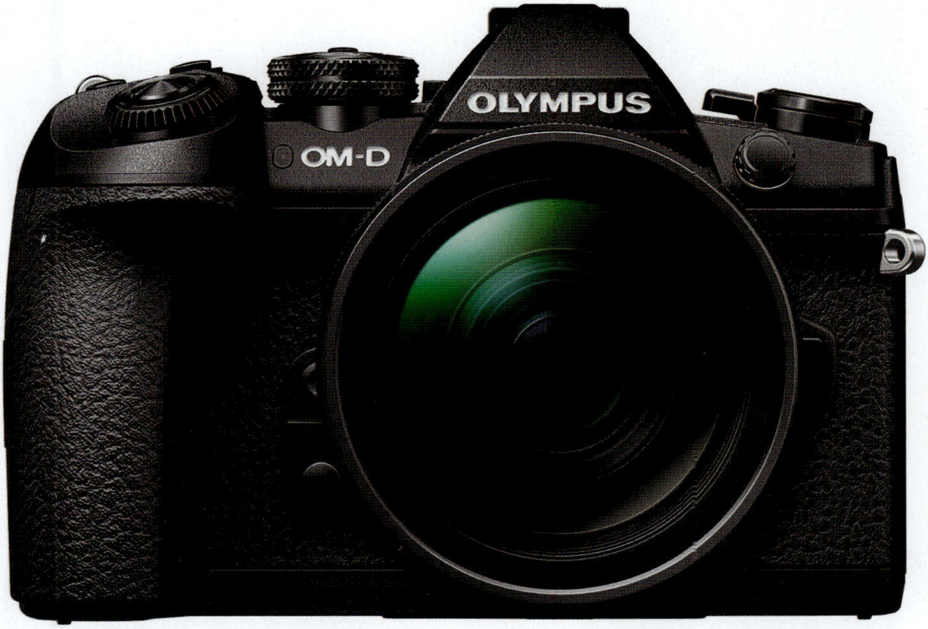

Figure 1.1: Olympus OM-D E-M1 Mark II front view

The small size of the camera makes it easy to fit a full photography system—including lenses, a battery pack, a flash unit, and accessories—in a small camera bag, allowing you to carry a full range of equipment without wearing yourself out.

The 20.4-megapixel imaging sensor; 2.36 million-dot interactive electronic viewfinder; 3.0-inch tilt, swivel, and touch live view display screen; 10–60 frames-per-second shooting rate; 5-axis sensor-shifting image stabilization; contrast and phase detection autofocus; 121 cross-type on-chip AF points; Digital ESP metering system; and 4K UHD video recording system allow you to take complete creative control of the scene in front of your lens.

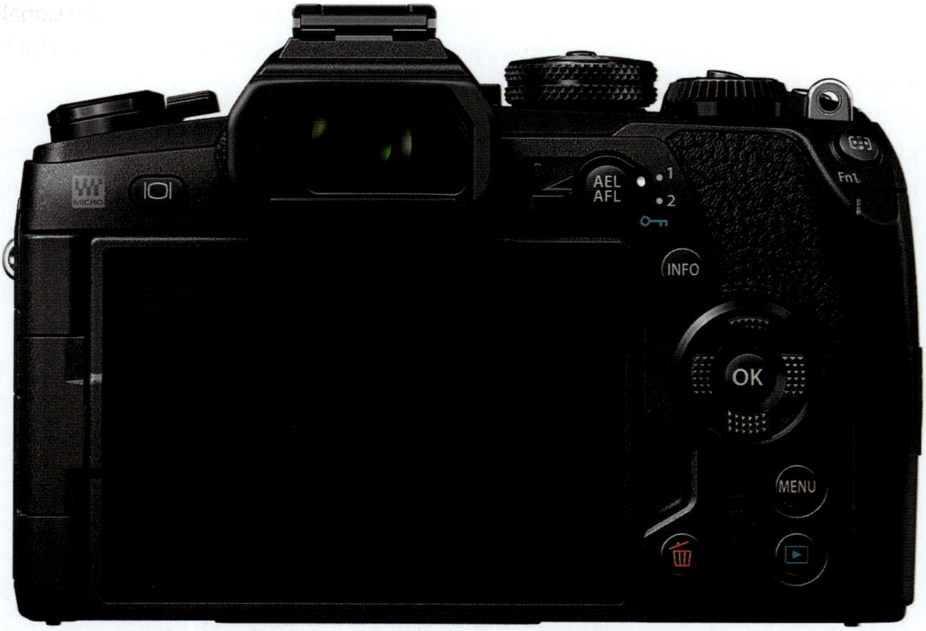

Figure 1.2: Olympus OM-D E-M1 Mark II back view

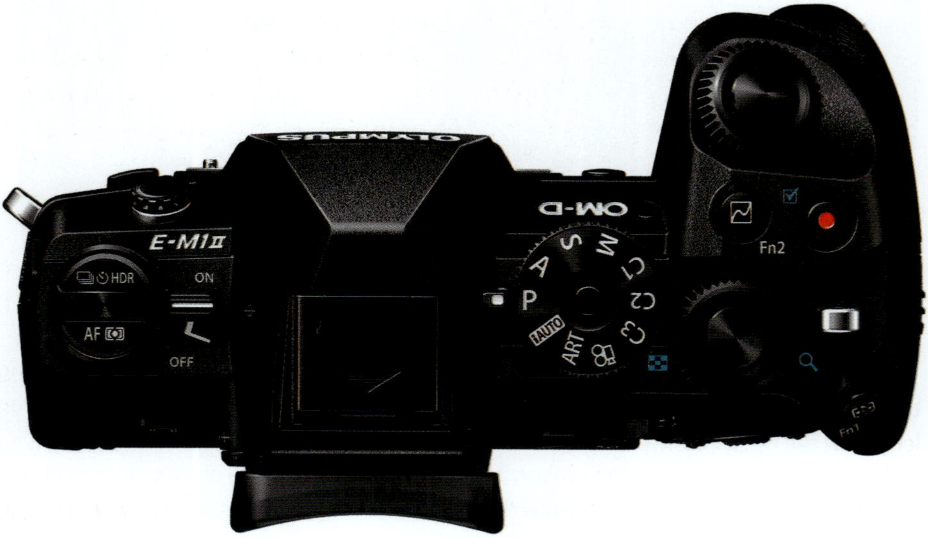

Figure 1.3: Olympus OM-D E-M1 Mark II top view

The E-M1II is one of the most configurable cameras ever created. The deep menu system and numerous programmable controls allow for custom configuration, making the E-M1II an ideal camera for photographers who want absolute control over every aspect of their photography—with full camera cooperation and ass stance.

On the other hand, the camera offers fully automatic modes that allow a new photographer to create outstanding images without excessive camera setup. You can start with the E-M1II as a new photographer and grow into the camera, gradually learning about custom features and relying less on automatic features over time.

This book explores your incredibly feature-rich camera in detail, covering virtually every button, dial, switch, and menu setting, and giving you how, when, and why information so that you can become a master of your new, powerful imaging instrument. Your passion for excellent photography can be fully expressed with your E-M1II. Let's take control of it!

How to Use This Book

The upcoming sections and chapters are best read with your camera in hand, ready for configuration. There are literally hundreds of things to configure on this advanced, mirrorless interchangeable-lens compact (MILC) camera.

This chapter will give new E-M1II users a place to start. Later, as you progress through the book, we'll look at all the buttons, switches, dials, and menu settings in detail. You will be able to fully master the operation of your Olympus OM-D E-M1 Mark II.

This book is a super user's manual that goes way beyond the small manual that comes with the camera. It covers not only how a certain function works (like the basic manual), but also when it is best to use certain features and why the features are best configured in particular ways. You will find a **Settings Recommendation** feature at the end of most sections, in which I offer suggestions for the best use of the various setting choices for different styles of photography.

There is an individual chapter for all of the visual display touch screens and for each menu system in the camera, giving you a detailed examination of virtually every aspect of the camera's control systems.

Because the E-M1II is a camera made primarily for advanced and professional users, this book assumes you have knowledge of basic things like depth of field; lens focal length and angle of view; and how the aperture, shutter speed, and ISO sensitivity control exposure.

If you need to brush up on these subjects, you can find a lot of helpful information in my book *Beyond Point-and-Shoot*. It assumes absolutely no previous knowledge of photography and covers the basics for new users of MILC and DSLR cameras. You can find out more about *Beyond Point-and-Shoot* at my website:
http://www.PictureAndPen.com/BeyondPS

I sincerely hope this book is useful to you and greatly expands your understanding of your new Olympus OM-D E-M1 Mark II camera.

Charge the Battery

When you first open the box that contains your new E-M1II, you should charge the camera's battery. The battery may have enough life in it for an hour or two of use, so it may not be critical to charge it immediately. However, for extended configuration and use, it is best to have a fully charged battery in the camera.

Super Control Panel or Live View Screen?

When you turn your new camera on, the first screen that appears on the rear monitor is the Super Control Panel (figure 1.4, image 1). This panel allows you to control things like the shutter speed, aperture, ISO, autofocus, and several other key camera functions. It is a very convenient screen, and we will consider it in detail in the chapter **Screen Displays for Camera Control**.

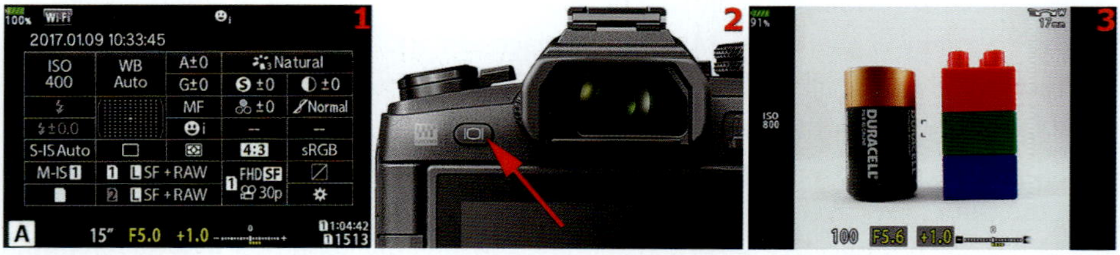

Figure 1.4: Switching between the Super Control Panel and Live View screen with LV button

When the Super Control Panel is displayed on the monitor, you will need to use the electronic viewfinder (EVF) to compose your pictures. If you want to use the Live View screen to compose your pictures instead of the EVF, you will need to press the LV button (figure 1.4, image 2). My camera's Live View screen is displaying my current subject, a battery and some Lego blocks in my light tent (figure 1.4, image 3). The LV button toggles between the Super Control Panel and the Live View screen, as shown in figure 1.4.

While the Super Control Panel is active you must use the EVF to compose and take pictures. While the Live View screen is active you can use either the Live View screen or the EVF to compose and take pictures.

If the Live View screen is active and you place your eye near the viewfinder, the E-M1II will instantly switch the subject display to the EVF and turn off the Live View screen. When you remove your eye from the EVF, the camera will immediately turn off the EVF and turn on the Live View screen.

Settings Recommendation: If you prefer to compose your images with the viewfinder and not hold the camera out at arm's length to compose with the Live View screen, you may want to leave the Super Control Panel active to have quick access to its settings. However, if you like to compose with the rear monitor (Live View), then you may want to leave the Live View screen active. To access the Super Control Panel while the Live View screen is active, simply press the OK button and it will appear.

Camera Main Menu System

The E-M1II has six primary menus that you may use to configure virtually all of the camera's functions. You can access these system menus by pressing the Menu button on the back of the camera while the Super Control Panel or Live View is active. Figure 1.5 shows all six primary menus, including the following:

- ***Shooting Menu 1:*** Contains functions used for shooting pictures, including picture modes (color and contrast control), image quality, aspect ratio, and frame rate speeds (10–60 frames per second).
- ***Shooting Menu 2:*** Continues with additional functions related to shooting pictures, including items such as bracketing, HDR, multiple exposure, distortion control, and anti-shock (counteracts shutter impact).
- ***Video Menu:*** Provides functions for shooting video, including video mode, image stabilization, button programming for video mode, display settings, and HDMI output (external video recorders).
- ***Playback Menu:*** Provides various functions to help you edit and view your still images (individual images or slide shows) on the monitor or a smart device (Wi-Fi connection to phone or tablet) and copy images between memory cards. Also allows in-camera creation of print orders for use with store kiosks and local inkjet printers.
- ***Custom Menu:*** Contains over 100 functions that allow you to configure the camera for different styles of photography, program the camera's buttons and levers, and control all aspects of how the camera's internal subsystems work.
- ***Setup Menu:*** Used to configure several items related to camera setup, such as date and time, menu display language, monitor brightness and color, internal viewfinder monitor timeout, Wi-Fi connection information, and Firmware upgrade version.

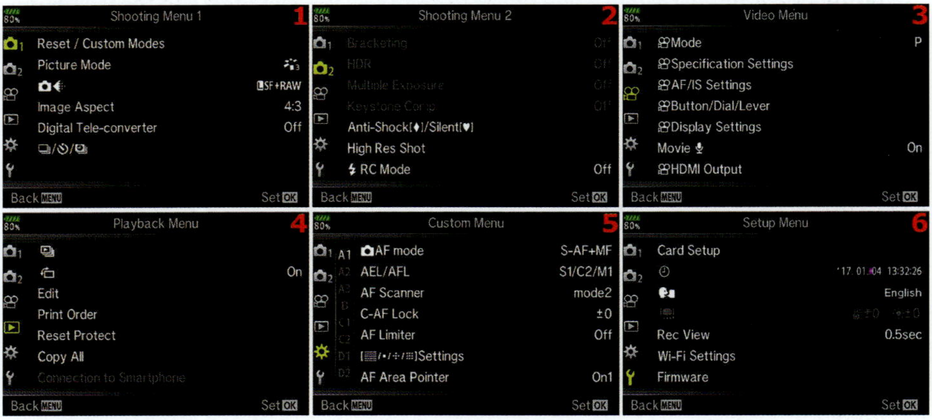

Figure 1.5: The E-M1 II has six primary menus

Each menu is represented by a small icon on the left side of the monitor and the name of the menu is located at the top of the screen. When a menu is active, the corresponding icon is green. Use the Arrow Pad to scroll up or down in the list of menus, and press right or left to enter or exit a menu.

When an item is not available for adjustment, it will be grayed-out. For example, I used HDMI output to capture the screens in figure 1.5, and because Bracketing, HDR, Multiple Exposure, and Keystone Comp. are not available when using the HDMI system to send a picture or video to an external device, they are grayed-out (figure 1.5, image 2). While this specific set of circumstances may not affect you often (unless you shoot a lot of video), this is a good example of what it looks like when an item is not available for adjustment.

When you see a grayed-out menu item, it is usually caused by the configuration of some other function with which that menu item has a relationship. Sometimes it can be difficult to figure out why a certain item is grayed-out. In this book, I will often provide an explanation for grayed-out items; however, please add yourself to my private Facebook group mentioned in the upcoming **Contacting the Author** section so that we can discuss thorny issues of this sort.

This book provides a detailed explanation of each menu item—including how, when, and why to configure each item—as well as suggested settings. Each main menu is covered in its own chapter. Let's get started!

Initial Camera Configuration

When you first acquire a new or used E-M1II camera, you will want to configure or at least check the camera's date, time, and location, along with several other functions that all new camera users should set up to match their needs. This section lists the most important camera settings for immediate configuration.

This section is not comprehensive because there are literally hundreds of settings you can customize and configure on the E-M1II camera. However, let me suggest some of the more important settings you may want to consider configuring before shooting for the first time.

Instead of repeating material found elsewhere in the book, I've listed the menu setting and the page number where you can find deeper information about that function. Place a bookmark here until you have examined and configured these basic functions. Afterward, you can use the camera for active picture-taking while you are studying its many features in this book.

Here are the most critical functions for immediate configuration:

- ***Super Control Panel versus Live Control:*** Pages 20, 73
- ***Date and Time:*** Page 594
- ***Language:*** Page 596
- ***ISO:*** Pages 22, 83, 140
- ***Metering mode:*** Pages 10, 50, 140, 594
- ***White Balance mode:*** Pages 23, 536
- ***Color Space:*** Pages 53, 546
- ***Picture Mode:*** Pages 28, 77, 479
- ***Super Fine (SF) JPEG mode:*** Pages 55, 532
- ***Still Picture image format:*** Page 173
- ***Autofocus mode:*** Page 403
- ***Manual focus assist modes:*** Pages 427, 428
- ***Image Stabilizer:*** Pages 45, 468
- ***Face Priority for autofocus:*** Pages 44, 418
- ***Autofocus illuminator light:*** Page 417
- ***Frames per second speed:*** Page 464
- ***High ISO Noise Filtration:*** Page 508
- ***Long Exposure Noise Reduction:*** Page 509
- ***Beep sound:*** Page 497
- ***Image review timeout:*** Page 598
- ***Image display rotation:*** Page 365
- ***Grid display:*** Page 574
- ***Battery gauge location:*** Page 98
- ***Touch Screen activation/deactivation:*** Page 582
- ***Playback screen types (image review):*** Page 474
- ***Live View screen types:*** Page 97
- ***Copyright and Artist Name for image metadata:*** Page 561
- ***Image file naming system:*** Page 555
- ***Eye detection sensor:*** Page 568
- ***Button function configuration (takes some time):*** Pages 67, 432
- ***Connection to your smartphone or tablet:*** Page 399

Now that you have configured your camera's initial functions, let's examine the various buttons, dials, and switches on the camera and briefly discuss the functionality of each one.

Camera Control Reference

This camera control reference is designed to help you locate and understand the purpose of each of the buttons, dials, and levers on the camera.

Many (if not most) of the buttons on the camera can be configured to offer alternate functionality. In fact, the E-M1II is *the* most configurable camera I have used in over 40 years of photography. You can truly customize this camera to work the way you prefer, for both external controls and internal functions.

The programmable camera controls can be programmed separately for still images and videos. I've created two downloadable documents that list all of the available Button Tasks for still images and videos: **Appendix A: Still Image Button Task Reference** and **Appendix B: Video Capture Button Task Reference**. You can find these two documents on the downloadable resources website:

www.rockynook.com/olympusem1markii

If you have a problem locating one of these buttons, please refer to the **External Control Location** section in the beginning of this book.

Let's examine each of the external camera controls in alphabetical order. We will examine each of the internal functions in later chapters.

Buttons

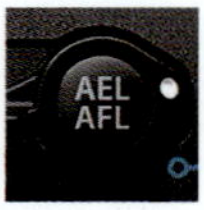

AEL/AFL button: The AEL/AFL button is fully programmable and can accept tasks listed in the appendices on the downloadable resources website (see the URL above). You can find instructions for how to assign a task to the AEL/AFL button on pages 435 (still photography) and 300 (video). Its factory default task is AEL/AFL, which locks autoexposure (AEL) and autofocus (AFL) when you press the button, and unlocks it when you press it again.

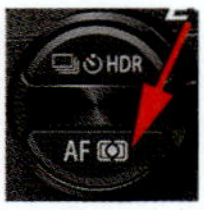

AF/Metering mode button: This button allows you to control the type of light meter and autofocus the camera will use. Press the button and turn the Front Dial to control the metering type. Press the button and turn the Rear Dial to control the autofocus modes. There is a limited amount of programmability for this button, tied in with the Lever functions in the Custom Menu, as described on page 456.

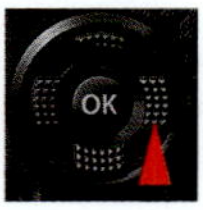

Arrow Pad buttons: The Arrow Pad buttons are normally used to scroll through camera menus, pictures, and various screens. The Arrow Pad has four buttons, including one each for up, down, left, and right (arrow points to right button). As you read through the instructions for configuring many of the camera functions in this book, you will often read "scroll to the right," or some other direction. This is a reference to using the Arrow Pad buttons. The Arrow Pad buttons have some programmability through Custom Menu functions, as described on page 438, and through Video Menu functions, as described on page 303. You can select from several tasks for the right and down Arrow Pad buttons. These tasks are listed in the appendices on the downloadable resources website.

Erase button: When you want to rid your camera's memory card of an unneeded picture or video, you can display it on the rear monitor, press the Erase button, answer Yes to the query, and press the OK button to delete the picture. This is not a programmable button.

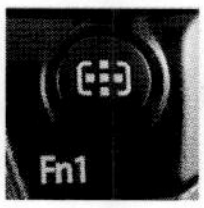

Fn1 button: The Fn1 button is fully programmable and can accept tasks listed in the appendices on the downloadable resources website. You can find instructions for how to assign a task to the Fn1 button on pages 433 (still photography) and 297 (video). Its factory default task is AF Area Select, which lets you choose an autofocus (AF) point to use from among the camera's 121 cross-type, on-chip AF points (with Micro Four Thirds lenses or older Four Thirds lenses used with an MMF-2 or MMF-3 lens adapter).

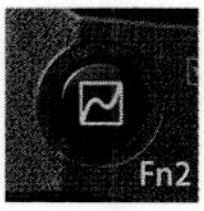

Fn2 button: The Fn2 button is fully programmable and can accept tasks listed in the appendices on the downloadable resources website. You can find instructions for how to assign a task to the Fn2 button on pages 433 (still photography) and 298 (video). Its factory default task is Multi Function, which lets you choose from one of seven specialized functions (e.g., Highlight&Shadow Control) by holding down the button and rotating the Rear Dial.

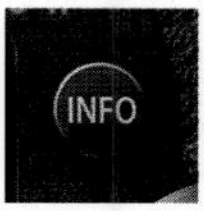

Info button: The Info button is used to enable or disable the menu help system. It is also used to scroll through and select various screen overlays for Live View or EVF shooting (e.g., Live Histogram, Level). Throughout this book, you will find that the Info button is used to choose various individual items within groups of items. This is not a programmable button.

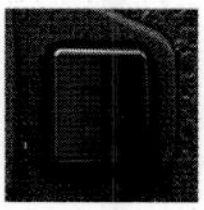

Lens release button: This non-programmable button has one function: releasing the lens lock so that you can change lenses. To remove a lens, press and hold the Lens release button while turning the lens in a counter-clockwise direction until it stops, then pull the lens straight out of the body. To mount a different lens, do not press the Lens release button. Insert the new lens by matching the orange dot on the top of the lens with the orange dot on the left side of the camera's lens mount. Turn the lens in a clockwise direction, without forcing it, until it clicks. It should turn very easily. The camera and lens is then ready to use.

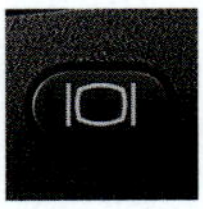

LV button: The LV button was discussed in a previous section of this chapter titled **Super Control Panel or Live View Screen?,** on page 6. The button is used to toggle between the Super Control Panel and the Live View screen on the rear monitor. It is also used to access the Flash Remote Control panel for wirelessly controlling multiple external flash units when *Shooting Menu 2 > [Flash] RC Mode* is set to On, as described on page 240. Additionally, this button is a fully programmable button, accepting the button tasks outlined in the appendices on the downloadable resources website. You can find instructions for how to assign a task to the LV button on pages 435 (still photography) and 303 (video).

Menu button: The Menu button is primarily used to access the menu systems (e.g., Shooting Menu 1, Setup Menu, Custom Menu). Press the Menu button when the rear monitor is active to open the Menu system. Scroll up or down with the Arrow Pad buttons to select one of the camera's menus, and then scroll to the right to access that menu. The Menu button is often used to cancel actions and to return to the main menu from within a function. This is not a programmable button.

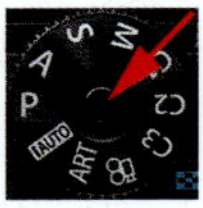

Mode dial lock button: This button is used for one thing only: to lock the Mode dial so that it cannot accidentally be moved from the current Mode dial setting (e.g., P, A, S, M). It works like the button on a retractable ball point pen—press it once to lock the Mode dial and press it again to unlock the Mode dial. This is not a programmable button.

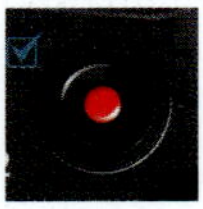

Movie button: The Movie button is fully programmable and can accept tasks listed in the appendices on the downloadable resources website. You can find instructions for how to assign a task to the Movie button on pages 454 (still photography) and 296 (video). Its factory default task is REC, which is used to start and stop the camera's video recording functions.

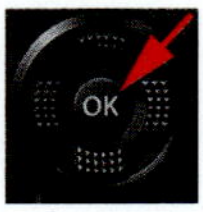

OK button: The OK button is used extensively to confirm configurations of camera functions. It can also be used to choose items. When you are done configuring a camera setting you will usually need to press the OK button to lock in your changes. You can also press the OK button to open the Live Control when the Live View screen is showing your subject (see configuration for this functionality on page 69). The Live Control allows you to select many of the camera's most important settings along the right side of the screen. You can use the Arrow Pad or camera dials to configure the selected Live Control item. Additionally, you can edit images by pressing OK when a picture is on the screen. This is not a programmable button.

One-Touch White Balance button: This button on the front of the camera is fully programmable and can accept tasks listed in the appendices on the downloadable resources website. You can find instructions for how to assign a task to the One-touch WB button on page 436 (still photography) and 301 (video). Its factory default task for still photography is One-touch WB, which lets you immediately take a white balance reading from a white or gray card and store it in one of the four Capture WB custom white balance storage areas, as described on page 539 (still photography) and 25 (video).

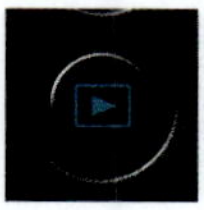

Playback button: This non-programmable button is for reviewing images and movies. You will press this button to examine images and videos saved on the camera's memory card. When you take an image, the camera defaults to a half-second display of an image after taking it. Therefore, unless you increase the image display time, which could interfere with using the EVF for follow-up shots (the just-taken image will display in the EVF), you will use the Playback button often to examine your images and videos.

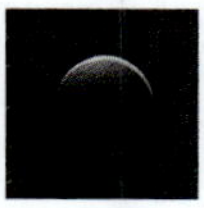

Preview button: The Preview button on the front of the camera is fully programmable and can accept tasks listed in the appendices on the downloadable resources website. You can find instructions for how to assign a task to the Preview button on page 437 (still photography) and 302 (video). Its factory default task for still photography is Preview, which lets you see the depth of field for the current aperture setting as you look at the EVF or Live View. The factory default assignment for the Preview button when you are capturing video is Magnify, which zooms in on the subject, enabling you to see fine details.

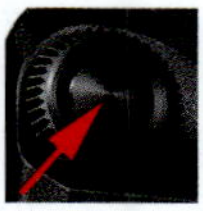

Shutter button: The Shutter button is primarily used to release the camera's shutter to take a picture (full press). It is also used to initiate autofocus (half press). The autofocus function can be relegated to the AEL/AFL button instead of the Shutter button for back-button focusing (a.k.a., Back button focus) as described on page 409. You can configure the Shutter button so that it starts and stops a video recording while in Movie Mode, as described on page 319.

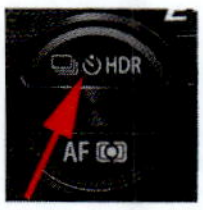

Sequential shooting/Self-timer/HDR button: This button allows you to control the camera's high dynamic range (HDR) system, along with the Sequential shooting frames-per-second rate (fps) and self-timer. Press the button and turn the Front Dial to control the HDR system. Press the button and turn the Rear Dial to control the Sequential shooting fps rate or to select the self-timer. There is a limited amount of programmability for these two buttons, tied in with the Lever functions in the Custom Menu, as described on page 456.

Next let's consider each of the cameras four dials and what they do.

Dials

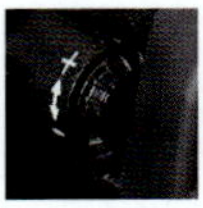

Diopter adjustment dial: The Diopter adjustment dial changes the optical power of a lens that's located in front of the camera's EVF so that you do not strain your eye when you are using the viewfinder. It works sort of like a pair of glasses to bring the image you see on the EVF into sharper focus for your eye; however, it does not correct for astigmatism. If you use the EVF and feel eyestrain or get a headache after using it, you should adjust the Diopter adjustment dial until the view is comfortable for you. You may have to use a different diopter setting for each eye.

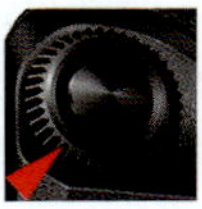

Front Dial: The Front Dial changes the aperture setting when the camera is set to Manual (M) mode on the Mode Dial. In other modes it is usually used to set +/- Exposure compensation. You can also use the Front Dial to zoom in and out of images displayed on the rear monitor. The Front Dial is sometimes used to select a single item from a list of items, such as subfunctions in the camera's menus. The Front Dial has a measure of programmability, as described on page 446 under the Custom Menu's Dial Function, and on page 313 under the Video Menu's [Movie] Dial Function. You can change which dial (Front or Rear) does what, and which direction you turn it to accomplish its task.

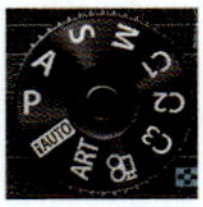

Mode Dial: The E-M1II is a multimode camera. It has a Mode Dial on top that allows you to change how the camera works. You can select from modes that turn your camera into a fully automatic (iAUTO, see page 70) point-and-shoot camera, or a fully manual (M), user-controlled camera, or various modes in between. In addition to the normal P, A, S, and M exposure modes, the Mode Dial offers various specialty modes including: ART mode (exotic filters), Movie mode (video recording, see page 136), and three programmable user controls C1, C2, and C3 (for selecting different camera configurations, see page 137). Some of the modes on the Mode Dial can be programmed to a degree with the Dial Function of the Custom Menu, as described on page 446. However, the Mode Dial itself is not programmable.

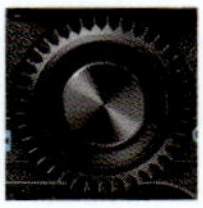

Rear Dial: The Rear Dial changes the shutter speed setting when the camera is set to Manual (M) mode on the Mode Dial. In other modes it is used to set the current controllable setting. For instance, when you use Aperture-priority (A) mode on the Mode Dial, you will use the Rear Dial to set the aperture. When you use Shutter-priority (S) mode on the Mode Dial, you will use the Rear Dial to set the shutter speed. When you are examining an image on the monitor, you can use the Rear Dial to advance to the next image or go back to the previous image. The Rear Dial can also be used as a substitute for the Arrow Pad buttons when moving in and out of functions in the camera's menus. The Rear Dial has a measure of programmability, as described on page 446 under the Custom Menu's Dial Function, and on page 313 under the Video Menu's [Movie] Dial Function. You can change which dial (Front or Rear) does what, and which direction you turn it to accomplish its task.

Finally, let's consider each of the camera's two levers and what they do.

Levers

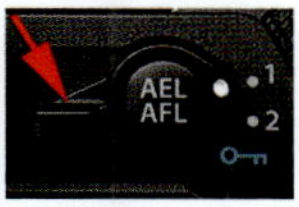

Lever: This Lever is designed to give the camera more than one basic way of doing things. You can configure some of the camera's functions to work one way when the Lever is set to position 1 and another way when the Lever is set to position 2. This is a programmable lever, with specific functionality, as described on page 454 (still photography) and 314 (video).

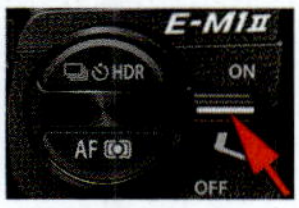

On/Off lever: This non-programmable lever has only one purpose: turning the camera on and off. If left in the On position, the camera will turn itself off after a specific period of time, which you can set with the *Custom Menu > D. Disp/[Sound]PC > Auto Power Off* function, as described on page 586. If the camera has shut down while the lever is in the On position, you will have to move the lever to the Off position and then back to On to bring the camera back to life.

Unusual Icons in Menu Names

Olympus uses unusual icons in some of its camera menus, in some cases making it hard to understand exactly what a menu selection means. For instance, in figure 1.6 you can see an icon that represents image quality at the point of both arrows in images 1 and 2.

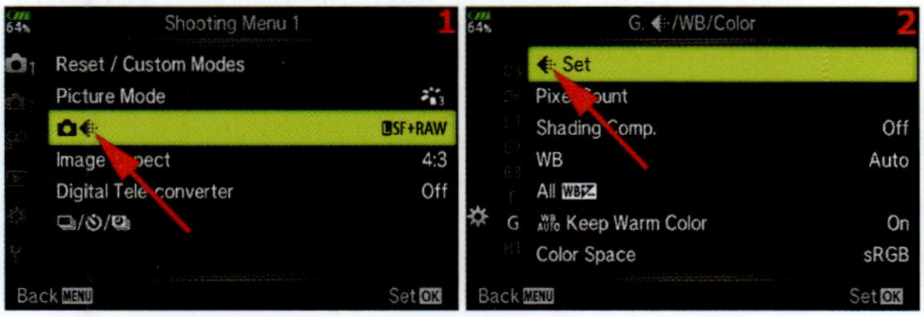

Figure 1.6: Unusual icons in menu names

You will see several different icons throughout the camera's menu system, some of which will be intuitive and others that are not. Because I do not have access to the Olympus icons, I have substituted words where an icon is used.

For example, the icon that represents the camera's image quality (figure 1.6) is called Record Mode by the Olympus user's manual. Therefore, when I refer to the image quality menu in this book I will use the words Record Mode in brackets, like this: [Record Mode].

In figure 1.6, image 2, you can see the same odd graphic used in a menu item that also contains the word Set. When I refer to the menu shown at the point of the red arrow in image 2, I will use: G. [Record Mode] Set.

Throughout the book, when you see a word in brackets as part of a menu name or function name, please remember that the word is used in place of the icon and represents the specific functionality that the icon is supposed to impart.

Contacting the Author

Please join my private Facebook group, Master Your Olympus (MYO), at the following web address:

https://www.facebook.com/groups/MasterYourOlympus/

Additionally, I have created a public Facebook site that allows members to freely associate with general Olympus camera users. It is called Olympus Digital Camera & Photo Enthusiasts (ODCPE), and is found here:

https://www.facebook.com/groups/ODCPE/

These two Facebook groups will allow us to stay in touch, display photographs created with our Olympus cameras, and learn from each other.

You will find a series of downloadable resources for this book, along with a list of any errata, at the following website:

http://www.rockynook.com/OlympusEM1Mark2

Author's Conclusion

Now that we have completed some basic camera configuration and discussed the external controls on the E-M1II, let's proceed into a detailed examination of the camera's various control screens. Many of these screens have selections that are touch sensitive, allowing you to choose that setting either with a touch of your finger or by using the Arrow Pad keys and scrolling around.

02 Screen Displays for Camera Control

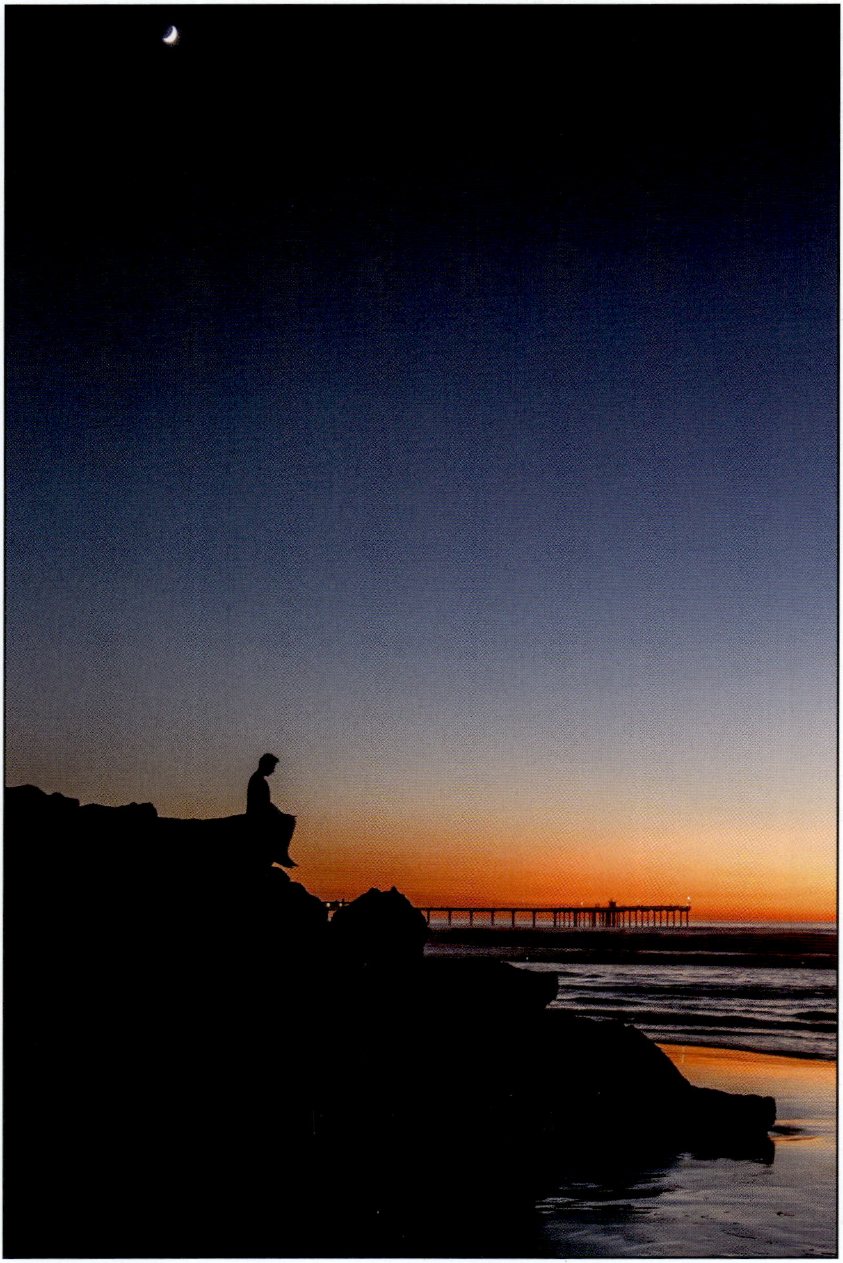

Image © Alan Hess

The Olympus OM-D E-M1 Mark II has very deep text menus to configure hundreds of camera settings, which we will consider in other chapters. The camera also has quite a few visual and touch screen displays for people who want to make basic camera adjustments with the built-in Live View monitor and touch screen.

The E-M1 II is unusual in that it presents you with multiple ways to configure your favorite settings. Many settings can be adjusted visually, with the screens discussed in this chapter, or by using the text-based menu system. In some cases the menus let you configure things more deeply and offer more settings than the visual screens. Therefore, as we discuss the individual settings on the visual touch screens in this chapter, there will often be references to later chapters with even deeper configuration settings in the menus.

We will also explore various controls that allow the camera to use the visual side of the user interface, such as the Exposure (P, A, S, M), iAUTO, and Art modes; the video recording system; high dynamic range (HDR) imaging; and the Metering system. This chapter is composed of three main sections:

- **PART 1: Super Control Panel** – An in-depth discussion of the convenient 28-section touch screen panel that provides a shortcut to several important camera functions.
- **PART 2: LV Super Control Panel, Live Control, Live Guide, and Art Menu** – Part 2 of this chapter consists of four main sections:
    1. **LV Super Control Panel:** An overview of the 28-section LV Super Control Panel, which is a transparent (you can see your subject through it) form of the non-Live View, opaque, Super Control Panel touch screen. This is available only in Live View mode.
    2. **Live Control:** An examination of the 14-section Live Control, which gives you a quick access point for some of the most often used camera functions.
    3. **Live Guide:** An exploration of the Live Guide system, which allows you to exercise creative control while using the camera's fully automatic iAUTO mode on the Mode Dial.
    4. **Art Menu:** Quick access to 14 Art filters you can apply to your pictures while using the ART mode on the Mode Dial.
- **PART 3: Other Live View, EVF, and Control Screens** – We will consider several visual touch screens that can be used to control things like Live View touch photography and image editing, Wi-Fi connection, Mode Dial control screens, and important electronic viewfinder (EVF) screens. Additionally, the camera has several miscellaneous controls screens that we will cover.

To start our exploration of the camera's visual touch interface, let's first examine the important touch screens you may use nearly every time you take pictures, depending on your style of photography.

Note: In the other chapters of this book, I use numbered, step-by-step instructions to describe how to use the menu screens and settings. In this chapter, I mostly use paragraphs instead of numbered steps because describing how to use a visual screen requires a lot of words. Using the step-by-step method would not have allowed me to break some of the descriptive paragraphs into sections, and would have made the text difficult to read.

PART 1: Super Control Panel

The Super Control Panel (figure 2.1) is one of the first screens the camera will display when a new E-M1II is turned on for the first time. To access the Super Control Panel if it is not displayed on the rear monitor, simply press the LV button at the left of the viewfinder.

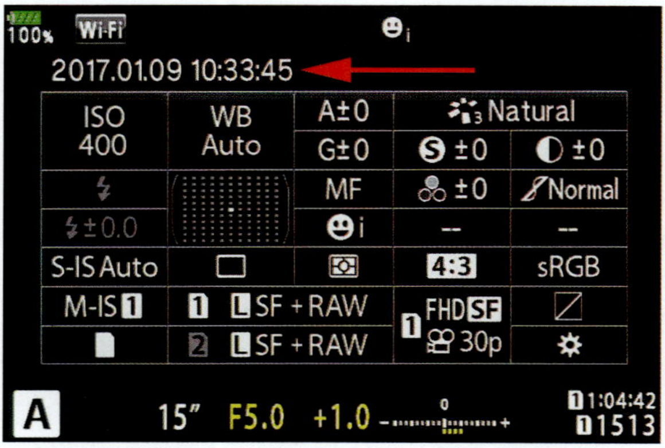

Figure 2.1: The Super Control Panel with nothing selected

As mentioned in chapter 1, **Camera Setup and Control Reference,** you will need to set the camera's date and time as one of the first setup steps. The red arrow in figure 2.1 points to the date and time on the Super Control Panel, which will be displayed in the format most used in your geographic area. If you have not yet set the date and time, it will not appear on the Super Control Panel. Use the instructions on page 594 to set the date and time.

The Super Control Panel is a non-Live View, visual form of a few of the camera's text menus, exposing some important settings for easy access. It contains 28 functions and settings that you can adjust, and each of them has a secondary settings screen.

If nothing is highlighted in green on the Super Control Panel, you must press the OK button once to activate the panel. If, instead, you try to use the Arrow Pad to move around the Super Control Panel, you will accidentally use the AF Area Select mode. Let's discuss this briefly.

Note: When you select an item on the Super Control Panel, that item's name will appear where the date and time are located on the inactive Super Control Panel shown in figure 2.1 (red arrow).

Accidentally Using AF Area Select Mode

When the Super Control Panel is showing on the screen but no function is highlighted in green (figure 2.2, image 1), pressing any of the Arrow Pad buttons opens AF Area Select mode (figure 2.2, image 2), allowing you to select one of the 121 AF points for targeted autofocus. You may have been expecting to scroll around in the Super Control Panel, and suddenly it disappears and a grid appears in its place.

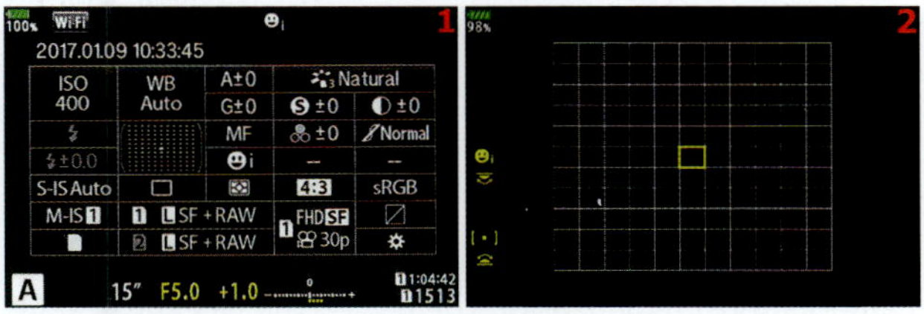

Figure 2.2: Using AF Area Select Mode with the Super Control Panel showing

If the AF point grid appears when you really wanted to use the Super Control Panel, simply press the OK button to select an AF point, and then press the OK button again to return to the Super Control Panel with one of its 28 functions highlighted in green. When a function is highlighted in green the panel is active and ready to use. If nothing is highlighted in green on the panel, the camera is still in AF Area Select mode, even though the Super Control Panel is showing.

This confuses many new E-M1II users until they finally understand what is happening. In fact, even after using Olympus cameras for several years, I still find myself opening the AF Area Select screen when I meant to move around the Super Control Panel. What at first appears to be an accident is actually a useful feature that allows you to quickly change AF points when you are using the viewfinder or the Live View monitor. We will discuss the AF Area Select mode later in this chapter (page 40).

Using Camera Controls

When the Super Control Panel is active, press the OK button, and one of the settings, usually ISO, will be highlighted in green. When any function is highlighted, you can scroll around the Super Control Panel with the Arrow Pad keys until the function you want to adjust is highlighted.

When a function is highlighted you can either turn the Front Dial to see the choices scroll by in the highlighted area, or you can press the OK button to enter the secondary screens for that Super Control Panel function. Turning the Rear Dial scrolls around in the Super Control Panel.

Using the Touch Screen

If you prefer, you can use the touch screen to access the features on the Super Control Panel. If nothing is highlighted in green on the Super Control Panel, you must double-tap the screen to wake it up. When it is awake, simply touch one of the settings to highlight it.

Double-tapping a highlighted function will open a secondary screen in which you may make adjustments. Secondary Super Control Panel screens are not touch sensitive, so you must use normal camera controls (e.g., Arrow Pad, Front Dial, and OK button) to change the settings. We will discuss this in more detail under the **Touch Screen** subheading, on page 101, later in this chapter.

Let's examine each of the functions in the Super Control Panel.

ISO Sensitivity

The ISO function changes the camera's sensitivity to light. The higher the ISO, the greater the sensitivity, and vice versa. Higher ISO sensitivities can add grainy digital noise to the darker areas of your image; therefore, keep the ISO as low as possible for the current lighting conditions.

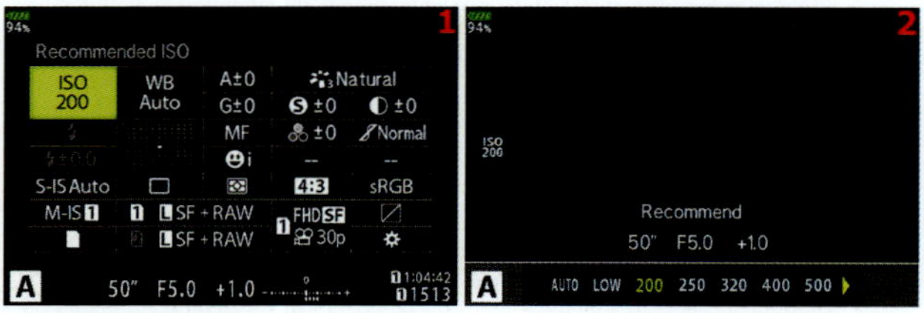

Figure 2.3: Choosing an ISO sensitivity value or AUTO

The camera recommends ISO 200 as a base—you will see Recommended ISO displayed on the Super Control Panel (where the date and time were previously) and Recommend displayed on the secondary screen when you have ISO 200 selected (figure 2.3). Of course, the ISO is variable, and you can change it to meet your needs.

To access the ISO sensitivity function, use the Arrow Pad keys to highlight the ISO position, as shown in figure 2.3, image 1. You can turn the Front Dial to select a new ISO sensitivity value immediately, or you can press the OK button to enter the secondary ISO screen (figure 2.3, image 2).

When the secondary ISO screen is active you will see a range of ISO sensitivity values at the bottom of the screen (figure 2.3, image 2). Use the Arrow Pad keys to scroll left or right and select an ISO sensitivity value, which will be highlighted. In figure 2.3, image 2, you can see that 200 is selected. The range of ISO values runs from LOW (ISO 100) to ISO 25600. You can also select AUTO, which allows the camera to select an ISO value depending on the ambient light conditions. AUTO is a great choice when you do not have time to adjust the ISO yourself. However, be aware that the camera will use high ISO values to get the picture in dark conditions, regardless of whether ISO noise is introduced. For the best quality, control the ISO sensitivity yourself.

When you have selected the ISO sensitivity value you want to use, press the OK button and the camera will return to the Super Control Panel with nothing selected.

Note: Olympus considers ISO 100 (LOW) to be an extended ISO value in the E-M1II. The recommended base ISO is 200. When LOW is selected you will see ISO Extension displayed on the main Super Control Panel (if it is active) and Extension displayed on the secondary ISO screen. This simply means that LOW approximates ISO 100, which is outside the normal ISO range for the camera. Do not worry, ISO LOW works great, and I use it much of the time to capture low-noise images when the ambient light allows it.

Settings Recommendation: I usually leave my camera set to ISO 200, and I find that it has low noise for everyday photography. When I shoot landscapes on a tripod, I often set it to LOW (ISO 100). The camera does well up to about ISO 1600, even though the Micro Four Thirds sensor is small. I would use ISO values above 1600 only in emergencies because the noise levels may become objectionable. You should test this for yourself to see where your noise tolerance lies.

White Balance

The E-M1II offers a wide range of preset white balance (WB) values, plus several custom WB settings, for a total of 13 WB settings.

As you may know, WB affects how the image records color in the ambient light. White should record as white; it should not have a tint. Other colors should be recorded as they appear in real life.

This is a very important setting for people who shoot JPEG files. It is difficult to change the hue of a JPEG image after the fact, and the change lowers the quality of the image due to compression losses when the file is modified and saved more than once.

A photographer who shoots in RAW does not have to worry as much about WB because it can be changed after the fact in computer software, with no damage to the image. However, it is still good for RAW shooters to use the best WB because it saves time in the post-processing workflow (the digital darkroom).

Let's see how to select a WB value from the Super Control Panel.

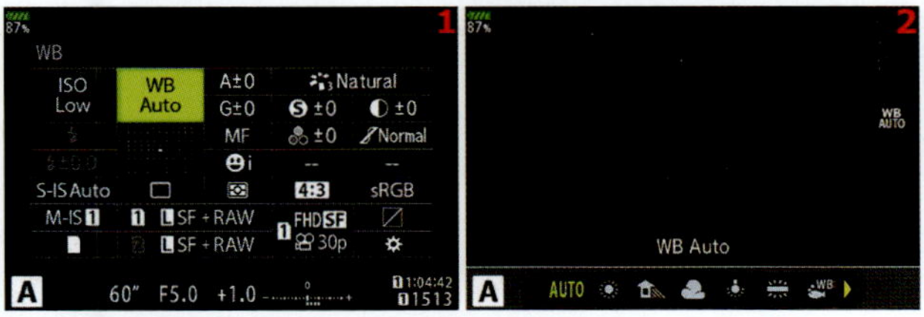

Figure 2.4A: Choosing a WB type

First let's examine where the WB function is located on the Super Control Panel. It is highlighted in figure 2.4A, image 1. Use the Arrow Pad keys to highlight that setting, and press the OK button to enter the secondary WB screen. Alternatively, you can turn the Front Dial to scroll through the 13 WB values shown at the bottom of the secondary screen without entering the secondary screen.

On the secondary screen (figure 2.4A, image 2) you can select a WB value by scrolling left or right with the Arrow Pad keys to highlight the WB value you want to use and then pressing the OK button to lock in a value. I chose AUTO.

There are several preset WB values, as follows (in order of appearance on the screen): AUTO WB; five named WB values for specific light types (Sunny, Shadow, Cloudy, Incandescent, Fluorescent); an Underwater WB; a Flash WB; four custom Capture WB values that you can use for ambient light readings from a gray or white card; and CWB (custom white balance), which allows you to directly set a Kelvin (K) WB value from 2000 (cool blue) to 14000 (warm red). For a detailed study of each of these WB types, see the **Custom Menu** chapter under the *Custom Menu > G. WB* function on page 536.

The Super Control Panel WB screen is a lite version of the function settings provided in the WB Custom Menu, as discussed on page 77. In this chapter we will discuss how to select settings. In the **Custom Menu** chapter we will discuss how, why, and when.

Fine-Tuning the Auto WB

Notice the A±0 and G±0 selections to the right of the WB function in figure 2.4A, image 1. These selections allow you to fine-tune the currently selected WB value if you want to change the hue. A stands for amber, and G stands for green.

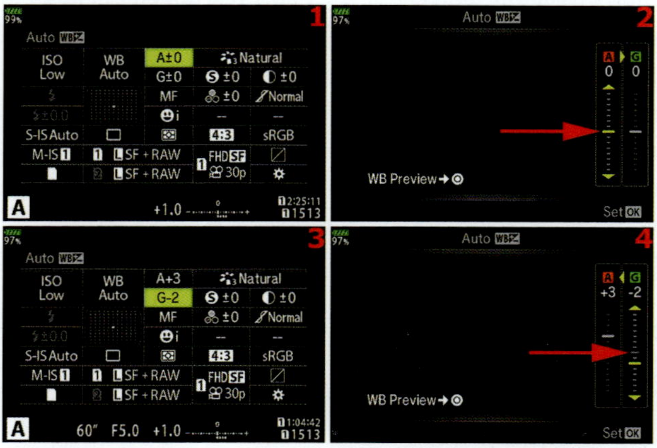

Figure 2.4B: Fine-tuning the amber and green white balance settings

Referring to figure 2.4B, select either the A±0 setting (image 1) or the G±0 setting (image 3), and then turn the Front Dial to adjust the WB fine-tuning value immediately, or press the OK button to enter the secondary screen (images 2 and 4). If you choose to use the secondary screen, move the indicator (red arrows) up (+) or down (-) with the Arrow Pad keys to select the WB adjustment.

In figure 2.4B, image 3, you will notice that the WB Auto adjustment is set for A+3 (add 3 amber) and G–2 (subtract 2 green). The same values are showing on the A and G indicators on the secondary screen in image 4. In image 2 the A indicator is selected and in image 4 the G indicator is selected. Notice how the small green up and down pointers appear at either end of the scale on the active indicator. Also, notice how the adjustment position bar is green instead of gray on the active indicator.

In figure 2.4B, image 2, the red arrow is pointing to the adjustment indicator for the A setting. The A setting can be fine-tuned over a range of 14 increments (A+7 to A-7). The G setting has the same 14-increment range. To move between the A and G settings in the secondary screen, press left and right on the Arrow Pad.

While using the secondary screen only (images 2 or 4), you may press the Movie button to take a temporary picture (WB Preview) with the adjusted WB setting and display it on the monitor. If you like the adjusted hue, press the OK button to Set the new value for the A fine-tuning value. In a similar manner, adjust the G setting (image 4). You can reset the fine-tuning by returning the green indicator bar back to 0 for both A and G.

Note: The WB setting shown in figure 2.4B is WB Auto. Therefore, the A and G adjustments apply only to WB Auto. You can select any of the available WB values for fine-tuning by selecting the WB Auto position and rotating the Front Dial. When the new WB type is selected, the A and G adjustments will apply to the new WB setting only.

Capture WB Ambient Light Reading

Let's examine how to do an ambient light reading from a white or gray card under the current light source, and assign it to one of the four Capture WB memory locations for taking pictures later under the same light source. The Capture WB memory locations store up to four separate WB values for your use under different types of light.

In figure 2.4C, image 1, the first of four Capture WB values has been selected by turning the Front Dial. Use this setting to select a previously captured and stored Capture WB ambient light reading or to create a new one and save it in a Capture WB memory location. If you have not yet created any Capture WB readings, read the following paragraphs.

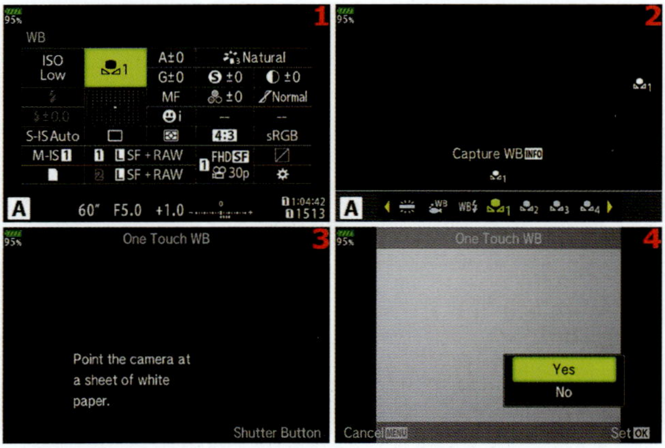

Figure 2.4C: Capturing an ambient WB reading from a gray or white card

To create and store a new Capture WB value, press the OK button when the WB location is selected on the Super Control Panel. Now scroll to one of the four Capture WB memory locations. You can identify the four Capture WB memory locations by their flower icons with numbers 1–4 (figure 2.4C, image 2). Notice also in image 2 that INFO is displayed after the Capture WB label. If you press the INFO button while one of the Capture WB memory locations is selected, the camera will prepare for a Capture WB reading from a white or gray card.

Figure 2.4C, image 3, shows the screen that appears next. It tells you to *Point the camera at a sheet of white paper*. You can also use a standard gray card. After you have positioned the white or gray card in front of the lens, press the Shutter button to take a picture. The camera does not store the picture on the memory card. Instead, it makes an accurate WB reading from the white or gray card. The camera will not attempt to focus on the card; it will simply fire the shutter.

Figure 2.4C, image 4, shows the screen after a successful Capture WB reading has been made. You can now decide whether you want to store the WB reading in the currently selected Capture WB location. To store the WB reading select Yes and press the OK button. If you do not want to save it, select No and press the OK button, or press the Menu button to cancel.

Your new Capture WB reading is now stored in the memory location you selected and has been applied to the camera for immediate or later use. Repeat this process to capture and store WB values in the other three Capture WB memory locations, if you need them.

CWB Custom WB Kelvin Value

If you know how to use direct Kelvin (K) WB values and want to input your own custom white balance (CWB), you can input a range from 2000 K (cool) to 14000 K (warm), which is a significantly broader range than many other camera brands. Let's see how it works.

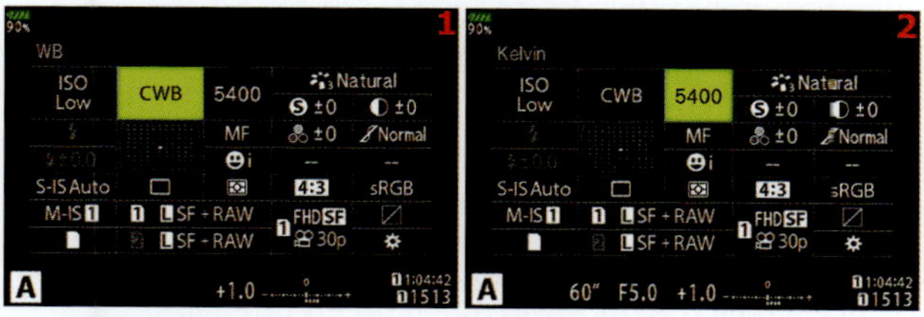

Figure 2.4D: Creating a custom white balance (CWB) reading

Select CWB by highlighting the WB function and turning the Front Dial until CWB appears (figure 2.4D, image 1).

Scroll to the right to select the K value (figure 2.4D, image 2), and rotate the Front Dial to select a K value between 2000 K (cool blue) and 14000 K (warm red). I chose 5400 K. Press the OK button to lock in the CWB setting.

An alternate way to set a CWB value is to use the WB secondary screen, as follows.

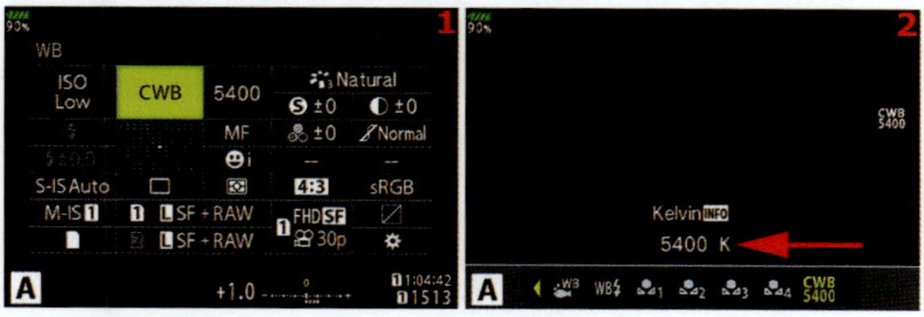

Figure 2.4E: Creating a custom white balance (CWB) reading with secondary screen

Highlight the WB function, as seen in figure 2.4E, image 1, and press the OK button to open the secondary WB screen (figure 2.4E, image 2).

Scroll until you find the CWB setting, which is located all the way to the right (the 13th setting). Press the INFO button to highlight the value (figure 2.4E, image 2, red arrow), and rotate the Front Dial to select a K value between 2000 K (cool blue) and 14000 K (warm red). I chose 5400 K. Press the OK button to lock in the CWB setting.

Settings Recommendation: The WB system in the E-M1II is quite flexible. I use AUTO WB most of the time. However, when I shoot without flash indoors, I have found that the camera makes somewhat warm images—sometimes a bit too warm under incandescent light. Therefore, I often find a white subject and do a One Touch WB reading so the color temperature more closely matches the light. (One-Touch WB is not available from the Super Control Panel. See page 436 for instructions.) You could also do a Capture WB ambient light reading, as previously described, or set the WB manually to something like Incandescent or Fluorescent when you are shooting under those light sources. For the best solution, shoot in a JPEG+RAW Image Quality mode, which allows you to change the WB of the RAW file after the fact (*Shooting Menu 1 > [Record Mode]*).

Picture Mode

Individual Picture Modes give images a specific look. There are 38 modes available under the Super Control Panel main and secondary screens. In this chapter, we will examine how to select these Picture Modes, but detailed configuration information is provided in the **Shooting Menu 1** chapter, under the **Picture Mode** heading on page 151. There we will discuss the how, when, and why of each Picture Mode in much greater detail.

Picture Modes permanently add stylish looks to JPEG images. RAW shooters can use the current Picture Mode setting or change Picture Modes after an image is taken, and then save the file as a JPEG with a new look.

Let's see how to select a Picture Mode, which also includes the camera's ART modes (otherwise found by selecting ART from the Mode Dial).

As shown in figure 2.4F, there are seven sections of the Super Control Panel devoted to the Picture Mode system. The currently selected Picture Mode—in this case, Monochrome—is shown in the top location. The six items below that provide various adjustments to the currently selected Picture Mode. The symbols shown and the names of the six items will vary somewhat, based upon which Picture Mode is currently selected on the Super Control Panel.

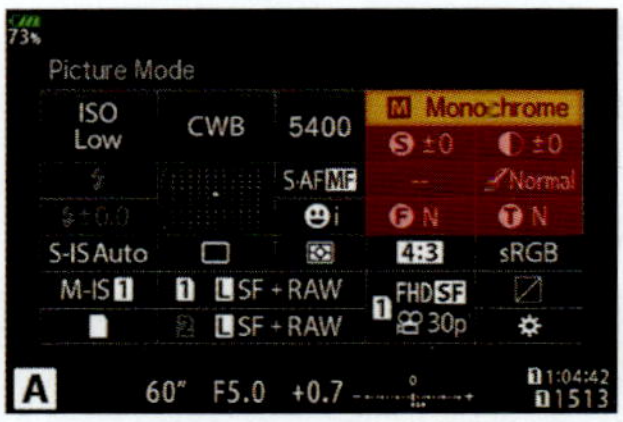

Figure 2.4F: The entire Picture Mode section of the Super Control Panel (in red)

First, let's consider how to select and make minor adjustments to a Picture Mode from the Super Control Panel. There are so many Picture Modes that it would be unnecessarily repetitive to discuss all 38 of them in this chapter. Please refer to the **Picture Mode** heading on page 151 for detailed configuration information.

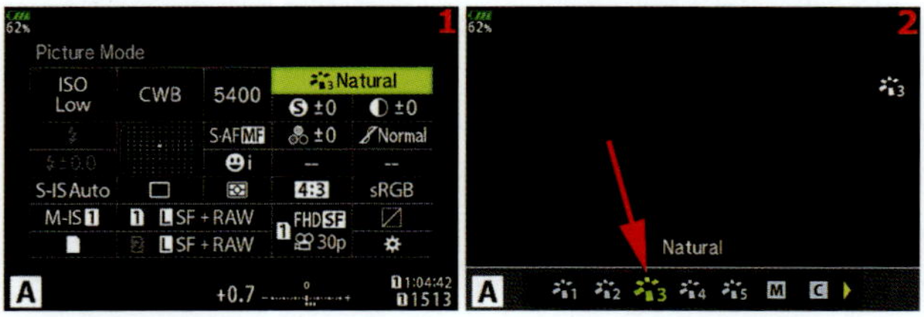

Figure 2.4G: Selecting a Picture Mode

In figure 2.4G, image 1, the Picture Mode function is highlighted and the Natural Picture Mode is currently selected. When you rotate the Front Dial, a series of 38 Picture Modes will scroll by. When the Picture Mode you want to use is shown in the highlighted area, it is selected.

Another way to select a Picture Mode is to highlight the Picture Mode location and press the OK button, which will open the secondary screen (figure 2.4G, image 2). Scroll left or right with the Arrow Pad and highlight the mode you want to use, then press the OK button to select it. I chose 3, which is the Natural Picture Mode.

Picture Mode: Sharpness, Contrast, Saturation, and Gradation

Most of the Picture Modes allow you to fine-tune several variables (up to six). Non-ART color Picture Modes provide four specific fine-tuning adjustments: Contrast, Sharpness, Saturation, and Gradation.

Let's see how to adjust these values for Picture Modes that allow it.

Sharpness

In figure 2.4H, image 1, you can see that 3 Natural Picture Mode is selected. In the highlighted area just below Natural, an S in a circle and a ±0 symbol is displayed. This is the Sharpness setting. Sharpness affects how well you can see fine details in an image.

When you adjust the Sharpness it applies only to the Picture Mode shown in the Super Control Panel (currently Natural); it does not affect any other Picture Modes. You can adjust the Sharpness over a range of four increments (+2 to –2) by turning the Front Dial (+2 to –2), or you can use a secondary screen to make the adjustment. With S±0 highlighted, press the OK button to open the secondary screen.

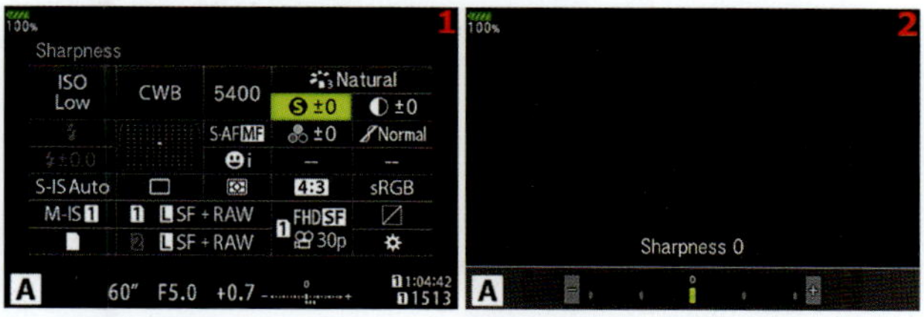

Figure 2.4H: Fine-tuning Sharpness

On the secondary screen (figure 2.4H, image 2), move the green indicator bar under the 0 to the left or right with the Arrow Pad keys (toward the – or + signs) to add or subtract Sharpness for that Picture Mode. Press the OK button to lock in your choice.

Contrast

In figure 2.4I, image 1, you can see that the 3 Natural Picture Mode is selected. The highlighted area just below Natural shows a circle that is half black and half white, and a ±0 symbol. This is the Contrast setting.

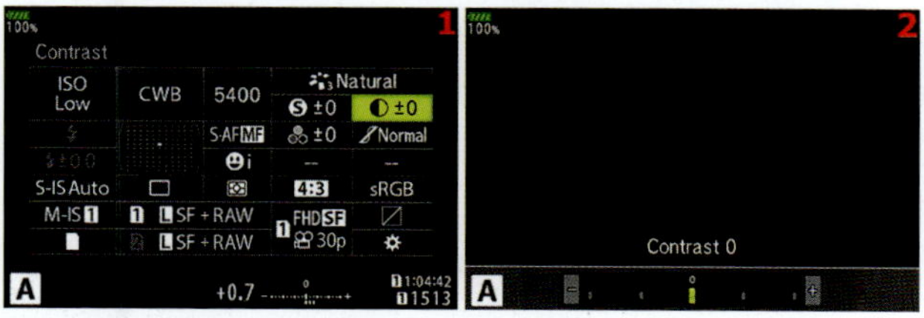

Figure 2.4I: Fine-tuning Contrast

Contrast affects the relationship between light and dark in the image. High-contrast images have very dark blacks, very bright whites, and strong colors. Low-contrast images often have weak light and dark areas and muted colors.

When you adjust the Contrast setting it applies only to the current Picture Mode shown in the Super Control Panel; it does not affect any other Picture Modes. You can adjust the Contrast over a range of four increments (+2 to –2) by turning the Front Dial, or you can use a secondary screen to make the adjustment. With the Contrast symbol highlighted, press the OK button to open the secondary screen.

On the secondary screen (figure 2.4I, image 2), move the green indicator bar under the 0 to the left or right with the Arrow Pad keys (toward the – or + signs) to add or subtract Contrast for that Picture Mode. Press the OK button to lock in your choice.

Saturation

In figure 2.4J, image 1, you can see that the 3 Natural Picture Mode is selected. A triad of small circles and ±0 is displayed in the highlighted area below Natural. This is the Saturation setting.

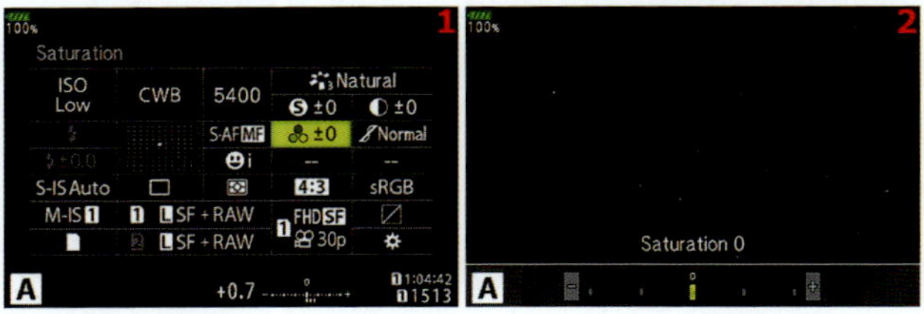

Figure 2.4J: Fine-tuning Saturation

Saturation affects how strong the colors in an image appear. A high-saturation image will have strong, bold colors; a low-saturation image will have weaker, muted colors.

When you adjust the Saturation setting it applies only to the current Picture Mode shown in the Super Control Panel; it does not affect any other Picture Modes. You can adjust the Saturation over a range of four increments (+2 to –2) by turning the Front Dial (+2 to –2), or you can use a secondary screen to make the adjustment. With the Saturation symbol highlighted, press the OK button to open the secondary screen.

On the secondary screen (figure 2.4J, image 2), move the green indicator under the 0 to the left or right with the Arrow Pad keys (toward the – or + signs) to add or subtract color Saturation for that Picture Mode. Press the OK button to lock in your choice.

Gradation

In figure 2.4K, image 1, you can see that the 3 Natural Picture Mode is selected. On a new E-M1II, a curves-adjustment symbol and the word Normal is displayed in the highlighted area below Natural; however, on a preowned camera it might show Auto, High, or Low (if the previous owner adjusted this value). This is the Gradation setting.

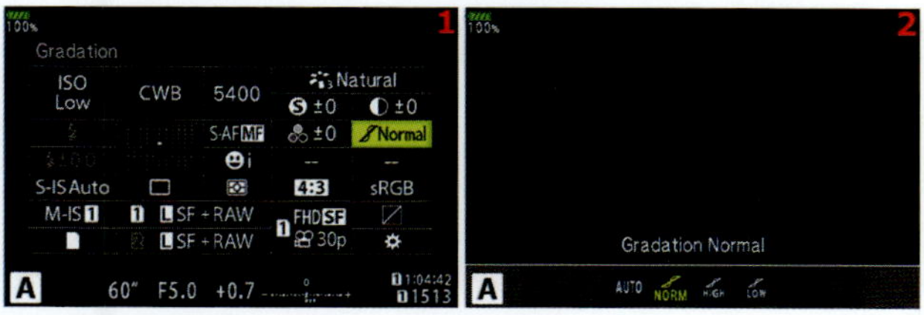

Figure 2.4K: Fine-tuning Gradation

Gradation affects the smoothness with which colors change into other shades. Here are the four Gradation settings and a brief description of each:

- **Auto:** The camera divides the image into detailed regions and adjusts the brightness for each region on an individual basis. The camera decides how to handle gradation, with special attention on resolving the smoothness between areas of very high contrast.
- **Normal** or **NORM:** This is the default. It provides a smooth look between contrast and color changes for everyday photography.
- **High:** This mode is best used for high-key subjects that tend to have very bright highlights and little darkness in the image.
- **Low:** This mode is best used for low-key subjects that tend to be dark and have few bright areas in the image.

When you adjust the Gradation it applies only to the current Picture Mode displayed in the Super Control Panel; it does not affect any other Picture Modes. You can adjust Gradation by simply turning the Front Dial until you see the Gradation setting you want to use, or you can use the secondary screen. With Normal (or another mode) highlighted, press the OK button to open the secondary screen.

On the secondary screen (figure 2.4K, image 2) you can adjust the Picture Mode Gradation by using the Arrow Pad keys to select one of the four available modes: AUTO, NORM, HIGH, and LOW. Press the OK button to lock in your choice.

Monochrome Picture Mode

The Monochrome Picture Mode is a little different than the color Picture Modes. It has the Sharpness, Contrast, and Gradation adjustments discussed in the previous subsections; however, it does not have the Saturation setting. Additionally, Monochrome adds a Color Filter system (called B&W Filter in previous Olympus cameras) for special effects and a color toning system called Monochrome Color (called Pict. Tone in previous Olympus cameras).

We have already discussed how the Sharpness, Contrast, and Gradation settings work (page 29). Now let's examine how the Color Filter and Monochrome Color settings operate. These two systems modify how the gray tones in the monochrome image are displayed, as if you were using glass filters (e.g., red, yellow) or special image processing (e.g., Sepia, Cyanotype).

Color Filter

In figure 2.4L, image 1, you can see that the M Monochrome Picture Mode is selected. Below that are the Sharpness, Contrast, and Gradation settings, with a dashed line where the Saturation setting would normally be. Below those settings is the one we are now concerned with, the Color Filter, identified by an F in a circle followed by a filter name (see upcoming list of filter names).

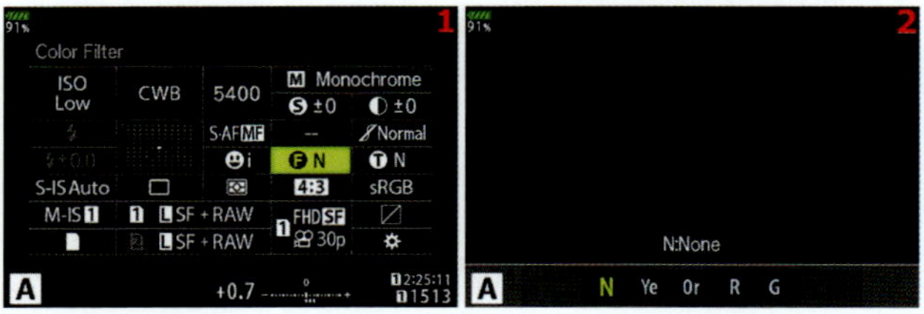

Figure 2.4L: Using the Color Filter mode

The Color Filter setting gives you four filter effects (Ye, Or, R, and G) that allow you to change how the camera records various colors and a None (N) setting, which uses no filter for a normal black-and-white image. Like glass lens filters that can be used to darken the sky or lighten the clouds, you can achieve similar effects with the four filters in the E-M1II. Here are the four Color Filter settings, with a brief description of each:

- **N (None):** Makes a normal black-and-white image.
- **Ye (Yellow):** Makes clearly defined white clouds and a sky with normal brightness.
- **Or (Orange):** Moderately emphasizes blue skies and sunset colors.
- **R (Red):** Strongly emphasizes red and crimson colors. Makes a blue sky with clouds seem dark and contrasty.
- **G (Green):** Strongly emphasizes green and red.

When Color Filter is selected, rotate the Front Dial and you will see the characters in the previous list appear on the screen (figure 2.4L, image 1). Stop turning the Front Dial when the filter you want to use is displayed.

You can also make a selection via a secondary screen, which you open by highlighting Color Filter and pressing the OK button. On the secondary screen (figure 2.4L, image 2) use the Arrow Pad keys to scroll to the filter you want to use, and then press the OK button to lock in your selection. Your choice affects the Monochrome Picture Mode only.

Monochrome Color

In figure 2.4M, image 1, you can see that the M Monochrome Picture Mode is selected. Below that, a circled T followed by a color name (N, S, B, P, and G) is highlighted. The T stands for tone—as in color tone—and the colors are described in the upcoming list.

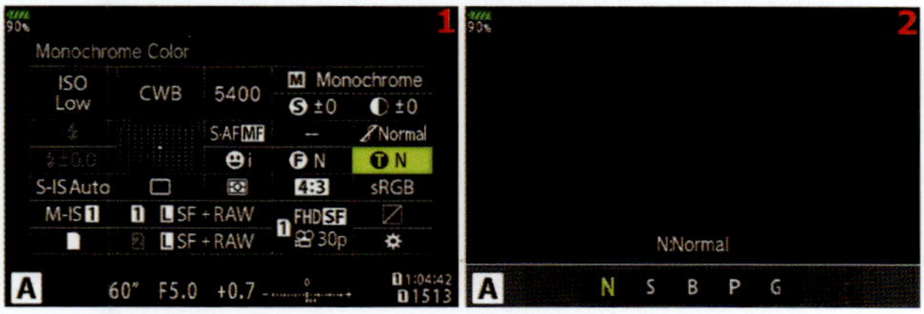

Figure 2.4M: Using the Monochrome Color setting

The Monochrome Color setting gives you four special effects that allow you to change how the camera displays the gray tones in each image. Here are the four Monochrome Color settings, with a brief description of each:

- **N (Normal):** Makes a normal black-and-white image.
- **S (Sepia):** Makes a monochrome image with a sepia (brownish) color.
- **B (Blue):** Makes a monochrome image with a light blue tint.
- **P (Purple):** Makes a monochrome image with a light purple tint.
- **G (Green):** Makes a monochrome image with a light green tint.

When Monochrome Color is selected, rotate the Front Dial and you will see the characters in the previous list appear on screen (figure 2.4M, image 1). Stop turning the Front Dial when the tone you want to use is displayed.

You can also make a selection via a secondary screen, which you open by highlighting Monochrome Color and pressing the OK button. On the secondary screen (figure 2.4M, image 2) use the Arrow Pad keys to scroll to the setting you want to use, and then press the OK button to lock in your choice. Your choice affects the Monochrome Picture Mode only.

Note: In this Picture Mode section we have considered how to select and modify a Picture Mode setting. As mentioned previously, there are 38 Picture Modes available on this camera! Each of these modes is discussed beginning on page 151.

As you scroll through the various Picture Modes, you will see the six settings below the Picture Mode location change their labels. Most of the time these labels are fairly easy to figure out; however, some may seem obscure. For the more difficult ones, see the Picture Mode discussion found on page 151 for more information.

Settings Recommendation: For everyday shooting I usually choose Natural Picture Mode. However, for some types of nature shooting I may use Vivid Picture Mode to make the colors pop. When I need the widest dynamic range for nature shooting, I may use the Muted Picture Mode, and then later increase the saturation and contrast manually for the best look. For portraits I often use Portrait Picture Mode to preserve natural-looking skin tones. When I am feeling adventurous, I even use some of the Art Modes. They can be quite fun! It's good that we have so many choices.

Picture Modes: JPEG versus RAW Files

The Picture Mode color scheme is permanently applied to a JPEG image. If you change your mind after taking a picture with a certain Picture Mode, you can modify the color of the JPEG image to some degree; however, modifying and resaving a JPEG file multiple times while tweaking the color may result in damage to the image (artifacts and color banding).

When you shoot in RAW (ORF) mode, Picture Mode settings are embedded into the image metadata (internal settings information), but are not permanently applied In this case, you can change Picture Modes after the fact and save the modified image as a new JPEG file with a completely different look. I use the Picture Mode settings, but I realize that the settings are not permanently applied to my RAW files; they are just displayed so I can see if I want to make adjustments. Changing Picture Modes or modifying the color balance directly and then resaving the image as a JPEG does not damage a RAW file.

Flash Mode

The E-M1II offers you a choice of seven flash modes. If you do not have a flash unit mounted in the camera's hot shoe, these settings will be displayed in a lighter color on the Super Control Panel, although they are still adjustable. Why not mount and turn on the small flash unit included with the camera before you read through this section? Let's examine each flash mode and see what it does:

- (*Fill in*): This is the primary flash mode for everyday use. The flash will fire each time you take a picture, and it will attempt to balance the flash output with ambient light to some degree (it fills in), but in most cases the flash unit provides the main illumination.
- (*Redeye*): This mode tries to cause the subject's pupils to contract by firing a preflash, blinking the red AF illuminator light on the camera body twice, and waiting for one second before the main flash fires. This may reduce the eerie red-eye look that can be seen in some pictures taken with flash.
- (*Flash Off*): The flash is off and will not fire.
- **SLOW** (*Red-Eye Slow*)**:** This mode executes the same actions as the Redeye mode mentioned previously; however, it also uses Slow flash, as described next. Basically, the camera fires a preflash to reduce red eye and also uses shutter speeds that can get very slow in dim ambient light. Therefore, this mode helps you use mostly ambient light to illuminate the subject, adds some fill light from the flash, and does red-eye reduction for good measure.
- **SLOW** (*Slow*): This mode fires the flash as soon as the first curtain of the shutter is fully open. Then, if the ambient light is dim, it allows the shutter to remain open to pull

in background light. If you are shooting in low light it is best to use a tripod for this mode (and other modes that use Slow), or at least brace yourself against a solid object when you take the picture. Otherwise, you may have a well-exposed subject with ghosting from camera movement after the flash fires. If a subject is moving when you use this mode, a ghosted trail may appear in *front* of the subject. Basically, Slow mode fires the flash at the beginning of the shutter speed time and allows the camera to continue gathering light for the rest of the time the shutter is open.

- **SLOW** (*Slow2*): This mode operates like Slow mode, except it fires the flash at the end of the shutter speed time, just before the second shutter curtain closes. In effect, the camera has already made an ambient light exposure before it fires the flash. For that reason, this mode is often called rear-curtain or second-curtain flash. If the subject is moving, a ghosted trail may appear *behind* the subject. Many people use this mode to imply motion in photographs.
- **FULL** (*Manual Value*): You can manually choose a flash power, as described in the paragraphs accompanying figure 2.5B. You can choose from the range of full power (Full) to 1/64 of full power. (See the upcoming **Manual Value Flash Mode** subsection for more information.)

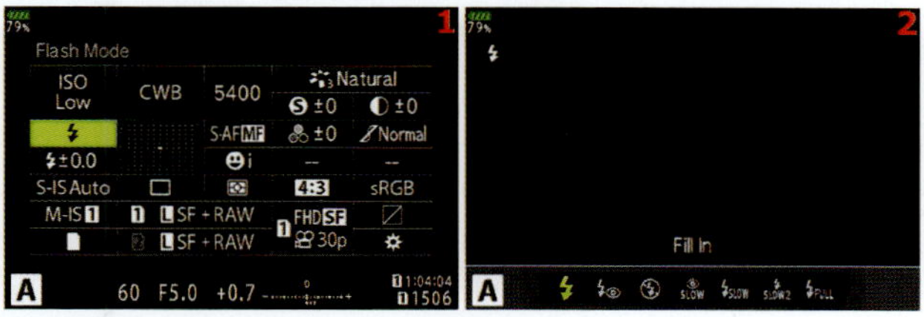

Figure 2.5A: Choosing a Flash Mode

In figure 2.5A, image 1, you can see that the Flash Mode position is highlighted. You can turn the Front Dial to scroll through the seven available modes (see previous list) and stop when the symbol of the mode you want to use is highlighted. If you don't know what the symbols mean, it may be best to use the secondary screen because it displays both the symbol and the name of the mode above the symbol area. Press the OK button to enter the secondary screen.

In figure 2.5A, image 2, the secondary screen is open. Along the bottom of the screen you can scroll left or right with the Arrow Pad keys to select the Flash Mode you prefer. The name of the mode will appear where you can see the words Fill In above the symbols in image 2. Press the OK button to lock in your chosen Flash Mode.

Manual Value Flash Mode

For studio shooters or individuals who prefer to very carefully control the flash output, Manual Value Flash Mode is available. This mode, as described in the previous list, allows you to manually choose a flash output power from a range of 1/64 power to Full power.

Let's see how to use the Manual Value mode.

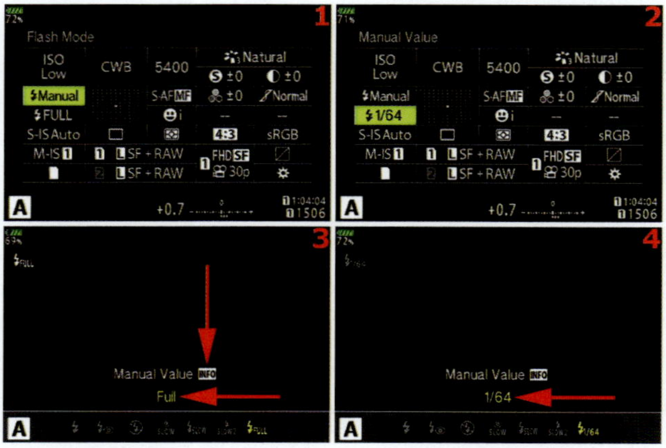

Figure 2.5B: Choosing a Manual Value for manual flash output control

In figure 2.5B, image 1, the Flash Mode position is highlighted. Either Rotate the Front Dial until Manual appears or press the OK button to open the secondary screen. With the secondary screen open, use the Arrow Pad keys to select the Manual Value mode, and then press the OK button.

Once you have the camera set to Manual Value flash mode, move the green highlight down one position to the flash output setting (where the word FULL appears in image 1). Rotate the Front Dial to select a new flash output value (figure 2.5B, image 2). You have a selection of several manual flash output levels, from FULL power to as low as 1/64th of full flash output.

Alternatively, you may also use the Flash Mode secondary screen to manually choose a flash output level. With Manual flash selected (figure 2.5B, image 1), press the OK button and the secondary screen will open (figure 2.5B, image 3). If this mode has not been moved from maximum flash output, the screen will display Manual Value with Full just beneath it. Notice that in image 3, the upper red arrow is pointing to the word INFO. Press the INFO button on the back of the camera to highlight the position shown at the tip of the lower red arrow (Full). You can now change the flash output level by rotating the Front Dial. I chose 1/64 power, which is the lowest power output setting (figure 2.5B, image 4).

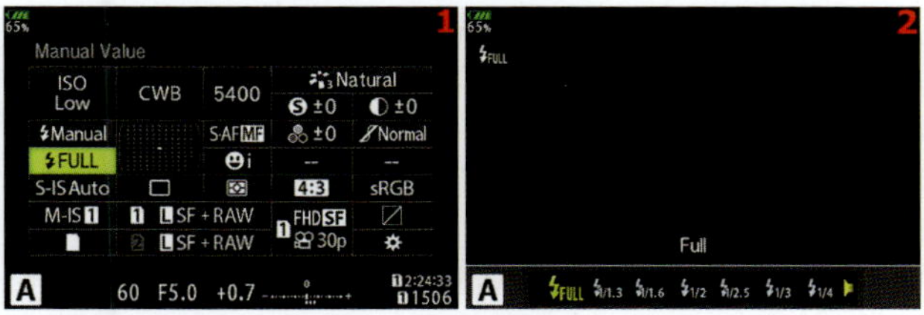

Figure 2.5C: Choosing a flash output level with a secondary screen

Finally, you can also use the flash output secondary screen to choose a flash output level. In figure 2.5C, image 1, the flash output setting is highlighted. Press the OK button and the secondary screen shown in figure 2.5C, image 2, will appear. Use the Arrow Pad keys to select a value in the list along the bottom of the screen. After you have chosen the value you want to use, press the OK button to lock it in.

Settings Recommendation: I use the Fill in flash mode most of the time. It seems to balance the flash well with ambient light, and the mode lets me, not the camera, decide when to use flash. The other modes (e.g., Slow, Slow2) are available for when you want special effects. Redeye seems to help somewhat for reducing the red-eye effect in portraits, but you should warn the subjects to stand still until after the second flash—first there is the preflash to reduce pupil size, then the main flash fires.

Flash Intensity Control (+/– Compensation)

Flash Intensity Control is similar to a flash compensation system. It is available in any flash mode except Manual (M).

If you are taking pictures and the background of the subject is exposed well but the subject is overexposed, you may want to dial back the power or intensity of the flash unit. If the subject is underexposed and the background is well exposed, you may want to increase the flash output to light the subject a little better. Flash Intensity Control gives you the power to do either. In effect, you are dialing in flash exposure compensation. Let's see how to adjust it.

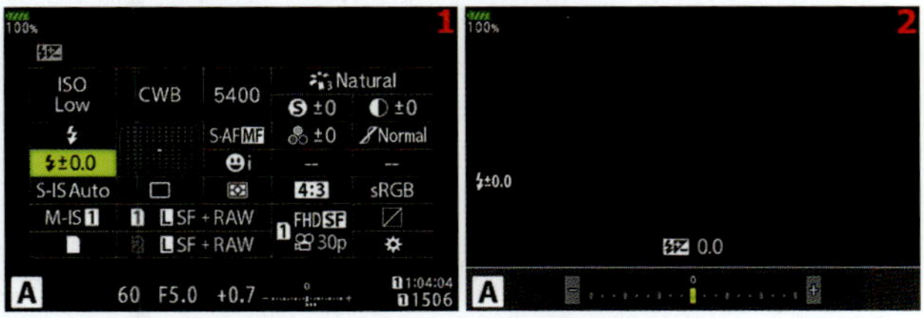

Figure 2.6: Choosing a Flash Intensity Control exposure compensation value

Select the Flash Intensity Control symbol, a small lightning bolt followed by ±0.0, as shown in figure 2.6, image 1. The 0.0 represents the EV value that can be dialed in, over a range of six EV steps (+3.0 to –3.0). Turn the Front Dial to change the flash intensity. You will see the EV value change to plus or minus, depending on which direction you turn the dial. As expected, turning the dial toward + makes the flash put out more power, and turning it toward – makes it put out less power. Stop turning the dial when you see the EV compensation value you want to use.

You can also use the secondary screen if you want a more visual representation of the flash intensity change. Press the OK button to open the secondary screen. Figure 2.6, image 2, shows the secondary screen with a 6-stop (EV step) scale (+3.0 to –3.0). Use the Arrow Pad keys to move the indicator bar left or right on the scale, toward the + or – signs. The positive or negative EV value will display where 0.0 is located in image 2. Press the OK button to lock in your flash intensity choice.

Settings Recommendation: I tend to shoot a little brighter than many photographers because I use RAW mode for the best image quality most of the time. When you use RAW (ORF) Image Quality mode, the image files have more overexposure headroom than you might think. Therefore, I generally leave the Flash Intensity Control set to +0.3, for a one-third stop overexposure. When you shoot JPEG files it is important to watch the histogram closely to prevent unrecoverable overexposure (highlight data loss), especially when shooting up close. You will need to experiment carefully with this setting to learn the personality of your particular flash unit under different circumstances.

AF Area (With ☺ Face Priority)

The AF Area mode affects which AF point, or points, are used when you initiate autofocus. You can select a single point anywhere in a grid of 121 AF points, or you can use a group of AF points. You can move the individual AF point or the group of AF points around the grid by pressing the Arrow Pad keys. This allows you to move one or more points to a particular area of the subject—such as an eye—as you view it on the Live View screen or through the electronic viewfinder (EVF) to ensure the best autofocus.

Additionally, the camera provides access to the ☺ Face Priority adjustment from the AF Area mode screen. The ☺ Face Priority mode allows you to choose different ways to detect human faces. We will discuss ☺ Face Priority in an upcoming section of this chapter, ☺ **Face Priority AF Mode** (page 44). The interface we will discuss here is another way to access the ☺ Face Priority system.

AF Area Adjustment

Let's first consider the AF Area mode adjustment. AF area mode determines how many AF points actively seek your subject when you press the Shutter button halfway down to initiate autofocus. Figure 2.7A, image 1, shows the AF Area mode location on the Super Control Panel. Image 2, shows the secondary screen for AF Area mode.

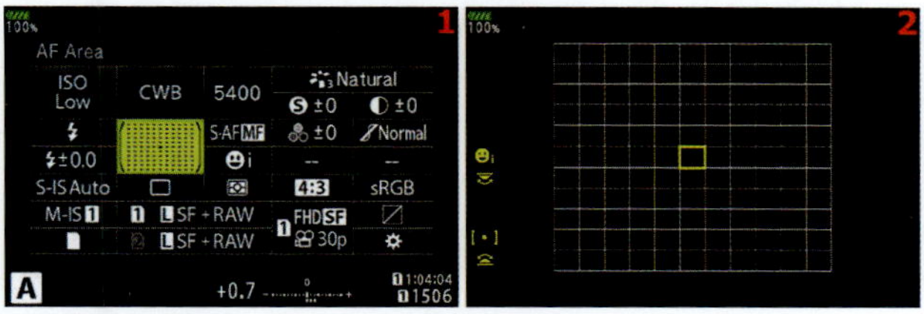

Figure 2.7A: Adjusting the AF Area mode

With the AF Area mode location highlighted on the Super Control Panel (figure 2.7A, image 1), turn the Front Dial to move the active AF point (or pattern) to the left or right in the grid. As the AF point scrolls off the edge of the tiny AF Area mode grid shown on the Super Control Panel, it will move up or down a row, according to which direction you are turning the Front Dial. If you have the time, you could scroll the miniature AF point through all 121 points; however, you may want to use the secondary screen instead to save time. Press the OK button to open the secondary screen (figure 2.7A, image 2).

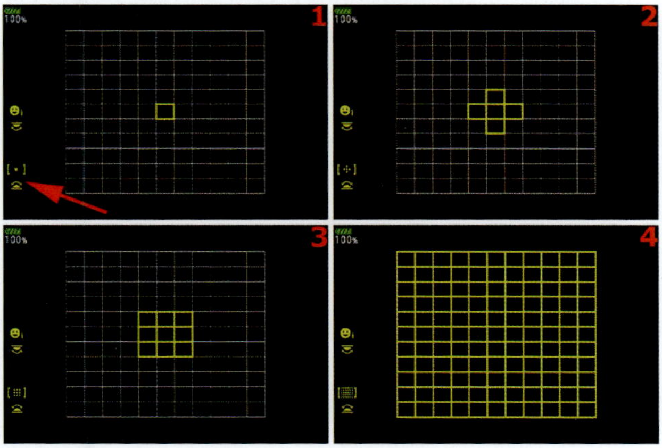

Figure 2.7B: Four AF point arrangements

In figure 2.7B, image 1, there is a red arrow pointing to the AF Area mode adjustment symbol. This informs you that you can turn the Front Dial to change the AF Area mode. The current mode shown on this screen uses one AF point that can be moved around the grid with the Arrow Pad buttons, allowing you to better focus on a particular part of your subject. Above the Front Dial icon, there is a symbol that shows the current AF Area mode pattern in square brackets. There are four AF Area modes available, as shown in figure 2.7B. Let's review each mode:

- **Single Target** (figure 2.7B, image 1): A single AF point that can be moved around the grid of 121 points with the Arrow Pad.

- **Five Target** (figure 2.7B, image 2): A plus-shaped pattern of five AF points, which can be moved around the grid of 121 points. This mode works well when you are attempting to focus on a smaller subject that might be moving in a small area, or for portraiture.
- **Nine Target** (figure 2.7B, image 3): A group of nine AF points that you can move around the grid. This mode works great for tracking a larger moving subject using certain AF Modes, such as C-AF+TR (page 404).
- **All Targets** (figure 2.7B, image 4): This is basically an automatic AF Area mode system. This mode uses all 121 points to determine which AF point(s) might give the best autofocus. It allows the camera to select the AF point without input from the photographer.

Select the mode you find most useful for your current needs and press the OK button to lock it in.

AF Area Select Button Task

If you prefer not to use the Super Control Panel to select an AF point type and size, there is a Button Task called AF Area Select that can be assigned to one of the programmable buttons (Button Functions) mentioned in the **Camera Setup and Control Reference** chapter.

In fact, the AF Area Select button task is already assigned to the Fn1 button by default. Therefore, if you have a brand new E-M1II, pressing the Fn1 button should open the AF Area mode screen, allowing you to choose the AF Area mode (and ☺ Face Priority settings, as described in the next subsection). Assigning Button Tasks is discussed on page 432.

☺ Face Priority Mode (On the AF Area Mode Screen)

☺ Face Priority mode lets you control when and how the camera detects faces during autofocus operations. In many cases, when a human face is present in the viewfinder or on the Live View screen, it is the subject. Therefore, you can choose to either make the camera extra sensitive to faces or turn this feature off.

When enabled, ☺ Face Priority mode can use an entire face, the pupil of the closest eye, or the pupil of the left or right eye of your subject. Let's look at how to select the various modes from the Super Control Panel.

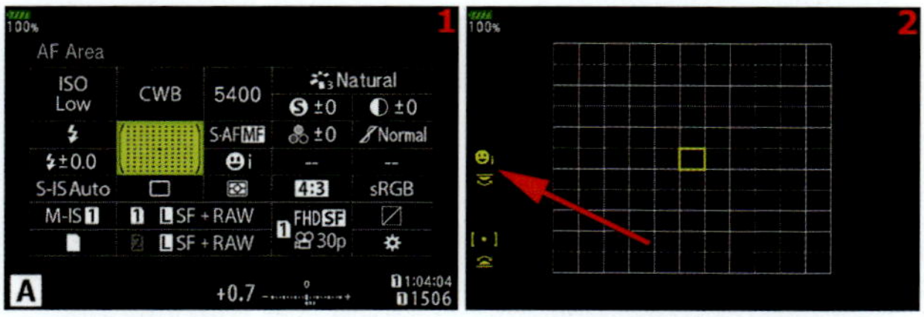

Figure 2.7C: Choosing a ☺ Face Priority mode and AF Area mode

Figure 2.7C, image 1, shows the AF Area mode selection highlighted. The ☺ Face Priority mode selections are on the AF Area mode secondary screen. Press the OK button to open the secondary screen.

In figure 2.7C, image 2 (red arrow), you can see the ☺ Face Priority icon on the AF Area mode screen. Rotate the Rear Dial to scroll through the ☺ Face Priority settings until you find the one you want to use. In figure 2.7C, ☺ Face Priority is set to ☺i (Face and Nearest Eye Priority). Here is a list of the five settings and what they do:

- **Off:** ☺ Face Priority is off.
- **☺:** The camera uses ☺ Face Priority for autofocus and exposure.
- **☺i:** The camera uses the pupil of the nearest eye for the best autofocus.
- **☺iR:** The camera uses the pupil of the right eye for the best autofocus.
- **☺iL:** The camera uses the pupil of the left eye for the best autofocus.

The ☺ Face Priority setting causes the camera to use the human faces it detects to calculate the best exposure, and, as mentioned previously, it varies the autofocus method depending on which mode you select. We will discuss this setting in more detail in the upcoming section titled ☺ **Face Priority AF Mode** on page 44.

Settings Recommendation: Most of the time my style of photography is well served with the normal single AF point from the Single Target mode shown in figure 2.7B, image 1, especially for landscape and nature photography. I may use the Five-Target mode when I am taking portrait pictures (figure 2.7B, image 2). The Nine-Target group mode comes in handy for actions shots (figure 2.7B, image 3), and I may use the full 121-point All Target mode when I am shooting at a party and don't want to bother with moving the AF point manually. All Target mode with ☺ Face Priority set to ☺i seems to work great at parties. Experiment with these modes to see which you like best in different styles of photography.

[Photo] AF Mode

The [Photo] AF Mode function provides six focus modes (figure 2.8, image 1). Five of them are for various types of autofocus, and one is for manual focus.

This subject is considered in more depth in the **Custom Menu** chapter under the **[Photo] AF Mode** subheading on page 404 (see *Custom Menu > A1. AF/MF > AF Mode*). In this chapter, we will examine how to select a [Photo] AF Mode from the Super Control Panel, and I'll provide a brief summary of how each mode works. Let's discuss each of the six modes:

- **Single AF (S-AF):** When you hold the Shutter button halfway down, the camera autofocuses on the subject, beeps once, and locks focus. In the top-right corner of the EVF (or Live View screen) you will see a small green dot. This indicates that the focus is good. If the subject moves, the focus may no longer be accurate; therefore, you must release the Shutter button and press it halfway again to update the focus. S-AF is best for static subjects or subjects that move very slowly. The AF point target indicator is a small green rectangle.

- **Continuous AF (C-AF):** Similar to S-AF, the camera will focus when you hold the Shutter button down, and it beeps when it has acquired good focus. It also displays the round green good-focus indicator at the top right of the camera screens. However, in this mode the E-M1II continuously autofocuses on whatever is in front of its lens. Unlike S-AF, the camera never really locks the focus permanently; it continues to seek the best autofocus at all times. If you change to a different subject, or if the subject moves, the camera will do its best to automatically update the focus. You may feel and hear the camera adjusting the lens as the focus changes. The AF point target indicator is a small green rectangle.
- **Manual focus (MF):** When you use MF mode you are entirely responsible for focusing the camera. The AF point target indicator is not used. Since the E-M1II does not have a split-prism screen to assist with focus, you may want to enable focus Peaking and/or Magnify under the *Custom Menu > A3. AF/MF > MF Assist > Peaking* [or *Magnify*] setting. Peaking makes it easy to see when the subject is in focus because it outlines the edges of the subject in white (or black) to indicate where the best focus is currently located. Peaking is discussed and samples are provided in the **Custom Menu** chapter under the **MF Assist** heading and the **Peaking** subheading on page 428. In the **MF Assist** section of that chapter I also discuss the **Magnify** function, which automatically zooms in to pixel-peeping levels when you turn the lens focus ring in manual mode, and it results in extremely accurate manual focus. Combining Peaking and Magnify makes manual focus easy.
- **Single AF + MF (S-AF+MF):** This mode is almost exactly like the S-AF mode, with its focus lock, beep, and round green good focus indicator. However, it offers one powerful extra feature: manual focus fine-tuning. After you press the Shutter button halfway and the camera has autofocused and locked focus on the subject (S-AF), you can fine-tune the focus with the lens focus ring (MF). If you have focus Peaking and Magnify enabled, as discussed in the previous paragraph, the camera will use those features during fine-tuning. The AF point target indicator is a small green rectangle. This is, by far, my favorite focus setting!
- **AF Tracking (C-AF+TR):** This mode is for autofocus with subject tracking. For general use this mode works like C-AF mode, with continuous autofocus updating. However, if the subject moves, and you are continuously holding the Shutter button halfway down, the camera will track the subject with a bigger focus point target indicator, while continuously updating the focus as the subject moves. To help you understand how to use this feature, select C-AF+TR, then focus on a small subject. Continue to hold the Shutter button halfway down and move the camera around, and you will see the AF point target indicator stay locked on the subject. It is effective at staying with a subject as long as the light is reasonably good and the subject is not moving too quickly. The AF point target indicator is a larger green square with bars sticking out of each side.

- **Preset MF (PreMF):** When you use this mode, the camera will remember a specific preset focus point, and will instantly return to that point when you press a programmed camera button. To store a preset focus point, follow these steps (***Note:*** This series of steps will be discussed in depth under the **Preset MF** subheading found on page 405):
  1. Place your camera on a tripod for most accurate use of this feature.
  2. Assign the Preset MF button task to one of the camera's programmable buttons, such as Fn1 (see page 405 for Preset MF button assignment information).
  3. Select PreMF from the Super Control Panel AF Mode secondary screen (figure 2.8, image 2).
  4. Your subject should now be displayed on one of the camera's screens.
  5. Press the INFO button to tell the camera to prepare for a focus preset.
  6. Manually focus the lens on the exact point on your subject that you want to store as a preset autofocus point.
  7. Press the OK button to record the preset focus point.
  8. Now when you press the programmable button that was assigned in step #1, the camera will focus at the point you stored as a preset.

Now let's examine how to select one of the focus modes.

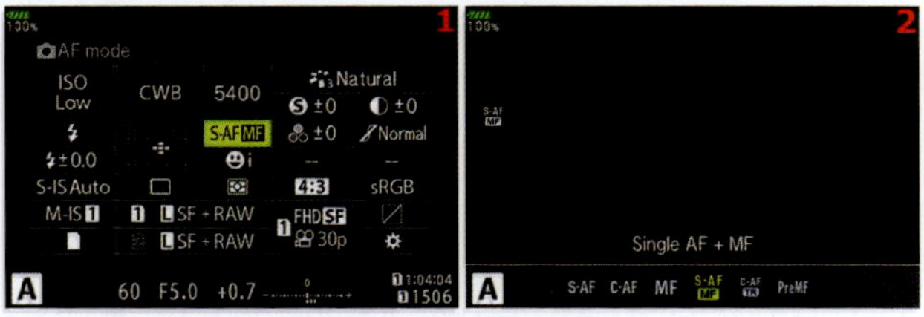

Figure 2.8: Choosing an Autofocus (AF) mode

In figure 2.8, image 1, you can see that the [Photo] AF Mode position is highlighted (S-AF+MF). Turn the Front Dial, and the six [Photo] AF Modes will scroll by. Stop scrolling when you see the mode you want to use. If you prefer to use the secondary screen to select a mode, press the OK button to open it.

Figure 2.8, image 2, shows the secondary [Photo] AF Mode screen with Single AF + MF selected. Use the Arrow Pad keys to scroll left or right until the mode you want to use is highlighted. Press the OK button to lock in the [Photo] AF Mode.

Note: If you are creating a preset autofocus point, as discussed in the previous list item Preset MF, you will need to use the secondary screen (figure 2.8, image 2) to store the preset. Also, you can change the [Photo] AF Mode by pressing the AF/Metering Mode button on top of the camera (to the left of the On/Off Lever) and turning the Rear Dial.

Settings Recommendation: I like to use S-AF+MF mode so I can use autofocus most of the time, but I can still turn the focus ring to enable manual focus, along with Peaking and Magnify. The S-AF mode is fine for slow shooting with well-defined, static subjects.

C-AF works quite well when I am shooting something like a wedding and the bride and groom are walking toward me. I use MF mode most often when I am taking macro shots and need to carefully control where the focus falls, due to the shallow depth of field in that type of photography. The tracking mode (C-AF+TR) works well for moving subjects, especially larger wildlife, people, cars, and airplanes. Small birds are harder to track because they move so quickly and tax the AF tracking system. However, even small bird photography is now much easier with the E-M1II.

☺ Face Priority Mode

☺ Face Priority mode is designed to make your camera extra sensitive to human faces. We previously discussed a different way to access these same ☺ Face Priority modes from the AF Area mode section of the Super Control Panel (page 44); however, this is a more direct way to access them from their own location on the Super Control Panel.

When this mode is enabled, the E-M1II will detect human faces, adjust the focus to capture them sharply, and tweak the camera's metering system to expose more accurately for human skin tones.

Additionally, you can select Face and Eye Priority (☺i) and even choose which eye to focus on (☺iR, ☺iL). When any type of ☺ Face Priority is active, the camera looks for human faces in the subject area and gives them priority for exposure. It then uses the selected type of ☺ Face Priority to decide how to autofocus. Let's examine the five available modes:

- **☺Off:** Face Priority is off.
- **☺:** The camera uses ☺ Face Priority for autofocus and exposure.
- **☺i:** The camera uses the pupil of the nearest eye for the best autofocus.
- **☺iR:** The camera uses the pupil of the right eye for the best autofocus.
- **☺iL:** The camera uses the pupil of the left eye for the best autofocus.

Let's examine how to select one of these modes.

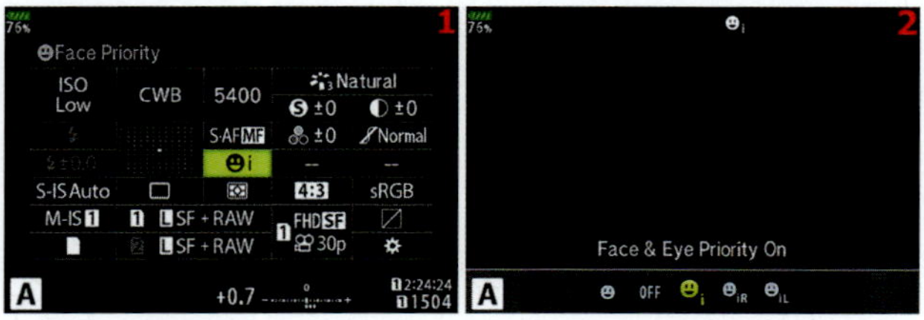

Figure 2.9: Selecting a Face & Eye Priority mode

In figure 2.9, image 1, you can see that ☺i (Face and Nearest Eye Priority) is turned on. Highlight the ☺ Face Priority position on the Super Control Panel. You can now use the Front Dial of the camera to scroll through the various modes. Stop scrolling when your favorite mode appears.

Alternately, you can use the secondary screen to select a mode. With the ☺ Face Priority position highlighted on the Super Control Panel, press the OK button to open the secondary screen. Figure 2.9, image 2, shows the ☺ Face Priority modes along the bottom of the screen. Use the Arrow Pad keys to scroll back and forth until the mode you want to use is highlighted. Press the OK button to lock in your choice.

Settings Recommendation: I have found that the camera works well with some form of ☺ Face Priority mode always active. It focuses normally on nonhuman subjects when no face is present, and it uses face detection only when it can detect human faces. I normally leave ☺i (Face and Nearest Eye Priority) set to On.

[Photo] Image Stabilizer

The 5-axis image stabilization (IS) system in the E-M1II is world-class and renowned as one of the best IS systems in any camera today. It will cut down on camera shake when you handhold the E-M1II, allowing you to use slower shutter speeds, smaller apertures, and lower ISOs while still getting sharp images. The camera body alone provides up to 5.5 stops of stabilization (i.e., you can handhold the camera with up to 5.5 steps slower shutter speed). When you use an M.Zuiko PRO lens that has built-in stabilization, the camera will use both the camera body stabilization and lens stabilization to provide up to 6.5 shutter speed steps of stabilization.

Since the primary IS system is built into the camera, it will work with any lens you use, including brands that require a non-intelligent adapter with no electronic connection to the camera. If you have Nikon or Canon (or other brand) lenses from one of your DSLRs, you can buy an inexpensive adapter to use them on the E-M1II.

Basically, the IS system will stabilize the image with virtually any lens that can be mounted on the camera. This subject will be examined in greater detail in the **Custom Menu** chapter under the **[Photo] Image Stabilizer** subheading on page 468 (*Custom Menu > C2. Release/[Stabilization Priority]/Image Stabilizer > [Photo] Image Stabilizer*). The following is a list of the various modes available in the Image Stabilizer menu:

- **Off:** No image stabilization is provided.
- **S-IS AUTO:** Olympus suggests this mode when you are unsure what you will be shooting and want to be prepared for any kind of movement. The camera automatically chooses the best type of image stabilization for the subject it detects. This is the factory default mode.
- **S-IS 1:** This is a general automatic mode that allows the Image Stabilizer to compensate in five directions (roll, pitch, yaw, vertical, and horizontal). It automatically corrects for movement in any or all of the directions (axes) at any time. It is not as sensitive to panning as S-IS AUTO.
- **S-IS 2:** The image stabilization system corrects only for the vertical axis (Vertical IS). Use this mode when you are panning the camera and are not concerned about horizontal

correction. If you are panning horizontally, such as at a car race, and are holding the camera in a horizontal (landscape) orientation, this mode may perform well for you.

- **S-IS 3:** The image stabilization system corrects only for horizontal camera shake (Horizontal IS). If you are panning horizontally, such as at a car race, and are holding the camera in a vertical (portrait) orientation, this mode may perform well for you.

Let's see how to configure the IS system.

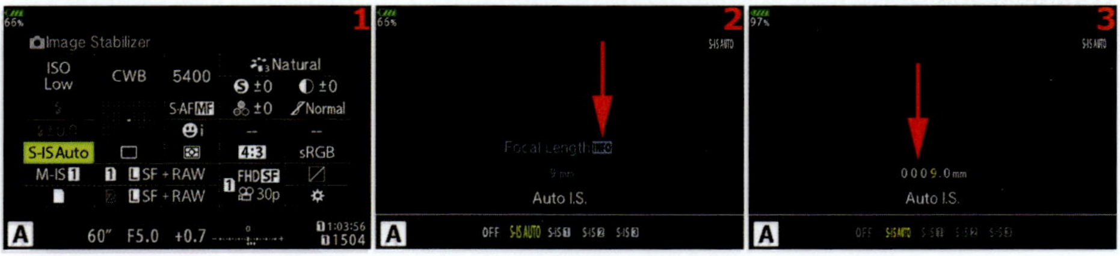

Figure 2.10: Choosing an image stabilization method

Figure 2.10, image 1, shows the [Photo] Image Stabilizer setting highlighted with S-IS AUTO selected. You can scroll through the five IS settings by turning the Front Dial. Stop turning the dial when the setting you want to use is highlighted. If you prefer to use the secondary screens, or if you are using a lens that is not a Micro Four Thirds or Four Thirds type that is attached to the camera with an adapter that does not have electronic connections for communication with the camera (a dumb adapter), press the OK button to open the secondary screen.

Figure 2.10, image 2, shows the [Photo] Image Stabilizer settings in a row at the bottom of the screen. Refer to the previous IS settings list and use the left or right Arrow Pad keys to move along the row until you highlight the setting you want to use. Press the OK button to lock in the setting. I selected Auto I.S. (S-IS AUTO). If you are using a Micro Four Thirds or Four Thirds lens, press the OK button and the IS system is ready to use. Skip the rest of this step and the next step. However, if you are using a dumb lens adapter with any type of lens, you will need to input the focal length of the mounted lens. Press the INFO button to move to the Focal Length screen.

Figure 2.10, image 3 (red arrow), allows you to register a focal length for a lens that is mounted on the camera with a dumb adapter. Press up or down on the Arrow Pad keys to select a focal length. The range of focal length choices are from 0mm to 1999mm. I chose 9mm in figure 2.10, image 3 (red arrow), which is the default. This focal length value is *not used* when you have a Micro Four Thirds lens mounted directly on the camera or when you mount a Four Thirds lens on a communicating (smart) adapter (e.g., an Olympus MMF-3). In those situations, the lens electronically communicates the focal length to the E-M1II body. After you have selected a value, press the OK button to lock it in.

Note: If you are using a zoom lens (not a prime lens) on a dumb adaptor you will have to estimate the focal length you will most often use and set that value in the screen shown in figure 2.10, image 3. If you use a different focal length than the one you entered, the IS system may not be quite as effective. However, since the 5-axis IS system is one of the best in the world, I am sure it will work quite well at any focal length you may use on a dumb adapter. You may want to experiment for the best results, especially at extreme angles of view, such as long telephoto or superwide. If you are using a tripod, Olympus recommends that you set IS to off.

There is a separate image stabilizer mode for capturing video. See the **[Video] Image Stabilizer** subheading on page 54.

Settings Recommendation: I have found that S-IS AUTO works beautifully for still images of any type. If you do a lot of panning, the S-IS AUTO mode is particularly effective. The camera allows you to disable certain types of IS directional correction (e.g., horizontal or vertical). Refer to the list of IS modes and select the mode that works best for your circumstances.

[Sequential][Self-Timer]

The [Sequential][Self-timer] system is composed of multiple parts: Single-frame, Sequential Shooting, Self-timer, Silent Shooting, Pro Capture, and High Res Shot.

These modes give you very flexible control over when and how the shutter is released for still image capture. In this chapter, I've provided a description of how each mode works, and we will examine how to select a mode. There is more comprehensive information provided for each of the [Sequential][Self-timer] modes in the **Shooting Menu 1** chapter under the **[Sequential]/[Self-Timer]/[Time Lapse]** heading on page 184. Let's briefly examine each of the modes and see how they work:

- **[Single]:** This mode causes the camera to take one picture each time you fully press the Shutter button. It uses the camera's mechanical shutter.
- **Silent [♥]:** This mode takes one picture each time you fully press the Shutter button, just like Single mode. However, it uses the electronic shutter instead of the mechanical shutter to eliminate noise from the shutter-release.
- **[Sequential] High (H):** The camera will take a continuous series of pictures at up to about 15 frames per second (fps) using the mechanical shutter. Focus, exposure, and white balance are fixed on the values determined for the first frame in the series.
- **[Sequential] H Silent [♥]:** The camera will take a continuous series of pictures at up to 60 fps (adjustable from 15 to 60 fps) using the electronic shutter (Silent). Focus, exposure, and white balance are fixed on the values determined for the first frame in the series. You can control the number of images captured per second (fps) with the *Custom Menu > C1. Release/[Sequential]/Image Stabilizer > [Sequential] H Settings > [♥ Sequential]* selection.
- **Pro Capture High (ProCapH):** This mode is similar to [Sequential] H Silent [♥] mode, except there are two parts to capturing a burst series of images. First, when you press and hold the Shutter button halfway down, the camera will capture a continuously

replaced series of up to 35 images (pre-shutter frames). Second, when you then press the Shutter button all the way down, the camera keeps the last 35 images captured just before you pressed the Shutter button all the way down, and it continues capturing images at up to 60 fps until you release the Shutter button. You can control the number of images that the camera uses in its Pro Capture High cycle (half Shutter button press) with *Custom Menu > C1. Release/[Sequential]/Image Stabilizer > [Sequential] H Settings > Pro Cap > Pre-shutter Frames* (1 to 35 images). You can also control the number of images captured per second (up to 60 fps) when the camera starts taking sequential images (full Shutter button press) with *Custom Menu > C1. Release/[Sequential]/Image Stabilizer > [Sequential] H Settings > Pro Cap > Max fps* (15 to 60 fps). Focus, exposure, and white balance are fixed on the values determined for the first frame in the series.

- **Sequential Low (L):** The camera will take a continuous series of pictures at up to 10 frames per second (1 to 10 fps). Focus, exposure, and white balance are fully active for each picture in the series, based on which AF Mode you have selected (e.g., S-AF, C-AF) and how you are using the autoexposure lock and autofocus lock (AEL/AFL) modes. You can control the number of images captured per second (fps) with *Custom Menu > C1. Release/[Sequential]/Image Stabilizer > [Sequential] L Settings > [Sequential]/♦ [Sequential]> Max fps* (1 to 10 fps).
- **[Sequential] L Silent [♥]:** The camera will take a continuous series of pictures at up to 18 fps using the electronic shutter (Silent). Focus, exposure, and white balance are fully active based on the AF Mode (e.g., S-AF, C-AF) and AEL/AFL mode selected. You can control the number of images captured per second with *Custom Menu > C1. Release/[Sequential]/Image Stabilizer > [Sequential] H Settings > ♥ [Sequential] Max fps* (1 to 18 fps).
- **Pro Capture Low (ProCapL):** This mode is similar to [Sequential] L Silent [♥] mode, except there are two parts to capturing a burst series of images. First, when you press and hold the Shutter button halfway down, the camera will capture a continuously replaced series of up to 35 images (pre-shutter frames). Second, when you then press the Shutter button all the way down, the camera keeps the pre-shutter frames captured just before you pressed the Shutter button all the way down, and it continues capturing images at up to 18 fps until you release the Shutter button. You can control the number of images the camera uses in its Pro Capture Low cycle (half Shutter button press) with *Custom Menu > C1. Release/[Sequential]/Image Stabilizer > [Sequential] L Settings > Pro Cap > Pre-shutter Frames* (1 to 35 images; defaults to 8 images). You can also control the number of images captured per second (up to 18 fps) when the camera starts taking sequential images (full Shutter button press) with *Custom Menu > C1. Release/[Sequential]/Image Stabilizer > [Sequential] L Settings > Pro Cap > Max fps* (10 to 18 fps). Focus, exposure, and white balance are fully active for each picture in the series, based on which AF Mode you have selected (e.g., S-AF, C-AF) and how you are using the autoexposure lock and autofocus lock (AEL/AFL) modes.

- **Self-timer 12 sec (12s):** The camera will take a single photograph 12 seconds after you press the Shutter button all the way down. The orange focus assist light on the front of the camera will shine solid for 10 seconds, then it will blink for 2 seconds before the shutter fires and the picture is taken.
- **Custom Self-timer (C):** This variable self-timer function allows you to select the number of seconds the camera will wait before firing (Timer), the number of images the camera will take when the self-timer expires (Number of Frames), and the period of time between each picture (Interval Length) if you have selected more than one picture with the Number of Frames setting. You can also choose whether or not to have the camera autofocus between each picture (Every Frame AF). Press the INFO button to access the individual settings within the Custom Self-timer secondary screen.
- **High Res Shot:** When you take a picture in this mode, the camera will capture eight images using its Silent electronic shutter and combine the images, in-camera, into one 50-megapixel image. Instead of the normal 20 MP at 5184 × 3888, the resulting combined image will be 50 MP at 8160 × 6120. The E-M1II achieves this result by using its sensor-shift technology to move the physical imaging sensor to all corners, across, and down an 8160 × 6120 frame, taking eight pictures as it moves, and then combining the images. Using a tripod is imperative for this mode, or you will have a blurry picture as your final result. The camera cannot use its normal Image Stabilization during this process, so it must be anchored down to something solid to get a sharp picture. It takes several seconds to capture the eight images and combine them into one big image. The camera will display a black screen with a progress bar as it captures and combines the images. If you see the symbol for High Res Shot blinking on the screen, it means the camera is unstable. Once you have pressed the Shutter button to start the process, wait for the progress bar to complete and the High Res Shot symbol to disappear from the screen before moving the camera. ***Note:*** There are other modes available besides the 50 MP mode, including a 25 MP mode, and two others. These modes will be discussed in greater detail in the **Shooting Menu 2** chapter under the **High Res Shot** heading (page 193). When you have selected High Res Shot on the Super Control Panel, the item just below its location on the panel (labeled 50MF) allows you to select the alternate modes, as does the menu setting at *Shooting Menu 1 > [Photo][Record Mode]*.

Now let's examine how to select one of the modes.

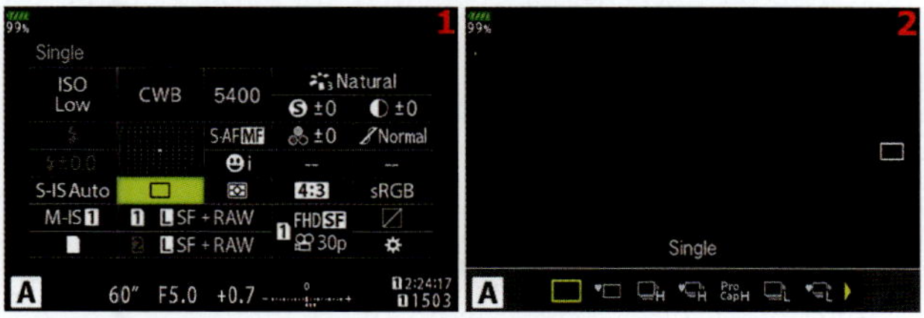

Figure 2.11: Choosing a Release mode

In figure 2.11 image 1, the Release Mode [Single] position is highlighted. Turn the Front Dial, and the 11 modes will scroll by. Refer to the previous list to determine which of the modes works best for your current needs. Stop scrolling on the mode you want to use. If you prefer to use the secondary screen to select a mode, press the OK button to open it.

Figure 2.11 image 2, shows the secondary screen with Single (Single-frame shooting) mode selected. Use the Arrow Pad keys to scroll left or right until you see the mode you want to use. Press the OK button to lock in your selection.

Note: You can also change the Release Mode by pressing the Sequential Shooting/Self-timer/HDR button on top of the camera (to the left of the On/Off lever) and turning the Rear Dial.

Settings Recommendation: I normally use Single mode because I do a lot of nature, landscape, and portrait work. I will often use the Silent modes when I am shooting a wedding, to keep from drawing attention to myself during the ceremony. I love the High Res Shot mode for landscapes (unless the wind is blowing hard, which can cause blurring). I don't do a lot of action shooting; however, if you do, there are few cameras currently on planet Earth that can match the E-M1II for high-speed image capture. You should take some time to experiment with each of these modes. Read this material carefully and try out each one. Once you have used each mode a few times, you will become more familiar with what to expect.

Metering

The Metering function gives you five different ways to obtain a correct exposure meter reading. Most people use the Digital ESP (matrix-type metering) setting because it is so amazingly good at providing a great exposure. However, for those who prefer other meter types, the camera is more than willing to provide! Let's examine each of the meter types and how to select them:

- **Digital ESP metering (ESP):** The camera meters the image with a matrix of 324 metered areas that cover the image frame. It uses complex mathematical computations to arrive at an excellent exposure. This metering mode works best for portraits when ☺ Face Priority is enabled.
- **Ctr-Weighted metering:** The camera averages the light between the subject and the background. It places more emphasis on exposure for the center area of the EVF or Live View screen, with less emphasis on parts of the scene that are farther away from the center.
- **Spot metering (Spot):** The camera uses a small circular area for metering, which coincides with the location of the active AF Point. This invisible circle is equivalent to 2 percent of the frame, and all metering takes place in this 2 percent area. You can move the Spot meter around the screen by moving the AF Point rectangle, positioning the active AF Point on any area of your subject to get a good exposure reading. If you prefer,

you can take multiple readings of different areas of the scene, determine the total light range, and set the exposure manually.

- **Spot Hilight (HI):** This type of metering is similar to standard Spot metering in that the camera uses a 2 percent area of the frame to meter. You can move the Spot meter around the screen by moving the AF Point rectangle. This metering mode is different from standard Spot metering because the camera tries to make white areas (highlights) stay white by increasing the exposure beyond a normal Spot reading to create a bright, high-key look.
- **Spot Shadow (SH):** This type of metering is also similar to normal Spot metering, using 2 percent of the frame. You can move the Spot meter around the screen by moving the AF Point rectangle. This metering mode is different from normal Spot metering because the camera tries to make dark areas (shadows) stay dark by decreasing the exposure below a normal Spot reading to create a low-key look.

Now let's see how to select one of the Metering modes.

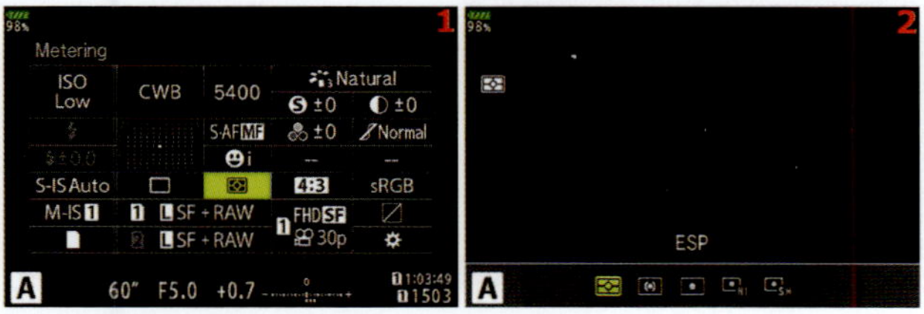

Figure 2.12: Choosing a Metering mode

In figure 2.12, image 1, the Metering position is highlighted. Turn the Front Dial, and the five modes will scroll by. Refer to the previous list to determine which of the modes works best for your needs. Stop scrolling on the mode you want to use. If you prefer to use the secondary screen to select a mode, press the OK button to open it.

Figure 2.12, image 2, shows the secondary Metering screen with Digital ESP metering mode selected. Use the Arrow Pad keys to scroll left or right until you see the mode you want to use. Press the OK button to lock in the mode.

Note: You can also change the Metering type by pressing the AF/Metering Mode button on top of the camera (to the left of the On/Off Lever) and turning the Front Dial.

Settings Recommendation: Digital ESP metering (ESP) is a very effective form of metering. I rarely need to use the other metering modes. Sometimes I might use the Spot meter to meter a bright subject against a darker background, but otherwise I am quite happy with ESP. Be sure to use a form of ☺ Face Priority when you are taking portraits with ESP. That seems to make the camera extra sensitive to exposing faces accurately, even if the background is dark and could cause some facial overexposure.

Aspect

The E-M1II is a Micro Four Thirds camera, which describes the aspect ratio of the sensor (4:3). Other camera brands have sensors with different aspect ratios. The Aspect function on the E-M1II allows you to change the normal 4:3 image aspect ratio to a different ratio that more closely matches the aspect ratios of other camera brands. In other words, the length and width of the image is cropped into a new relationship. The five available ratios are 4:3, 16:9, 3:2, 1:1, and 3:4.

The new Aspect ratio changes the final shape of the image, which means the camera must crop the picture. Therefore, use a different ratio only when you have special needs.

Image Aspect ratio is discussed in more detail in the **Shooting Menu 1** chapter under the **Image Aspect** subheading on page 181, including samples of the different ratios.

Let's examine how to select one of the five image Aspect ratios.

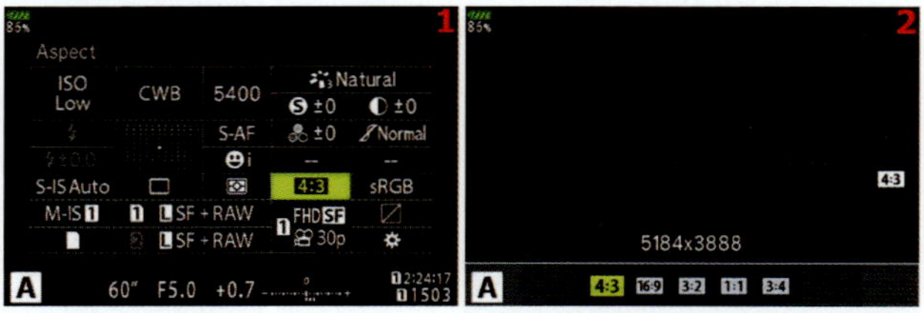

Figure 2.13: Choosing an image Aspect ratio

Figure 2.13, image 1, shows the Aspect position highlighted on the Super Control Panel with the 4:3 Aspect ratio selected. To select a different Aspect ratio, turn the Front Dial and the Aspect ratios will scroll by. Stop scrolling when the ratio you want to use is highlighted. You can also use the Aspect secondary screen to select an Aspect ratio. Press the OK button to open the secondary screen.

Figure 2.13, image 2, shows a list of five Aspect ratios across the bottom of the screen. There is also a handy guide above the line of ratios that shows the pixel dimensions of the corresponding Aspect ratio. I chose the default 4:3 Aspect, which displays pixel dimensions of 5184 × 3888. You can determine the megapixel (MP) rating of each Aspect ratio by multiplying the pixel dimensions. For instance, 5184 × 3888 = 20,155,392, or just over 20 MP. If you scroll through the rest of the settings and multiply the pixel dimensions, you will see that every ratio except 4:3 results in images of less than 20 MP. That is, Aspect settings other than 4:3 create smaller images due to cropping. Choose the Aspect you want to use by scrolling left or right with the Arrow Pad keys, highlighting the ratio you want to use, and pressing the OK button to lock in the Aspect.

Note: As you change Aspect ratios, the electronic viewfinder (EVF) and Live View monitor displays will adjust to the new shape so you can accurately shoot with the new Aspect. As a test, change the Aspect ratio, and then hold your camera up to your eye or examine the Live View monitor to see the difference in the image size and shape.

Settings Recommendation: I rarely change the Aspect ratio of the image with this function. I prefer to simply crop the image after the fact in my computer. However, if you need a specific Aspect ratio but don't have time to crop your images, the camera is ready to provide the ratio you need with no hassle and only minor image quality loss.

Color Space

The Color Space setting allows you to change the color gamut that your camera uses. That means the camera can capture colors over a narrower or wider range. Adobe RGB can capture color over a wider range than sRGB. Adobe RGB can capture about 50 percent of the color range that an average human eye can see, whereas sRGB can capture about 35 percent.

However, there are other factors to consider before you select a Color Space setting. For instance, websites, basic home inkjet printing, and retail color printing labs normally use sRGB because most amateur shooters use that camera setting. Commercial printers (books and magazines) and stock photo agencies prefer Adobe RGB.

This subject in considered in greater detail in the **Custom Menu** chapter under the subheading **Color Space** on page 546 (*Custom Menu > G. [Record Mode]/WB/Color > Color Space*). Please read that section to more fully understand the consequences of selecting one Color Space setting over the other. Here's how to select one of the Color space settings.

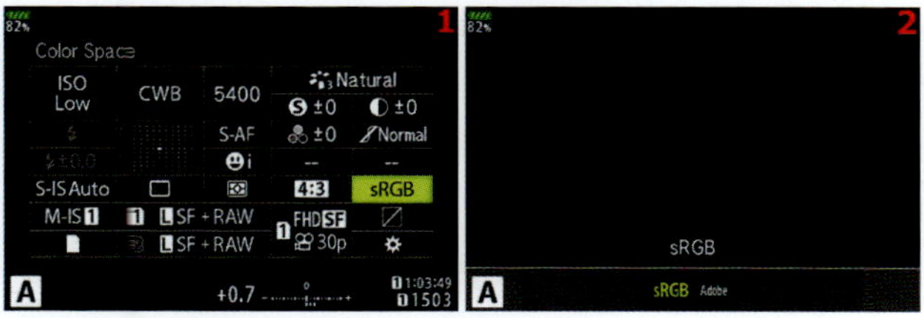

Figure 2.14: Choosing a Color Space

In figure 2.14, image 1, you can see that the Color Space function is selected. When it is highlighted, use the Front Dial to toggle between the two Color Spaces (sRGB or Adobe). Stop turning the dial when your favorite appears. Alternately, you can use the secondary screen to select a Color Space, as described next.

Figure 2.14, image 2, shows the Color Space selections along the bottom of the screen. Use the Arrow Pad keys to scroll back and forth until the mode you want to use (sRGB or Adobe RGB) is highlighted. Press the OK button to lock in your choice.

Settings Recommendation: As a stock photographer who licenses images online, I generally use the Adobe RGB Color Space because it maps well to CMYK offset printing that is used by commercial printers. Most stock sites expect you to submit images with the Adobe RGB Color Space. However, when I am shooting snapshots for online use, I use sRGB because it better matches the requirements of websites and home color inkjet printers.

[Video] Image Stabilizer

The [Video] Image Stabilizer function is similar to the [Photo] Image Stabilizer function—discussed on page 45—except that it is for video capture only. There are two [Video] Image Stabilizer modes, plus Off. Let's examine each of them:

- **Off:** Image stabilization will not be used while recording a video.
- **M-IS1:** The camera attempts to stabilize small camera movements by using the sensor-shift (VCM) mechanism along with electronic correction in the form of pixel shifting. This method will provide the most stable video, but may add a little jumpiness to the display if there is excessive camera movement.
- **M-IS2:** The camera attempts to stabilize small camera movements by using the sensor-shift (VCM) mechanism alone. No pixel-shifting electronic correction is used.

Now let's examine how to select one of the modes.

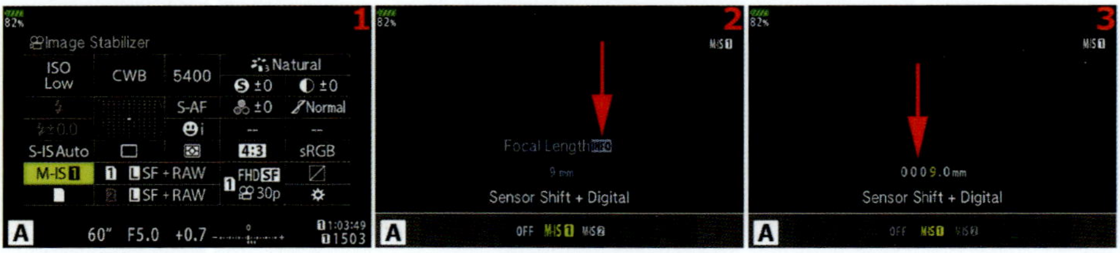

Figure 2.15: Selecting an Image Stabilization method for use during video capture

Figure 2.15, image 1, shows the [Video] Image Stabilizer setting on the Super Control Panel. You can rotate the Front Dial until the mode you want to use (M-IS1 or M-IS2) is displayed, or you can press the OK button to access the secondary screens (images 2 and 3).

The first secondary screen (image 2) shows the modes—Off, M-IS1 (Sensor Shift + Digital), and M-IS2 (Sensor Shift Only)—on the bottom of the screen. Use the Arrow Pad to choose the mode you want to use and press the OK button to lock it in.

If you are not using an M.Zuiko lens, or you are using a different-brand lens that cannot communicate electronically with the camera, you should provide the focal length of the lens. Press the INFO button (figure 2.15, image 2, red arrow) and use the Arrow Pad to input a focal length (figure 2.15, image 3, red arrow). Your focal length choices range from 0 mm to 1999 mm. If you are using a zoom lens, input the focal length you use most frequently. Image stabilization should still work reasonably well at the other available focal lengths on your zoom lens. (Please experiment with your lens before doing important work). Press the OK button when you have entered a focal length.

Settings Recommendation: I normally use the M-IS1 setting when I am capturing videos. However, I am aware that I may see an odd sliding or jumping motion in the video if I move the camera excessively. Both the M-IS1 and M-IS2 stabilization modes do a great job with stabilization. A good way to test the two modes is to walk down the road while recording a video. Switch between the two modes so that you can get a good look at how the camera responds when pixel-shifting (electronic correction) is enabled (M-IS1) and disabled (M-IS2). The appearance of the videos will help you decide which is most appropriate for your use.

[Photo][Record Mode] (Image Quality)

The [Photo][Record Mode]—or Image Quality—function allows you to choose the JPEG image quality for your still pictures. You can shoot in various JPEG sizes and pixel counts, including Large (L), Middle (M), and Small (S). You can also choose from several JPEG compression levels, including Super Fine (SF), Fine (F), Normal (N), and Basic (B).

This chapter will discuss how to choose an Image Quality for taking still pictures. However, there is a lot to discuss in making these choices. There is deeper information on this subject available in the **Shooting Menu 1** chapter under the **[Photo][Record mode]** subheading (page 173). Be sure to read that information before you shoot too many important images so you can make the best image quality choices.

On the Super Control Panel menus, you will see JPEG size and compression rate names combined. For instance, a Large-size, Fine-compression rate JPEG will be listed as LF, and a Medium-size, Normal-compression rate JPEG will be shown as MN.

The size for RAW mode, or the RAW file in a combination mode (e.g., LF+RAW), is always Large (L) with a 5184 × 3888 pixel ratio. RAW files always contain all available image data and cannot be resized in-camera. JPEG images have adjustable sizes, pixel counts, and compression rates.

The E-M1II has two SD memory card slots, unlike earlier cameras in the OM-D series. Therefore, there are two settings on the Super Control Panel for Image Quality, one for each card (figure 2.16A). The top item is for card slot 1 (top SD card slot in the camera) and the bottom item is for card slot 2 (bottom SD card slot in the camera).

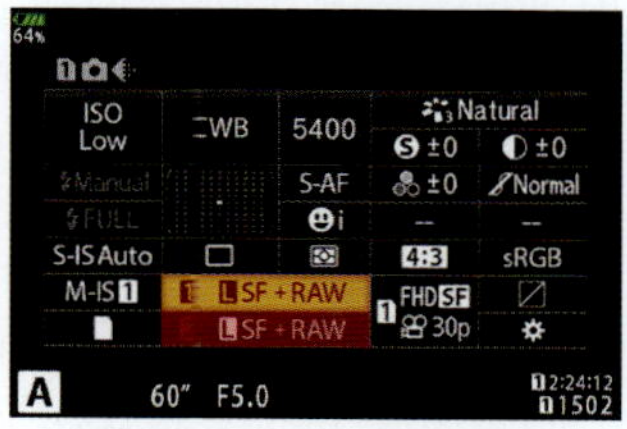

Figure 2.16A: Independent Image Quality settings for the two card slots (1 and 2)

Initially, the camera is set so that the two cards are independent of each other. One of the SD cards must be assigned to accept images, while the other card stays empty until assigned for use. The camera defaults to using only the top card (slot 1). You can change the card relationship for your camera by going to *Custom Menu > H1. Record/Erase > Card Slot Settings > Save Settings*. Instructions for how to do this can be found in the **Custom Menu** chapter under the **Card Slot Settings** subheading (page 549). You can also make these card relationship changes by using the [Photo] Save Settings function on the Super Control Panel, which is discussed in an upcoming section in this chapter (page 61).

For the purpose of understanding how to set the Image Quality on the Super Control Panel, we will consider only the top position in this section. The way the camera is initially configured from the factory is for the two memory cards to use exactly the same Image Quality settings. Therefore, if you make a change on the Super Control Panel for card 1, the same settings will automatically be entered into the Super Control Panel for card slot 2. Just keep in mind that you can separate this process so that the two cards can act independently, with different Image Quality settings (see page 55). At this point, it would benefit you to review the **Card Slot Settings** information on page 549 before continuing.

Let's see how to select an image quality for the SD card in card slot 1.

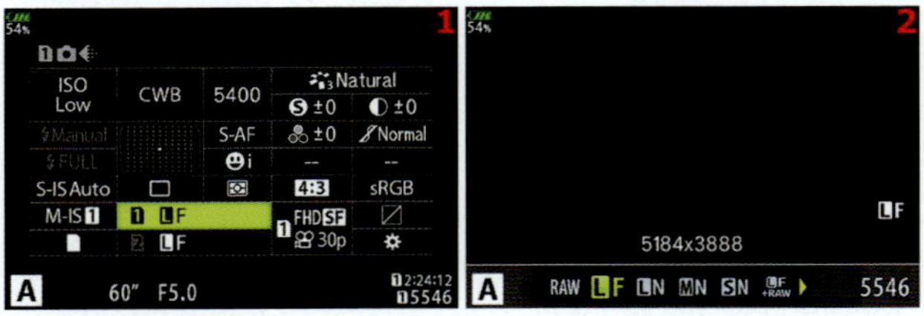

Figure 2.16B: Choosing an Image Quality setting

Figure 2.16B, image 1, shows the Image Quality position highlighted with Large Fine (LF) JPEG image quality selected. You may select one of the nine Image Quality settings by turning the Front Dial until the mode you want is displayed in the highlighted position. If you want to use the secondary screen to select a new Image Quality, press the OK button to open the secondary screen.

Figure 2.16B, image 2, shows the Image Quality secondary screen. You will find nine Image Quality choices along the bottom of the screen. Use the Arrow Pad keys to scroll left or right until the mode you want to use is highlighted, then press the OK button to lock in the mode.

Note: When it is enabled in the Custom Menu, there is also a JPEG Large Super Fine (LSF) Image Quality [Record Mode]. It will not appear in any of the Image Quality menus unless you enable it with the *Custom Menu > G. [Record Mode]/Color/WB > [Record Mode] Set* function. Enabling this option is discussed in the **Custom Menu** chapter under the **[Record Mode] Set** subheading on page 532.

Settings Recommendation: Because of its smaller sensor, I want my E-M1II to capture the best possible quality, so I most often use the RAW setting. However, shooting in RAW requires that I post-process the files and later convert them to JPEGs. If I need to give images to someone quickly, I may use the LSF+RAW setting and shoot both file types at the same time. This gives me the best of both worlds: a RAW file for when I have time to make a masterpiece, and a JPEG file for immediate use.

Even if you do not know how to post-process RAW files, I suggest that you capture both RAW and JPEG files so you will have an uncompressed original (RAW) file for especially good images later, when you have learned the needed post-processing skills. Shooting a

Large Super Fine JPEG (LSF) and a RAW file at the same time is as easy as selecting it from the Super Control Panel menu. Just look for LF+RAW or LSF+RAW. The camera will write both file formats to the memory card at the same time. The Large Super Fine (LSF) JPEG setting will be available *only* after you enable it, as previously described.

[Video] [Record Mode]

The E-M1II has an advanced video recording system with Cinematic 4K (C4K), 4K UHD, and lower resolution video capability (i.e., 1080p Full HD and 720p HD). There is an entire menu in the camera devoted to recording video, aptly named Video Menu. In this chapter, we will discuss how to choose these video modes, but there is a much deeper discussion of how the individual modes work in the **Video Menu and My Clips** chapter (page 249).

The camera also offers a [Video] [Record mode] function on the Super Control Panel (figure 2.17, image 1). The seven settings can be seen in this location when you rotate the Front Dial, or along the bottom of the secondary screen that appears when you press the OK button (figure 2.17, image 2). While you can select a [Video] [Record Mode] setting directly from the Super Control Panel, its individual subsettings are adjustable only on the secondary screen. With a setting highlighted on the secondary screen, press the INFO button to modify its subsettings. Following is a description of each of the seven settings:

- **Shooting Clips:** This first mode is designed to let you shoot short (1–8 second) video clips for uploading to social media websites. The three available *Movie Resolutions* are: 4K (2160p), FHD (1080p), and HD (720p). There are three *Compression/Bit Rates* available: SuperFine (26 Mbps), Fine (14 Mbps), and Normal (10 Mbps). There are five *Frame Rates* available: 60p, 50p, 30p, 25p, and 24p (availability of each Frame Rate depends on the Movie Resolution selected). With relatively low bit rates (high compression), this mode is clearly designed to make unedited video clips for uploading to the Internet. You cannot record a full-length video in this mode, with its *Clip Recording Time* limitation of 1 to 8 seconds (1s, 2s, 4s, and 8s).
- **Settings 1 to 4:** The next four settings are identical, allowing you to set up four separate video capture configurations for quick changes in the field. The available *Movie Resolutions* for each setting are: 4K (2160p), FHD (1080p), and HD (720p). The available *Compression/Bit Rates* are: ALL-Intra (no inter-frame compression at 202 Mbps), Super-Fine (52 Mbps), Fine (30 Mbps), and Normal (18 Mbps). The available *Frame Rates* are: 60p, 50p, 30p, 25p, and 24p (availability of each Frame Rate depends on the Movie Resolution selected). The camera allows you to record a video up to 29 minutes long or up to 4 GB in file size, whichever comes first. Use these four settings to configure your four favorite video capture methods and select between them at will.
- **Custom:** This mode is like an all-in-one mode that allows you to configure a setting for special circumstances. You have more choices in this mode than in any of the other modes. You can choose to adjust Movie Resolution, Compression/Bit Rate, Frame Rate, Clip Recording Time, and Slow or Fast Motion:

a. *Movie Resolutions* include: C4K (Cinematic 4K or 4096 × 2160 in 17:9 aspect ratio), 4K (UHD or 3840 × 2160 in 16:9 aspect ratio), FHD (1920 × 1080 in 16:9 aspect ratio), and HD (1280 × 720 in 16:9 aspect ratio).

b. *Compression/Bit Rates* include: ALL-Intra (237 Mbps in C4K, or 202 Mbps in normal 4K), SuperFine (52 Mbps), Fine (30 Mbps), and Normal (18 Mbps).

c. *Frame Rates* include: 60p, 50p, 30p, 25p, and 24p (availability of each Frame Rate depends on the Movie Resolution selected).

d. *Clip Recording Times* include: Off (29 minutes maximum), 1s, 2s, 4s, and 8s.

e. *Slow or Fast Motion* provides: Slow Fast Off (normal speed); seven fast-motion speeds: x1.2, x1.25, x2, x2.5, x3.75, x5, x10; and two slow-motion speeds: x0.5, x0.6.

   Custom mode provides a one-stop-shop for you to choose any combination of [Video] [Record Mode] the camera offers.

- **Motion JPEG** (or M-JPEG): This is an older HD format (720p) that provides excellent quality video but produces *huge* files. Each individual frame of the video is an individually compressed (just under 1 MP) JPEG image. This mode will fill up your memory card(s) very quickly.

Now let's consider how to select and configure one of these modes.

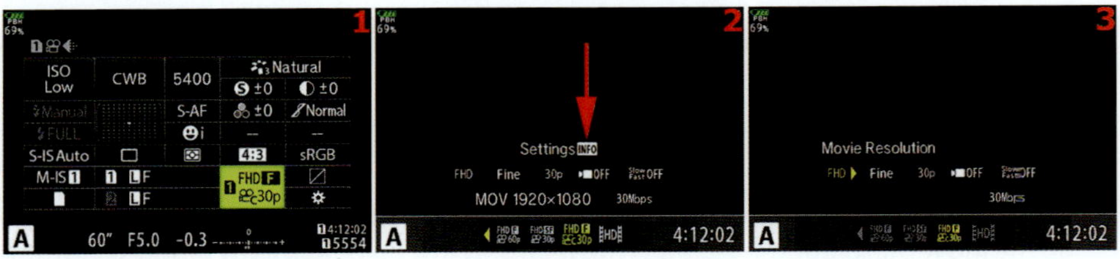

Figure 2.17: Choosing a [Video] [Record Mode]

Figure 2.17, image 1, shows the [Video] [Record mode] function highlighted in green. You can rotate the Front Dial to select one of the preconfigured modes, or you can press the OK button to open the secondary screen, where you can select or change the settings for a particular mode.

Figure 2.17, image 2, shows the secondary screen for the Custom mode. Notice that you can press the INFO button (red arrow) to access the five subsettings for the Custom mode (image 3): Movie Resolution, Compression/Bit Rate, Frame Rate, Clip Recording Time, and Slow or Fast Motion. Movie Resolution is currently selected in image 3. You can scroll to the left or right with the Arrow Pad to select another subsetting for the Custom mode.

Press the OK button when you have finished configuring the [Video] [Record Mode] and the camera will use it for your video recordings until you choose a different setting.

Settings Recommendation: I leave my camera set to the Custom mode so that I can use my favorite [Video] [Record Mode] or make adjustments to its subsettings quickly. I tend to shoot mostly 1080p video of family and friends, so I need video less than some enthusiasts might. If you need to shoot different types of video without taking much time to configure modes, then you should configure each of the individual Settings 1 to 4 with a different video recording specification. For example, Setting 1 could be 4K with the best bit rate and 30p frame rate; Setting 2 could be set to FHD (1080p) at a SuperFine bit rate and 60p frame rate; and Setting 3 could be set to FHD at a Fine bit rate and 30p frame rate. The four settings (1–4) allow you to configure the camera for four different ways of recording video, with the Custom setting providing a fifth. I do not use the Motion JPEG (HD) setting because 720p is too small for me and I do not like the giant video files M-JPEG creates. I also rarely use the Shooting Clips mode that lets you create 1–8 second, high-compression video clips. If you shoot a lot of video for social media, you may love this mode.

Please try each mode and carefully examine how it looks when you are shooting static-subject video and moving-subject video. The E-M1II's video system is rather advanced compared to its predecessors, which means there are lots of new things to learn! Be sure to read over the **[Movie] Specifications Settings** section of the **Recording Movies, Video Menu, and My Clips** chapter (page 283) to get an even deeper explanation of these new video modes.

Highlight&Shadow Control

The Highlight&Shadow Control function provides you with a way to visually adjust the shadows, midtones, and highlights in a live image prior to capture. You will immediately see how each adjustment affects the live image on the camera monitor. Let's see how it works.

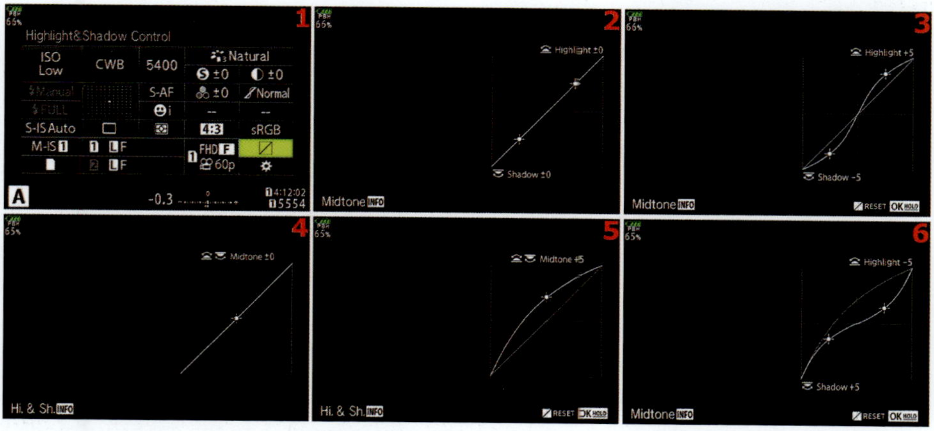

Figure 2.18: Visually adjusting the Highlights, Shadows, and Midtones before capture

Figure 2.18, image 1, shows the location of the Highlight&Shadow Control. This control is available for making adjustments to a live image on the camera's rear monitor only. If you try to put the camera up to your eye, the controls will disappear. Therefore, choose the function and press the OK button to open the secondary screen for live-image fine-tuning. Have your camera in hand as we make these adjustments.

Note: I photographed these screens with the lens cap on so that you can see the controls with maximum contrast. When you are using this control, the screens shown in figure 2.18, images 2–6, will display your subject instead of a black background. When you use the control, you will see exactly how each adjustment affects the image you are preparing to capture.

Figure 2.18, image 2, shows the initial secondary screen, with the Highlight and Shadow adjustment control. To adjust the Highlights in the currently displayed image, press up or down on the Arrow Pad and you will see the plus-shaped (+) indicator on Highlight side of the grid move up or down. Note how the highlights in your image change as you move the indicator in up to seven increments (+/–) in either direction (14 increments total).

Next, press left or right on the Arrow Pad and you will see the Shadow adjustment indicator move while the shadow detail in your image changes. Figure 2.18, image 3, shows that I have moved the Highlight indicator to +5, and the Shadow indicator to –5. Again, you will be doing this with a live image on the screen so you can immediately see how the adjustment affects the exposure of the subject.

In image 3, you can also see a straight diagonal line underneath the Highlight and Shadow curve. This diagonal line represents the midtones in the image and is also adjustable.

Notice in the bottom left corner of figure 2.18, image 3, that you can press the INFO button to open the Midtone adjustment screen shown in image 4. This separate Midtone adjustment also immediately affects the live image. You can adjust it in up to seven +/– increments (14 increments total). In figure 2.18, image 5, you can see that the Midtone adjustment is set to +5.

You can toggle between the Shadow&Highlight and Midtone adjustment screens by pressing the INFO button. You will see each of the adjustments on the same grid, with the currently selected adjustment in brighter white and with the plus-shaped indicator(s). Figure 2.18, images 5 and 6, show both sides of the INFO button screen toggle.

When you're pleased with the way your image looks, press the OK button to save the setting, and then press the Shutter button to take the picture with your adjustments in place.

If you want to clear the adjustments so that future images are not affected, open the secondary screen and hold down the OK button until the Highlight&Shadow and Midtone adjustments are reset back to +/– 0.

Settings Recommendation: I use this function when I am shooting a contrasty static macro image. I first set the exposure the normal way (according to the exposure mode I am using: P, A, S, or M), and then fine-tune the highlights, shadows, and midtones with this control. Of course, using this control takes more time, so it is best for slower forms of photography.

[Photo] Save Settings

The [Photo] Save Settings function allows you to specify where your camera saves the images you take. In other words, it lets you choose which memory card combination the camera will use when it saves an image you just captured.

The E-M1II defaults to saving all images to the memory card in the top slot (Slot 1) and ignores the card in the bottom slot (Slot 2), but you can change this relationship if you wish. Let's take a look at all of the available settings.

- **Standard:** If there is only one memory card in the camera, the camera will save all images to that card (of course). If there are two cards in the camera, the E-M1II will save all images to whichever card slot is specified in *Custom Menu > H1. Record/Erase > Card Slot Settings > [Photo] Save Slot*. You can select from 1 (Slot 1) or 2 (Slot 2). This mode provides for only one Image Quality format, such as Large Fine (LF) JPEG, or a combined format, such as LF+RAW, to be used at one time. You can choose which card (Slot 1 or Slot 2) will save your videos by selecting the *[Video] Save Slot* setting at the same Custom Menu location. When the selected memory card becomes full for either capture type (photo or video), you cannot save any more pictures or videos. You can use the Standard mode to direct all images to one of the memory cards and all videos to the other memory card, or you can direct all images and videos to just one of the memory cards. ***Note:*** The Super Control Panel's Card Slot Settings secondary screen (Figure 2.19A, image 2) is the same as the *Custom Menu > H1. Record/Erase > Card Slot Settings* screen.
- **Auto Switch:** This mode is very similar to Standard mode. When the card you've chosen for [Photo] Save Slot is full, the camera will automatically switch to the other memory card, allowing you to continue taking images until both cards are full. You may use only one Image Quality format (or one combined format, such as LF+RAW) at a time. This setting *does not apply to capturing video*—it applies only to still image capture. The camera will *not* switch to the other memory card when it runs out of space for recording video. Instead, the video will merely stop recording when the card becomes full. If you attempt to capture another video without changing to a memory card that has sufficient space, you will see an error message on the monitor telling you the card is full.
- **Dual Independent ↓**: You can select a different Image Quality format for each memory card. In other words, if you choose Large Fine JPEG (LF) for Slot 1 and RAW for Slot 2, when you press the Shutter button, the camera will capture and save a Large Fine (LF) JPEG file to card slot 1, and it will also save a RAW (ORF) file to card slot 2. If either card becomes full, you can *no longer take pictures,* even if there is space available on the other memory card.
- **Dual Independent ↑**: This mode works the same as Dual Independent ↓ (previous list item) in that you can choose a different Image Quality format for each memory card. However, if either card becomes full, you may *continue taking pictures,* as long as there is space available on the other memory card.

- **Dual Same ↓**: This mode lets you choose a certain Image Quality format for both cards to receive at the same time. Whatever Image Quality you choose is written to both cards simultaneously. If either memory card becomes full, you may *no longer take pictures*.
- **Dual Same ↑**: This mode works the same as Dual Same ↓ (previous list item) in that you can choose a certain Image Quality format for both cards to receive at the same time. However, if either memory card becomes full, you may *continue taking pictures*, as long as the other memory card has available space.

Now let's consider how to use these modes.

Using the Standard and Auto Switch Modes

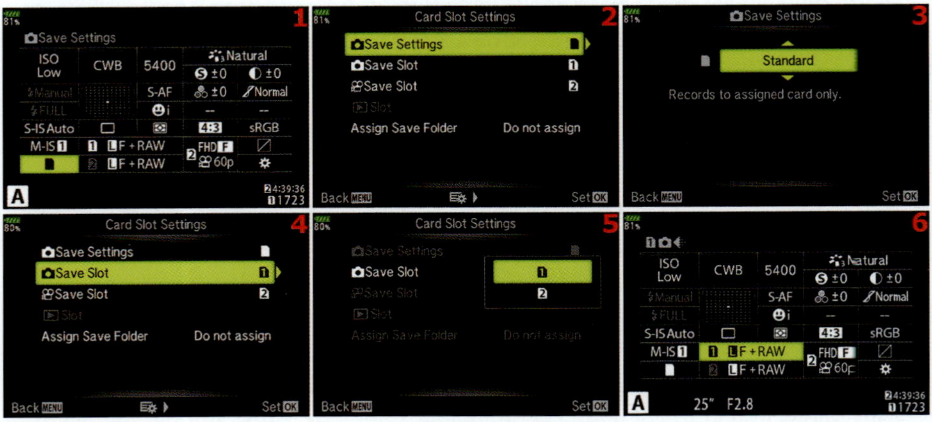

Figure 2.19A: Using Standard mode (or Auto Switch mode)

Figure 2.19A, image 1, shows the [Photo] Save Settings location on the Super Control Panel. You can use the Front Dial to scroll through all of the settings discussed in the previous list, stopping on the one you want to use. However, these settings require additional configuration, so let's start by examining the secondary screens needed to configure the Standard and Auto Switch modes. Press the OK button to open the initial secondary screen.

Figure 2.19A, image 2, shows the Card Slot Settings secondary screen. Use the Arrow Pad to highlight [Photo] Save Settings and scroll to the right.

Figure 2.19A, image 3, shows the [Photo] Save Settings screen with Standard showing in the up/down menu. Select Standard or Auto Switch and press the OK button to Set the mode. The camera will switch back to the Card Slot Settings screen (figure 2.19A, image 4). Scroll down to [Photo] Save Slot, and then scroll to the right.

Figure 2.19A, image 5, displays the small window that opens, offering you the choice of card slot 1 or card slot 2. Choose the card slot that contains the card to which you want to save photos and press the OK button to Set the choice.

Both Standard and Auto Switch work the same way, except that Auto Switch allows the camera to automatically switch to the other memory card if the card you selected under [Photo] Save Slot runs out of space. The Standard mode will *not* automatically switch, and you will see a *Card Full* error instead. Now that you have selected the mode and slots to use, you should select an Image Quality for the still images you will capture in this mode. Press the MENU button to return to the Super Control Panel.

Figure 2.19A, image 6, shows the two Image Quality settings—one for each card. The top Image Quality selection for card slot 1 is highlighted in green, with the location for card slot 2 directly below it. You will note that both card slots have the same Image Quality mode showing. Since the Standard and Auto Switch modes use only one assigned card slot, you cannot select a different Image Quality mode for card slot 1 and card slot 2. If you change either of the two Image Quality settings, the opposite setting will change to the same value. Now you can go ahead and take your pictures.

Using the Dual Independent Modes (↑↓)

Following are the methods used to configure [Photo] Save Settings for the two Dual Independent modes.

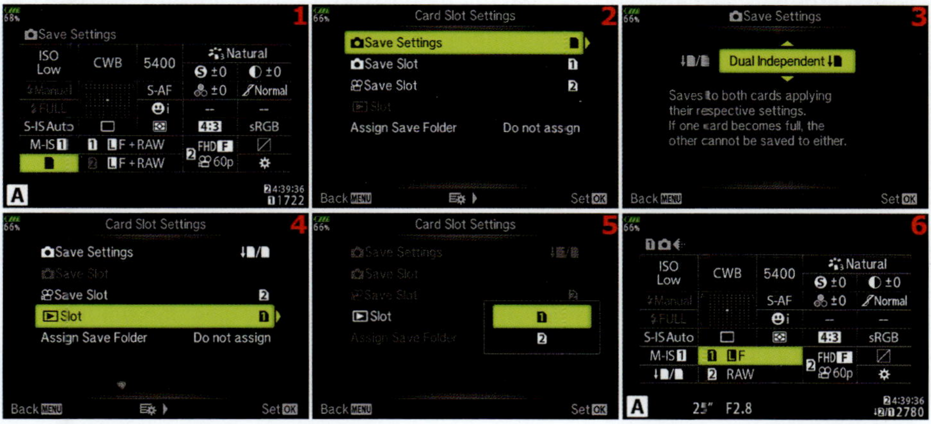

Figure 2.19B: Using the Dual Independent modes

With the [Photo] Save Settings location highlighted on the Super Control Panel (figure 2.19B, image 1), press the OK button to open the initial secondary screen.

Figure 2.19B, image 2, shows the Card Slot Settings secondary screen. Use the Arrow Pad to highlight [Photo] Save Settings and scroll to the right.

Figure 2.19B, image 3, shows the [Photo] Save Settings screen with Dual Independent ↓ showing in the up/down menu. Select Dual Independent ↓ or Dual Independent ↑ and press the OK button to Set the mode. The camera will switch back to the Card Slot Settings screen (figure 2.19B, image 4). From that screen select the [Playback] Slot setting and scroll to the right.

When you use either of the Dual Independent modes, the camera will display the images from only one of the cards during image Playback. Figure 2.19B, image 5, shows the small window that appears when you scroll to the right on the [Playback] Slot setting. Choose the card slot (1 or 2) from which you want to display images when you press the camera's Playback button.

The images will look the same regardless of which card slot you choose. The only difference is that they may be in different image formats (e.g., RAW versus JPEG; see the next paragraph about Image Quality). However, one of the cards may have images on it that the other does not, so you may prefer to display images from one card over the other. You can switch the Playback image display between the two cards at any time with the [Playback] Slot setting. Press the MENU button to return to the Super Control Panel.

Figure 2.19B, image 6, shows the two Image Quality settings—one for each card. The top Image Quality selection for card slot 1 is highlighted in green, with the location for card slot 2 directly below it. You will note that the two card slots have different Image Quality modes showing. You may select a particular Image Quality mode for card slot 1 and a different Image Quality mode for card slot 2. There are differences when you are using either of the two modes, as follows:

a) **Dual Independent ↓:** If you selected this mode in figure 2.19B, image 3, and you run out of card space on *either* of the memory cards, the camera will refuse to take any more pictures until you insert a memory card with more space. If you attempt to take more pictures, you will see a *Card Full* warning on the monitor.
b) **Dual Independent ↑:** If you selected this mode in figure 2.19B, image 3, and you run out of card space on either of the memory cards, the camera will continue taking pictures, provided that the other memory card still has space. The Image Quality format that will be written after one card becomes full matches the assigned format for whichever memory still has space. For example, if you have card slot 1 assigned to receive Large Fine (LF) JPEGs and card slot 2 assigned to receive RAW files, and the memory card in card slot 1 becomes full, the camera will stop attempting to write LF JPEG files to card slot 1, but will continue writing RAW files (only) to card slot 2.

Now you can take your pictures.

Using the Dual Same Modes (↑↓)

Following are the methods used to configure [Photo] Save Settings for the two Dual Same modes.

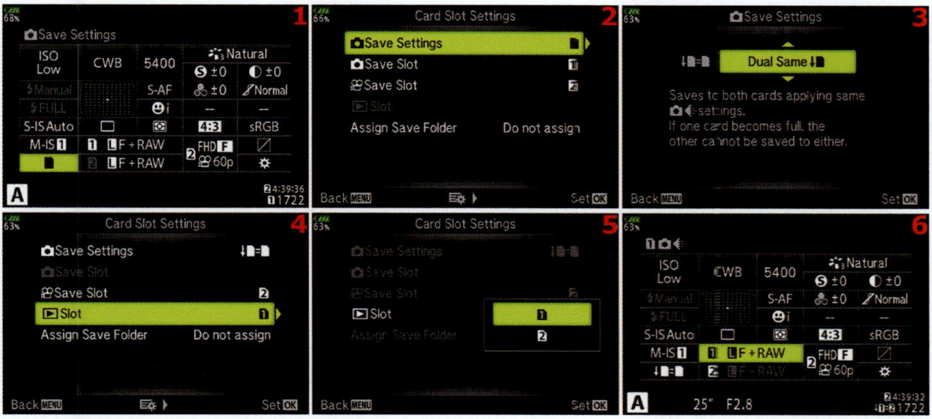

Figure 2.19C: Using the Dual Same Modes

With the [Photo] Save Settings location highlighted on the Super Control Panel (figure 2.19C, image 1), press the OK button to open the initial secondary screen.

Figure 2.19C, image 2, shows the Card Slot Settings secondary screen. Use the Arrow Pad to highlight [Photo] Save Settings and scroll to the right.

Figure 2.19C, image 3, shows the [Photo] Save Settings screen with Dual Same ↓ showing in the up/down menu. Select Dual Same ↓ or Dual Same ↑ and press the OK button to Set the mode. The camera will switch back to the Card Slot Settings screen (figure 2.19C, image 4). From that screen select the [Playback] Slot setting and scroll to the right.

When you use either of the Dual Same modes, the camera will display the images from only *one* of the cards during image Playback. Figure 2.19C, image 5, shows the small popup window that will appear when you scroll to the right on the [Playback] Slot setting. Choose the card slot (1 or 2) from which you want to display images when you press the camera's Playback button.

The images will look the same regardless of which card slot you choose. The only difference is that they may be in different image formats (e.g., RAW versus JPEG). However, one of the cards may have images on it that the other does not, so you may prefer to display one card over the other. You can switch the Playback image display between the two cards at any time with the [Playback] Slot setting. Press the MENU button to return to the Super Control Panel.

Figure 2.19C, image 6, shows the two Image Quality settings—one for each card. The top Image Quality selection for card slot 1 is highlighted in green, with the location for card slot 2 directly below it. You will note that both card slots have the same Image

Quality mode showing. You cannot select a different Image quality mode for card slot 1 and card slot 2—that's why they call this mode Dual *Same*. The camera writes the same image format to both cards. If you change either of the two Image Quality settings, the opposite setting will change to the same value. The differences between the two modes are as follows:

a) **Dual Same ↓:** If you selected this mode in figure 2.19C, image 3, and you run out of card space on *either* of the memory cards, the camera will refuse to take any more pictures until you insert a memory card with more space. If you attempt to take more pictures, you will see a *Card Full* warning on the monitor.
b) **Dual Same ↑:** If you selected this mode in figure 2.19C, image 3, and you run out of card space on *either* of the memory cards, the camera will continue taking pictures, provided that the other memory card still has space.

Now you can take your pictures.

Settings Recommendation: After careful consideration, with regard to my preferred style of photography (landscapes), I selected Dual Independent ↑ mode. This mode allows me to use more than one Image Quality format, and will keep on shooting when one of the cards gets full.

However, if you do not need to use different Image Quality formats, you could use Auto Switch to allow the camera to continue writing pictures to the secondary memory card after the primary card becomes full. This is like the "overflow" method on many cameras.

Using the Dual Same ↑ mode is like the backup method on many cameras, in that it takes the same picture and writes it to both cards. I generally avoid any mode that limits me to writing to just one card at a time (Standard), or stops accepting images when one of the two memory cards is full (Dual Independent ↓ and Dual Same ↓).

Read this chapter section over carefully and try to fully understand how these modes work. You will be able to use them all for one style of photography or another. If you don't want to take the time to learn these modes in detail, just remember to use modes with the up arrow. Always climb up ↑, never fall down ↓.

Memory Card Compatibility

The E-M1II camera is compatible with the following memory card types: SD, SDHC, SDXC, and Eye-Fi. However, the memory card slots are compatible with different types of cards. The top slot (slot 1) is compatible with the faster UHS-II memory cards, while the bottom slot (slot 2) is compatible with UHS-I memory cards. For best results, use the top slot—with a UHS-II card—when you are recording 4K UHD video or shooting with a still-image Release Mode, such as ProCapture (extremely high-speed continuous burst shooting). Slower card types will probably work okay, but there is a slight chance that you may drop video frames or miss photo frames. Test this carefully before doing commercial or important work.

Button Function

In the Camera Setup and Control Reference chapter we examined each of the external controls on the camera body. Recall that many of the buttons are programmable; that is, you can assign a task to the button and change it to another task later. The Button Tasks for making still images are listed in **Appendix A: Still Image Button Task Reference**, which can be found on the downloadable resources webpage: www.rockynook.com/olympusem1markii.

The Button Function location on the Super Control Panel is a shortcut to the *Custom Menu > B. Button/Dial/Lever > Button Function* settings. These Button Function settings allow you to assign Button Tasks directly to the programmable buttons. We will cover the Button Function task assignments in greater detail in the **Custom Menu** chapter, under the **Button Function [Programmable Buttons] (B)** subheading on page 432.

Since the full description of how to use this function is lengthy, there is no need to repeat it here. This section will give a brief explanation of how to do a single button assignment. Please refer to the later material for a complete description of all the available Button Tasks for each programmable button on your camera, lens, and HLD-9 power battery holder.

Important Note: Olympus uses the term *Button Function* to describe the physical button to which a task can be assigned. The functionality that can be assigned to the button (what it does) is called a *Button Task* (my words, to make it easier to understand). Therefore, in this book you will read that a particular Button Task has been assigned to a certain Button Function, which simply means the physical button (Button Function) has been given a task (Button Task) to do when you press the button. As previously mentioned, there is a list of Button Tasks in Appendix A on the downloadable resources webpage.

Let's see how to assign a Button Task to the Fn1 Function.

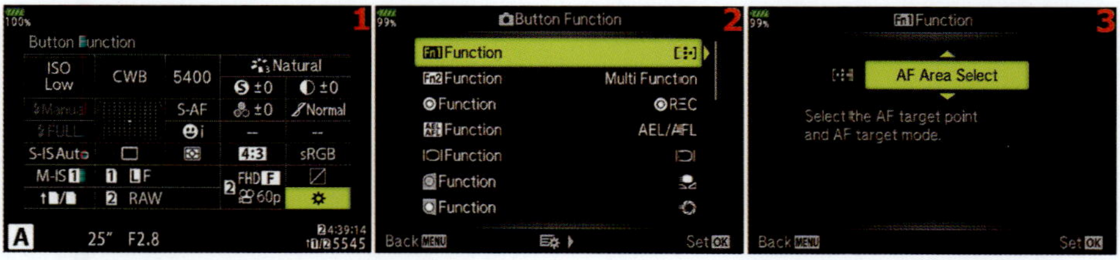

Figure 2.20: Assigning a Button Task (e.g., AF Area Select) to a Button Function (e.g., Fn1)

In figure 2.20, image 1, you can see that the Button Function position is highlighted. You *cannot* scroll through the various Button Functions (e.g., Fn1, Fn2) by turning the Front Dial. Instead, you must press the OK button to open the secondary screen showing all the available Button Functions.

Figure 2.20, image 2, shows the Button Function selection menu. On this screen you will find a list of 16 Button Functions. Highlight the one to which you want to assign a

Button Task and scroll to the right. In this example we are working with the Fn1 Function.

Figure 2.20, image 3, displays an up/down menu that you can scroll through by pressing up or down on the Arrow Pad keys. There are many Button Tasks listed in this up/down menu. Refer to Appendix A on the downloadable resources webpage for a list of Button Tasks that you can assign to the Fn1 Function. Not all tasks are available for all buttons. After you have assigned a Button Task, the task will execute when you press the Fn1 button on the back of the E-M1II. You can see in figure 2.20, image 3, that I selected the Button Task called [+] AF Area Select. Choose a Button Task from the menu, and then press the OK button to lock in the task for the Fn1 Function.

Follow the same process to assign a task to each of the buttons on the camera, lens, and optional HLD-9 power battery holder (if you have one), referring to the Appendix A for an explanation of each Button Task.

Settings Recommendation: This camera is very flexible and powerful due to the large number of tasks you can assign to the individual buttons, dials, and levers. You will spend a lot of time examining and making decisions about which Button Task to assign to which Button Function. Please get used to calling the camera buttons *Button Functions,* not just buttons, at least when you are making task assignments. That's what Olympus does, and if you do not understand this, it will be difficult to configure your camera later. The same goes for the dials and levers. They are called Dial Functions and Lever Functions instead of just dials and levers. The entire B. Button/Dial/Lever section of the Custom Menu is devoted to assigning various tasks to Button, Dial, and Lever *Functions*.

In part two of this chapter, we will consider another set of screens called Live Control, which many people prefer over the Super Control Panel.

PART 2: LV Super Control Panel (Live SCP), Live Control, Live Guide, and Art Menu

The E-M1II is no slouch when it comes to providing screens you can use to adjust the camera. In addition to the Super Control Panel, there are four important Live View function screens: the LV Super Control Panel (referred to as Live SCP in the camera menu), Live Control, Live Guide, and Art Menu (figure 2.21A). The Live Control is disabled by default, but we will enable it.

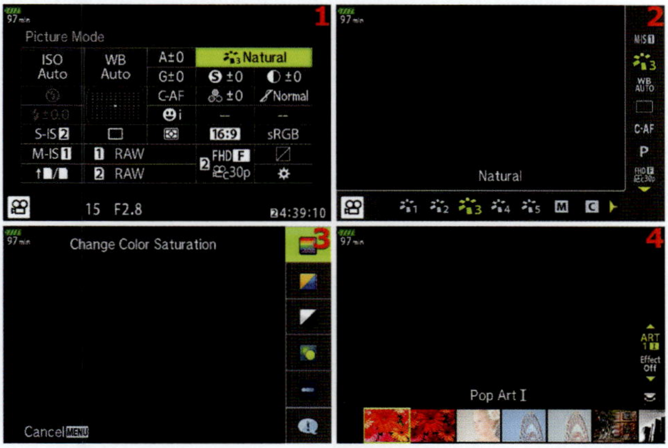

Figure 2.21A: (1) LV Super Control Panel, (2) Live Control, (3) Live Guide, and (4) Art Menu

To access these four Live View function screens you must make sure they are enabled on your camera. Before we discuss how to use each screen, let's examine the Custom Menu function that allows you to enable or disable each screen.

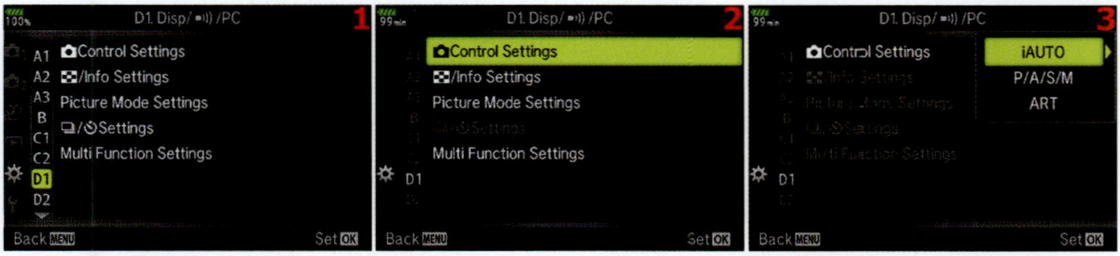

Figure 2.21B: Custom Menu screens to access the four Live View function screen settings

Open the menu system by pressing the MENU button on the back of the camera. The Custom Menu is represented by the gear symbol on the left side of the menu screen—the fifth menu from the top. Highlight D1 and scroll to the right (figure 2.21B, image 1).

Figure 2.21B, image 2, shows section D1 of the Custom Menu. Highlight [Photo] Control Settings and scroll to the right. This will open the small popup menu shown in image 3, from which you can select which of the four Live View function screens will appear when you use each of the Mode Dial settings: iAUTO, P/A/S/M, and ART. Not all four Live View function screens are available for every setting on the Mode Dial.

Enabling or Disabling Specific Live View Function Screens

The following subsections describe how to enable or disable each of the Live View function screens for each of the Mode Dial settings.

iAUTO Function Screens

The iAUTO setting allows you to select which of three available Live View function screens are active when the Mode Dial is set to iAUTO mode. iAUTO mode is the camera's point-and-shoot mode, allowing you to take great pictures without worrying too much about camera settings. The camera will decide how to make a good exposure. However, you may control some of the camera settings with the three available Live View function screens under iAUTO: Live Guide, Live Control, and LV Super Control Panel. Let's see how to enable the screens.

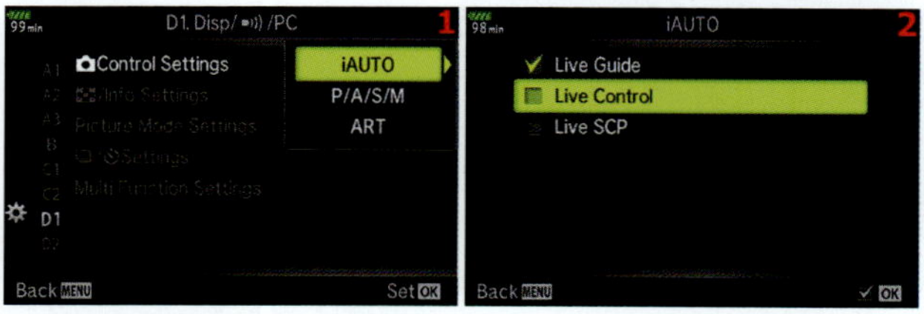

Figure 2.21C: Enabling Live View function screens under iAUTO mode

Figure 2.21C begins where figure 2.21B left off. In image 1 you see that iAUTO is highlighted. Scroll to the right to access the three iAUTO Live View function screen selections: Live Guide, Live Control, and LV Super Control Panel (Live SCP) (figure 2.21C, image 2).

To enable a Live View function screen, highlight it and press the OK button to put a check mark in the box next to the name. To disable a function screen, press the OK button again to remove the check mark. In image 2, you can see that Live Guide is enabled, but Live Control and LV Super Control Panel (Live SCP) are disabled. Put a check mark in the boxes of any function screens you want to use when the camera is set to iAUTO. You can scroll through the enabled screens by pressing the INFO button when in iAUTO mode.

Settings Recommendation: Many people *do not* enable the Live Control and LV Super Control Panel for iAUTO mode because it is a mode that's primarily used for fun shooting, not making a lot of camera adjustments. I enable only the Live Guide for iAUTO mode.

P/A/S/M Function Screens

The P/A/S/M setting allows you to select which of two available Live View function screens are active when you have the Mode Dial set to one of the four exposure modes (P, A, S, or M): Live Control and LV Super Control Panel. Live Control defaults to off, while LV Super Control Panel defaults to on. Let's see how to enable or disable the screens.

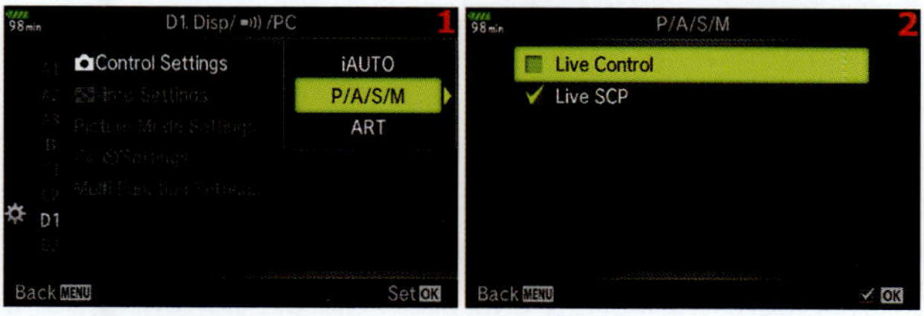

Figure 2.21D: Enabling Live View function screens under the P, A, S, M modes

Figure 2.21D begins where figure 2.21B left off. In image 1 you see that the P/A/S/M mode is highlighted. Scroll to the right to access the two Live View function screen selections: Live Control and LV Super Control Panel (Live SCP) (figure 2.21D, image 2).

To enable a Live View function screen, highlight it and press the OK button to put a check mark in the box next to the name. To disable a function screen, press the OK button again to remove the check mark. In image 2, you can see that LV Super Control Panel (Live SCP) is enabled, but Live Control is disabled. Put a check mark in the boxes of any function screens you want to use when the camera is set to P/A/S/M. You can scroll through the enabled screens by pressing the INFO button when in P, A, S, or M mode.

Settings Recommendation: Many people appreciate the functionality of the Live Control screen, which provides a subset of the 28 functions and settings found on the Super Control Panel and the LV Super Control Panel. I always enable the Live Control. Most of the time I prefer it over the LV Super Control Panel. The Live Control provides 14 of the most-used camera adjustments in a format that makes it easy to change the settings. I like that I can have both the Live Control and LV Super Control Panel screens available in Live View mode and toggle between them by pressing the INFO button.

ART Function Screens

The ART setting allows you to select which of three available Live View function screens are active when you have the Mode Dial set to the ART mode: Art Menu, Live Control, and LV Super Control Panel. Live Control and LV Super Control Panel default to off, while Art Menu defaults to on. Let's see how to enable or disable the screens

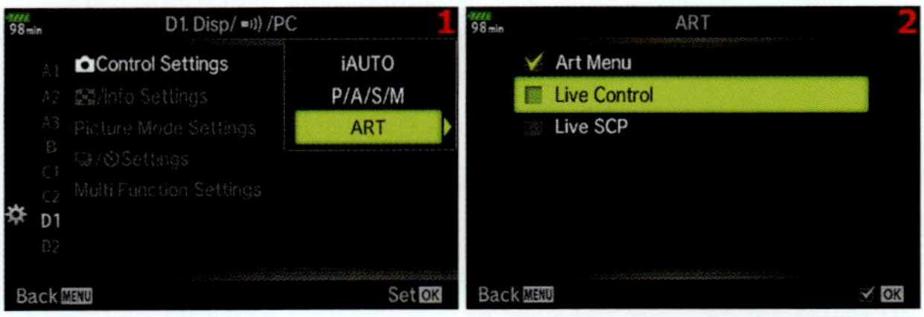

Figure 2.21E: Enabling Live View function screens under ART mode

Figure 2.21E begins where figure 2.21B left off. In image 1 you see that the ART mode is highlighted. Scroll to the right to access the three Live View function screen selections: Art Menu, Live Control, and LV Super Control Panel (Live SCP) (figure 2.21E, image 2).

To enable a Live View function screen, highlight it and press the OK button to put a check mark in the box next to the name. To disable a function screen, press the OK button again to remove the check mark. In image 2, you can see that Art Menu is enabled, but Live Control and LV Super Control Panel (Live SCP) are disabled. Put a check mark in the boxes of any function screens you want to use when the camera is set to ART. You can scroll through the enabled screens by pressing the INFO button when in ART mode.

Settings Recommendation: Many people use ART mode as a highly creative mode and may want to access more camera settings than in other modes. I generally enable all three of the Live View function screens, especially the Live Control, so that I can scroll through all of the available camera settings when I am being especially creative with the ART mode. The Art Menu (figure 2.21A, image 4) allows you to choose from 29 Art Filters to flavor your images in various ways.

Now let's take a closer look at all four of the different Live View function screens.

LV Super Control Panel (Live SCP)

The LV Super Control Panel (figure 2.22) is a Live View version of the Super Control Panel. It is the default control screen that appears when you are using Live View to view your subject on the monitor and then press the OK button.

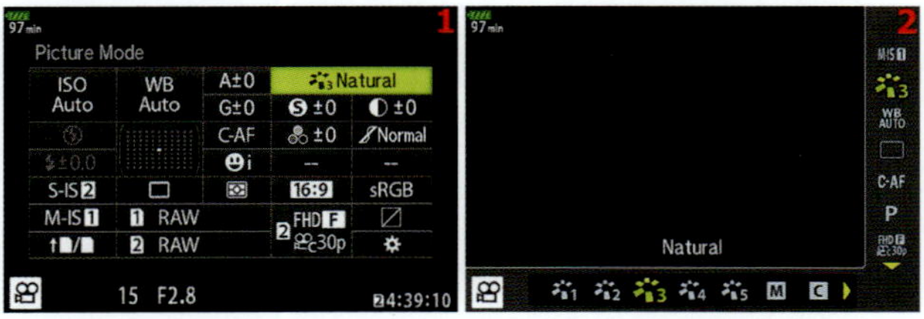

Figure 2.22: The LV Super Control Panel and a secondary screen

There are no major differences between the Super Control Panel and the LV Super Control Panel. They have the same functions and secondary screen settings. What you learned in Part 1 of this chapter applies equally to the LV Super Control Panel. Thus, there is no need to discuss any of the functions shown on the LV Super Control Panel since we already covered them in detail in our discussion of the Super Control Panel.

Why Is There an LV Super Control Panel and a Super Control Panel?

Many of you may question why there is a LV Super Control Panel and a Super Control Panel. Basically, Olympus feels that a version of the Super Control Panel is the best interface for accessing 28 camera functions and settings. If you are not using Live View and you turn on your camera, the Super Control Panel is there on the monitor. If you press the LV button and switch into Live View mode, you can press the OK button and the LV Super Control Panel shows up.

The question is, how do *you* feel? If you are enjoying the use of the touch-screen Super Control Panel, then you can leave the camera configured the way it comes from the factory. The LV Super Control Panel or Super Control Panel will be available to you immediately. If, however, you prefer the less full-featured but more targeted Live Control, you can use it instead of the LV Super Control Panel. The Live Control will not replace the Super Control Panel, but it will replace the LV Super Control Panel when you press the INFO button—if the Live Control has been enabled (as previously discussed). We will discuss the Live Control in more detail in the upcoming Live Control subsection.

Live Control

The Live Control is another convenient way to access the most-used camera settings. It contains a subset of the settings found on the Super Control Panel and LV Super Control Panel, but the user interface is different.

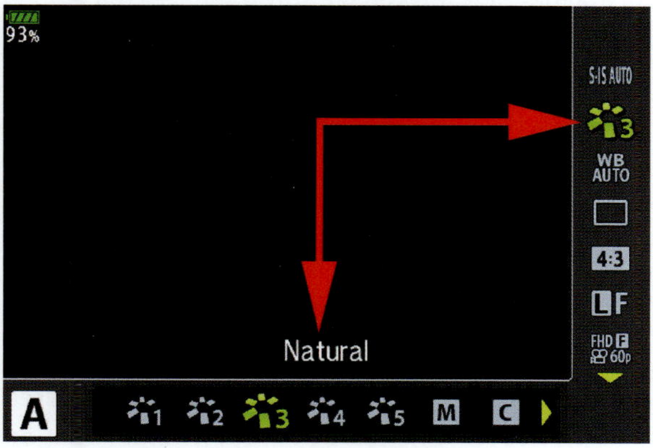

Figure 2.23A: Live Control functions (right side)

Figure 2.23A shows the Live Control with the Picture Mode function selected (top red arrow). Notice that on the right side of the Live Control screen there are a series of icons. These are the 14 camera functions that you can access via the Live Control. You can scroll up and down with the Arrow Pad to select one of the functions.

All of the settings for the selected function will appear at the bottom of the Live Control screen (Figure 2.23A, bottom red arrow), rather than on a secondary screen like you see with the Super Control Panel. You can scroll left and right along the bottom of the screen with the Arrow Pad to select one of the settings for the selected function.

As you proceed through the 14 Live Control functions, keep in mind that Live Control is just another front end to a subset of the same functions that are accessed via the Super Control Panel. To avoid repeating material, the Live Control information in this chapter will be limited to how to access the settings for each of the 14 Live Control functions. Also provided are page number cross-references to later chapters where each setting is configured in detail.

Note: The Live Control's functions and settings are not touch sensitive.

Should I Use the Live Control?

The Live Control is a very convenient camera control system. In some ways it is more convenient than the Super Control Panel, although it is less comprehensive. While the non-Live View Super Control Panel will be used mostly by photographers who dislike Live View and would rather use the electronic viewfinder (EVF) to take pictures, the Live Control (or the LV Super Control Panel) is for those who don't mind having both Live View and the EVF available at all times. Interestingly, unlike with previous Olympus cameras, the Live Control is *not enabled* on the camera by default; instead, the previously discussed LV Super Control Panel shows up. You must enable the Live Control in the camera's Custom Menu (see the next subsection, **Enabling the Live Control**).

If you are satisfied with using the Super Control Panel and do not want to use the Live Control, you can access the same 14 functions via the Super Control Panel or the regular camera menu system. However, if you have used previous Olympus cameras and have learned to enjoy the simplicity of the Live Control, then you should follow the next subsection to enable it.

Live Control and the Super Control Panel are mutually exclusive. When you select one of them, the other is temporarily disabled. To switch between the Live Control (once enabled) and the Super Control Panel, you will press the LV button. Now let's examine how to enable the Live Control.

Enabling the Live Control

The Live Control is available only after you enable it in the Custom Menu. We discussed how to enable the Live Control under the **iAUTO Function Screens, P/A/S/M Function Screens,** and **ART Function Screens** subsections starting on page 71. In review, let's go through this process step-by-step and enable the Live Control for the P/A/S/M modes (figure 2.23B), which are the modes used most often by enthusiasts and pros.

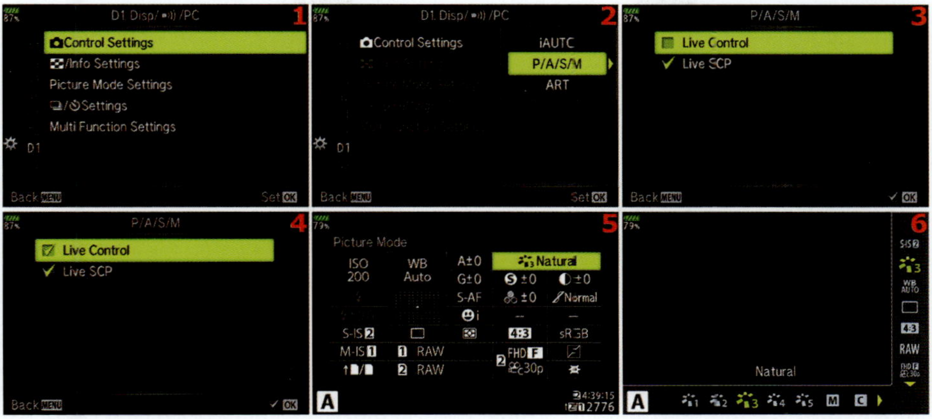

Figure 2.23B: Enabling the Live View and Live Control screens

Use these steps to enable the Live Control for the P/A/S/M exposure modes on the Mode Dial:

1. Press the LV button (to the left of the viewfinder) to enter Live View mode. This is necessary or you will not be able to see the Live Control once it is enabled. The LV Super Control Panel and the Live Control are mutually exclusive. They cannot be enabled at the same time. Let's proceed into the Custom Menu to enable the Live Control.
2. Figure 2.23B, image 1, shows the Custom Menu's D1 section. Highlight [Photo] Control Settings and scroll to the right.
3. A small window with a list of exposure modes will pop up on the screen (figure 2.23B, image 2). As discussed in previous chapter subsections, you must enable the Live Control individually for the P/A/S/M, iAuto, and Art modes. Highlight P/A/S/M and scroll to the right.
4. The P/A/S/M screen will now appear with Live Control and LV Super Control Panel (Live SCP) selections (figure 2.23B, image 3). The LV Super Control Panel is already enabled. Highlight the Live Control setting and press the OK button to put a check mark in the box.
5. The Live Control is now available for use (figure 2.23B, image 4). Press the MENU button to finish the operation, and you will return to the screen with the popup box (figure 2.23B, image 2). Follow the same steps to enable the Live Control for the other two settings (iAUTO and ART), if you wish.
6. Once both the Live Control and LV Super Control Panel are enabled, press the MENU button four times to return to the normal Live View screen (or press the Shutter button halfway). When you are sure that you are looking at the Live View screen and you can

see your subject on the monitor, press the OK button. The LV Super Control Panel will appear, as seen in figure 2.23B, image 5. Now press the INFO button and the camera will replace the LV Super Control Panel with the Live Control (figure 2.23B, image 6).

At this point, your camera will display the Live Control when it is in Live View mode and you press the OK button. You can toggle between the Live Control and the LV Super Control Panel with the INFO button. The camera will remember which screen you prefer and use it until you switch to the other.

Individual Live Control Screens

Now let's go over each of the 14 Live Control functions. Use the Arrow Pad to scroll up or down in the list of functions on the right side of the Live Control screen. When a function is highlighted it is selected and its settings appear along the bottom of the screen.

We will not go into detail on each of the individual settings found at the bottom of the Live Control screen because we have already considered those same settings in **Part 1: Super Control Panel,** and we will consider them in much greater detail in later chapters. To prevent massive material duplication (and tedious reading), I will provide page number cross-references for each function on the Live Control screen.

Let's start at the top of the Live Control function menu with the Image Stabilization function.

Image Stabilization

The E-M1 II's 5-axis Image Stabilizer compensates for camera shake in five axes: ro l, pitch, yaw, vertical, and horizontal. With this feature enabled, you can handhold your camera at much slower shutter speeds.

Scroll left or right with the Arrow Pad to choose one of the individual settings of the Image Stabilizer system. Figure 2.23C shows that the S-IS AUTO setting is selected.

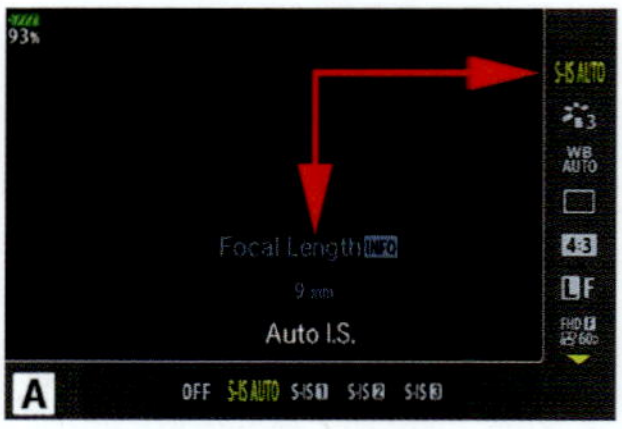

Figure 2.23C: Image Stab lizer function (right arrow) and settings (bottom arrow)

Deeper Information: This function is examined in much greater detail in the **Custom Menu** chapter under the **[Photo] Image Stabilizer** subheading on page 468.

Settings Recommendation: I have found that S-IS AUTO works well for still images of any type. If you do a lot of panning, the S-IS AUTO mode is particularly effective. The camera allows you to disable certain types of IS directional correction (e.g., horizontal or vertical). Refer to the list of IS modes on page 468 and select the mode that works best for your circumstances.

Picture Mode

Individual Picture Modes apply a specific look to JPEG images. RAW shooters can use the current Picture Mode setting or change Picture Modes after the image has been taken, and then save the file as a JPEG with a new look. There are 38 Picture Modes available at the bottom of the Live Control screen, including several Art Modes.

Scroll left or right with the Arrow Pad to choose one of the individual settings of the Picture Mode system. Figure 2.23D shows that the Natural (3) setting is selected.

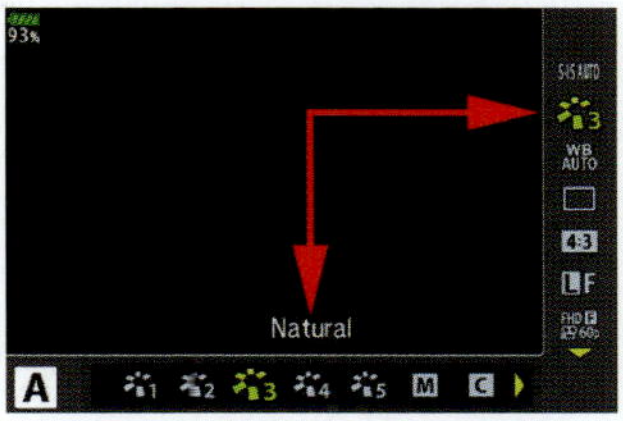

Figure 2.23D: Picture Mode function (right arrow) and settings (bottom arrow)

Deeper Information: In the **Shooting Menu 1** chapter, under the **Picture Mode** heading on page 151, we will discuss the how, when, and why of each Picture Mode in much greater detail. Additionally, you can fine-tune the Sharpness, Contrast, Saturation, and Gradation of several Picture Controls. You can also refer to the **Super Control Panel** section earlier in this chapter, under the subheading **Picture Mode: Sharpness, Contrast, Saturation, and Gradation** on page 29, for more information.

Settings Recommendation: For everyday shooting, I usually choose Natural Picture Mode. However, for some types of nature shooting I may use Vivid Picture Mode to make the colors pop. When I need the widest dynamic range for nature shooting, I may use the Muted Picture Mode, and then later increase the saturation and contrast manually for the best look. For portraits, I often use Portrait Picture Mode to preserve natural-looking skin tones. When I am feeling adventurous, I even use some of the Art Modes.

White Balance (WB)

The E-M1II offers several preset White Balance (WB) values (e.g., Sunny, Cloudy, Incandescent). In addition, you can take an ambient light reading (Capture WB), directly input a Kelvin (K) color temperature (Custom White Balance, or CWB), or let the camera determine the WB (AUTO). There are a total of 13 WB settings.

Scroll left or right with the Arrow Pad to choose one of the individual settings of the White Balance system. Figure 2.23E shows that the WB Auto setting is selected.

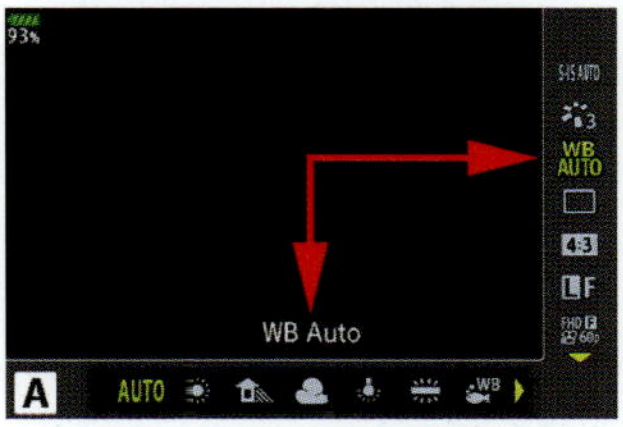

Figure 2.23E: WB function (right arrow) and settings (bottom arrow)

Deeper Information: For a detailed study of each of these WB types see the **Custom Menu** chapter under the *Custom Menu > G. [Record Mode]/WB/Color > WB* function on page 536. The Live Control WB screen is another version of the function settings provided in the WB Custom Menu. In this chapter we've discussed how to select settings. In the **Custom Menu** chapter we will discuss how, why, and when.

Settings Recommendation: The WB system in the E-M1II is pretty flexible. I use AUTO WB most of the time. The range of choices at your fingertips guarantees that you can use an accurate WB and capture true colors. Why not take time to shoot some pictures with the various WB values to see how the camera changes the color balance? It's also a good idea experiment with taking an ambient Capture WB reading from a white or gray card (page 539). This can be a vital step if you find yourself in a situation where you must carefully control the color.

[Sequential][Self-Timer]

The camera's [Sequential][Self-timer] system is designed to let you control the style and rate of image capture when you are shooting in bursts. It also lets you control remote shooting with specialized Self-timer controls.

Scroll left or right with the Arrow Pad to choose one of the individual settings of the [Sequential][Self-timer] system. Figure 2.23F shows that the Single setting is selected.

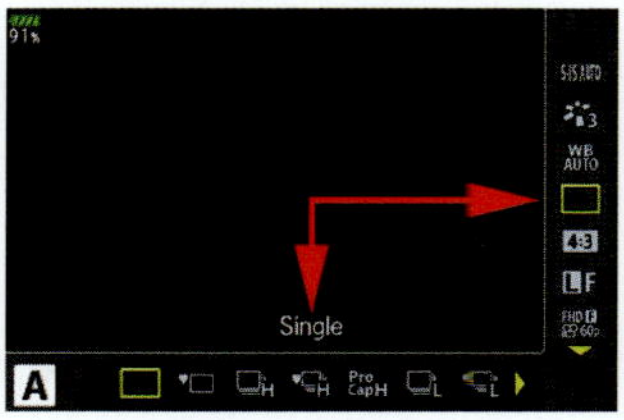

Figure 2.23F: Release Mode function (right arrow) and settings (bottom arrow)

Deeper Information: These modes are considered in more detail in the **Shooting Menu 1** chapter under the **[Sequential]/[Self-Timer]/[Time Lapse]** subheading on page 184.

Settings Recommendation: As a nature and portrait photographer, I normally use single-frame shooting. However, if I'm shooting a sporting event with fast-moving players, I often switch to Sequential High (H) burst shooting mode and continuous AF (C-AF), which gives me a shooting speed of up to 18 frames per second with active autofocus between each frame (60 fps without active AF). The new Pro Capture mode allows you to capture the peak of the action by shooting up to 35 frames in advance of a series of action shots. When it is time to use the Self-timer, I normally choose the 12s setting and take a single picture. However, if I want to be creative and use the Self-timer for multiple frames, I often use the Self-timer Custom setting.

Aspect

The E-M1II is a Micro Four Thirds camera, which describes the aspect ratio of the sensor (4:3). Other camera brands have sensors with different aspect ratios. The Aspect function on the E-M1II allows you to change the Micro Four Thirds (4:3) standard image aspect ratio to various other aspect ratios that more closely match the ratios of other brands. In other words, the length and width of the image is cropped into a new relationship. The five available ratios are 4:3, 16:9, 3:2, 1:1, and 3:4.

The new aspect ratio changes the final shape of the image, which means the camera must crop the picture. Therefore, use a different ratio only when you must.

Scroll left or right with the Arrow Pad to choose one of the individual settings of the Aspect system. Figure 2.23G shows that the 4:3 (5184×3888) setting is selected.

Note: When you change to a different Aspect setting, the electronic viewfinder (EVF) and Live View screen will adjust to the new shape so you can accurately shoot with the new aspect ratio.

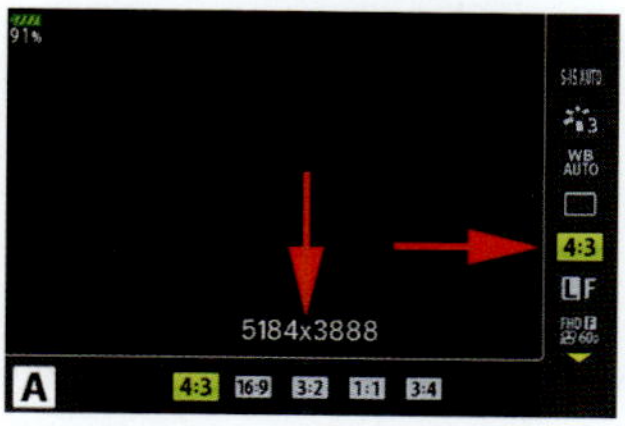

Figure 2.23G: Aspect (ratio) function (right arrow) and settings (left arrow)

Deeper Information: The Aspect settings are discussed in more detail in the **Shooting Menu 1** chapter under the **Image Aspect** subheading on page 181. Picture samples of the different ratios are also provided.

Settings Recommendation: I rarely change the aspect ratio of the image with this function. I prefer to simply crop the image after the fact in my computer. However, if you need a specific aspect ratio but don't have time to crop your images, the camera is ready to provide the ratio you need with no hassle and only minor image quality loss.

[Photo][Record Mode] (Image Quality)

This flexible function allows you to choose the Image Quality for your pictures. You can shoot in RAW (ORF) mode or in various JPEG sizes and pixel counts, including Large (L), Middle (M), and Small (S). You can also choose from several JPEG compression levels, including Super Fine (SF), Fine (F), Normal (N), and Basic (B).

On the Live Control Image Quality settings, you will see JPEG size and compression rate names combined. For instance, a Large-size, Super Fine compression rate JPEG will be listed as LSF, and a Large-size, Fine compression rate JPEG will be listed as LF.

The size for the RAW mode, or the RAW file in a combination mode (e.g., LF+RAW), is always Large (L) with a 5184 × 3888 pixel ratio. Of course, different aspect ratios (previous subsection) for JPEG images will cause the image pixel size to vary somewhat (page 181).

Scroll left or right with the Arrow Pad to choose one of the individual settings of the Image Quality system. Figure 2.23H shows that the LF (Large Fine JPEG) setting is selected.

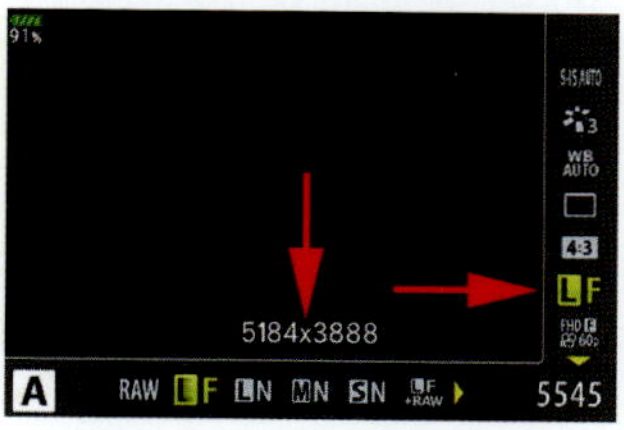

Figure 2.23H: Image Quality function (right arrow) and settings (left arrow)

Deeper Information: There is deeper information on this subject in the **Shooting Menu 1** chapter under the **[Photo][Record Mode]** subheading on page 173. Be sure to read that information before you shoot too many important images so you can make the best image quality choices.

Note: The JPEG Super Fine (SF) Record Mode is available only when it is enabled in the Custom Menu. It will not show up in any of the Image Quality menus unless you enable it. Instructions are provided in the **Custom Menu** chapter under the **[Record Mode] Set** subheading on page 532.

Settings Recommendation: Because of its smaller sensor, I want my E-M1II to capture the best possible quality, so I most often use the RAW setting. However, shooting in RAW requires that I post-process the files and later convert them to JPEGs. If I need to give images to someone quickly, I may use the LSF+RAW setting and shoot both file types at the same time. This gives me the best of both worlds: a RAW file for when I have time to make a masterpiece, and a JPEG file for immediate use. For fun shooting, you may decide to set your camera to one of the JPEG modes so you don't have to store extra RAW files, and you will still have great images to e-mail, print, or use on social media sites.

[Video] [Record Mode]

This function allows you to choose the Movie Resolution (C4K, 4K, FHD, HD), Compression/Bit Rate (ALL-intra, SuperFine, Fine, Normal), and Frame Rate (60p, 50p, 30p, 25p, 24p) for your video recordings. Plus, you can choose whether to record longer segments (up to 29 minutes, 59 seconds) or short clips (from 1 to 8 seconds), and whether to use Fast or Slow Motion.

Scroll left or right with the Arrow Pad to choose one of the individual settings of the Video Recording system. Figure 2.23l shows that the FHD (MOV 1920×1080) Movie Resolution, Fine Compression/Bit Rate, and 60p Frame Rate are selected.

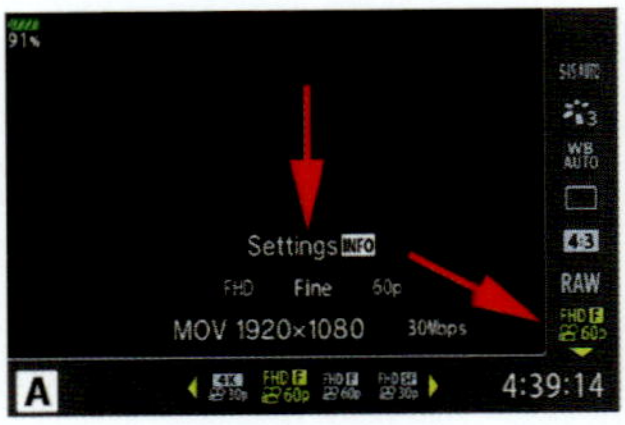

Figure 2.23l: [Video][Record Mode] function (right arrow) and settings (left arrow)

Deeper Information: These settings will be discussed in detail in the **Recording Movies, Video Menu, and My Clips** chapter under the **[Movie] Specification Settings** subsection on page 283.

Settings Recommendation: I normally shoot video in the FullHD format because I want great quality and a reduced file size. However, when I am shooting important video, such as a beautiful nature series in the Great Smoky Mountains of Tennessee and North Carolina, I often max out the camera's video specifications to full Cinema 4K (C4K), with the best bit rates and frame rates. I carry several extra memory cards and batteries on those days.

If you want to learn how to post-process video, you may want to shoot some short videos with a Motion JPEG AVI type selected (HD). It is much easier to work with these videos in basic video editing software because every frame contains a small compressed JPEG picture. However, since this mode is limited to 720p and makes huge files, I would use it only for experimentation.

Editing videos that use H.264 MPEG-4 AVC compression is more difficult because of the way the video is stored in each frame. The individual frames store only things that have changed (the motion), and the entire scene is recorded as key frame every few frames. To work with this type of video in editing software, you must have experience working with H.264 MPEG-4 AVC compressed videos.

If all you want to do is shoot great video, I suggest that you experiment with the formats that have the MOV container type to get the smallest file sizes.

Flash Mode

The E-M1II offers you a choice of seven flash modes that allow you to vary the timing and power of the flash system. The E-M1II does not have a built-in, popup flash, but Olympus has provided the tiny FL-LM3 unit (guide number of 9.1 at ISO 100) in the box, which mounts onto the camera's hotshoe. Also, the optional Olympus FL-900R flash unit (guide number of 58 at ISO 100) became available when the E-M1II was released. And, of course, there are several older Olympus (e.g., FL-600R) and aftermarket flash units available. Here is how to choose a flash mode.

Scroll left or right with the Arrow Pad to choose one of the individual settings of the Flash Mode system. Figure 2.23J shows that the Fill In setting is selected.

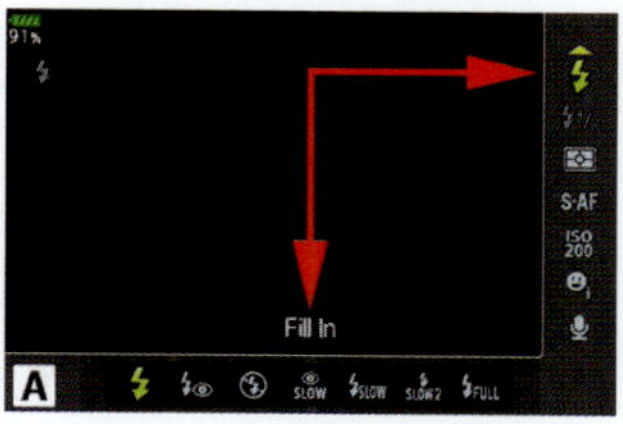

Figure 2.23J: Flash Mode function (right arrow) and settings (bottom arrow)

Deeper Information: The seven Flash Modes are covered in detail in this chapter in **Part 1: Super Control Panel** under the **Flash Mode** subheading on page 34.

Settings Recommendation: I use the Fill In flash mode most of the time. It seems to balance the flash well with bright ambient light, and it provides the main light source when ambient light is dim. The other modes (e.g., Slow, Slow2) are available for when you want special effects. Redeye mode seems to help somewhat for reducing the red-eye effect in portraits. If you are shooting in a studio and want to carefully control flash output, you should experiment with the manual flash setting.

Flash Intensity Control (+/– Compensation)

Flash Intensity Control is similar to a flash compensation system. If you are taking pictures and the background of the subject is exposed well but the subject is overexposed, you may want to dial back the power or intensity of the flash unit. If the subject is underexposed and the background is well exposed, you may want to increase the flash output to light the subject a little better. Flash Intensity Control gives you the power to do either. In effect, you are dialing in flash exposure compensation.

Scroll left or right with the Arrow Pad to move the small green indicator bar in the compensation scale at the bottom of the screen. You can select from a six EV-step range (–3.0 to +3.0 EV). Figure 2.23K shows that the 0.0 EV setting is selected (no compensation).

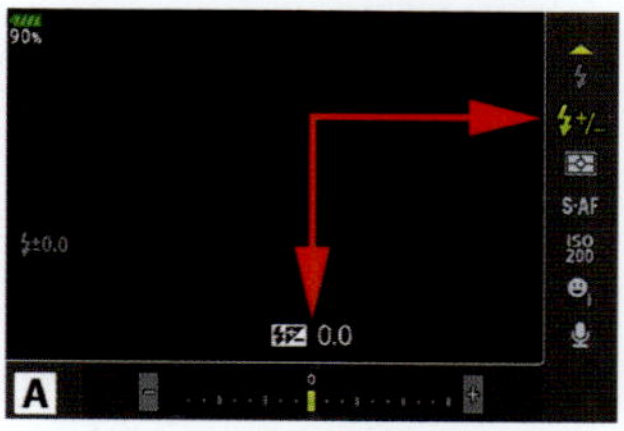

Figure 2.23K: Flash Intensity Control funct on (right arrow) and settings (bottom arrow)

Deeper Information: The flash intensity/compensation system is covered in detail in this chapter in **Part 1:**

Super Control Panel under the **Flash Intensity Control (+/– Compensation)** subheading on page 37.

Settings Recommendation: I tend to shoot a little brighter than many photographers because I use RAW mode for the best image quality most of the time. When you use RAW (ORF) Image Quality mode, the picture files have more overexposure headroom than you might think. Therefore, I sometimes set the Flash Intensity Control to +0.3, for a one-third stop overexposure. When you shoot JPEG files it is important to watch the histogram closely to prevent unrecoverable overexposure (highlight data loss), especially when shooting up close.

Metering

The E-M1II has five light metering styles that allow you great flexibility in how you expose your images.

Scroll left or right with the Arrow Pad to choose one of the individual settings of the Metering system. Figure 2.23L shows that the ESP setting is selected.

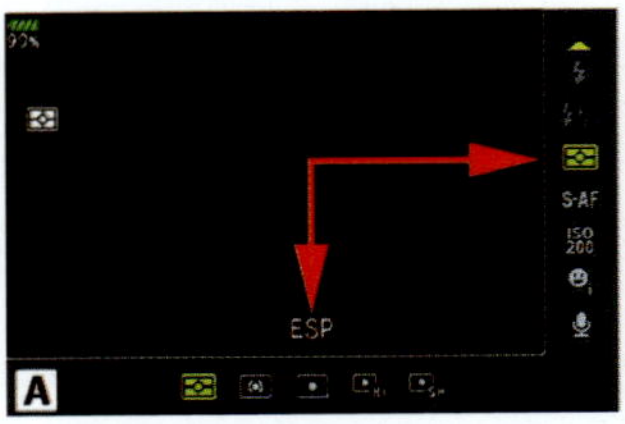

Figure 2.23L: Metering function (right arrow) and settings (bottom arrow)

Deeper Information: We will consider the Metering mode types in more detail in the **Custom Menu** chapter under the **Metering** subheading on page 522.

Settings Recommendation: Digital ESP metering (ESP) is a very effective form of metering. I rarely have to use the other metering modes. Sometimes I might use the Spot meter to meter a bright subject against a darker background, but otherwise I am quite happy with ESP. Be sure to use a form of ☺ Face Priority when you are taking portraits with ESP. That seems to make the camera extra sensitive to exposing faces accurately, even if the background is dark and could cause some facial overexposure.

[Photo] AF Mode

The AF Mode function provides several focus methods. Four of them are for autofocus and one is for manual focus. Also, one of the autofocus methods will allow focus tracking.

Scroll left or right with the Arrow Pad to choose one of the individual settings of the AF Mode system. Figure 2.23M shows that the Single AF (S-AF) setting is selected.

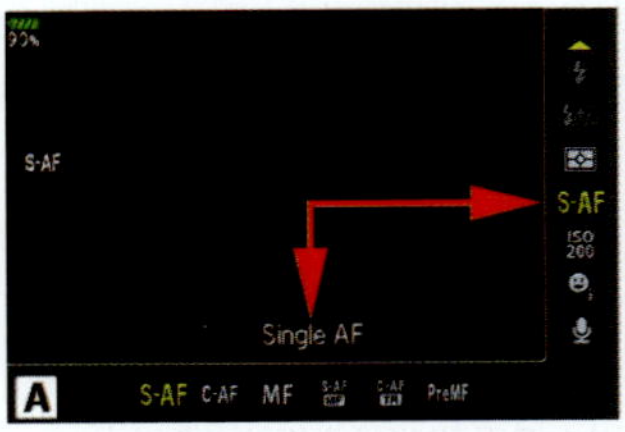

Figure 2.23M: [Photo] AF Mode function (right arrow) and settings (bottom arrow)

Deeper Information: This subject is considered more thoroughly in the **Custom Menu** chapter under the **[Photo] AF Mode** subheading on page 404.

Note: Since the E-M1II does not have a split-prism screen to assist with Manual focus (MF), you may want to enable focus Peaking and/or Magnify. Peaking makes it easy to see when the subject is in focus because it outlines the edges of the subject in one of four selectable colors (red, yellow, black, or white) to indicate where the best focus is currently located. Peaking is discussed and samples are provided in the **Custom Menu** chapter under the **Peaking Settings** subheading (page 491) and the **MF Assist** subheading (page 426). In the **MF Assist** section I also discuss the **Magnify** function, which automatically zooms in to pixel-peeping levels when you turn the lens focus ring, and it results in extremely accurate manual focus. Combining Peaking and Magnify makes manual focus easy.

Settings Recommendation: I like to use S-AF+MF mode so I can use autofocus most of the time, but still engage and turn the manual focus ring to enable manual focus (for lenses that allow it), along with Peaking and Magnify. The S-AF mode is fine for slow shooting with well-defined, static subjects. C-AF works quite well when I am shooting something like a wedding and the bride and groom are walking toward me. I use MF mode most often when I am taking macro shots and need to carefully control where the focus falls, due to the shallow depth of field in that type of photography. The tracking mode (C-AF+TR) works well for moving subjects, especially larger wildlife, cars, and airplanes. You can even use the PreMF setting to use a preset focus point. Very flexible!

ISO Sensitivity

The ISO function changes the camera's sensitivity to light. The higher the ISO, the greater the sensitivity, and vice versa. Higher ISO sensitivities can add grainy digital noise to the darker areas of your image; therefore, keep the ISO as low as possible for the current lighting conditions.

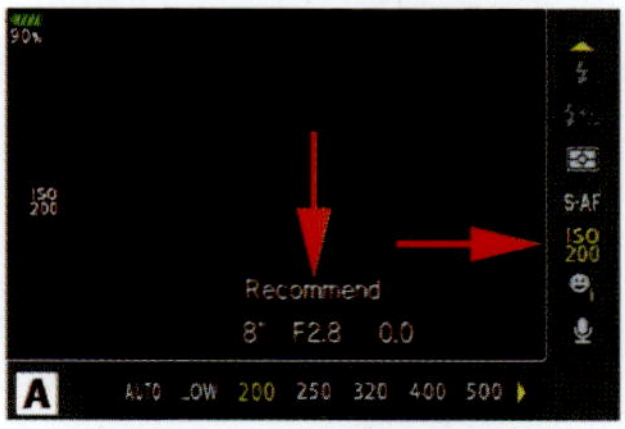

Figure 2.23N: ISO function (right arrow) and settings (left arrow)

Scroll left or right with the Arrow Pad to choose one of the individual settings of the ISO system. You can choose AUTO (camera decides the ISO), LOW (~ISO 100), or a range of settings all the way up to ISO 25600. Figure 2.23N shows that the ISO 200 setting is selected.

Deeper Information: ISO Sensitivity is covered in detail in this chapter in **Part 1: Super Control Panel** under the **ISO Sensitivity** subheading on page 22.

Note: Olympus considers ISO 100 (LOW) to be an extended ISO value in the E-M1II. The recommended base ISO is 200. When LOW is selected you will see Extension displayed at the bottom of the screen. This simply means that LOW approximates ISO 100, which is outside the normal ISO range for the camera. Do not worry, ISO LOW works great, and I use it much of the time to capture low-noise landscape and portrait images when the ambient light allows it.

Settings Recommendation: I usually leave my camera set to ISO 200 because it has low noise for everyday photography. When I shoot landscapes on a tripod, I often set it to LOW (ISO 100). The camera does well up to about ISO 3200, even though the Micro Four Thirds sensor is small. I would use ISO values above 3200 only in emergencies because the noise levels may become objectionable. You should test this for yourself to see where your noise tolerance lies.

☺ *Face Priority*

The ☺ Face Priority AF mode is designed to make your camera extra sensitive to human faces. When this mode is enabled, the E-M1II will detect human faces, adjust the focus to capture them sharply, and tweak the ESP metering to expose more accurately for human skin tones.

Additionally, you can select Eye Priority and even choose which eye to focus on. When any type of ☺ Face Priority is active, the camera looks for human faces in the subject area and gives them priority for exposure. It then uses the selected type of ☺ Face Priority to decide how to autofocus.

Scroll left or right with the Arrow Pad to choose one of the individual settings of the ☺ Face Priority system. Figure 2.23O shows that the ☺i (Face & Eye Priority) setting is selected.

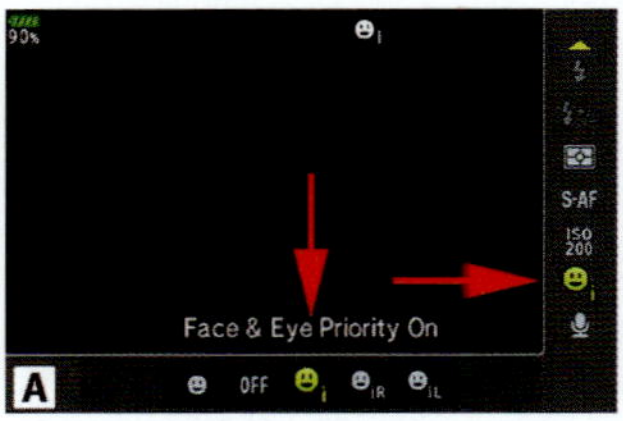

Figure 2.23O: ☺ Face Priority function (right arrow) and settings (left arrow)

Deeper Information: This subject is considered in more detail in the **Custom Menu** chapter, under the ☺ **Face Priority** subheading on page 418.

Settings Recommendation: I have found that the camera works well with some form of ☺ Face Priority mode always active. It focuses normally on nonhuman subjects when no face is present, and it uses face detection only when it can detect human faces. I normally leave ☺i (Face & Eye Priority) set to On.

Movie [Sound]

This simple function turns the camera's built-in stereo sound recorder on or off when you are recording videos. If you are recording sound with an external digital audio recorder, you may not want the camera to record sound at all. Or you may be shooting a family video and do want to record stereo sound.

Scroll left or right with the Arrow Pad to choose one of the individual settings of the Movie [Sound] system. Figure 2.23P shows that the ON setting is selected.

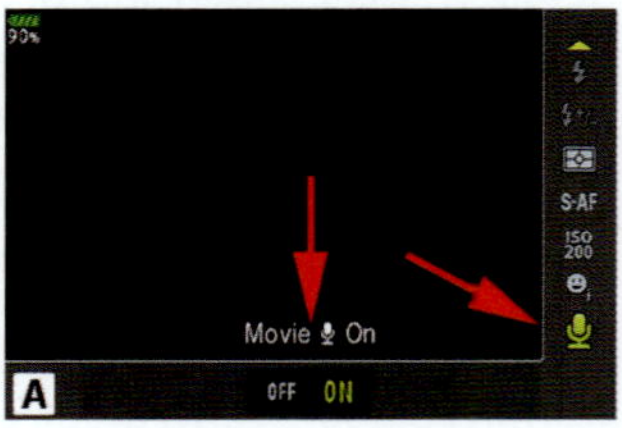

Figure 2.23P: Movie Sound function (right arrow) and settings (left arrow)

Deeper Information: The Video Menu provides an expanded version of this simple setting. While this setting allows you to turn sound on and off, the Video Menu's **Movie [Sound]** > **On** function (page 328) allows you to control many aspects of Video [Sound] recording.

Settings Recommendation: I leave the Movie [Sound] recorder turned on all the time. I do not use an external audio recorder often; therefore, I want my camera to use the built-in stereo mic system (found on either side of the EVF on top of the camera). If you shoot professional video, you should familiarize yourself with the six settings under the Video Menu's **Movie [Sound] On** function (go to *Video Menu > Movie [Sound] > On* and scroll to the right).

Next, let's consider the Live Guide function screen that you may want to use when the camera is in iAUTO exposure mode on the Mode Dial.

Live Guide

When you place your E-M1II in iAUTO mode on the Mode Dial, it becomes a point-and-shoot camera. You press the Shutter button, and the camera does the rest. You can relax and take pictures without worrying about camera settings. Even for a professional photographer, a fully automatic mode is welcome at certain times.

Not every picture you take is destined to be a masterpiece, some are just for fun. When you're at a party taking snapshots, as long as the image looks nice, who cares how it got that way? Using a fully automatic mode is good for fun photography, but it is not available on many professional cameras.

Try iAUTO mode when you are taking snapshots and see if you enjoy using it. The camera software is capable of making nice images for sharing on social media sites, and the built-in Wi-Fi makes it easy to transfer the pictures.

Why the Live Guide System?

The Live Guide system allows you to make visual adjustments to the exposure, color balance, and look of your image—directly on the Live View screen—without knowing anything about camera functions like white balance, exposure metering, aperture, or shutter speed. It is a visual system for those just learning to use a more accomplished camera, or for knowledgeable photographers to use while teaching others basic photography principles.

Using the Live Guide Menu Items

In addition to offering complete camera automation in iAUTO mode, the E-M1II—continuing with the idea that everything should be configurable—also provides a way to fine-tune the images that are taken with fully automatic settings.

Note: For the graphics that follow, I used live camera screens; however, I left the lens cap on so that you can see the various screen settings more clearly. When you use the Live Guide system, you will see and adjust your image via Live View on the monitor or in the Electronic Viewfinder (EVF). Where my graphical screens show a dark background, yours will display a live subject.

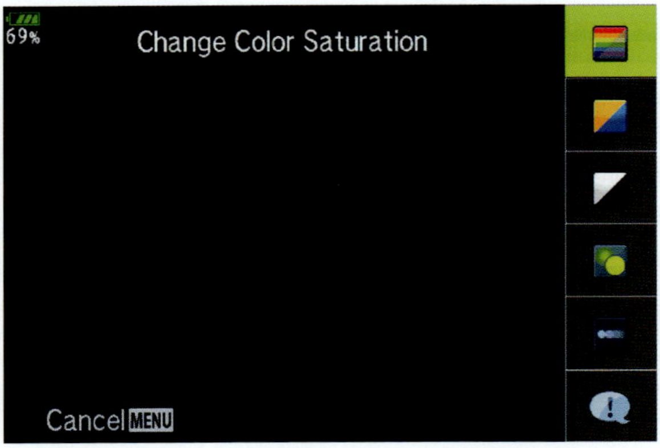

Figure 2.24A: The Live Guide Menu (six items)

There are six Live Guide menu items, as seen on the right side of Figure 2.24A. Here are brief descriptions of what each guide does (top to bottom):

- **Change Color Saturation:** Visually change the color saturation of a subject just before you make the picture.
- **Change Color Image:** Visually change the color temperature of a subject just before you make the picture. You can make the color warmer (more red) or cooler (more blue).
- **Change Brightness:** Visually change the brightness of a subject just before you make the picture.
- **Blur Background:** Change the lens aperture by moving the adjustment slider while visually previewing the depth of field (zone of sharp focus) just before you make the picture.
- **Express Motions:** Visually control the shutter speed by moving the adjustment slider.
- **Shooting Tips:** Get tips on various photographic subjects, including Child, Pet, Flower, and Cuisine photography. You will also find screens for suggestions on framing an image and using camera accessories.

Let's now consider how to use the Live Guide system, and then look at each Live Guide menu item in more detail.

Set the Mode Dial to iAUTO (figure 2.24B, image 1). You will see a small tab at the right side of the Live View screen (figure 2.24B, image 2, red arrow). When you touch the tab, the Live Guide system will open. You can also open the Live Guide system by pressing the OK button when the Live View screen shows your subject.

Figure 2.24B, image 3, displays the six Live Guide selections on the right side of the screen. The Change Color Saturation guide is currently selected and is highlighted in green at the top of the menu. We will use this guide as an example.

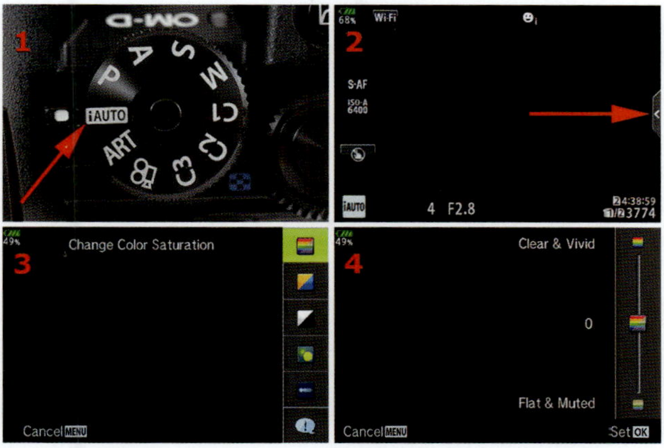

Figure 2.24B: Using the Live Guide system (image 2)

If you slide your finger up and down the screen over the Live Guides, the highlighted area will follow your finger and stop when you lift it. You can simply touch one of the six Live Guide icons—or press the OK button with the icon highlighted—to open that guide's secondary screen. Each of the six menu items shown in image 3 has its own secondary screen(s).

Figure 2.24B, image 4, shows the secondary screen for the Change Color Saturation guide. Notice the slider on the right of the screen, which is currently at the zero (0) position. Slide the indicator up to increase saturation or down to reduce saturation. You will see the saturation in your image change on the Live View screen as you move the indicator.

Each of the other guides has a similar secondary screen, allowing you to see the adjustments you're making via Live View before you take the picture. When the effect looks good, remove your finger and press the OK button to Set the effect.

You can combine the effects of several Live Guides by simply adjusting each one via its secondary screen. You can tell that a certain Live Guide effect has been adjusted and is in force if there is a green check mark next to the menu item. In figure 2.24C, you can see that Change Color Saturation, Change Brightness, and Blur Background all have check marks.

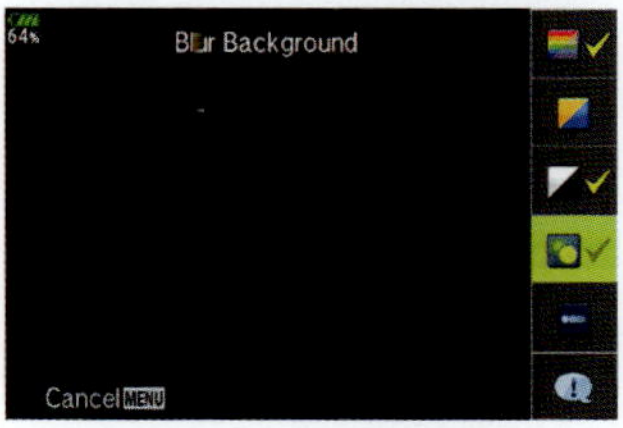

Figure 2.24C: Combined Live Guide effects

All of the items that have check marks are active and affecting the current Live View subject. These settings will remain in effect for the current shooting session until you touch the Menu symbol on the lower-left corner of the Live Guide screen, press the Menu button on the camera, or turn the camera off.

Now let's consider each of the six Live Guide menu items in more detail. Use the guides individually or cumulatively to adjust the appearance of a live subject on the monitor or in the EVF.

Change Color Saturation

Change the color saturation on an image just before you take the picture. This allows you to make autumn scenes even more vivid or reduce the color saturation for a muted look.

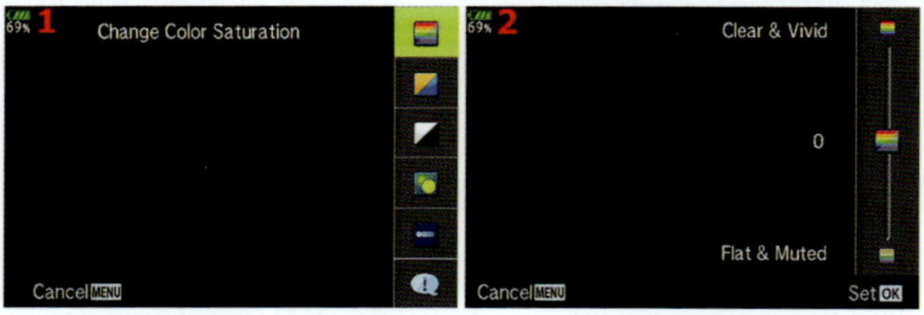

Figure 2.24D: Change Color Saturation (similar to changing Picture Modes)

Select the top menu choice, as seen in figure 2.24D, image 1, and press the OK button. Using the screen seen in figure 2.24D, image 2, move the slider up toward Clear & Vivid (more saturation) or down toward Flat & Muted (less saturation). Press the OK button to Set the value, and then take your pictures. The camera will stay set to the color saturation level you chose until you press the Menu button, touch the Menu symbol on the bottom-left corner of the screen, or turn the camera off.

Change Color Image

Change the color temperature of an image just before you take the picture. You can make the color warmer (more red) or cooler (more blue). This is a fast way to modify the camera's white balance visually.

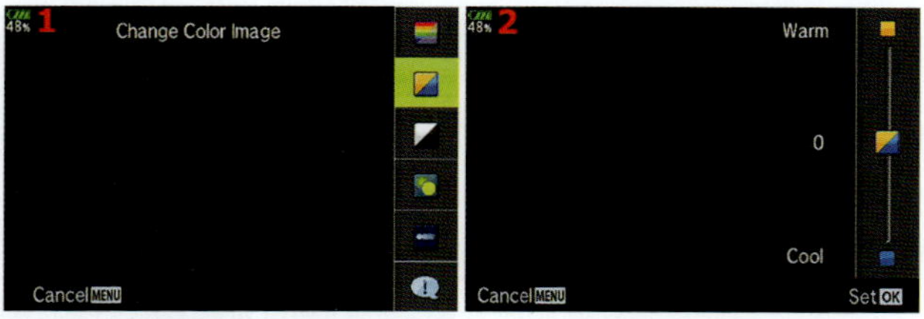

Figure 2.24E: Change Color Image (similar to adjusting the white balance)

Select the menu choice second from the top, as seen in figure 2.24E, image 1, and press the OK button. Using the screen seen in figure 2.24E, image 2, move the slider up toward Warm (reddish) or down toward Cool (bluish). Press the OK button to Set the value, and then take your pictures. The camera will stay set to the color temperature you chose until you press the Menu button, touch the Menu symbol on the bottom-left corner of the screen, or turn the camera off.

Change Brightness

Change the brightness of an image in real time, just before you take the picture. This setting allows you to control the exposure of an image by revealing more detail in the shadow areas (making the image brighter) or reducing the highlights (making the image darker). This works like regular +/– exposure compensation.

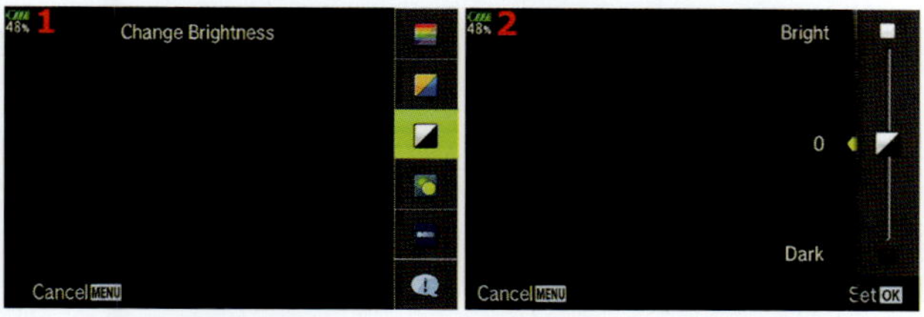

Figure 2.24F: Change Brightness (similar to exposure compensation)

Select the menu choice third from the top, as seen in figure 2.24F, image 1, and press the OK button. Using the screen seen in figure 2.24F, image 2, move the slider up toward Bright or down toward Dark. Press the OK button to Set the value, and then take your pictures. The camera will stay set to the brightness level you chose until you press the Menu button, touch the Menu symbol on the bottom-left corner of the screen, or turn the camera off.

Blur Background

Change the lens aperture by moving the adjustment slider up or down while visually previewing depth of field (zone of sharp focus) in front of and behind your subject, just before you take the picture. A large aperture (Blur) will have less depth of field, blurring the background and foreground, while a small aperture (Sharp) will have more depth of field, sharpening the background and foreground. The camera automatically adjusts shutter speed and ISO sensitivity to keep the exposure accurate while you are adjusting the aperture with the slider.

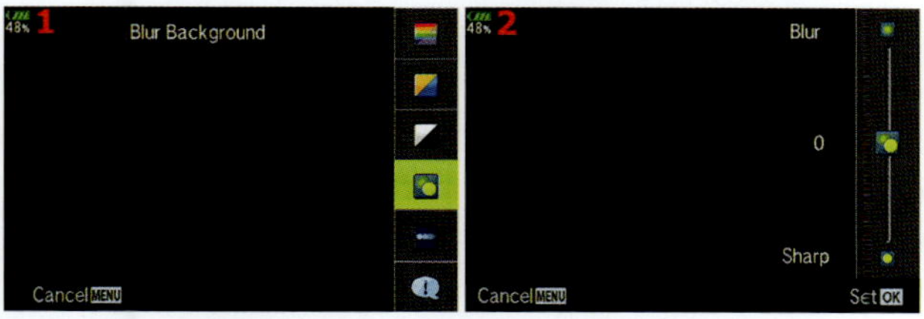

Figure 2.24G: Blur Background (similar to adjusting the aperture)

Select the fourth menu choice from the top, as seen in figure 2.24G, image 1, and press the OK button. Using the screen seen in figure 2.24G, image 2, move the slider up toward Blur or down toward Sharp. Press the OK button to Set the value, and then immediately take your pictures. The camera will stay set to the visual depth of field value you chose until you press the Menu button, touch the Menu symbol on the bottom-left corner of the screen, or turn the camera off.

Settings Recommendation: Blur Background is a useful method to visually adjust the depth of field in an image. This function may be used by macro shooters to adjust close-up images with very shallow depth of field, or by a portrait photographer who wants to make sure there is enough depth of field to have a subject's face fully in focus. By moving the slider, you will be able to see the depth of field changing on the camera's monitor or in the viewfinder. Consider this function to be a super-powered depth of field preview button. A new photographer can control the zone of sharpness in an image without fully understanding depth of field because it is done visually. An experienced photographer can use this function for the luxury of fine-tuning depth of field in an accurate visual way.

Express Motions

Control the camera's shutter speed by moving the adjustment slider. The camera will give you no indication of what shutter speed you are using. However, by moving the adjustment slider toward the Blurred Motion choice, you are progressively slowing down the shutter speed. By moving the slider toward Stop Motion, you are progressively making the shutter speed faster. The camera automatically adjusts the aperture and ISO sensitivity to keep the exposure accurate while you are adjusting the aperture with the slider.

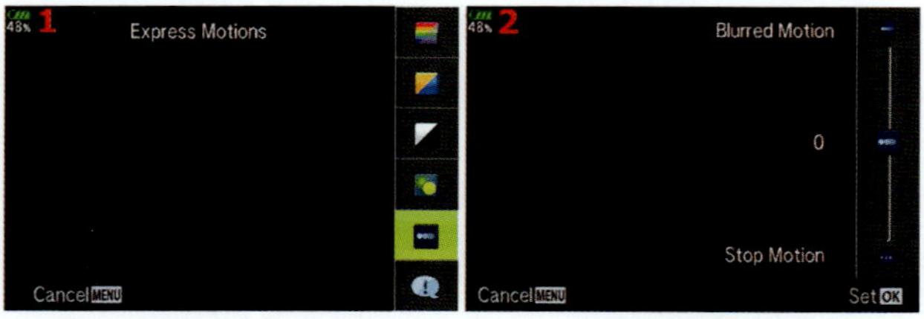

Figure 2.24H: Express Motions (similar to adjusting the shutter speed)

Select the fifth menu choice from the top, as seen in figure 2.24H, image 1, and press the OK button. Using the screen seen in figure 2.24H, image 2, move the slider up toward Blurred Motion or down toward Stop Motion. Press the OK button to Set the value, and then immediately take your pictures. The camera will stay set to the shutter speed you chose until you press the Menu button, touch the Menu symbol on the bottom-left corner of the screen, or turn the camera off.

Note: If you are shooting in low light and move the setting toward Blurred Motion, the camera may drop to a shutter speed so slow that you will be unable to successfully take a sharp picture while handholding the camera. Be prepared to use a tripod if the ambient light is dim. You will need to test this by firing a few test shots. At the time this book was written, the E-M1II has better image stabilization than any other current camera (that I know of). Therefore, you may be able to handhold the camera with the settings pushed toward Blurred Motion in lower ambient light. However, even with good image stabilization, any subject movement will be blurry. Please test this function carefully under the current lighting conditions when you are shooting important work.

Settings Recommendation: By varying the shutter speed you will be able to express subject motion, allowing blur with Blurred Motion or stopping action with Stop Motion. The speed of the shutter speed is less apparent visually since it is used only during the exposure. However, the effect of this function *can* be seen on the monitor or in the viewfinder to a degree. It appears that the camera uses its silent electronic shutter to give you somewhat of a preview of the effect of moving the slider; however, the full effect on the actual image will be best seen after the image is taken.

If you are shooting something like a waterfall and want to have wispy blurred water, you can move the adjustment slider toward Blurred Motion and take your picture, experimenting visually with the results. If you are shooting action, you can set the camera toward Stop Motion and visually see how much the slider needs to be moved based on the resulting preview and final pictures.

Shooting Tips

Obtain special instruction from the camera on various photographic subjects including Child, Pet, Flower, and Cuisine Photography. You will also find screens with suggestions for framing an image and using camera accessories.

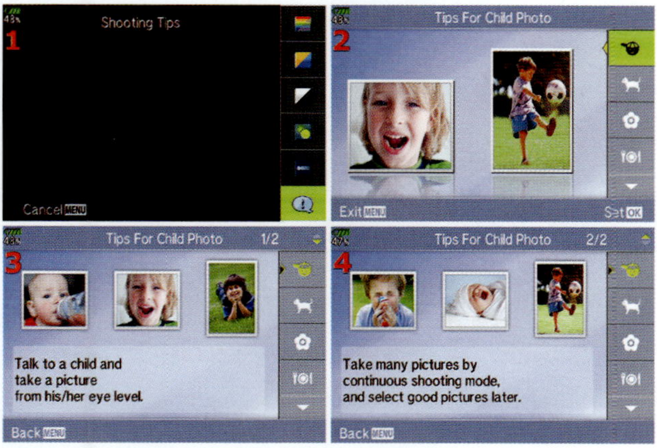

Figure 2.24l: Shooting Tips for various styles of photography

Select the last menu choice on the Live Guide menu—the Shooting Tips selection—as seen in figure 2.24l, image 1, and press the OK button to open the secondary screen.

In figure 2.24I, image 2, you can see four of the six available Shooting Tips icons, each with a small picture that represents the type of tip it provides. The other two menu choices are accessed by scrolling down with the Arrow Pad. Scroll up and down to select the type of instruction you want to receive. Pay attention to the text at the top of the screen, which describes the type of tips (i.e., Tips For Child Photo). Press the OK button to enter the chosen Shooting Tips screen. Each screen is very simple and requires little explanation. In each of the six upcoming graphics (figures 2.24J to 2.24O) you will see the individual screens for Shooting Tips. We will use figure 2.24I as our sample, but all six of the Shooting Tips screens work the same way. Press the OK button to open the actual Shooting Tips screen.

Figure 2.24I, image 3, shows one of the actual Shooting Tips screens. Each Shooting Tips selection has more than one screen full of tips for that subject. There are from two to four instructional screens for each selection, as shown by a number at the top right of the actual tips screens (1/2, 1/3, or 1/4). You can access each successive tips screen by scrolling down. If you reach the last screen in the series for a particular Shooting Tips selection and continue scrolling down, the next Shooting Tips type will appear. In fact, you could simply select the screen shown in figure 2.24I, image 3, and keep scrolling down until you have read all available Shooting Tips for all types of photography.

Following are six graphics that show the selection screen and the first screen of tips for each Shooting Tips type.

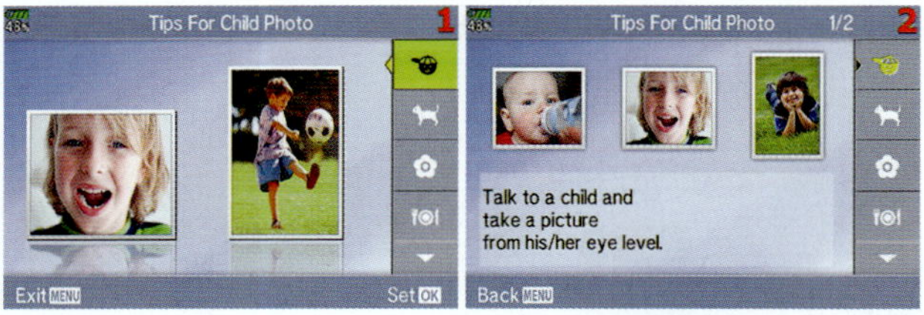

Figure 2.24J: Tips for Child Photo (two information screens)

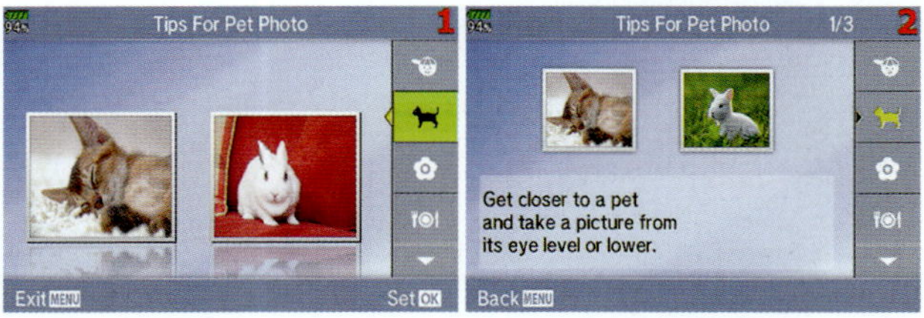

Figure 2.24K: Tips for Pet Photo (three information screens)

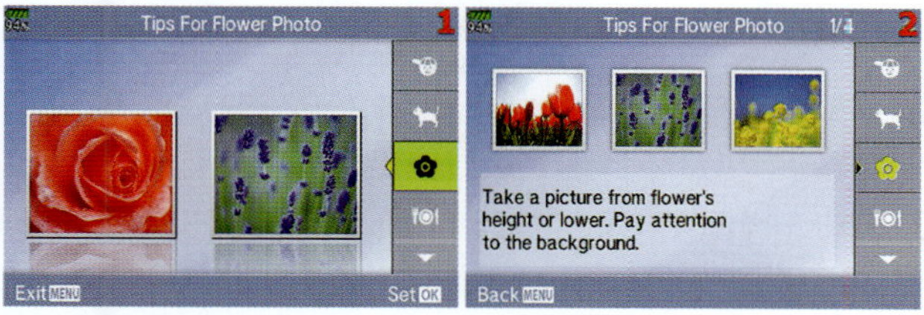

Figure 2.24L: Tips for Flower Photo (four information screens)

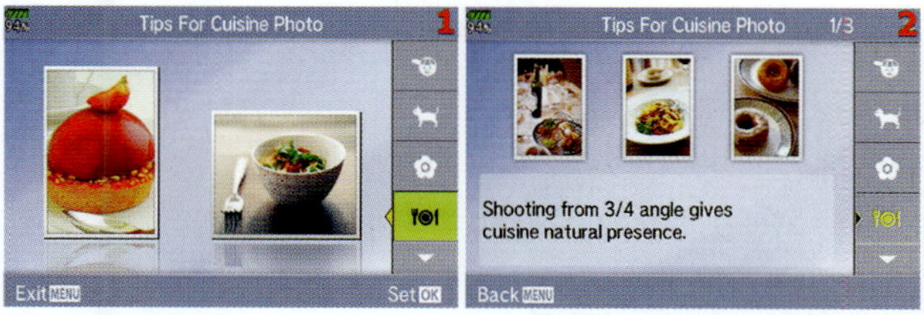

Figure 2.24M: Tips for Cuisine Photo (three information screens)

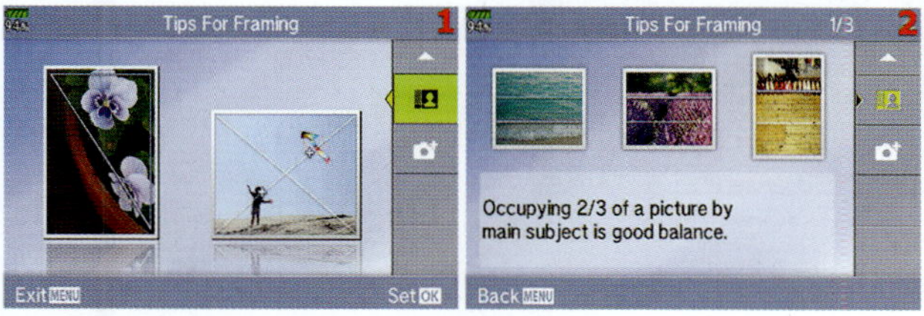

Figure 2.24N: Tips for Framing (three information screens)

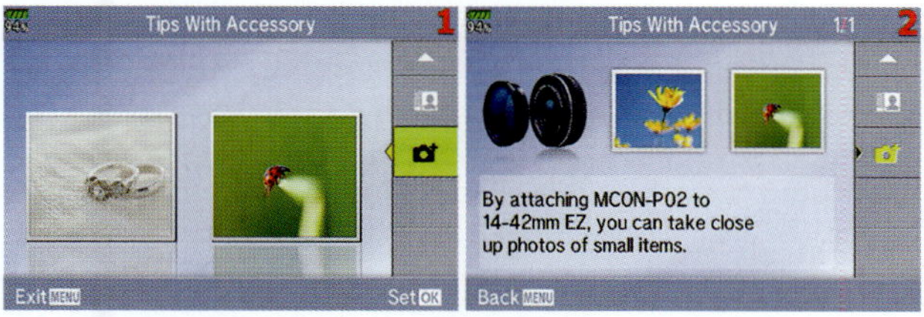

Figure 2.24O: Tips With (Camera) Accessory (one information screen)

Settings Recommendation: These Shooting Tips are rather basic but do have good suggestions for the types of photography discussed. The number of actual tips is quite limited, thereby limiting the overall usefulness of this particular function.

Now let's examine the Art Menu found when your camera is set to the ART position on the Mode Dial.

Art Menu

The Art Menu (figure 2.25A) provides 15 Art Filter types that you can use to flavor your JPEG images in-camera. Most of the filter types have more than one version, so you will see filters named Pop Art I, Pop Art II, Grainy Film I, Grainy Film II, and so on. Some Art Filter types even have three versions. In all, you can access 29 filter versions within these 15 Art Filters.

Note: Art Filters cannot be applied to RAW (ORF) images, only to JPEG pictures

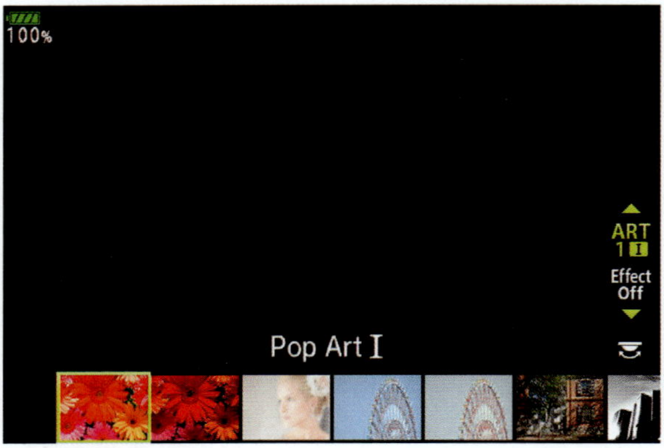

Figure 2.25A: The ART Menu

Following is a list of the filter names and a description of each. Try them out and see which ones appeal to you!

Filter Name	Description
Pop Art I, II	This mode is like the Vivid Picture Mode on steroids. All colors are saturated to the max, and contrast is raised to an even higher level than in Vivid Mode. One of the Pop Art modes is best when you are in a playful mood and want to create an exciting image. The intense colors will not be close to reality, but who needs reality when you are having fun?
Soft Focus	This mode provides a high-key and blurred effect. The contrast is very low, and there is an overall softness like fine gauze. The subject appears sharp, but it is covered with blur. The effect looks a bit like when you see yourself in a foggy mirror. It has a bright glowing effect that is sharp and blurry at the same time.
Pale&Light Color I, II	This mode washes out all the colors and lowers the contrast so blacks become grays. You might think of this as being opposite of Pop Art or Vivid Modes. It gives an image a high-key, cooler, and pastel look.
Light Tone	This mode is similar to the Pale&Light Color Mode in that it lowers contrast and desaturates colors. However, instead of having a somewhat cool (bluish), high-key look, the colors look like they are overlaid with gray film and have a darker, low-key look. Light Tone makes the image look like the effect you see when an overdone high dynamic range (HDR) image has too few shadows.

Filter Name	Description
Grainy Film I, II	This mode provides an extremely high-contrast black-and-white effect. All colors become extra-dark shades of gray, and most highlight details become pure white. This mode would be great for shooting a bare tree in a snow-covered field on a misty, overcast day. This mode creates stark images and is best for low-contrast scenes because it will obliterate any detail in strongly colored or bright scenes by adding extreme contrast to the picture.
Pin Hole I, II, III	This mode has a relatively saturated look like Vivid Mode, but it adds a heavy vignette effect to the corners of the image, as if the light rapidly diminishes. It's as though you were using a pinhole camera to make the image, except the picture is nice and sharp. Primarily, Pin Hole provides a vignette effect.
Diorama I, II	A diorama is a three-dimensional miniature in which small artificial objects are arranged and photographed to resemble real life. You can use Diorama Mode to create a reverse diorama, where real- ife places like city scenes can be made to look artificial. This mode creates a band of sharpness either in a horizontal or vertical direction (it's adjustable), and everything outside of the band is blurred, making the picture seem like it has a very limited depth of field. To create a Diorama, use the instructions found in the **Shooting Menu 1** chapter under the **Diorama** subheading on page 157 (*Shooting Menu 1 > Picture Mode*).
Cross Process I, II	This mode imitates an old method of developing film in chemicals that were designed for different types of film. Often there are odd colors and higher than normal contrast. Images shot with Cross Process have a green cast and high contrast.
Gentle Sepia	This mode converts all colors to monochrome and adds a warm, brownish effect that resembles less-saturated sepia toning. It could be used with old-fashioned clothing to imitate antique portrait pictures, or you could shoot a nature scene with this mode and make it look like a bygone era.
Dramatic Tone I, II	This mode is unusual. It creates a low-key tone where normal highlights are darkened and dark tones are lightened. Bright colors are somewhat muted, and detail is maintained, even in dark areas. There is strong contrast without being overly bright. The look is dramatic and unlike anything I have seen from other camera brands.
Key Line I, II	This mode converts the edges of the subject and the borders of contrast changes (color gradations) into line drawings. It maintains a lot of detail, unlike the cartoonish look from some other cameras. The color is mostly maintained, although it is more pastel and muted, and blacks become quite gray.
Watercolor I, II	This mode gives colors and edges a watercolor effect that tends to blow out highlights and dark areas. Most detail is lost in a normal exposure, so experiment with underexposure when you use this mode. Dark tones and extreme highlights seem to turn stark white and disappear completely from the image, and other colors become pale and washed out.
Vintage I, II, III	The Vintage Art Filter allows you to tint the image in such a way that it appears to be a faded, color-shifted image you would expect to see after a print has been hanging on a wall for many years.
Partial Color I, II, III	The Partial Color Picture Mode is designed to let you use a previously configured Partial color setup. To choose a partial color, see the **Shooting Menu 1** chapter under the **Partial Color** subheading on page 158 (*Shooting Menu 1 > Picture Mode*). After you have configured a Partial Color, only that color will display, and other colors will appear as monotone shades.

Filter Name	Description
ART BKT	This mode takes a single picture with no special effects, and then creates 14 copies of the picture and applies each ART filter (version I only). Therefore, taking one picture will result in 15 pictures being created. But wait, there's more! If you apply all Picture Modes—including the Art filters—at *Shooting Menu 2 > Bracketing > On > ART BKT > On,* one Shutter button press will result in 38 pictures being created, as the camera enthusiastically applies up to 37 selected Picture Modes and Art Filters to your single image. Be careful when using this mode because you could end up with a huge number of images very quickly. Please see the information in the **Shooting Menu 2** chapter under the subheading **Bracketing** on page 201 for deeper information about ART mode bracketing.

Now let's examine the controls and screens needed to choose one of the Art Filters.

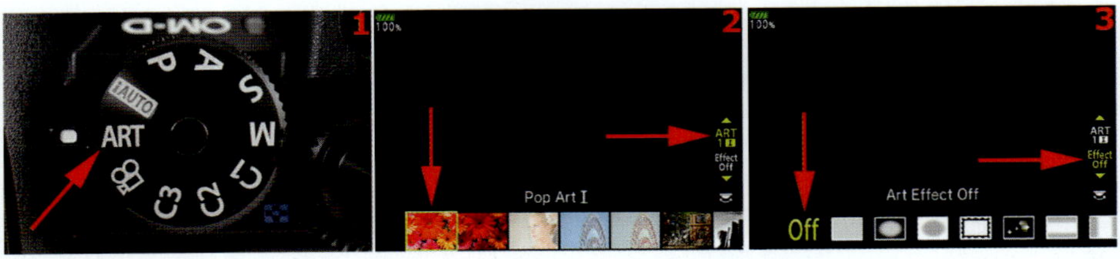

Figure 2.25B: The ART Menu and its Effects selections

Make sure your camera is set to ART mode on the Mode Dial (figure 2.25B, image 1).

When you open the Live View screen or peer through the electronic viewfinder (EVF), you will see the screen shown in figure 2.25B, image 2, except that your subject will appear instead of the black background. Any filter you choose will immediately affect the subject so that you can choose a look you enjoy.

Scrolling up or down with the Arrow Pad on the screen shown in figure 2.25B, image 2, will provide you with the Art Filter or a special Effect that can be applied to that filter. In image 2 the right arrow is pointing to the name of the Art Filter. In image 3 I have scrolled down (right arrow) and selected the Effects section for the Pop Art I filter. The arrows on the left point to the name of the Art Filter (image 2) or Effect (image 3). Basically, scrolling up or down toggles between the currently selected Art Filter and a set of Effects (e.g., Frame, Pin Hole, White Edge) that can be applied to that filter. You should see your Art Filter choice and the Effect you have chosen immediately applied to the subject on the camera screen. Press the OK button to select the Art Filter and any Effect you have added, and then take your pictures.

Deeper Information: This chapter provides a simple introduction to the Art Filters and shows you where they are located on the camera. Art Filters are just specialized Picture Modes under a different name. The Art Filters are discussed in much deeper detail in the **Shooting Menu 1** chapter under the **Picture Mode** subheading on page 151. The ART BKT filter is considered in the **Shooting Menu 2** chapter under the **Bracketing** subheading on page 201. The ART selection on the Mode Dial is just another way to access the Art

Filters and Effects. You may also use the same Picture Modes, Art Filters, and Effects from the camera's Menu system, Super Control Panel, LV Super Control Panel, and Live Control. That's no less than five human-to-camera interfaces for one set of functions. One thing is for sure, Olympus gives you multiple ways to access most of the camera's functions.

Settings Recommendation: If you would like to add special effects to your images but do not like processing images in your computer, the camera provides these filters for your convenience. Some are mild and others are quite drastic. If you experiment with the filters, I'm sure you'll find some you really like.

Now let's examine the various icons you will find on the Live View screen and in the electronic viewfinder (EVF), which is usually a duplicate of the Live View screen.

PART 3: Other Live View, EVF, and Control Screens

Electronic Viewfinder (EVF) and Live View Screen Styles

The 1,037k dot resolution, 3.0 inch (7.6 cm) Live View screen on the back of the camera and the 2.35 M dot resolution electronic viewfinder (EVF) usually have the same appearance. You can select from three EVF styles, as shown in figure 2.26A.

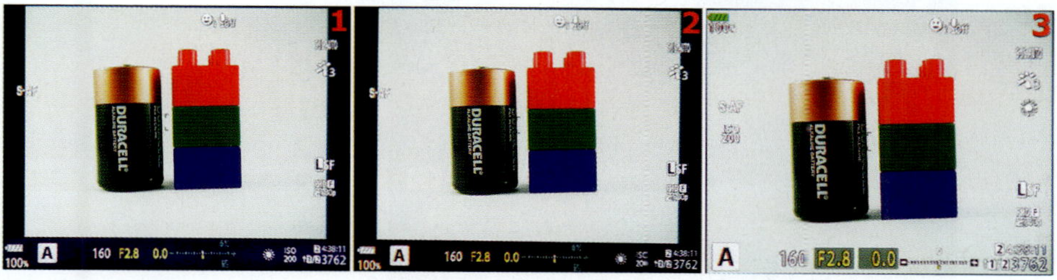

Figure 2.26A: EVF screen styles 1, 2, and 3

Two of the three EVF styles are very similar (figure 2.26A, images 1 and 2). They have sparse screens that display only information that is absolutely necessary. Because they are similar to displays from the old film days, they are considered retro styles.

Style 1 has a blue band at the bottom of the screen with white and yellow text (image 1), and Style 2 has a black bar with white and yellow text (image 2). Both of these styles limit information mostly to the bottom bar, although they display some of the symbols shown in figure 2.26B in upper areas of the screen.

Style 3 (figure 2.26A, image 3) is the default EVF style. It is modern and magnifies the subject more for ease of viewing, plus it displays more symbols and text while you shoot. Style 3 matches the Live View monitor—except for specific symbols related to touching the screen (e.g., Wi-Fi symbol)—so when you switch from the EVF to the Live View monitor, there will be virtually no change in the appearance of the screen. This cuts down on confusion when you are shooting quickly.

To change to a different EVF style, use the *Custom Menu > I. EVF > EVF Style* function, as discussed in the **Custom Menu** chapter under the **EVF Style** subheading on page 571.

Figure 2.26B is a screen that reflects EVF Style 3 and the normal Live View screen. EVF Styles 1 and 2 have similar symbols. Most photographers leave the camera set to Style 3 so the EVF and Live View screen will match.

Let's discuss the symbols you will see on the EVF and Live View screens. Besides the EVF screens we have just considered, there are four Live View screens that use the same screens as EVF Style 3. You can switch between the four Live View styles by pressing the INFO button repeatedly.

Again, if you are using EVF Style 1 or 2, then the Live View and the EVF screens will differ. If you are using EVF Style 3, the EVF and Live View screens will look the same.

First, we will look at the default Live View and EVF Style 3 screen with its many symbols (figure 2.26B). This is the Live View and EVF screen that you will see when the camera is new and nothing has been changed. For the first screen, I left the lens cap on so that it's easy to see the default symbols displayed on the screen.

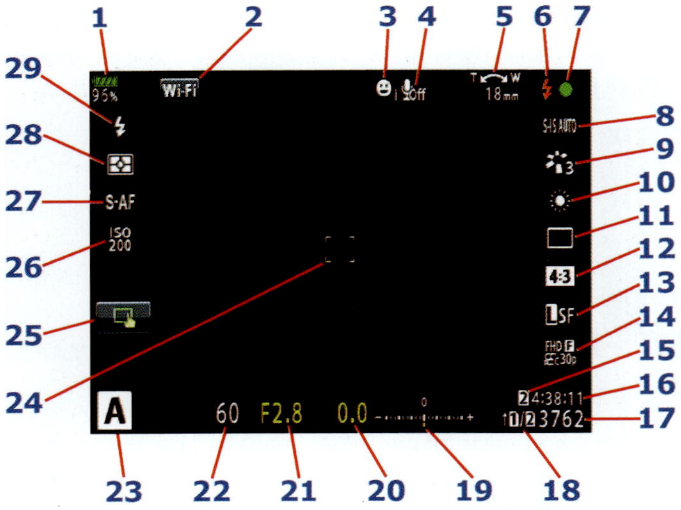

Figure 2.26B: Live View and EVF screen symbols (EVF Style 3)

Each of the numbered items in figure 2.26B are identified in the following list:

1. **Battery level:** Shows the current power level available in the camera or HLD-9 power battery holder. When an HLD-9 power battery holder is mounted, you will see a tiny PBH between the green battery symbol and the percentage number. PBH stands for power battery holder and indicates that the battery in the HLD-9 power battery holder is being used before the battery in the camera (see page 583). If PBH is not displayed, the battery symbol refers to the battery in the camera.
2. **Wi-Fi:** Enables the Wi-Fi system upon your touch.
3. ☺ **Face Priority:** Displays the current Face Priority mode setting.

4. **Movie Sound:** Shows whether the video sound recording system is enabled or disabled.
5. **Lens focal length:** Displays the focal length of the lens as you turn the zoom ring. Also shows the direction to turn the lens for telephoto (T) and wide angle (W).
6. **Flash:** Shows the status of the flash unit that is mounted on the Hot shoe. It blinks while the flash unit is recharging and shines solid when the flash unit is ready.
7. **AF confirmation mark:** Lets you know when the autofocus system has acquired good focus.
8. **Image Stabilizer:** Confirms the Image Stabilizer (IS) mode.
9. **Picture Mode:** Confirms which Picture Mode the camera is using.
10. **White Balance**: Confirms the White Balance mode.
11. **Release Mode:** Confirms the following shutter-release modes: Sequential shooting, Self-timer, Anti-Shock, Silent, and Pro Capture.
12. **Aspect:** Confirms the image Aspect ratio.
13. **Image Quality:** Confirms the image quality mode for still images: JPEG [Record Mode] and RAW mode.
14. **Video Mode:** Confirms the Movie Resolution (e.g., C4K, 4K, FHD), Compression/Bit Rate (e.g., ALL-intra, SuperFine, Fine), and Frame Rate (e.g., 60p, 30p, 24p).
15. **Movie Save Slot:** Displays the card slot number (1 or 2) for saving your video recordings.
16. **Video recording time:** Reports the hours, minutes, and seconds of available video recording time for the current Movie Save Slot memory card (see #15).
17. **Image capacity:** Reports the available image capacity for the current memory card.
18. **[Photo] Save Settings:** Displays how the camera saves still images to the two memory cards (e.g., Dual Independent, Dual Same, Standard).
19. **Exposure Compensation and Flash Intensity indicator scale:** If a yellow line of dots appears below the scale, it indicates the amount of the current Exposure Compensation. If a white line of dots appears above the scale, it shows the amount of the Flash Intensity setting.
20. **Numerical Exposure Compensation value:** Shows the current Exposure Compensation value (–5.0 to +5.0).
21. **Aperture:** Confirms the current aperture.
22. **Shutter speed:** Confirms the current shutter speed.
23. **Shooting mode:** Shows the current shooting mode on the Mode Dial (e.g., P, A, S, M).
24. **AF point indicator:** Shows the currently active moveable AF point.
25. **Touch screen operations control:** Confirms the current touch screen mode. Use it to select other touch screen modes.
26. **ISO sensitivity:** Confirms the current ISO sensitivity level and ISO mode.
27. **AF mode:** Confirms the current autofocus (AF) mode.
28. **Metering mode:** Confirms the current Metering mode.
29. **Flash Mode:** Confirms the current Flash Mode.

Now let's consider the four Live View screen styles and EVF Style 3 screen with the lens cap off. The limited symbols shown on the following screens are the same as those in the previous list. Figure 2.26C, image 1, is the same screen as is shown in figure 2.26B, but the lens cap has been removed. You can access the screens shown in images 2, 3, and 4 by pressing the INFO button repeatedly.

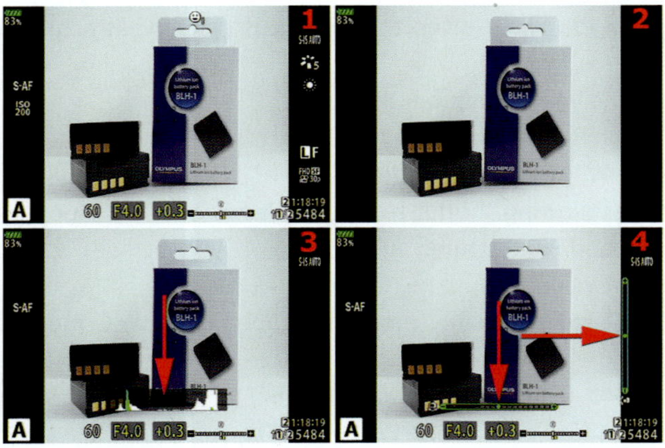

Figure 2.26C: All four Live View Screens (change with the INFO button)

Figure 2.26C, image 1, shows the default screen for Live View and EVF Style 3 viewing. Press the INFO button to move to the next screen style.

Figure 2.26C, image 2, displays a very sparse style for when you don't want the distraction of screen information overlays. Press the INFO button again to move to the next screen style.

Figure 2.26C, image 3, shows a screen containing a true Live Histogram. The histogram will change with any exposure changes you make, giving you instant feedback on any over- or underexposure situations. This is a very useful screen for those who like to use the histogram for supplementing the light meter.

The availability of a Live Histogram is one of the better features of a mirrorless camera. Cameras with mirrors can give you only an after-the-fact histogram when you use the optical viewfinder. The Live Histogram on the E-M1II is a powerful feature, and will help you judge exposure with great accuracy. If the histogram is cut off on the left side of the graph window, the image may be too dark. If it is cut off on the right, the image may be too light. If it is cut off on both ends of the histogram window, the scene has too much light range to be recorded fully in one image; therefore, you should use high dynamic range (HDR) imaging (combining multiple images with different exposures into one picture), or you can expose for the highlights and let the shadows go dark. Using the exposure meter and Live Histogram together makes for some very accurate exposures. Press the INFO button to move on.

Figure 2.26C, image 4, displays the camera's leveling system. When the horizontal and vertical level gauges are green, the camera is perfectly level. When one or both turn white, the camera is off level. Either of the two gauges will turn white and the little dot(s) at the point of the red arrows in image 4 will move when the camera is no longer level. The vertical level gauge measures tilting the lens up and down (pitch), while the horizontal gauge measures rotating the camera left and right (roll), like when you turn the steering wheel on your car. There is no yaw measurement (moving the lens left or right while the camera remains level). Use the horizontal gauge to level your camera on a tripod or when handholding for perfectly level horizons. Use the vertical gauge to level the camera with things like building edges and other vertical lines.

Note: When the Live View screen or EVF is active, pressing one of the Arrow Pad keys opens the AF Area Select screen, with its grid of 121 AF points, which allows you to move the AF point indicator (#24) to a location on the subject, such as an eye. Try it!

There are many additional symbols that can appear on the Live View screen, besides the ones you see in figure 2.26B. Many of these symbols will not show up until certain settings are changed to something different than their factory defaults. This chapter considers the most important settings you will see on the Live View screen. For a detailed look at *all* available symbols (approximately 44 of them), please refer to page 20 of the E-M1II User's Manual (2016.9 version), under the "Information displays while shooting" heading.

Touch Screen

The three-inch touch screen on the back of your E-M1II can be quite useful. You can use the touch screen to execute various camera functions, including the following:

- Set certain camera settings through the Super Control Panel (or LV Super Control Panel)
- Initiate autofocus only or initiate autofocus and also take a picture
- Zoom in up to 14x to see extreme detail for focusing before taking a picture
- Zoom in to view details of an image you just took (pixel peeping)
- Swipe to view pictures on the monitor
- Zoom in and out on pictures you are viewing on the monitor
- Enable or disable the wireless LAN (Wi-Fi) function
- Use the Live Guide system when iAUTO is selected on the Mode Dial

Let's examine the main functions the touch screen offers and see how they work.

Enabling or Disabling the Touch Screen

Some photographers may not want to use the touch screen. You can disable it by setting the *Custom Menu > J1. [Photo] Utility > Touchscreen Settings* function to Off (figure 2.27).

Many E-M1II users enjoy using the touch screen. Most of us have become used to smartphones and tablets, and the practice of touching a screen to execute an app or function is becoming second nature. However, keep this function in mind if you want to enable or disable the touch screen in the future. The default setting is On.

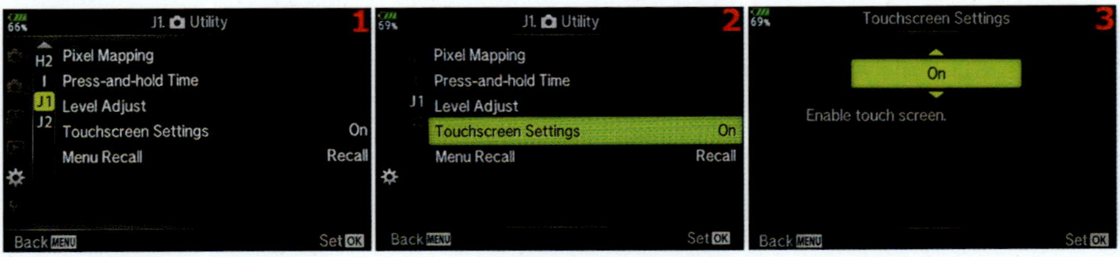

Figure 2.27: Enabling or disabling the touch screen (default is On)

Use these steps to enable or disable the touch screen:

1. Select J1. Utility from the Custom Menu and scroll to the right (figure 2.27, image 1).
2. Select Touchscreen Settings from the J1. Utility menu and scroll to the right (figure 2.27, image 2).
3. Press up or down on the Arrow Pad keys to use the up/down menu. Select On to enable the touch screen and Off to disable it (figure 2.27, image 3). Press the OK button to Set your choice.

Settings Recommendation: There are certain times when accidentally touching the screen could cause you to take a picture. For instance, let's say you are a photojournalist and are using the tilt & swivel screen while you hold the camera over your head to see above a crowd. You have the touch screen enabled, and while you adjust the angle of the screen you accidentally touch it, causing the camera to take a picture or focus on something other than the subject. In that kind of situation, disabling the touch screen makes sense.

However, for most of us, the touch screen offers excellent features and is enjoyable to use. After all, we are using one of the most high-tech cameras ever invented. Why not use it to the fullest? Other photographers are jealous that their cameras don't have a touch screen. Your E-M1II does!

Now let's consider how to use the touch screen.

Touching the Super Control Panel or LV Super Control Panel

In this chapter we have already considered how to use the two versions of the Super Control Panel, but we examined them mostly from the perspective of using external controls. Let's briefly examine how to use either of the Super Control Panels from the touch screen.

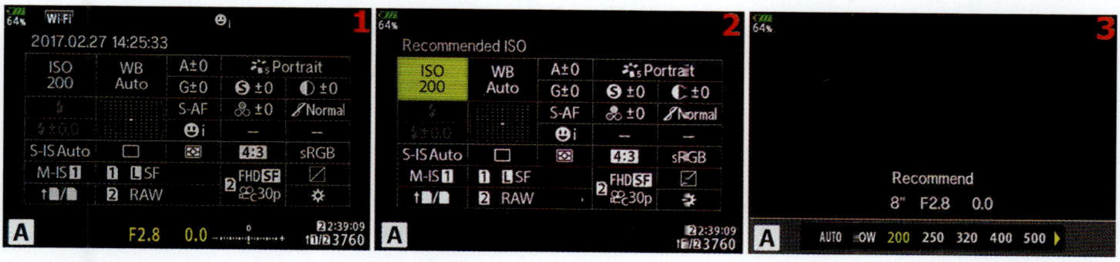

Figure 2.28: Using the touch screen with the Super Control Panel

Figure 2.28, image 1, shows the Super Control Panel when the camera is first turned on. The screen has nothing highlighted and awaits your OK button press to select one of the settings. However, you are not limited to just pressing the OK button; you can also use the touch screen to select a setting on the Super Control Panel. While the Super Control Panel is in the state seen in image 1—with no setting highlighted—touching the screen does nothing. However, if you first double-tap the screen on the setting you want to use, the screen will unlock and that function will be highlighted. After that you can touch other functions and they will be highlighted immediately. [***Note:*** The LV Super Control Panel works in a similar way, except that it always appears with some function highlighted (similar to figure 2.28, image 2). To choose a different function simply touch that function on the LV Super Control Panel screen.]

Figure 2.28, image 2, shows that I have double-tapped (Super Control Panel) or single-touched (LV Super Control Panel) the ISO function to highlight it. I could simply touch a different function and it would become highlighted. While a function is highlighted you can turn the Front Dial to scroll through the settings for that function and stop when the one you want to use is highlighted, or you can double-tap the function to open its secondary screen (figure 2.28, image 3). You must then use physical camera controls to select settings from the secondary screen. Unfortunately, the secondary screens are not touch sensitive.

Settings Recommendation: Double-tapping the Super Control Panel or touching the LV Super Control Panel is easy and fast. It prevents me from accidentally using the Arrow Pad keys and opening the Super Control Panel's default AF Area Select setting instead of scrolling around on the Super Control Panel as I expected. Remember that any time you use the Arrow Pad keys on the Super Control Panel with no function highlighted, the camera defaults to showing you the 121-point AF grid so you can select an AF point for autofocus. I keep forgetting this and find myself grinding my teeth when I discover I have, yet again, opened the AF Area Select screen when I didn't mean to.

To save myself some aggravation, I simply double-tap the Super Control Panel or single-touch the LV Super Control Panel to select the function I want to adjust, and then I use the physical camera controls to make the adjustments.

Touch Focusing with Drag and Zoom In

The camera touch screen has two modes for autofocus. The first one allows you to touch any area of the screen to focus on a certain area of the subject, drag the focus to somewhere else on the screen, or zoom in over an adjustable range (3x to 14x) to see extreme subject detail for very accurate focus. The second one lets you take a picture by touch (instead of with the Shutter button), which I will discuss in the upcoming subsection **Touch Focusing and Taking a Picture**.

Let's see how to use the touch screen for high-detail autofocus or manual focus. Figure 2.29 is the Live View screen with the lens cap on to show maximum contrast. Normally you will see your subject on this screen behind an overlay of the symbols. Have your camera in hand while you walk through these steps to make sure you understand how to use the touch features correctly.

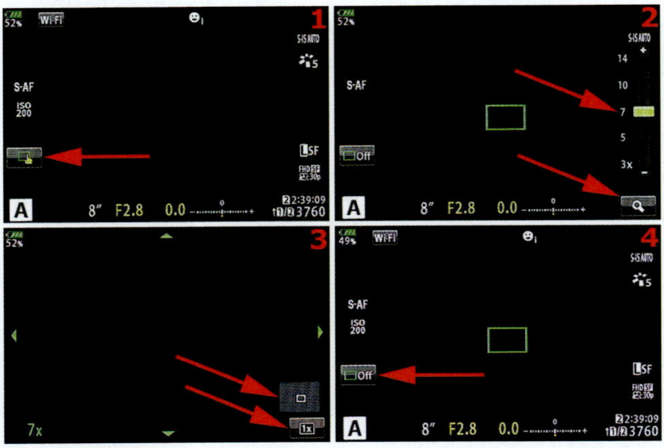

Figure 2.29: Using Autofocus with the zoom-in touch screen method

On the screen shown in figure 2.29, image 1, repeatedly tap the symbol shown at the red arrow until you see the hand and finger touching a green rectangle. This represents the touch focus only mode. After the symbol is selected, touch the portion of the subject that you want to have in sharpest focus. The camera will autofocus at that location and display a green AF target rectangle that shows where you touched.

You can now do one of several things: press the Shutter button and take a picture, change the size of the AF target rectangle and drag it to any point on the screen with your finger, or make the camera zoom in for extreme detail focusing.

With figure 2.29 as a guide, let's consider each of these actions:

- **Take a picture:** In figure 2.29, image 2, touch the screen to focus on a particular area of the subject, then press the Shutter button all the way down to take a picture.
- **Drag the AF target rectangle:** Hold your finger on the green AF target rectangle in the middle of figure 2.29, image 2, and drag it to any point on the Live View screen.

Then lift your finger and reapply it to activate autofocus, and then press the Shutter button to take a picture.

- **Zoom in for extreme focus detail:** The top red arrow in figure 2.29, image 2, points to the zoom scale on the Live View screen. This scale appears for only a few seconds and then disappears. You can touch the screen again to make it reappear. With your finger, you can slide the indicator from 3x to 14x, and you will see the AF target change size to match. This changes the area inside the AF target rectangle and makes it more or less sensitive to the exact area it is focusing on. The 14x position is extremely sensitive to detail and uses a very small AF target rectangle that covers a very small area of the subject. The 3x position uses a much larger AF target area and makes the AF target rectangle less sensitive to specific details in the subject because autofocus is based on a larger area. You can drag the resized AF target rectangle with your finger to a different area of the subject. Then you can refocus by lifting your finger and touching the screen again, or you can simply take a picture with the Shutter button. You can also move the AF target area on the Live View screen with the Arrow Pad keys. If you want to confirm the area that the camera is using for autofocus, you can touch the magnifying glass symbol at the bottom-right corner of the screen (figure 2.29, image 2, bottom red arrow). If the symbol has disappeared, touch the screen again to make it reappear. The magnifying glass symbol will make the camera zoom in and display the subject at whatever magnification you previously selected.

When you touch the magnifying glass symbol at the bottom-right corner of figure 2.29, image 2, the zoomed-in view will be displayed on the screen (figure 2.29, image 3), and the zoom level you selected will be indicated in green at the bottom-left of the screen (I chose 7x). You can move the zoomed view around by sliding your finger on the screen. A small white rectangle will appear in a larger gray rectangle; this shows you where in the image your AF target is located (figure 2.29, image 3, top red arrow). The small white rectangle represents the AF target area within the screen, and the gray rectangle represents a full-size view of the subject on the Live View screen. Touch focus does not work when the lens is zoomed in; you must press the Shutter button halfway down to autofocus, then press it the rest of the way down to take a picture. Or you can touch the 1x symbol at the bottom right of the screen (figure 2.29, image 3, bottom red arrow) to return to the normal 1:1 view before you take the picture. Be sure not to move the camera, or the autofocus may be out of date when you zoom back out. If the 1x button is not displayed, touch the screen again to make it appear.

Now that you have touch focused, zoomed in and out, and taken a picture, it is time to leave the special mode that allows you to zoom in. If you don't, the AF target rectangle will stay on the screen in whatever size you previously chose. To exit touch focus mode, touch the symbol shown in figure 2.29, image 4 (red arrow). The symbol is a green rectangle followed by the word Off. The camera will now return to normal operation.

Settings Recommendation: The touch focus, drag, and zoom method is a fast way to get a zoomed-in view of a subject that requires high-detail focusing. It works for both autofocus and when you are manually focusing. Touch focus does not work when you focus manually, but the zooming feature does. When you use Manual focus while zoomed in from the touch screen, the camera does not show focus Peaking, even if it is enabled for normal manual focus. Learn to use this method for when you really need it, such as during macro shooting.

Touch Focusing and Taking a Picture

We discussed how to use touch focus in the previous subsection. Now we will look at the second mode for the touch screen. It works like the built-in camera on a smartphone or tablet. You can focus on a particular area of the subject by touching that area, and then you take the picture. However, the E-M1II does it in a slightly different way. Instead of separating the focus and picture-taking actions, it combines the two. When you touch an area of the subject on the Live View screen, the camera will immediately autofocus and take a picture. Let's examine how it works.

Figure 2.30 shows a Live View screen with the lens cap on for maximum contrast. The red arrow points to the symbol that indicates you can touch the screen to focus and take a picture. It looks like a hand with a finger touching the side of a button. If a different symbol is displayed, tap it repeatedly until the correct symbol appears.

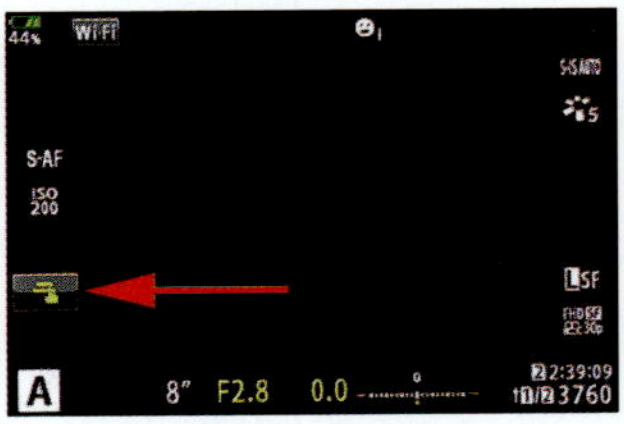

Figure 2.30: Enabling the touch function

To focus and take a picture with the Live View screen, compose the picture and touch the area of the subject that you want to focus on. The camera will autofocus on that area then take a picture.

Settings Recommendation: Taking a picture with the touch method is simpler than using a smartphone camera app. All you have to do is lightly touch the screen, and the camera will autofocus and snap the picture. This is convenient for some types of shooting, such as when you use the tilted screen over the top of a crowd or low to the ground for macro shooting. Give it a try!

Touch Screen Image Viewing

The touch screen system makes it easy for you to do full-frame, indexed, or calendar playback of images on your memory card. It works like a smartphone or tablet for full-frame image viewing, where you swipe left or right to view pictures. You cannot pinch or spread two fingers to zoom in and out, but the E-M1II has an easy-to-use zoom slider.

You can also select one or more images for protection to prevent the *Setup Menu > Card Setup > 1* (or *2*) *> All Erase* function and the Delete (red trash can) button from removing the images (formatting the memory card will still remove them, though).

Additionally, you can create a Share Order to mark images for sharing with your tablet or smartphone after you install the Olympus Image Share (OI.Share) app.

Let's see how to use the touch screen image viewing system.

Full-Frame Image Viewing

Using the touch system to view your images is the ultimate in simplicity. You simply pull up an image and swipe left or right to view other pictures.

In figure 2.31A, image 1, you can see the Playback button. Press it to open the full-frame image viewing system. As the arrows in figure 2.31A, image 2, indicate, you can swipe left or right to change to a different picture. Give it a try!

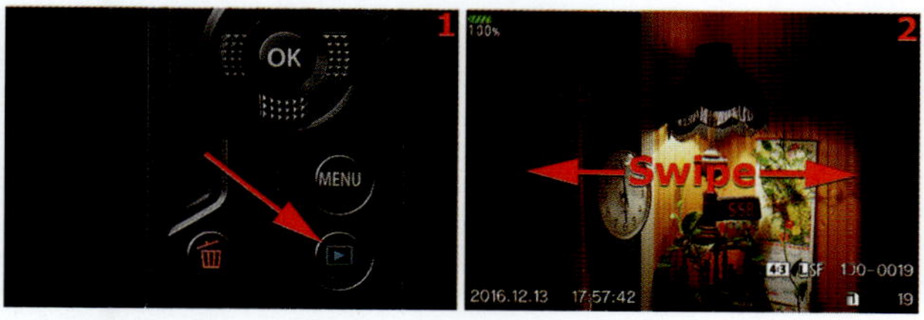

Figure 2.31A: Full-frame image viewing with the swipe method

Note: When a picture is displayed on the monitor in full-frame Playback mode, you can also turn the Front Dial, or press the left or right Arrow Pad keys, to scroll through your pictures.

Zooming In and Out on a Full-Frame Image

You can zoom in and out on the image displayed on the monitor with magnifications from 1x (full frame) to 14x. Let's see how.

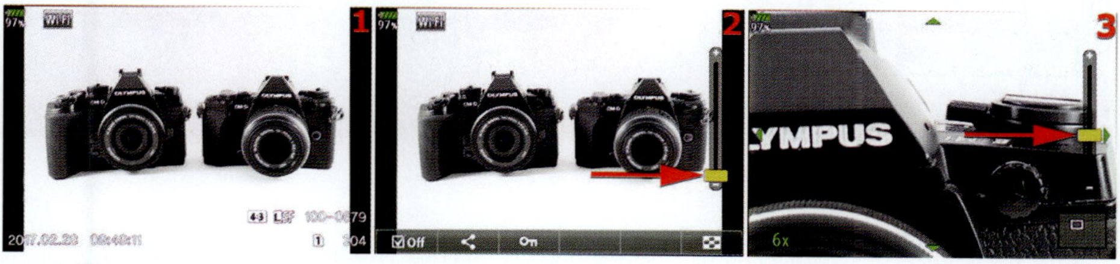

Figure 2.31B: Zooming in on an image

Figure 2.31B, image 1, shows a picture of my E-M1 and E-M5 Mark II, taken with my E-M1II. To zoom in, touch the screen. A control bar will appear on the bottom of the screen, along with a sliding zoom control on the right (figure 2.31B, images 2 and 3, red arrows). Use your finger to slide the zoom control up or down. You can also use your finger to scroll around in the frame to locate the area you want to view closely.

In figure 2.31B, image 2, the zoom indicator is at the bottom of the scale, which is the 1x full-frame position. The 1x designation does not show on the screen. In image 3 the zoom indicator is at the middle of the scale at the 6x zoom position. The zoom magnification of 6x is displayed in green at the bottom left of the monitor (figure 2.31B, image 3). At 6x, the E-M1 camera in the image is much larger and you can see more detail. Zooming in to 14x brings in very fine detail so you can see if the image is sharp.

Note: When you view a full-frame picture on the monitor, you can turn the Rear Dial counterclockwise to zoom in. This can be a faster way to zoom in. After you zoom in on a picture, you can scroll around the frame with the Arrow Pad keys, as indicated by green arrow tips on each edge of the frame.

Index and Calendar Image Viewing

If you want to scroll through 25 image thumbnails instead of a single image in full-frame mode, you can use Index viewing. When the Index is displayed, you can scroll around within the thumbnails to find an image you want to view in full-frame mode.

Additionally, you can view a monthly Calendar that shows one thumbnail for each day you took pictures. Days with no pictures do not have a thumbnail. Let's see how to use these features.

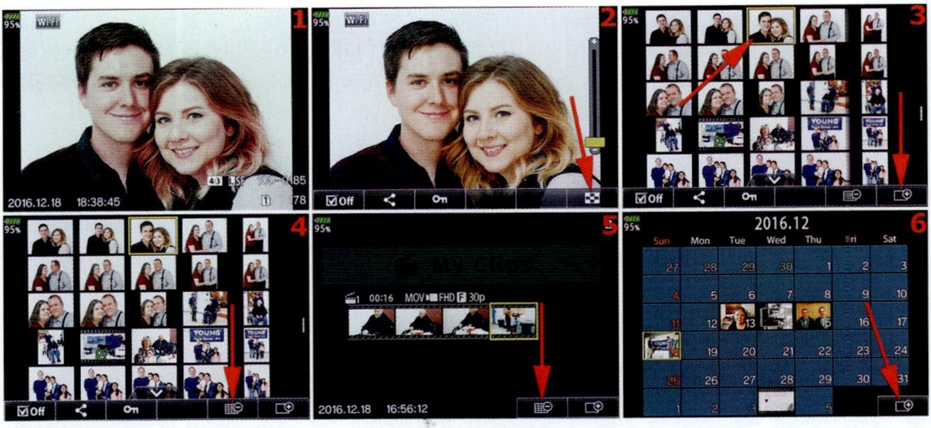

Figure 2.31C: Using the Index and Calendar

Figure 2.31C, image 1, shows a full-frame picture. To use the Index and Calendar system, touch the monitor to open the control bar on the bottom of the screen (figure 2.31C, image 2). The Index symbol is on the right end of the control bar. Touch it to open the Index of 25 thumbnails (figure 2.31C, image 3).

In figure 2.31C, image 3, notice that the current image of the young couple is at the top red arrow. When the Index is open you can tap any thumbnail to open the corresponding image to a full-frame size. To scroll through additional thumbnails, slide your finger up or down on the screen. Or you can use the Arrow Pad keys to scroll around within the thumbnails, then press the OK button to open an image to full size. In figure 2.31C, image 3, the bottom red arrow is pointing to the symbol that returns the display back to full-frame mode with the control bar at the bottom of the monitor.

Note: Touching an image in Index view will open it to full-frame size only if the symbol at the left end of the control bar says Off with a check mark (figure 2.31C, image 3). If the symbol says On with a check mark, touching a thumbnail will mark the corresponding image for other functions, such as deletion protection (Protect), sharing with a smart device (Share Order), or targeted multi-image deletion (Erase selected). We will discuss each of these functions in upcoming subsections.

The Calendar symbol is shown in figure 2.31C, image 4 (red arrow). Touch this symbol to open Calendar mode.

If there are any 1–8 second video "clips" (My Clips; not full videos) on the current memory card, an intermediate screen that displays only those video clips will appear (figure 2.31C, image 5). If there are no video clips available, Calendar mode will be displayed instead (figure 2.31C, image 6). Skip the next paragraph if you have no video clips on your memory card and the Calendar mode is displayed.

If there are video clips available, you cannot touch a video clip to play it (firmware 1.0), but you can touch a clip to highlight it. To play the video clip, you must press the OK button, which will open a window with various choices, including Play. Touch the Calendar symbol at the red arrow in figure 2.31C, image 5, and the Calendar mode will display. If the Calendar symbol has disappeared, which it does after a couple of seconds, just touch elsewhere on the screen and it will reappear. (***Note:*** We consider the video My Clips system in more detail on page 339.)

Figure 2.31C, image 6, shows the Calendar mode. December 2016 is displayed (2016.12), and you can see that I took pictures only on December 13, 14, 15, and 18, along with January 4, 2017. Each of those dates shows an image thumbnail. If you touch the thumbnail for a certain day within the current month, the Calendar will open to full-frame mode and the first image or video you took on that day will be displayed. You can swipe up or down on the Calendar to see other months.

If you touch an image that is shown in the first few days of the following month, the camera will not respond. You must swipe up or down to move between available months. In the bottom-right corner of image 6 (red arrow), you can see the symbol that returns the camera to full-frame mode. If the symbol is not displayed, touch the screen anywhere other than on a thumbnail, and it will reappear for a few seconds.

Note: When you view a full-frame picture on the monitor, turning the Rear Dial *clockwise* opens the Index and Calendar modes, which can be faster. If you use the Rear Dial to enter the Index or Calendar mode, the control bar will be condensed into a tab at the bottom center of the screen. Touch the tab to open the control bar. If you turn the Rear Dial *counter-clockwise* when a full-frame image is showing on the monitor, the camera will zoom in on the image for detailed viewing.

Protecting an Image from Accidental Deletion

When you are taking pictures, some will be excellent and others will not be as good. While you are deleting some of the less desirable images, you may accidentally delete an image you want to keep, then you have to stop using that card until you run an image recovery program on it. To avoid this scenario, you can protect your excellent images against deletion immediately after you take them.

The protection function of the E-M1II allows you to select one or many images and mark them against deletion. The camera will not delete the image, even if asked to, unless you format the card. Let's see how it works.

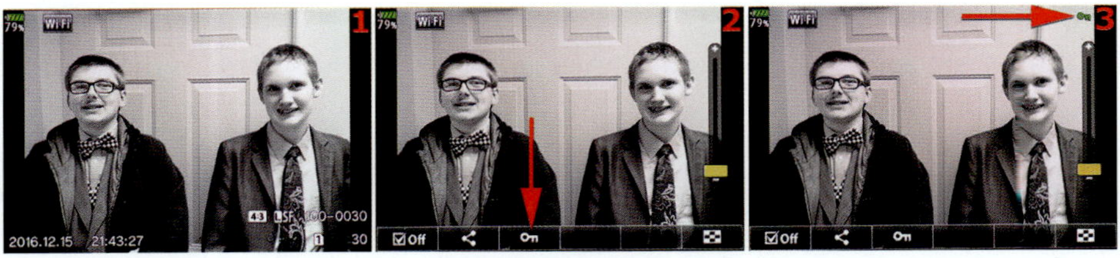

Figure 2.31D: Setting deletion protection on an individual image

Press the Playback button to display an image from the memory card (figure 2.31D, image 1), then touch the monitor to open the control bar at the bottom of the screen.

Figure 2.31D, image 2 (red arrow), shows the control bar. The arrow points to a key symbol that you can touch to add or remove protection for the currently displayed image.

Figure 2.31D, image 3 (red arrow), shows the green Protect (key) symbol that appears when you touch the symbol on the control bar. You can toggle protection on and off by repeatedly touching the key symbol on the control bar. When the key symbol is displayed at the top-right corner of the image, the image is protected from deletion (except during card formatting).

Now let's examine how to protect multiple images while using the Index format for viewing thumbnails on the monitor.

Protecting Multiple Images from Accidental Deletion

If you would like to set deletion protection on a group of images, the camera gives you an interface that makes it relatively easy to do so. You will use the 25-image Index display to select images by touching their thumbnails then setting protection. Let's see how.

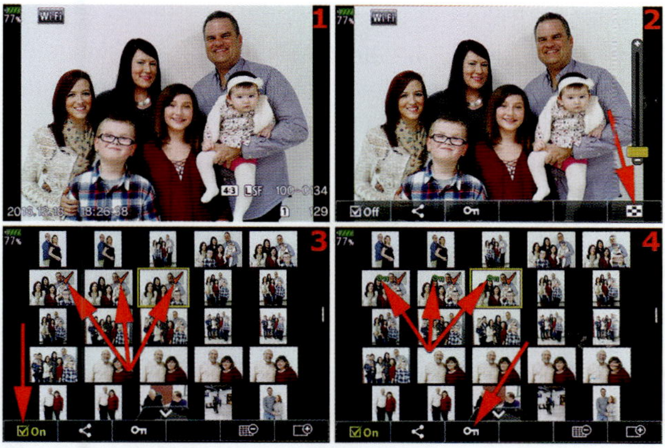

Figure 2.31E: Setting deletion protection on multiple images

Press the Playback button to display a picture from the memory card (figure 2.31E, image 1), then touch the monitor to open the control bar at the bottom of the screen.

Figure 2.31E, image 2, shows the open control bar, and the red arrow points to the Index symbol. Touch the symbol to open the 25-image thumbnail Index.

Figure 2.31E, image 3, shows the open Index. The left red arrow points to a symbol with a check mark and the word On. Notice in figure 2.31E, image 2, that the same symbol is a check mark with the word Off. By touching this symbol repeatedly you can toggle it from On to Off. When On is selected you can touch multiple images, and a red check mark will appear in the upper-right corner of each thumbnail you touch, indicating that the image is selected. If you touch a thumbnail with Off displayed, the camera will open the thumbnail to a full-frame display. Therefore, to select multiple images for protection (add red check marks), be sure that On with a check mark is displayed at the left end of the control bar. In figure 2.31E, image 3, the three red arrows on the right are pointing to three consecutive images that I want to protect from deletion. These three images are checked and ready for the next step.

After you have selected the images you want to protect, touch the Protect key symbol (figure 2.31E, image 4, right red arrow). The key symbol will appear on all images with red check marks (figure 2.31E, image 4, three red arrows on right). Now lightly touch the Shutter button, and the camera will switch back to the Live View screen. Your selected images are protected.

Note: To unprotect a group of protected images, you can use an item on the Playback Menu to reset all protected images at once: *Playback Menu > Reset Protect* (select Yes under Reset Protect, then press the OK button). This is faster than unprotecting individual images.

There is another way to apply protection to individual pictures, which we will discuss in a later section of this chapter on page 120. It involves using the menu that pops up when you press the OK button while a single image is displayed on the monitor.

Creating a Share Order

The E-M1II allows you to import images into an app called Olympus Image Share (OI.Share). You can use the camera's Wi-Fi system to send images to your smartphone or tablet. When you use the Share Order function to create a Share Order, OI.Share will ask if you want to import marked images when you connect the camera to a smart device.

Single-Image Share Order

Let's examine how to create a single-image Share Order and how to use it to import pictures.

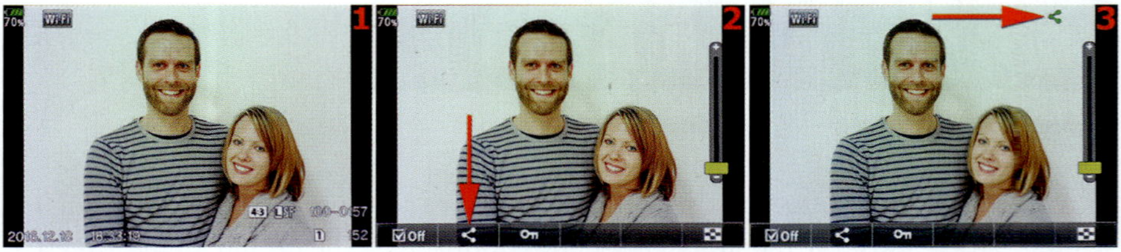

Figure 2.31F: Creating a Share Order for a single image

Press the Playback button to display an image (figure 2.31F, image 1), then touch the monitor to open the control bar at the bottom of the screen.

In figure 2.31F, image 2 (red arrow), the control bar is open. The arrow points to the share symbol that adds the image to the current Share Order or automatically creates a new one. Touch the share symbol.

The share symbol appears on the image when you touch it on the control bar (figure 2.31F, image 3, red arrow). You can toggle the Share Order for that image by repeatedly touching the share symbol on the control bar. When the share symbol is displayed on the image, it is in the current Share Order, and it will automatically be shared with a smart device through the OI.Share app.

Multiple-Image Share Order

Now let's examine how to add multiple images to a Share Order while using the Index format for viewing thumbnails on the monitor.

Press the Playback button to display a picture from the memory card (figure 2.31G, image 1), then touch the monitor to open the control bar at the bottom of the screen.

Figure 2.31G, image 2, shows the control bar open, and the red arrow points to the Index symbol. Touch the symbol to open the 25-image thumbnail Index.

Figure 2.31G, image 3, shows the open Index. The left red arrow points to a symbol with a check mark and the word On. Notice in figure 2.31G, image 2, that the same symbol is a check mark with the word Off. By touching this symbol repeatedly you can toggle it from On to Off. When On is selected you can touch multiple images, and a red check mark will appear in the upper-right corner of each thumbnail you touch, indicating that the image is selected. If you touch a thumbnail with Off displayed, the camera will open the thumbnail to a full-frame display. In figure 2.31G, image 3, the three red arrows on the right are pointing to three consecutive images that will be added to a Share Order for transmission through OI.Share. These three images have their red check marks and are ready for the next step.

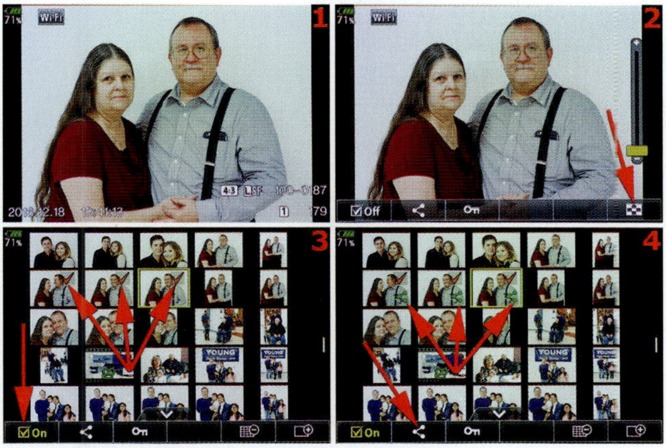

Figure 2.31G: Creating a Share Order for multiple images

After you have selected the images you want to add to the Share Order, touch the share symbol in the control bar (figure 2.31G, image 4, left red arrow). The share symbol will appear on images that have red check marks (figure 2.31G, image 4, three red arrows on the right). Now lightly touch the Shutter button, and the camera will switch back to the Live View screen. Your selected images are in a Share Order and are ready to share as soon as you connect OI.Share to your camera's Wi-Fi system.

Note: To remove all images from the existing Share Order, you can use an item on the Setup Menu to reset all shared images at once: *Setup Menu > Wi-Fi Settings > Reset share Order* (select Yes under Reset share Order and press the OK button). This is faster than removing individual images from the Share Order.

Importing Images from a Share Order

An upcoming subsection called **Wireless LAN (Wi-Fi) System** explains how to use the Wi-Fi system to connect the E-M1II with a tablet or smartphone (page 339). Figure 2.31H shows several screenshots of OI.Share during the process of importing images marked in a Share Order.

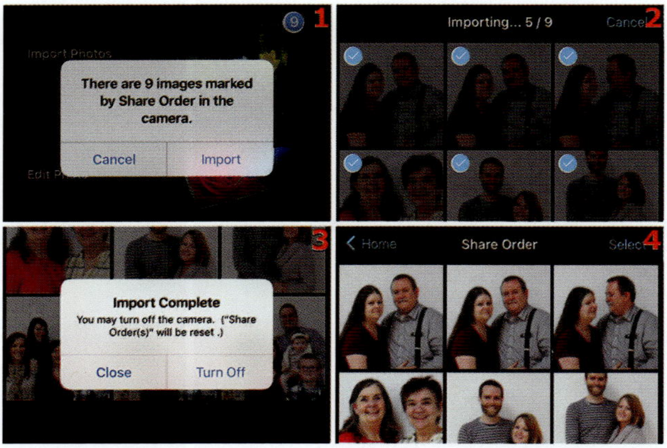

Figure 2.31H: Importing from a Share Order to the OI.Share app

Figure 2.31H, image 1, shows the OI.Share app on an iPhone as it responds to the existence of a Share Order. The app finds the Share Order on the memory card and automatically offers to import marked files.

Figure 2.31H, image 2, shows OI.Share in the process of importing images in the Share Order.

Figure 2.31H, image 3, displays the OI.Share app screen after it has completed importing the images. You may have OI.Share turn off the camera if you'd like.

Figure 2.31H, image 4, is the screen you will see once the Share Order has been fully downloaded and is ready for use. Touch a thumbnail to do something with it.

Note: As mentioned previously, we will discuss how to connect the camera and the OI.Share app in an upcoming subsection (page 141).

Other Important Control Screens

The E-M1II has a few additional screens that you can use to configure various camera functions. Let's consider them!

Playback of Images

Viewing images on the monitor (Playback) is one of the more convenient things about shooting digitally. You can see the success or failure of each image as you take it—instant gratification! Olympus makes it very easy to zoom in and examine detail in an image. If the image is substandard, simply delete it. If it is spectacular, then set things like Protection (page 120) and Sharing (page 120).

Think of the amount of money saved compared to shooting with film in the good old days. With 35mm film, each frame cost real money (up to $1). With digital, you can shoot until you're satisfied, with no additional expense!

The camera offers three Playback screens. The default screen has minimal shooting information (e.g., aperture, shutter speed, ISO), an additional screen shows detailed shooting info, and a third screen provides a very clean look at an image with virtually no information overlays.

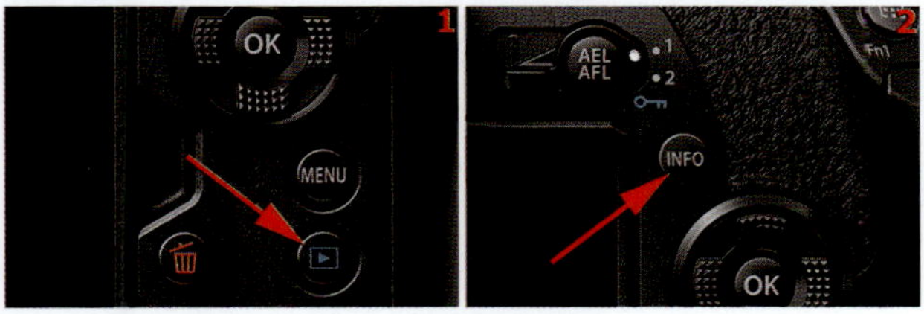

Figure 2.32A: Controls for Playback of images

There are two controls you will use to access pictures and change Playback screens. Figure 2.32A, image 1, shows the Playback button, which you press to start viewing images on the monitor. To change Playback screens, press the INFO button (image 2).

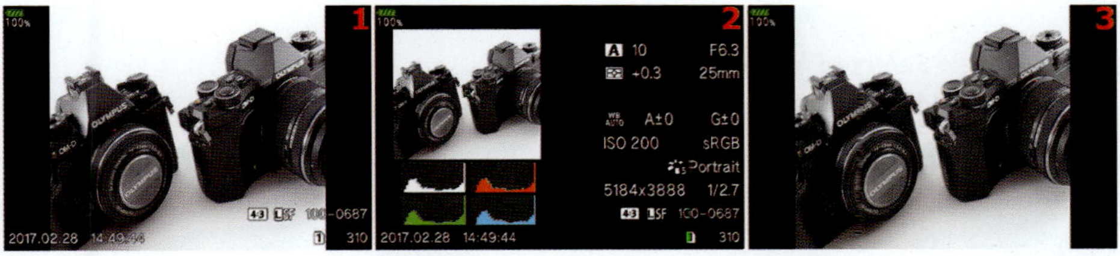

Figure 2.32B: Viewing images on the monitor

Figure 2.32B shows the three available Playback screens. Image 1 is the default Playback screen with basic shooting information, such as the image Time, Date, and image number. Image 2 shows the detailed Playback screen, with much more shooting information and a smaller version of the image displayed in the left top corner. Image 3 shows the clean screen, with virtually no overlays, so that you can get a good look at the image and zoom in and out without having information overlays obscure details in the picture.

Erasing Images

Not every picture you take will be a masterpiece. Some will be okay and others should be deleted. Let's see how we can get rid of the substandard images.

Erasing a Single Image

The camera allows you to delete a single image very quickly. Any image that is displayed on the screen and is not marked with the image protection key symbol can be deleted by using the following steps.

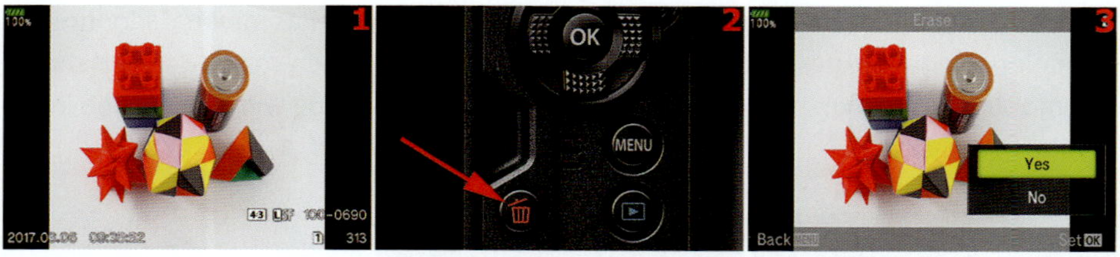

Figure 2.33A: Erasing a single image that is displayed on the monitor

Figure 2.33A, image 1, is an unsuccessful image. The first step to delete an unwanted image is to display it on the monitor as shown.

Figure 2.33A, image 2, shows the Erase button, which has a red trash can symbol. Press the Erase button once.

Figure 2.33A, image 3, shows the menu that opens after you have pressed the Erase button. You have the choice of Yes or No. Select Yes and press the OK button to delete the current image, or press No to cancel.

Next let's see how to delete a few selected images by using the Index thumbnail system.

Erasing a Few Selected Images

If you need to delete a few images to save space, you can use the camera's multi-image deletion method. It allows you to use the Index thumbnail system to examine 25 images at a time and choose several for deletion. Let's examine how it works.

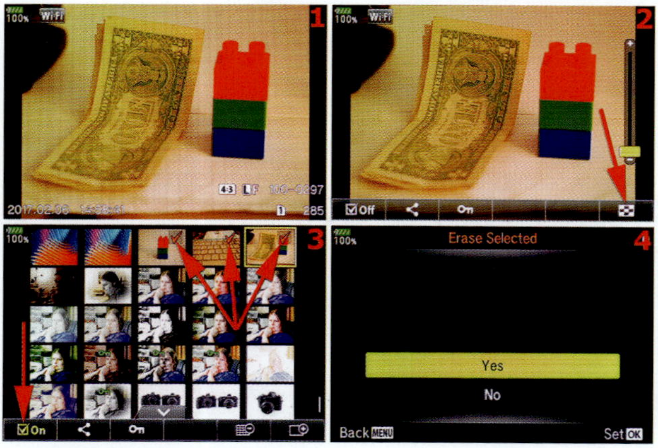

Figure 2.33B: Erasing a few selected images

Press the Playback button to display a picture on the monitor (figure 2.33B, image 1), then touch the monitor to open the control bar at the bottom of the screen.

Figure 2.33B, image 2, shows the open control bar, and the red arrow points to the Index symbol. Touch the symbol to open the 25-image thumbnail Index.

Figure 2.33B, image 3, shows the open Index. The left red arrow points to a symbol with a check mark and the word On. When On is selected you can touch multiple images, and a red check mark will appear in the upper-right corner of each thumbnail. Be sure that On is selected for this function because if you touch a thumbnail with Off displayed, the camera will open the thumbnail to a full-frame display. In figure 2.33B, image 3, the three red arrows at the top right are pointing to three consecutive images that we will delete. I touched these thumbnails to make the red check marks appear. After you select (touch) the images you want to delete, press the Erase button with the trash can icon (figure 2.33A, image 2).

Figure 2.33B, image 4, shows the confirmation screen that appears after you press the Erase button. To delete the images, select Yes and press the OK button, or select No to cancel.

Note: There are two other, more radical, ways to erase all images on the memory card: All Erase and Format. All Erase deletes all images that are not marked with a Protect key symbol, and Format erases all images on the memory card regardless of protection. All Erase is discussed on page 592, and Format is discussed on page 593.

Working with Images In-Camera

Some people do not enjoy working with computers, yet they want to shoot in RAW format and convert their images to JPEGs, or even edit JPEGs, in-camera. The E-M1II gives you a fully featured post-processing system that you can use without a computer. You can shoot RAW images, or JPEG+RAW images, and later post-process the RAW image in the camera and save the processed image to the memory card.

Additionally, the camera has several other functions that allow you to do various things with the pictures on the memory card. You can edit, share, protect, voice annotate, rotate, overlay, print, erase, or create a slideshow with images you have already taken—all without using a computer.

The functions described in this section are available in two places: first, by pressing the OK button when an image is displayed on the monitor; and second, by using the function selections that are available when you press the Menu button. Several of these settings, such as the image editing functions, are rather comprehensive and require lengthy explanations. This section will give you an overview of these functions and will direct you to deeper information that is provided elsewhere in this book.

RAW Data Edit

RAW Data Edit allows you to convert a file from RAW to JPEG in-camera. If you prefer to shoot RAW files for maximum image quality and you quickly need a JPEG for some reason, you can create one without using a computer. This item will not appear on the RAW/JPEG menu when a JPEG-only image is displayed on the monitor.

Let's look at an overview of how to access the RAW file editing system from the visual screens, then refer to the deeper information that is provided later in this book.

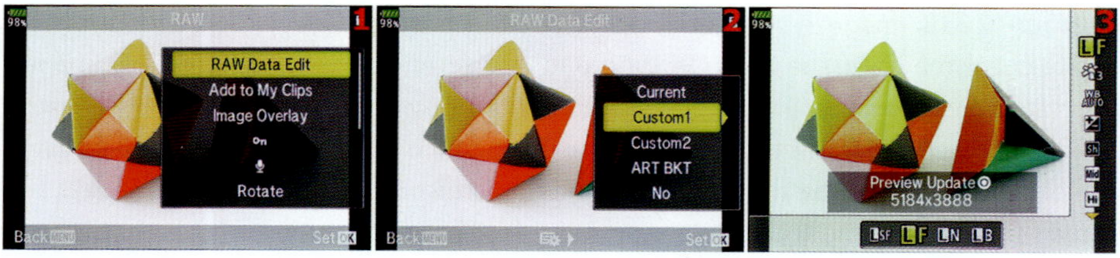

Figure 2.34A: Using the RAW Data Edit in-camera post-processing functions

Figure 2.34A, image 1, shows the RAW Data Edit menu, which will appear when a RAW file is viewed on the monitor and the OK button is pressed once. Highlight RAW Data Edit, and then press the OK button.

Figure 2.34A, image 2, shows the RAW Data Edit menu with its five image conversion choices. Select a menu item and scroll to the right. We will use Custom1 as our example.

Several of the choices have secondary screens, such as the one seen in figure 2.34A, image 3. These screens allow you to manipulate all aspects of the image—with up to 11 JPEG conversion settings, as seen on the right side of the screen shown in image 3—and then resave the RAW file as a new JPEG image without making any changes to the original RAW file.

Deeper Information: This is a rather deep menu system with many individual subfunctions. These same functions are also accessible from the Playback Menu under the Edit selection. To learn more about the deep capabilities of the RAW Data Edit functions, please see the **Playback Menu** chapter, under the **Edit** subheading, on page 366.

JPEG Edit

The JPEG Edit function lets you make in-camera changes to your JPEG image files then save them as new files. It works only with JPEG files. This item will not appear on the RAW/JPEG menu when a RAW-only image is displayed on the monitor.

Let's examine how to access the JPEG file editing system from the visual screens, then refer to the deeper information that is provided later in this book.

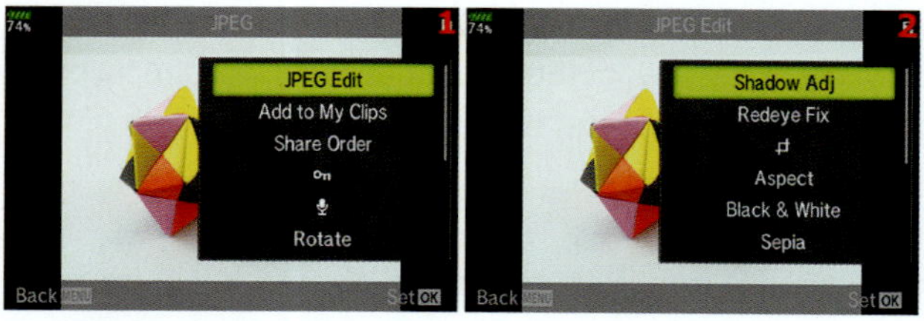

Figure 2.34B: Editing JPEG images

Display a JPEG file on your camera monitor and press the OK button button to open the JPEG menu (figure 2.34B, image 1). Then highlight JPEG Edit and press the OK button.

Figure 2.34B, image 2, shows the JPEG Edit menu. There are a total of nine choices (scroll down to see all of them) that allow you to manipulate, resize, and resave the JPEG image as a new JPEG file, without making any changes to the original JPEG image.

Deeper Information: This is a deep menu system with nine individual subfunctions. These same functions are also accessible from the Playback Menu, under the Edit selection. To learn about the deep capability found in the JPEG Edit functions, please see the **Playback Menu** chapter, under the **Edit** subheading, on page 366.

Add to My Clips

My Clips is a camera feature that allows you to combine short video clips, images, and music into a single movie. We will consider how to create short video clips and assemble everything in the **Video Menu and My Clips** chapter, under the **My Clips Movie Creation** section (page 339).

The *Add to My Clips* function allows you to insert JPEG images between videos in the current My Clips session. Let's see how to do it.

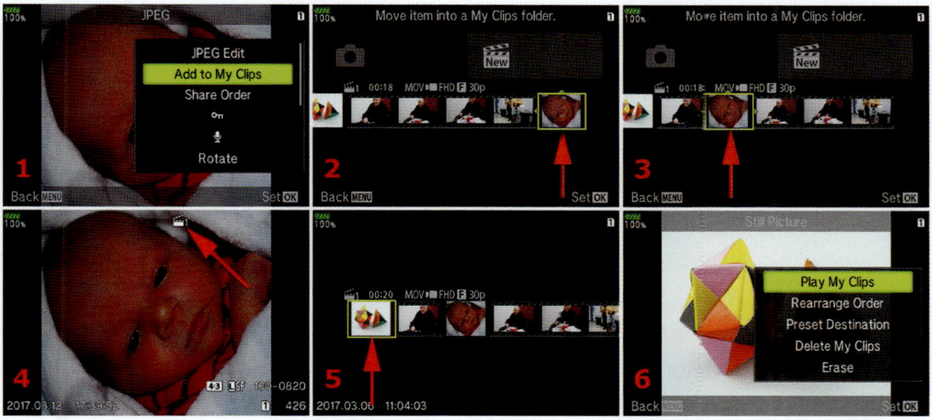

Figure 2.34C: Adding an image to an existing My Clips session

For these steps to work, you must already have a series of videos shot in a sequence (same size and type) using the 1 to 8 second Clip Recording Time video style on the memory card (see **My Clips Movie Creation** on page 339).

Display an image on the monitor that you would like to insert between movie clips and press the OK button to open the photo editing menu (figure 2.34C, image 1). Highlight Add to My Clips on the menu and press the OK button.

The Move item into a My Clips folder screen will appear, with the selected image at the far-right end of the group of My Clips videos (figure 2.34C, image 2, red arrow). Use the Arrow Pad to scroll the image to the left until it is in between two movie clips. Then press the OK button to insert the image. (When the first of the two clips finishes playing, the image will be displayed briefly, and then the next video clip will play.)

Figure 2.34C, image 4, shows the symbol that appears on any images you have inserted into a My Clips video movie.

With the marked image still displayed on the monitor, rotate the Rear Dial *clockwise* two clicks. The first click of the dial will display the 25-image index of thumbnails, and the second click will display the current My Clips folder with the movies and images you've assembled (figure 2.34C, image 5). Move to the first video in the My Clips session and press the OK button to open the menu.

Highlight Play My Clips and press the OK button (figure 2.34C, image 6). All the video clips and images will now play like an integrated movie (up to 15 minutes long).

Share Order

This chapter previously considered how to create a Share Order for individual images and groups of images (page 112). This function is another way the camera allows you to add individual images to an existing Share Order or to create a new one. When new images are added to a Share Order, the OI.Share app will automatically import them to your smartphone or tablet when you open the app and connect it to your camera with the Wi-Fi system. Let's examine how it works.

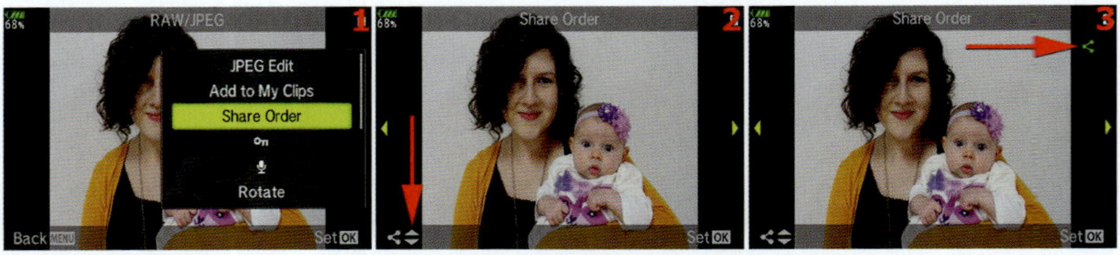

Figure 2.34D: Adding an image to a Share Order for sharing with a smart device

Display an image you would like to add to a Share Order on the monitor and then press the OK button to open the editing menu (figure 2.34D, image 1). Select Share Order from the menu and press the OK button to open the Share Order screen.

Figure 2.34D, image 2, shows the Share Order screen that allows you to add or remove an image from a Share Order. Press up or down with the Arrow Pad keys to add the image to a Share Order (red arrow). A share symbol will appear in the upper-right corner of the image when it is shared (figure 2.34D, image 3, red arrow). You can toggle this symbol on or off—to add or remove the image from a Share Order—by pressing up or down on the Arrow Pad again.

Scroll to the right or left with the Arrow Pad keys to select other images to add or remove from a Share Order.

Protecting Images

Previously in this chapter we discussed how to protect an individual image or a group of images from deletion (page 110). This function is an additional way to protect or unprotect individual images. When you add protection to an image, the camera will refuse to delete it except when you format the memory card. Let's see how it works.

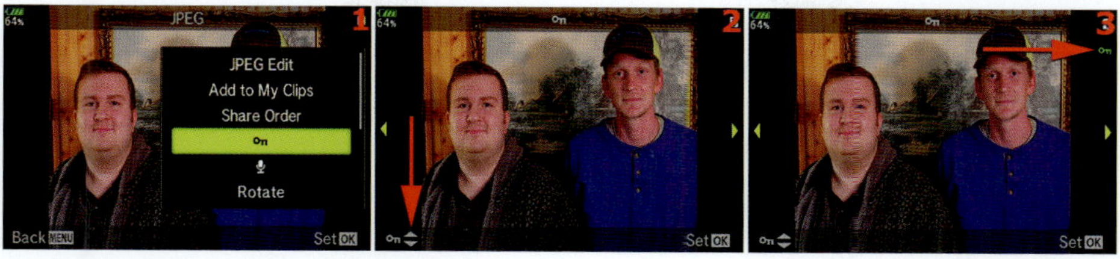

Figure 2.34E: Protecting an image from deletion

Display an image you would like to protect on the monitor and then press the OK button to open the editing menu (figure 2.34E, image 1). Select the Protect key symbol from the menu and press the OK button to open the Protect screen.

Figure 2.34E, image 2, shows the Protect screen that allows you to protect or unprotect the image. Press up or down with the Arrow Pad to toggle protection (red arrow). A small key symbol will appear in the upper-right corner of the image when it is protected (figure 2.34E, image 3, red arrow).

Scroll to the right or left with the Arrow Pad keys to select other images to which you want to add or remove deletion protection.

Audio Recording

Audio Recording allows you to add a voice message up to 30 seconds long to an image file while you view it on the camera monitor.

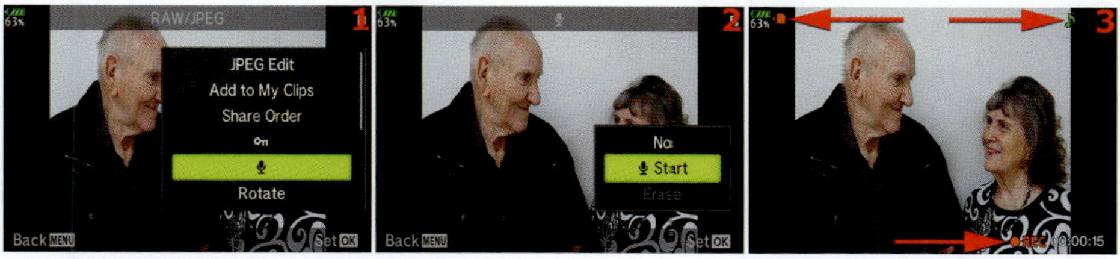

Figure 2.34F: Adding a voice message to an image file

Choose the image to which you want to add the Audio Recording and press the OK button to open the editing menu (figure 2.34F, image 1). Highlight the microphone symbol and press the OK button again.

Figure 2.34F, image 2, shows the screen that allows you to cancel (No), record (Start), or Erase an Audio Recording for the displayed image. Highlight Start and press the OK button to begin recording your voice annotation.

Figure 2.34F, image 3, shows two symbols and a timer. The symbol at the top-left arrow is the card access symbol, which will blink during the recording process. The symbol at the top-right arrow is a small music note symbol. The note symbol informs you that a voice message is attached to the image. It will stay with the image when you view it on the camera unless you Erase the Voice Annotation. The bottom-right arrow points to a red REC symbol, which indicates that a message is being recorded. To the right of the REC symbol is a counter (currently at 00:00:15, or 15 seconds), which makes it look like you can record a long message, but the camera will stop recording at exactly 30 seconds.

Rotate Image

The Rotate Image function allows you to change how an image is displayed on the camera monitor. This function does not appear to affect images after you export them to an external device; on such a device, images are displayed as they were taken.

If a picture has a vertical orientation and you would rather display it horizontally on the camera monitor, use the following steps.

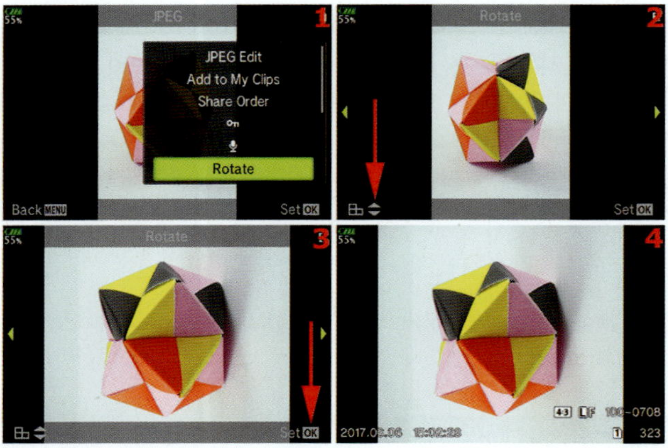

Figure 2.34G: Rotating images for in-camera display

Figure 2.34G, image 1, shows a vertical image that would also look good as a horizontal image. With the image displayed on the monitor, press the OK button to open the editing menu. Choose Rotate and press the OK button.

Figure 2.34G, image 2 (red arrow), shows that pressing the up or down keys on the Arrow Pad will rotate the image. You can rotate the image a full 360 degrees in 90 degree increments by pressing up or down on the Arrow Pad.

When you are happy with the orientation of the image, press the OK button to Set the direction (figure 2.34G, image 3).

The image will be displayed in the selected orientation when you view it on the camera monitor (figure 2.34G, image 4).

Slideshow

When you have a card full of great pictures, you may want to share a slideshow with friends and family. The camera makes it easy and allows you to display timed still images or movies with background music, if you choose.

You have full control over which images are displayed, as well as the time intervals between JPEG images (a slideshow does not work with RAW files) and videos. You can also download several songs from Olympus to use as background music (BGM).

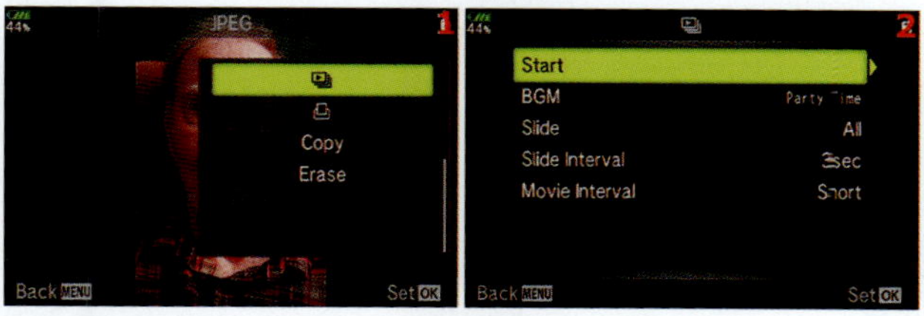

Figure 2.34H: Starting a Slideshow with default settings

It is extremely easy to start a slideshow with default values. Display any image on the monitor, and it will be the first one in the slideshow. Press the OK button to open the menu and scroll down to the first item on the second menu page. Figure 2.34H, image 1, shows the JPEG menu with the Slideshow symbol highlighted. Press the OK button again to open the secondary menu, which is a duplicate of the screen found under the Playback Menu.

As seen in figure 2.34H, image 2, select Start and scroll to the right, or press the OK button with Start highlighted, and the camera will start a slideshow of JPEG images and videos with a three-second (3sec) delay between each image and video. The default is to play only a few seconds of videos then move on to the next item.

You can modify the settings in figure 2.34H, image 2, including the following: background music (BGM); whether the slideshow should include images only, videos only, or both images and videos (Slide); Slide Interval time; and Movie Interval (short or full video play).

To stop a slideshow, press the Menu button or Playback button, or lightly press the Shutter button.

Deeper Information: Each of the items in figure 2.34H, image 2, are fully explained in the **Playback Menu** chapter, under the **[Slideshow]** subheading, on page 359.

Print Order

You can use Print Order to print JPEG images without doing much more than taking pictures and then inserting the memory card on which they are saved into a Digital Print Order Format (DPOF) compatible printing device. The printing device will read the Print Order and output the number of prints you specify.

The Print Order function will not allow you to select RAW images, only JPEGs. We will now examine an overview of setting up a basic Print Order for a single image.

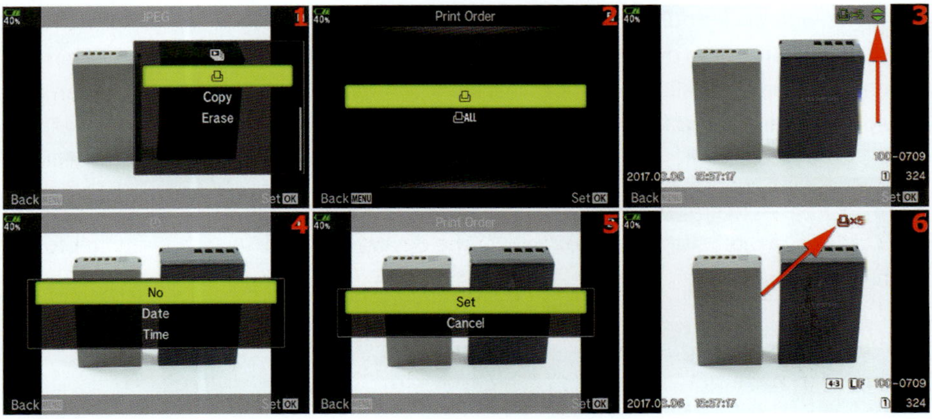

Figure 2.34l: Creating a DPOF Print Order for an individual image

On the camera monitor, display an image you want to print, then press the OK button to open the editing menu and select the Print Order symbol (figure 2.34l, image 1). Press the OK button again to open the next screen.

Figure 2.34l, image 2, shows the Print Order menu. You can choose a single image by selecting the [Print] symbol or [Print] All to mark all images for printing. Make your choice from the menu and press the OK button to move to the next screen.

In figure 2.34l, image 3, you can see a small control in the top-right area of the screen. This control allows you to choose the number of prints you want for this image; the available range is 1 print (x1) to 10 prints (x10). Select the number of prints by pressing up or down on the Arrow Pad keys. Press the OK button to Set the number and move to the next screen.

In figure 2.34l, image 4, you can select No, Date, or Time. Select No if you do not want to use a Date or Time stamp. Select one or both of the other options to add a Date and Time stamp to your printed image. With your choice highlighted, press the OK button to move to the next screen.

Figure 2.34l, image 5, allows you to select Set to confirm your choices, which means this image will be added to the Print Order on the memory card, or you can select Cancel to stop the process.

Figure 2.34l, image 6, shows the Print Order symbol on our sample picture. The red arrow points to a red symbol that is identical to the Print Order symbol in figure 2.34l, image 1 (other than color).

When you remove the memory card from the camera and insert it into a DPOF-compatible printing device, the device's software will offer you various choices based on what it finds in the Print Order.

Deeper Information: The Print Order processes for both single- and multiple-image Print Orders are covered in much greater detail in the **Playback Menu** chapter, under the **Print Order** subheading, on page 123.

Copy

The Copy function on the photo editing menu allows you to copy images from a memory card in one card slot to the card in the other slot, if there is space available on *both* cards. (***Note:*** If you do not have two memory cards in the camera, the Copy selection will not appear on the photo editing menu.) There are three ways to copy an image:

- Copy the image from the source card to the destination card using the default folder the camera will create automatically.
- Create a brand-new, user-numbered folder on the destination card just before copying the image to it.
- Copy the image to a folder you previously created on the destination card.

Let's consider how to use these methods and copy an image.

Choosing Source and Destination Memory Card Slots

You have control over which card is considered the source card and which is the destination card. Use the following screen from the Super Control Panel (or LV Super Control Panel) to choose the source memory card slot and the destination card, which, of course, must be the only other available memory card slot.

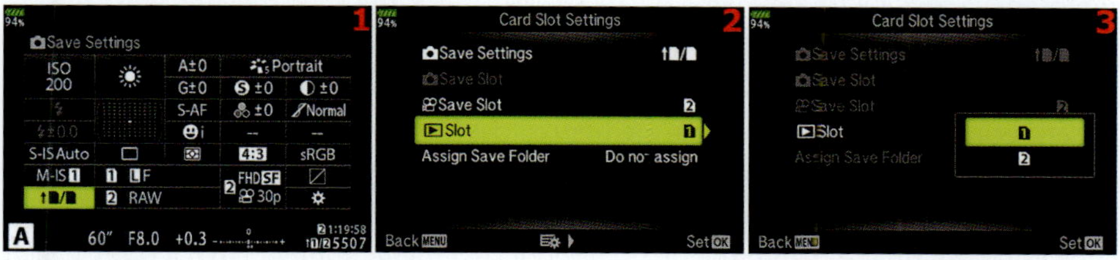

Figure 2.34J: Choosing the source and destination memory cards for copying images

Figure 2.34J, image 1, shows the [Photo] Save Settings function on the LV Super Control Panel. When this is selected, press the OK button to open the Card Slot Settings secondary screen.

Highlight the [Playback] Slot setting (figure 2.34J, image 2) and scroll to the right. This setting controls which card is the source card.

Choose a source card slot from the popup list (1 or 2; figure 2.34J, image 3). The other memory card will automatically be the destination card. Press the OK button to lock in your choice.

Note: If you prefer to use the camera's menu system to choose a source and destination card, you may use the following menu path to access the same [Playback] Slot function: *Custom Menu > H1. Record/Erase > Card Slot Settings > [Playback] Slot.*

Choosing or Creating a Folder on the Destination Card

When you copy an image, you are copying from a folder on the source card to a folder on the destination card. You can choose whether to use a default folder created by the camera, create a new folder, or select a different existing folder on the destination card. Let's see how to do each of these options.

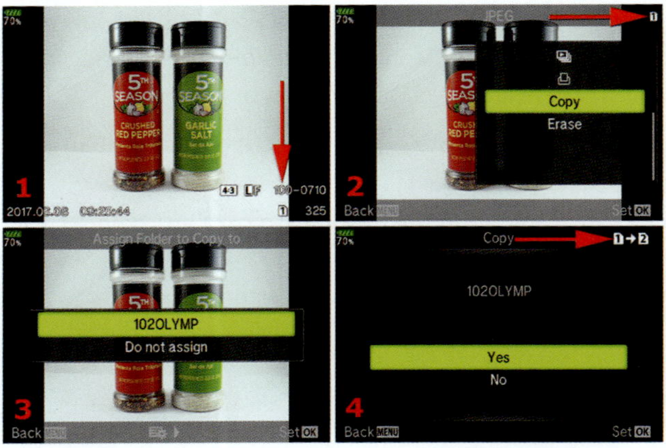

Figure 2.34K: Using the camera's default destination folder

Using camera-chosen folder names: Display the image you want to copy on the camera's monitor. Notice in figure 2.34K, image 1 (red arrow), that the folder number is 100, which represents a folder with the name of: 100OLYMP. This is the source folder. Press the OK button to open the photo editing menu.

Figure 2.34K, image 2, shows the Copy selection on the menu. Notice at the point of the red arrow in image 2 that the source memory card is listed—in this case, card slot 1. Highlight Copy on the photo editing menu and press the OK button to open the next screen.

The Assign folder to Copy to menu will appear (figure 2.34K, image 3). There are two choices shown on the menu. The first is a suggested folder number (102OLYMP), which will vary according to existing folders on the source and destination memory cards. The second choice on the menu is Do not assign, which tells the camera to decide which destination folder to use. Highlight one of the two choices on the menu and press the OK button to open the Copy screen.

Figure 2.34K, image 4, shows the Copy screen. Select Yes to copy the image from the source to the destination memory card and folder. A *Busy* screen will appear briefly while the image is copied (not shown). To Cancel the operation, select No and press the OK button.

If you would prefer to create a new folder with a folder number you supply, you can do so with the following steps.

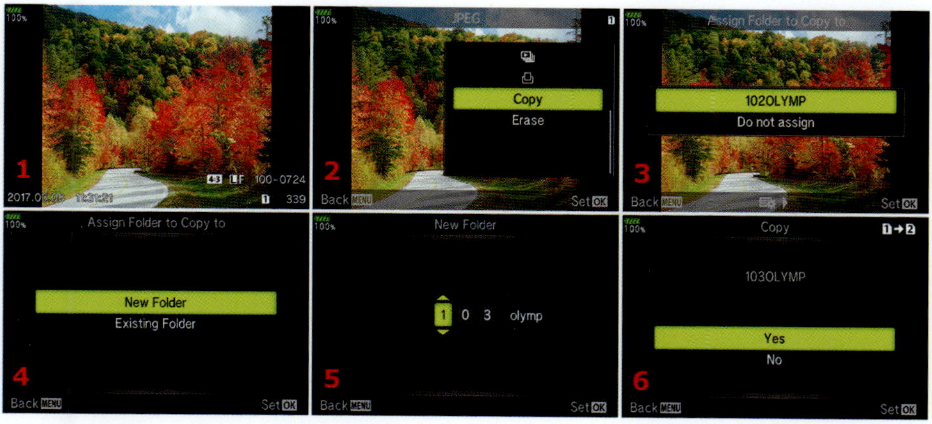

Figure 2.34L: Creating a new folder with your own folder number

Using a folder name that you choose: Choose an image you want to copy (figure 2.34L, image 1) then press the OK button to open the photo editing menu.

Highlight Copy on the menu (figure 2.34L, image 2) and press the OK button to open the next screen.

The Assign folder to Copy to menu will appear (figure 2.34L, image 3). There are two choices shown on the menu. The first is again a suggested folder number (102OLYMP), which will vary according to existing folders on the source and destination memory cards. If instead of pressing the OK button, you scroll to the right with the folder name highlighted, the camera will offer you additional choices.

Figure 2.34L, image 4, shows the Assign Folder to Copy to screen with two choices: New Folder and Existing Folder. Select New Folder and press the OK button.

The New Folder screen will open with a small up/down menu for each of the first three characters in the new folder name (figure 2.34L, image 5). You can select a new folder number from 100 to 999. If the folder already exists on the destination memory card, the camera will simply use it. If the folder does not exist on the destination card, the camera will create it. You cannot change the text portion of the folder name, which defaults to OLYMP. Use the Arrow Pad to change the three numerals to a number you want to use, and then press the OK button to Set the number.

The camera will now open the Copy screen (figure 2.34L, image 6), which is the final step before copying the image file to the folder on the destination card. Select Yes from the menu and press the OK button to copy the image to the selected folder. A *Busy* screen will appear briefly while the image is copied (not shown). To cancel the operation, select No and press the OK button.

Finally, you can choose an existing folder instead of creating one. Let's see how.

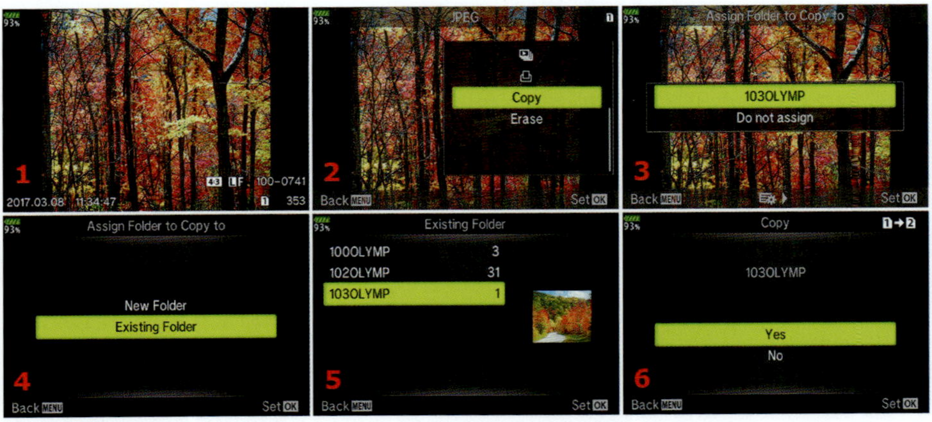

Figure 2.34M: Choosing an existing folder from a list of available folders

Choosing an existing folder: Choose an image you want to copy (figure 2.34M, image 1) then press the OK button to open the photo editing menu.

Highlight Copy on the menu (figure 2.34M, image 2) and press the OK button to open the next screen.

The Assign Folder to Copy to menu will appear (figure 2.34M, image 3). There are two choices shown on the menu. The first is again the suggested folder number (102OLYMP), which will vary according to existing folders on the source and destination memory cards. If instead of pressing the OK button, you scroll to the right with the folder name highlighted, the camera will offer you additional choices.

Figure 2.34L, image 4, shows the Assign Folder to Copy to screen with two choices: New Folder and Existing Folder. Select Existing Folder and press the OK button.

The camera will now display the Existing Folder screen with a choice of folders that already exist on the destination memory card (figure 2.34M, image 5). My camera's destination memory card has three available folders (100OLMYP, 102OLYMP, and 103OLYMP). To the right of the folder name in image 5, you will see the number of images in each folder (3, 31, and 1), along with a thumbnail of one or more images that already exist in the folder. Highlight the folder to which you want to copy the image and press the OK button.

The camera will now open the Copy screen (figure 2.34M, image 6), which is the final step before copying the image file to the folder on the destination card. Select Yes from the menu and press the OK button to copy the image to the selected folder. A *Busy* screen will appear briefly while the image is copied (not shown). To cancel the operation, select No and press the OK button.

Note: If you prefer, you can duplicate these operations by using the following camera menu path instead of the photo editing menu: *Custom Menu > H1. Record/Erase > Card Slot Settings > Assign Save Folder.*

Erase

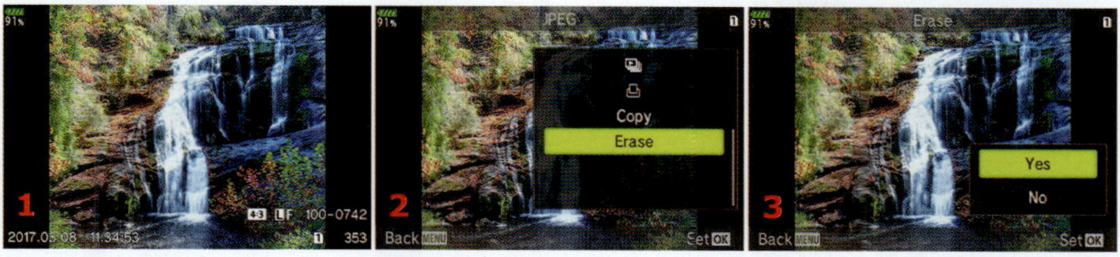

Figure 2.34N: Deleting a single image (RAW or JPEG) or video

Display an image or video that you no longer want on the monitor and press the OK button to open the photo editing menu (figure 2.34N, image 1).

Select Erase from the photo editing menu (figure 2.34N, image 2) and press the OK button to start the deletion process.

In figure 2.34N, image 3, you can see a small menu with the choices of Yes or No. Choose Yes and press the OK button to immediately delete the displayed image or video, or select No to cancel.

Mode Dial Setting Control Screens

The Mode Dial on top of the E-M1II has 10 settings. Each setting has a control screen that lets you use the camera in specific ways.

Let's examine each mode briefly. They will be used throughout the rest of this book as we discuss how they relate to photography with the E-M1II and individual camera settings.

Manual (M) Mode

Manual (M) is the ultimate mode for taking your time and getting it right. For photographers who want complete control of their cameras, M mode is best. The camera makes no decisions about the exposure triangle (shutter speed, aperture, and ISO sensitivity) for still pictures, leaving it up to the photographer to take full creative control of the exposure. You control the shutter speed with the Rear Dial and the aperture with the Front Dial.

Let's examine the control screens you use in M mode.

Figure 2.35A, image 1, shows the Mode Dial set to Manual (M) mode. With this mode you have full control of the shutter speed, aperture, and ISO, as well as exposure compensation. Notice in images 2–4 that an M appears in the lower-left corner of the Live View screen.

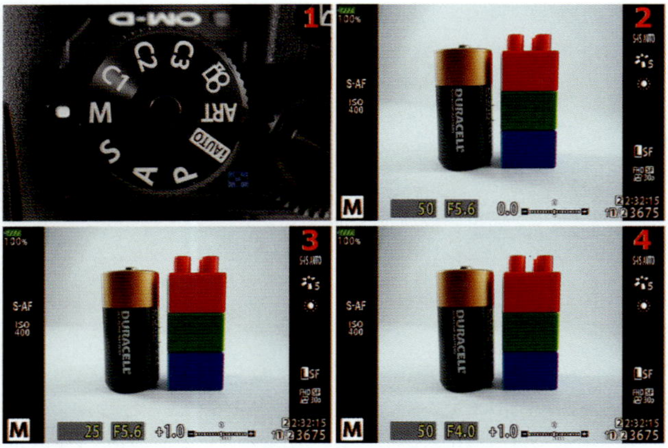

Figure 2.35A: Using Manual (M) mode on the Mode Dial

Figure 2.35A, image 2, shows a good exposure of my battery and blocks. The exposure control settings are displayed at the bottom of the screen (50, F5.6, 0.0). Notice that both the shutter speed (50) and aperture (F5.6) settings are in dark rectangles, which means you have manual control of the settings. The current shutter speed is 1/50 sec (50) and is *controlled with the Rear Dial*. The current aperture is f/5.6 (F5.6) and is *controlled with the Front Dial*. Notice that to the right of 0.0, at the bottom of image 2, there is a –/+ exposure indicator that is currently zeroed out. There is a tiny square under the 0 point of the scale, and there are no other tiny squares along the bottom of the scale. This indicates that the exposure is good, and the camera is ready for you to press the Shutter button and take a picture.

Figure 2.35A, image 3, shows that I have adjusted the shutter speed by 1 EV step (1 stop). It was set to 1/50 sec (50) in image 2, and now it is set to 1/25 sec (25). Turn the Rear Dial to change the shutter speed. Also, notice that since I added an extra stop (+1.0) of exposure, the –/+ exposure indicator now displays +1.0, and there are several tiny squares under the –/+ exposure scale (image 3). The squares are extending toward the first major division on the + side of the scale, which represents 1 stop overexposure. The camera gives you both a numerical (e.g., 0.0, +1.0) value and a –/+ scale value. The numerical value can register a maximum of 3 stops (+3.0) overexposure and 3 stops underexposure (–0.3). The –/+ scale registers the same 3 stops. If you exceed 3 stops (3 EV steps) of over- or underexposure, the numerical exposure value and the squares under the –/+ scale blink rapidly.

Figure 2.35A, image 4, shows that I have restored the shutter speed to 1/50 sec (50) and adjusted the aperture from f/5.6 (F5.6) to f/4 (F4.0). You adjust the aperture with the Front Dial. Notice also that since 1/50 sec at f/5.6 is the correct exposure for this subject (image 2), and my camera is set to 1/50 sec at f/4 in image 4, the numeric exposure value and –/+ scale are both again registering 1 stop of overexposure (+1.0 EV).

Basically, you can use either the aperture or shutter speed to dial in the best exposure. This allows you to use the aperture to control depth of field and the shutter speed to control motion.

After you have the exposure set the way you want it, take your pictures. Next let's consider Shutter priority (S) mode for photographers who need to control motion.

Note: When you turn the Front and Rear Dials to change the shutter speed and aperture, each click of the dial changes the exposure by an amount equal to the value in the EV Step function at *Custom Menu > E1. Exp/ISO/BULB/[Meter] > EV Step*. The factory default is 1/3 EV (1/3 stop) for each click. However, if you prefer, you can set the value to 1/2 EV or 1 EV per click in the EV Step function.

Shutter Priority (S) Mode

Shutter priority (S) mode is for photographers who shoot moving subjects and need to stop action, such as for sports photography. It is also used by photographers who need to blur motion, such as when shooting a waterfall.

S mode is a semiautomatic mode; the photographer takes manual control of the shutter speed, and the camera provides automated aperture control, maintaining correct exposure values.

Let's see how to adjust the camera in S mode.

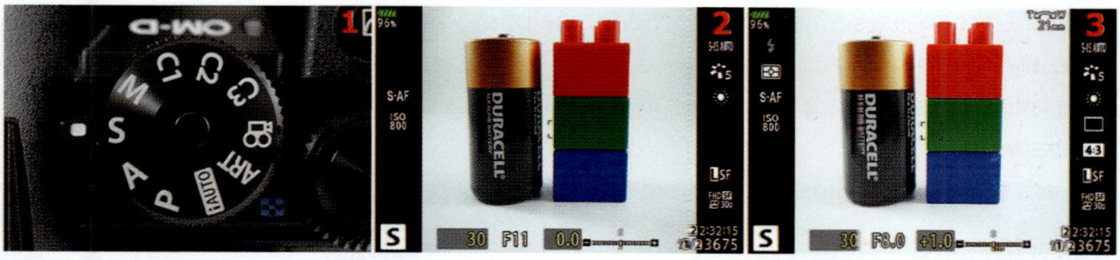

Figure 2.35B: Using Shutter priority (S) mode

Figure 2.35B, image 1, shows the Mode Dial set to Shutter priority (S) mode. Again, when you use S mode you have full control of the shutter speed, and the camera automatically adjusts the aperture, so the exposure is always accurate. Notice in images 2 and 3 that an S appears in the lower-left corner of the Live View screen.

Figure 2.35B, image 2, shows a good exposure of my battery and blocks. You can see the exposure control settings at the bottom of the screen (30, F11, 0.0). The current shutter speed is set to 1/30 sec (30) and is *controlled with the Rear Dial*. Notice that the shutter speed (30) is in a dark rectangle and the aperture (F11) is not. This indicates that you have manual control of the shutter speed, and the camera automatically controls the aperture. Also, notice that the 0.0 setting (exposure compensation) is in a dark rectangle, which means you can control it and override the camera's automatic exposure value by adding or subtracting light. You control –/+ exposure compensation with the Front Dial. You can dial in exposure compensation over a range of 10 EV steps (–5.0 to +5.0). The –/+ scale shows the current compensation value in either a negative or positive direction.

Note: Be careful when you use exposure compensation because Live View can fool you. If the aperture number starts to blink on the monitor, the camera cannot provide additional compensation. The Live View monitor may continue to brighten or darken, but no light is being added or subtracted to the image (also see the next **Note**).

In figure 2.35B, image 3, I dialed in +1.0 EV of exposure compensation. The camera adjusted the aperture from F11 (image 2) to F8.0 (image 3) to provide one additional EV step of exposure. After you have the exposure set the way you want it, take your pictures.

Note: While you are making shutter speed adjustments with the Rear Dial, you may see the aperture number start to blink. This means the camera has reached its maximum or minimum aperture and cannot open or close the aperture any further, even though the monitor may brighten or darken. If this happens, you may want to consider using ISO AUTO so the camera can increase or decrease the ISO sensitivity to maintain a good exposure. Do not let the image you see on the Live View screen fool you when the aperture number is blinking.

Aperture Priority (A) Mode

Aperture priority (A) mode is for photographers who need to control the depth of field (zone of sharp focus), such as in portrait or landscape photography.

The A mode is a semiautomatic mode; the photographer manually controls the aperture, and the camera automatically controls the shutter speed, maintaining correct exposure values. Basically, a good exposure will be maintained when the camera and photographer work together.

Let's see how to adjust the camera in A mode.

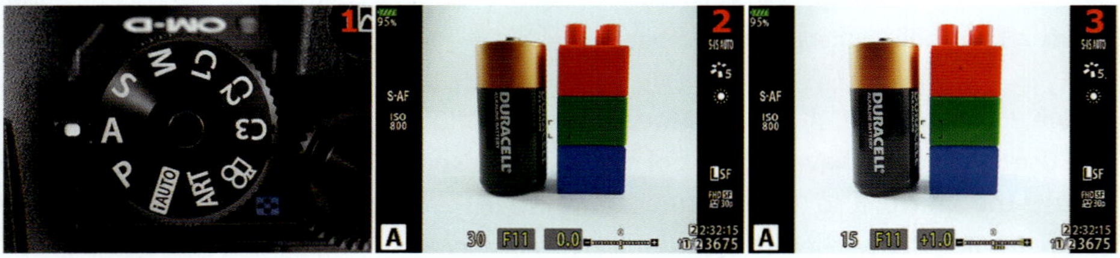

Figure 2.35C: Using Aperture priority (A) mode

Figure 2.35C, image 1, shows the Mode Dial set to Aperture priority (A) mode. When you use this mode you have full control of the aperture, and the camera automatically adjusts the shutter speed so the exposure is accurate. When you use A mode at small apertures be sure the shutter speed does not get too slow to handhold. With the 5-axis Image Stabilizer (IS) built in to the E-M1II, you may be able to get sharp pictures down to 1 second (1") unless you are a shaky person (some have reported less and some have reported more). When you shoot at slow shutter speeds, use a monopod or tripod for the best results.

Notice in images 2 and 3 that an A appears in the lower-left corner of the Live View screen when you use A mode.

Figure 2.35C, image 2, shows a good exposure of my battery and blocks. You can see the exposure control settings at the bottom of the screen (30, F11, 0.0). The aperture is set to f/11 (F11) and is *controlled with the Rear Dial*. Notice that the aperture setting (F11) is in a dark rectangle and the shutter speed setting (30) is not. This indicates that you have manual control of the aperture, and the camera automatically controls the shutter speed. Also, notice that the 0.0 setting (exposure compensation) is in a dark rectangle, which means you can control it and override the camera's automatic exposure value by adding or subtracting light. You control –/+ exposure compensation with the Front Dial. You can dial in exposure compensation over a range of 10 EV steps (–5.0 to +5.0). The –/+ scale shows the current compensation value in either a negative or positive direction.

Note 1: Be careful when you use exposure compensation because Live View can fool you. If the shutter speed number starts to blink on the monitor, the camera cannot provide additional compensation. The Live View monitor may continue to brighten or darken, but no light is being added or subtracted to the image (also see **Note 2**).

In figure 2.35C, image 3, I dialed in +1.0 EV of exposure compensation. The camera adjusted the shutter speed from 30 (image 2) to 15 (image 3) to provide one additional EV step of exposure. After you have the exposure set the way you want it, take your pictures.

Note 2: While you are making aperture adjustments with the Rear Dial, you may see the shutter speed number start blinking. This means the camera has reached its maximum 1/8000 second (8000) or minimum 60 second (60") shutter speed and cannot adjust the shutter speed any further, even though the monitor may brighten or darken. If this happens, you may want to consider using ISO AUTO so the camera can increase or decrease the ISO sensitivity to maintain a good exposure. Do not let the image you see on the Live View screen fool you when the shutter speed number is blinking.

Program (P) Mode

Program (P) mode is a throwback to when full automation first arrived on cameras. In the olden days, P mode was similar to today's iAUTO mode. P mode provides fully automatic control of the shutter speed and aperture and lets the photographer concentrate on taking pictures. In a sense, the camera becomes a point-and-shoot camera when you use P mode.

However, unlike iAUTO mode, where the camera takes complete control of all aspects of getting the picture, P mode allows you to have some control for special circumstances. You can take control of the aperture by turning the Rear Dial and overriding the camera's aperture choice. This allows you to shoot without thinking about camera settings, but when you need to, you can override the camera's aperture setting with one of your own; the camera still controls the shutter speed.

When you override the aperture setting with the Rear Dial, you place the camera into a special version of the Program mode, called Program shift (Ps) mode. Ps mode is very similar to A mode, which we considered in the previous chapter subsection.

Let's see how to use P mode and Ps mode.

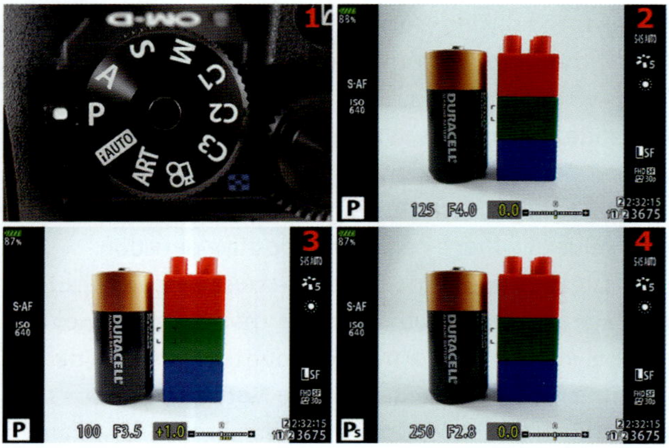

Figure 2.35D: Using Program (P) and Program shift (Ps) modes

Figure 2.35D, image 1, shows the Mode Dial set to Program (P) mode. Notice in images 2 and 3 that a P appears in the lower-left corner of the Live View screen when you use Program mode, and Ps appears when you use Program shift mode (image 4). Also notice that in images 2–4 the shutter speed and aperture numbers are not in dark rectangles (unlike M, S, and A modes). This indicates that the camera automatically controls the shutter speed and aperture in P mode, even though you can override the aperture setting in Ps mode.

In figure 2.35D, image 2, the shutter speed of 1/125 sec (125) and aperture of f/4 (F4.0) are just right for a good exposure. At this point I could take the picture and not worry about any of the settings. The camera is in control.

In figure 2.35D, image 3, I used the Front Dial to add +1.0 EV exposure compensation. The camera changed the shutter speed from 1/125 sec (125) to 1/100 sec (100) and the aperture from f/4 (F4.0) to f/3.5 (F3.5). This maintains a balanced exposure with +1.0 EV of compensation.

In figure 2.35D, image 4, I removed the exposure compensation value and overrode the aperture setting by turning the Rear Dial. The camera changed the P in the bottom-left corner to Ps. It is now using Program shift mode, allowing me to shift the programmed exposure to one more closely matching what I would like to use. I chose an aperture of f/2.8 (F2.8), which is 1 EV step more exposure than f/4 (image 2), or double the light. The camera changed the shutter speed from 1/125 sec (image 2) to 1/250 sec (image 4), or half the time, to compensate for the extra stop of light I added by opening the aperture. Double the light for half the time is an equivalent exposure, except the new settings will result in a shallower depth of field (larger aperture) and faster shutter speed. To exit Ps mode, turn the Rear Dial until the camera displays the original shutter speed. When you are ready, take your pictures.

iAUTO Mode

iAUTO mode is the camera's point-and-shoot mode. It is great for those who want to take pictures without having to worry about camera settings. In this mode, the camera controls the shutter speed, aperture, and ISO sensitivity, relieving you of that responsibility.

Because this is a fully automatic mode, you can just take pictures and enjoy your photography. The camera is very capable of making excellent images with no help, so this mode is a great one to use when you are just learning to operate a more complex camera and you want to make sure you get some good pictures.

That said, being an Olympus camera, the E-M1II gives you ways to take control if you want to with the Live Guide menu, which is always available when you are using iAUTO mode. We previously discussed the Live Guide menu in this chapter starting on page 85. The Live Guide may be used to override the camera's automatic settings in a visual way. This is useful for an inexperienced photographer.

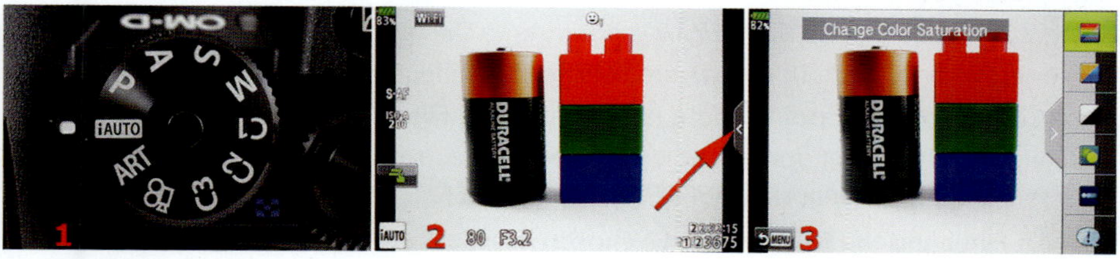

Figure 2.35E: Using iAUTO mode

Figure 2.35E shows the iAUTO setting on the Mode Dial (image 1), along with the Live Guide Menu system (image and 3). Set your camera to this mode and go take images worry-free. If you want to experiment with the appearance of the not-yet-taken image shown on the monitor, simply touch the little tab shown at the red arrow in image 2 and the Live Guide menu will appear (image 3). You can use the six functions from the menu to change the currently displayed subject in various ways (saturation, tint, brightness, background blur, and motion control) before you take the picture.

Deeper Information: Please see the subsection titled **Using the Live Guide Menu Items** (page 85), which discusses using the Live Guide system to change how iAUTO mode renders your photographs.

ART Mode

As previously discussed in in Part 2 of this chapter, the ART mode setting allows you to apply various special effects (up to 37) to your images. The ART selection on the Mode Dial is yet another way to access the camera's ART filters. Since we have considered these same filters when we were previously examining the camera's other function interfaces, let's see how to access and use ART filters from the Mode Dial.

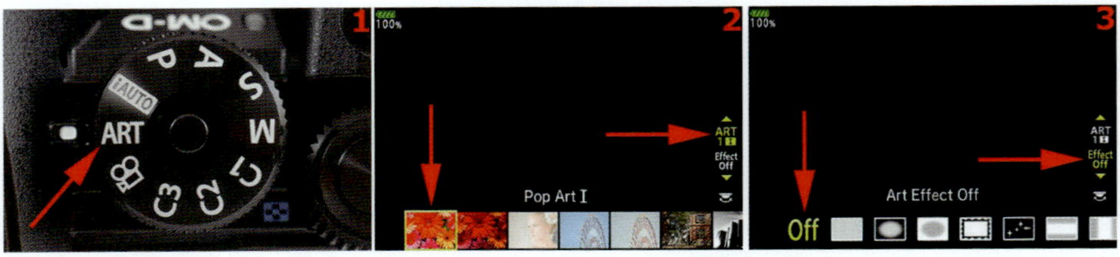

Figure 2.35F: The ART Menu and its Effects selections

Make sure your camera is set to ART mode on the Mode Dial (figure 2.35F, image 1).

When you open the Live View screen or peer through the electronic viewfinder (EVF), you will see the screen shown in figure 2.35F, image 2, except you will see your subject rather than a black background. Any filter you choose will immediately affect the subject so you can choose a look you enjoy.

Scrolling up or down with the Arrow Pad on the screen shown in figure 2.35F, image 2, will provide you with the Art Filter or a special Effect that can be applied to that filter. In figure 2.35F, image 2, the right arrow is pointing to the name of the Art Filter. In image 3, I have scrolled down (right arrow) and selected the Effects section for the Pop Art I filter. The arrows on the left point to the name of the Art Filter (image 2) or Effect (image 3). Basically, scrolling up or down toggles between the currently selected Art Filter and a set of Effects (e.g., Frame, Pin Hole, White Edge) that can be applied to that filter. You will see your Art Filter and the Effect you have chosen immediately applied to the subject on the camera screen. Press the OK button to select the Art Filter and any Effect you have added, and then take your pictures.

Deeper Information: Art Filters are discussed in much deeper detail in the **Shooting Menu 1** chapter under the **Picture Mode** subheading on page 151. The ART BKT filter is considered in the **Shooting Menu 2** chapter under the **Bracketing** subheading on page 201.

Movie Mode

The E-M1II has a full-featured video recording system that lets you create Cinematic 4K, 4K UHD, Full HD, and HD videos. It's easy to use the [Movie] mode. Let's see how.

Figure 2.35G, image 1, shows my camera set to [Movie] mode on the Mode Dial. This lets the camera act like a standard video recorder for everyday family events.

Figure 2.35G, image 2, displays the video recording screen when video recording is not active. The camera is ready to record a video and all the controls are active (control explanations on page 257).

Figure 2.35G, image 3, shows the Movie button, which has a red dot. When the screen shown in image 2 is on the monitor and you are ready to record a video, press the Movie button.

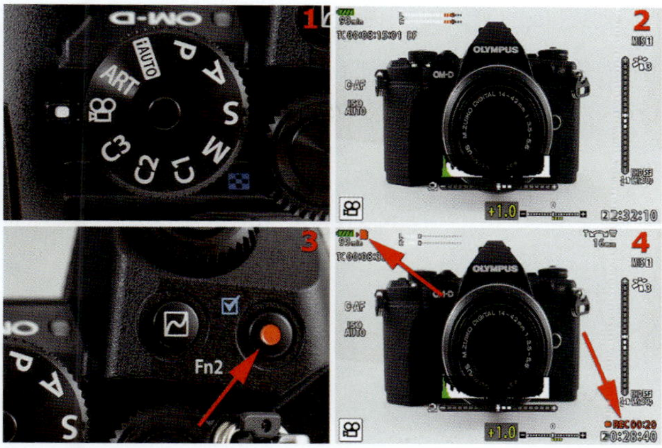

Figure 2.35G: Starting a video recording

Figure 2.35G, image 4, shows a video being recorded. Notice in the lower-right corner that there is a red dot followed by a REC symbol. It appears any time you are recording a video. Just to the right of the REC symbol is a timer that counts the recording time, which can be up to 29 minutes per video recording. I have recorded a video that is 20 seconds long (00:20). At the top-left corner of the screen, the card access symbol will blink as video is written to the memory card.

After you are finished recording a video, press the Movie button again to stop recording. This is a very basic way to record video. You can gain greater control over video recording by configuring the camera for more advanced operations.

Deeper Information: See the **Recording Movies, Video Menu, and My Clips** chapter on page 249 for detailed information on recording videos.

Custom Modes (C1, C2, and C3)

There are three Custom Modes available on the Mode Dial. These three modes allow you to save up to three complete camera configurations, which you can immediately recall by simply selecting C1, C2, or C3 on the Mode Dial.

As you step through the menu chapters of this book, you will be configuring up to hundreds of settings. When you have the camera configured just the way you like it for a certain style of photography, use the following steps to save the configuration to one of the Custom Modes (e.g., C1). Later, you can reconfigure the camera for a different style of photography and save that configuration to a different Custom Mode (e.g., C2).

You have three Custom Mode settings that give you the ability to customize how your E-M1II operates, and then change it on the fly, without having to make internal camera configuration changes. Use the following steps to configure each of the three modes (C1, C2, and C3).

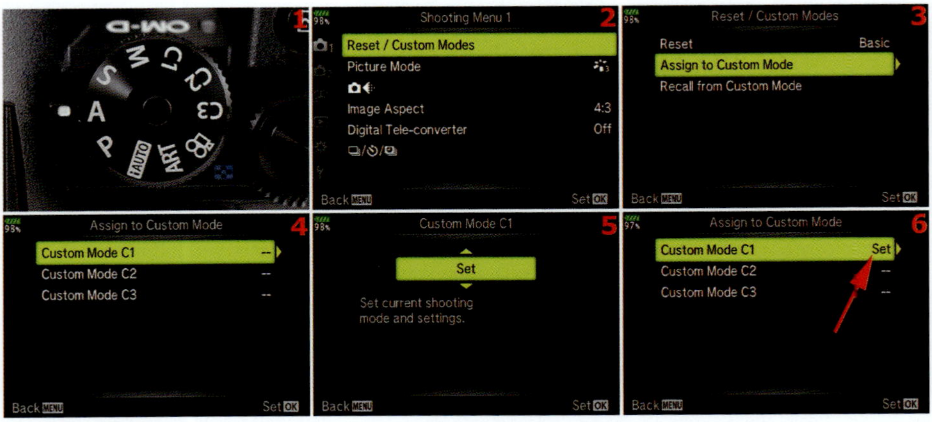

Figure 2.35H: Configuring Custom Mode C1

Following are the steps to configure one of the Custom Modes. We will use C1 as our example Custom Mode:

1. Set your camera's Mode Dial to one of the P, A, S, or M modes (figure 2.35H, image 1). *Do not set the Mode Dial to iAUTO, ART, [Movie], C1, C2, or C3 mode!* The camera will remember which mode you set the Mode Dial to when you save the configuration, and it will use that exposure mode when you select C1 later. Let me repeat this for emphasis: You *do not* set the camera to C1, C2, or C3 to save a configuration. You must have the Mode Dial set to one of the P, A, S, or M modes before moving to the next step.
2. Configure your camera with any other settings you would like to save.
3. Press the MENU button and choose Reset/Custom Modes from Shooting Menu 1 (figure 2.35H, image 2), then scroll to the right with the Arrow Pad.
4. Highlight Assign to Custom Mode (figure 2.35H, image 3) and scroll to the right.
5. Choose the Custom Mode you want to use (e.g., Custom Mode C1) and scroll to the right (figure 2.35H, image 4).
6. From the up/down menu, choose Set and press the OK button (figure 2.35H, image 5). The E-M1II will immediately save the current detailed camera setup to Custom Mode C1. The screen will reflect that Custom Mode C1 has a saved configuration by displaying the word Set at the end of the line after Custom Mode C1, as seen in figure 2.35, image 6 (red arrow).

Now that you have saved a camera configuration to Custom Mode C1, you can completely reconfigure the camera and save the new configuration to C2, and then another configuration to C3. You may store up to three detailed camera configurations, which can be instantly recalled by simply selecting C1, C2 or C3. Very useful technology!

Settings Recommendation: I set my camera's configuration for nature photography and save that configuration to C1. I then reconfigure the camera for sports and action shooting and save that configuration to C2. Finally, I configure my camera for events (graduations, weddings, etc.) and portrait shooting and save that configuration to C3. This Custom Modes system is quite flexible and useful, allowing you to configure your camera in multiple ways for multiple styles of photography.

Buttons and Levers with Control Screens

There are a couple of buttons and one lever on the camera that have their own control screens. As a conclusion to this control screen chapter, let's consider the special screens used by the [Sequential]/[Self-timer]/HDR button, the AF/[Metering] button, and the Fn Lever.

[Sequential]/[Self-Timer]/HDR Button Control Screen

The Sequential/Self-timer/HDR button allows you to access three separate systems at any moment: Sequential shooting mode, Self-timer mode, and high dynamic range (HDR) mode. Let's see how it works.

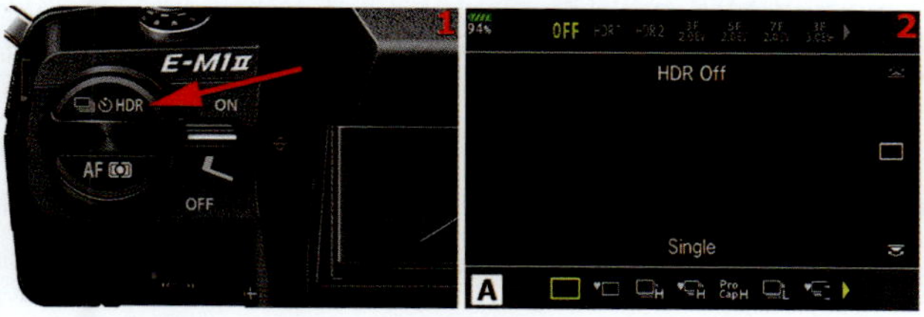

Figure 2.36: Accessing Sequential shooting, Self-timer, and HDR modes

Figure 2.36, image 1, shows the [Sequential]/[Self-timer]/HDR button on the top-left of the camera. Press this button to open a secondary adjustment screen.

Figure 2.36, image 2, shows the multipurpose secondary screen with settings at the top and bottom. Turn the Front Dial to control the HDR system. Turn the Rear Dial to control the [Sequential] shooting and [Self-timer] modes. After you have selected the settings you want to use, press the OK button.

Deeper Information: The [Sequential] shooting and Self-timer modes were discussed earlier in this chapter under both the **Super Control Panel** (page 20) and **Live Control** (page 69) sections. Refer to those sections to review how to use the [Sequential] shooting and [Self-timer] modes.

The HDR system is covered extensively in the **Shooting Menu 2** chapter under the **HDR** subheading on page 218.

AF/[Metering] Button Control Screen

The AF/[Metering] button allows you to quickly access the autofocus (AF) and [Metering] modes. Let's examine how to access them.

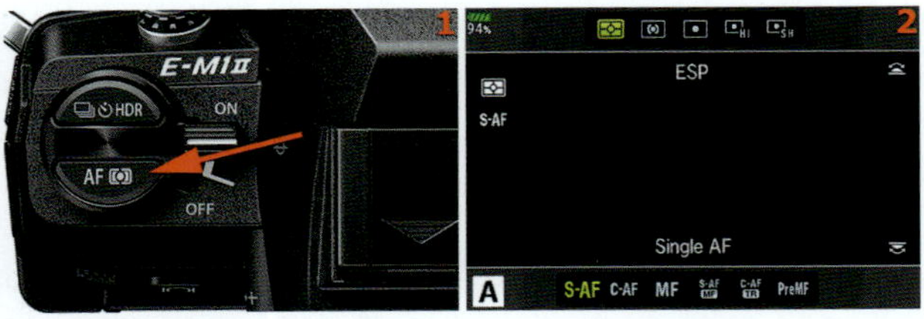

Figure 2.37: Accessing the Metering and AF modes

Figure 2.37, image 1, shows the AF/[Metering] button. Press this button to open the secondary screen.

Figure 2.37, image 2, shows the secondary screen with the [Metering] modes along the top and the AF modes along the bottom. Turn the Front Dial to select the [Metering] mode. Turn the Rear Dial to select the AF mode. After you have made your selections, press the OK button.

Deeper Information: The [Metering] modes are covered in detail under the **Super Control Panel** section (page 20) and **Live Control** section (page 69) of this chapter. They are also covered in the **Custom Menu** chapter, under the **Metering** subheading, on page 522.

The AF modes are covered in detail under the **Super Control Panel** section (page 20) and **Live Control** section (page 69) of this chapter. They are also covered in the **Custom Menu** chapter under the **[Photo] AF Mode** subheading on page 404.

Lever Control Screen

The Lever on the back of the camera allows you to quickly access the White Balance (WB) and ISO sensitivity control screens. Let's examine how to access them.

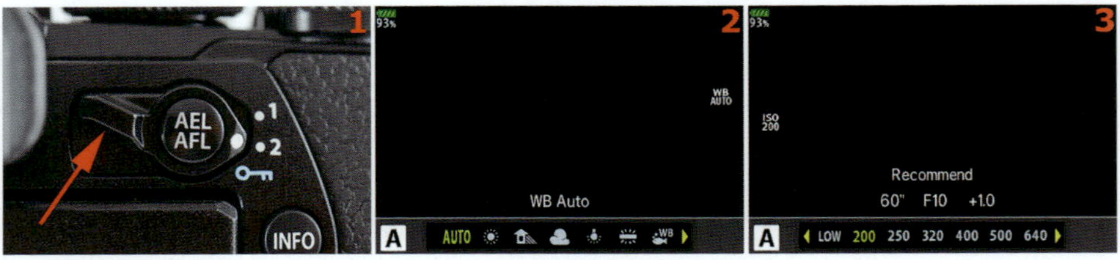

Figure 2.38: Accessing the ISO sensitivity and WB systems

You will normally leave the Fn Lever on the camera set to the first (1) position. However, while you are taking pictures, you can quickly access the ISO sensitivity and WB systems. Flip the Fn Lever to the second (2) position (figure 2.38, image 1) and turn the Rear Dial to open the WB control screen (image 2), or the Front Dial to open the ISO sensitivity control screen (image 3). If you want to switch to the opposite control screen (WB versus ISO, or vise versa), the camera must be back in normal Live View mode (or Super Control Panel mode). At that point, you can turn the opposite dial to open the other control screen.

When either of the secondary control screens are open, turning either Dial will scroll through the values for that control screen, or you can use the Arrow Pad to scroll. Stop on the value you want to use. After you have made your selections, press the OK button.

Deeper Information: The ISO sensitivity modes are covered in detail under the **Super Control Panel** section (page 20) and **Live Control** section (page 69) of this chapter.

The WB modes are covered in detail under the **Super Control Panel** section (page 20) and **Live Control** section (page 69) of this chapter. They are also covered in the **Custom Menu** chapter under the **WB** subheading on page 535.

Wireless LAN (Wi-Fi) System

One of the powerful features of the E-M1II is its ability to communicate with a smartphone or tablet (smart device). You can use a smart device to control the camera, change settings, and take pictures. You can also transfer pictures to your smart device.

Let's examine how to use the touch screen on your camera to start a Wi-Fi session.

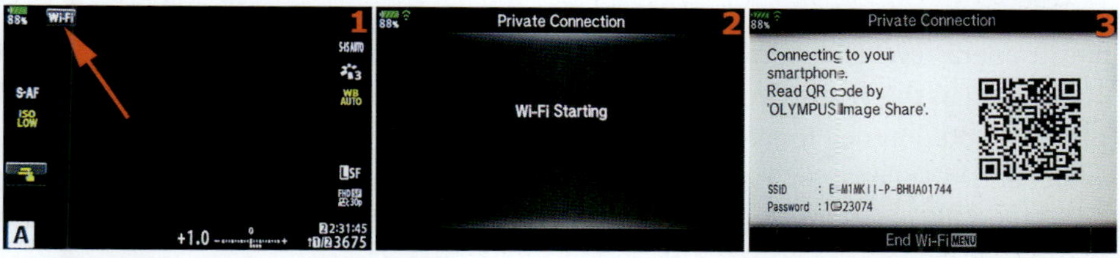

Figure 2.39: Initiating a Wi-Fi session

In figure 2.39, image 1, you can see the Wi-Fi symbol on the Live View screen. Touch the symbol to start a Wi-Fi session.

Figure 2.39, image 2, shows the screen that appears while the Wi-Fi system is activating.

Figure 2.39, image 3, shows a Private Connection screen that lets you know a Wi-Fi session is active and the camera is ready for connection.

Following are the steps to connect your smart device to your camera:

1. Open the Olympus Image Share (OI.Share) app on your smart device.
2. Use the Easy Setup button at the bottom of the OI.Share app screen to scan the QR code on the Private Connection screen on the camera (figure 2.39, image 3).
3. Install the resulting Profile on your smart device.
4. Connect to the E-M1MKII-P-NNNNNNNNN Wi-Fi connection under the Wi-Fi settings on your smart device.
5. Go back into the OI.Share app and use it to access your pictures.

Deeper Information: Using the Wi-Fi system is a rather detailed subject. The previous discussion explains how to start the process of making an initial Wi-Fi connection by using the touch screen and some basic connection information. However, the camera and smart device interface process and the use of OI.Share requires a lengthy description. Please refer to the **Playback Menu** chapter under the **Connection to Smartphone (or Tablet)** subheading on page 399 for complete information. We will consider how to make a wireless connection between your smart device and camera, along with configuration information for the OI.Share app.

Author's Conclusions

This chapter has introduced the many control screens you will see while you are using the Super Control Panel, LV Super Control Panel, Live Control, Live Guides, Live View, EVF, and button/lever control screens. Many of these screens are discussed in greater detail throughout this book as they are applied to the hundreds of choices in the camera menus.

The next several chapters will be devoted to a deep examination of the E-M1II menu system, including the Shooting Menu 1 and 2, Video Menu, Playback Menu, Custom Menu, and Setup Menu.

The number of settings in the E-M1II makes it one of the most configurable, and complex, cameras available today. That complexity is manageable when you have a good guide, such as this book. Keep your camera in-hand as you work through this book and continue your journey to mastery of the Olympus OM-D E-M1II professional, mirrorless interchangeable-lens camera (MILC). Now, let's look at those deep menus!

Settings Recommendation: The camera has a help system that is active when you use the camera's text-based menus. Although the help system is useful, it can sometimes get in the way of the menu selections. You can toggle the help system off and on by pressing the INFO button when a menu is active. I use the help system when I have forgotten what a symbol means. When I am finished, I turn the help system off again.

03 Shooting Menu 1

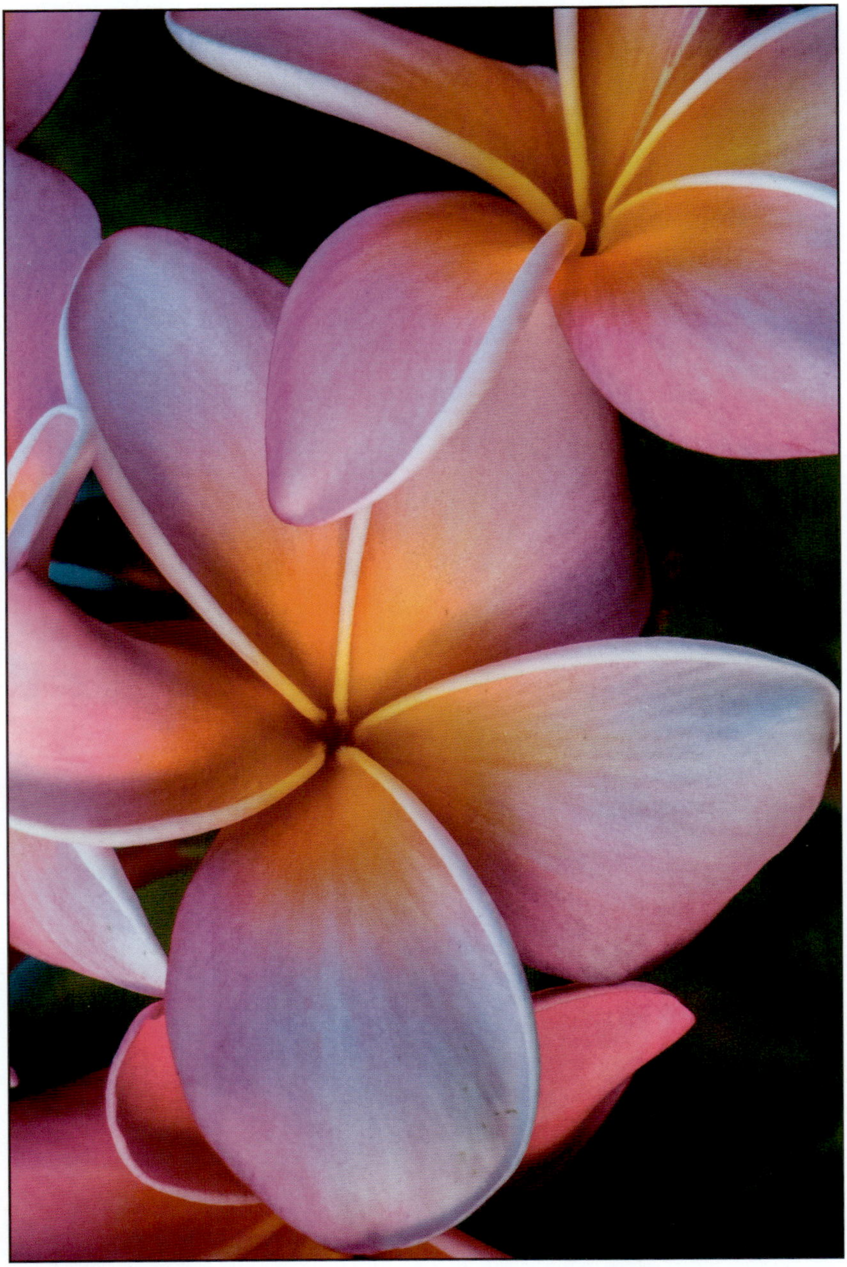

Image © Alan Hess

Shooting Menu 1 is the first in a series of camera configuration menus that we will consider in great detail. The E-M1II is the most configurable camera I've ever owned! With that powerful flexibility comes a great deal of complexity. Unfortunately, the user's manual provided with the camera is inadequate at helping one understand how to work with all these menus and their functions.

Therefore, this book is filled with hands-on knowledge derived from hundreds of hours of experimentation. You could probably do the same as me and struggle through the process of figuring it all out, but now you don't have to. I've done it for you. At the very least, I hope that *Mastering the Olympus OM-D E-M1 Mark II* helps you better understand and enjoy your new camera.

Now, let's get started on all of these functions. It is best if you have your camera in hand and work through the functions one by one. Even if you don't think you need a certain function right now, why not take some time to at least examine each menu item? Then, if your needs change, you will remember that your camera can do a certain thing and you can research how to configure it for that need.

As discussed in the previous chapter, you can use the Custom Modes—C1, C2, and C3 on the Mode Dial—to configure this camera in three different ways. For instance, the configuration you create as you go through this chapter could be saved to Custom Mode C1, and then you could do another configuration for C2, and another for C3. As you progress through your first configuration, make some notes in the book's margins or on a separate sheet of paper to keep track of how you might configure a certain function differently for the next Custom Mode.

Figure 3.1 shows the menu we will consider in this chapter: Shooting Menu 1. Let's examine these menu items in detail and determine how you might best use them. We will start at the top of Shooting Menu 1 and work our way down the menu.

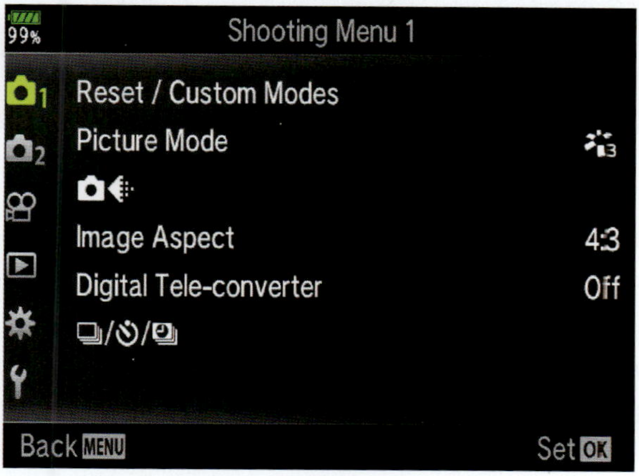

Figure 3.1: Shooting Menu 1

Reset/Custom Modes

There are three Custom Modes available on the Mode Dial. These three modes allow you to save up to three complete camera configurations, which are then available for for immediate recall when you select C1, C2, or C3 on the Mode Dial.

As you step through the menu chapters of this book, you will be configuring up to hundreds of settings. When you have the camera configured just the way you like it for a certain style of photography, use the steps in the following section to save the configuration to one of the Custom Modes (e.g., C1). Later, you can reconfigure the camera for a different style of photography and save that configuration to a different Custom Mode (e.g., C2).

You'll notice that there are two other settings in the Reset/Custom Modes function—*Reset* and *Recall from Custom Mode*. In order to use either of these two settings, there needs to be a configuration already saved in one of the Custom Modes. Therefore, we will start by considering how to save our current camera configuration to Custom Mode C1, and then we will examine the Reset and Recall from Custom Mode functions.

Assign to Custom Mode

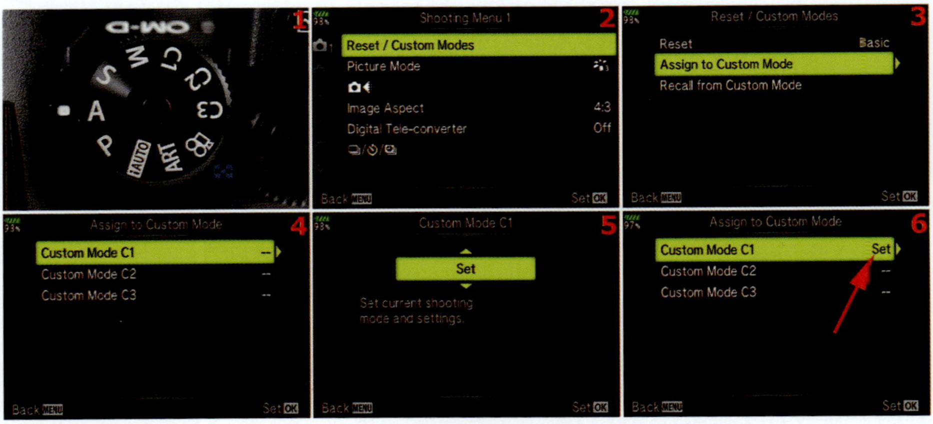

Figure 3.2A: Configuring Custom Mode C1

Following are the steps to configure one of the Custom Modes. We will use C1 as our example Custom Mode:

1. Set your camera's Mode Dial to one of the P, A, S, or M modes (figure 3.2A, image 1). *Do not set the Mode Dial to* iAUTO, ART, [Movie], C1, C2, *or* C3 *mode!* The camera will remember which mode you selected on the Mode Dial when you save the configuration, and it will use that exposure mode when you select C1 later. Let me repeat this for emphasis: You *do not* set the camera to C1, C2, or C3 to save a configuration. You must have the Mode Dial set to one of the P, A, S, or M modes before moving to the next step.

2. Press the MENU button and choose Reset/Custom Modes from Shooting Menu 1 (figure 3.2A, image 2) and scroll to the right with the Arrow Pad.
3. Highlight Assign to Custom Mode (figure 3.2A, image 3) and scroll to the right.
4. Choose the Custom Mode you want to use (e.g., Custom Mode C1) and scroll to the right (figure 3.2A, image 4).
5. From the up/down menu, choose Set and press the OK button (figure 3.2, image 5).
6. The E-M1II will immediately save the current detailed camera setup to Custom Mode C1. The screen will reflect that Custom Mode C1 has a saved configuration by displaying the word Set at the end of the line after Custom Mode C1, as seen in figure 3.2A, image 6 (red arrow).

Now that you have saved a camera configuration to Custom Mode C1, you can completely reconfigure the camera and save the new configuration to C2, and then another configuration to C3. You may store up to three detailed camera configurations, which are then available for instant recall when you select C1, C2, or C3. Very useful technology!

Note: There is an extensive Menu Directory list in the camera user's manual on pages 165–176. This list shows which camera settings can be saved or reset with the *Reset/Custom Modes* function. It also shows which settings can be reset to the factory defaults when you use the *Reset/Custom Modes* > *Reset* > *Basic* (or *Full*) function. The Menu Directory is several pages long and quite dense because it lists virtually every function in the camera. When you look up a function in the list, note whether there is a check mark under the column labeled *1. If there is a check mark, that function can be saved in one of the Custom Modes; if there is not a check mark, it cannot be saved. If there is a check mark under the column labeled *2, you can reset those marked settings with the *Full* reset selection. If there is a check mark under the column labeled *3, you can reset those marked settings with the *Basic* reset selection.

Recall from Custom Mode

This setting has the same effect as choosing Custom Mode C1, C2, or C3 on the Mode Dial; it is simply a different access point. For example, if you select Custom Mode C1 on the Mode Dial, the camera will immediately overwrite the current settings with the settings saved to Custom Mode C1. Likewise, if you go to *Shooting Menu 1* > *Reset/Custom Modes* > *Recall from Custom Mode,* and select Custom Mode C1 from the menu, the camera will overwrite the current camera settings with the settings saved to Custom Mode C1.

This may have you wondering what will happen if the Mode Dial is set to C2 or C3 and you use the *Recall from Custom Mode* setting to recall Custom Mode C1. In this case, the E-M1II will immediately overwrite its current settings with the settings from C1, including the shooting mode (P, A, S, M). It will use those settings to take pictures until you move the Mode Dial to another position. If you then choose a different Custom Mode position on the Mode Dial (C1, C2, or C3), the camera will immediately switch to that Custom Mode's settings.

If, instead, you choose one of the other non-custom Mode Dial settings (e.g., P, A, S, M), the camera will continue using the settings you loaded with *Recall from Custom Mode,* except that it will use the shooting mode that is currently selected on the Mode Dial (P, A, S, M) instead of the shooting mode that is saved to the Custom Mode (C1, C2, C3). In fact, any time the Mode Dial is set to one of the P, A, S, or M modes, and then you use the *Recall from Custom Mode* setting to recall a saved Custom Mode, the camera will recall all of the saved settings for that Custom Mode except for the shooting mode (P, A, S, M). Instead, it will use the shooting mode you currently have selected on the Mode Dial, along with the recalled Custom Mode settings.

Let's examine how to recall a Custom Mode with Shooting Menu 1.

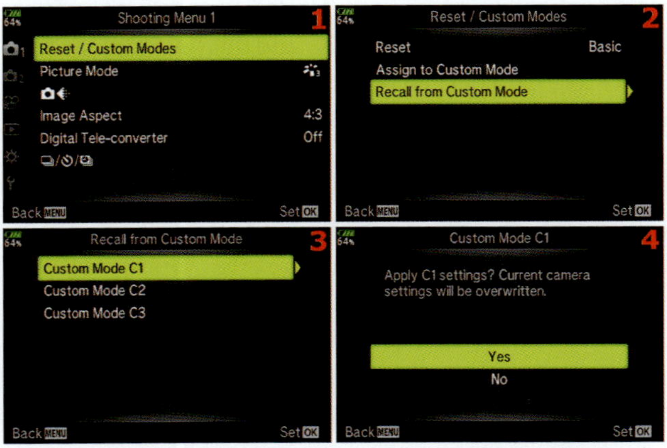

Figure 3.2B: Using the Recall from Custom Mode setting

Use the following steps to recall a Custom Mode via Shooting Menu 1:

1. Choose Reset/Custom Modes from Shooting Menu 1 and scroll to the right (figure 3.2B, image 1).
2. Highlight Recall from Custom Mode and scroll to the right (figure 3.2B, image 2).
3. Select the Custom Mode you want to recall and then scroll to the right (figure 3.2B, image 3). We are using Custom Mode C1 as our example.
4. Highlight Yes and press the OK button to recall the Custom Mode (C1) or select No and press the OK button to cancel (figure 3.2B, image 4).

Again, when you use this method to recall a Custom Mode instead of selecting it from the Mode Dial, the camera will *not* use the shooting mode (P, A, S, M) you originally saved under that Custom Mode. Instead, it will use the shooting mode currently selected on the Mode Dial—unless, of course, you have one of the Custom Modes dialed in, in which case the camera *will* use the saved shooting mode. However, I must ask, why set the camera to a Custom Mode on the Mode Dial, and then use the Shooting Menu to recall that same Custom Mode or a different one? I suppose the recall setting is useful for recalling a Custom Mode at any time, except that it is even easier to simply select a Custom Mode from the Mode Dial!

Note: You cannot use the *Recall from Custom Mode* setting to recall a Custom Mode when the Mode Dial is set to iAUTO, ART, or Movie modes. It works only when the Mode Dial is set to P, A, S, M, C1, C2, or C3 modes.

Reset

There may come a time when you would like to start fresh with the camera's configuration. You can fully reset the camera (other than things like Time & Date) by using the Full reset method, or you can partially reset the camera by using the Basic reset method. Let's examine both of these reset methods.

Basic or Full Reset

As previously mentioned, the E-M1II user's manual has a massive chart that lists the default for each camera setting, along with the user's manual page number for each setting (see user's manual pages 165–176). It also lists the settings that can be saved under a Custom Mode (C1, C2, C3), and specifies which functions will be restored to factory settings with the Full and Basic reset. You may want to refer to this chart as you consider the save, recall, and reset settings for the Custom Modes. Let's examine how to do a Basic and Full reset for your E-M1II settings.

Note: A Basic reset will *not* delete your carefully crafted Custom Modes (C1, C2, C3). However, a Full reset *will* delete them. Be very careful! If you do a Full reset, you will lose virtually all of your camera settings as the E-M1II is returned to factory default settings!

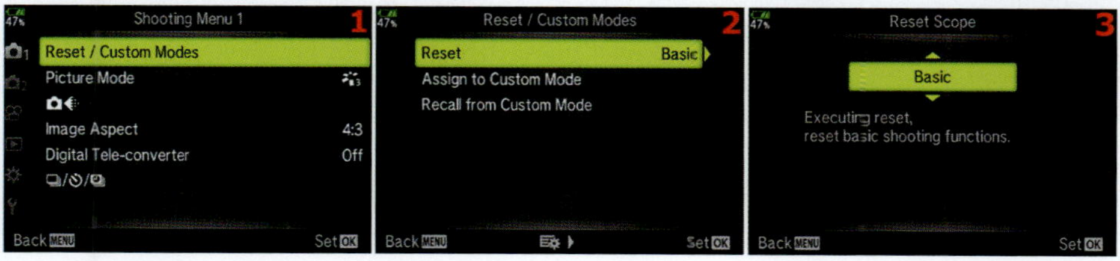

Figure 3.2C: Resetting the camera to factory default settings

Use the following steps to reset the camera to factory default settings for all (Full) or some (Basic) of the camera's current settings:

1. Choose Reset/Custom Modes from Shooting Menu 1 and scroll to the right (figure 3.2C, image 1).
2. Highlight Reset and scroll to the right (figure 3.2C, image 2).
3. Choose Basic or Full from the up/down menu (figure 3.2C, image 3). Full resets the majority of the camera's functions, including the Custom Modes (C1, C2, C3). Refer to the *2 column on the chart found on pages 165–175 in the E-M1II user's manual. Basic

resets only some of the camera's functions. These are listed in the *3 column on pages 165–175 of the user's manual. Pages 175–176 lists the defaults that will be stored in the Custom Modes when you do a Full reset. Once you have chosen Basic or Full from the up/down menu, press the OK button to reset the camera's functions. The reset occurs immediately once you press the OK button; there is no extra screen that asks for permission.

In addition to a Full or Basic reset you can also reset a single Custom Mode.

Resetting a Single Custom Mode

Since the camera offers you three Custom Modes (C1, C2, C3), you have a wide choice of camera configurations. However, after some time, you may find that you no longer need one of the Custom Modes, or you may want to change it extensively for a different style of photography. In that case, it is good to reset the Custom Mode you want to reconfigure so you can start from the beginning.

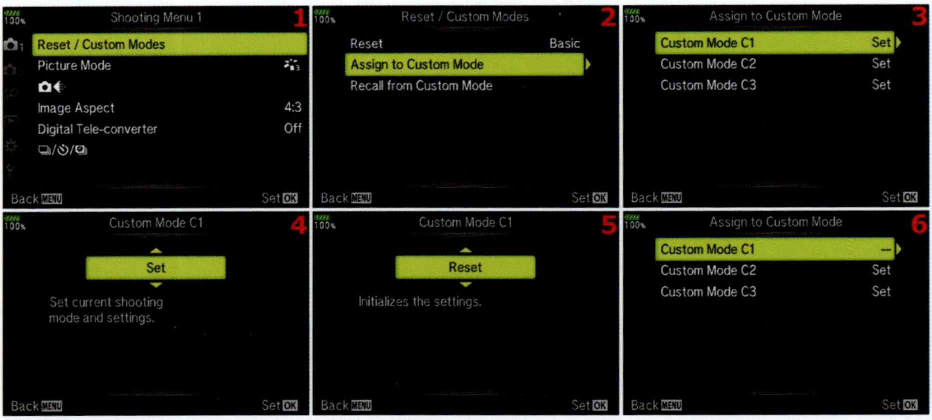

Figure 3.2D: Resetting an individual Custom Mode

Use the following steps to reset an individual Custom Mode (C1, C2, C3):

1. Choose Reset/Custom Modes from Shooting Menu 1 and scroll to the right (figure 3.2D, image 1).
2. Highlight Assign to Custom Mode and scroll to the right (figure 3.2D, image 2).
3. Highlight the Custom Mode you want to reset to factory defaults (figure 3.2D, image 3). We are resetting Custom Mode C1 as an example. Notice that the word Set is shown to the right of each Custom Mode. This signifies that each mode has been configured previously. If a mode does not have saved settings, you will see two dashes (--) instead of Set. Once you have highlighted the mode you want to reset, scroll to the right.
4. You will be presented with an up/down menu with two choices, Set and Reset (figure 3.2D, image 4). If you choose Set, you will overwrite any settings already saved

there, which is not what we currently want to do. Instead, choose Reset from the up/down menu (figure 3.2D, image 5), which will reset the single C1 mode. Press the OK button and the camera will immediately reset the Custom Mode with no further warnings.

Once you have successfully reset the Custom Mode (in the case of our example, C1) you will notice that the Set word no longer appears next to the Custom Mode on the Assign to Custom Mode screen, but that a double-dash symbol -- is showing instead (figure 3.2D, image 6). The double-dash means that the Custom Mode is set to factory default settings. It has been successfully reset.

Settings Recommendation: I set my camera's Custom Mode configuration for nature photography and save that configuration to C1. I then reconfigure the camera for sports and action shooting and save that configuration to C2. Finally, I configure my camera for events (e.g., graduation, wedding) and portrait shooting and save that configuration to C3. This Custom Modes system is quite flexible and useful, allowing you to configure your camera in multiple ways for multiple styles of photography.

Picture Mode

Picture Mode allows you to choose one of 38 adjustable image effects for each shooting session. If you have ever used film, you know that there are distinct looks to each film type. No two films produce color that looks the same.

Picture Mode gives you the ability to impart a specific look to your images as if you were using different types of film or simply wanted to create special effects. You can use the Picture Modes as they are provided from the factory, or you can fine-tune Contrast, Sharpness, Saturation, and Gradation.

The Picture Mode settings you choose are applied permanently to JPEG images as soon as you press the Shutter button. Modifying and resaving a JPEG image causes gradual damage because of data losses that occur during compression, so be sure to select the best Picture Mode setting when you shoot.

When you shoot in RAW (ORF) mode, Picture Mode settings are *not* permanently applied to the image. Instead, the Picture Mode information is saved in the metadata of the image. The camera and your computer will display each RAW image with the Picture Mode settings temporarily applied; however, unlike with JPEG images, settings can be changed after the fact with RAW images with no damage. See the **[Photo] [Record Mode]** section later in this chapter to find out how to choose an image quality mode.

There are five basic Picture Modes that you will use frequently, and there are 33 additional Creative and Art Picture Modes. This abundance of special effect modes gives you freedom to express yourself creatively with your pictures, from stoic to wildly overblown.

The images on the next few pages show the full range of Picture Modes. In each image, the mode is set to the default level with no adjustments, except for the last three images

(Partial Color I, II, and III), for which I made an adjustment to choose a particular color. We will consider how to adjust the modes after we examine them.

Now, let's discuss each of the available modes and how they affect your images. In a printed book it is hard to reproduce the sometimes subtle shade variations in the various Picture Modes; therefore, you should take a picture in each mode and examine how each one looks on your computer or tablet. As we consider each of the Picture Modes, you will learn a lot more about them if you can see a sample on your tablet or monitor.

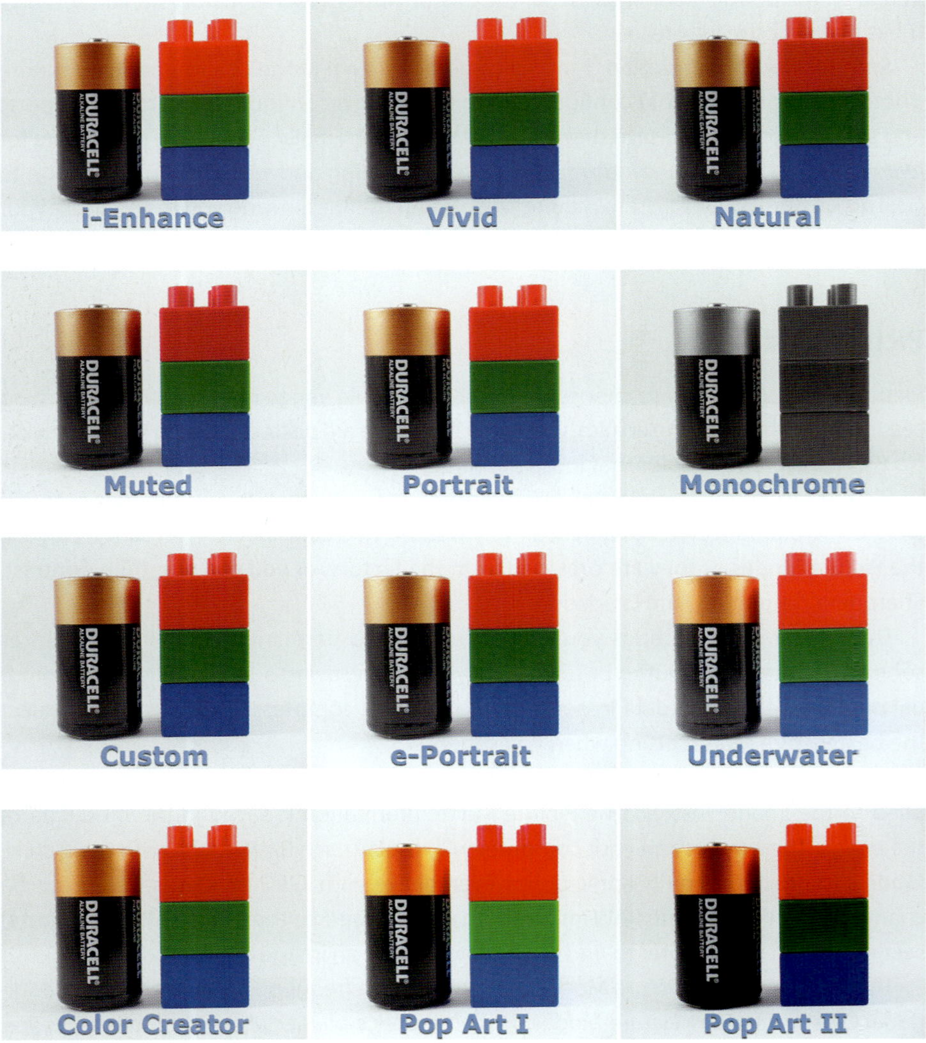

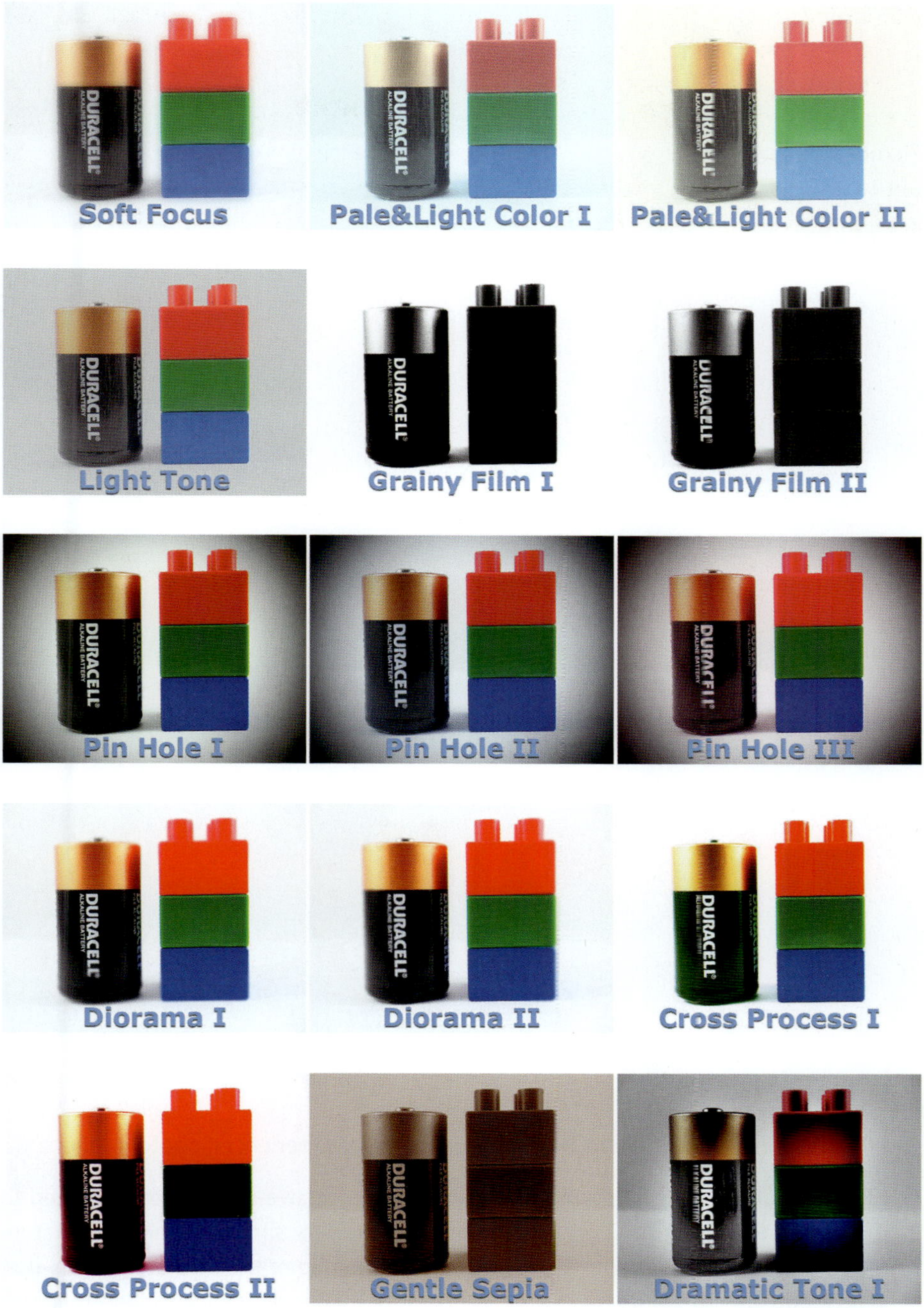
Soft Focus
Pale&Light Color I
Pale&Light Color II
Light Tone
Grainy Film I
Grainy Film II
Pin Hole I
Pin Hole II
Pin Hole III
Diorama I
Diorama II
Cross Process I
Cross Process II
Gentle Sepia
Dramatic Tone I

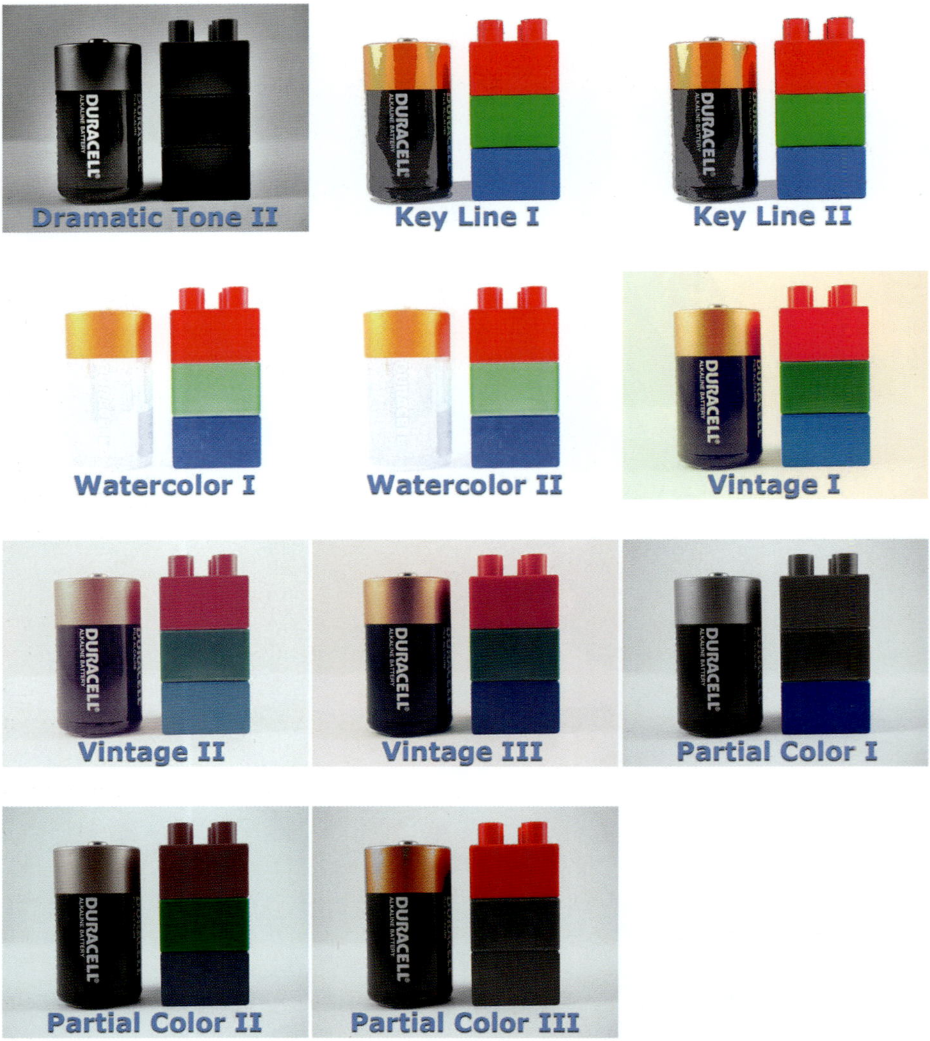

Basic Picture Modes

The five basic Picture Modes will be used most often by experienced photographers:

- **i-Enhance:** This mode gives your images "more impressive-looking results suited to the scene," according to Olympus. The effect looks very similar to the Vivid Picture Mode, with a little less contrast. It will provide the snap of the saturated colors that Vivid Mode provides, but it will have a little more dynamic range due to slightly lighter blacks. From the description provided by Olympus, it seems the camera software may provide a little extra smarts so it can adjust to the scene in front of your lens.

- **Vivid:** This mode adds saturation and contrast to your images and creates pictures with deeply saturated color, dark blacks, and white whites. This mode is great for landscapes when there's a lot of color, such as in the spring and autumn. Vivid Mode will make colors pop.
- **Natural:** This mode gives a more balanced look to your images, with color and contrast that is not too intense or muted. This is an excellent mode for general photography, and many photographers will use it much of the time. It has enough saturation and contrast to create a beautiful image without going overboard.
- **Muted:** This Picture Mode is best for an image that will be post-processed later in a computer. It is a balanced setting that applies minimal camera processing so you can do more with the image during post-processing. The Muted Picture Mode has less saturation and weaker shadows, so the image will be less contrasty—that is, there will be more shadow and highlight detail.
- **Portrait:** This mode gives a more natural texture and coloration to skin. It is similar to the Muted Picture Mode, with emphasis on making sure that skin tones are rendered in a pleasing way. Skin tones get the most emphasis with Portrait Picture Mode, so it may be best for individuals and groups of people.

The upcoming Picture Modes may be used by people who want to add special effects inside the camera, without using a computer. They are variations on the five basic Picture Modes, with strong changes in the Contrast, Sharpness, Saturation, and Gradation adjustments. These 33 special effect Picture Modes can save time and help you have fun with your camera.

Settings Recommendation: For JPEG shooting I normally use one of the basic Picture Modes. I usually use the Natural setting. Remember that a Picture Mode is applied to a JPEG image immediately and irreversibly, but you can change the Picture Mode of a RAW image after you shoot it, so it doesn't really matter which mode you select. Your RAW conversion software will try to display the image the way you took it, but you can change it without much trouble.

We will look at the five Creative Modes and the 23 Art Picture Modes next. Many advanced photographers do not use Art Picture Modes because they would rather create their own art in Photoshop, Lightroom, or other imaging software. However, some of the Art Picture Modes included with the E-M1II are great fun, even for jaded professionals. If you would normally not consider using scene or effects modes with other camera brands, take a few minutes to play around with the E-M1II's Art Picture Modes. You might find something that you will use often, like I did!

Creative Modes

The five Creative Modes allow you to do specialized things with your photography, such as shoot black-and-white images, smooth skin tones, manipulate color, shoot underwater, and even create your own Custom Picture Mode. Here are the five Creative Modes:

- **Monochrome:** This mode allows black-and-white photography lovers to shoot in that style. Monochrome Mode provides images with dark shadows and pleasing whites and grays. In fact, the monochrome images straight from the camera are perfectly usable and require little adjustment, unlike black-and-white images from some other cameras. You can use the image as a base for contrast and brightness adjustments, and few other post-processing adjustments are needed.
- **Custom:** This mode allows you to choose one of the five basic Picture Modes as a base, and then adjust the mode's Contrast, Sharpness, Saturation, and Gradation until it is just right for your needs. The camera will remember your adjustments and use them when you select this mode. We will examine how to adjust and save a Custom Mode in an upcoming subsection.
- **e-Portrait:** This mode is designed for when you are shooting portraits. According to Olympus, the e-Portrait Mode produces "smooth skin textures," whereas the basic Portrait Mode produces "beautiful skin tones." The camera does special in-camera post-processing (skin smoothing) on portraits made with e-Portrait Mode, as described in the upcoming subsection called **Using e-Portrait Picture Mode**. Comparing regular Portrait Mode pictures with e-Portrait Mode pictures does reveal a difference. The e-Portrait Mode gives a distinctly smoother appearance to the skin. Which do you like best: "beautiful skin tones" or "smooth skin textures"? Try both Portrait and e-Portrait Modes and see which you prefer.
- **Underwater:** This special mode is similar to Vivid Mode, except that it makes colors appear somewhat brighter. It tends to strengthen the color saturation to make colors look less muted when you shoot through water. Use this mode when you are shooting underwater with your E-M1II inside an Olympus PT-EP14 Underwater Housing unit.
- **Color Creator:** This mode lets you make on-the-fly adjustments to hue and saturation. If the image in your viewfinder or on the monitor does not show the hue or saturation you would like to see, you can make adjustments by using a color wheel. If the image seems a little cool, you can simply dial in some red to warm it up (either a little or a lot); if the color seems too muted, you can change the saturation from almost nothing to extremely saturated. We'll discuss how to do this in an upcoming subsection.

Art Picture Modes

The Art Picture Modes give you great freedom in creating nonstandard photography. You can create special overall looks, such as pastel or wildly saturated colors, extreme grain, high- and low-key images, and specialized blurring. In addition to the Art Picture Modes, you may also apply special effects, color filters, and colorized tints, each of which we will examine.

Don't completely discount these Art Picture Modes if you make a living with photography. There are some interesting effects that may be useful even for imaging professionals. For enthusiast photographers, the Art Picture Modes can provide a refreshing break from reality.

Here is a list of the 28 Art Picture Mode choices. There are only 14 Art Picture Modes, but several of the modes come in multiple varieties (e.g., Pop Art I, II), providing 28 different looks:

- **Pop Art I, II:** These two modes are like the Vivid Mode on steroids. All colors are saturated to the max, and contrast is raised to an even higher level than in Vivid Mode. These modes are best when you are in a playful mood and want to create an exciting image. The intense colors will not be close to reality, but who needs reality when you are having fun?
- **Soft Focus:** This mode provides a high-key and blurred effect. The contrast is very low, and there is an overall softness like fine gauze. The subject appears sharp, but it is covered with blur. The effect looks a bit like when you see yourself in a foggy mirror. It has a bright glowing effect that is sharp and blurry at the same time
- **Pale&Light Color I, II:** These two modes provide pastel colors and lower the contrast so blacks become grays. You might think of these as being the opposite of the Pop Art or Vivid Modes. They give an image a high-key, cooler, pastel lock.
- **Light Tone:** This mode is similar to the Pale&Light Color Mode in that it lowers contrast and desaturates colors. However, instead of having a somewhat cool (bluish), high-key look, the colors look like they are overlaid with gray film and have a darker, low-key look. Light Tone makes the image look like the effect you see when an overdone high dynamic range (HDR) image has too few shadows.
- **Grainy Film I, II:** These two modes provide an extremely high-contrast black-and-white effect. All colors become extra-dark shades of gray, and most highlight details become pure white. These modes are great for shooting something like a bare tree in a snow-covered field on a misty, overcast day. They create stark images and are best for low-contrast scenes because they tend to reduce detail in strongly colored or bright scenes by adding extreme contrast to the picture
- **Pin Hole I, II, III:** These three modes have a relatively saturated look like Vivid Mode, but they add a heavy vignette effect to the corners of the image, as if the light rapidly diminishes. It's as though you were using a pinhole camera to make the image, except the picture is nice and sharp. Primarily, the Pin Hole modes provide a strong vignette effect, with some mild differences in color tint between the three modes.
- **Diorama I, II:** A diorama is a three-dimensional miniature in which small artificial objects are arranged and photographed to resemble real life. You can use the two Diorama Modes to create a reverse diorama, where real-life places like city scenes can be made to look artificial. These modes create a band of sharpness either in a horizontal (mode I) or vertical (mode II) direction, and everything outside of the sharp band is blurred, making the picture seem like it has a very limited depth of field.
- **Cross Process I, II:** These two modes imitate an old method of developing film in chemicals that were designed for a different type of film. Often there are odd colors and higher than normal contrast. Images shot with Cross Process Mode I have a green cast, while mode II provides a reddish tint. Both modes provide rather high contrast.

- **Gentle Sepia:** This mode converts all colors to monochrome and adds a warm, brownish effect that resembles less-saturated sepia toning. It could be used with old-fashioned clothing to imitate antique portrait pictures, or you could shoot a nature scene with this mode and make it look like a bygone era.
- **Dramatic Tone I, II:** These two modes are unusual. They both create a low-key tone where normal highlights are darkened and dark tones are lightened. Dramatic Tone mode I is in color and mode II is in black-and-white. Image detail is maintained, even in dark areas. There is strong contrast without being overly bright. The look is very dramatic and unlike anything I have seen from other camera brands.
- **Key Line I, II:** These two modes convert the edges of the subject and the borders of contrast changes (color gradations) into line drawings. They maintain a lot of detail, unlike the cartoonish look from some other cameras. The color is mostly maintained, although it is more pastel and muted, and blacks become quite gray. Mode II is somewhat higher in contrast than mode I.
- **Watercolor I, II:** These two modes give colors and edges a watercolor effect that tends to blow out highlights and dark areas. Most detail is lost in a normal exposure, so experiment with underexposure when you use this mode. Dark tones and extreme highlights seem to turn stark white and disappear completely from the image, and other colors become pale and washed out. Mode I is a bit higher in contrast than mode II.
- **Vintage I, II, III:** These three modes vary levels of contrast and tinting to create different vintage looks. The colors are what you would expect to see from an old print that's been hanging on a wall or in an album for a long time. The various filters allow for creativity within the range of vintage looks.
- **Partial Color I, II, III:** These three modes are basically identical. Each gives you a color wheel from which you can choose a particular color or range. Once you've chosen a color, all other colors are rendered in monochrome shades. Therefore, with the three modes, you can emphasize three different primary colors and then switch between them for a different look.

There are also eight special effects modes, called "Add Effects," that can be added to Art Picture Modes. All of the Art Picture Modes will allow you to apply from one to eight of these Add Effects (e.g., Soft Focus Effect, Pin Hole Effect).

Art Picture Mode Add Effects

The following eight Add Effects allow you to modify how a particular Art Picture Mode looks. Not all Add Effects are available for each Art Picture Mode. You will need to examine each mode to see which Add Effects are available.

- **Off:** No extra effects are added to the image.
- **Soft Focus Effect:** A dreamy blur effect is added to the image.
- **Pin Hole Effect:** The corners of the image are darkened to pure black.
- **White Edge Effect:** The corners of the image are brightened to pure white.

- **Frame Effect:** A white frame is added to the image, and a processed-film look is added to the edges of the picture inside the frame.
- **Star Light Effect:** A four-point star effect is added to points of light in the image.
- **Blur Effect: Top and Bottom:** A band of sharpness extends horizontally through the middle of the image and the top and bottom of the image are blurred.
- **Blur Effect: Left and Right:** A band of sharpness extends vertically through the middle of the image and the left and right sides of the image are blurred.

Giving you even more opportunities for creativity, there are also "Color Filters," available for the monochrome Art Picture Modes.

Color Filters

Following are five Color Filters that can be applied to the monochrome Art Filters (i.e., Grainy Film I, II and Dramatic Tone II). Let's examine what these filters accomplish.

- **N:** The Neutral filter creates a normal black-and-white image, with colors rendered as shades of gray, but the image will have a much higher contrast and be far grainier than an image shot in Monotone Picture Mode.
- **Ye:** The Yellow filter creates a black-and-white image that lightens reds, darkens blues, and has little affect on greens.
- **Or:** The Orange filter creates a black-and-white image that somewhat darkens reds and greens; it more heavily darkens blues.
- **R:** The Red filter creates a black-and-white image that lightens reds, somewhat darkens greens, and more heavily darkens blues.
- **G:** The Green filter creates a black-and-white image that darkens reds, lightens greens, and darkens blues.

Finally, there are special image tinting capabilities, called "Monochrome Color" for the monochrome Art Picture Modes. Let's examine the tinting capability.

Monochrome Color (Tints)

Following are five Monochrome Color tints that can be applied to the monochrome Art Picture Modes (i.e., Grainy Film I, I, III and Dramatic Tone II).

- **N:** The Neutral tone creates a grainy, high-contrast black-and-white image with no special toning.
- **S:** The Sepia tone gives an image a light brown tone that resembles the sepia images introduced in the 1880s.
- **B:** The Blue tone creates an image with a bluish color, similar to the cyanotype images that were introduced in the 1840s.
- **P:** The Purple tone adds a light purple color to an image.
- **G:** The Green tone adds a light green color to an image.

In upcoming sections we will discuss how to apply these special effects, filters, and tints to each of the Art Picture Modes (and the normal Monochrome Picture Mode).

Choosing, Fine-Tuning, and Using Picture Modes

Now that we have examined each of the Picture Modes, let's see how to select one and fine-tune it. Plus we'll see how to use the modes that allow special configuration choices, such as Monotone, Custom, and Color Creator.

Selecting a Picture Mode

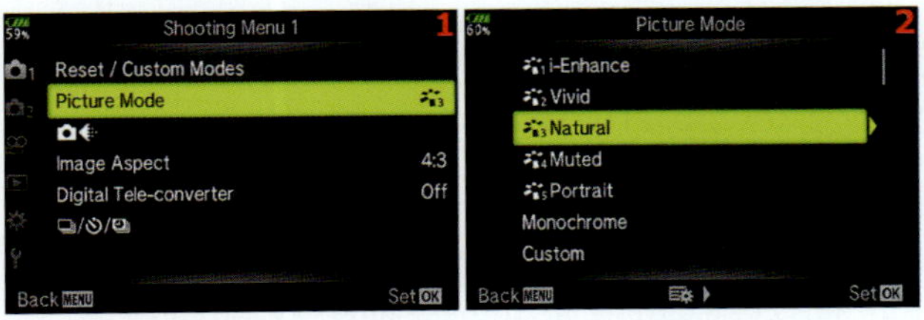

Figure 3.3A: Selecting a Picture Mode

Use these steps to select a Picture Mode:

1. Choose Picture Mode from Shooting Menu 1 and scroll to the right (figure 3.3A, image 1).
2. Highlight the Picture Mode you want to use and press the OK button. Natural is selected in figure 3.3A, image 2. The camera will switch back to the main Shooting Menu 1 screen, and you can take your pictures. As described in the next subsection, you can fine-tune the control if you want to change one of its parameters.

Fine-Tuning a Basic Picture Mode

Fine-tuning allows you to change the internal values of a Picture Mode. You can adjust Contrast, Sharpness, Saturation, and Gradation.

Contrast controls the ratio between dark and light in the image and extends or reduces the amount of detail. Sharpness lets the camera add or take away sharpness in the image. Saturation controls how vivid the colors look. Gradation modifies how the camera handles light and dark tones, such as a normal, bright (high-key), or dark (low-key) look.

Let's fine-tune a basic Picture Mode, using Natural as an example.

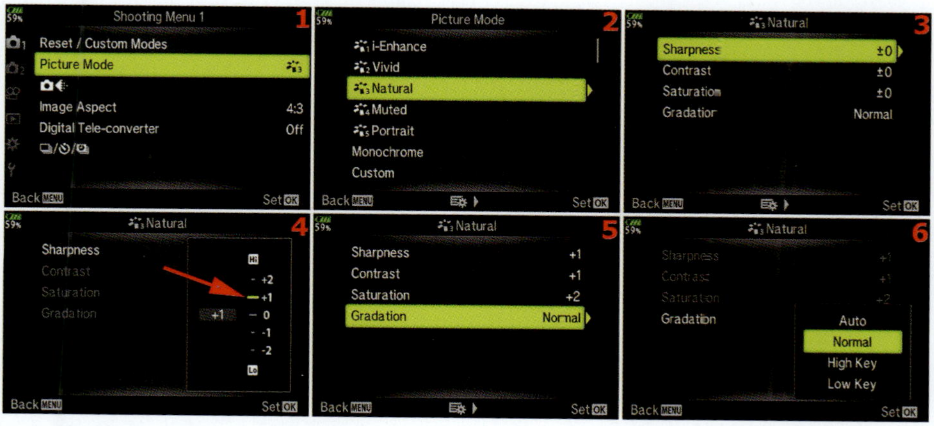

Figure 3.3B: Fine-tuning a Picture Mode

Use the following steps to fine-tune a basic Picture Mode (i-Enhance, Vivid, Natural, Muted, and Portrait):

1. Choose Picture Mode from Shooting Menu 1 and scroll to the right (figure 3.3B, image 1).
2. Select the Picture Mode you want to fine-tune and scroll to the right (figure 3.3B, image 2). I decided to fine-tune Natural.
3. Sharpness, Contrast, and Saturation are adjusted the same way, so only the screens for Sharpness are shown. Gradation is different, and we will consider it in steps 5 and 6. Highlight Sharpness, Contrast, or Saturation and scroll to the right (figure 3.3B, image 3).
4. Set the value on the scale from Hi (+2) to Lo (–2), or leave it at 0 for no change. In figure 3.3B, image 4, Sharpness +1 is selected (red arrow). If you want to modify Contrast or Saturation, repeat steps 3 and 4. In figure 3.3B, image 5, you can see that I set Sharpness to +1, Contrast to +1, and Saturation to +2. Experiment with the values to see how they affect your images. Press the OK button any time to save the setting. To change Gradation, move on to steps 5 and 6.
5. Choose Gradation from the menu and scroll to the right (figure 3.3B, image 5).
6. Choose one of the four values—Auto, Normal, High Key, or Low Key—and press the OK button (figure 3.3B, image 6). The four values have the following effects:
   - **Auto:** Lets the camera choose the Gradation
   - **Normal:** Makes a regular picture with no unusual Gradation changes
   - **High Key:** Shifts the picture toward bright values
   - **Low Key:** Shifts the picture toward dark values

The i-Enhance Picture Mode adds another setting called Effect (figure 3.3C, image 1). It controls the level of enhancement (High, Standard, Low) to the image. There are two additional screens for i-Enhance:

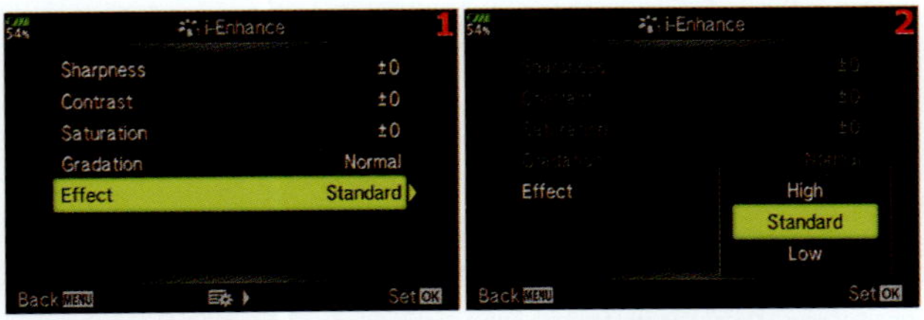

Figure 3.3C: The Effect setting for i-Enhance Mode

1. Select Effect from the menu and scroll to the right (figure 3.3C, image 1).
2. Highlight one of the three enhancement levels—High, Standard, or Low—and press the OK button to choose it (figure 3.3C, image 2). Experiment with this setting by taking pictures with all three enhancement levels.
3. When you have i-Enhance configured, scroll to the left until you return to the Picture Mode screen, then press the OK button to select the current Picture Mode. The camera will return to the Shooting Menu 1 screen with the symbol of the current mode displayed. Take your pictures.

Using Monochrome Picture Mode

Monochrome Picture Mode allows you to get creative with black-and-white images. You can use built-in color filters for changing the contrast, and you can even add toning, such as sepia, blue (cyanotype), and several others. Let's examine how to use Monochrome Mode.

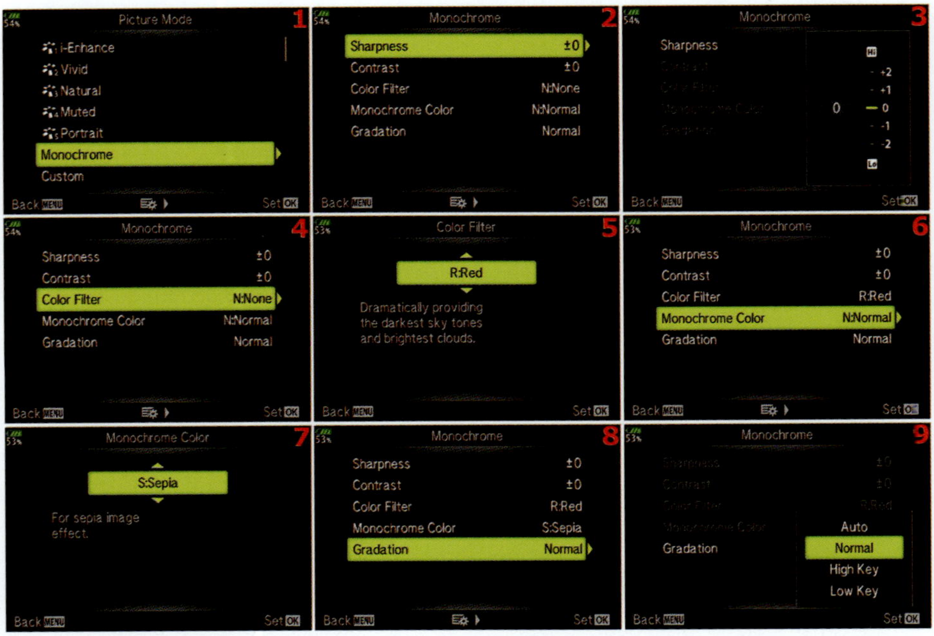

Figure 3.3D: Monochrome Mode

Use these steps to control Monochrome Mode:

1. Select Monochrome from the Picture Mode menu (on Shooting Menu 1) and scroll to the right (figure 3.3D, image 1).
2. Choose Sharpness or Contrast and scroll to the right (figure 3.3D, image 2).
3. Sharpness and Contrast are adjusted using the same method. I'll use Sharpness as an example. The menu that opens for Sharpness or Contrast allows you to increase or decrease the setting, up to two levels in either direction. Set the value on the scale from Hi (+2) to Lo (–2), or leave it at 0 for no change. Press the OK button to choose a value (figure 3.3D, image 3).
4. Select Color Filter from the menu and scroll to the right (figure 3.3D, image 4).
5. You can now choose one of the following Color Filter values from the up/down menu (figure 3.3D, image 5):
   - **N:None:** Provides a standard monochrome image
   - **Ye:Yellow:** Increases the contrast between the sky and clouds, but not as much as the R:Red filter
   - **Or:Orange:** Removes some of the foggy bluish haze when you use a telephoto lens for a distant subject
   - **R:Red:** Creates dark skies and bright clouds for maximum sky contrast
   - **G:Green:** Improves skin tones for portraits
6. Next, if you want to add a colored tone to your image, select Monochrome Color and scroll to the right (figure 3.3D, image 6).
7. Choose one of the following values from the Monochrome Color up/down menu (figure 3.3D, image 7):
   - **N:Normal:** Provides a standard monochrome image
   - **S:Sepia:** Adds a warm brown tone to a monochrome image, which resembles an antique sepia look
   - **B:Blue:** Adds a blue tone to a monochrome image, similar to the old-fashioned cyanotype look
   - **P:Purple:** Adds a purple tone to a monochrome image
   - **G:Green:** Adds a green tone to a monochrome image
8. To set the Gradation level, choose Gradation from the menu and scroll to the right (figure 3.3D, image 8).
9. Choose one of the four values—Auto, Normal, High Key, or Low Key—and press the OK button (figure 3.3D, image 9):
   - **Auto:** Lets the camera choose the Gradation
   - **Normal:** Makes a regular monochrome picture with no unusual Gradation changes
   - **High Key:** Shifts a monochrome picture toward bright values
   - **Low Key:** Shifts a monochrome picture toward dark values
10. When you have Monochrome fully configured, scroll to the left until you return to the Picture Mode screen, then press the OK button to select the current Picture Mode. The camera will return to the Shooting Menu 1 screen with the symbol of the current mode (M) displayed. Take your pictures.

Using Custom Picture Mode

Custom Picture Mode allows you to create your own Picture Mode and tweak it for your style of photography. Since Custom Mode lets you control the appearance of an image in exquisite detail, let's carefully examine each step.

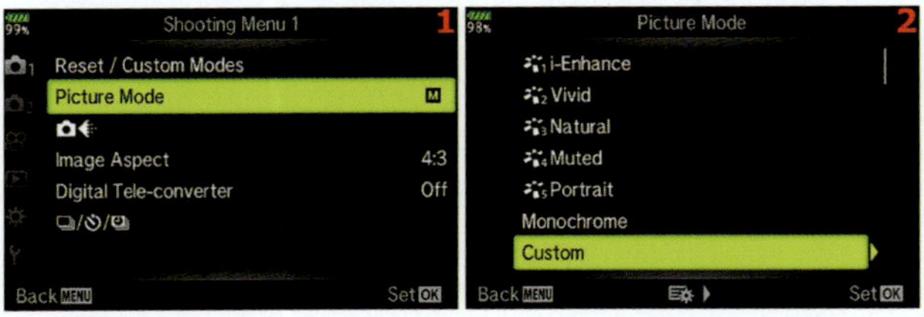

Figure 3.3E: Creating a Custom Picture Mode, step 1

1. Choose Picture Mode from Shooting Menu 1 menu and scroll to the right (figure 3.3E, image 1).
2. Select Custom from the Picture Mode menu and scroll to the right (figure 3.3E, image 2).

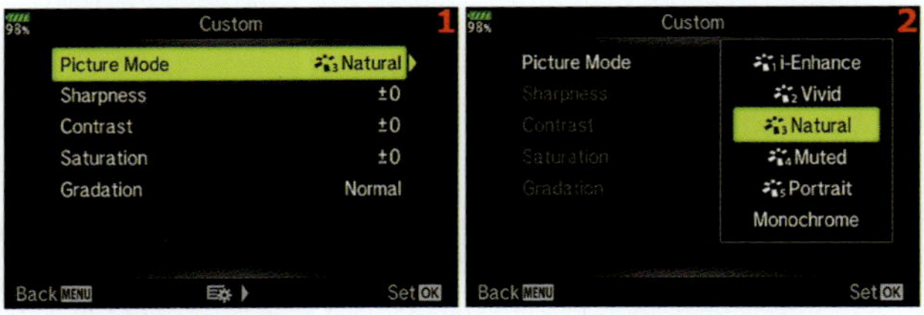

Figure 3.3F: Creating a Custom Picture Mode, step 2

3. Choose Picture Mode from the Custom Menu and scroll to the right (figure 3.3F, image 1).
4. Highlight one of the five basic Picture Modes or the Monochrome Picture Mode as the base for your Custom Picture Mode. I highlighted Natural. Press the OK button to select the mode (figure 3.3F, image 2).

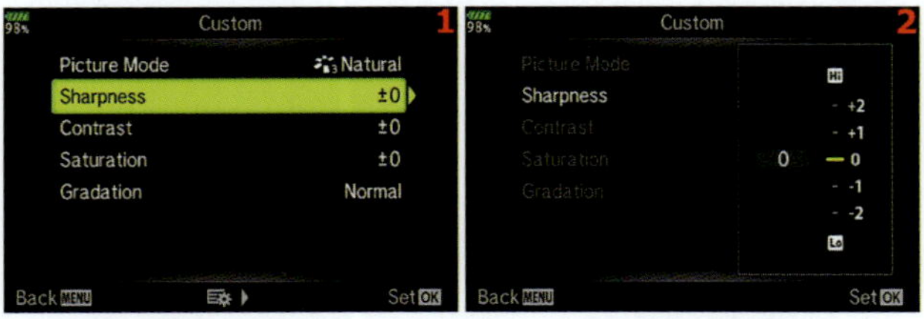

Figure 3.3G: Creating a Custom Picture Mode, step 3

5. Sharpness, Contrast, and Saturation are adjusted the same way, so I'll use Sharpness as an example. Highlight Sharpness, Contrast, or Saturation and scroll to the right (figure 3.3G, image 1).

6. Set the value on the scale from Hi (+2) to Lo (–2), or leave it at 0 for no change. In figure 3.3G, image 2, I selected Sharpness 0. If you want to modify Contrast or Saturation, repeat steps 5 and 6. Press the OK button to save the setting.

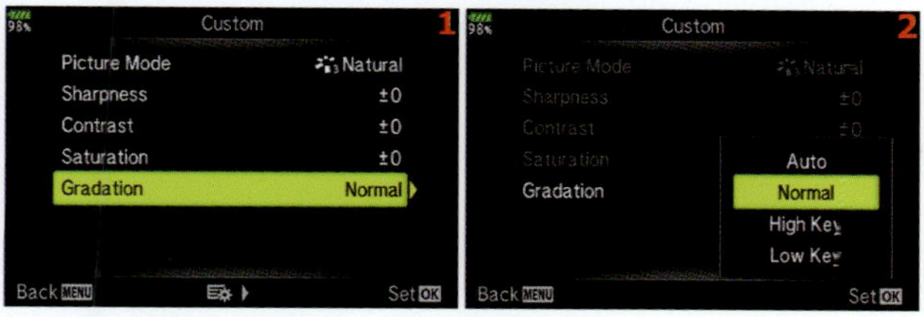

Figure 3.3H: Creating a Custom Picture Mode, step 4

7. To set the Gradation, choose Gradation from the menu and scroll to the right (figure 3.3H, image 1).
8. Choose Auto, Normal, High Key, or Low Key and press the OK button (figure 3.3H, image 2):
   - **Auto:** Lets the camera choose the Gradation
   - **Normal:** Makes a regular picture with no unusual Gradation changes
   - **High Key:** Shifts the picture toward bright values
   - **Low Key:** Shifts the picture toward dark values
9. When you have the Custom Picture Mode fully configured, scroll to the left until you return to the Picture Mode screen, then press the OK button to select the current Picture Mode. The camera will return to the Shooting Menu 1 screen with the symbol of the current mode displayed. Take your pictures.

Using e-Portrait Picture Mode

The e-Portrait Picture Mode is designed to make skin look smooth and translucent. It imitates the look of skin-smoothing plug-ins for Photoshop and is designed for taking pictures of faces. When you take a picture in e-Portrait Mode, the camera takes longer to write the image to the memory card, so the card access symbol will flash a little longer than usual.

Because the camera does internal image post-processing on skin tones, e-Portrait Mode cannot be used when you shoot video or if you bracket your images, whereas Portrait Picture Mode can be used in both of these situations because it doesn't perform post-processing to smooth the skin. You cannot adjust e-Portrait Mode.

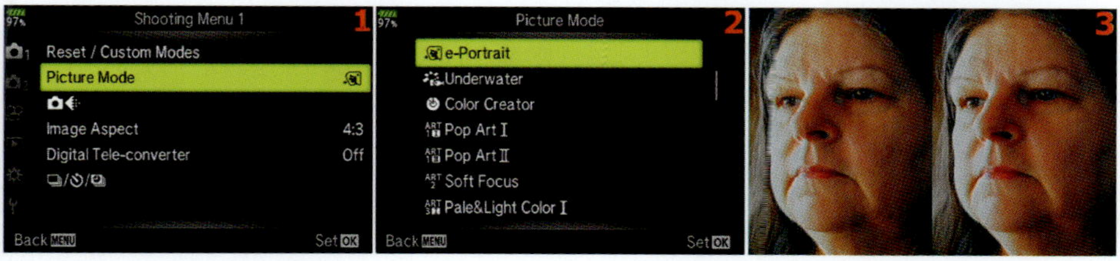

Figure 3.3I: e-Portrait Mode

Use these steps to select e-Portrait Mode:

1. Choose Picture Mode from Shooting Menu 1 and scroll to the right (figure 3.3I, image 1).
2. Highlight e-Portrait on the Picture Mode menu and press the OK button to select it (figure 3.3I, image 2). The camera will return to the Shooting Menu 1 screen and display the e-Portrait Mode symbol. Take your pictures.

Note: In figure 3.3I, image 3, you can see a before *(left)* and after *(right)* comparison of e-Portrait Mode. The image on the right has smoother skin tones.

Using Color Creator Picture Mode

Color Creator allows you to adjust the color of the subject by using a color wheel that controls hue and saturation while you look at the subject through the viewfinder or on the monitor.

First, let's examine how to choose Color Creator from the Picture Mode menu. Then we will consider the steps to make on-the-fly color adjustments.

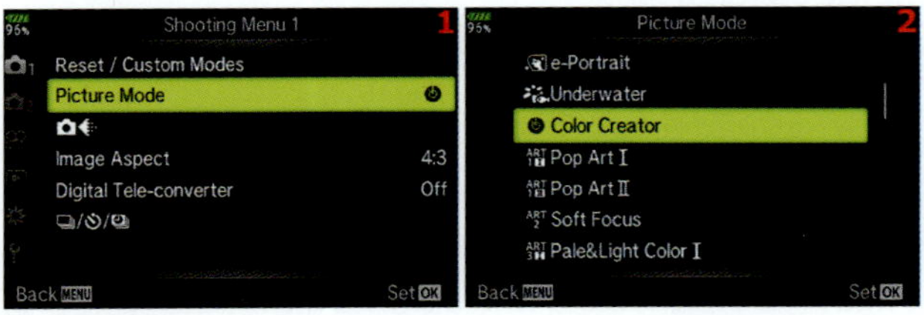

Figure 3.3J: Selecting Color Creator from the Picture Mode menu

Use these steps to prepare your subject for special color photography:

1. Choose Picture Mode from Shooting Menu 1 and scroll to the right (figure 3.3J, image 1).
2. Highlight Color Creator and press the OK button to choose it (figure 3.3J, image 2). The camera will return to Shooting Menu 1. Take your pictures.

Now we will use the Super Control Panel to bring up the Color Creator wheel on the viewfinder or monitor (you can also select it from the Live Control or LV Super Control Panel). It is important that you have your camera in your hand as you follow along with these instructions; otherwise, they will make little sense. It is much easier to understand what happens if you watch it unfold on your camera monitor or in the viewfinder.

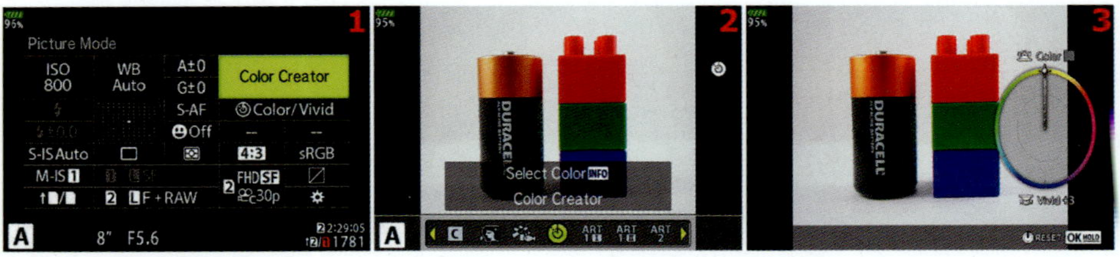

Figure 3.3K: Selecting Color Creator from the Super Control Panel

Here are the steps to select Color Creator from the Super Control Panel:

1. Open the Super Control Panel (or LV Super Control Panel) and highlight the Picture Mode location (figure 3.3K, image 1). Rotate the Front Dial until Color Creator shows on the panel (image 1), or press the OK button and select the Color Creator from the secondary screen (figure 3.3K, image 2).
2. Press the INFO button to open the Color Creator adjustment wheel (figure 3.3K, image 3).

Now we will adjust the hue and saturation of the colors in the image by using the Color Creator wheel. Your camera will display the scene in front of the lens, and you will see the effect of the color change when you move the dials.

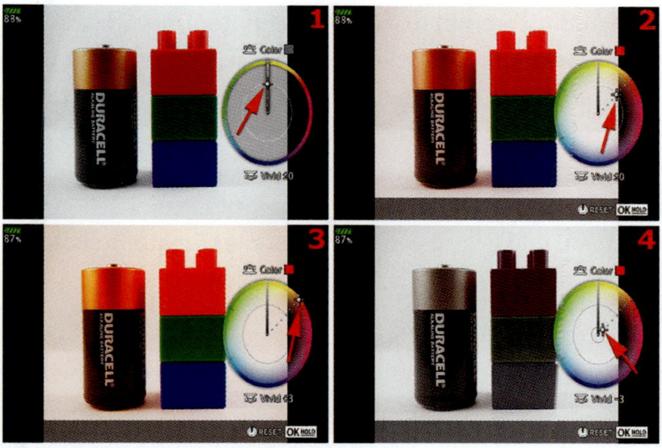

Figure 3.3L: Using the Color Creator wheel to change hue and saturation

Use the following steps to create special color tints in your image. Figure 3.3L begins where figure 3.3K left off, with the Color Creator adjustment wheel shown in the viewfinder or on the monitor and a subject in the background. If the Color Creator has not been adjusted in the past, you will see the wheel's default appearance (figure 3.3L, image 1). This is a neutral setting on the color wheel.

1. Turn the Front Dial to adjust the hue. As you do so, you will see a dotted line, move in the direction you turned the dial (figure 3.3L, image 2, red arrow). In my example, I turned the Front Dial three or four clicks clockwise until the dotted line pointed toward the beginning of the red portion of the wheel. As you rotate the dial, watch the subject carefully in the viewfinder or on the monitor. Its hue will change as you rotate through the red, green, blue, and yellow portions of the wheel. The dotted line will travel 360 degrees around the wheel until it is back at the 12 o'clock position, which represents neutral. You can see a small box to the right of the word Color at the top of the wheel. As you rotate the Front Dial and the dotted line travels around the wheel, you will see that square change color to indicate the hue that will be added to your

image when you take a picture. The color red is selected in figure 3.3L, image 2, as evidenced by the small red Color box and the obvious overall red tint in image 2.

2. After you have chosen a hue, use the Rear Dial to control the saturation in the image. When you turn the Rear Dial counterclockwise, you will see the saturation dot (with two horizontal lines and two vertical lines extending outward) move toward the edge of the color wheel, which increases the saturation in the image (figure 3.3L, image 3, red arrow). When you turn the Rear Dial clockwise, moving the dot toward the center of the circle, the saturation will be decreased. You will see a smaller ring inside the Color Creator wheel that follows the dot as you move it. To be clear, when the dot is closer to the middle of the Color Creator wheel, the saturation decreases; when the dot is closer to the outside of the Color Creator wheel, the saturation increases. You will see the word Vivid with a number below the Color Creator wheel. The vividness, or saturation, will vary from –4 (monochrome) to +3 (very saturated), as indicated by the small number after the word Vivid. Our example in figure 3.3L, image 3, is at Vivid +3, or full saturation. In figure 3.3L, image 4, the saturation is dialed all the way down to just above monochrome (Vivid –3). One more click of the Rear Dial would take us to Vivid –4, or full monochrome.
3. Make your adjustments and then press the OK button to accept the color scheme. It will be applied to all the images you make until you reset the Color Creator to neutral. Take your pictures.

Note: To reset the Color Creator to neutral, press and hold the OK button for about two seconds until the Color Creator resets to neutral hue and saturation, as shown in figure 3.3L, image 1.

Settings Recommendation: If you want to regularly change the hue and saturation in your images, experiment with the Color Creator. If you leave it at neutral, your images will be less saturated and have lower contrast, and they will be easier to work with in post-processing on your computer. If you modify the hue and saturation in Color Creator, remember to change the camera to a different Picture Mode when you are done.

And remember, if you shoot RAW (ORF) images, it's easy to change the color and contrast afterwards, so it doesn't matter which Picture Mode you choose. We'll discuss this a little more in the **[Photo][Record Mode]** section later in this chapter.

Applying Art Picture Modes, Add Effects, Color Filter, and Monochrome Color

As previously mentioned, there are 14 Art Picture Modes available in the E-M1II, many of which have multiple variations, providing a total of 28 distinct artistic looks. If you like to convey different moods in your pictures and do not like post-processing RAW files on a computer, you might enjoy these Art Picture Modes.

Each Art Picture Mode was examined in this chapter on page 94. To access the Art Picture Modes, you can use the shortcut of setting the Mode Dial to ART, pressing the OK button, and selecting one of the 28 options—along with several special effects available under each mode. Or, you can go to *Shooting Menu 1 > Picture Mode* to select Art Picture Modes. This section provides more detail on how the modes and effects work for both choices.

Let's examine each of the special effects (called "Add Effects") that can be applied to Art Picture Modes, and then we'll discuss how to apply the effects to your upcoming pictures.

Art Picture Modes on the Mode Dial

The Mode Dial has an ART Mode position that opens up the Art Picture Modes and special effects for quick access. Most Art Picture Modes allow you to apply Add Effects, and the monochrome-style Art Picture Modes (i.e., Grainy Film I, II and Dramatic Tone II) allow you to apply Color Filters and Monochrome Color (tints).

We will use Dramatic Tone II (Art 10) as our sample in this section because it allows you to apply Add Effects, Color Filters, and Monochrome Color (figure 3.3M). You will use the same steps to apply available effects, filters, and tints to any Art Picture Mode that allows for them.

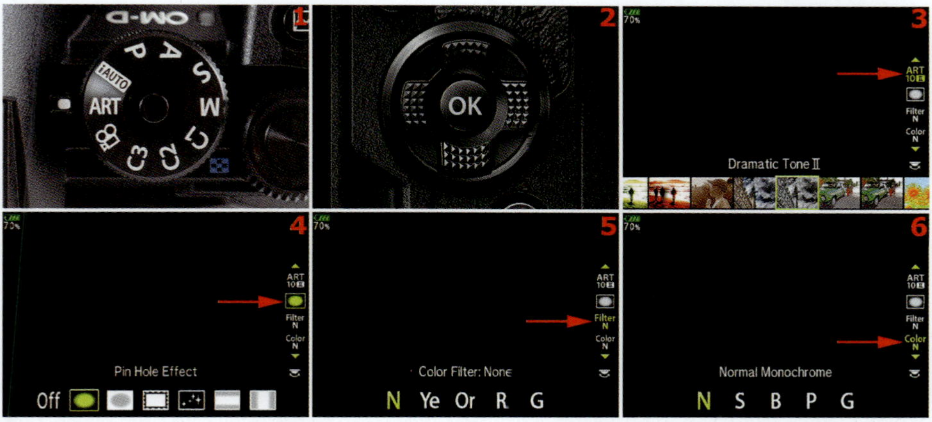

Figure 3.3M: Applying Art Picture Modes and effects from the Mode Dial and secondary screen

Use the following steps to select an Art Picture Mode and Add Effect, along with a Color Filter and Monochrome Color (when available):

1. Set the camera's Mode Dial to the ART position (figure 3.3M, image 1).
2. Once you've selected the ART position, the screen shown in figure 3.3M, image 3 will be displayed (except you will see your subject on the screen; my graphic was created with the lens cap on). If you see your subject but not the Art Picture Mode secondary screen, press the OK button (figure 3.3M, image 2). The currently selected Art Picture Mode and special effects are shown on the right side of the screen, and the options for each are displayed along the bottom of the screen (figure 3.3M, image 3).

3. Notice in figure 3.3M, image 3, that the red arrow is pointing to ART10 (II). This represents the Dramatic Tone II Art Picture Mode (page 156), which is selected at the bottom of the secondary screen (image 3). If you scroll left or right with the Arrow Pad when this screen is active, you can select from the 28 Art Picture Mode options. If you scroll up or down with the Arrow Pad, you will be able to select Add Effects, Color Filters, and Monochrome Color. Most of the Art Picture Modes will offer only Add Effects, and will not offer Color Filters or Monochrome Color. We are using Dramatic Tone II as our sample because this monochrome-style Art Picture Mode offers all of the special effects. Scroll down with the Arrow Pad.
4. Figure 3.3M, image 4, shows that the Pin Hole Effect is selected. The red arrow points to the symbol for the currently selected Add Effect, and the bottom of the screen offers up to eight Add Effects (page 158). The number of available Add Effects varies depending on which Art Picture Mode is selected—some modes offer all eight, others offer only one or two. Scroll left or right with the Arrow Pad to see how the different Add Effects change the look of the subject on the screen. Stop scrolling when the effect you want to use is highlighted.
5. Figure 3.3M, image 5, displays the Color Filter (page 159) choices, which are available for monochrome-style Art Picture Modes only. Most Art Picture Modes will not have the Color Filter selections available. For those that do, scroll left or right to choose a Color Filter. Color Filters affect how various colors in your subject are represented by light or dark gray tones, instead of colors. Scroll down with the Arrow Pad (if available).
6. The final choices on the secondary screen for the monochrome-style Art Picture Modes are the Monochrome Color selections (page 159). These provide overall tints for the image, such as Normal Monochrome (normal black-and-white), Sepia Monochrome (brownish), Blue Monochrome, Purple Monochrome, and Green Monochrome. The entire image is tinted by the Monochrome Color selections.
7. Once you have selected your modes and special effects, simply take your pictures.

Again, Color Filter (step 5) and Monochrome Color (step 6) are available only for certain monochrome-style Art Picture Modes (i.e., Grainy Film I, II and Dramatic Tone II). The other Art Picture Modes will have only the Add Effects (step 4) choices. Therefore, skip steps 5 and 6 for Art Picture Modes that do not display the Color Filters or Monochrome Color selections.

Next let's examine how to select the Art Picture Modes and other effects from the *Shooting Menu 1 > Picture Mode* screens.

Art Picture Modes in Shooting Menu 1 (Picture Mode)

The 28 Art Picture Modes are also available via the *Shooting Menu 1 > Picture Mode* menu. Let's examine how to select these modes and effects from the Picture Mode menu. We'll use Dramatic Tone II Art Picture Mode as our example once again (figure 3.3N).

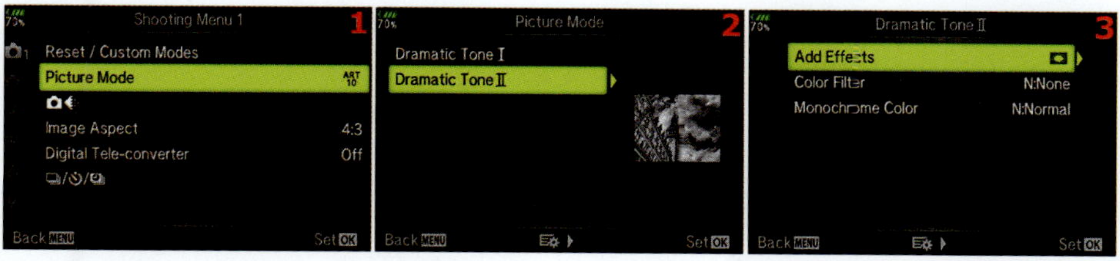

Figure 3.3N: Applying Art Picture Modes and effects from *Shooting Menu 1 > Picture Mode* screens

Use the following steps to select an Art Picture Mode from the Picture Mode menu, and then apply an Add Effect, Color Filter, and Monochrome Color setting (when available):

1. Choose Picture Mode from Shooting Menu 1 and scroll to the right (figure 3.3N, image 1).
2. Highlight your favorite Art Picture Mode under the Picture Mode menu (figure 3.3N, image 2). We will use Dramatic Tone II as our example mode. Press the OK button to select it for immediate use in default mode, which applies the Art Picture Mode with no Add Effects. If you want to change the Add Effects, Color Filter, or Monochrome Color settings (if available) before you take pictures, scroll to the right and proceed to step 3 (figure 3.3N, image 3).

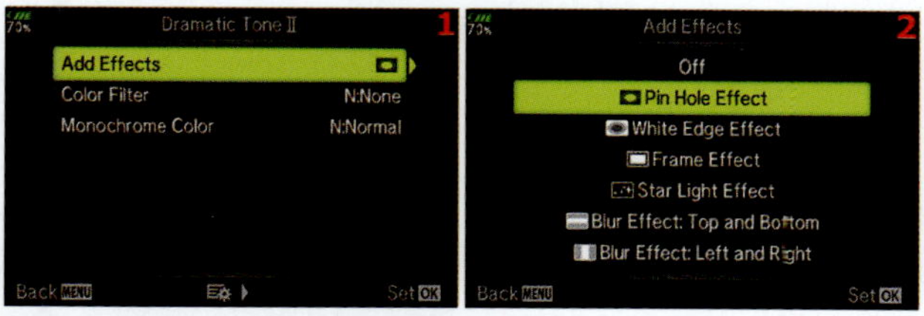

Figure 3.3O: Choosing an Add Effects type

3. Figure 3.3O, image 1, begins where figure 3.3N, image 3, left off. Select Add Effects from the menu and scroll to the right.
4. Scroll up or down to highlight one of the Add Effects types, or Off (figure 3.3O, image 2), as described in the Add Effects list (page 158). Choose an Add Effects type by pressing the OK button, which will set the effect and return to the previous screen.

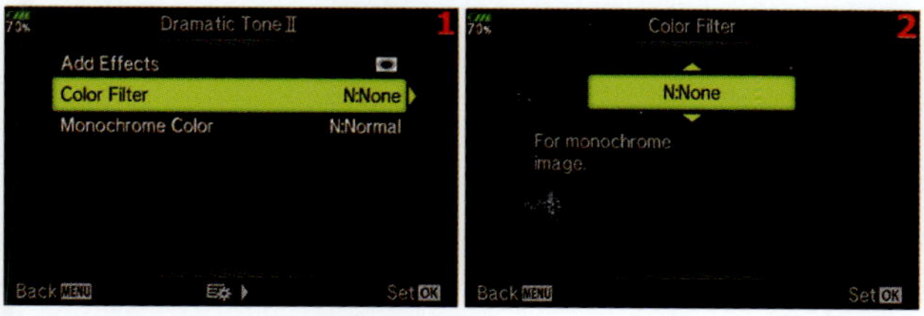

Figure 3.3P: Choosing a Color Filter type

5. Figure 3.3P, image 1, begins where figure 3.3N, image 3, left off. If available, select Color Filter from the menu and scroll to the right. (***Note:*** This selection is available for only a few monochrome-style Art Picture Modes. Skip steps 5 and 6 if Color Filter is not available for the Art Picture Mode you've selected.)
6. Scroll up or down to highlight one of the Color Filter types (figure 3.3P, image 2), as described in the Color Filter list (page 159). Select your Add Effects type by pressing the OK button, which will set the effect and return to the previous screen.

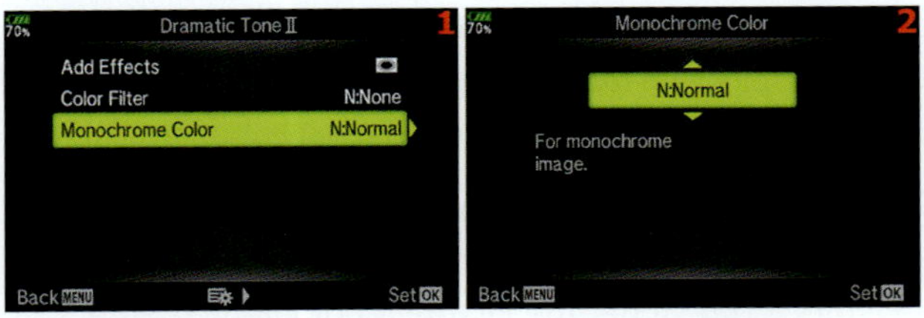

Figure 3.3Q: Choosing a Monochrome Color type

7. Figure 3.3Q, image 1, begins where figure 3.3N, image 3, left off. If available, select Monochrome Color from the menu and scroll to the right. (***Note:*** This selection is available for only a few monochrome-style Art Picture Modes. Skip steps 7 and 8 if Monochrome Color is not available for the Art Picture Mode you've selected.)
8. Scroll up or down to highlight one of the Monochrome Color types (figure 3.3Q, image 2), as described in the Monochrome Color list (page 159). Select your Monochrome Color type by pressing the OK button, which will set the effect and return to the previous screen.
9. When you are finished making adjustments, scroll to the left until you return to the Picture Mode screen (figure 3.3R), and then press the OK button to select the Art Picture Mode you have been adjusting. The camera will return to the Shooting Menu 1 screen with the symbol of the current mode displayed. Take your pictures.

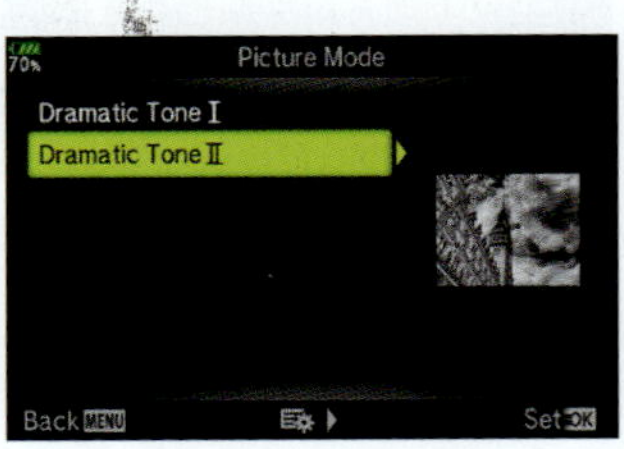

Figure 3.3R: Highlight the Art Picture Mode you have been adjusting and press OK

Again, most Art Picture Modes will not have Color Filter or Monochrome Color available, in which case you should skips steps 5–8.

Art Picture Mode Bracketing

As if the E-M1II is not amazing enough, it has one of the most unusual functions I have ever seen in a camera. You can take a single picture and the camera will make 14 duplicates while you watch. It applies each of the 14 Art Picture Modes to a single new image (version I only). You end up with the original image plus 14 pictures that display each Art Picture Mode. It takes only a few seconds and gives you a wide variety of images to choose from.

This function is not part of the menu-based *Shooting Menu 1 > Picture Mode* system. It is available only when you select ART from the Mode Dial on top of the camera, press the OK button, and select ART BKT from the secondary screen. See the **ART BKT** subheading in the **Shooting Menu 2** chapter, on page 202, for information about how to use the Art Picture Mode bracketing function.

[Photo][Record Mode]

[Photo][Record Mode] provides the basic file formats, or Image Quality, your camera uses for taking still pictures. Basically, the camera can capture still images in several varieties of JPEG, or in ORF files, which is the Olympus RAW image format. Let's examine the still image formats.

Still Image Formats

There are two still image formats available in the E-M1II: JPEG and RAW (ORF). We will examine both of these formats and discuss their pros and cons, but first let's see how to select a format.

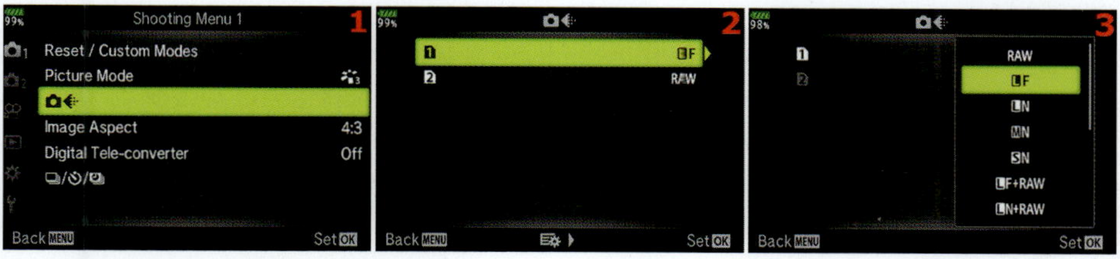

Figure 3.4A: Selecting a JPEG format

Use the following steps to choose a JPEG image format:

1. Select [Photo][Record Mode] (the symbols look like a camera and a fading diamond) from Shooting Menu 1 and scroll to the right (figure 3.4A, image 1).
2. You may run a different format for each of the memory cards in your camera (Slot 1 and Slot 2). Choose card slot 1 or 2 from the [Photo][Record Mode] menu and scroll to the right (figure 3.4A, image 2).
3. You will see five basic modes and four combination modes (figure 3.4A, image 3). If the camera is set to the defaults, the basic modes are RAW, LF, LN, MN, and SN. (The menu shown in figure 3.4A, image 3, can be configured to reflect the modes you use most frequently. We will discuss how to change it in the note after these steps.) The JPEG+RAW combination modes create both a RAW file and a JPEG file each time you take a picture. The default selections for the combination modes are LF+RAW, LN+RAW, MN+RAW, and SN+RAW. You can't see the last two combination modes in figure 3.4A, image 3, because you must scroll down to access them. We will talk more about RAW images in the next subsection. Highlight one of the basic or combination formats and press the OK button to select it. I chose Large Fine or (LF).

Note: There is another setting called Super Fine (SF). It is not enabled when your camera is new. Large Super Fine (LSF) creates even better images—with less compression—than Large Fine (LF). To make LSF available, you must adjust a setting under the Custom Menu, then LSF will appear instead of LF on the menu in figure 3.4A, image 3. In the *Custom Menu > G. [Record Mode]/WB/Color > [Record Mode] Set* function, change any of the settings to SF, as shown in figure 3.4B (see the next subsection).

Image Size, Pixel Count, and JPEG Compression Ratios

The E-M1II gives you a choice of several RAW or JPEG image sizes, including Large (L), Middle (M), and Small (S), and several pixel counts too (e.g., 5184 × 3888). You can also choose from several JPEG compression levels, including Super Fine (SF), Fine (F), Normal (N), and Basic (B). JPEG files have a certain compression ratio, depending on the compression rate (SF, F, N, and B). Table 3.1 lists the image sizes, pixel counts, compression rate names, and the compression ratio for that type of JPEG.

For instance, the Fine (F) compression ratio is 1:4, which means the file size will be approximately 25 percent of the original file size (1 ÷ 4 = 0.25). The Normal (N) compression ratio is 1:8, which means the compressed JPEG is about 12.5 percent of the original file size (1 ÷ 8 = 0.125). JPEG files are compressed with *lossy* compression, which means a large portion of the image data is thrown away. A 1:4 compression ratio, with a file size that is only 25 percent of the original file size, results in a permanent loss of 75 percent of the image data. That's why you must take accurate JPEG pictures so you don't have to post-process them later. When you change and resave a JPEG image, more compression is applied to an already compressed image and even more data is thrown away. It is not a good idea to change and resave a JPEG image more than once or twice. Otherwise, compressions losses will damage the image and lead to issues like excessive JPEG artifacts and color banding.

On the other hand, RAW files are compressed with automatic (you can't change it) lossless compression that keeps all data and still compresses the image by 20 to 40 percent, depending on the complexity of the subject. The lossless compression of a RAW file does not throw away any data. Therefore, you can modify and resave a RAW file over and over with no data loss. You cannot disable the lossless compression on RAW files. Don't worry, though, because the lossless compression of a RAW file is like the familiar ZIP format on your computer. All the original data returns when the file is uncompressed. Your RAW conversion software will decompress the RAW file without your intervention.

On your camera menus, you will see the size and compression rate names combined for JPEG settings. For instance, a Large-size, Fine-compression rate JPEG will be listed as LF, and a Medium-size, Normal-compression rate JPEG will be shown as MN.

Size	Pixel Count	Compression Rate for JPEG			
Large (L)	5184 × 3888	Large Super Fine (LSF) Ratio = 1:2.7	Large Fine (LF) Ratio = 1:4	Large Normal (LN) Ratio = 1:8	Large Basic (LB) Ratio = 1:12
Middle (M)	3200 × 2400 2560 × 1920 1920 × 1440 1600 × 1200	Middle Super Fine (MSF) Ratio = 1:2.7	Middle Fine (MF) Ratio = 1:4	Middle Norma (MN) Ratio = 1:8	Middle Basic (MB) Ratio = 1:12
Small (S)	1280 × 960 1024 × 768	Small Super Fine (SSF) Ratio = 1:2.7	Small Fine (SF) Ratio = 1:4	Small Normal (SN) Ratio = 1:8	Small Basic (SB) Ratio = 1:12

Table 3.1: JPEG format size, pixel count, and compression (see figure 3.4C)

Table 3.1 lists the available image sizes, pixel counts, and compression ratios in the E-M1II. The pixel size for RAW mode is always Large (L) 5184 × 3888. RAW files always contain all available image data and cannot be resized in-camera. JPEG images have adjustable sizes, pixel counts, and compression rates.

Figure 3.4B shows how to use the *Custom Menu > G. [Record Mode]/WB/Color > [Record Mode] Set* function to change the default choices for the compression rate (SF, F, N, and B). After you make a change on the Custom Menu screen shown in figure 3.4B, image 2, *Shooting Menu 1 > [Photo][Record Mode]* will offer you the compression choices you chose in the Custom Menu, instead of the factory default settings. Before making the change in the Custom Menu, your camera most likely offers you the following compression rates: LF, LN, MN, and SN.

Why settle for a Large Fine (LF) JPEG when a Large Super Fine (LSF) JPEG is available? I set my camera to use LSF, LF, MF, and SF. However, you may have a need for a normal (N) or basic (B) JPEG. The camera gives you the ability to make any of those settings available to the *Shooting Menu 1 > [Photo] [Record Mode]* function by changing the settings in the *Custom Menu > G. [Record Mode]/WB/Color > [Record Mode] Set* function (figure 3.4B).

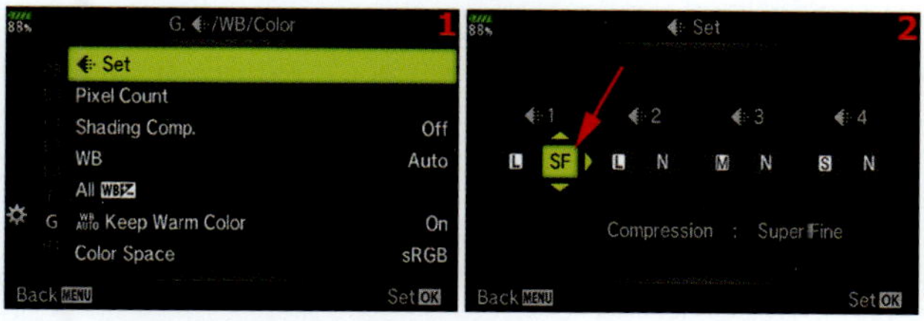

Figure 3.4B: Changing the default compression rate

The compression rate for JPEGs shown in table 3.1 is controlled through the Custom Menu, as shown in figure 3.4B. You can modify any of the four JPEG settings shown in figure 3.4B, image 2, and the new settings will replace the old ones. Large Super Fine (LSF) is selected in figure 3.4B, image 2. Your selections will also appear in other camera menus that offer JPEG size and compression settings (such as the menu shown in figure 3.4A, image 3). This is discussed in more detail in the **Custom Menu** chapter under the **[Record Mode] Set** subheading on page 532.

You can also choose a different pixel count if you need to shoot a smaller megapixel (MP) size than the camera's native 5184 × 3888 pixel count (20.4 MP). Only JPEG images are affected by changing the pixel count. Figure 3.4C shows the screens used to choose a different MP size for your JPEG pictures *(Custom Menu > G. [Record Mode]/WB/Color > Pixel Count)*.

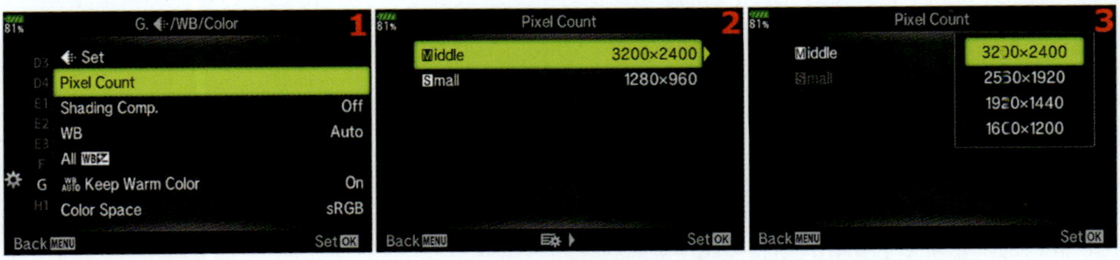

Figure 3.4C: Choosing a smaller MP size for your images

You can control the pixel count for both Middle (M) and Small (S), as shown in table 3.1, with the Custom Menu (figure 3.4C). This is discussed in more detail in the **Custom Menu** chapter under the **Pixel Count** subheading on page 534.

Now, let's examine the two available formats and see how they work.

JPEG Format

JPEG format is used by people who want excellent image quality but have little time for, or interest in, post-processing or converting images to another format. They want to use images immediately with no major adjustments.

The JPEG format applies your chosen camera settings to the image when it is taken. The image comes out of the camera ready to use, as long as you have exposed it properly and have configured all the other settings appropriately.

Since JPEG is a lossy format—because image compression permanently throws data away—you cannot modify and save a JPEG file more than a time or two before compression losses begin to degrade the image. Therefore, make sure to shoot JPEG images correctly in the first place.

The compression rate of a JPEG image affects the overall image quality. Super Fine mode will give you the best looking picture since the compression ratio is rather low. Each higher compression rate, Fine through Basic, throws away more color information, but the smaller file takes up less room on your camera's memory card(s) and in your computer. You will need to balance your desire for image quality with your available storage space.

Photographers who shoot a lot of images or don't have time to post-process RAW often shoot JPEGs. That encompasses a lot of photographers.

Nature photographers might want to use RAW (ORF) format since they often have more time for processing images and wringing the last drop of quality out of them, but event or journalist photographers on deadlines may not have the time for, or interest in, processing images, so they often use the JPEG format.

Here are the pros and cons of capturing JPEG images:

JPEG positives

- Allows for the maximum number of images on a memory card and computer hard drive.
- Allows for the fastest transfer from the camera memory buffer to a memory card.
- Compatible with everything and everybody in imaging.
- Uses the printing industry standard of 8 bits.
- Produces high-quality, first-use images.
- No special software is needed to use the image right out of the camera (no post-processing).
- Immediate use on websites with minimal processing.
- Easy transfer across the Internet and as e-mail attachments.

JPEG negatives

- JPEG is a lossy format.
- You cannot manipulate a JPEG image more than once or twice before it begins to degrade to an unusable state. Every time you modify and save a JPEG image, it loses more data and quality because of data compression losses.

Settings Recommendation: Because JPEG images are compressed, even the largest files do not take up that much space. Therefore, when I shoot JPEGs I use Large Super Fine (LSF) most of the time. The only time I would use a higher compression rate is if I were running out of card space on an important shoot. Computer hard drives are cheap these days. Why limit the quality of your images just to save some storage space?

RAW (ORF) Format

RAW (ORF) is the image purist's mode of choice. It's important that you understand that RAW files are not really images—yet. The RAW format is merely a container that stores a small sample JPEG file, black-and-white image data, color information markers, and camera setting markers. The RAW file must be converted to another file type before you can use it.

When you take a picture in RAW format, the camera records the raw image data from the sensor and stores markers for how the camera's color, sharpening, contrast, saturation, and so forth are set, but it does not apply the camera setting information to the image. In your post-processing software, the image will appear on-screen with the settings you initially configured in your E-M1II (or a best estimate). However, these settings are applied temporarily so you can see them on your camera and computer screens.

If you don't like the white balance you selected when you took the picture, simply apply a new white balance and the image will appear as if you had used that setting when you captured the image. If you used Natural Picture Mode and now want to use Vivid Picture Mode, you can apply it before the final conversion, and it will be as if you used it when you shot the picture.

This is quite powerful! Virtually no camera settings are applied to a RAW file permanently. During post-processing you can apply completely different settings to the image and it will look like you used those settings when you took the picture. This allows a lot of flexibility later. You simply cannot do that with a JPEG file without causing compression damage.

RAW (ORF) is generally used by photographers who are concerned with maximum image quality and who have time to convert the images. When you shoot a RAW image, it is saved on the memory card in your camera, and later in your computer, as a file ending in ORF.

Here are the pros and cons of RAW (ORF) format:

RAW (ORF) positives

- Allows the manipulation of image data to achieve the highest-quality image available from the camera.
- All original details stay with the image for future processing needs.
- No conversions, sharpening, sizing, or color rebalancing will be performed by the camera. Your image data is untouched and pure!
- You can convert ORF files to any other image format by using your computer's much more powerful processor instead of your camera's processor.
- You have much more control over the final look of the image since you, not the camera, make the final decisions about the appearance of the image.
- The ORF file's 14-bit format stores maximum color information for later use.

RAW (ORF) negatives

- Not often compatible with the publishing industry, except after conversion to another format.
- Requires post-processing with proprietary Olympus software or third-party software.
- Larger file sizes are created, so you must have more storage media.
- There is no industry-standard RAW format. Each camera manufacturer has its own proprietary format. Adobe has developed a generic RAW format called digital negative (DNG) that is becoming an industry standard. You can use various types of software, such as Adobe Lightroom, to convert your RAW images to DNG if you desire.
- The industry standard for home and commercial printing is currently 8 bits, not 14 bits.

Steps for RAW Conversion in Olympus Viewer 3 Software

Here are the basic steps to convert a RAW (ORF) file into JPEG or TIFF format with the free Olympus Viewer 3 software (method may vary in later versions of the software):

1. Transfer the images from your camera to your computer.
2. Select a folder full of E-M1II images from the Folder pane on the left side of the Olympus Viewer 3 software. When you see images on the computer screen in Olympus Viewer 3, you will see the word RAW in the upper-right corner of the RAW (ORF) images (or R+J when there is both a RAW and a JPEG image). You will also see the filename appended by ORF below the image (e.g., PC180263.ORF)
3. Right click the RAW image and select Open Edit Window.
4. On the right side of the screen under the Histogram display, you will see two tabs: Edit and Raw. Both of these screens allow you to change all sorts of things in the RAW image before you save it as a JPEG (or other format). The Raw tab even lets you change things like Picture Mode and White balance.
5. Make your changes, and the computer will update the image immediately after each change. The changes won't be permanently saved until you save the file as another format.
6. When you are done adjusting the image, open the File menu and select Export. The Export Image window will open.
7. Select a file name, Format (JPEG, TIFF), JPEG compression, and Resize for converting the image. Use Exif-JPEG or Exif-TIFF if you want to preserve the EXIF data in the image metadata (e.g., lens, focal length, shutter speed, aperture, ISO setting).
8. Select Export by Batch Processing from the drop-down menu next to the Save button. In the right-lower corner the software will show a progress bar that says Processing… and the number of images being converted in parenthesis (you can convert multiple images in one batch).
9. Finish will appear where Processing… was previously, with a solid orange progress bar, after your images have been converted.

Settings Recommendation: I use the RAW (ORF) format most of the time. I think of a RAW file like I thought of my slides and negatives a few years ago. It's my original image that must be saved and protected. I am primarily a nature photographer, so I make time to post-process each important image. You may not have time for that, or maybe you're not interested in post-processing. In that case JPEG images may be more reasonable for your shooting style. The format you use most often will be dictated by your time constraints and digital workflow.

If you normally shoot JPEGs, experiment with the free Olympus Viewer 3 software by converting a few RAW images as previously described.

Combined JPEG+RAW Shooting (Two Images at Once)

Some photographers use one of the four [Record Mode] settings (partially shown in figure 3.4A, image 3). These JPEG+RAW modes save two images at the same time: one JPEG and one RAW. Here are the factory default settings for the combined format shooting:

- LF+RAW
- LN+RAW
- MN+RAW
- SN+RAW

These settings give you the best of both worlds because the camera saves an ORF file and a JPEG file each time you press the Shutter button.

You can use the RAW (ORF) file to store all the image data and later process it into a masterpiece, and you can use the JPEG file immediately with no adjustment.

The JPEG+RAW modes have the same features as their stand-alone modes. In other words, a RAW file in a JPEG+RAW mode works like a RAW file in RAW (ORF) mode, and a JPEG file in a JPEG+RAW mode works like a JPEG SF, F, N, or B file on its own.

Keep in mind that you can change the default settings for the combined modes by changing the *Custom Menu > G. [Record Mode]/WB/Color > [Record Mode] Set* function values for JPEG compression (figure 3.4B). The JPEG compression modes you choose appear both in the camera menus for standard JPEG files and for the combined shooting modes.

Image Format Recommendation

Which format do I prefer? Why, RAW, of course! But it does require a bit of commitment to shoot in this format. RAW (ORF) files are not yet images and must be converted to another format for use. After they are converted, they can provide the highest-quality images your camera can possibly create.

When you shoot in RAW, the camera is simply an image-capturing device and you are the image manipulator. You decide the final format, compression ratio, size, color balance, and so forth. In RAW (ORF) mode, you get the best image your camera can produce. It is not modified by the camera software and is ready for your personal touch. No camera processing allowed!

If you get nothing else from this section, remember this: by letting your camera process images in *any* way, it modifies or throws away data. There is a finite amount of data for each image that can be stored in your camera, and later in your computer. With JPEG, your camera optimizes the image according to JPEG compression algorithms created by an Olympus programmer. Data is thrown away permanently, in varying amounts.

If you want to keep *all* the image data that was recorded with your images, you must store your originals in RAW format. Otherwise you'll never be able to access the original data to change how it looks. A RAW file is the closest thing to a film negative or transparency that your digital camera can make. That's important if you would like to modify the image later. If you are concerned with maximum quality, you should probably shoot and store your images in RAW format. Later, when you have the urge to make another masterpiece out of the original RAW image file, you'll have *all* your original data intact for the highest-quality image.

Image Aspect

The Image Aspect ratio of a picture is the ratio of the sides to each other. When the length of the sides change, the horizontal to vertical ratio changes.

The easiest way to understand Image Aspect is to see a group of images that were taken with the five available Image Aspect ratios, which are 4:3, 3:4, 1:1, 3:2, and 16:9.

I tried to maintain the size of the birdhouse in the images shown in figure 3.5A so you can see how the ratio affects the image frame. The E-M1II camera uses 4:3 as the default ratio. Many other camera brands use 3:2 as the default, which results in longer and more narrow images.

You can choose from five Image Aspect ratios (figure 3.5A). Be aware that changing the Image Aspect ratio also changes the megapixel rating of the image.

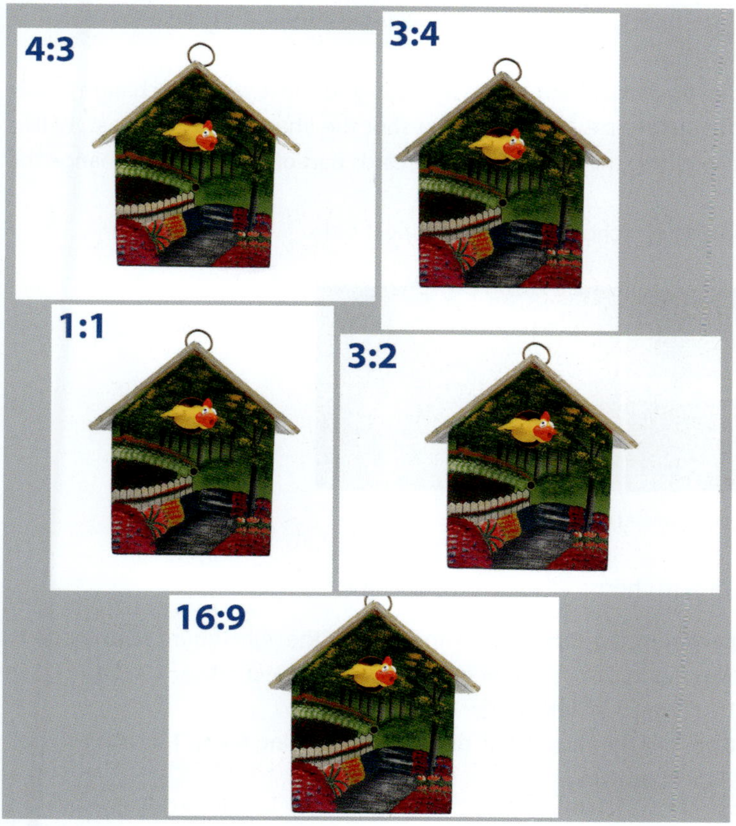

Figure 3.5A: Comparison of Image Aspect ratios

Image Aspect ratios apply only to JPEG images. When you shoot RAW images, the camera will store a reference to the ratio in the metadata, and it will display the aspect ratio as a smaller frame inside the normal 4:3 image border.

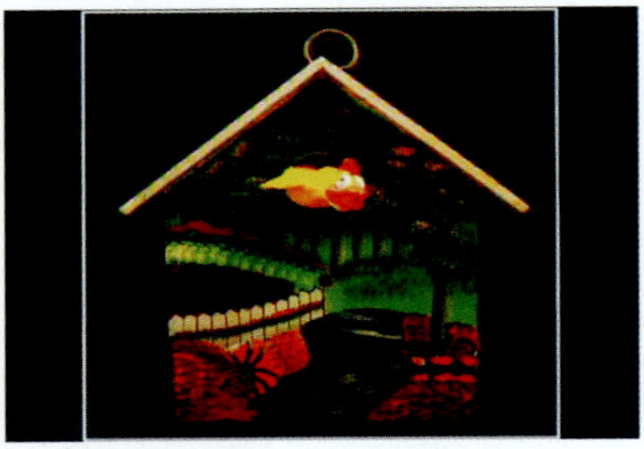

Figure 3.5B: RAW image displaying a 1:1 Image Aspect ratio frame

Figure 3.5B shows a RAW image with the 1:1 Image Aspect ratio frame. The normal 4:3 image is displayed on the camera screens and in the Olympus Viewer 3 software. When you view the image, it has a temporary frame that outlines the chosen aspect ratio, which, in this case, is 1:1.

If you later decide you do not want to use the ratio you chose, you can change it later without affecting the image size, but only if you shot the image in RAW format. With a JPEG you would have to crop the image, which discards part of the image, to change the aspect ratio.

Now, let's examine how to choose an Image Aspect ratio.

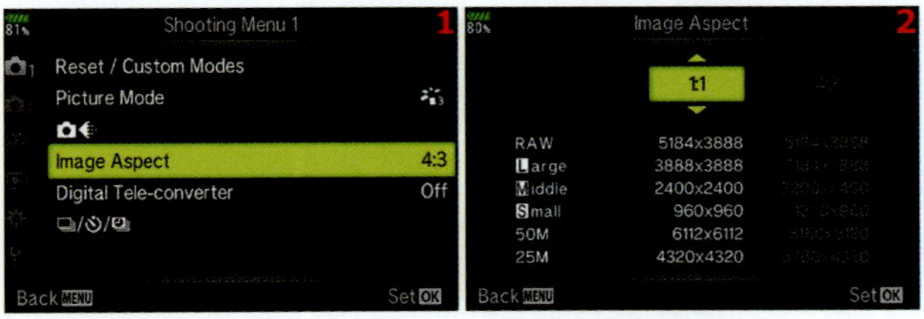

Figure 3.5C: Choosing an Image Aspect ratio

Use the following steps to choose an Image Aspect ratio:

1. Select Image Aspect from Shooting Menu 1 and scroll to the right (figure 3.5C, image 1).
2. Using the up/down menu, select one of the five Image Aspect ratios: 4:3, 3:4, 1:1, 3:2, or 16:9. I chose 1:1 (figure 3.5C, image 2).
3. Press the OK button, and the camera will display the Shooting Menu 1 screen with the selected Image Aspect showing.

Determining the Megapixel Size for a New Image Aspect Ratio

In figure 3.5C, image 2, you can see that pixel dimensions are displayed for each Image Aspect ratio you choose (below the up/down menu). The pixel dimensions of a RAW image will not change because the camera saves all the image data when you shoot in RAW (ORF).

However, you will see the Large, Middle, and Small JPEG pixel dimensions change with each Image Aspect ratio change. You can compare the new dimensions with the dimensions of the normal 4:3 Image Aspect ratio because they are displayed on the right side of the screen.

You can determine the megapixel size of the new image by multiplying the numbers in the pixel dimensions. For instance, in figure 3.5C, image 2, a Large JPEG is 3888 × 3888 when you use the 1:1 Image Aspect ratio. Multiply the numbers to find the megapixel size of the image:

$$3888 \times 3888 = 15{,}116{,}544$$

The image will have a size of just over 15 MP (15.1 MP). This number will vary with each Image Aspect ratio.

Settings Recommendation: Image Aspect ratios are useful primarily for people who shoot a lot of JPEG images and don't want to crop the image later. Basically, the camera crops the image for you, in-camera, when you select an Image Aspect ratio other than the default of 4:3. If you shoot in RAW most of the time, you can safely ignore this function. RAW shooters are accustomed to post-processing their images, and adjusting the aspect ratio (cropping) is a common post-processing step.

Digital Tele-Converter

Digital Tele-converter makes the camera function as if the mounted lens has a longer focal length than it really does.

Let's say you have a 12–40mm lens on the camera. Normally the maximum zoom would be 40mm. However, when you enable the Digital Tele-converter you can zoom to 80mm instead of 40mm. Although this may seem appealing, the 2x zoom factor is *not an optical zoom*. Instead, the camera crops the image so it looks like the scene is twice as close. It then saves the image at the normal size with a loss of image quality. You could do the same thing by enlarging the image in your computer then cropping it.

Let's see how to use this function in case you want to experiment with it.

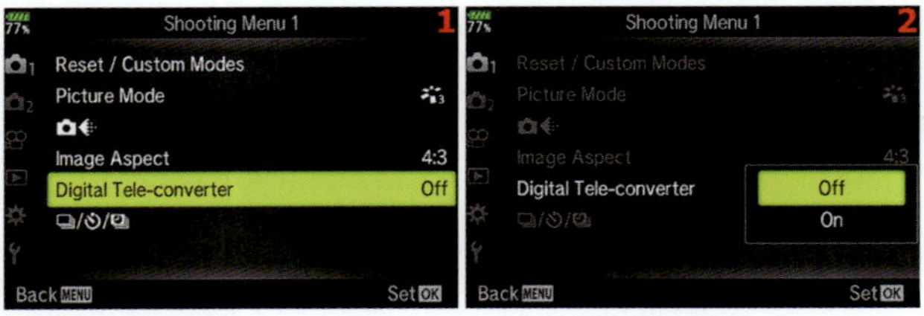

Figure 3.6: Enabling or disabling Digital Tele-converter

Use the following steps to use the Digital Tele-converter:

1. Select Digital Tele-converter from Shooting Menu 1 and scroll to the right (figure 3.6, image 1).
2. Choose On or Off from the small pop-up menu (figure 3.6, image 2).
3. Press the OK button to lock in your selection.

If you are shooting JPEG files, the camera will artificially double the focal length of your lens by cropping the image in-camera. Your 12–40mm lens becomes a 24–80mm lens, and the images will have significantly lower quality when they are enlarged.

If you are shooting in RAW mode, the camera captures all the image data and puts a frame around the area the Digital Tele-converter would have captured. The frame is displayed on the camera screens and in the Olympus Viewer 3 software. However, a RAW image is still a RAW image, and all the data is available.

Settings Recommendation: Unless you are in the woods without a long telephoto lens and you see Bigfoot or a yeti that you must photograph, I would leave this function alone. Just shoot the image normally and crop it later in your computer. This type of function is offered on the cheapest point-and-shoot cameras, but cropping an image from the center of a picture and then enlarging it destroys the image quality.

[Sequential]/[Self-Timer]/[Time Lapse]

The Sequential Shooting, Self-Timer, and Interval Shooting/Time Lapse system is composed of multiple parts, including Single-frame, Sequential Shooting, Self-Timer, Silent Shooting, Pro Capture, and High Res Shot. It also encompasses a complete Interval Shooting/Time Lapse system for time exposures that can be used to assemble short time lapse movies.

Let's first consider how each of the [Sequential] and [Self-Timer] modes work, and then we will consider how [Time Lapse] shooting works.

[Sequential] and [Self-Timer] Modes

The 11 sequential shooting and self-timer modes give you flexible control over when and how you release the shutter for still image capture.

[Single]

The Single mode causes the camera to take one picture each time you fully press the Shutter button. It uses the camera's mechanical shutter.

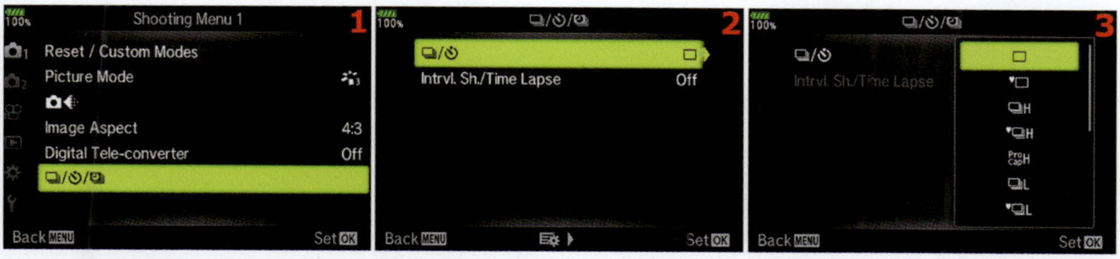

Figure 3.7A: Selecting Single mode

Use the following steps to select Single mode:

1. Highlight the [Sequential]/[Self-Timer]/[Time Lapse] menu item on Shooting Menu 1 and scroll to the right (figure 3.7A, image 1).
2. Select [Sequential]/[Self-Timer] and scroll to the right (figure 3.7A, image 2).
3. Choose the Single mode symbol from the menu and press the OK button to lock in your choice (figure 3.7A, image 3). Take your pictures.

Silent [♥]

The Silent mode causes the camera to take one picture each time you fully press the Shutter button, just like Single mode. However, the camera uses its electronic shutter instead of its mechanical shutter so there is no shutter-release noise.

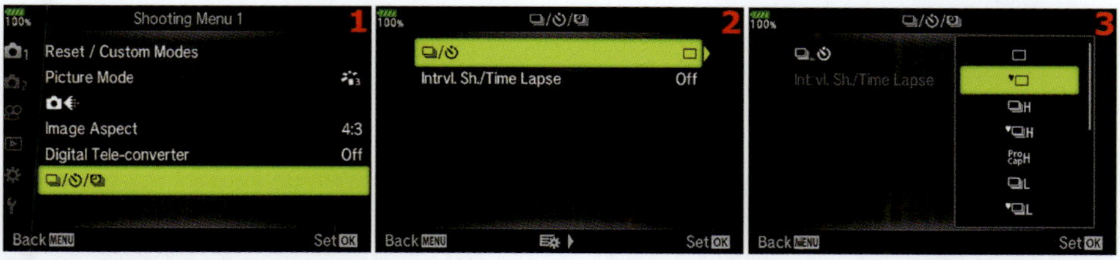

Figure 3.7B: Selecting Silent mode

Use the following steps to select Silent mode:

1. Highlight the [Sequential]/[Self-Timer]/[Time Lapse] menu item on Shooting Menu 1 and scroll to the right (figure 3.7B, image 1).

2. Select [Sequential]/[Self-Timer] and scroll to the right (figure 3.7B, image 2).
3. Choose the Silent mode symbol from the menu and press the OK button to lock in your choice (figure 3.7B, image 3). Take your pictures.

[Sequential] H (High)

When you are using the Sequential High mode, the camera will take a continuous series of pictures at up to about 15 frames per second (fps) using the mechanical shutter.

Focus, exposure, and white balance *are fixed* on the values determined for the first frame in the series.

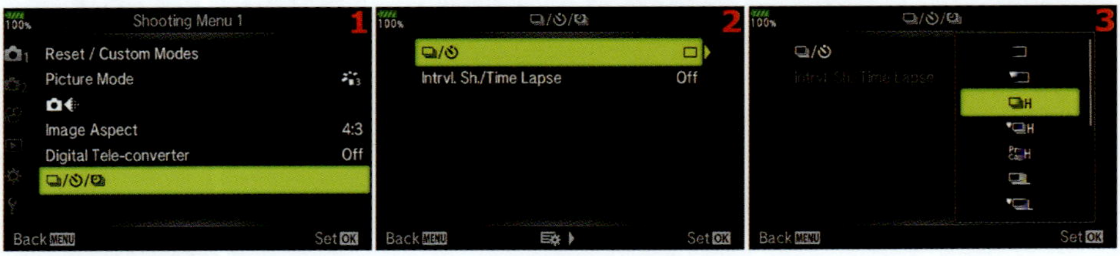

Figure 3.7C: Selecting Sequential High mode

Use the following steps to select Sequential High mode:

1. Highlight the [Sequential]/[Self-Timer]/[Time Lapse] menu item on Shooting Menu 1 and scroll to the right (figure 3.7C, image 1).
2. Select [Sequential]/[Self-Timer] and scroll to the right (figure 3.7C, image 2).
3. Choose the Sequential High mode symbol from the menu and press the OK button to lock in your choice (figure 3.7C, image 3). Take your pictures.

[Sequential] H Silent [♥]

When you are using the Sequential High Silent mode, the camera will take a continuous series of pictures at up to 60 fps (adjustable from 15 to 60 fps) using the electronic shutter (Silent).

Focus, exposure, and white balance *are fixed* on the values determined for the first frame in the series.

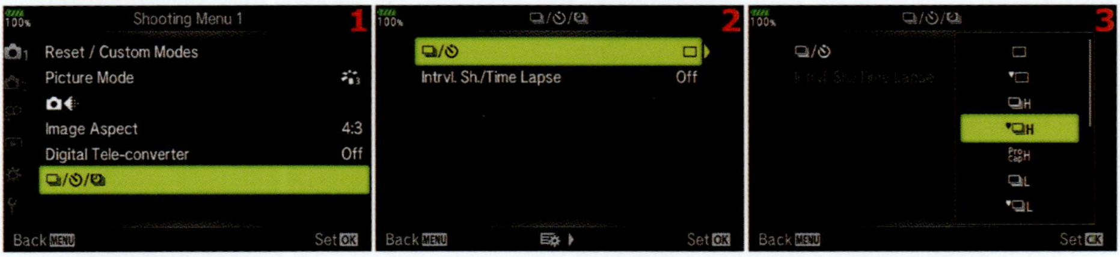

Figure 3.7D: Selecting Sequential High Silent mode

Use the following steps to select Sequential High Silent mode:

1. Highlight the [Sequential]/[Self-Timer]/[Time Lapse] menu item on Shooting Menu 1 and scroll to the right (figure 3.7D, image 1).
2. Select [Sequential]/[Self-Timer] and scroll to the right (figure 3.7D, image 2).
3. Choose the Sequential High Silent mode symbol from the menu and press the OK button to lock in your choice (figure 3.7D, image 3). Take your pictures.

You can control the number of images captured per second (fps) with the *Custom Menu > C1. Release/[Sequential]/Image Stabilizer > [Sequential] H Settings > [♥ Sequential] > Max fps* setting (see page 465).

Pro Capture High (ProCapH)

This mode is similar to [Sequential] H Silent [♥] mode except that there are two parts to capturing a burst series of images. First, when you press and hold the Shutter button *halfway down* the camera will capture a continuously replaced series of 1 to 35 images (pre-shutter frames). Second, when you then press the Shutter button *all the way down* the camera keeps the pre-shutter frames, and then it continues capturing images at a rate of 15 to 60 fps until you release the Shutter button.

Focus, exposure, and white balance *are fixed* on the values determined for the first frame in the series.

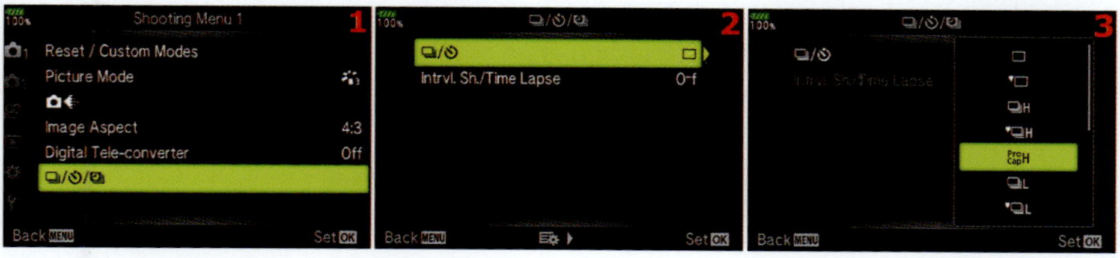

Figure 3.7E: Selecting Pro Capture High mode

Use the following steps to select Pro Capture High (ProCapH) mode:

1. Highlight the [Sequential]/[Self-Timer]/[Time Lapse] menu item on Shooting Menu 1 and scroll to the right (figure 3.7E, image 1).
2. Select [Sequential]/[Self-Timer] and scroll to the right (figure 3.7E, image 2).
3. Choose the Pro Capture High (ProCapH) mode symbol from the menu and press the OK button to lock in your choice (figure 3.7E, image 3). Take your pictures.

You can control the number of images that the camera uses in its Pro Capture High cycle (half Shutter button press) with the *Custom Menu > C1. Release/[Sequential]/Image Stabilizer > [Sequential] H Settings > Pro Cap > Pre-shutter Frames* setting (1 to 35 images, see page 467).

You can also control the number of images captured per second (up to 60 fps) when the camera starts taking sequential images (full Shutter button press) with the *Custom Menu > C1. Release/[Sequential]/Image Stabilizer > [Sequential] H Settings > Pro Cap > Max fps* setting (15 to 60 fps, see page 464).

[Sequential] L (Low)

The camera will take a continuous series of pictures at a rate of 1 to 10 frames per second.

Focus, exposure, and white balance *are fully active* for each picture in the series, based on which AF Mode you have selected (e.g., S-AF, C-AF) and how you are using the autoexposure lock and autofocus lock (AEL/AFL) modes.

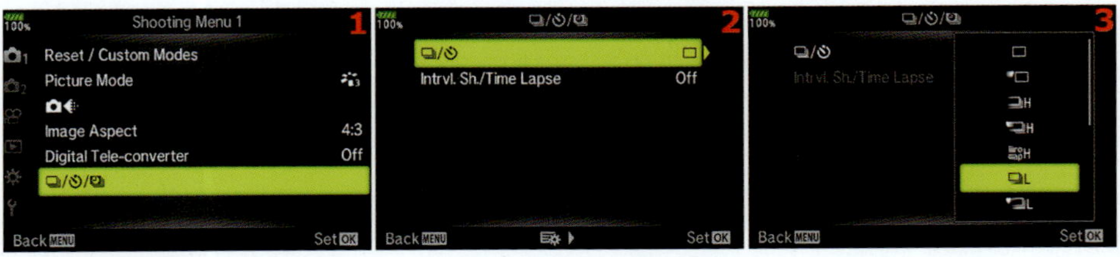

Figure 3.7F: Selecting Sequential Low mode

Use the following steps to select Sequential Low mode:

1. Highlight the [Sequential]/[Self-Timer]/[Time Lapse] menu item on Shooting Menu 1 and scroll to the right (figure 3.7F, image 1).
2. Select [Sequential]/[Self-Timer] and scroll to the right (figure 3.7F, image 2).
3. Choose the Sequential Low mode symbol from the menu and press the OK button to lock in your choice (figure 3.7F, image 3). Take your pictures.

You can control the number of images captured per second (fps) with the *Custom Menu > C1. Release/[Sequential]/Image Stabilizer > [Sequential] L Settings > [Sequential]/♦ [Sequential]> Max fps* setting (1 to 10 fps, see page 461).

[Sequential] L Silent [♥]

The camera will take a continuous series of pictures at a rate of 1 to 18 fps using the electronic shutter (Silent).

Focus, exposure, and white balance *are fully active* based on the AF Mode (e.g. S-AF, C-AF) and AEL/AFL mode selected.

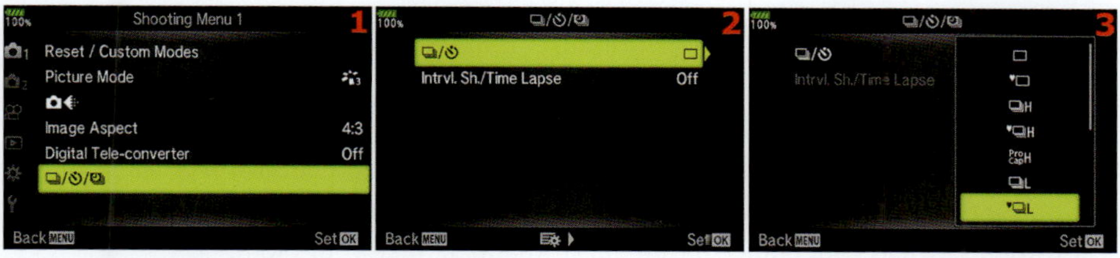

Figure 3.7G: Selecting Sequential Low Silent mode

Use the following steps to select Sequential Low Silent mode:

1. Highlight the [Sequential]/[Self-Timer]/[Time Lapse] menu item on Shooting Menu 1 and then scroll to the right (figure 3.7G, image 1).
2. Select [Sequential]/[Self-Timer] and scroll to the right (figure 3.7G, image 2).
3. Choose the Sequential Low Silent mode symbol from the menu and press the OK button to lock in your choice (figure 3.7G, image 3). Take your pictures.

You can control the number of images captured per second with the *Custom Menu > C1. Release/[Sequential]/Image Stabilizer > [Sequential] H Settings > ♥ [Sequential] > Max fps* selection (1 to 18 fps, see page 465).

Pro Capture Low (ProCapL)

This mode is similar to [Sequential] L Silent [♥] mode except that there are two parts to capturing a burst series of images. First, when you press and hold the Shutter button *half-way down* the camera will capture a continuously replaced series of 1 to 35 images (pre-shutter frames), with the default set to 8 frames per second. Second, when you then press the Shutter button *all the way down* the camera keeps the pre-shutter frames, and then it continues capturing images at a rate of 10 to 18 fps until you release the Shutter button.

Focus, exposure, and white balance *are fully active* for each picture in the series, based on which AF Mode you have selected (e.g., S-AF, C-AF) and how you are using the auto-exposure lock and autofocus lock (AEL/AFL) modes.

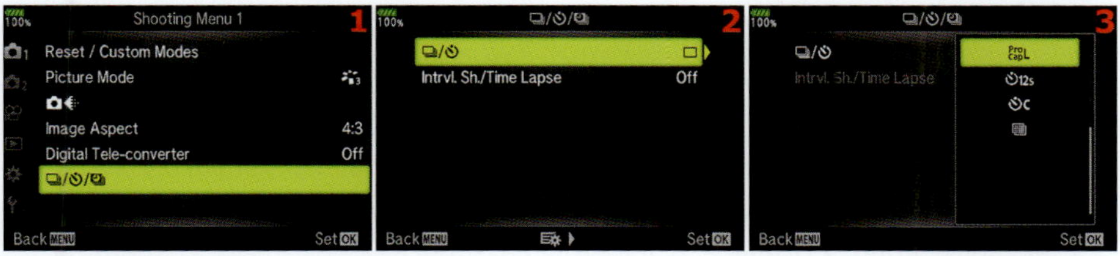

Figure 3.7H: Selecting Pro Capture Low mode

Use the following steps to select Pro Capture Low (ProCapL) mode:

1. Highlight the [Sequential]/[Self-Timer]/[Time Lapse] menu item on Shooting Menu 1 and scroll to the right (figure 3.7H, image 1).
2. Select [Sequential]/[Self-Timer] and scroll to the right (figure 3.7H, image 2).
3. Choose the Pro Capture Low (ProCapL) mode symbol from the menu and press the OK button to lock in your choice (figure 3.7H, image 3). Take your pictures.

You can control the number of images that the camera uses in its Pro Capture Low cycle (half Shutter button press) with the *Custom Menu > C1. Release/[Sequential]/Image Stabilizer > [Sequential] L Settings > Pro Cap > Pre-shutter Frames* setting (1 to 35 images, although it defaults to 8 images; see page 463).

You can also control the number of images captured per second (up to 18 fps) when the camera starts taking sequential images (full Shutter button press) with the *Custom Menu > C1. Release/[Sequential]/Image Stabilizer > [Sequential] L Settings > Pro Cap > Max fps* setting (10 to 18 fps, see page 463).

[Self-Timer] 12s (12 Seconds)

The camera will take a single photograph 12 seconds after you press the Shutter button all the way down. The orange focus assist light on the front of the camera will shine solid for 10 seconds, and then it will blink for 2 seconds before the shutter fires and the picture is taken.

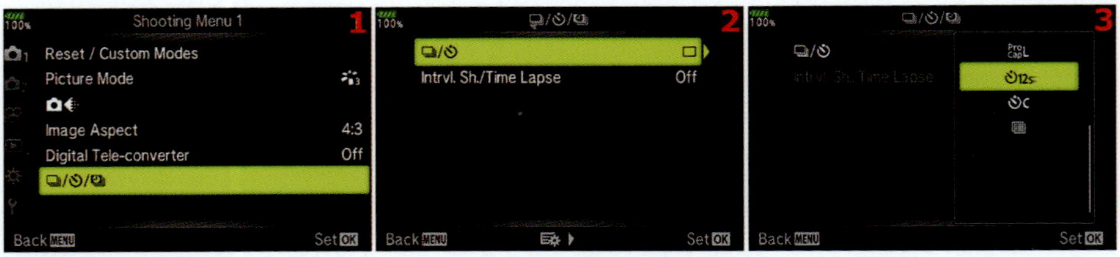

Figure 3.7I: Selecting Self-Timer 12 second mode

Use the following steps to select Self-timer 12 second (12s) mode:

1. Highlight the [Sequential]/[Self-Timer]/[Time Lapse] menu item on Shooting Menu 1 and scroll to the right (figure 3.7I, image 1).
2. Select [Sequential]/[Self-Timer] and scroll to the right (figure 3.7I, image 2).
3. Choose the Self-timer 12s symbol from the menu and press the OK button to lock in your choice (figure 3.7I, image 3). Take your pictures.

Custom Self-Timer (C)

This variable self-timer function allows you to select the number of seconds the camera will wait before firing (Timer), the number of images the camera will take when the self-timer expires (Number of Frames), and the period of time between each picture (Interval Length) if you have selected more than one picture with the Number of Frames setting. You can also choose whether or not the camera will autofocus between each picture (Every Frame AF). Press the INFO button to access the individual settings within the secondary screen of the Custom Self-timer.

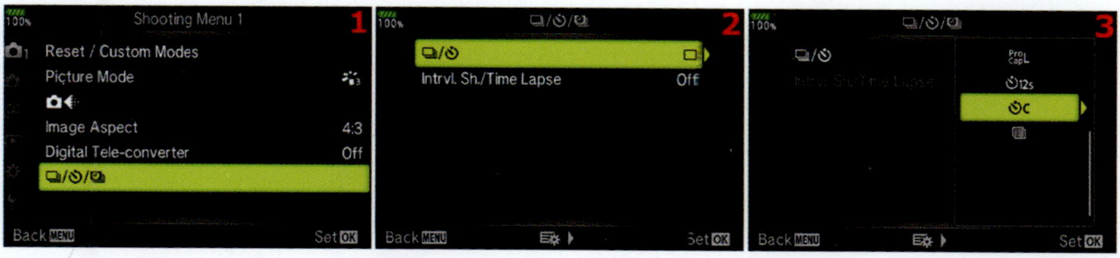

Figure 3.7J: Using the Custom Self-timer

Use the following steps to configure the Custom Self-timer mode:

1. Highlight the [Sequential]/[Self-Timer]/[Time Lapse] menu item on Shooting Menu 1 and scroll to the right (figure 3.7J, image 1).
2. Select [Sequential]/[Self-Timer] and scroll to the right (figure 3.7J, image 2).
3. Choose [Self-Timer] C from the menu and scroll to the right (figure 3.7J, image 3).

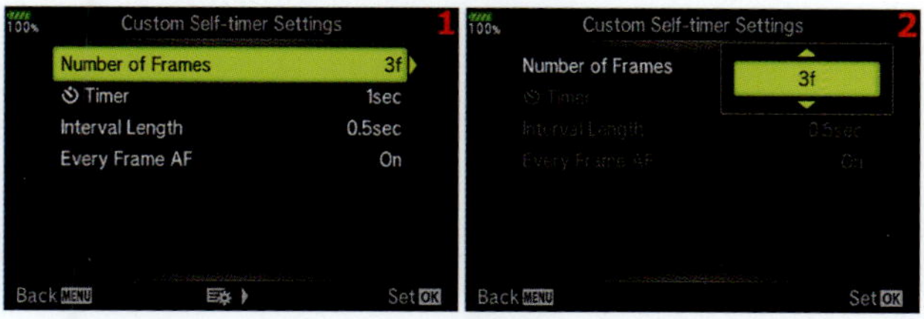

Figure 3.7K: Setting the Number of Frames

4. Choose Number of Frames from the Custom Self-timer Settings menu and scroll to the right (figure 3.7K, image 1).
5. Use the up/down menu to select the number of images you want to take (figure 3.7K, image 2). You can choose to capture from 1 to 10 frames (1f to 10f). Press the OK button to lock in the value.

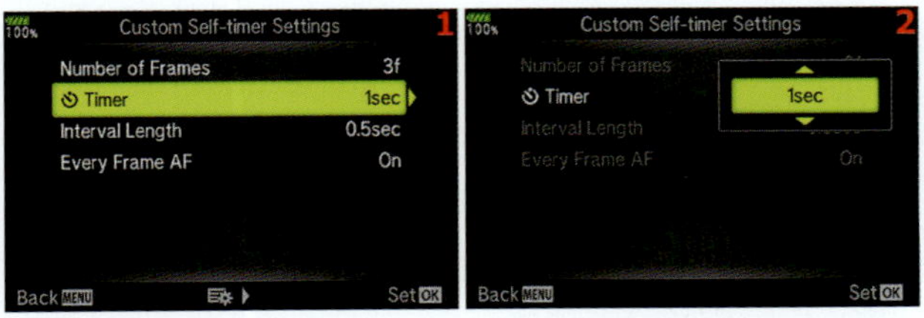

Figure 3.7L: Setting the self-timer delay (delay before camera fires the first frame)

6. Select [Self-timer] Timer from the Custom Self-timer Settings menu and scroll to the right (figure 3.7L, image 1).
7. Set the self-timer delay—the time-out period before the camera takes the first picture—by choosing the number of seconds before the camera releases the shutter (figure 3.7L, image 2). Use the up/down menu to select a value from 1 second to 30 seconds (1sec to 30sec). Press the OK button to lock in the value.

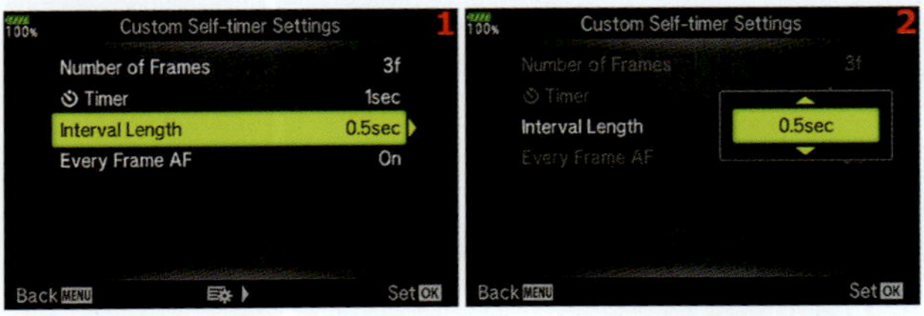

Figure 3.7M: Setting the Interval Length (delay between multiple pictures)

8. Choose Interval Length from the Custom Self-timer Settings menu and scroll to the right (figure 3.7M, image 1). The Interval Length sets the time delay between each of the pictures taken, if you selected more than 1 frame under Number of Frames (steps 4 and 5).
9. Use the up/down menu to choose a value from ½ second to 3 seconds (0.5sec to 3sec). Press the OK button to lock in the value.

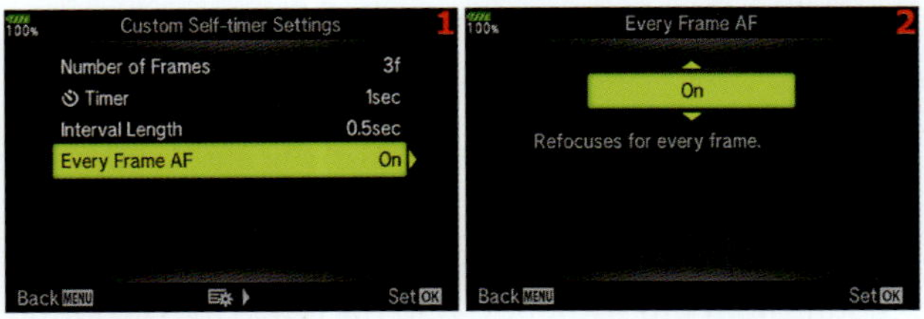

Figure 3.7N: Setting Every Frame AF (autofocus)

10. Choose Every Frame AF from the Custom Self-timer Settings menu and scroll to the right (figure 3.7N, image 1). This setting lets you choose whether or not the camera will autofocus on each frame or only on the first frame in the series.
11. Choose On or Off from the up/down menu. On means that the camera will refocus on each picture, whereas Off means it will focus only on the first image. Press the OK button to lock in the value.

High Res Shot

When you take a picture in this mode, the camera will capture eight images using its Silent electronic shutter, and then combine the images in-camera into one approximately 80-, 50-, or 25-megapixel image, according to the Image Quality mode you select. Instead of the normal 20 MP image at 5184 × 3888, the resulting combined image will be significantly larger (see table 3.2).

The E-M1II achieves this result by using sensor-shift technology to move the physical imaging sensor to create a larger-than-normal frame. The camera takes eight pictures as it moves the sensor, and then combines the images into one large image.

It takes several seconds for the E-M1II to capture the eight images and combine them into one big image, so it is imperative that you mount your camera on a tripod when you are using this mode, or you will end up with a blurry picture. The camera cannot use its normal Image Stabilization during this process.

The camera will display a black screen with a progress bar once it has captured and begun combining the images. Before you take the High Res Shot, you may see the symbol for High Res Shot blinking on the screen. If so, this means the camera is unstable. Stabilize the camera before proceeding. Once you have pressed the Shutter button to start the process, wait for the progress bar to complete and the High Res Shot symbol to disappear from the screen before moving the camera.

You can choose from four different Image Quality sizes for High Res Shots. Table 3.2 contains a list of the Image Quality choices along with the corresponding pixel ratio, megapixel size, and image file(s) produced for each option.

Image Quality	Pixel Ratio	Megapixel Size	Image Files Produced
50MF	8160 × 6120	49.9 MP	1 JPEG
25MF	5760 × 4320	24.9 MP	1 JPEG
50MF + RAW	10368 × 7776	80.6 MP	1 JPEG, 1 ORF, 1 ORI
25MF + RAW	5760 × 4320	24.9 MP	1 JPEG, 1 ORF, 1 ORI

Table 3.2: High Res Shot information

In table 3.2, you will note that the camera produces a single, large, combined JPEG file when you use one of the 50MF or 25MF Image Quality choices.

However, the E-M1II produces multiple files when you select one of the "+ RAW" settings (i.e., 50MF + RAW or 25MF + RAW). The JPEG in the trio of files is a combined JPEG, the ORF file is a combined RAW file, and the ORI file is a single RAW file, with no combination.

Note: If you want to, you can rename the ORI file to a new file name with an ORF extension and it will perform as a normal RAW file. All three files have the same file name except for the three-character ending (e.g., 120921.JPG, 120921.ORF, 120921.ORI). Therefore, if you want to rename the ORI file to an ORF file, you will need to change the file name so that it no longer matches the current file name; otherwise, you may overwrite the combined ORF file with the renamed ORI file.

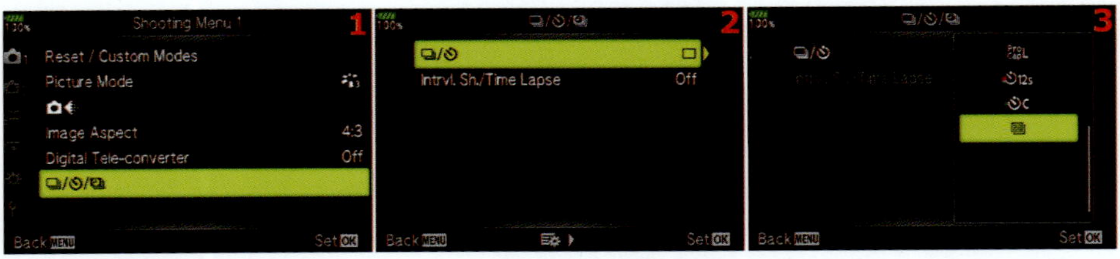

Figure 3.7O: Selecting High Res Shot

Use the following steps to select High Res Shot mode:

1. Highlight the [Sequential]/[Self-Timer]/[Time Lapse] menu item on Shooting Menu 1 and scroll to the right (figure 3.7O, image 1).
2. Select [Sequential]/[Self-Timer] and scroll to the right (figure 3.7O, image 2).
3. Choose the High Res Shot symbol from the menu and press the OK button to lock in your choice (figure 3.7O, image 3).

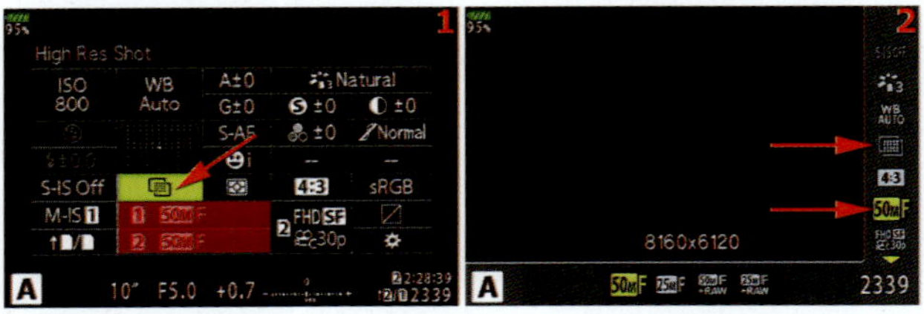

Figure 3.7P: Choosing the Image Quality of the High Res Shot

4. Now that you have selected the High Res Shot mode, you need to choose an Image Quality. Your choices are shown in table 3.2. Figure 3.7P, image 1, shows the Image Quality setting on the Super Control Panel (or LV Super Control Panel), highlighted in red. There are two places for selecting the Image Quality (one for each memory card). To make an Image Quality choice, highlight one of the memory cards (1 or 2) and turn the Front Dial (or press the OK button to enter the secondary screen).

   In the Live Control screen shown in figure 3.7P, image 2, the top red arrow points to the High Res Shot symbol, indicating that the mode is selected. The lower red arrow shows where to select the Image Quality when using the Live Control. Along the bottom of the screen in image 2, you will see the four Image Quality choices you may select by pressing left or right with the Arrow Pad.
5. Once you have selected the Image Quality mode you will use, set your camera on a tripod and take your large pictures. This method is best used for subjects with very little or no movement in the frame.

Settings Recommendation: I normally use Single mode because I do a lot of nature, landscape, and portrait work. When I am shooting a wedding, I will often use the Silent modes to keep from drawing attention to myself during the ceremony. I love the High Res Shot mode for landscapes (unless the wind is blowing hard, which can cause blurring). I don't do a lot of action shooting; however, if you do, there are few cameras currently available that can match the E-M1II for high-speed image capture. You should take some time to experiment with each of these modes. This is a complex system, but once you have used each mode a few times, you will become more familiar with what to expect.

[Time Lapse] (Interval Shooting)

The Time Lapse function allows you to automatically take a series of images—from 1 to 999—over a period of time and later use the images individually or combine them into a Time Lapse Movie. Maybe you would like to shoot a series of images during an event or shoot star trails overnight with a sunrise at the end. There are many creative ways you can use Time Lapse. The Time Lapse system has four internal settings:

- **Frame:** This setting allows you to choose from 1 to 999 still images during the automatic shooting interval. They can be used individually or combined into a Time Lapse Movie.
- **Start Waiting Time:** This setting allows you to choose a time delay before the first Time Lapse picture is taken, from 1 second to 99 hours, 99 minutes, and 99 seconds after you press the Shutter button.
- **Interval Length:** This setting configures how much delay occurs between pictures after the Start Waiting Time expires. You may select from 0 seconds to 99 hours, 99 minutes, and 99 seconds between frames.
- **Time Lapse Movie:** If this setting is Off, the camera records each frame in the Time Lapse picture series as an individual picture and does nothing else. If this setting is On, the camera will take each picture, and at the end of the Time Lapse series it will combine all the pictures into a time lapse Movie. With either setting, you will have all the still pictures at the end. If Time Lapse Movie is On, you have the added benefit of a movie along with the still images. ***Note:*** Be sure to turn this On if you want a movie, otherwise you will have to combine the frames into a movie in post-processing software, such as Olympus Viewer 3. You can't make a movie in-camera from existing images, except at the end of the Time Lapse series.
- **Movie Settings:** Allows you to set the Movie Resolution and Frame Rate of the time lapse Movie. Refer to table 3.3 for Movie Resolution and Frame Rate setting values.

The Movie Resolution affects the pixel size of the movie: HD is 1280 × 720, FullHD is 1920 × 1080, and 4K UHD is 3840 × 2160. All resolutions use the 16:9 aspect ratio. Generally, the human eye is sensitive to flicker when using Frame Rates slower than about 1/10 second. Therefore, it is best to use 10 or 15 fps whenever possible to prevent flicker in your time lapse Movie. The 4K setting, unfortunately, allows only 5 fps. Keep in mind that the higher the Frame Rate, the more pictures required to maintain a certain Movie length. In other words, it will require three times more images to create a 30-second Movie at 15 fps than at 5 fps. Experiment with this before using the Time Lapse feature commercially!

Now let's examine how to configure these settings so you can make some Time Lapse Movies!

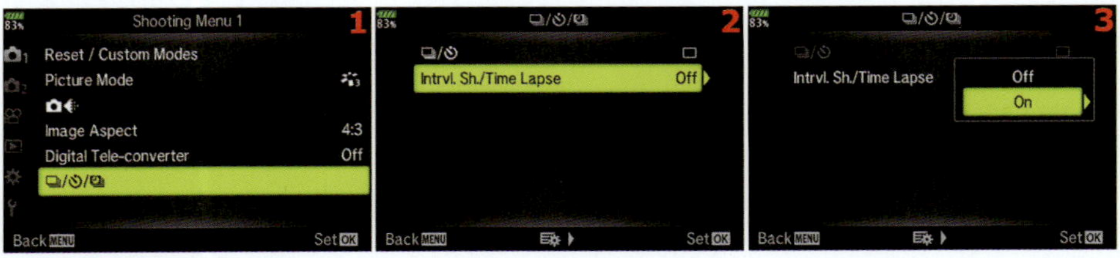

Figure 3.8A: Starting the Time Lapse sequence

Use the following steps to configure a Time Lapse shooting session:

1. Select [Sequential]/[Self-timer]/[Time Lapse] from Shooting Menu 1 and then scroll to the right (figure 3.8A, image 1).
2. Choose Intrvl. Sh./Time Lapse from the [Sequential]/[Self-timer]/[Time Lapse] menu and scroll to the right (figure 3.8A, image 2).
3. A small window will open and allow you to choose Off or On (figure 3.8A, image 3). To configure the Time Lapse system, highlight On and scroll to the right.

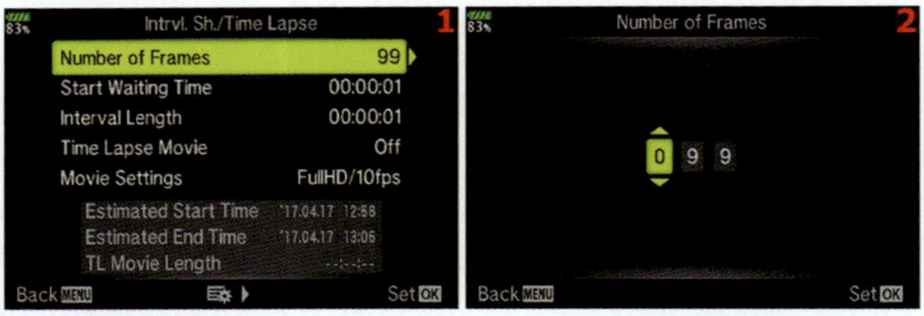

Figure 3.8B: Choosing the number of images in the Time Lapse series (1–999)

4. Choose Number of Frames from the Intrvl. Sh./Time Lapse menu and scroll to the right (figure 3.8B, image 1).
5. Use the three up/down menus to select the Number of Frames (pictures) for the Time Lapse series, from 001 to 999 (figure 3.8B, image 2). The factory default is 099 images.

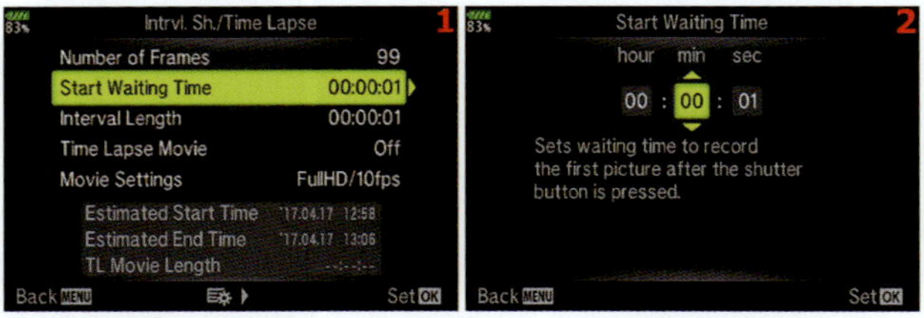

Figure 3.8C: Choosing when the Time Lapse series will start

6. Choose Start Waiting Time from the Intrvl. Sh./Time Lapse menu and scroll to the right (figure 3.8C, image 1).

7. Use the three up/down menus to set an hour (hour), minute (min), and second (sec) delay, from 00:00:00 to 99:99:99, before the first Time Lapse frame is taken (figure 3.8C, image 2). The factory default is 00:00:01.

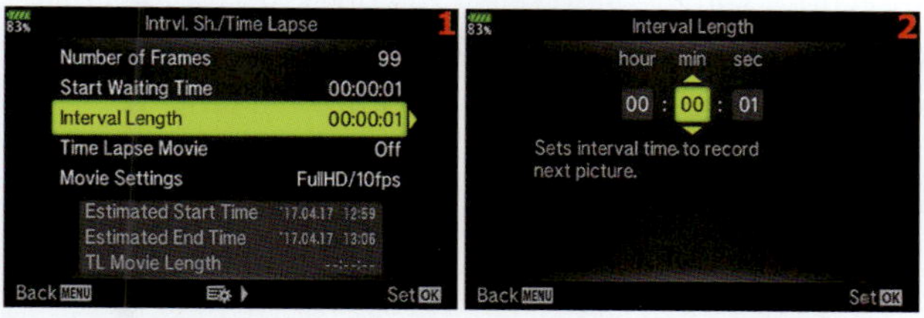

Figure 3.8D: Choosing the delay between frames of the Time Lapse series

8. Choose Interval Time from the Intrvl. Sh./Time Lapse menu and scroll to the right (figure 3.8D, image 1).
9. Use the three up/down menus to set an hour (hour), minute (min), and second (sec) delay, from 00:00:00 to 99:99:99, between each frame of the Time Lapse sequence (figure 3.8D, image 2). The factory default is 00:00:01. Remember that you set the Number of Frames in the Time Lapse sequence in steps 3 and 4 (figure 3.8B). The Interval Length is the delay between each frame. It begins as soon as the first frame has been taken.

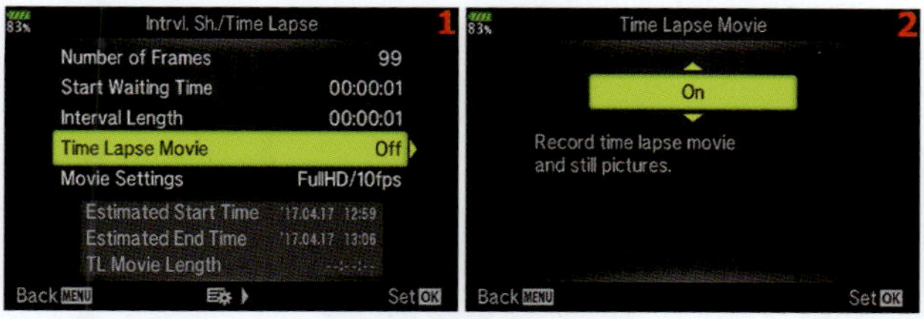

Figure 3.8E: Choosing whether to combine images into a Time Lapse Movie

10. Choose Time Lapse Movie from the Intrvl. Sh./Time Lapse menu and scroll to the right (figure 3.8E, image 1).
11. Use the up/down menu to select On or Off (figure 3.8E, image 2). On means the camera will take still Time Lapse images plus make a Time Lapse Movie at the end of the image capture sequence, and Off means it will take still images and *not* make a movie.

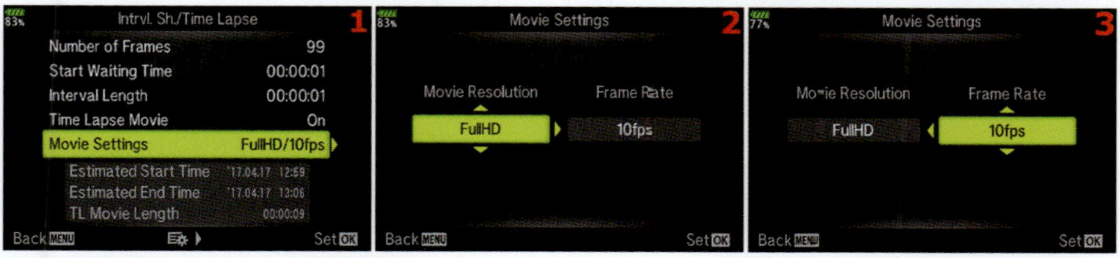

Figure 3.8F: Selecting the Movie quality

12. Choose Movie Settings from the Intrvl. Sh./Time Lapse menu and scroll to the right (figure 3.8E, image 1).
13. There are two up/down menus, Movie Resolution and Frame Rate. Refer to table 3.3 and use the Movie Resolution up/down menu to select the pixel size for the images you want to assemble into a Movie (figure 3.8F, image 2).
14. Scroll to the right and select a Frame Rate from the up/down menu shown in figure 3.8F, image 3.
15. Press the OK button to Set your choices, and then go shoot the Time Lapse sequence.

Movie Resolution	Frame Rates (fps)
HD (720p)	5, 10, 15, and 30 fps
FullHD (1080p)	5, 10, and 15 fps
4K (2160p or UHD)	5 fps

Table 3.3: Movie Resolution and Frame Rate for Movie Settings

Power Sources for Long Time Lapse Sequences

Be sure you have a fully charged battery before you start a time lapse sequence. A single battery may not last through a longer series of images. Serious time lapse shooters have both a battery pack and an AC adapter for long-term time lapse sequences (figure 3.8G).

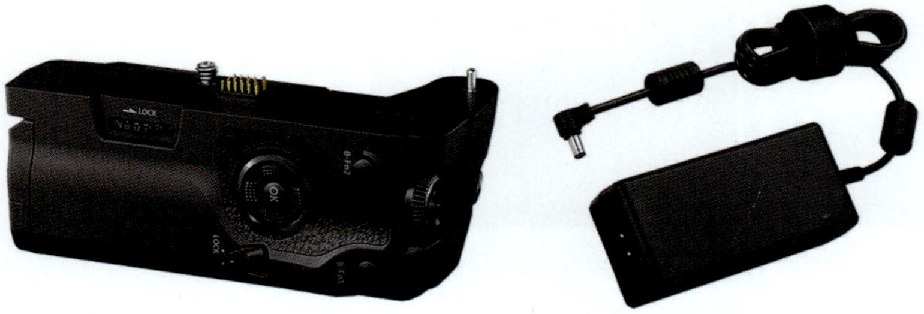

Figure 3.8G: Olympus HLD-9 battery pack (*left*) and Olympus AC-5 AC adapter (*right*)

Many people use the Olympus HLD-9 battery pack so they can use two internal BLH-1 lithium ion (li-ion) batteries. They use an Olympus AC-5 AC adapter for an even longer time lapse series and more frames. The AC-5 adapter plugs in to the HLD-9 battery pack, not the camera itself. You therefore need to purchase both items shown in figure 3.8G.

Settings Recommendation: This camera makes it very easy to create short or long time lapse still-image sequences and movies. If you want to assemble your own time lapse movie outside the camera, you can use the provided Olympus Viewer 3 (or later) software. Or you can let the camera do it all for you. If you have always wanted to make some cool time lapse movies, you now have an easy way to do it. Why not try it tonight?

Author's Conclusion

This is one complex little camera! However, with complexity comes great configurability and power. The next chapter will consider functions on Shooting Menu 2, which lets you control things like Bracketing, HDR, Multiple Exposure, and High Res Shot.

04 Shooting Menu 2

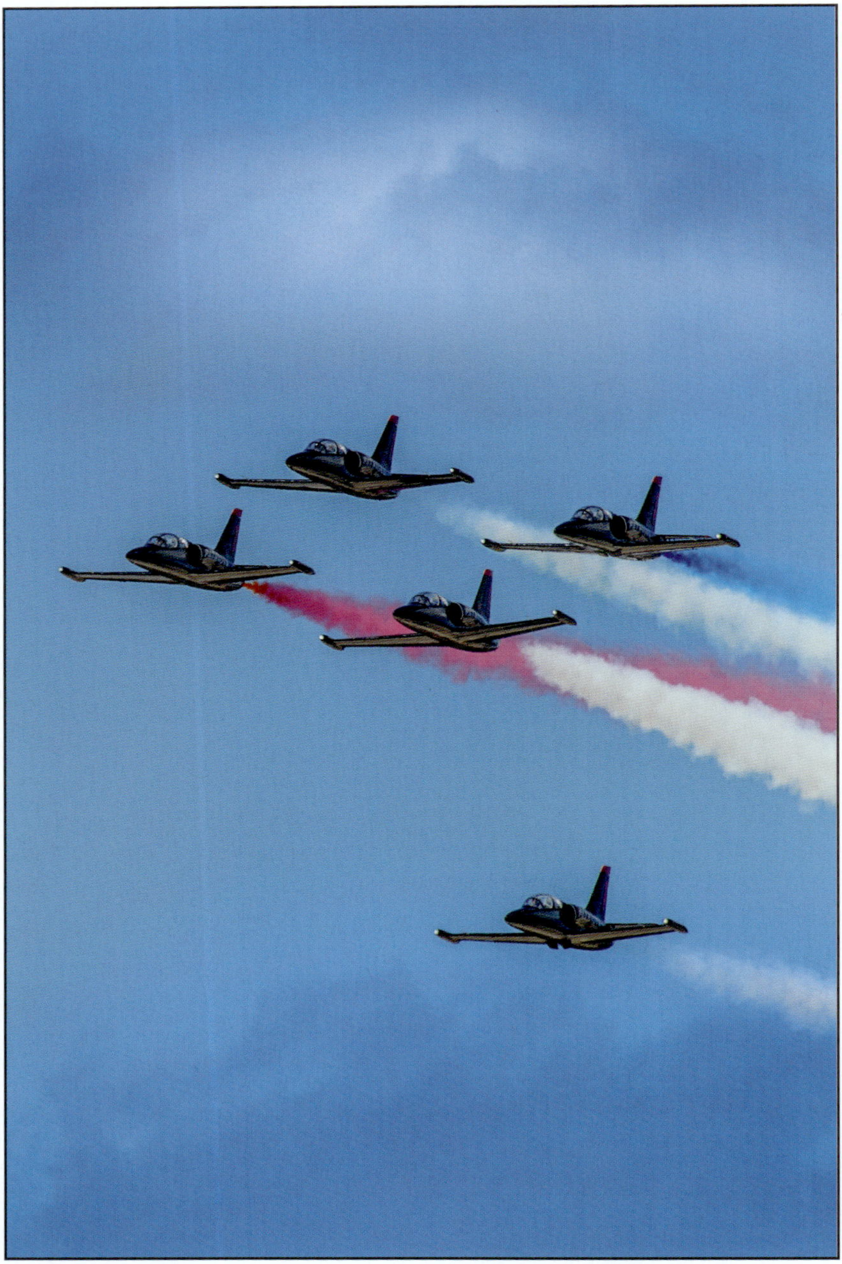

Image © Alan Hess

Shooting Menu 2 is a continuation of Shooting Menu 1. It contains advanced functions that control how the camera takes pictures.

Figure 4.1 shows the seven main functions found in Shooting Menu 2. As we proceed through this chapter, be sure to have your camera in hand and make adjustments as you work through each section.

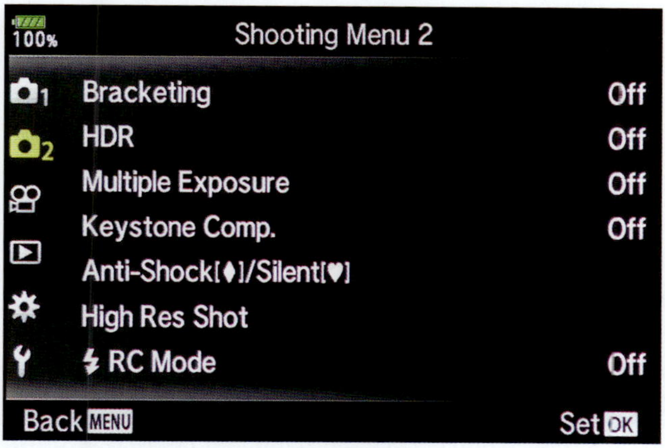

Figure 4.1: A preview of Shooting Menu 2

Let's consider each of the functions available under Shooting Menu 2.

Bracketing

Bracketing is when you take multiple images of the same subject using different settings, either to guarantee at least one balanced picture or to combine multiple pictures for various effects.

The E-M1II provides six bracketing methods that cover virtually all types of image bracketing: Auto Exposure (AE BKT), White Balance (WB BKT), Flash (FL BKT), ISO sensitivity (ISO BKT), Art (ART BKT), and Focus (Focus BKT).

This section describes how to configure bracketing. You will often have to return to this menu to configure how bracketing works, even though you can select it with external controls. First let's consider how the camera shoots individual frames in a bracketed series.

Shooting a Bracketed Series of Images

There are several choices available for shooting a bracketed series of frames:

- **[Single-Frame] shooting:** If you are using [Single-Frame] shooting, one picture in the bracket series will be taken with each full press of the Shutter button.

- **[Sequential] H or L:** If you switch to [Sequential] H or [Sequential] L mode, you can hold down the Shutter button and the camera will shoot only the number of images in the bracket, then it will stop.
- **[Self-timer] Custom:** For hands-off bracketing while the camera is on a tripod, you may use the Custom Self-timer (C) mode while AE BKT is enabled. You simply set the Timer setting (e.g., 5sec delay) and the Interval Length setting (e.g., 0.5sec between frames) to whatever you want, and you set the Number of Frames setting (e.g., 7f) to match the number of frames in the bracket. The camera will wait for the Timer delay to expire, shoot one of the bracketed frames, wait for the Interval Time to shoot the next frame, and continue this sequence until the series is completed. [See **Custom Self-Timer (C),** on page 191, to learn how to use the self-timer.]

The shooting methods for bracketing in the previous list apply only to AE BKT, and FL BKT.

For ISO BKT the camera will repeat the series of three bracketed images over and over, for as long as you hold down the Shutter button.

For WB BKT and ART BKT, you take only one picture and the camera creates multiple copies of that picture and applies effects.

Focus BKT automatically uses **[Sequential] H Silent [♥]** mode (page 480) to fire off all the frames when you are using Focus Bracketing or Focus Stacking. You simply hold down the Shutter button until the camera stops taking pictures. This should result in sharper pictures since you are not required to press the Shutter button several times. We will discuss this further in an upcoming section.

When you take pictures in brackets that allow you to control individual frames, the camera always shoots frames with exposure variations in this order: *normal exposure > underexposure > overexposure*. For example, if you choose to shoot a seven-frame bracket (7f) in AE BKT, the camera will shoot the bracket in this sequence: *normal exposure > underexposure 1 > underexposure 2 > underexposure 3 > overexposure 1 > overexposure 2 > overexposure 3*.

Now, let's consider the six bracketing types and see what each does.

AE BKT (Auto Exposure Bracketing)

Auto Exposure bracketing allows you to shoot from two to seven images in a bracket. The exposure of each shot varies by 0.3, 0.7, or 1.0 EV steps. Later you can select the best image from the series or combine the images into one high dynamic range (HDR) image.

Let's examine how to select and use AE BKT.

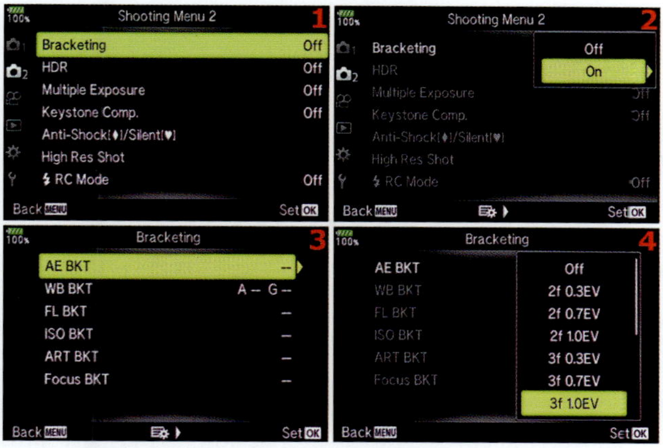

Figure 4.2A: Using Auto Exposure bracketing (AE BKT)

Use these steps to configure AE BKT:

1. Choose Bracketing from Shooting Menu 2 and scroll to the right (figure 4.2A, image 1).
2. A small menu will open and allow you to select Off or On. Highlight On and scroll to the right (figure 4.2A, image 2). Or you can disable AE BKT by selecting Off and pressing the OK button (then skip the rest of these steps)
3. Highlight AE BKT and scroll to the right (figure 4.2A, image 3).
4. A menu will open with many bracketing choices that look like this: 3f 1.0EV (figure 4.2A, image 4). The first two characters represent the number of frames in the bracket, from two to seven frames (2f to 7f). The second group of characters represent the EV variation between images in the bracket. Your choices are 1/3 EV step (0.3EV), 2/3 EV step (0.7EV), and 1 EV step (1.0EV). If you choose 3f, 5f, or 7f, skip step 5 and go directly to step 6. If you choose 2f, move on to step 5 because the three 2f choices bring up an extra screen. 7f is limited to 0.3EV and 0.7EV.

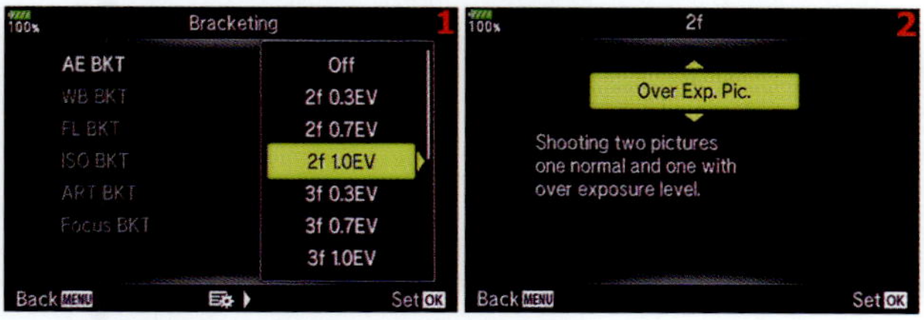

Figure 4.2B: A 2f exposure variance is selected

5. If you choose any of the three 2f choices, you will need to decide if the second image in the bracket will be overexposed (Over Exp. Pic.) or underexposed (Under Exp. Pic.). Figure 4.2B shows the screens you use to make your selection Image 1 is the same as figure 4.2A, image 4, except 2f has been selected. Use the up/down menu shown in figure 4.2B, image 2, to choose either an overexposed image (Over Exp. Pic.) or an

underexposed image (Under Exp. Pic.) for the second picture in the 2f bracket series. Press the OK button to lock in your choice, and take your pictures. If you use a 2f setting, skip step 6.

6. To use one of the 3f, 5f, or 7f settings, highlight the one you wish to use and press the OK button. The camera will then display your choice on the Bracketing screen next to AE BKT (figure 4.2A, image 3). Press the OK button again and the popup menu will display with On and Off, as seen in figure 4.2A, image 2. Select On and press the OK button again to lock in your selection. Take your pictures.

Note: Be sure to disable AE BKT (select Off) when you are done taking exposure-bracketed pictures.

Settings Recommendation: If you are shooting a two- or three-frame bracket it may be best to choose a 1.0EV setting. That will result in enough difference among the exposures to combine them or choose the best one. When you shoot a five- or seven-frame bracket, so much extra light is captured that you may get by with smaller variations between the images (e.g., 0.3EV or 0.7EV). Experiment with this to see what works for you. Auto Exposure bracketing is a useful tool for HDR shooters and people who want to have the best exposure and don't mind the extra shots.

WB BKT (White Balance Bracketing)

White Balance (WB) bracketing lets you shoot one image and have the camera bracket the WB on the Amber–Blue (A–B) axis, the Green–Magenta (G–M) axis, or a combination of both axes (A–B + G–M).

You can select two, four, or six steps of color change for the A–B or G–M axis, or you can apply two, four, or six steps of color change to the combined A–B + G–M axes. The camera will create two WB-modified copies of the original image for each single-axis bracket (three images per axis), or eight copies plus the original image for the combined-axes bracket (nine images total). Tables 4.1–4.3 demonstrate this in an easy-to-understand pattern.

This function may seem complex, but you don't have to fully understand it to successfully bracket the white balance of your image. You can simply fire off a bracket and look at the resulting images to choose the one you like. However, it's more efficient to understand what happens when you use WB bracketing.

First let's discuss how to configure WB BKT, then we will look at the WB bracket system in more detail.

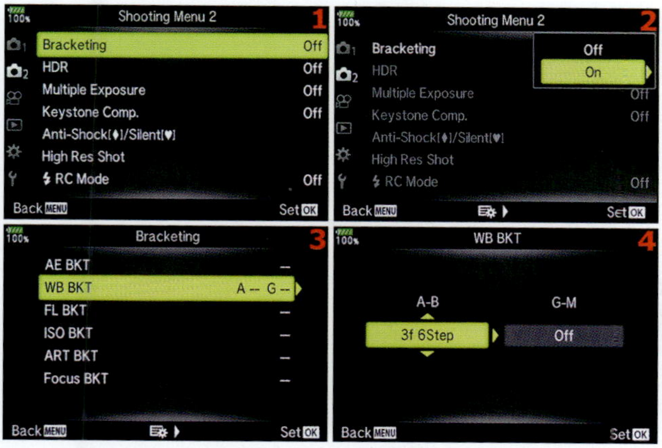

Figure 4.2C: Using White Balance bracketing (WB BKT)

Use these steps to configure WB BKT:

1. Choose Bracketing from Shooting Menu 2 and scroll to the right (figure 4.2C, image 1).
2. A small window will open where you can choose Off or On. Highlight On and scroll to the right (figure 4.2C, image 2). Or you can disable WB BKT by selecting Off and pressing the OK button (and skipping the rest of these steps).
3. Highlight WB BKT and scroll to the right (figure 4.2C, image 3).
4. You will see two up/down menus (figure 4.2C, image 4). One is for the A–B axis and the other is for the G–M axis. You can choose two steps (3f 2Step), four steps (3f 4Step), or six steps (3f 6Step) of color change. The 3f simply means the camera will create three images per axis. Select a value for one or both of the axes (A–B, G–M) and press the OK button. The screen shown in figure 2.4C, image 2, will reappear. Highlight On and press the OK button again to lock in your WB BKT configuration. I chose to bracket the A–B axis only, using three frames (3f), and I used six steps (6Step) of color changes for maximum color shift in the bracket.
5. Take a single picture and the camera will create color-shifted copies to complete the bracketed series (refer to tables 4.1–4.3).

Note: Be sure to turn WB BKT off when you are done bracketing.

Tables 4.1–4.3 show the pattern the camera uses for White Balance bracketing. The tables demonstrate only the two-step version (3f 2Step) of WB BKT. All three bracketing variations use the same pattern with wider color steps or more intense color changes. As you increase the bracket from two steps (2Step) to four steps (4Step) to six steps (6Step), the color changes become more saturated. Therefore, you can substitute 4 or 6 for 2 in the tables and see that the 2Step, 4Step, and 6Step patterns work the same.

A–B axis bracket (3f 2Step)		
Image number	A–B	G–M
1	A +0	G +0
2	A –2	G +0
3	A +2	G +0

Table 4.1: The WB BKT A–B pattern (notice that G–M stays at 0)

G–M axis bracket (3f 2Step)		
Image number	A–B	G–M
1	A +0	G +0
2	A +0	G –2
3	A +0	G +2

Table 4.2: The WB BKT G–M pattern (notice that A–B stays at 0)

A–B + G–M axes bracket (3f 2Step)		
Image number	A–B	G–M
1	A +0	G +0
2	A +0	G –2
3	A +0	G +2
4	A –2	G +0
5	A –2	G –2
6	A –2	G +2
7	A +2	G +0
8	A +2	G –2
9	A +2	G +2

Table 4.3: The WB BKT combined A–B + G–M pattern

Settings Recommendation: This complex-sounding WB bracketing system is not as hard as it looks. Just remember that you can simply create the bracket and then select the image you like best. If none of them are color shifted enough for your liking, use more steps in the bracket—that is, switch from 3f 2Step to 3f 4Step, or even 3f 6Step. And remember, press the Shutter button only *once* for each WB bracketed shot!

FL BKT (Flash Bracketing)

Flash bracketing varies the light output of the flash over three frames (3f) so you can get the best exposure. You can select bracket levels of 0.3EV, 0.7EV, or 1.0EV, which gives you a difference of as little as 1/3 stop, and as much as 1 stop, between the images in the bracket.

The bracketing order for the three frames is *normal* > *underexposed* > *overexposed*. The camera will take a normal exposure with the flash and then two more exposures with under- and overexposure; the amount depends on the bracket levels you selected.

Let's examine how this works.

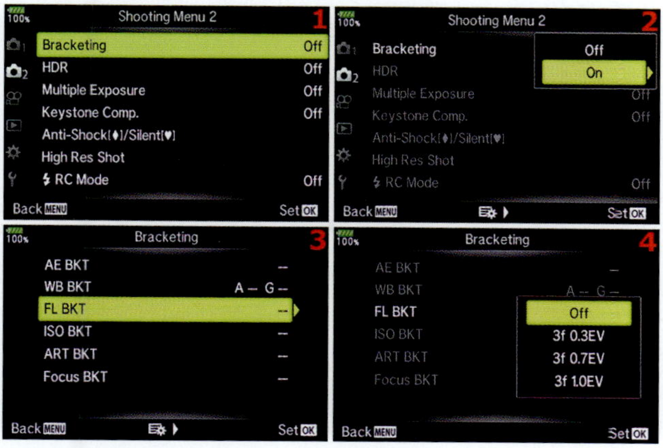

Figure 4.2D: Using Flash bracketing (FL BKT)

Use these steps to configure FL BKT:

1. Choose Bracketing from Shooting Menu 2 and scroll to the right (figure 4.2D, image 1).
2. A small window will open and allow you to select Off or On. Highlight On from the menu and scroll to the right (figure 4.2D, image 2). Or you can disable FL BKT by selecting Off and pressing the OK button (and skipping the rest of these steps).
3. Highlight FL BKT on the Bracketing menu and scroll to the right (figure 4.2D, image 3).
4. You will now see a small popup menu with four choices (figure 4.2D, image 4). The available selections are Off three frames with a variance of 1/3 EV (3f 0.3EV), three frames with a variance of 2/3 EV (3f 0.7EV), and three frames with a variance of 1 EV (3f 1.0EV). Highlight your selection and press the OK button. The camera will then display your choice on the Bracketing screen next to FL BKT (in place of the -- symbol shown in figure 4.2D, image 3). Press the OK button again and the popup menu will display with On and Off, as seen in figure 4.2D, image 2. Select On and press the OK button again to lock in your selection. Take your pictures.

Note: Be sure to disable FL BKT when you are done taking flash bracketed pictures.

Settings Recommendation: The recharge cycle time of your flash unit will determine how quickly you can fire the three bracketed images in the series. When I used the FL-LM3 flash included with the camera, it took at least one second before I could fire the second and third images in the bracket. Evidently, the small flash unit takes a little longer to recharge itself for the next shot. However, when I used my Olympus FL-600R flash unit, I could fire the flash bracket series with no delay between the images.

A larger flash unit will perform better when you need rapid flash bracketing. If you can wait a moment between shots, the small included flash will suffice for closer subjects.

ISO BKT (ISO Bracketing)

ISO bracketing allows you to bracket three frames with bracket levels of 0.3EV, 0.7EV, or 1.0EV for two of the pictures. The bracketing order for the three frames is *normal > underexposed > overexposed*.

The camera will take a picture at the ISO sensitivity you selected. You can then take two more pictures with different ISO settings: one underexposed and another overexposed. The amount of under- and overexposure depends on the EV you select.

There are two things you need to be aware of when you use ISO bracketing:

- **Continuous bracketing:** With other types of bracketing, when you use Sequential H or Sequential L modes and hold down the Shutter button, the E-M1II will take only the number of frames in the bracket and then stop taking pictures. However, with ISO BKT the camera will *not* stop taking pictures when it reaches the end of the bracket. If you hold down the Shutter button in Sequential H or Sequential L modes, the camera will continue firing at full speed until the image buffer is full, and the three-frame bracketing sequence will repeat. This feature allows you to bracket rapidly moving subjects while you track them with your camera.
- **Nothing lower than Low ISO:** If you have your camera set to Low ISO, which is below ISO 200 and is equivalent to ISO 100, it will not be able to shoot the underexposed frame of the bracket. Instead you will have two normal (Low or ISO 100) exposures and one overexposed image in the three-frame bracket (*normal > normal > overexposed*). Obviously, the camera cannot go below its lowest ISO value to capture an underexposed image.

Now, let's see how to configure ISO bracketing.

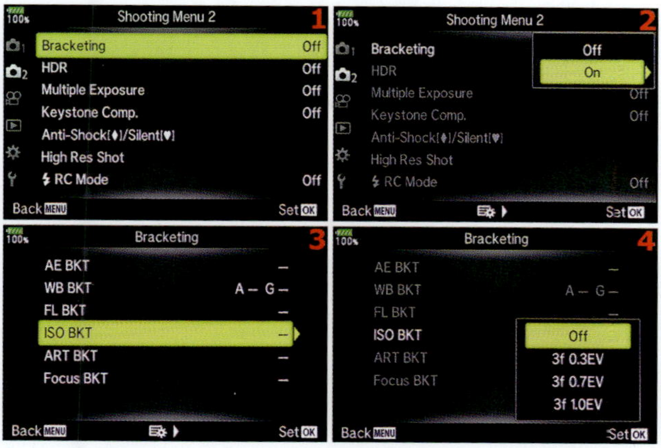

Figure 4.2E: Using ISO Bracketing (ISO BKT)

Use these steps to configure ISO BKT:

1. Choose Bracketing from Shooting Menu 2 and scroll to the right (figure 4.2E, image 1).
2. A small window will open where you can select Off or On. Highlight On and scroll to the right (figure 4.2E, image 2). Or you can disable ISO BKT by selecting Off and pressing the OK button (and skipping the rest of these steps).
3. Highlight ISO BKT on the Bracketing menu and scroll to the right (figure 4.2E, image 3).
4. You will see a small popup menu with four choices (figure 4.2E, image 4). The available selections are three frames with a variance of 1/3 EV (3f 0.3EV), three frames with a variance of 2/3 EV (3f 0.7EV), and three frames with a variance of 1 EV (3f 1.0EV). Highlight your selection and press the OK button. The camera will then display your choice on the Bracketing screen next to ISO BKT (figure 4.2D, image 3). Press the OK button again and the popup menu will display with On and Off, as seen in figure 4.2D, image 2. Select On and press the OK button again to lock in your selection. Take your pictures.

Note: Be sure to disable ISO BKT when you are finished.

Settings Recommendation: For subjects that have a lot of contrast, you will want to use a wider range of EV in the ISO BKT, such as 3f 1.0EV. For lower-contrast subjects you may be able to fine-tune the exposure by using 3f 0.3EV. Experiment with this setting so you'll know how to use it when you need to make sure you get a good exposure.

ART BKT (Art Mode Bracketing)

When you use Art bracketing from the Art selection on the camera's Mode dial, the camera will make copies of a picture and apply each of the Art Picture Modes you select (shown in figure 4.2G). You can take just one picture and the camera will bracket, or copy, it and apply each of the selected Art Picture Modes to the copies. This results in numerous copies of the original image with a different filter applied to each one.

You can choose from the 28 listed Art Modes (e.g., Pop Art I, Soft Focus, Grainy Film II) for ART BKT, and even add the normal Picture Modes (e.g., Vivid, Natural, Muted) and the more creative Picture Modes (e.g., Monochrome, Color Creator, Custom) to the bracket, creating up to 9 additional images. That's up to 37 copies of a single image with all sorts of filters applied. Imagine that many pictures from a single shot—perhaps too many!

Let's see how to select the filters you would like to use in the ART bracket.

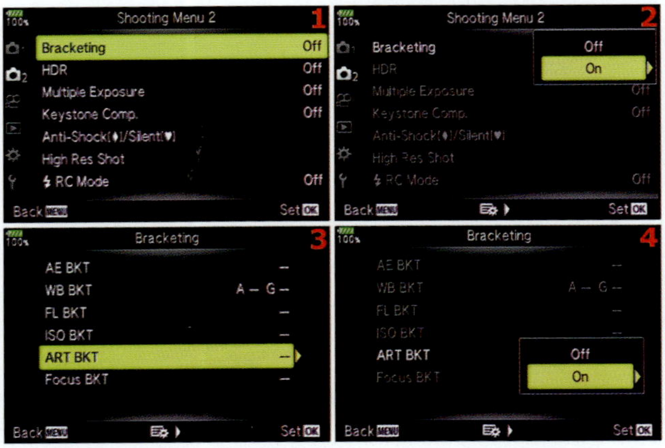

Figure 4.2F: Using Art Mode Bracketing (ART BKT)

Use these steps to configure ART BKT:

1. Choose Bracketing from Shooting Menu 2 and scroll to the right (figure 4.2F, image 1).
2. A small window will open where you can select Off or On. Highlight On and scroll to the right (figure 4.2F, image 2). Or you can disable ART BKT by selecting Off and pressing the OK button (and skipping the rest of these steps).
3. Highlight ART BKT on the Bracketing menu and scroll to the right (figure 4.2F, image 3).
4. You will see a small popup menu with two choices: On and Off (figure 4.2F, image 4). Highlight On and scroll to the right.

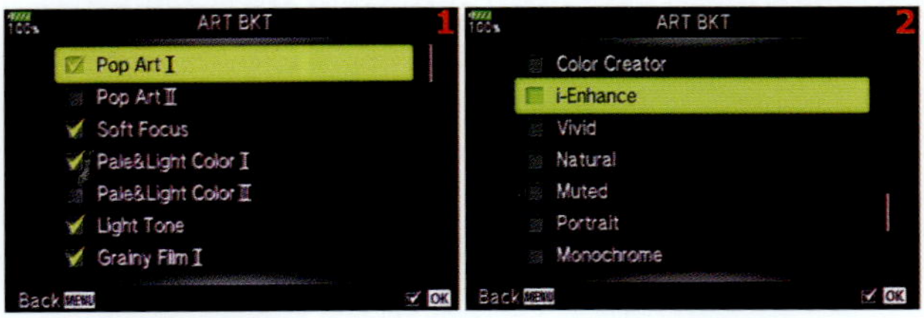

Figure 4.2G: Choosing an ART or Basic Filter

5. The camera will display a list of 37 ART BKT choices, some checked and some not checked, as partially seen in figure 4.2G, images 1 and 2. Scroll up or down and press the OK button to add or remove a check mark next to any of the Art Modes and Picture

Modes. A check mark means that mode will be added to the Art bracket. When you are done checking and unchecking modes, press the Menu button to return to the screen in figure 4.2F, image 4. Be sure On is highlighted and press the OK button again. The camera will return to the menu shown in figure 4.2F, image 3, except On will be displayed after ART BKT. Press the OK button once more and the camera will return to the screen in figure 4.2F, image 2. Select On and press the OK button a final time to enable Bracketing, and the camera is ready to use.

6. Take a *single* picture. The red card write symbol will flash in the upper-left corner of the viewfinder or monitor until all the copies (up to 37) are created. You will see each image displayed briefly—with a different filter applied—as it is created.

Note: Be sure to turn off ART BKT or you will create up to 37 pictures each time you press the Shutter button.

Settings Recommendation: This bracketing method is fun a time or two, but then you might wonder why you're using it. About the only time I use ART BKT is when I want to show off the prowess of this camera. I usually say something like, "I bet your camera won't do this!"

Unless you want a smorgasbord of arty pictures to choose from, this function may not be too useful. Try it a time or two and see what you think. And remember, if you shoot in RAW mode, any of these filters can be applied after the fact in the Olympus Viewer 3 software.

Focus BKT (Focus Bracketing and Focus Stacking)

Focus BKT comes in two parts: Focus Bracketing and Focus Stacking. Although the two work similarly, they produce very different results. Let's discuss each of these two powerful bracketing functions individually.

Focus Bracketing

The Focus BKT function allows you to take a series of shots with different focus points. You will establish the beginning focus point by initiating autofocus. The camera will then move the focus toward infinity for each successive shot, thereby providing a range of images with different autofocus points. For example, you may focus on a subject's eye, and then let the camera shoot several images with different points of focus, allowing you to choose from the best focus for that subject.

You will choose the number of shots, the focus differential (how far to move the focus between shots), and a flash charge time (to allow time for the flash to recycle). Let's examine how to configure Focus Bracketing.

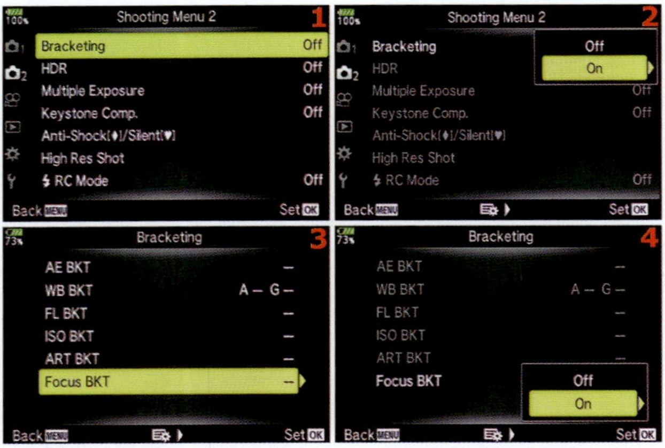

Figure 4.2H: Using Focus Bracketing (Focus BKT)

Use the following steps to configure Focus Bracketing:

1. Choose Bracketing from Shooting Menu 2 and scroll to the right (figure 4.2H, image 1).
2. A small window will open where you can select Off or On. Highlight On and scroll to the right (figure 4.2H, image 2). Or you can disable Focus BKT by selecting Off and pressing the OK button (and skipping the rest of these steps).
3. Highlight Focus BKT on the Bracketing menu and scroll to the right (figure 4.2H, image 3).
4. You will see a small popup menu with two choices: On and Off (figure 4.2H, image 4). Highlight On and scroll to the right.

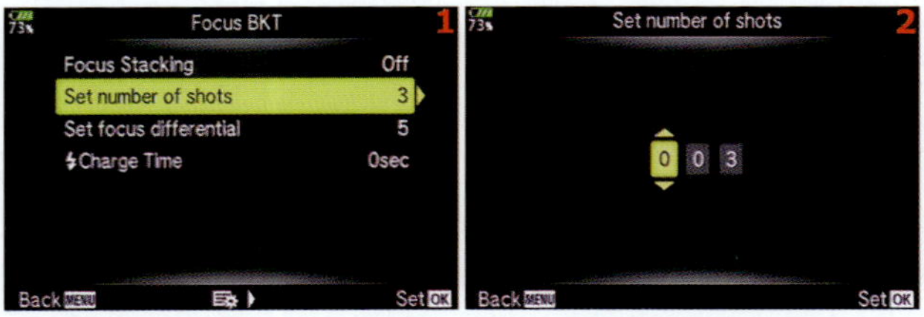

Figure 4.2I: Selecting the number of shots for the Focus Bracketing series

5. Ignore the Focus Stacking item on the Focus BKT menu for now. We will consider Focus Stacking in the next subsection. Choose Set number of shots and scroll to the right (figure 4.2I, image 1).
6. The Set number of shots setting allows you to choose the number of individual images you will take in this Focus Bracketing series (figure 4.2I, image 2). Use the three individual up/down menus to choose the number of shots, selecting a number between 0 and 9 for the first two up/down menus, and between 3 and 9 for the last up/down menu. You can choose anywhere from 3 (003) to 999 images for the bracketed series. You cannot take less than three shots (003) for this series.

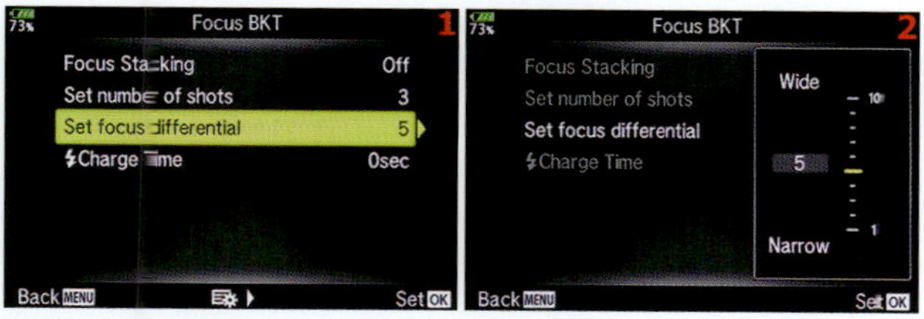

Figure 4.2J: Setting a focus differential (how much to move the focus between images)

7. Next you must set the amount the camera will move the focus position between shots. Highlight Set focus differential and scroll to the right (figure 4.2J, image 1).
8. Use the focus differential slider to choose a forward focus movement amount (figure 4.2J, image 2). Remember, as the camera takes the Focus Bracketing series, the focus will move toward infinity only (away from you) for each shot. If you want the camera to move the focus position in a narrow band (small increments), move the yellow bar toward 1 (Narrow). If you would rather have wider spacing between the focus positions for each shot, move the yellow bar toward 10 (Wide). Press the OK button to lock in the focus differential.

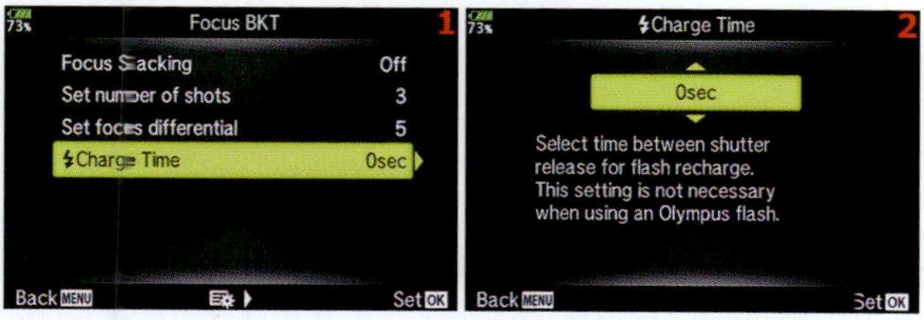

Figure 4.2K: Setting a Charge Time to allow the flash to recycle between shots

9. If you are using a non-Olympus flash unit, you may need to consider flash recycle time. An Olympus flash unit coordinates with the camera, so it should not require this setting. To set a flash charge time for a non-Olympus flash unit, choose [Flash] Charge Time from the Focus BKT menu and scroll to the right (figure 4.2K, image 1).
10. Use the up/down menu to select the number of seconds the camera should wait before firing the next image in the Focus Bracketing series (figure 4.2K, image 2). You can choose a time ranging from 0 seconds (0sec) to 30 seconds (30sec). When you have selected the flash charge time you want to use, press the OK button to lock in the value.

Note: The camera will use [Sequential] H Silent [♥] mode to release the shutter. You only need to press the Shutter button one time, and the camera will automatically take all the pictures in the bracketed series. You do not need to hold down the Shutter button.

A flash unit will not fire unless you have *Shooting Menu 2 > Anti-Shock[♦]/Silent[♥] > Silent[♥]Mode Settings > Flash Mode* (page 234) set to *Allow*. Therefore, if you want to use a flash unit, please configure that setting.

Settings Recommendation: Focus Bracketing is a good function for those who absolutely must have the proper focus on their subject. Portraiture and even things like product shooting may benefit from bracketing the focus. It's well worth it to experiment with this function!

Focus Stacking

The Focus Stacking function allows you to capture closeup images with much greater depth of field than you could normally capture in one image.

The Focus Stacking process moves the focus backward and then forward from the initial focus point. Focus Stacking differs from Focus Bracketing in that the camera will take only 8 shots, instead of up to 999. Also, at the end of the Focus Stacking series, the camera combines the eight images into one image, with virtually everything in focus. The E-M1II keeps all eight of the individual images, plus the final combined image.

You can use the Set focus differential (how far to move the focus forward) and [Flash] Charge Time (non-Olympus flash recharge time) settings in the same way you did in the previous subsection. This gives you finer control over how you work with macro shots.

As an example, I used Focus Stacking to shoot a series of photographs of an Olympus lens cap. In figure 4.2L, you will see the progression of the focus as it moves backward and forward. I started the series by focusing on the "M" in OLYMPUS (figure 4.2L, image 1). When I pressed the Shutter button *once,* the camera automatically captured all eight pictures (image 1 to image 8) shown in figure 4.2L, and combined them into the final picture (image 9).

It is best to set the initial focal point somewhere in the center of the subject, instead of on an edge, because during the stacking process, the focal point first moves toward the camera by two steps, and then away from the camera by six steps (see red arrows in figure 4.2L). The Olympus user's manual implies that the center may be better as a starting position with these words: "*The focus position is automatically shifted based on the center of the focal position and 8 frames are captured in a single shot.*"

Notice that the camera cropped the edges of the final picture (9) so that all eight pictures would fit in the final combined picture's 5184 × 3888 frame. The subject in the final picture appears somewhat larger (narrower field of view) than the eight individual pictures.

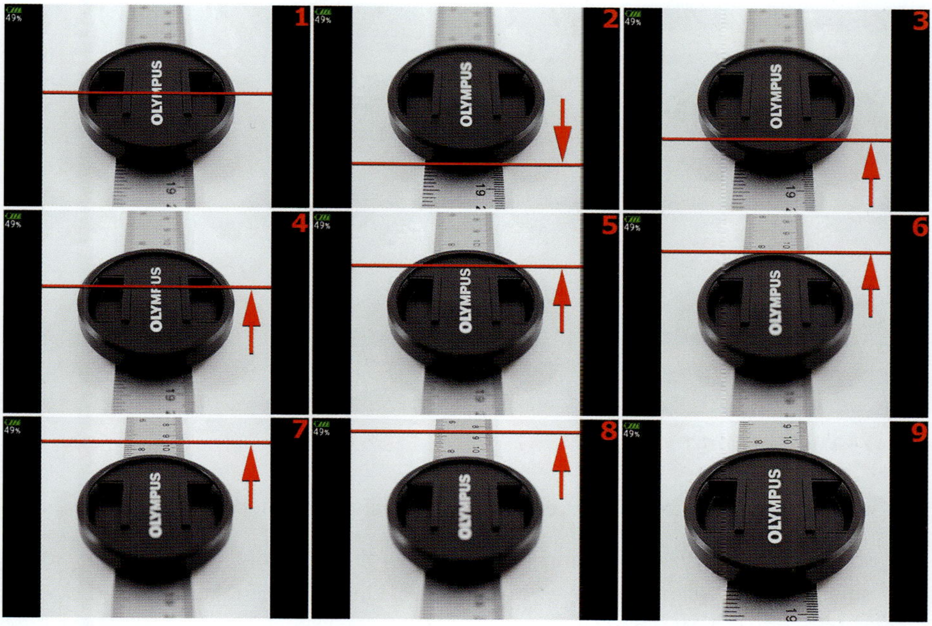

Figure 4.2L: Focus Stacking example

To make it easier to visualize the focus stacking (moving focal point) process, I added a red line across each of the 8 images, showing the focal point location in each image (figure 4.2L). The red arrows show the direction in which the focal point moved for each shot. Notice that the movement of the focal point between images 3 and 4 is more substantial than between the other images. This is because the focal point centered around the M on the lens cap was already captured in image 1. Therefore, the camera didn't waste a shot taking a picture it already had; it skipped the M position (center point of subject) as it passed by.

You can see that there are no blurry (out of focus) areas in the final image (9)—it is sharp from front to back. Interestingly, I took this series handheld (braced) at f/4.0 in my light tent to make the depth of field (zone of sharp focus) surrounding the focal point easier to see. Imagine what you could do with f/8 or f/11 (much greater depth of field) on a tripod!

It takes the camera about one second to shoot the entire eight-frame series and combine the images because it uses the Silent (♥) electronic shutter in high-speed (H) mode. Therefore, unless your subject is moving rapidly, you could use this feature handheld for many images. For best results with a macro lens and extreme closeups, use a tripod and smaller apertures.

Let's see how to configure a Focus Stacking session.

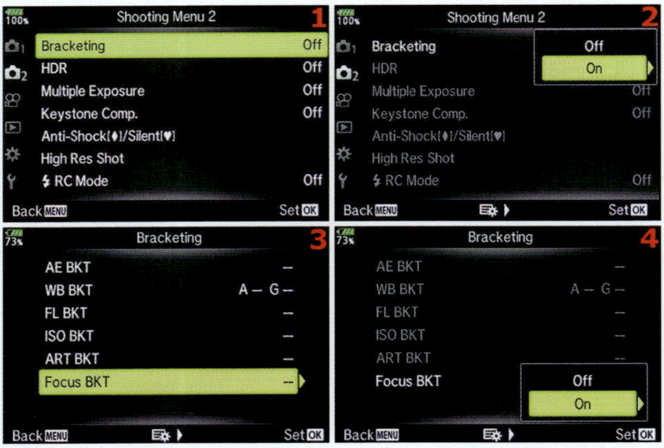

Figure 4.2M: Configuring Focus Stacking

Use the following steps to configure the Focus Stacking operation:

1. Choose Bracketing from Shooting Menu 2 and scroll to the right (figure 4.2M, image 1).
2. A small window will open where you can select Off or On. Highlight On and scroll to the right (figure 4.2M, image 2).
3. Highlight Focus BKT on the Bracketing menu and scroll to the right (figure 4.2M, image 3).
4. You will see a small popup menu with two choices: On and Off (figure 4.2M, image 4). Highlight On and scroll to the right.

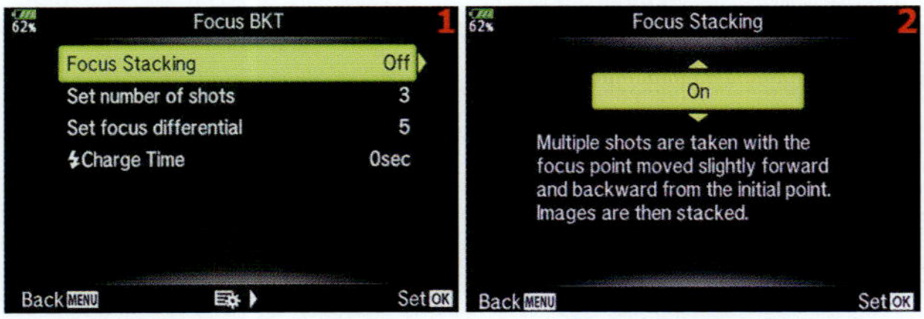

Figure 4.2N: Enabling Focus Stacking

5. Highlight Focus Stacking on the Focus BKT menu and scroll to the right (figure 4.2N, image 1).
6. Choose On from the Focus Stacking up/down menu and press the OK button to enable stacking (figure 4.2N, image 2).

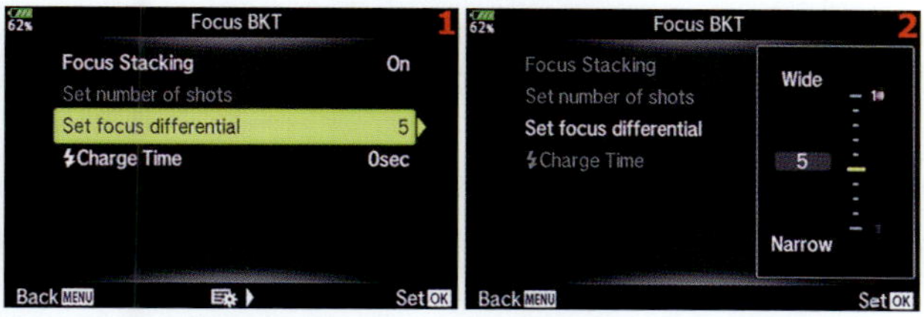

Figure 4.2O: Setting a focus differential (how much to move the focus between images)

7. Next you must set the amount the camera will move the focus position between shots. Highlight Set focus differential and scroll to the right (figure 4.2O, image 1).
8. Use the focus differential slider to choose a forward focus movement amount (figure 4.2O, image 2). If you want the camera to move the focus positions in a narrow band (small increments), move the yellow bar toward 1 (Narrow). If you would rather have wider spacing between the focus positions for each shot, move the yellow bar toward 10 (Wide). I used the default 5 position for the 8 example images in figure 4.2L. For a subject smaller than my lens cap, and especially when using a macro lens on a tiny subject, you may want to narrow the focus differential. When you are shooting larger subjects handheld, you could make the focus differential wider for more focus coverage. Press the OK button to lock in the focus differential value.

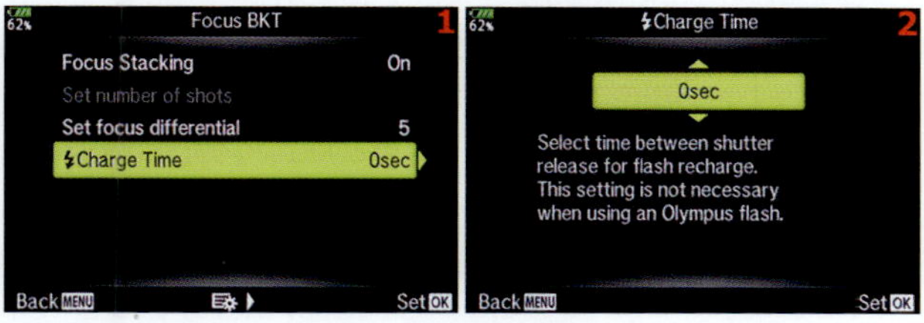

Figure 4.2P: Setting a Charge Time to allow the flash to recycle between shots

9. If you are using a non-Olympus flash unit, you may need to consider flash recycle time. An Olympus flash unit coordinates with the camera, so it should not require this setting. To set a flash charge time for a non-Olympus flash unit, choose [Flash] Charge Time from the Focus BKT menu and scroll to the right (figure 4.2P, image 1).
10. Use the up/down menu to select the number of seconds that the camera should wait before firing the next image in the Focus Bracketing series (figure 4.2P, image 2). You can choose a time ranging from 0 seconds (0sec) to 30 seconds (30sec). When you have selected the flash charge time you want to use, press the OK button to lock in the value.

Note: As with Focus Bracketing (previous subsection), the camera will use [Sequential] H Silent [♥] mode to release the shutter. You only need to press the Shutter button *one* time, and the camera will automatically take all eight of the pictures in the bracketed series. You do not need to hold down the Shutter button.

A flash unit will not fire unless you have *Shooting Menu 2 > Anti-Shock[♦]/Silent[♥] > Silent[♥]Mode Settings > Flash Mode* (page 234) set to *Allow*. Therefore, if you want to use a flash unit, please configure that setting.

Settings Recommendation: Focus Stacking is a wonderful function for those who shoot a lot of macro (closeup) images. Any time you need a deeper depth of field for a non-moving subject, this function can help you. Please take the time to learn how to use this powerful function. Your photography will benefit and you will make images that others simply cannot make.

Bracketing Chaos

Be sure to disable *all* forms of bracketing within their respective configuration screens when you are done with that bracketing type. If you don't, *the camera will stack the bracketing methods* and use them at the same time.

Suppose you have AE BKT and ART BKT enabled simultaneously. The camera will create three AE BKT pictures with the *normal > underexposure > overexposure* AE bracketing, and it will also create up to 37 ART BKT images for each of the three AE BKT images. The camera will apply each AE BKT to every ART BKT image, and you could end up with dozens of images. Imagine what would happen if you have several bracketing methods turned on at the same time and take pictures—bracketing chaos!

Some forms of bracketing are mutually exclusive to other forms of bracketing. If you have a certain bracketing type enabled, another bracketing type will disable the previously selected type. Experiment by trying to enable multiple bracketing types and you will see what I mean.

Be careful with these bracketing methods. I have not seen any warnings when multiple bracketing types are enabled at the same time. This could be useful if that is your intention, but I am afraid that many people will forget to turn them off and will get results they never expected. Be aware that bracketing chaos is entirely possible!

HDR

High dynamic range (HDR) imaging allows you to shoot several images of the same scene, with different exposures, and combine them into one image, either immediately in-camera or later during post-processing. The result is an image with a massive dynamic range that is more like what the human eye can see than what a camera can normally capture in just one image. For example, in figure 4.3A, notice how the combined 5-image HDR picture shows more detail in the areas behind the cabin and on the front porch.

The camera offers two modes that automatically combine the images in-camera (HDR1 and HDR2). Five other modes shoot three, five, or seven images with different exposure values. You can combine them into a single HDR image during post-processing on your computer.

HDR can be quite useful for static subjects when maximum shadow and highlight detail are important. However, it's important to be careful with HDR because it can make an image look artificial and gaudy if overdone. Some people like the no-shadow effect, but others just roll their eyes at the shadowless look. With the wide range of HDR capability in the E-M1II, you have a choice.

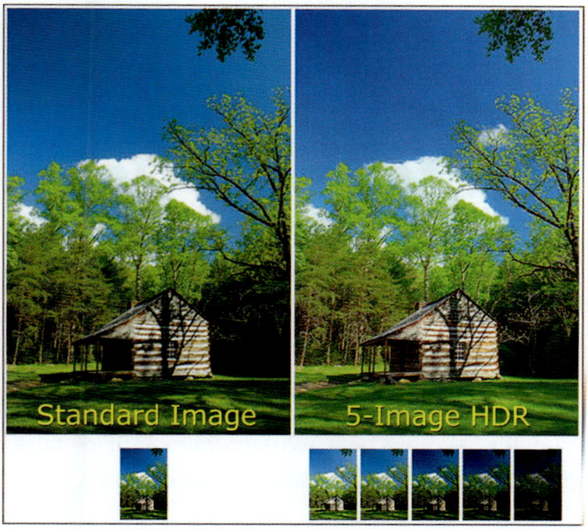

Figure 4.3A: A Standard picture compared to a five-image HDR picture

HDR1 and HDR2

If you have the camera set to RAW and enable the HDR1 or HDR2 setting, the camera will switch to a JPEG+RAW mode (if it is not already set to such a mode) and capture a normal RAW image; it will also combine the separate JPEG images into one HDR image. The result is two images: one RAW and one combined HDR JPEG.

If the camera is set to a JPEG mode, it will take three to seven pictures as JPEGs only and combine them into a single HDR JPEG.

Following are descriptions of each in-camera, automatic HDR mode:

- **HDR1:** The camera takes four images in rapid succession and combines them, in-camera, to create an HDR image that does not overdo the HDR look. It keeps some shadow contrast so the image does not look overprocessed. It looks more like a well-exposed image with a wider dynamic range than normal.
- **HDR2:** The camera takes four images in rapid succession and combines them, in-camera, to create a painterly, overprocessed HDR image with very light shadows that contain much more detail than normal.

Note: The HDR1 and HDR2 modes use ISO 200, the Picture Mode is set to Natural, and the Color Space is set to sRGB. The slowest available shutter speed you can choose as a base is 4 seconds. The longest available exposure for a single image during the bracketed image series is 15 seconds. Continuous autofocus (C-AF) will not function, so the camera automatically switches to Single autofocus (S-AF).

The Other Five HDR Modes

If you want to combine your own HDR images in your computer, the camera is ready to provide what you need with HDR1 and HDR2.

In addition to the two automatic HDR modes, five other HDR modes create individual images with various exposure levels so you can combine them yourself in software like Photomatix Pro or Photoshop:

- **3f 2.0EV:** Creates three frames (3f) with 2 EV steps between each frame (2.0EV). It uses the *normal > underexposure > overexposure* method of exposing the images.
- **5f 2.0EV:** Creates five frames (5f) with 2 EV steps between each frame (2.0EV). It uses the *normal > underexposure > underexposure > overexposure > overexposure* method of exposing the images.
- **7f 2.0EV:** Creates seven frames (7f) with 2 EV steps between each frame (2.0EV). It uses the *normal > underexposure > underexposure > underexposure > overexposure > overexposure > overexposure* method of exposing the images.
- **3f 3.0EV:** Creates three frames (3f) with 3 EV steps between each frame (3.0EV). It uses the *normal > underexposure > overexposure* method of exposing the images.
- **5f 3.0EV:** Creates five frames (5f) with 3 EV steps between each frame (3.0EV). It uses the *normal > underexposure > underexposure > overexposure > overexposure* method of exposing the images.

The camera will use whichever image quality mode you select—RAW or JPEG—to create the individual files.

If you are shooting in a JPEG+RAW mode, the camera will create all the HDR images for each mode. If you select 3f 2.0EV and shoot in JPEG+RAW mode, the camera will create two normally exposed images (one JPEG and one RAW), two underexposed images (one JPEG and one RAW), and two overexposed images (one JPEG and one RAW).

Let's examine how to configure the HDR system.

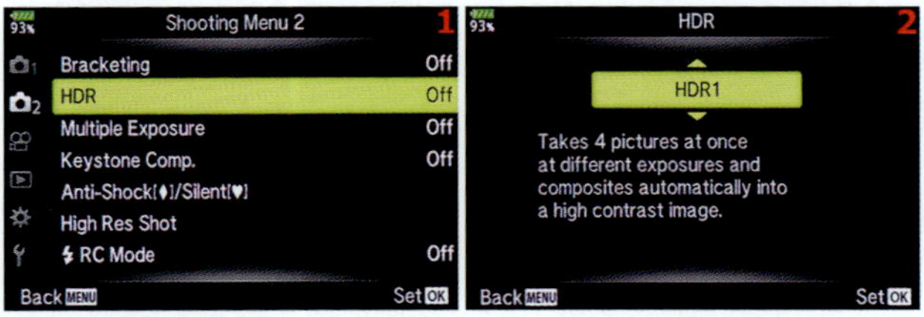

Figure 4.3B: Selecting and using an HDR mode

Use the following step to enable an HDR mode:

1. Choose HDR from Shooting Menu 2 and scroll to the right (figure 4.3B, image 1).
2. Use the up/down menu to select one of the HDR types (figure 4.3B, image 2). Your choices include HDR1 and HDR2, the five other HDR modes discussed in the previous list, and Off.
3. Press the OK button to lock in the HDR mode of your choice. When you are ready to take your HDR images, set the camera up on a tripod and press the Shutter button *once*. The camera will use [Sequential] H mode to automatically capture all the frames in the HDR series.

Note: The HDR mode will remain enabled until you select Off from the up/down menu and press the OK button. Be sure to turn off HDR mode when you are done.

Also, you cannot use the Self-timer to start capturing the HDR image series. For hands-off shutter release, consider using the Olympus RM-CB2 Remote Cable Release.

Settings Recommendation: You can let the camera combine the images for you, or you can combine them yourself in your computer. I find myself using the HDR1 or HDR2 automatic modes when I am just enjoying photography and want extra range in a certain image. It is very convenient to have the camera do it for you. However, when I am shooting landscapes and am concerned about maximum image quality, I prefer to do my own image combining and tone mapping with Photomatix Pro or Photoshop.

Fortunately, the camera lets us choose how we use HDR—for fun or for professional results.

Multiple Exposure

Multiple Exposure in the E-M1II lets you shoot two separate images and combine them into one image. This process differs from HDR because the exposures of the two images are the same.

There are three ways to use Multiple Exposure:

- **Multiple Exposure without Auto Gain:** Two images are taken with a standard exposure for each, then they are combined in-camera.
- **Multiple Exposure with Auto Gain:** Two images are taken at one-half exposure for each, then they are combined in-camera.
- **Multiple Exposure with Overlay:** You choose a RAW image from the memory card and then take another picture. The camera combines the image from the memory card with the new picture. You can repeat this action to add new exposures to the combined image. Just choose the combined image from the memory card again and shoot another new picture.

Standard Multiple Exposure with and without Auto Gain

The process is harder to describe than to perform. The camera displays the two images on the monitor or in the viewfinder, then you visually line up the two images you want to combine. After you learn about the Multiple Exposure options, the process is easy.

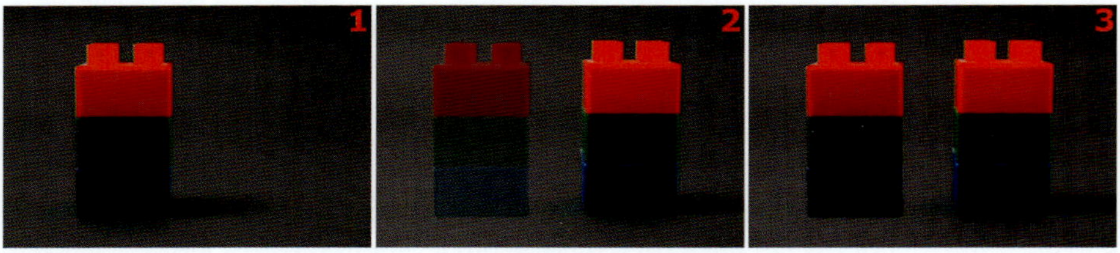

Figure 4.4A: A simulation of combining two images in-camera

Figure 4.4A is a simulation of how to combine two images. Image 1 is the first exposure and image 2 is the second exposure—image 1 still shows up as a shadowy figure that overlays the live image. Image 3 is the combined image after you press the Shutter button. While you are shooting image 2, you can still see image 1 in your viewfinder or on the camera monitor, so it is easy to align the elements before you press the Shutter button. Use the following steps to try it.

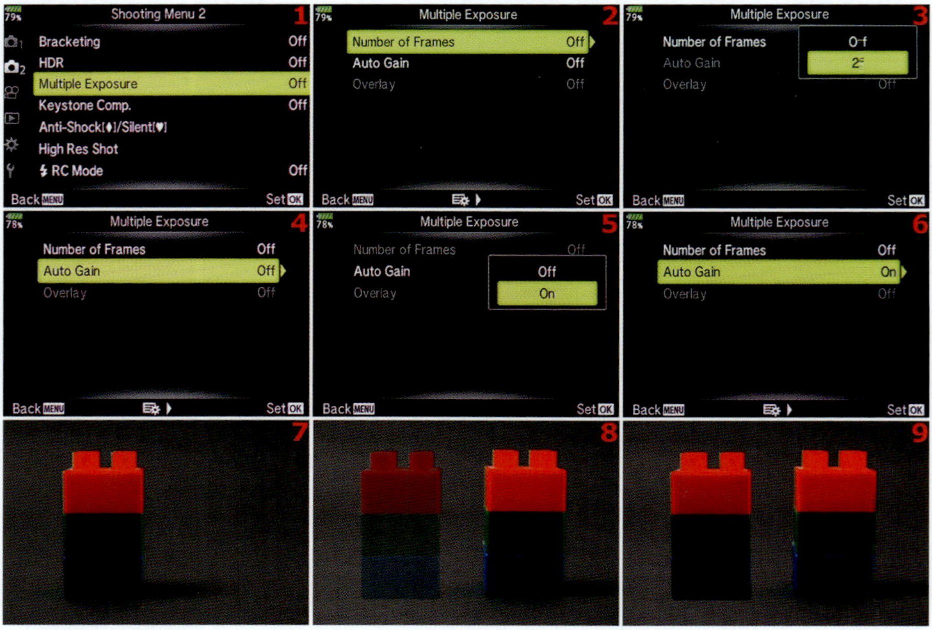

Figure 4.4B: Combining two images in-camera

Use these steps to create a Multiple Exposure:

1. Choose Multiple Exposure from Shooting Menu 2 and scroll to the right (figure 4.4B, image 1).
2. Select Number of Frames from the Multiple Exposure menu and scroll to the right (figure 4.4B, image 2).
3. A small window will open where you can choose Off or 2f (figure 4.4B, image 3). Activate the Multiple Exposure system by highlighting 2f and pressing the OK button. The camera is now ready to take two frames (2f) that will be combined.
4. Select Auto Gain from the Multiple Exposure menu and scroll to the right (figure 4.4B, image 4).
5. A small window will open with two choices: Off and On (figure 4.4B, image 5). Auto Gain affects how the exposure for the two images is made. If you enable Auto Gain (On), the camera will take the two images at half their normal exposure, which will make the background look normal after the two images are combined (because each image has half the needed exposure), and the subjects may be a little transparent. If you do not enable Auto Gain (Off), the camera exposes the two images normally, which will create a much brighter background in the final combined image. Choose On or Off and press the OK button (figure 4.4B, image 6).
6. Now you can take the two pictures that the camera will combine. Figure 4.4B, image 7, shows what was displayed in my viewfinder and on my camera monitor for the first picture. I snapped the picture.
7. Figure 4.4B, image 8, shows what was displayed in my viewfinder and on my camera monitor, including the shadowy figure of the first picture, as I framed the next shot. I moved my camera around until the two images were lined up the way I wanted them, and then I pressed the Shutter button.
8. The camera overlaid the two images and combined them (figure 4.4B, image 9).

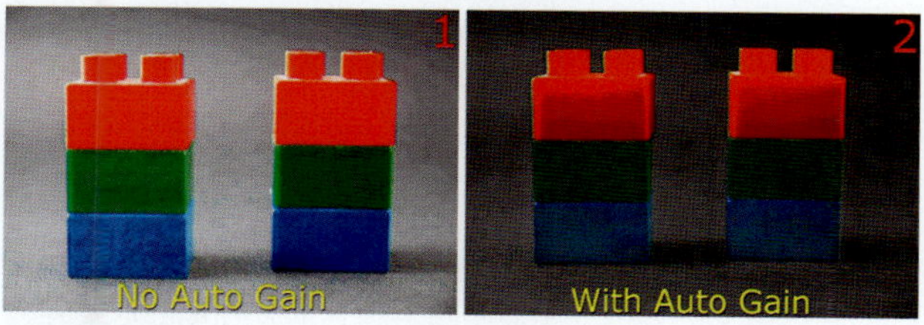

Figure 4.4C: Multiple Exposures without Auto Gain (*image 1*) and with Auto Gain (*image 2*)

In a printed book it is difficult to accurately simulate the steps because you cannot see the images being created. However, figure 4.4C shows the results of a Multiple Exposure operation without Auto Gain (image 1) and with Auto Gain (image 2).

Next, let's consider how to use the Multiple Exposure Overlay system.

Multiple Exposure with Overlay

The Multiple Exposure Overlay function allows you to choose a RAW image from the memory card and take a new picture that overlays it. The two exposures are then combined (figure 4.4D).

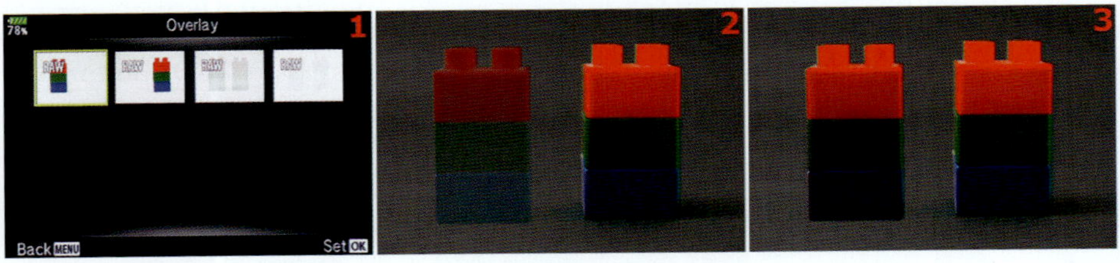

Figure 4.4D: Choosing a RAW image and then overlaying a new picture

This is similar to a normal Multiple Exposure, except the first image already resides in RAW format on the memory card. You choose from a list of images on the camera monitor, and then take the second image for the Multiple Exposure.

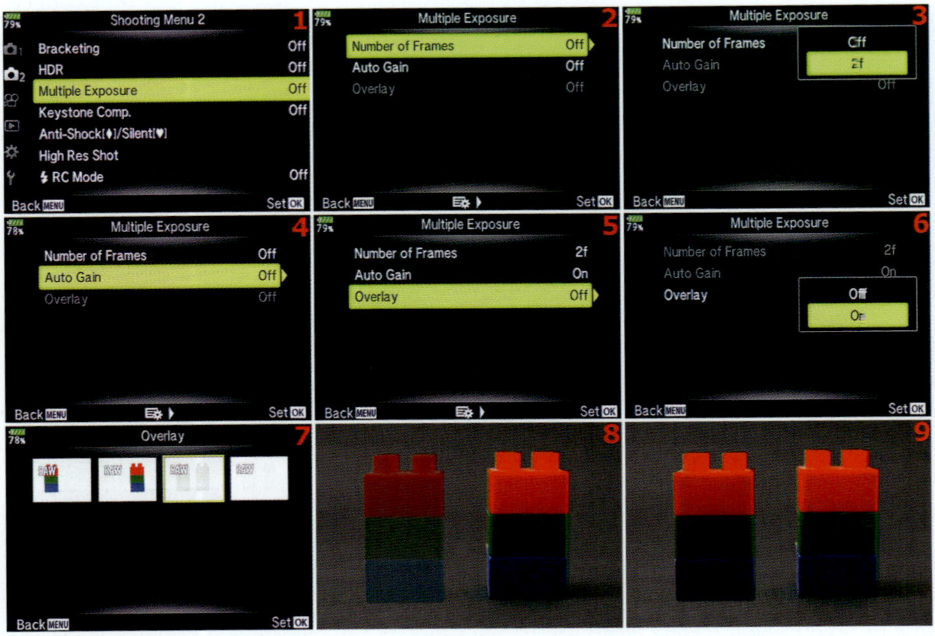

Figure 4.4E: Using the Multiple Exposure Overlay system

Use the following steps to overlay an existing RAW image with a new exposure. Make sure you shoot in RAW mode!:

1. Choose Multiple Exposure from Shooting Menu 2 and scroll to the right (figure 4.4E, image 1).
2. Select Number of Frames from the Multiple Exposure menu and scroll to the right (figure 4.4E, image 2).
3. A small window will open and allow you to choose Off or 2f (figure 4.4E, image 3). Activate the Multiple Exposure system by highlighting 2f and pressing the OK button. The camera is now ready to combine two frames (2f).
4. Select Auto Gain from the Multiple Exposure menu and scroll to the right (figure 4.4E, image 4). I left out the next two screens to keep the figure to a manageable size, but choose On or Off, depending on whether you want to use Auto Gain.
5. Scroll down and select Overlay from the Multiple Exposure menu then scroll to the right (figure 4.4E, image 5).
6. Enable Overlay by selecting On from the small window, then press the OK button (figure 4.4E, image 6).
7. Now you will see a list of all the RAW images on your memory card (figure 4.4E, image 7). A yellow rectangle will surround one of the RAW images. Move the rectangle to the image you want to use as the base for the overlay to select it. I chose a stack of blocks positioned on the left side of the frame.
8. The RAW image you selected in step 7 will be faintly displayed on the monitor or in the viewfinder (figure 4.6E, image 8). You will also see the current scene in front of your lens, similar to my simulation in image 8. Compose the current subject in relation to the RAW image and press the Shutter button.
9. The camera will combine the current subject with the RAW image (figure 4.4E, image 9). You can keep taking pictures and the camera will continue to combine them. You can see the combined image on the monitor or in the viewfinder before you press the Shutter button, so you can make some creative compositions.

Note: Remember that you can combine many exposures into one image. Start at step 7 (figure 4.4E, image 7) and choose a previously combined RAW image to be the base for the Multiple Exposure Overlay, then take a new picture to add to the Multiple Exposure.

Settings Recommendation: Multiple Exposures and Overlays are a lot of fun. You could take a picture of one person and create a twin using Multiple Exposure. Or you could take a RAW picture and later overlay a different subject (or two).

Keystone Comp.

Keystone Comp. makes your E-M1II act like one of those big view cameras, with its tilts, swings, and excellent distortion correction. You use the function while you view the subject on the monitor, not later in post-processing. Keystone Comp. allows you to correct the odd leaning-backward perspective distortion you see when you point a wide-angle lens upward to capture a tall subject (vertical plane tilt). Additionally, you can use this function to correct perspective distortion on a horizontal plane (swing). The results of this powerful function are easier to see than describe, so let's examine how it works.

In figure 4.5A you can see a battery and building blocks in a normal, straight-on configuration. Notice that there are two adjustable indicators on the screen (red arrows). The top red arrow points to the tilt control, which allows you to tilt the top or bottom of the image toward or away from you. Tilt correction is applied with the Rear Dial. The bottom red arrow points to the swing control, which allows you to swing the left or right side of the image toward or away from you. Swing correction is applied with the Front Dial.

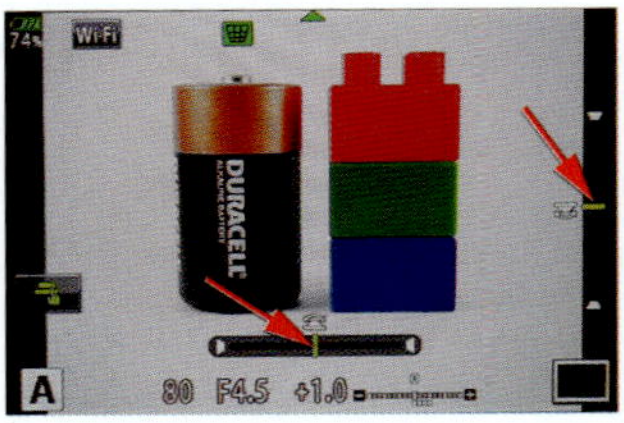

Figure 4.5A: Normal subject view with Keystone comp. function set to On

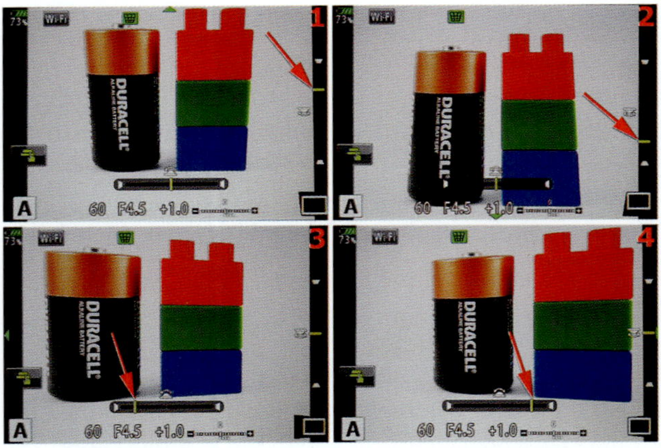

Figure 4.5B: Making adjustments to the subject with the Keystone Comp. function

In figure 4.5B I used the tilt-swing features of the Keystone Comp. function to make the subject swing left and right or tilt front to back—without moving the camera.

In image 1 the tilt indicator is at the top of the scale, and the camera is tilting the top edge of the image toward you. The bottom of the image stays the same.

In image 2 the tilt indicator is at the bottom of the scale, and the camera is tilting the bottom edge of the image toward you. The top of the image stays the same.

In image 3 the swing indicator is at the left side of the scale, and the camera is swinging the left side of the image toward you. The right side of the image stays the same.

In image 4 the swing indicator is at the right side of the scale, and the camera is swinging the right side of the image toward you. The left side of the image stays the same.

Keystone Comp. Correction

In figure 4.5C you can see a picture in which I used some vertical Keystone Comp. correction to make the fire tower stand up straighter. I was standing below the tower with my wide-angle lens pointed upward.

In the first frame the tower seems to be leaning away at the top. That's because the wide-angle lens is magnifying closer objects (the base of the tower) more than distant objects (the top of the tower).

In the second frame, notice how the camera has pulled the top of the image forward, cutting off the edges of the frame to compensate, and thus enlarging the subject a little. When you use this live function, you can see if the subject is cut off due to cropping, and you can make composition adjustments before you take the picture.

In the second frame, the fire tower is straighter, with a more normal perspective. I enjoyed using Keystone Comp. much more than I expected. It corrects distortion without blurring the subject.

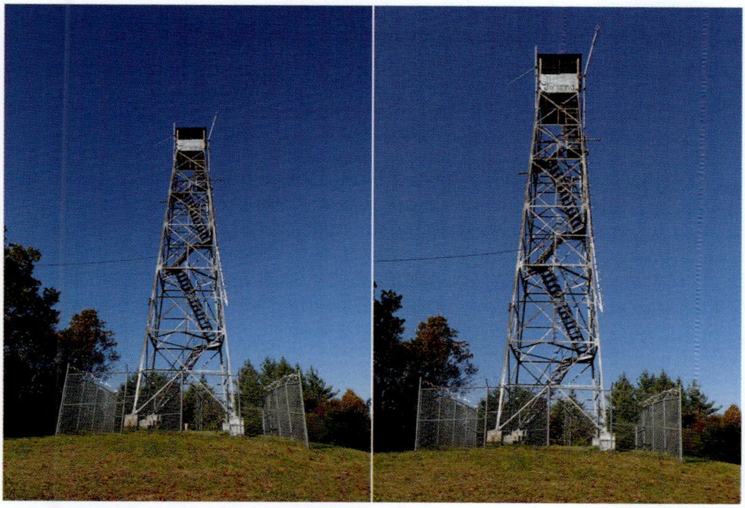

Figure 4.5C: Keystone comp. correction in action

Now let's examine how to enable and disable Keystone Comp.

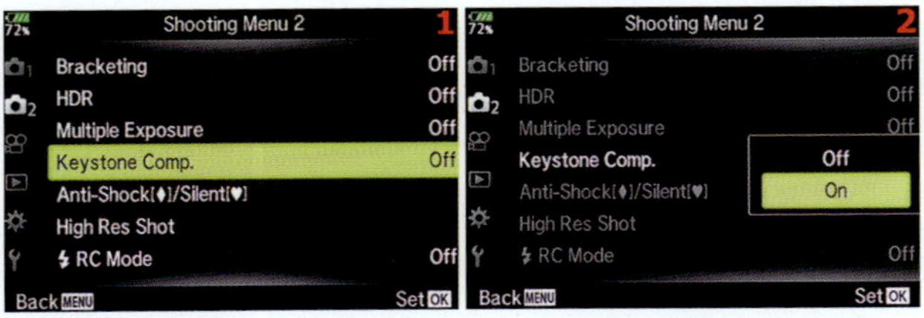

Figure 4.5D: Enabling or disabling Keystone Comp.

Use the following steps to use the Keystone Comp. function:

1. Select Keystone Comp. from Shooting Menu 2 and scroll to the right (figure 4.5D, image 1).
2. A menu will open (figure 4.5D, image 2). Scroll to choose Off or On. If you choose On, the camera will switch the Live View screen to Keystone Comp. mode, with the tilt-swing indicators (figure 4.5B). When the camera is in this mode you can't easily change the exposure because the Front Dial and Rear Dial are tied up with Keystone Comp. adjustments. Therefore, it's important to set the exposure correctly before you enter Keystone Comp. mode to take a picture.
3. Press the OK button to lock in your selection.

Settings Recommendation: Although this tilt and swing method is not quite up to the standards of a view camera's tilt and swing system or an optical tilt-shift lens, it is a quick way to add some distortion correction on the fly. It tends to stretch the edges of images, so I don't use this function for large adjustments. However, for a little tweaking it's fun to use.

Anti-Shock [♦]/Silent [♥]

The Anti-Shock [♦] function is designed to cut down on sharpness-robbing vibrations caused by small camera movements at the time of exposure. The act of pressing the Shutter button with your finger causes camera vibrations that can produce image blurring at slow shutter speeds. If you have your camera on a tripod, you can set a delay value before the shutter fires, allowing time for vibrations to die down after you have pressed the Shutter button. You can choose delay values from the Anti-Shock [♦] menu from 0 seconds to 30 seconds.

The Silent [♥] function causes the camera to use its silent electronic shutter instead of its somewhat noisier and more shock-prone mechanical shutter. You can also choose a delay time for the Silent [♥] function to prevent blurring of the image by photographer- or camera-induced vibrations.

Anti-Shock [♦] and Silent [♥] are mutually exclusive. You cannot select both modes at the same time.

Let's examine how to use these two functions and a couple of related subfunctions to create very sharp images at slow shutter speeds.

Anti-Shock [♦]

When you are capturing images using a shutter speed slower than 1/320 second and you have Anti-Shock [♦] enabled, the camera uses electronic first-curtain shutter release mode to help stop vibrations. You can set a timeout from 0 seconds to 30 seconds before the shutter fires, allowing time for vibrations to die down after you press the Shutter button.

Note: To use Anti-Shock [♦] mode, you must have enabled its use in *Custom Menu > D1. Disp/[Sound]/PC > [Sequential]/[Self-timer] Settings* (figure 4.6A). There you will find several [Sequential]/[Self-timer] settings that normally do not show on the camera's selection screens. If you select the extra anti-shock settings, they will immediately appear in the [Sequential]/[Self-timer] selection screens along with the normal [Sequential]/[Self-Timer] settings. Enabling these extra settings will be discussed in the chapter **Custom Menu,** under the **[Sequential]/[Self-Timer] Settings** subheading (page 480). In this chapter, we will enable the [♦] [Single] mode so that we can take pictures with an Anti-Shock [♦] delay enabled.

Please note that in addition to [♦] [Single] mode, there are also four other Anti-Shock [♦] modes: [♦] [Sequential] L, [♦] [Self-timer] 2s, [♦] [Self-timer] 12s, and [♦] [Self-timer] C. Again, you won't see any of the Anti-Shock [♦] modes on the [Sequential]/[Self-timer] settings screens until you have enabled them in Custom Menu D1 (figure 4.6A). Let's see how.

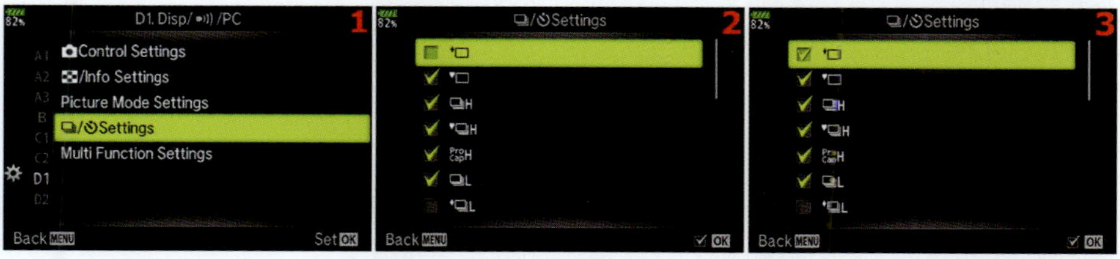

Figure 4.6A: Adding [♦] [Single] mode to the [Sequential]/[Self-timer] screens

Use these steps to add [Sequential]/[Self-timer] [♦] [Single] mode (or up to four others) to the [Sequential]/[Self-timer] settings and to use an Anti-Shock [♦] delay to prevent vibrations:

1. Highlight [Sequential]/[Self-timer] Settings on the D1. Disp/[Sound]/PC screen in the Custom Menu and scroll to the right (figure 4.6A, image 1).
2. On the [Sequential]/[Self-timer] Settings menu, you will find 19 items (figure 4.6A, image 2). Only some of them will be checkmarked on a new E-M1II camera. The items that do not have check marks will not show in the [Sequential]/[Self-timer] selection screens. Highlight the top item, which represents the [♦] [Single] mode, and press the OK button to place a check mark in the box (figure 4.6A, image 3).

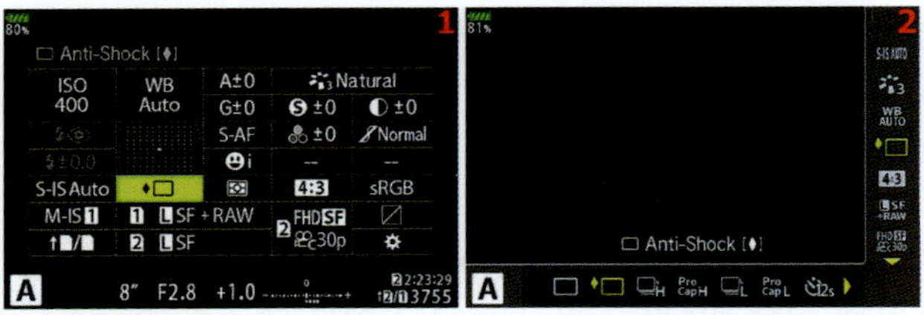

Figure 4.6B: Selecting [♦] [Single] mode from the Super Control Panel or Live Control

3. In figure 4.6B, image 1, I selected the Anti-Shock [♦] [Single] mode on the Super Control Panel. In image 2, you can see the same selection on the Live Control. The Anti-Shock [♦] [Single] mode would not be available for selection on either of these two [Sequential]/[Self-timer] selection screens, or on the screen opened with the [Sequential]/[Self-timer]/HDR button on top of the camera, if I had not put a check mark in the box in Custom Menu D1 (figure 4.6A, image 3). Select Anti-Shock [♦] [Single] mode from your [Sequential]/[Self-timer] screen of choice (figure 4.6B). Now let's enable the Anti-Shock [♦] delay.

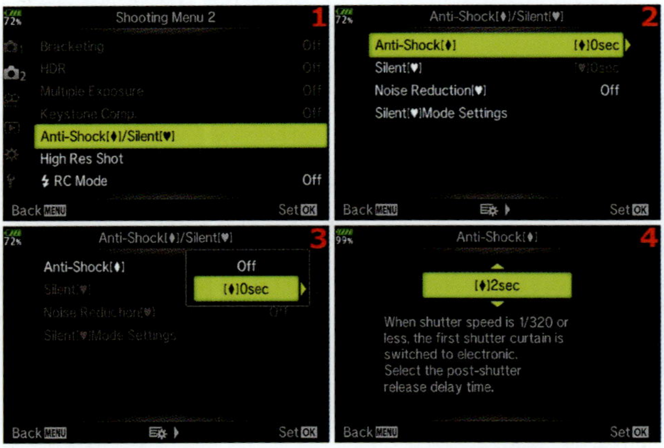

Figure 4.6C: Choosing a shutter-release delay or anti-shock setting

4. Select Anti-Shock [♦]/Silent [♥] from Shooting Menu 2 and scroll to the right (figure 4.6C, image 1).
5. Highlight Anti-Shock [♦] from the Anti-Shock [♦]/Silent [♥] menu and scroll to the right (figure 4.6C, image 2).
6. A small menu will pop up with two selections: Off and a time value ([♦]0sec for first-time use; figure 4.6C, image 3). Choose the [♦]0sec value and scroll to the right to select a new time value, or select Off to disable Anti-Shock [♦].
7. As seen in figure 4.6C, image 4, you will use the up/down menu to select a vibration-suppressing shutter delay, from [♦]0sec (0 seconds) to [♦]30sec (30 seconds). I chose [♦]2sec (2 seconds) in image 4.
8. Press the OK button to Set your chosen value.

Now you have enabled the Anti-Shock [♦] Single setting on the Super Control Panel (and Live Control), and you have selected the Anti-Shock [♦] shutter delay. You may take your pictures with a multi-second delay for vibration suppression.

Note: When you are shooting in Anti-Shock [♦] mode with a shutter speed faster than 1/320 second (e.g., 1/500 second, 1/2000 second) the camera will use its mechanical shutter only. However, when you are using a shutter speed slower than 1/320 second (e.g., 1/250 second, 1/30 second), the camera will use its electronic first-curtain shutter instead of the mechanical shutter. This tends to reduce the chance of vibration with slower shutter speeds, maximizing sharpness.

Silent [♥]

When you are using Silent [♥] mode, you can introduce a delay starting from the time you press the Shutter button. The shutter will not fire until the delay expires. This will help you get sharper pictures while using Silent [♥] mode.

Please note that in addition to [♥] [Single] mode, there are also four other available Silent [♥] modes: [♥] [Sequential] L, [♥] [Self-timer] 2s, [♥] [Self-timer] 12s, and [♥] [Self-timer] C. You won't see any of the Silent [♥] modes on the [Sequential]/[Self-timer] settings screens until you have enabled them in Custom Menu D1 (figure 4.6D). Let's see how.

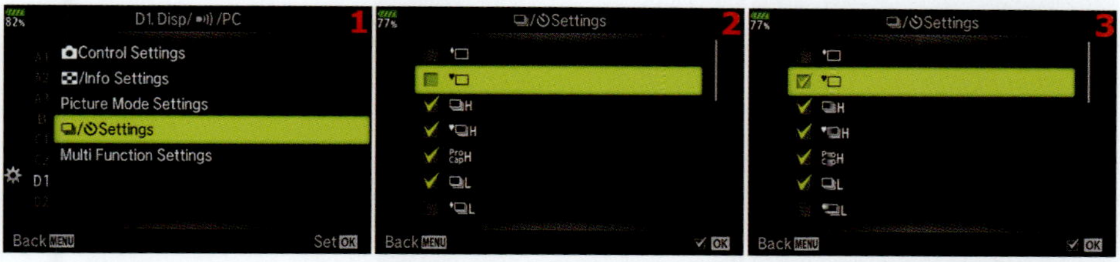

Figure 4.6D: Adding [♥] [Single] mode to the [Sequential]/[Self-timer] screens

Use these steps to add [Sequential]/[Self-timer] [♥] [Single] mode (or up to four others) to the [Sequential]/[Self-timer] settings and to use a Silent [♥] delay to prevent vibrations:

1. Highlight [Sequential]/[Self-timer] Settings on the D1. Disp/[Sound]/PC screen in the Custom Menu and scroll to the right (figure 4.6D, image 1).
2. On the [Sequential]/[Self-timer] Settings menu, you will find 19 items (figure 4.6D, image 2). Only some of them will be checkmarked on a new E-M1II camera. The items that do not have check marks will not show in the [Sequential]/[Self-timer] selection screens. Highlight the second item on the list, which represents the Silent [♥] [Single] mode, and press the OK button to place a check mark in the box (figure 4.6D, image 3).

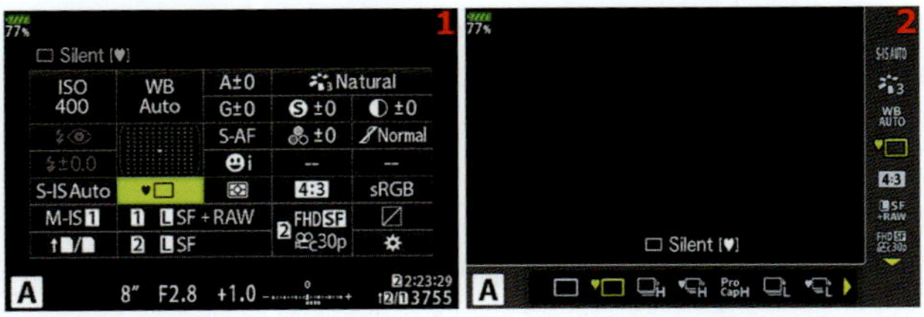

Figure 4.6E: Selecting [♦] [Single] mode from the Super Control Panel or Live Control

3. In figure 4.6E, image 1, I selected the Silent [♥] [Single] mode on the Super Control Panel. In image 2, you can see the same selection on the Live Control. The Silent [♥] [Single] mode would not be available for selection on either of these two [Sequential]/[Self-timer] selection screens, or on the screen opened with the [Sequential]/[Self-timer]/HDR button on top of the camera, if I had not put a check mark in the box in Custom menu D1 (figure 4.6D, image 3). Select Silent [♥] [Single] mode from your [Sequential]/[Self-timer] screen of choice (figure 4.6E). Now let's enable the Silent [♥] delay.

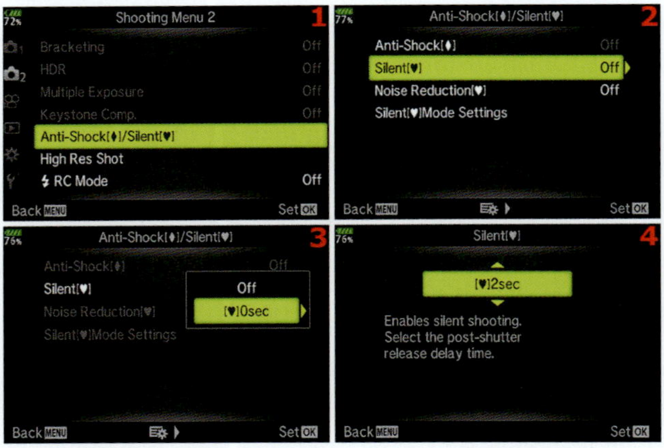

Figure 4.6F: Choosing a shutter-release delay or silent mode setting

4. Select Anti-Shock [♦]/Silent [♥] from Shooting Menu 2 and scroll to the right (figure 4.6F, image 1).
5. Highlight Silent [♥] from the Anti-Shock [♦]/Silent [♥] menu and scroll to the right (figure 4.6F, image 2).
6. A small menu will pop up with two selections: Off and a time value ([♦]0sec for first time use; figure 4.6F, image 3). Choose the [♦]0sec value and scroll to the right, or select Off to disable Silent [♥].
7. As seen in figure 4.6F, image 4, you will use the up/down menu to select a vibration-suppressing delay, from [♥]0sec (0 seconds) to [♥]30sec (30 seconds). I chose [♥]2sec (2 seconds) in image 4.
8. Press the OK button to Set your chosen value.

Now you have enabled the Silent [♥] [Single] setting on the Super Control Panel (and Live Control), and you have selected the Silent [♥] shutter delay. You may take your pictures with a multi-second delay for vibration suppression.

Noise Reduction [♥]

If you are using Silent [♥] mode and shooting long exposures, you might end up with some noise in your images due to the sensor getting warm (fog), or some bright spots (often red) in the picture from a few hot pixels. If you enable Noise Reduction [♥], the camera will use the black-frame subtraction noise-reduction method to remove noise from your images. Long-exposure noise is not the same as the noise that results from high-ISO shooting. It is safe to leave long-exposure noise reduction turned on all the time because it does not blur the image to reduce noise. We will discuss this type of noise reduction in greater detail in a later chapter (page 509).

Unfortunately, when you're using this Noise Reduction [♥] function in combination with shutter speeds of 5 seconds or longer, you will hear four mild shutter sounds as the camera uses the black-frame subtraction method to shoot a second image with the shutter closed. If you keep the camera's shutter speed under 5 seconds, you can shoot with no shutter sound in Silent [♥] mode, even though Noise Reduction [♥] is enabled.

Let's examine how to enable long-exposure Noise Reduction [♥].

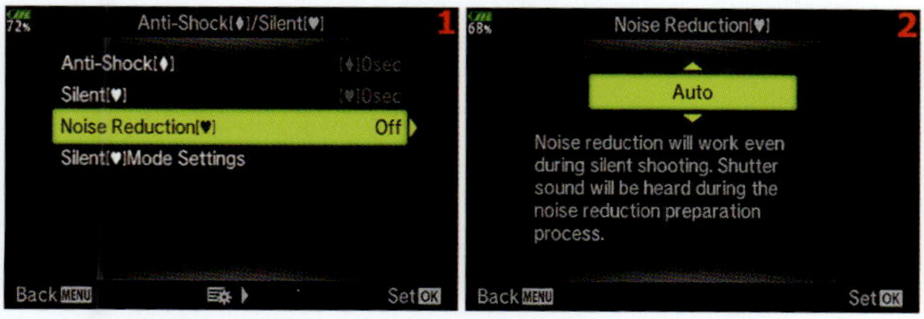

Figure 4.6G: Enabling long-exposure Noise Reduction [♥]

Use the following steps to select automatic long-exposure noise reduction in Silent [♥] mode:

1. Choose Noise Reduction [♥] from the Anti-Shock [♦]/Silent [♥] menu and scroll to the right (figure 4.6G, image 1).
2. Use the up/down menu to select Auto for automatic long-exposure noise reduction in Silent [♥] mode, or Off to disable it (figure 4.6G, image 2).
3. Press the OK button to lock in the setting.

Settings Recommendation: I leave the Noise Reduction [♥] function turned on all the time. That way, if I decide to do some star trails or other long exposures in Silent [♥] mode, I know my camera is ready to reduce the foggy amp noise and remove the hot pixels that generally appear in digital images during long exposures.

Silent [♥] Mode Settings

This function allows you to get serious about reducing noise or light that might attract a raging beast (or bride) to you for disturbing the quiet. Not only can you turn off sound, but you can also disable the focus assist light and any non-Olympus flash you might have forgotten to dismount. Let's see how.

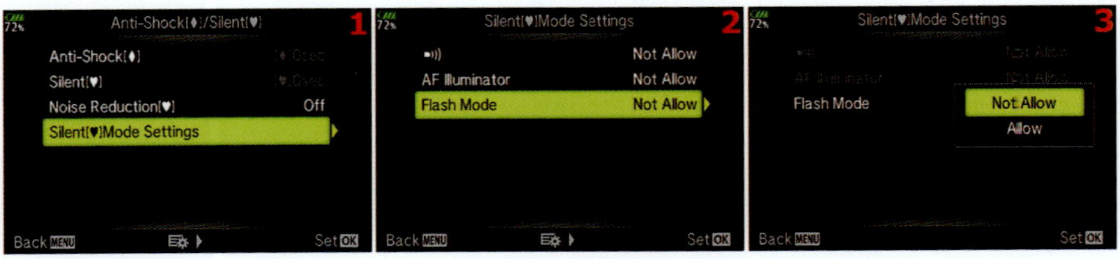

Figure 4.6H: Disable all light and sound when using Silent [♥] mode

Use the following steps to disable light and sound that might call attention to you or disturb those around you while the camera is in Silent [♥] mode:

1. Choose Silent [♥] Mode Settings from the Anti-Shock [♦]/Silent [♥] menu and scroll to the right (figure 4.6H, image 1).
2. Highlight [Sound], AF Illuminator, or Flash Mode on the Silent [♥] Mode Settings menu and scroll to the right (figure 4.6H, image 2). They all work the same way. I used Flash Mode as the example. Flash Mode applies only to non-Olympus flash units.
3. You will now see a popup menu with two choices: Not Allow and Allow. Select Not Allow to disable a particular feature, or Allow to enable it, according to your needs.
4. Press the OK button to Set the value.

Settings Recommendation: If I am shooting macro shots or handheld shots with slow shutter speeds that are especially prone to being degraded by camera vibrations, I often use an Anti-Shock [♦] delay to reduce or eliminate vibrations. Silent [♥] works in a similar manner to Anti-Shock [♦] mode, except that it uses the silent electronic first-curtain shutter in all situations. There may be even less vibration when the camera uses the silent electronic shutter, compared to the mechanical shutter; however, in all situations, pressing the Shutter button is a major cause of vibrations. Using Anti-Shock [♦] mode—or Silent [♥] mode when no shutter noise is wanted—will help you keep your images sharp at slow shutter speeds. Be sure to use a tripod!

When I am shooting on a tripod I use an electronic cable release, such as the Olympus RM-CB2 Remote Cable Release, to prevent camera vibrations from damaging my shot. I also like to use at least a 2-second delay to allow camera vibrations to die down before I release the shutter. Although a mirrorless camera is not as susceptible to vibrations as a DSLR, it is still wise to use a tripod and hands-off shutter release to make the sharpest possible pictures.

I leave Noise Reduction [♥] turned on all the time because I like long-exposure noise reduction when I shoot images with a shutter speed longer than 5 seconds.

I use the Silent [♥] Mode Settings functions according to my needs at the time. When I am shooting pictures of a bear, I certainly don't want my camera drawing attention to me.

High Res Shot

High Res Shot mode allows you to create extra-large JPEG and RAW files with up to more than double the normal megapixel (MP) rating.

When you take a picture in this mode, the camera will capture eight images using its Silent electronic shutter, and then combine the images in-camera into one approximately 80-, 50-, or 25-megapixel image, according to the Image Quality mode you select. Instead of the normal 20 MP image at 5184 × 3888, the resulting combined image will be significantly larger (see table 4.4).

The E-M1II achieves this result by using sensor-shift technology to move the physical imaging sensor to create a larger-than-normal frame. The camera takes eight pictures as it moves the sensor, and then combines the images into one large image.

It takes several seconds for the E-M1II to capture the eight images and combine them into one big image, so it is imperative that you mount your camera on a tripod when you are using this mode, or you will end up with a blurry picture. The camera cannot use its normal Image Stabilization during this process.

The camera will display a black screen with a progress bar once it has captured and begun combining the images. Before you take the High Res Shot, you may see the symbol for High Res Shot blinking on the screen (figure 4.7D, image 2). If so, this means the camera is unstable. Stabilize the camera before proceeding. Once you have pressed the Shutter button to start the process, wait for the progress bar to complete and the green High Res Shot symbol to disappear from the screen before moving the camera.

You can choose from four different Image Quality sizes for High Res Shots. Table 4.4 contains a list of the Image Quality choices along with the corresponding pixel ratio, megapixel size, and image file(s) produced for each option.

Image Quality	Pixel Ratio	Megapixel Size	Image Files Produced
50MF	8160 × 6120	49.9 MP	1 JPEG
25MF	5760 × 4320	24.9 MP	1 JPEG
50MF + RAW	10368 × 7776	80.6 MP	1 JPEG, 1 ORF, 1 ORI
25MF + RAW	5760 × 4320	24.9 MP	1 JPEG, 1 ORF, 1 ORI

Table 4.4: High Res Shot information

In table 4.4, you will note that the camera produces a single, large, combined JPEG file when you use one of the 50MF or 25MF Image Quality choices.

However, the E-M1II produces multiple files when you select one of the "+ RAW" settings (i.e., 50MF + RAW or 25MF + RAW). The JPEG in the trio of files is a combined JPEG, the ORF file is a combined RAW file, and the ORI file is a single RAW file, with no combination.

You may have noticed in table 4.4 that the 50 MF + RAW setting produces an 80.6 MP ORF file (10368 × 7776). The camera does not show this pixel size on its image detail screen (figure 4.7D, image 6); instead, it reports that the ORF file is 8160 × 6120 (~50 MP). However, if you open the huge ORF file in Photoshop or Olympus Viewer 3, you will find that it has pixel dimensions of 10368 × 7776. The reason Olympus does not report the ORF file as being 80.6 MP is because its image detail really contains only about 50 MP in quality, due to the pixel-shifting method that was used to capture it. Therefore, Olympus underreports the file size.

If you want to, you can rename the ORI file to a new filename with an ORF extension and it will perform as a normal 5184 × 3888 RAW file. All three files have the same file name, except for the three-character ending (e.g., 120921.JPG, 120921.ORF, 120921.ORI). Therefore, if you want to rename the ORI file to an ORF file, you will need to change the file name so that it no longer matches the current file name; otherwise, you may overwrite the combined ORF file with the renamed ORI file.

Note: If you leave High Res Shot set to Off and do not select a High Res Shot delay time, as described in the following steps 1–4, many of the upcoming camera screens examined in figures 4.7B and 4.7C will simply not work. Basically, this High Res Shot function on Shooting Menu 1 is the first place to go to enable the High Res Shot process. You can leave High Res Shot enabled all the time (I do) and simply not select it until needed. Now let's examine the steps to set up a High Res Shot.

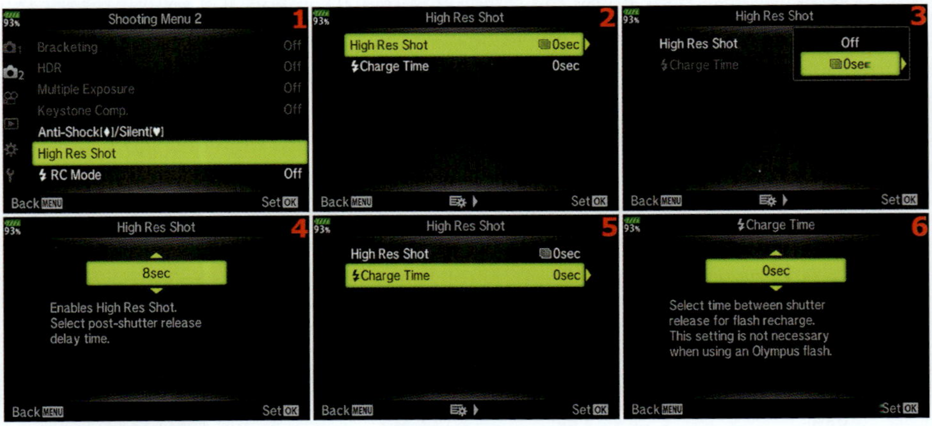

Figure 4.7A: Selecting High Res Shot

Use the following steps to configure your E-M1II for making a High Res Shot:

1. Select High Res Shot from Shooting Menu 2 and scroll to the right (figure 4.7A, image 1).

2. Highlight High Res Shot on the High Res Shot menu and scroll to the right (figure 4.7A, image 2).
3. Choose the [High Res Shot] 0sec selection from the popup menu and scroll to the right to select a delay value (figure 4.7A, image 3). Or, if you would rather not use a delay value to reduce vibrations, simply highlight 0sec, press the OK button, and skip step 4. (***Note:*** Since High Res Shot is all about getting maximum image detail, it would be a shame to limit that detail by shaking the camera. It's a good idea to use some delay time to allow vibrations to dissipate before the shutter fires.)
4. Select a delay time from the up/down menu (figure 4.7A, image 4). This delay time will allow any camera vibrations to settle down after you have pressed the Shutter button and before the camera takes the picture. You can select from no delay (0sec) to 30 seconds (30sec), with several intermediate delay values. In the example, an 8-second delay (8sec) is selected.
5. If you are using a non-Olympus flash unit, you may need to consider flash charge time. An Olympus flash unit coordinates with the camera, so it should not require the use of this setting. If you do not need time for the flash to recharge, skip to step 7. To set a flash charge time for a non-Olympus flash unit, choose [Flash] Charge Time from the High Res Shot menu and scroll to the right (figure 4.7A, image 5).
6. Use the up/down menu to select the number of seconds that the camera should wait before capturing the image, so that the flash has time to recycle (figure 4.7A, image 6). You can choose from 0 seconds (0sec) to 30 seconds (30sec). When you have selected the [Flash] Charge Time you want to use, press the OK button to lock in the value.

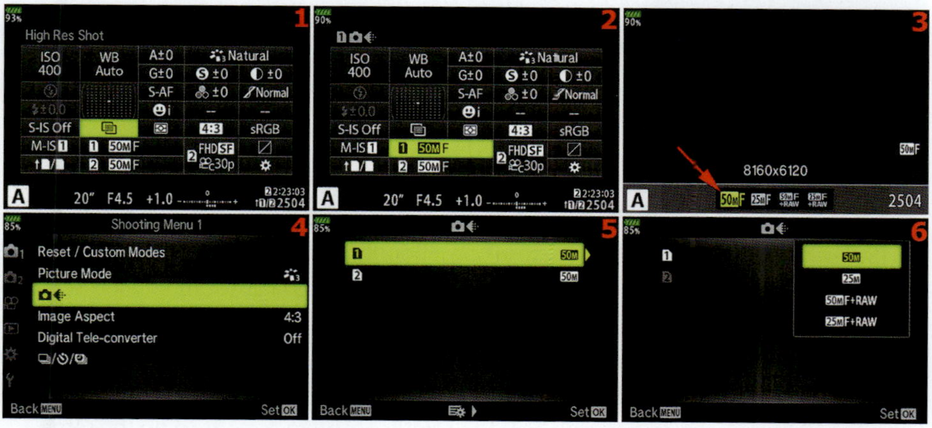

Figure 4.7B: Choosing the Image Quality of the High Res Shot

7. Figure 4.7B shows two separate ways to choose a [Photo][Record Mode] (Image Quality) value for your High Res Shot. Figure 4.7B, images 1–3, show how to use the Super Control Panel to select a 50MF High Res Shot Image Quality. If you want to use the Super Control Panel or LV Super Control Panel to select the Image Quality value, choose the [Photo][Record Mode] location, as seen in figure 4.7B, image 1. Select

the High Res Shot symbol by turning the Front Dial (image 1). Next, scroll down one position and select one of the memory card locations (1 or 2, as seen in figure 4.7B, image 2), and press the OK button to open a secondary screen (figure 4.7B, image 3). From the secondary screen choose one of the High Res Shot Image Quality values (refer to table 4.4). Our example choice in figure 4.7B, image 3, is the 50MF JPEG setting (8160 × 6120) for an ~50 MP JPEG image. If you used the Super Control Panel to select the Image Quality value, you can skip step 8, which describes how to use Shooting Menu 1 to do the same thing.

8. Figure 4.7B, images 4–6, describe how to use Shooting Menu 1 to select an Image Quality setting for the High Res Shot. Highlight [Photo][Record Mode] on Shooting Menu 1 and scroll to the right (figure 4.7B, image 4). Choose one of the memory card slots (1 or 2) and scroll to the right (figure 4.7B, image 5). Select one of the four Image Quality settings (e.g., 50M) from the popup menu and press the OK button to lock in the value.

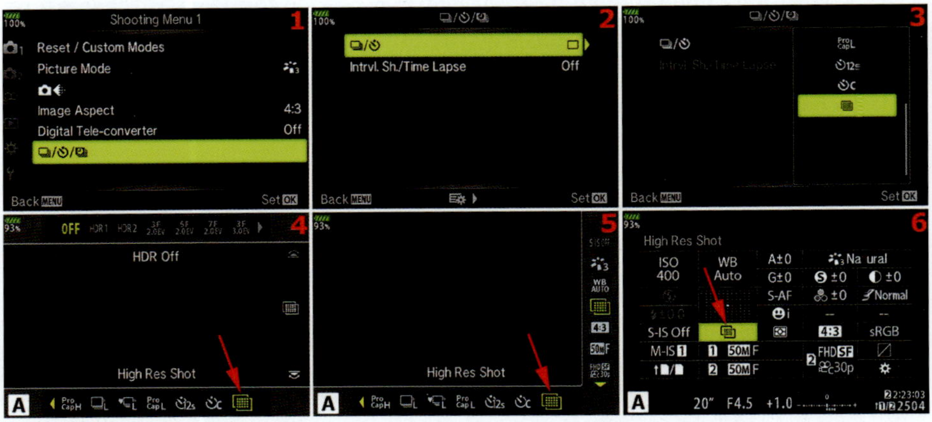

Figure 4.7C: Selecting High Res Shot mode

9. Figure 4.7C shows the various ways you can choose High Res Shot mode via different camera screens. First, let's use Shooting Menu 1 to choose the mode. Highlight [Sequential]/[Self-timer]/[Time Lapse] on Shooting Menu 1 and scroll to the right (figure 4.7C, image 1). Select the [Sequential]/[Self-timer] subset menu and scroll to the right (figure 4.7C, image 2). Choose the High Res Shot mode symbol from the bottom of the popup menu and press the OK button to lock in your choice (figure 4.7C, image 3). If you used Shooting Menu 1 to select High Res Shot mode, you can skip steps 10 and 11, which describe how to use other camera screens to do the same.

10. Figure 4.7C, image 4, shows the screen that appears when you press the [Sequential]/Self-timer]/HDR button on top of the camera. You will find the High Res Shot symbol at the far right end of the menu bar on the bottom of the screen. Turn the Rear Dial or use the Arrow Pad keys to make your selection.

11. Figure 4.7C, image 5, shows the Live Control screen you can access by pressing the OK button when your subject is displayed on the rear monitor (or in the EVF), if you have

the Live Control enabled (page 69). Otherwise, if you do not have the Live Control enabled, you can use the Super Control Panel (page 20), or the LV Super Control Panel (page 69), to access the same High Res Shot mode symbol (figure 4.7C, image 6). Simply turn the Front Dial to change the symbols until the High Res Shot symbol appears. Following are the screens you will see while capturing a High Res Shot.

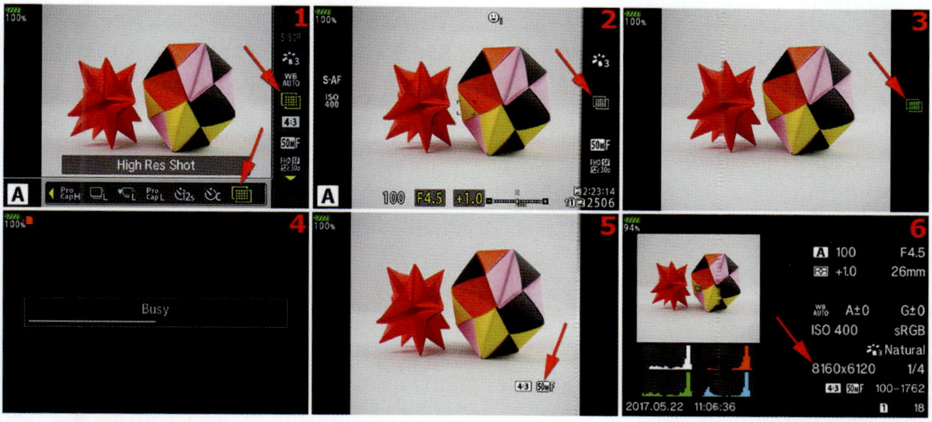

Figure 4.7D: Capturing a High Res Shot image

12. Figure 4.7D, image 1, shows the Live Control with the High Res Shot mode symbol selected. Use the Live Control, Super Control Panel, LV Super Control Panel, [Sequential]/[Self-timer]/HDR button, or Shooting Menu 1 to select the High Res Shot symbol, as described in previous steps.
13. It is very important that the camera is mounted on a solid tripod or other stable platform, or you will be unable to use High Res Shot effectively. In figure 4.7D, image 2, the red arrow is pointing at the High Res Shot symbol. If this symbol is blinking, the camera is not stable enough to create a High Res Shot. Stabilize the camera until the symbol stops blinking.
14. Once you have pressed the Shutter button, your camera will start its High Res Shot delay countdown (see figure 4.7A to set the delay). While the delay is counting down, the screen will go black, except for the green High Res Shot symbol seen in figure 4.7D, image 3. Once the High Res Shot delay has expired you will see the screen shown in figure 4.7D, image 3, with your subject in the background, of course. This screen is displayed while the camera captures the eight frames needed to make the High Res Shot. Do not move the camera during image capture, which can last for several seconds.
15. As soon as the eight frames have been captured, the camera starts merging them into the final High Res Shot. During the merge process, the camera will display a Busy screen with a progress bar (figure 4.7D, image 4).
16. Following the Busy screen, the camera will briefly display the screen shown in figure 4.7D, image 5. Then it will return to the normal shooting screen, ready to take

more High Res Shot images. Be sure to select a mode other than High Res Shot when you are finished.

17. Figure 4.7D, image 6, shows the Playback screen in information mode (press the INFO button when a picture is displayed on the monitor to use the image information screen). Notice that the camera shows you the High Res Shot pixel ratio, along with normal shooting information.

Settings Recommendation: I love the High Res Shot mode for landscapes (unless the wind is blowing hard, which can cause blurring). There are many types of static photography that will benefit from added image resolution. Although it may seem a little complex in the beginning, after you have taken a few High Res Shots, it will become second nature. While this mode might not fully match the resolution of a true 50 MP sensor, it can add lots of extra detail for many subjects. Try it out—I think you'll like it.

[Flash] RC Mode

[Flash] RC Mode allows you to use the separate FL-LM3 flash unit that is included in the box with the camera as a controller for an external, off-camera flash unit, such as the Olympus FL-900R, FL-600R, FL-300R, and STF-8. Those four Olympus flash units are recommended in the user's manual, on page 152, as the best flash units for wireless remote control.

You can control up to three banks of multiple flash units, or just one or two external flashes, for much nicer flash light than direct on-camera flash.

We will examine how to make the E-M1II interface with an Olympus FL-600R flash unit and set it up to fire wirelessly as a slave, while using the small, hotshoe-mounted FL-LM3 flash unit as a master. First, let's set up the camera, and then we'll configure the external flash unit(s).

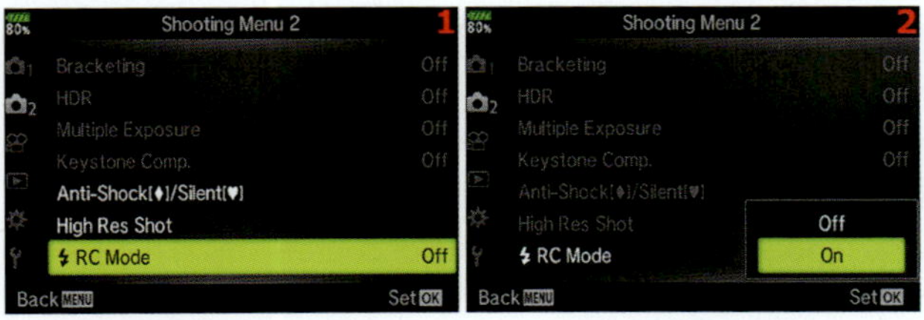

Figure 4.8A: Enabling RC Mode

1. Mount the FL-LM3 flash unit on the camera hot shoe, make sure it is locked into place, and switch the FL-LM3 On/Off lever to On.
2. Press the Menu button, choose [Flash] RC Mode from Shooting Menu 2, and scroll to the right (figure 4.8A, image 1).

3. A small window will open and allow you to choose Off or On (figure 4.8A, image 2). To configure and use [Flash] RC Mode, select On and press the OK button. The live view screen will appear on the camera monitor, but we are not ready to shoot. We need to configure a specialized flash-only Super Control Panel for remote-controlled flash.

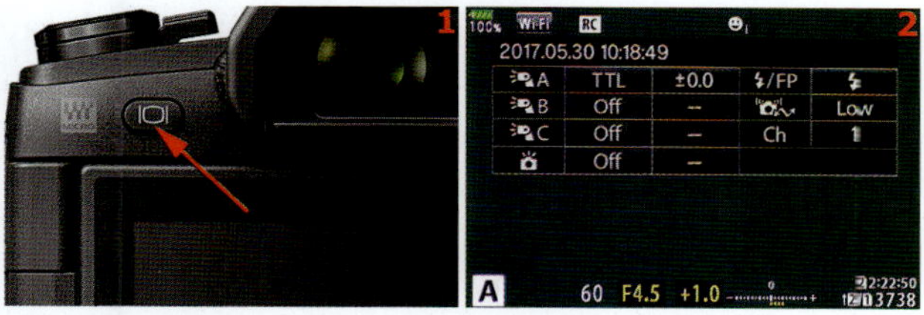

Figure 4.8B: Opening the special flash-only Super Control Panel with the LV button

4. Press the LV button (figure 4.8B, image 1) to switch out of Live View and open the flash-only Super Control Panel (figure 4.8B, image 2). This version of the Super Control Panel is devoted to RC flash control and differs from the normal Super Control Panel. You will see this panel only when [Flash] RC Mode is On. We will use this panel to set up our camera to interface with and control an Olympus FL-600R flash unit. ***Note:*** If you do not see the Super Control Panel shown in figure 4.8B, image 2, after you press the LV button, you will need to press the INFO button to bring it up. You can switch between the normal Super Control Panel and the flash-only Super Control Panel by pressing the INFO button when [Flash] RC Mode is set to On.

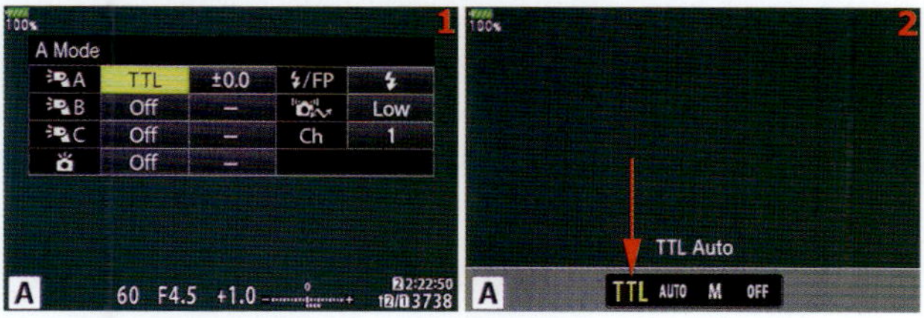

Figure 4.8C: Configuring flash bank A

5. Figure 4.8C, image 1, shows three flash control bank settings (A, B, and C) and a fourth setting (camera symbol). Each of the A, B, and C banks may control one or many flash units; you can set up complex lighting arrangements and control them wirelessly. Each bank can be configured separately for different lighting effects in various areas of your scene. We will configure only bank A in this example, but the other banks work the same way. Highlight TTL (figure 4.8C, image 1, yellow box) and press the OK button. This opens the TTL Auto window, which has four choices: TTL, Auto, M, and Off (figure 4.8C, image 2). You can change the flash mode for the remote slave flash by selecting a mode:
   - **TTL mode:** The TTL mode, which is also known as TTL Auto, uses through-the-lens (TTL) technology to automatically create excellent exposures from any combination

of flash units on that bank. The flash units send out a nearly imperceptible preflash immediately before the main flash fires. This lets the camera and flash combination balance the light so you don't have to calculate lighting ratios; you just set it to TTL and take pictures.

- **Auto mode:** The Auto mode is an older non-TTL technology that is included for people who are accustomed to using an older type of flash unit. It works pretty much the same as TTL mode, without the preflash that helps the camera and flash unit more accurately balance the light. You can safely ignore Auto mode unless you want to experiment with it. The flash exposures may not be as accurate as those in TTL mode.
- **M mode:** M or Manual mode is designed for photographers who are accustomed to using flash units in studios. You can control the power settings for each bank individually, from 1/1, or full power, to as low as 1/128 power. Many people are used to working with flash units this way, so this mode is familiar to them. It is often necessary to calculate flash ratios when you use this mode because there is no automation.
- **Off:** When you choose Off, a flash bank is disabled and does nothing. If you have a group of flash units set up to use this bank, you can temporarily disable the bank—for light testing purposes—by setting it to Off.

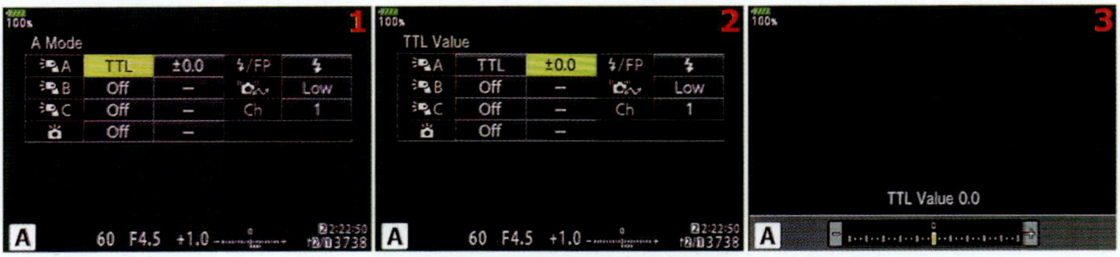

Figure 4.8D: Preparing bank A for using TTL mode

6. Now, let's examine how to choose and prepare each of the three active settings in the previous list (TTL, Auto, and M). Remember, you set each flash bank (A, B, or C) individually so you can organize them separately. First we will look at TTL mode and discuss how to make an exposure compensation for bank A. Choose TTL from the panel (figure 4.8D, image 1) and scroll to the right until ±0.0 is highlighted (figure 4.8D, image 2). Now press the OK button and the screen shown in figure 4.8D, image 3, will appear. You can enter a – or + exposure compensation value, and any flash unit on this bank will use that compensation. Scroll to the left or right to move the yellow-green indicator (in image 3 it is directly below the tiny 0 on the –/+ scale). Scroll left for underexposure (down to –5.0 EV TTL Value) and right for overexposure (up to +5.0 EV TTL Value). Press the OK button and that EV will be used by all flash units on that bank (in this case, bank A). If you want no exposure compensation, leave the TTL Value set to 0.0. Next let's consider how to use Auto mode.

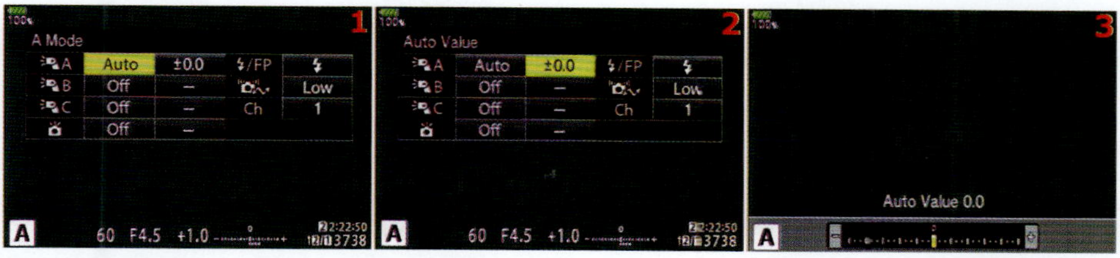

Figure 4.8E: Preparing bank A for AUTO mode

7. Choose Auto from the panel (figure 4.8E, image 1) and scroll to the right until ±0.0 is highlighted (figure 4.8E, image 2). Press the OK button and the screen shown in figure 4.8E, image 3, will appear. You can enter a – or + exposure compensation value, and any flash unit on this bank will use that compensation. Scroll to the left or right to move the yellow-green indicator (in image 3 it is directly below the tiny 0 on the –/+ scale). Scroll left for underexposure (down to –5.0 EV Auto Value) and right for overexposure (up to +5.0 EV Auto Value). Press the OK button and that EV will be used by all flash units on that bank (in this case, bank A). If you want no exposure compensation, leave the Auto Value set to 0.0. Now let's look into Manual (M) mode.

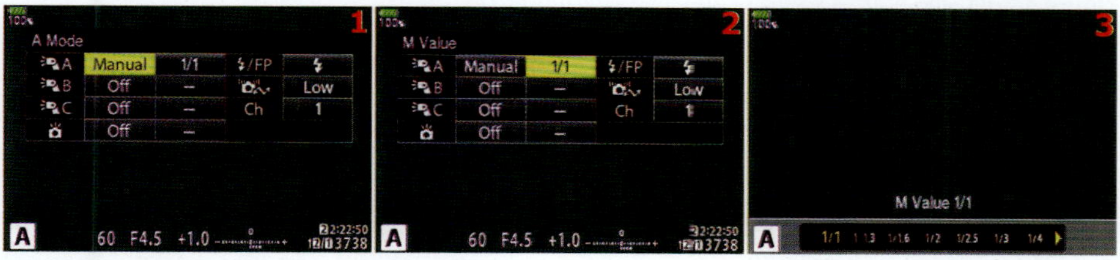

Figure 4.8F: Preparing bank A for M mode

8. Choose Manual from the panel (figure 4.8F, image 1) and scroll to the right until 1/1 is highlighted (figure 4.8F, image 2). Press the OK button and the screen shown in figure 4.8F, image 3, will appear. You can enter an M Value from 1/1 to 1/128, which corresponds to the power output of every flash unit on the bank (in this case, bank A). Scroll left for more flash power (up to 1/1, or full power) or right for less flash power (down to 1/128). Press the OK button and that power level will be used by all flash units on that bank.

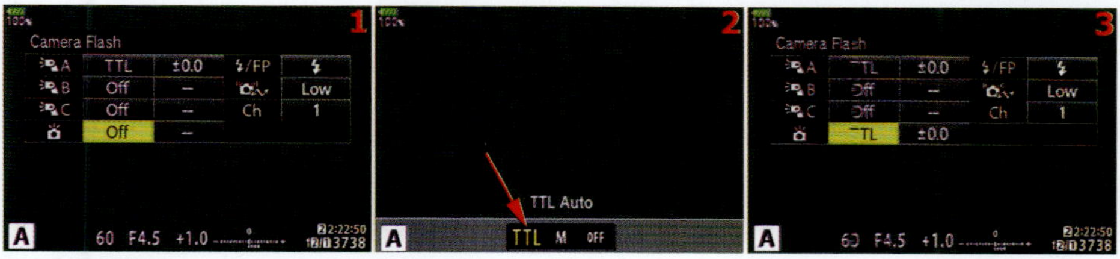

Figure 4.8G: Adding fill light with the FL-LM3 flash unit

9. Now you must decide if you want the tiny FL-LM3 flash unit to add light to the image. The default is Off, as shown in figure 4.8G, image 1. That means the small FL-LM3 master flash will not provide a flash burst like the slave units do. If it did, it would provide direct flash, which may not be what you want. Be careful that the FL-LM3 does not add unwanted light to your image (e.g., eyeglass reflections). If it does, use a smaller aperture or move the camera farther away from your subject. If you do want the FL-LM3 flash to provide extra fill light, you can set it to TTL or M mode (figure 4.8G, images 2 and 3) and it will behave like the bigger slave units. When the FL-LM3 flash unit provides light to the scene, it has its own bank without an A, B, or C label. Now let's consider flash sync speed.

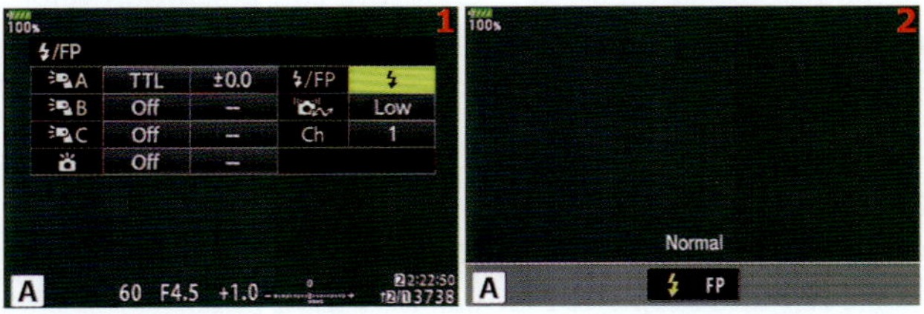

Figure 4.8H: Using normal x-sync or Super FP sync mode

10. Your camera will typically use a Normal maximum x-sync shutter speed of 1/250 second. However, that may not work if you are shooting outside and want to use a wider aperture and faster shutter speed. The camera can use a faster sync speed called Super FP (focal plane) high-speed sync mode (figure 4.8H, image 1) or FP mode. The upcoming sidebar titled **Super FP Sync Mode** describes how that mode works. You might want to shoot at f/2.8 in direct sunlight for a shallow depth of field, and use a shutter speed of up to 1/8000 second, while still using fill flash to reduce shadows. Most of the time this setting can stay at the Normal x-sync setting (maximum 1/250 second shutter speed), which is indicated by the lightning bolt symbol in figure 4.8H, image 2. You can select FP if you want to experiment with Super FP high-speed sync mode (up to 1/8000 second shutter speed).

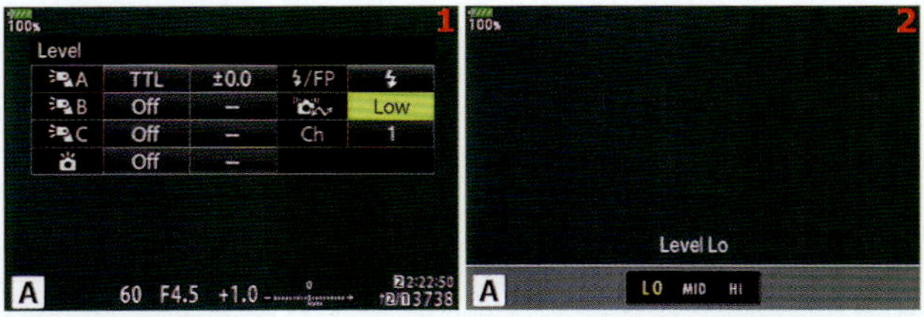

Figure 4.8I: Changing the power level of the master flash communication light output

11. When ambient light conditions are very bright or the slave flash units are farther away from the camera, you may need to increase the light output from the preflash of the master flash, which is how it communicates with the slave units (figure 4.8I). You can't

leave it set to Hi all the time because the Hi setting may cause the preflash to produce enough light to interfere with your lighting arrangement. You will need to experiment with this setting, especially if some or all of the slave flash units are not responding to the master flash. You many need to increase the power from Level Lo to Level Mid or even to Level Hi.

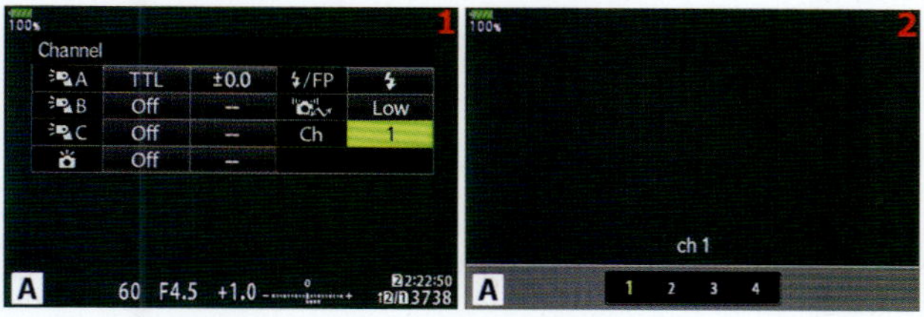

Figure 4.8J: Choosing a communication channel for the master and slaves

12. The master flash unit communicates with the slave units on one of four channels (ch 1–4); therefore, the master unit and each slave unit must be set to the same channel. The factory default is ch 1, so if you do not modify the channel setting, the flash system is ready to go (figure 4.8J, image 1). But if you buy a flash unit that has been changed, or if another photographer is working nearby, you may need to change the channel. You can choose from ch 1 to ch 4 and then press the OK button (figure 4.8J, image 2). I left the camera (master flash) set to ch 1 and I'll need to set the sample FL-600R slave unit to the same channel for each bank, which we will do in the next few steps. (***Note:*** Steps 13–15 will vary with different Olympus and aftermarket flash units.)

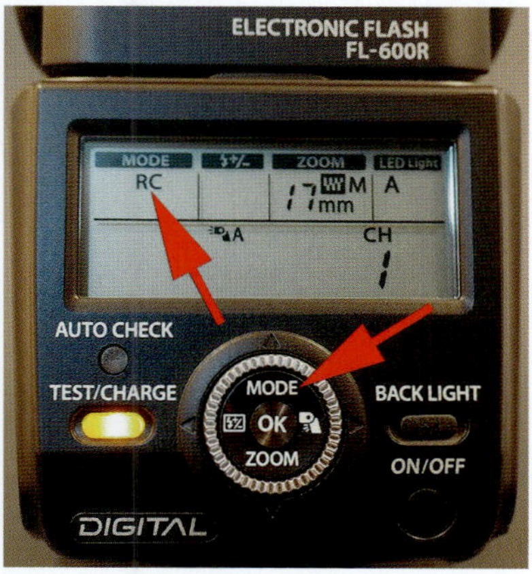

Figure 4.8K: Preparing an Olympus FL-600R flash unit for slave control

13. In this step we will prepare an Olympus FL-600R flash unit to use the correct bank and channel so it can receive communications from the preflash of the FL-LM3 flash unit. First we must set the flash unit to RC mode (figure 4.8K, top arrow). Turn the flash unit on and press the silver ring above MODE (figure 4.8K, bottom arrow) until you see A flashing under the MODE label on the flash unit's LCD display. Turn the silver ring two clicks clockwise until RC appears under MODE (figure 4.8K, top arrow). Press the OK

button on the flash unit to set RC mode. The accessory light on the front of the FL-600R unit will flash every few seconds to let you know it is in remote control (RC) mode and is ready to be used as a slave.

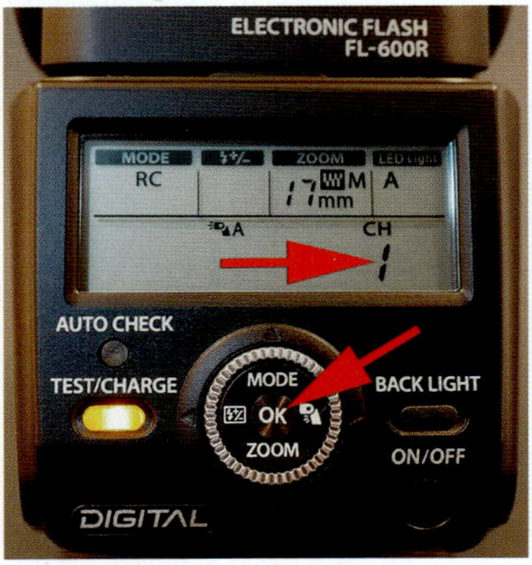

Figure 4.8L: Matching the slave unit channel to the master flash unit channel

14. Now we must match the communication channel of the slave to the channel of the master. Press the OK button on the FL-600R flash (figure 4.8L, bottom arrow) and you will see RC start flashing under the MODE label of the flash unit's LCD. Press the bottom of the silver ring below the OK button and the number under CH will start flashing on the LCD (figure 4.8L, top arrow). Turn the silver ring until the slave flash unit's channel (CH) number matches the channel you chose for the master flash unit in step 12. I left the FL-600R flash set to CH 1, which matches the master flash unit's ch 1. When you are done, press the OK button on the flash unit to set the channel.

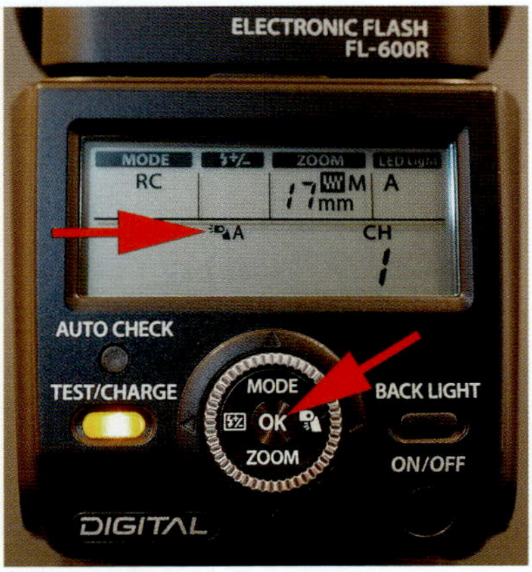

Figure 4.8M: Choosing a bank (A, B, or C) for your slave flash unit

15. The final step is to decide which bank (A, B, or C) to put the slave flash unit on. In our example, we prepared only bank A, and we left banks B and C set to Off. Therefore, we must set this FL-600R slave unit to bank A. It happens to be on bank A already (figure 4.8M, top arrow) because that is the factory default. However, let's discuss how

to change it. Press the OK button on the flash unit (figure 4.8M, bottom arrow) and RC will start flashing under the MODE label on the flash unit's LCD. Press the bottom of the silver ring to move down, then press left on the silver ring to move to the bank label. (***Note:*** If something else besides RC is flashing on the LCD, simply press down, up, left, or right on the silver ring to move to the bank location shown in figure 4.8M, top arrow.) When the bank letter is flashing, rotate the silver ring to select a different bank (A, B, or C). When you are done, press the OK button on the flash unit. Raise the small master flash, position the slave flash, and start taking pictures.

Settings Recommendation: Keep in mind that we have configured only bank A, and the camera has three banks. You could have a large number of flash units configured in different lighting positions and with different power levels, all controlled by your FL-LM3 master flash unit. That tiny flash has a lot of power. It can control a virtually unlimited number of external flash units that are placed at a reasonable distance from the camera. It is quite a creative lighting system, isn't it?

Super FP Sync Mode

The E-M1II has an additional mode that lets it exceed the normal flash sync speed of 1/250 second. It is called Super FP (focal plane) sync mode. Normally, both the front and rear shutter curtains must be out of the way before the flash fires. Super FP sync mode lets you use shutter speeds all the way up to 1/8000 second. At these speeds, the rear shutter curtain follows the front shutter curtain so closely that only a traveling narrow, horizontal slit exposes the sensor at any given time.

When you select a sync speed faster than 1/250 second, the camera fires the flash in a series of short pulses instead of one big flash. The pulses fire as the narrow shutter curtain slit moves across the face of the sensor. The faster the shutter speed, the less power the flash can manage. You must be able to depend on ambient light in addition to flash when you use Super FP sync mode, especially at higher shutter speeds. However, this lets you use faster lenses (e.g., f/1.4, f/2.8) wide open in bright light, due to the very fast shutter speed. You can expose properly with a very shallow depth of field, even though the light is very bright.

Author's Conclusions

Have you ever seen so many functions in one camera? I have never seen a camera with so many configuration possibilities. The advantage is that all of these functions let you do almost any type of photography you can think of. And all of this power is packed into such a diminutive camera. Do you like your E-M1II as much as I like mine?

The next chapter discusses the seven primary video functions used to control the powerful video recording capability built into your camera. Let's make some movies!

05 Recording Movies, Video Menu, and My Clips

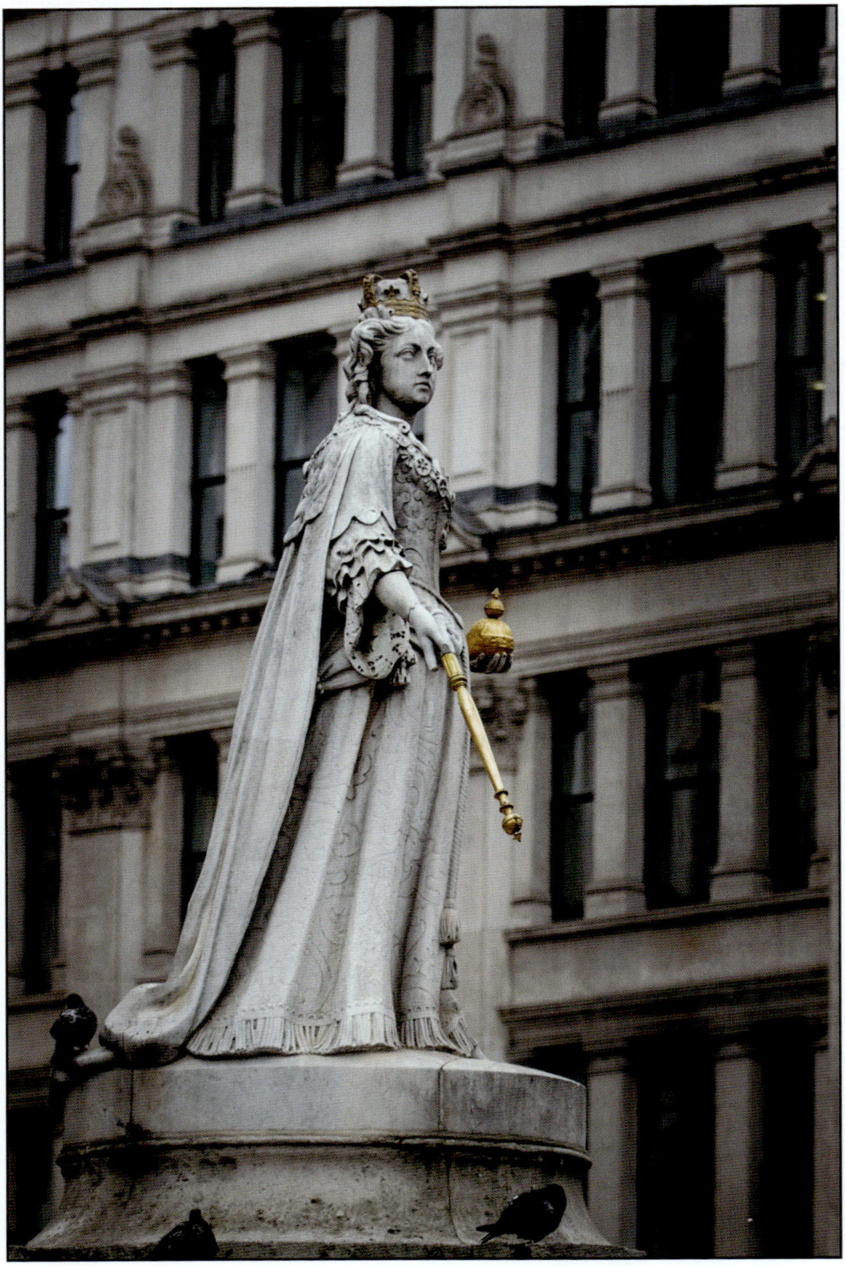

Image © Alan Hess

Compared to its predecessors, the Olympus OM-D E-M1 Mark II has significant video capture advancements. In addition to Motion JPEG, the E-M1II also offers High Definition (HD; 720p), Full HD (1080p), 4K Ultra HD (2160p with a 16:9 ratio), and Cinematic 4K (C4K; 2160p with a 17:9 ratio). The image stabilization built into the camera makes it easy to capture high-quality, very stable video—even when you're walking—with no extra stabilization equipment.

This chapter is divided into three sections:

- **Part 1:** A reference for choosing the best video formats along with initial camera setup information for capturing video.
- **Part 2:** An in-depth reference for the seven specific Video Menu functions you will use to configure the camera for advanced video capture.
- **Part 3:** A look at the E-M1II's My Clips system, through which short video clips (1 to 8 seconds each) and still images can be combined in-camera into a movie up to 15 minutes in length.

Now let's examine the various functions that allow you to configure your camera for superior video capture.

PART 1: Basic Video Recording Information

Let's start by discussing some of the video formatting information you will need to know. Then we'll examine how to make videos without a lot of camera configuration by using the video setting on the Mode Dial.

Technical Video Format Information

The E-M1II offers a series of video settings that allow you to make movies up to 29 minutes long or 4 GB in size, per segment. Or you can send a clean, uncompressed (4:2:2), 8-bit video stream through the HDMI port to an external video recorder (see Atomos.com). When you use an external recorder, the recording time and file size of the video are limited only by the storage size of the external recorder.

As previously mentioned, the camera has five video Record Modes: Motion JPEG, HD, Full HD, Ultra HD, Cinematic 4K. For in-camera recording to a memory card, the E-M1II uses one of two selectable compressed-video formats: H.264 MPEG-4 AVC or Motion JPEG.

The standard 16:9 aspect ratio is used by the Motion JPEG, HD, Full HD, and 4K recording formats. This aspect ratio matches today's computer monitors, some smart devices, and most HDTVs.

C4K uses the 17:9 aspect ratio, which matches the widescreen aspect ratio used by digital cinema cameras and projectors. The C4K 17:9 ratio is a standard format of the Digital

Cinema Initiatives specification—a joint venture by Disney, Fox, Paramount, Sony Pictures Entertainment, Universal, and Warner Bros. Studios.

For most of the Record Modes, there are variable frame and bit rates. Frame rates can vary from 24 to 60 frames per second using the progressive (p) recording method (24p to 60p). Bit rates can vary from 10 Mbps (megabits per second) to 237 Mbps. The bit rates have the following names: All-Intra (A-I), SuperFine (SF), Fine (F), and Normal (N). Olympus does not provide information on the Bit Rate for Motion JPEG.

Note: Deeper information on these technical items will be provided in Part 2 of this chapter when we consider the actual configuration of the various Movie Record Modes (page 285). Please see table 5.1 for a quick summary of these facts.

Record Mode	Pixel Ratio/ Frame Rate	Aspect Ratio	Bit Rate for A-I, SF, F, and N	Compression, Format, and Container	Video Length/ Size
Cinematic 4K (C4K)	4096×2160 at 24p	17:9	237 Mbps	H.264, MPEG-4 AVC, MOV	29 min/4 GB
Ultra HD (4K)	3840×2160 at 24p, 25p, 30p	16:9	102 Mbps	H.264, MPEG-4 AVC, MOV	29 min/4 GB
Full HD	1920×1080 at 24p, 25p, 30p	16:9	202, 52, 30, 18 Mbps	H.264, MPEG-4 AVC, MOV	29 min/4 GB
HD	1280×720 at 24p, 25p, 30p, 50p, 60p	16:9	102, 26, 24, 10 Mbps	H.264, MPEG-4 AVC, MOV	29 min/4 GB
Motion JPEG	1280×720 at 30p	16:9	Info not available	Compressed JPEG, AVI	29 min/2 GB

Table 5.1: Technical Video Format Information

Using table 5.1 as a guide, choose the video format you will find the most useful. You have a wide range of options! Now let's discuss how to apply the options to the camera before recording video.

Seven Video Settings

There are seven video settings available under the [Video][Record Mode] section of the Super Control Panel, LV Super Control Panel, and Live Control. When you press the OK button with your subject on the monitor, the Super Control Panel, LV Super Control Panel, or Live Control will appear—according to how you configured your camera in chapter 2.

You can switch between the LV Super Control Panel and the Live Control by pressing the INFO button, and you can access the Super Control Panel by pressing the LV button to the left of the viewfinder eyepiece. Since the Super Control Panel and LV Super Control Panel are almost identical, we will use the LV Super Control Panel as our example (figure 5.1A). We will also examine the Live Control (figure 5.1B).

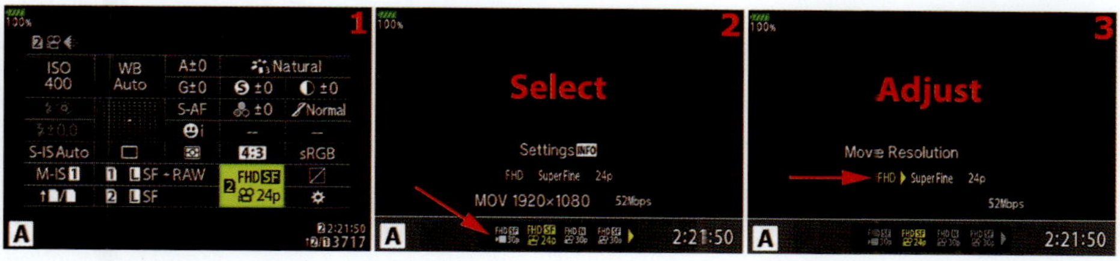

Figure 5.1A: Seven video settings on the Super Control Panel or LV Super Control Panel

Use these steps to select and adjust a video setting via the LV Super Control Panel or Super Control Panel:

1. Press the OK button to open the LV Super Control Panel (or Super Control Panel). Select the [Video][Record Mode] location (figure 5.1A, image 1), and then press the OK button again to enter the secondary screen.
2. On the secondary screen, scroll left or right with the Arrow Pad to highlight one of the seven video settings (figure 5.1A, image 2). This selects the video setting, making it active.
3. With a video setting highlighted, press the INFO button to open the adjustment screen, which is where you will adjust the Movie Resolution, Compression/Bit Rate, Frame Rate, and Clip Recording Time for that particular video setting (figure 5.1A, image 3). Scroll left or right with the Arrow Pad to select a subsetting, and then up or down to change its value. Press the OK button to lock in the video setting for recording a video.

Note: Clip Recording Time is adjustable only for video settings 1 and 6, and is available for when you want to capture 1–8 second My Clips videos. We will discuss how to use the My Clips feature in part 3 of this chapter (page 339).

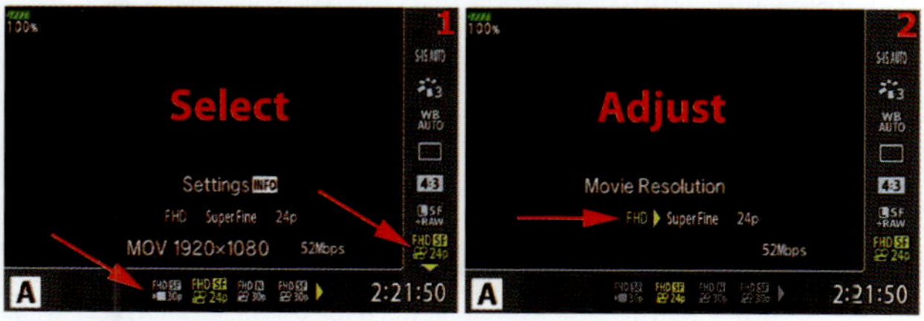

Figure 5.1B: Seven video settings on the Live Control

Use these steps to select and adjust a video setting via the Live Control:

1. Press the OK button to open the Live Control (if previously selected as the interface you wanted to use). Scroll up or down with the Arrow Pad until you highlight the [Video][Record Mode] setting on the right side of the screen (figure 5.1B, image 1, right arrow). Then scroll left or right with the Arrow Pad to select one of the seven video settings (left arrow). When a mode is highlighted, it is selected.

2. Press the INFO button when the Live Control screen is active to access the subsettings for the currently selected video setting (figure 5.1B, image 2). You will use screen 2 to adjust the Movie Resolution, Compression/Bit Rate, Frame Rate, and Clip Recording Time for the selected video setting. Scroll left or right to select a subsetting, and then up or down to change its value. Press the OK button to lock in the video setting for recording a video.

Note: You can adjust the Clip Recording Time only when using video settings 1 and 6.

Exploring the Seven Video Settings

The first of the seven video settings (from left to right) is used for shooting short My Clips videos, which range from 1 to 8 seconds in length. These clips can later be combined with pictures into a movie up to 15-minutes long. The Clip Recording Time subsetting is available for this video setting. With this setting you can record HD, Full HD, and 4K UHD video (table 5.1).

Video settings two through five are designed to allow you to set up four different video formats so that you can switch between them quickly when you need different styles of video. Basically, settings two through five are repetitions of the same setting that you can configure differently. There is no Clip Recording Time for these four settings. With these four settings you can record HD, Full HD, and 4K UHD video.

Video setting six is a Custom video setting that allows you to configure all aspects of video capture in one place. You can adjust Movie Resolution, Compression/Bit Rate, Frame Rate, Clip Recording Time, and Slow or Fast Motion. Slow or Fast Motion rates will vary according to the base Frame Rate (e.g., 24p, 30p). Some Frame Rates (e.g., 60p) will not allow Slow or Fast Motion. Any Slow or Fast Motion value below x1.0 (e.g., x0.5) is slow motion. Any value above x1.0 (e.g., x1.2) is fast motion.

Video setting seven, Motion JPEG, is a high-quality video mode with very large file sizes. Each video frame is a small JPEG file. There are no adjustments for a Motion JPEG video. Some individuals who like to do a lot of video post-processing like to use Motion JPEG because each video frame can be post-processed so easily. Each frame of a Motion JPEG video uses regular JPEG compression instead of the H.264 B-frame compression used by the other six video settings. However, with Motion JPEG you are limited to 720p video and the file sizes are larger than most people will want to deal with. If you experiment with this video mode, you may want to limit yourself to short videos (or use large memory cards).

Note: You can also adjust Movie Resolution, Compression/Bit Rate, Frame Rate, Clip Recording Time, and Slow or Fast Motion from *Video Menu > [Video] Specification Settings > [Video][Record Mode],* by scrolling to the right on each Record Mode and using the provided controls (page 285).

Recording Videos

The E-M1II provides a relatively simple interface for capturing video. Using the knowledge of video settings and formatting you've gained from the previous subsection, let's examine the steps used to prepare your E-M1II for recording videos. Once you have seen an initial configuration you will be prepared to use your camera effectively.

First-Time Configuration for Video Capture

We will now proceed, step-by-step, through a configuration of the camera for high-quality video capture. You could pick up the camera at any time, put it in iAUTO mode on the Mode dial, and press the Movie Button to record your movie. However, that is equivalent to using a point-and-shoot camera to take still pictures. While there are appropriate times to use a point-and-shoot for both still images and video capture, I suspect that you are more interested in learning how to use the camera for superior-quality video capture. Therefore, let's consider each part of the configuration process, using all of the features provided by Olympus.

To start capturing video, use the following steps:

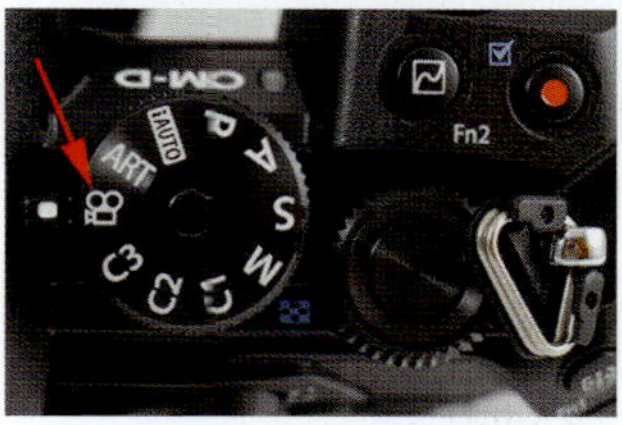

Figure 5.1C: Use Movie Mode for full control of the video capture process

1. Set the camera to Movie Mode on the Mode Dial (figure 5.1C). In this mode, the camera offers on-the-fly exposure control through a touch-based Silent Shooting Menu, which we will consider in an upcoming subsection. You cannot fully adjust the aperture, shutter speed, and ISO *during* a video recording unless you use the Silent Shooting Menu. (***Note:*** You can record videos without setting the Mode Dial to Movie Mode; however, the aperture, shutter speed, and ISO will need to be set before the video recording starts and cannot be changed during the recording.) Also, by using the Movie Mode setting, you enable the use of several special effects that can be applied to the video during capture. We will discuss the special effects in an upcoming subsection.

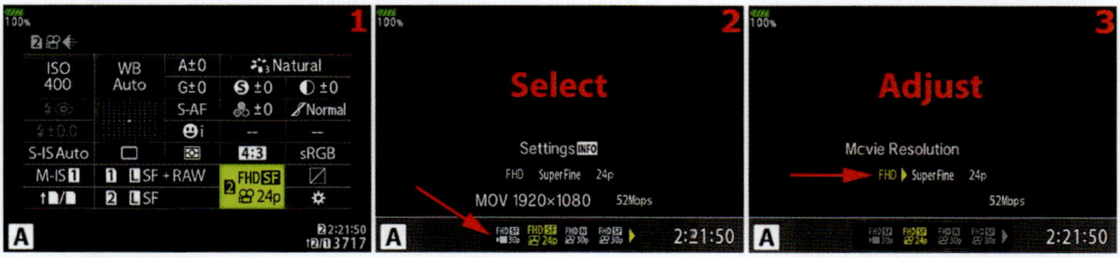

Figure 5.1D: Selecting a video mode and adjusting its subsettings

2. As discussed in the previous **Seven Video Settings** subsection (page 252), use the Super Control Panel, LV Super Control Panel, or Live Control to choose a video setting for recording (figure 5.1D). In this example, we'll use the LV Super Control Panel. To recap:
   a. Choose [Movie][Record Mode] from the screen (figure 5.1D, image 1), and press the OK button to open the secondary screen.
   b. Scroll left or right with the Arrow Pad to select one of the seven video settings (figure 5.1D, image 2). When the setting you want to use is highlighted, press the INFO button on the back of the camera.
   c. Scroll left or right to select a subsetting—Movie Resolution, Compression/Bit Rate, and Frame Rate—and then scroll up or down to adjust the subsetting (figure 5.1D, image 3). Refer to table 5.1 for information about each subsetting (page 250). Press the OK button to lock in the video setting.

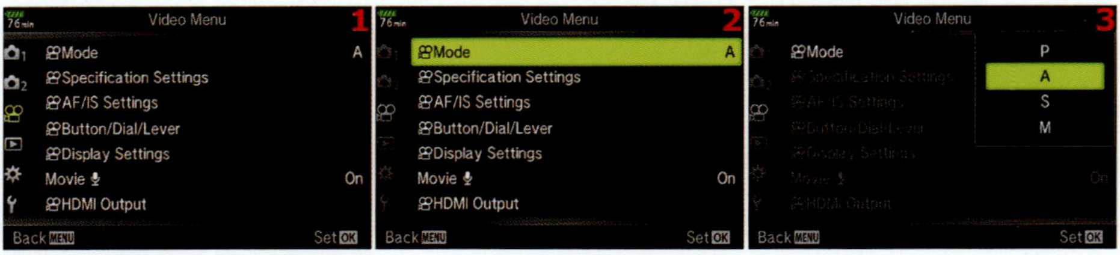

Figure 5.1E: Choosing an exposure mode while using Movie Mode on the Mode Dial

3. Press the Menu button on the back panel of the camera and scroll down to the Video Menu (figure 5.1E, image 1). Scroll to the right to select functions from the menu.
4. Highlight [Movie] Mode and scroll to the right (figure 5.1E, image 2).
5. Select an exposure mode type (P, A, S, or M) from the popup menu (figure 5.1E, image 3). Your choices are Program mode (P), Aperture-priority mode (A), Shutter-priority mode (S), and Manual mode (M). The P mode lets the camera control the aperture, shutter speed, and ISO sensitivity. The A mode lets you control the aperture, while the camera controls the shutter speed and ISO sensitivity. The S mode lets you control the shutter speed, while the camera controls the aperture and ISO sensitivity. The M mode lets you control the aperture, shutter speed, and ISO sensitivity. We will use Aperture-priority (A) mode as our example. A full explanation of these modes is provided in the **[Movie] Mode** section on page 282. [***Note:*** You must use the touch-based Silent Shooting Menu (page 263) to manually select and adjust any aspect of the four exposure modes (P, A, S, and M).] Choose the mode you want to use from the menu shown in figure 5.1E, image 3, and press the OK button to lock in the setting.

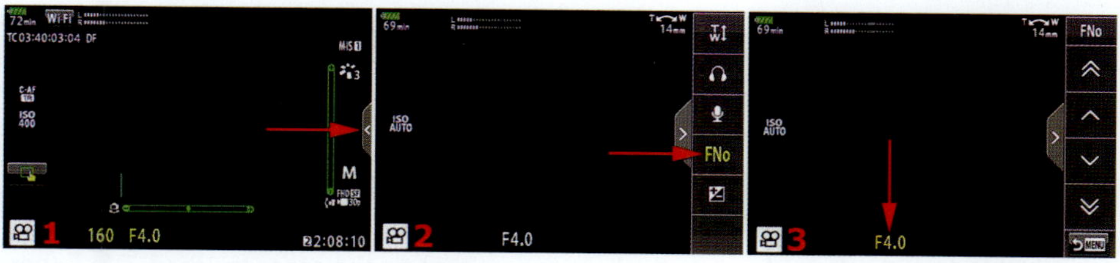

Figure 5.1F: Using the Silent Shooting Menu (page 263)

6. If the movie recording screen is not on the monitor, press the Shutter button halfway until the screen shown in figure 5.1F, image 1, is displayed (make sure the camera is in Movie Mode on the Mode Dial). Notice the small tab sticking out from the right side of the screen (image 1, red arrow). Touch that tab with your fingertip, and the Silent Shooting Menu will open on the monitor. [***Note:*** The Silent Shooting Menu is discussed in detail in the upcoming **Silent Shooting Menu** section (page 263).]
7. The Silent Shooting Menu will appear on the right side of the screen (figure 5.1F, image 2). It offers several items according to which exposure mode (P, A, S, or M) you selected previously. Note that FNo (f/number) is available on the menu because we selected Aperture-priority (A) mode in a previous step. Touch FNo (image 2, red arrow) with your fingertip and its adjustment menu will open.
8. At the bottom of the FNo adjustment screen, you can see the aperture (F4.0) displayed (figure 5.1F, image 3, red arrow). Pay careful attention to the following sentence: The aperture can be silently adjusted *before* you start recording video and *during* a video recording from the Silent Shooting Menu when you have previously selected Aperture-priority (A) mode. To adjust the aperture, touch the up or down arrow tips on the right side of the screen (image 3, under FNo). The double up/down arrow tips adjust the aperture very quickly, while the single up/down arrow tips adjust the aperture more slowly. You can use the tiny MENU touch button at the bottom of the FNo column to return to the previous screen for other adjustment types. [***Note:*** When you use the Silent Shooting Menu's touch controls to adjust the exposure modes, you will avoid any noise or vibration that would be caused by adjusting external controls. That said, when the Silent Shooting Menu is open (image 2 or 3), you can also adjust the current exposure setting by turning the noisy Front or Rear Dial, if you prefer.]

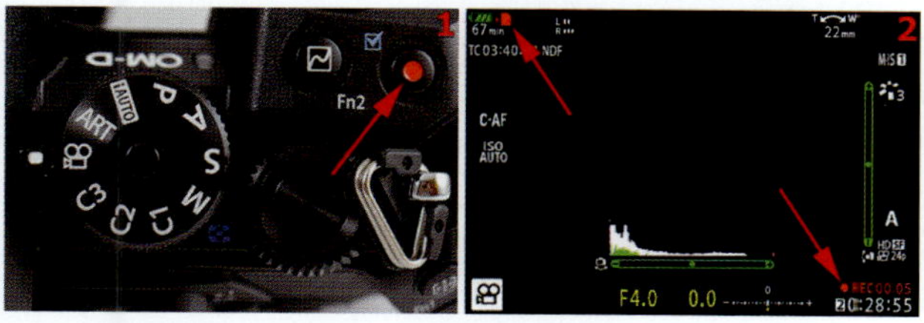

Figure 5.1G: Start recording a video

9. The camera is ready to record a video. Frame your subject and press the Movie Button (figure 5.1G, image 1) to start the recording.
10. The movie recording screen will appear (figure 5.1G, image 2). For the example, I left the lens cap on for maximum symbol contrast. Normally, the subject will appear where there is currently a black background. You will note that there are two red arrows on the screen. The top-left arrow points to the SD card activity symbol, which will blink while the video is actively being written to the memory card. The lower-right arrow points to the record (REC) symbol, followed by the time counter (00:05). The counter shows how many minutes and seconds (MM:SS) you have recorded so far. Please refer to figure 5.1H (page 257) for a description of each symbol on the movie recording screen.

Note: All video modes that start with MOV (e.g., MOV 1920 x 1080, as seen in figure 5.1D, image 2) use H.264 MPEG-4 AVC format in a MOV "container." A container is simply a file format used to contain the video, sound, and other formatting information in a single file that can be played on a playback device. You will see the container name as three letters at the end of the video file name (e.g., videoname.mov or videoname.avi).

The video mode that starts with *Motion JPEG* uses Motion JPEG format in an AVI container. Refer to table 5.1 to review the limitations of each mode.

Also, if you record a video that exceeds 4 GB in size, the camera will automatically split the movie into multiple segments of up to 4 GB each. It will automatically continue recording the next segment as soon as one 4 GB segment is complete.

Settings Recommendation: You must decide which video formats you will use most often. When this book was written, the broadcast standards for most HDTV video was still 720p, with some 1080p available (e.g., YouTube, Netflix). However, 4K is rising very rapidly, and the best videos are currently captured and viewed in 4K. If you are shooting video commercially, you will definitely want to use 4K. However, be prepared to use very large memory cards due to the extra-large file sizes that will result from shooting 4K. No less than 64 GB SD cards will do, and 128 GB or 256 GB are even better.

If you are shooting family video and have small-capacity memory cards, shooting in 720p or 1080p is perfectly fine for now. However, keep in mind that in five or ten years, your videos will appear tiny and pixelated on the latest super-high-definition display screens, even in 1080p. If you can afford to shoot 4K, do so now for your best video. This never stops, and even 8K video is on the horizon!

One thing you need to carefully experiment with when you shoot video is the Image Stabilizer. This function is configured via *Video Menu > [Video] AF/IS Settings > [Video] Image Stabilizer*. (See page 295 for more information on handheld video stabilization.) If you are shooting video while you are walking straight forward or are not waving the camera from side to side, stabilization works amazingly well to keep the image stable. But if your video requires panning from side to side, you may not want to use image stabilization. The camera will attempt to correct the panning motion until it runs out of room to adjust, and then it will make a little jump in your video. This looks strange and might even ruin the video. You will have to try it and see if the panning motion jumps are acceptable to you.

Be sure to select the destination memory card slot you want to use for saving video files by adjusting the *Custom Menu > H1. Record/Erase > Card Slot Settings > [Video] Save Slot* function (page 552).

Exploring the Movie Recording Screen

The movie recording screen (seen previously in figure 5.1G, image 2) has 21 main symbols and a few others that may occasionally appear. Let's examine the screen's primary symbols so that you will recognize them during use.

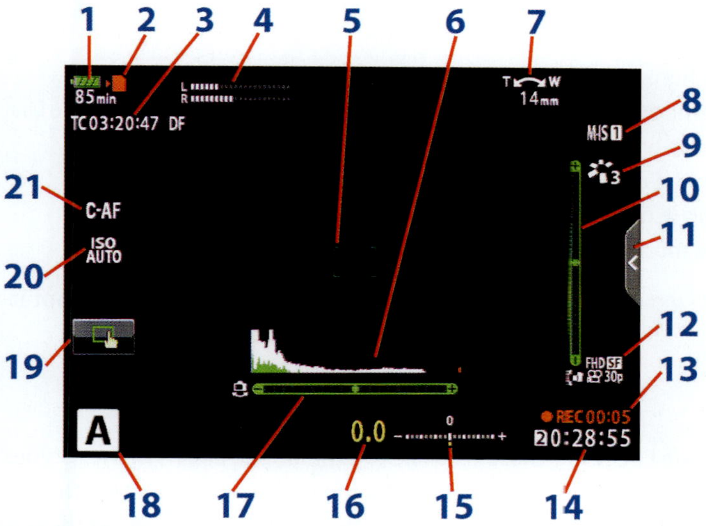

Figure 5.1H: Movie recording screen symbols

Following is an explanation for each of the symbols on the movie recording screen (figure 5.1H):

1. Battery time capacity (how long the battery will last while recording; e.g., 85 mins).
2. Card access is active. This red card symbol will blink while the video is being recorded and written to the memory card.
3. Time Code: a clock that counts in video frames. This feature allows professional videographers—who often record video and sound on separate devices—to synchronize the sound and video from different recording devices very precisely during video post-processing.
4. Left (L) and right (R) stereo mic input levels.
5. Current focus point location.
6. Live histogram display.

7. Current lens angle of view, which can be adjusted on the fly to telephoto (T) or wide-angle (W).
8. Video stabilization mode (page 258).
9. Picture Mode (page 151).
10. Vertical artificial horizon (green when level).
11. Silent Shooting Menu (provides several touch-screen video functions).
12. Current video mode settings.
13. Current recording time, in minutes and seconds (MM:SS).
14. Number of hours, minutes, and seconds (H:MM:SS) available on the memory card in the selected card slot (1 or 2). The card slot in use (2) is displayed in a tiny SD card symbol at the beginning of the time counter, just before the hour value.
15. Exposure compensation –/+ indicator in 1/3 EV steps.
16. Exposure compensation in digital format (e.g., 1.0).
17. Horizontal virtual horizon (green when level).
18. Current exposure mode (P, A, S, M), or video special effects mode when the Mode Dial is set to Movie Mode (video camera symbol).
19. Video touchscreen on and off control.
20. Current ISO setting (e.g., ISO 400, AUTO).
21. Current autofocus mode (e.g., S-AF, C-AF, MF).

Now let's consider a few more interesting functions you may want to use when capturing video.

Movie Effects

The E-M1II has five Movie Effects for those who like to experiment. Effects of these types are normally applied during video post-processing (grading) on your computer, after the video has already been recorded. However, for those who simply want to have a little fun, you might want to experiment with adding some special effects during a video recording. Here is a description of each effect, followed by an explanation of how to select them.

Five Movie Effect Descriptions

A. ***Apply Art Filter*** (Picture Mode): This effect lets you select one of the Art Filters (or any other Picture Mode) on the fly, and the effects of that filter are applied to the video immediately. This effect can be combined with any of the other effects.

B. ***Art Fade*** and ***Old Film*** (combined effect): This adds an interesting vignetting (fading) effect, along with simulated damage (scratches) and dust, to scenes and transitions. When turned on, this effect stays on until disabled. It can be used with the Apply Art Filter and Movie Tele-converter effects, but not with the Multi Echo or One Shot Echo effects.

C. ***Multi Echo:*** This effect applies after-images. If you are videoing a moving object, this will add a trail behind the object as it moves along. It "echos" the current image continuously in a blurry stream behind the movement. When turned on, this effect stays on until disabled. It can be used with the Apply Art Filter and Movie Tele-converter effects, but not with the Art Fade and Old Film or One Shot Echo effects.

D. ***One Shot Echo:*** This effect is similar in scope to the Multi Echo effect, except that it applies only one after-image and then turns off. Your subject will be briefly duplicated in a transparent sort of way and then return to normal. This effect can be used with the Apply Art Filter and Movie Tele-converter effects, but not with the Art Fade and Old Film or Multi Echo effects.

E. ***Movie Tele-converter:*** This effect allows you to temporarily crop the image (zoom in) so that the subject is greatly enlarged, with a loss of some image quality. This is done digitally without changing the focal length of the lens. In other words, the effect is a digital crop that lets you silently zoom in very quickly. The camera stays zoomed in until you zoom back out. This effect can be executed while any of the other effects are active.

Now let's examine how to select and use each of the effects.

Enabling Movie Effect

Before you can use the five Movie Effects in the previous list (A–E), you must enable Movie Effect in the Video Menu. Let's see how.

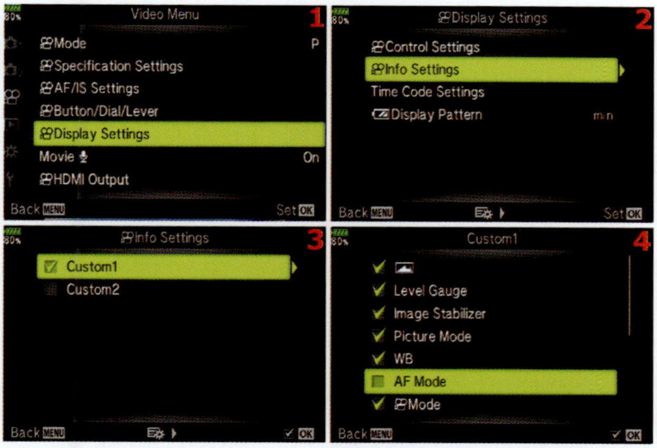

Figure 5.2A: Enabling Movie Effects

To enable Movie Effects, use the following steps:

1. Select [Movie] Display Settings from the Video Menu and scroll to the right (figure 5.2A, image 1).
2. Choose [Movie] Info Settings from the [Movie] Display Settings menu and scroll to the right (figure 5.2A, image 2).
3. Highlight Custom1 on the [Movie] Info Settings menu and scroll to the right (figure 5.2A, image 3).

4. At the bottom of the list of Custom1 choices, you will find Movie Effect, with no check mark in its box. Place a check mark in the box by highlighting Movie Effect and pressing the OK button. Once the check mark is in the box, lightly touch the Shutter button (half press) to exit the screen. Movie Effect is now enabled.

Selecting a Movie Effect

Once you have enabled Movie Effect in the Video Menu and have placed the camera in Movie Mode (video camera icon) on the Mode Dial, the movie recording screen we discussed previously (figure 5.1H) adds five small touch controls at the bottom of the screen (figure 5.2B, image 2, A–E). Each touch control allows you to turn an effect on or off. Let's see how they work!

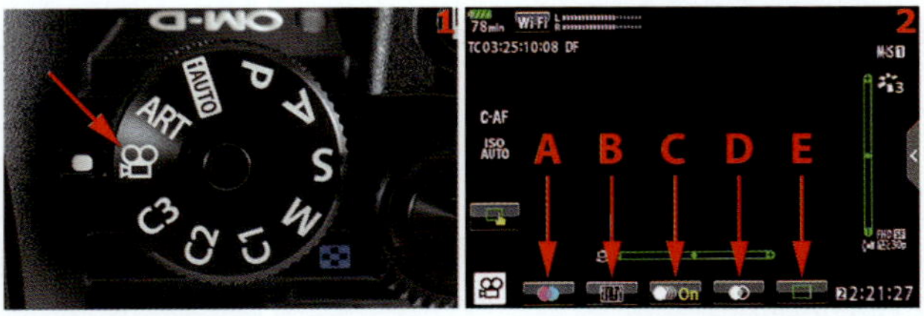

Figure 5.2B: Enabling Movie Mode and the Movie Effect touch controls

In the next five subsections, I've lettered the touch controls to match the associated descriptions in the previous list of movie effects. Keep in mind that you can use the touch controls to apply effects before and during a recording session. Let's discuss each of the touch controls and see how to use them.

Apply Art Filter (A)

The Apply Art Filter effect allows you to apply an Art Filter or change to a different Picture Mode before you start recording or while recording.

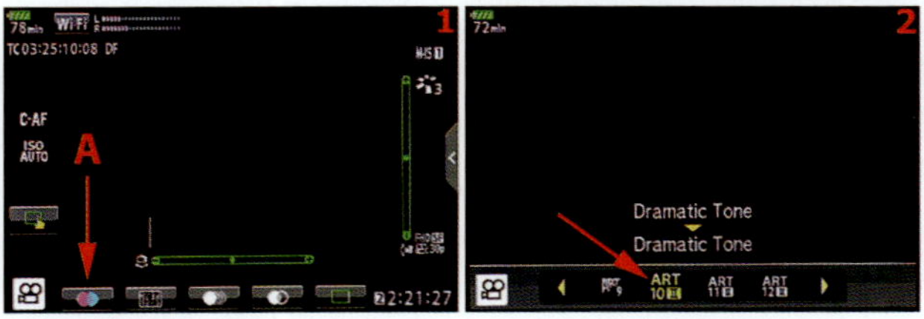

Figure 5.2C: Using the Apply Art Filter effect

Figure 5.2C, image 1, shows the Apply Art Filter (A) touch control. When you touch it the secondary screen shown in image 2 will appear. Touch the yellow left or right arrows on the bottom row until the Art Filter or Picture Mode you want to use appears. Touch the filter or mode name and the camera will immediately switch back to the video with the new filter or mode active.

Art Fade and Old Film (B)

The Art Fade and Old Film effect is fun! I wouldn't overuse it, but adding a fade-in and -out (vignette) effect along with dust and scratches can give your video an old-timey look, especially if you use Monochrome Picture Mode (black-and-white). You should try this one. Be sure to wear some out-of-date clothes!

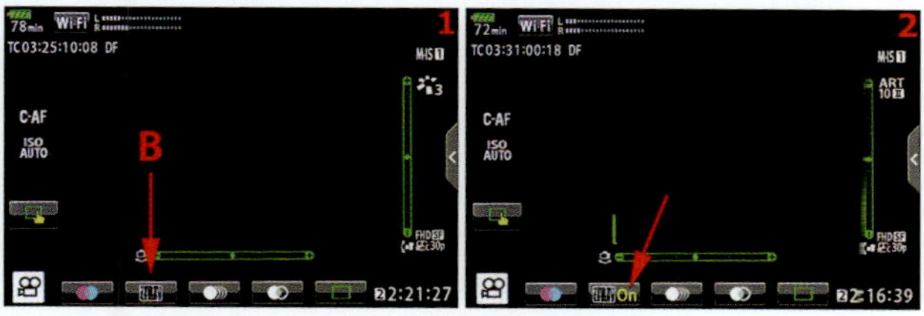

Figure 5.2D: Using the Art Fade and Old Film effect

Figure 5.2D, image 1, shows the Art Fade and Old Film (B) touch control. When you touch it the word On will appear on the right side of the touch control, as shown in image 2 (red arrow). If you are recording a video, you will see the video fade in the corners, and scratches will appear in various places. You can turn this on before you start recording the video, or you can enable it after the recording has started. Touch the control (B) again to turn it off. Have some fun with this one!

Note: The Olympus user's manual implies that Art Fade and Old Film are separate effects (page 37). Furthermore, the manual shows the touch control for Apply Art Filter as if it enables a standalone Art Fade effect, which is not correct, and the Apply Art Filter effect (previous subsection) is not even mentioned. In actuality, a single touch on touch control B (figure 5.2B, image 1) enables or disables both Art Fade and Old Film simultaneously, while a touch on touch control A enables or disables the Apply Art Filter effect. Therefore, I combined Art Fade and Old Film under touch control B in this book, according to how it actually exists in the camera. If this differs from what you see in your user's manual, Olympus may have updated the manual. My user's manual is dated 2016.9 (September 2016) on the back cover.

Multi Echo (C)

The Multi Echo effect applies to moving objects in the video frame (or the entire frame if you move the camera). This will give you a sharp view of the moving subject, with a trail (echo) of blurry after-images following the subject.

This same type of effect is often used in still photography to imply movement. However, in a video, which already has real movement, it provides a weird effect that some will appreciate and others will dismiss outright. Experiment with this effect and see if it makes you happy.

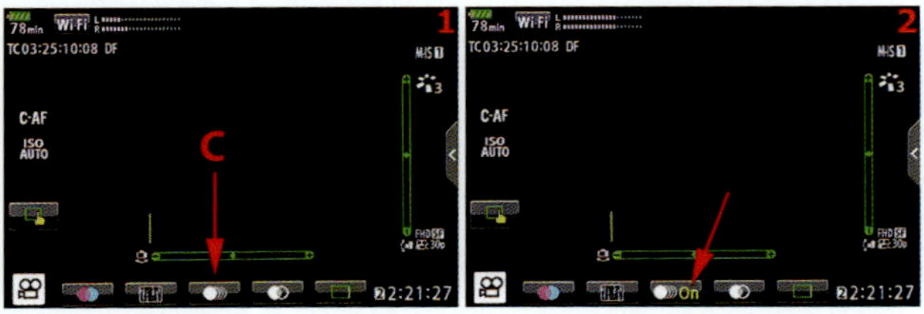

Figure 5.2E: Using the Multi Echo effect

Figure 5.2E, image 1, shows the Multi Echo (C) touch control. When you touch it the word On will appear on the right side of the touch control, as shown in image 2 (red arrow). If you are recording a video, you will see an after-image trail following any moving subjects. When using this effect, it is best to hold the camera still, allowing only the subject to move. If you move the camera, the entire frame will be blurry and filled with after-images. You can turn this on before you start recording the video, or you can enable it after the recording has started. Touch the control (C) again to turn it off.

One Shot Echo (D)

The One Shot Echo effect creates a single after-image of your subject, and then it turns off. It works like the Multi Echo effect, except there is only one echo (no after-image trail).

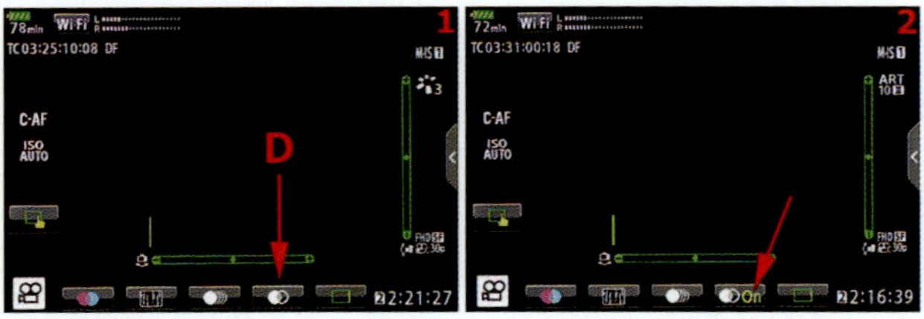

Figure 5.2F: Using the One Shot Echo effect

Figure 5.2F, image 1, shows the One Shot Echo (D) touch control. When you touch it the word On will appear briefly on the right side of the touch control, as shown in image 2 (red arrow). If you are recording a video, you will see a single after-image of any moving subject(s) for each touch of the (D) control. This effect is designed to be used when needed and lasts for only one echoed frame; then it disables itself. Use repeatedly as needed.

Movie Tele-Converter (E)

The Movie Tele-converter effect provides you with a digital zoom that will crop the video into a small, framed area that can be moved around with the Arrow Pad before zooming in.

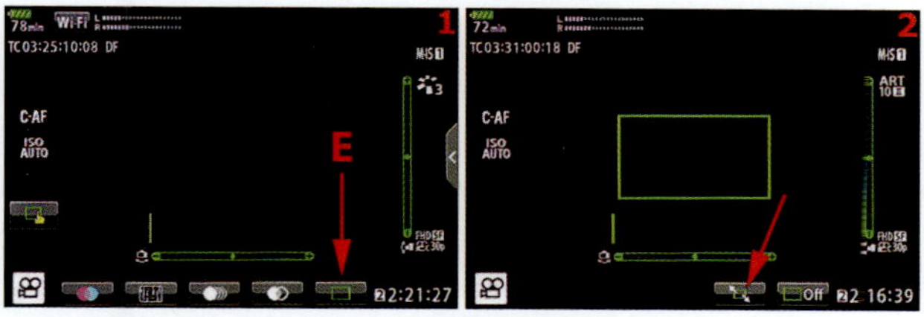

Figure 5.2G: Using the Movie Tele-converter effect

Figure 5.2G, image 1, shows the Movie Tele-converter (E) touch control. When you touch it, the available touch controls will change, as shown in image 2 (red arrow). All of the touch controls for the other effects will disappear and a small zoom-in-and-out control (image 2, red arrow) will appear to the left of the (E) touch control. The word Off will also appear on the (E) touch control.

The green rectangle in the middle of the screen in image 2 outlines the area that will be visible when you touch the zoom-in-and-out touch control. Touch the control repeatedly to zoom in and out. You can use the Arrow Pad to move the green crop rectangle to a different area in the frame before you zoom in. Touch the (E) touch control again to disable the digital Tele-converter.

Silent Shooting Menu

In addition to the Movie Effect controls (page 258) that appear only when you set the Mode Dial to Movie Mode (small video camera icon), the camera also has a touch control menu that is always available on the right side of the movie recording screen (figure 5.3A). The touch-based Silent Shooting Menu varies its settings depending on whether the camera is set to Movie Mode on the Mode Dial or not. It provides seven functions that affect how you record video. Six of the functions are available when you are using Movie Mode and four are available outside of Movie Mode. Following is a list of the seven functions.

Touch Menu for Video Recording

A. ***Telephoto/Wide-angle (T/W):*** Allows you to use touch controls on the movie recording screen to control the focal length of any mounted Olympus "Digital" lens that can be electronically zoomed (e.g., M.Zuiko ED 14–42mm F3.5–5.6 EZ pancake-style, compact lens). This function is available both when using Movie Mode and when not.

B. ***Headphone Volume:*** Provides touch controls on the movie recording screen to control the headphone volume. This function is available both when using Movie Mode and when not.

C. ***Microphone Volume:*** Provides touch controls on the movie recording screen to control the microphone volume. This function is available both when using Movie Mode and when not.

D. ***Shutter Speed (SS):*** Allows you to adjust the shutter speed of the camera before or during a video recording. This function is available only when using Movie Mode on the Mode Dial, with *Video Menu > [Movie] Mode* set to Shutter-priority (S) mode or Manual (M) mode.

E. ***Aperture (FNo):*** Allows you to adjust the aperture before or during a video recording. This function is available only when using Movie Mode on the Mode Dial, with *Video Menu > [Movie] Mode* set to Aperture-priority (A) mode or Manual (M) mode.

F. ***ISO:*** Allows you to change the light sensitivity of the camera's imaging sensor before or during a video recording. This function is available only when using Movie Mode on the Mode Dial, with *Video Menu > [Movie] Mode* set to Manual (M) mode.

G. ***Exposure Compensation (–/+):*** Allows you to directly and visually change the exposure compensation, adding (+) or subtracting (–) exposure, by using touch controls on the movie recording screen. This function is available both when using Movie Mode and when not, when *Video Menu > [Movie] Mode* is not set to Manual (M) mode. There is not enough room on the Silent Shooting Menu screen for seven items, so the camera drops the Exposure Compensation (–/+) setting. Therefore, you won't find this setting when you select Manual (M) for the exposure mode.

Now let's examine the Silent Shooting Menu, which lives under a small tab on the right side of the movie recording screen (figure 5.3A, image 1).

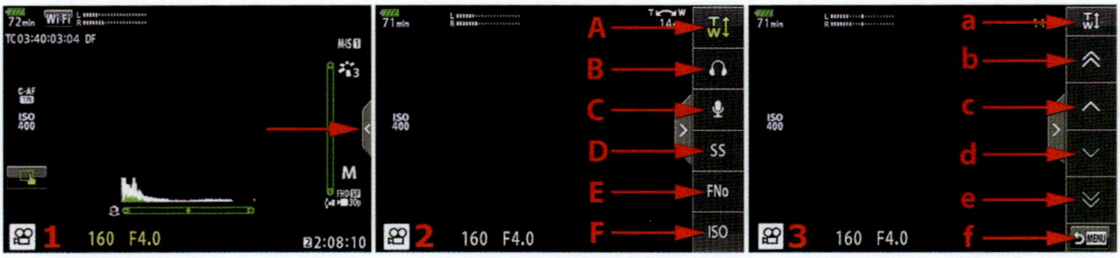

Figure 5.3A: Using the Silent Shooting Menu for video

Use the following steps to adjust items on the Silent Shooting Menu:

1. Touch the tab on the right side of the movie recording screen (figure 5.3A, image 1, red arrow) to open the Silent Shooting Menu and access the functions we discussed in our previous list.
2. Figure 5.3A, image 2, shows the Silent Shooting Menu that opens on the right side of the screen. Notice that it has several symbols, which I've labeled with arrows and

letters that match six of the items in the previous list (A–F). The top item on the menu is the (A) Telephoto/Wide Angle (T/W) setting. The five symbols below the T/W symbol are (B) Headphone Volume, (C) Microphone Volume, (D) Shutter Speed, (E) Aperture, and (F) ISO sensitivity. [***Note:*** (G) Exposure Compensation –/+ is not shown because it is not available when Manual (M) exposure mode is selected. Olympus allocated only six spots on the Silent Shooting Menu.] These items will vary according to the exposure mode you have selected in *Video Menu > [Movie] Mode* (P, A, S, M). We'll use the T/W menu item as our sample initially, but we will consider each potential menu item in more detail in the next seven subsections. Touch the menu item you want to adjust and the next screen will open.

3. The adjustment screen is similar for all seven of the menu functions (figure 5.3A, image 3). The symbol of the currently selected menu item (a) is displayed at the top of the adjustment bar that runs up and down the right side of the screen. The next four symbols that look like arrow tips (b–e) are up and down symbols that allow you to adjust the current function. The double-arrow symbols (b and e) adjust the setting quickly, while the single-arrow symbols (c and d) adjust the setting slowly. At the very bottom of the adjustment bar is a small touch control labeled Menu (f). If you touch the Menu control the camera will return to the previous screen (figure 5.3A, image 2) so that you can select a different menu item to adjust [A, B, C, D, E, F, or G (see list in previous subsection)].

Now let's examine each menu item individually.

Telephoto/Wide-Angle (T/W)

The T/W function allows you to zoom in and out with any lens that allows electronic zooming. You will not have to physically touch the lens to make it zoom in and out; instead, you will change the focal length of the lens electronically by using touch controls on the monitor (figure 5.3B). Zooming electronically is much less likely to shake the camera, although with some lenses, it could introduce a little noise.

If you have an electronic-zoom lens, experiment with the T/W function to see how it works. Normal, non-electronic-zoom lenses will not activate the T/W function and it will remain grayed out and unavailable on the menu.

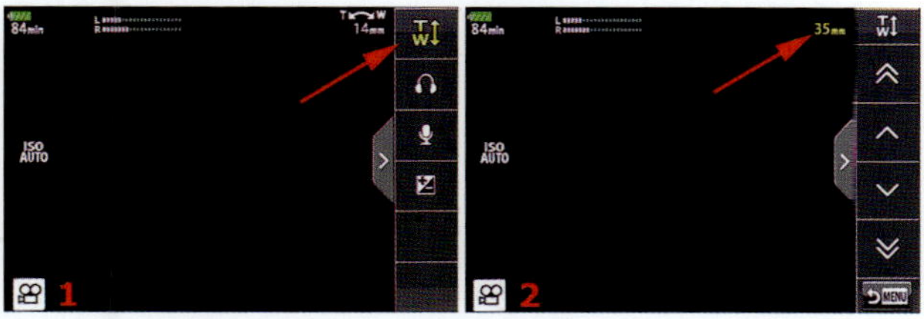

Figure 5.3B: Zooming in and out with an electronic-zoom lens

Use the following steps to zoom in and out electronically with the touch controls:

1. Touch the little tab shown in figure 5.3A, image 1, and the screen shown in figure 5.3B, image 1, will open. Select the T/W menu item by touching it, and the T/W control screen will open.
2. Figure 5.3B, image 2, shows the T/W control screen. Touch the upward double-arrow symbol to rapidly zoom toward the telephoto focal-length range. If you want to zoom more slowly, use the upward single-arrow instead. The downward double-arrow causes the camera to quickly zoom toward a wide-angle focal-length setting, while the downward single-arrow makes it zoom more slowly. The zoom values can be adjusted according to the widest wide-angle value (e.g., 14 mm) and longest normal or telephoto value (e.g. 42 mm) of focal lengths within the current zoom lens.

Headphone Volume

The cool little E-M1II provides a headphone jack, unlike many lesser cameras (and some expensive smartphones). You can control the headphone volume with the Silent Shooting Menu (figure 5.3C).

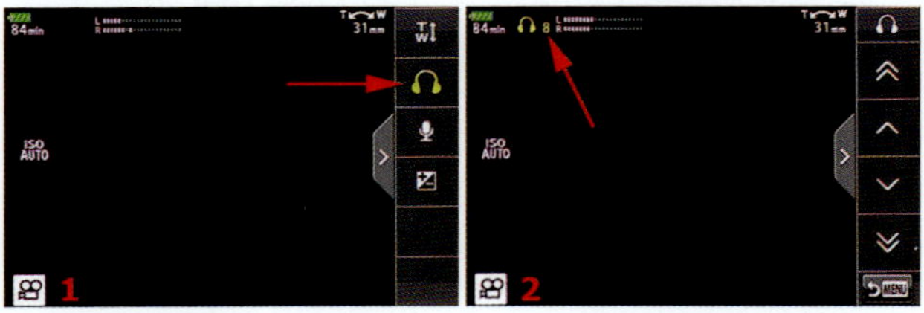

Figure 5.3C: Adjusting the headphone volume

Use the following steps to adjust the headphone volume:

1. Touch the little tab shown in figure 5.3A, image 1, and the screen shown in figure 5.3C, image 1, will open. Select the [Headphone] menu item by touching it, and the [Headphone] control screen will open.
2. Figure 5.3C, image 2, shows the [Headphone] control screen. Touch the upward double-arrow symbol to rapidly increase the volume. If you want to increase the volume more slowly, use the upward single-arrow instead. The downward double-arrow lowers the volume quickly, while the downward single-arrow lowers it more slowly. Notice the [Headphone] symbol in the top-left corner of figure 5.3C, image 2. The small number following the symbol (8) represents the headphone volume. The volume may be adjusted within a range of 1 to 16.

Microphone Volume

When you are using the camera's built-in stereo microphone, or have mounted an external microphone, you will need to control the input volume. The Silent Shooting Menu makes that easy (figure 5.3D).

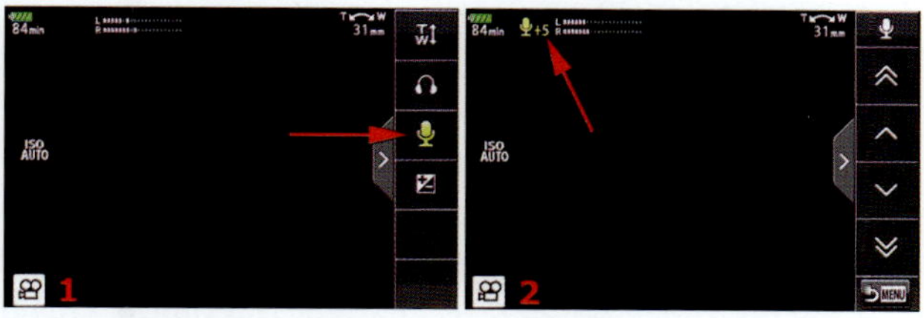

Figure 5.3D: Adjusting the microphone volume

Use the following steps to adjust the microphone volume:

1. Touch the little tab shown in figure 5.3A, image 1, and the screen shown in figure 5.3D, image 1, will open. Select the [Microphone] menu item by touching it, and the [Microphone] control screen will open.
2. Figure 5.3D, image 2, shows the [Microphone] control screen. Touch the upward double-arrow symbol to rapidly increase the input volume. If you want to increase the input volume more slowly, use the upward single-arrow instead. The downward double-arrow lowers the input volume quickly, while the downward single-arrow lowers it more slowly. Notice the [Microphone] symbol in the top-left corner of figure 5.3D, image 2. The small number following the symbol (+5) represents the microphone input volume. The input volume can be adjusted within a range of –10 to +10.

Shutter Speed (SS)

Many videographers recommend that the shutter speed be set to approximately double the video capture frames-per-second (fps) rate (Frame Rate, see table 5.1 on page 250), although it can be varied for special effects. For instance, if you are capturing video at 30 fps (e.g., 1080/30p), you should use a shutter speed of 1/60 second. Or at 24 fps you should use 1/50 second. You can change the shutter speed before or during a video recording (figure 5.3E). Let's see how to make the adjustment.

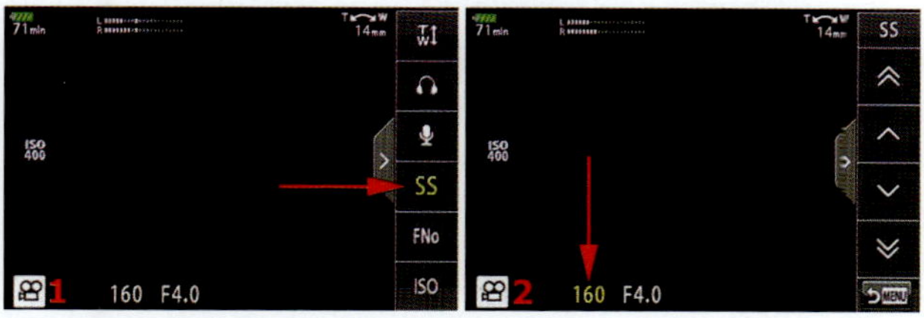

Figure 5.3E: Adjusting the shutter speed (SS) with touch controls

Use the following steps to adjust the shutter speed (SS):

1. Touch the little tab shown in figure 5.3A, image 1, and the screen shown in figure 5.3E, image 1, will open. If *Video Menu > [Movie] Mode* is set to Shutter-priority (S) mode or Manual (M) mode, the SS item will appear on the Silent Shooting Menu. Select SS by touching it, and the SS control screen will open.
2. Figure 5.3E, image 2, shows the SS control screen. Touch the upward double-arrow symbol to rapidly increase the shutter speed (make it faster). If you want to increase the shutter speed more slowly, use the upward single-arrow instead. The downward double-arrow reduces the shutter speed quickly (makes it slower), while the downward single-arrow reduces the shutter speed more slowly. Notice the shutter speed number 160 (1/160 second) at the bottom of figure 5.3E, image 2. The shutter speed may be adjusted within a range of 1/24 second (24) to 1/8000 second (8000).

Aperture (FNo)

When you're recording a video, you may wish to use a smaller aperture opening to capture a large depth of field (zone of sharpness), such as when you're videoing a beautiful scene in the mountains; or you may prefer to use a shallow depth of field to blur the background and call attention to your subject, such as when you're videoing a couple walking hand-in-hand down a path. The aperture f/number may be changed before or during a video recording (figure 5.3F). Let's examine how to adjust the aperture.

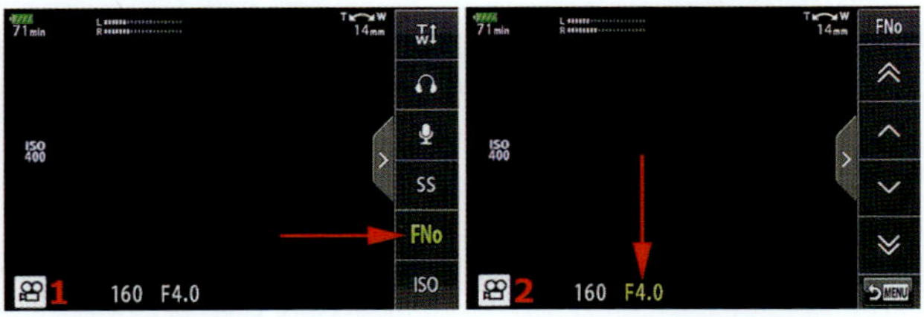

Figure 5.3F: Adjusting the aperture (FNo)

Use the following steps to adjust the aperture (FNo):

1. Touch the little tab shown in figure 5.3A, image 1, and the screen shown in figure 5.3F, image 1, will open. If *Video Menu > [Movie] Mode* is set to Aperture-priority (A) mode or Manual (M) mode, the FNo item will appear on the Silent Shooting Menu. Select FNo by touching it, and the FNo (aperture) control screen will open.
2. Figure 5.3F, image 2, shows the FNo control screen. Touch the upward double-arrow symbol to rapidly increase the aperture f/number (make the aperture opening smaller). If you want to increase (stop down) the aperture more slowly, use the upward single-arrow instead. The downward double-arrow decreases the aperture f/number quickly (making the aperture opening larger), while the downward single-arrow decreases (opens up) the aperture f/number more slowly. Notice the aperture f/number (F4.0)

at the bottom of figure 5.3F, image 2. The aperture can be adjusted within the range from the maximum aperture opening (smallest aperture f/number—e.g., F1.4, F2.8) for the current lens to the minimum aperture opening (largest aperture f/number—e.g., F16, F22) for the lens.

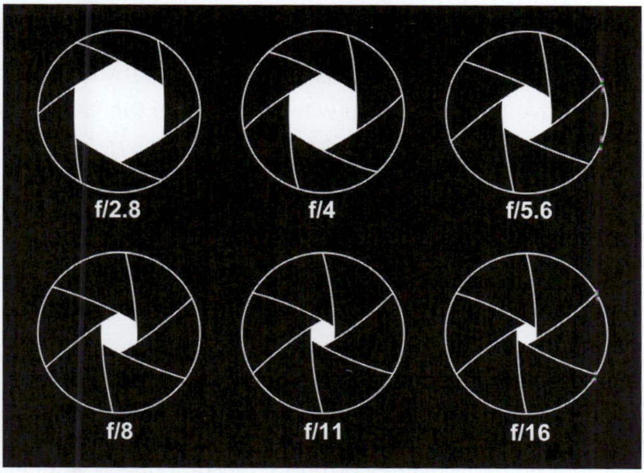

Figure 5.3G: Aperture f/numbers may seem backward

Aperture review: While examining figure 5.3G, remember that aperture f/numbers may seem backward. The smaller aperture f/number, such as f/2.8, represents the larger physical aperture opening (hole), and the larger aperture f/number, such as f/16, represents the smaller physical aperture opening.

ISO

A powerful feature of the E-M1II is that it allows you to adjust the imaging sensor's light sensitivity (ISO) on the fly. For instance, you may move from a darker area to a lighter area, in which case you would need to close the aperture somewhat to prevent overexposure. The ISO sensitivity can be changed before or during a video recording with the Silent Shooting Menu (figure 5.3H). Let's consider how to do it.

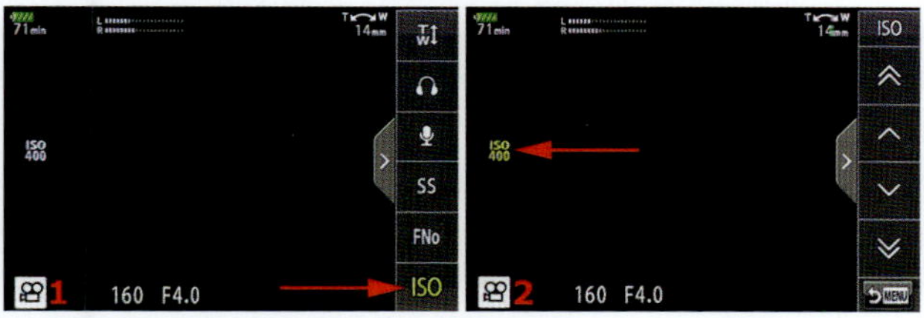

Figure 5.3H: Adjusting the ISO sensitivity

Use the following steps to adjust the ISO sensitivity:

1. Touch the little tab shown in figure 5.3A, image 1, and the screen shown in figure 5.3H, image 1, will open. If *Video Menu > [Movie] Mode* is set to Manual (M) mode, the ISO item will appear on the Silent Shooting Menu. Select ISO by touching it, and the ISO sensitivity control screen will open.
2. Figure 5.3H, image 2, shows the ISO sensitivity control screen. Touch the upward double-arrow symbol to rapidly increase the ISO sensitivity (make the Micro Four Thirds imaging sensor more sensitive to light). If you want to increase the ISO more slowly, use the upward single-arrow instead. The downward double-arrow reduces the ISO sensitivity quickly, while the downward single-arrow reduces the ISO more slowly. Notice the ISO sensitivity number (ISO 400) on the left side of figure 5.3H, image 2. The ISO sensitivity can be adjusted within a range of ISO 200 to ISO 6400.

Exposure Compensation (–/+)

The Exposure Compensation (–/+) function allows you to use touch controls to add or subtract exposure from the current video recording (figure 5.3I). Use it to brighten or darken the video as needed. You will instantly see the effects of the Exposure Compensation adjustment in the live histogram on the movie recording screen and in the appearance of the video itself.

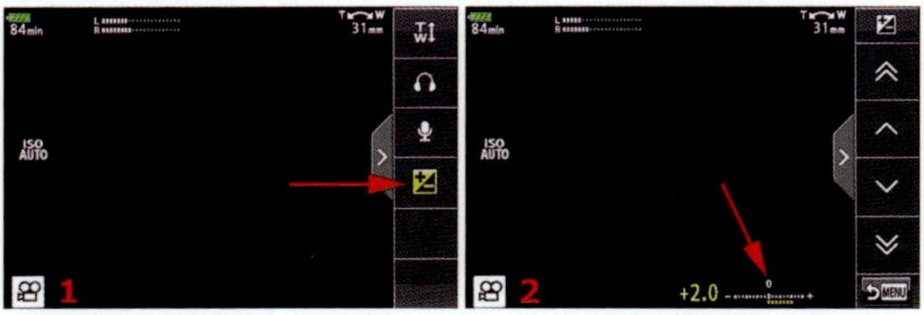

Figure 5.3I: Using exposure compensation while recording video

Use the following steps to adjust the exposure during a video recording:

1. Touch the little tab shown in figure 5.3A, image 1, and the screen shown in figure 5.3I, image 1, will open. Select the Exposure Compensation [+/–] menu item by touching it, and the [+/–] control screen will open. This item will appear on the Silent Shooting Menu only when you do *not* have the camera set to Manual (M) mode in *Video Menu > [Movie] Mode*.
2. Figure 5.3I, image 2, shows the [+/–] control screen. You can override the camera's light meter by using Exposure Compensation to add or subtract exposure. Touch the upward double-arrow symbol to rapidly increase the amount of light entering the camera (overexposure). If you want to increase the exposure more slowly, use the upward single-arrow instead. The downward double-arrow reduces the exposure quickly (underexposure), while the downward single-arrow reduces the exposure more slowly.

Notice the exposure indicator scale at the bottom of figure 5.3I, image 2, which shows that I have my camera set to 2 EV steps of overexposure. The small number to the left of the scale (+2.0) is the EV step value in numerical form. The exposure can be adjusted in 1/3 EV steps within a range of –3.0 EV to +3.0 EV.

Touch Focus and Moving the AF Point

The E-M1II provides a way to move the AF point by touching the movie recording screen. This method may help to prevent the camera shake that could occur if you were to move the AF point with the Arrow Pad while recording video.

If you have the autofocus set to S-AF (Single autofocus), you will need to refocus the camera after you move the AF point by pressing the Shutter button halfway down. However, if you have the autofocus set to C-AF (Continuous autofocus), the camera will automatically refocus on the new area you have selected. It may be a good idea to use C-AF when you are positioning the AF point by touch.

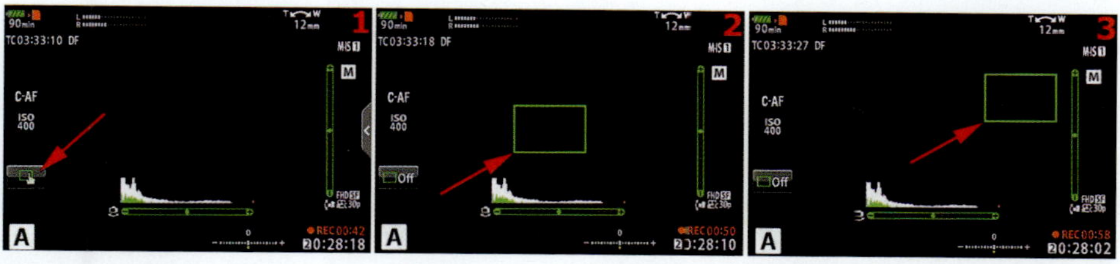

Figure 5.4: Moving the AF point by touching the movie recording screen

Use the following steps to relocate the AF point on the movie recording screen (use touch focus when using C-AF):

1. In figure 5.4, image 1, you can see the small AF touch button control on the bottom-left area of the screen (red arrow). We know that it is active because the tiny AF point rectangle in the touch button is green. If you touch this button, it will disable the AF point touch function. When the function is inactive, the symbol will change to a grayed-out circle with a slash (not shown). Make sure the function is active and proceed to the next step.
2. Now if you touch the screen while recording a video, you will see the green AF point rectangle appear (figure 5.4, image 2, red arrow). That rectangular area is where the camera gets the best focus. You can move this green focus rectangle by touching elsewhere on the movie recording screen. In figure 5.4, image 3, I simply touched the upper right area of the movie recording screen and the AF point immediately jumped to that point.

Since I captured the screenshots shown in figure 5.4 with the lens cap on, you cannot see any subject on my movie recording screens. However, your screen will show your actual subject, allowing you to touch different areas of the subject for best focus results. Again, if you do not have autofocus set to C-AF, the camera will not refocus when you move the AF point by touch. To most effectively use touch focus, I suggest enabling C-AF. You can touch the small AF touch button control to turn off the touch focus at any time, as signified by the word Off in the touch button.

Using the Movie Playback Menu

After you have recorded a few videos, there are several things you may want to do with them, such as play, trim, share, protect, copy, or erase them. The Movie Playback Menu allows you to do all of this without using a computer. Let's consider each of the items on the Movie Playback Menu.

Play Movie

You can play a video on the monitor of your E-M1II to determine its quality or simply to enjoy it immediately. The monitor is large enough for two or three people to watch the video together. Let's see how to use the Playback Menu to play a video.

Figure 5.5A: Playing a movie on the camera's monitor

Use the following steps to watch a video on the camera's monitor:

1. Scroll through the pictures and videos on the monitor until you locate the video you want to play (figure 5.5A, image 1). Press the OK button to open the Movie Playback Menu. Highlight Play Movie and press the OK button again.
2. The video will start playing immediately. While it is playing you can raise or lower the headphone (or rear speaker) volume with the up and down Arrow Pad keys (figure 5.5A, image 2, red arrow).
3. If you want to scroll backward or forward in the video, first press the OK button to pause the video, and then press the left or right Arrow Pad key to scroll backward or forward (figure 5.5A, image 3, red arrow). When the video is paused, you can press up on the Arrow Pad to jump back to the beginning of the video, or down to jump to the end.

Note: When you Play a video that has automatically been split into multiple 4 GB sections, the camera will offer you a menu with the following items:

- ***Play from Beginning:*** Plays a split movie all the way through, automatically jumping from one 4 GB segment to the following segment.
- ***Play Movie:*** Allows you to play individual 4 GB segments as standalone movies.

Movie Edit

The Movie Edit function allows you to trim a video from the beginning or the end, but not from the middle. Let's examine how to trim a movie to delete unneeded scenes from the beginning or end.

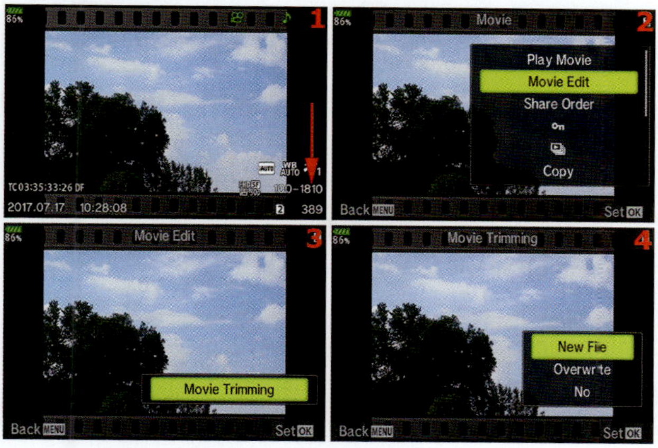

Figure 5.5B: Movie Trimming

Use the following steps to trim a movie:

1. Scroll through the pictures and videos on the camera's monitor until you locate the video you want to trim (figure 5.5B, image 1). We are working from an original, unedited video. Please note that its number is 1810 (image 1, red arrow).
2. Press the OK button to open the Movie Playback Menu (figure 5.5B, image 2). Highlight Movie Edit and press the OK button again.
3. A popup box will open with Movie Trimming already highlighted (figure 5.5B, image 3). Press the OK button to continue.
4. A menu will appear with three items: New File, Overwrite, and No (figure 5.5B, image 4). You must now make a decision about how the edited video will be written to the camera's memory card. If you choose New File, the camera will save the edited video with a new filename (e.g., 1811) and leave the original, unedited video (e.g., 1810) intact. If you select Overwrite, the E-M1II will overwrite the original, unedited video with the edited video (thereby deleting the original video). Be careful with this setting because you will lose your longer original video. Finally, if you select No, the camera will simply

return to the previous screen, with Movie Trimming highlighted (figure 5.5B, image 3). Often the best choice is New File, which allows you to keep the original, unedited video (e.g., 1810), and create a new, edited copy, too (e.g., 1811). In the next few steps we will edit (trim) the original video and save the edited copy. Select New File and press the OK button to move to the next steps (figure 5.5C).

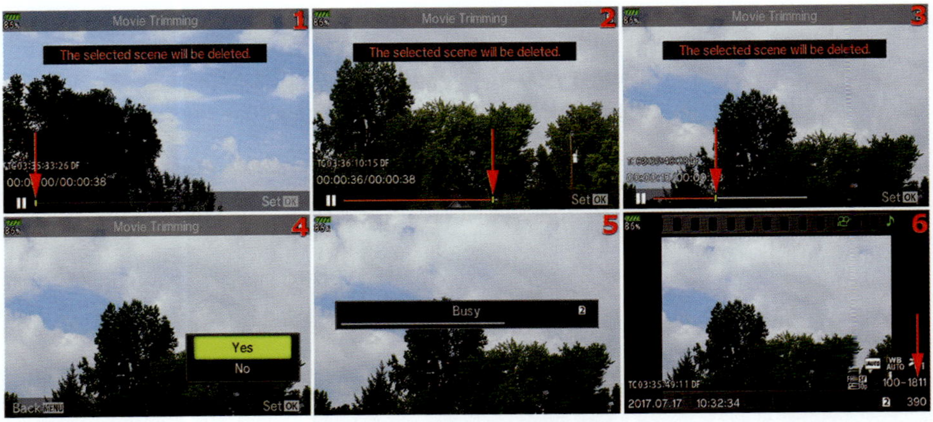

Figure 5.5C: Deleting selected frames from the beginning of the video

5. Figure 5.5C begins where figure 5.5B ends. In figure 5.5C, image 1, you can see that the yellow frame indicator is positioned at the very first frame (far left) of the video (red arrow). At this point you can choose to delete frames from the beginning of the video (figure 5.5C), or from the end of the video (figure 5.5D). Let's consider how to delete frames from the beginning of the video first, and then we will go over how to remove frames from the end. To begin the trimming process, press the OK button while the screen shown in figure 5.5C, image 1, is active. The screen displayed in figure 5.5C, image 2, will appear. Notice how the yellow frame indicator has jumped to near the end of the video. All frames represented by the area of the indicator shown in red will be deleted soon.
6. Scroll to the left with the Arrow Pad while watching the individual frames of the video scroll by on the monitor. When you reach the point at which you want to delete all previous frames, stop scrolling with the Arrow Pad. The frames represented by the red area to the left of the yellow frame indicator are now ready to be deleted (figure 5.5C, image 3). Press the OK button to start the deletion process.
7. A menu will open with a choice of Yes or No (figure 5.5C, image 4). If you choose Yes, the frames in the red area to the left of the indicator in image 3 will be deleted. Highlight No to cancel and return to the previous screen, or Yes to delete the selected frames. Press the OK button to finalize the deletion.
8. A Busy screen with a progress indicator will appear while the frames are trimmed from the beginning of the video (figure 5.5C, image 5). It will take a few seconds to delete

the selected frames and write the edited video with the new filename to the memory card (if New File was selected in figure 5.5B, image 4), or to overwrite the source video (if Overwrite was selected).

9. Since we selected New File previously, the camera has created a new file named 1811 (figure 5.5C, image 6, red arrow), leaving the source video (1810) unharmed. Now let's see how to delete frames from the end of the video (figure 5.5D).

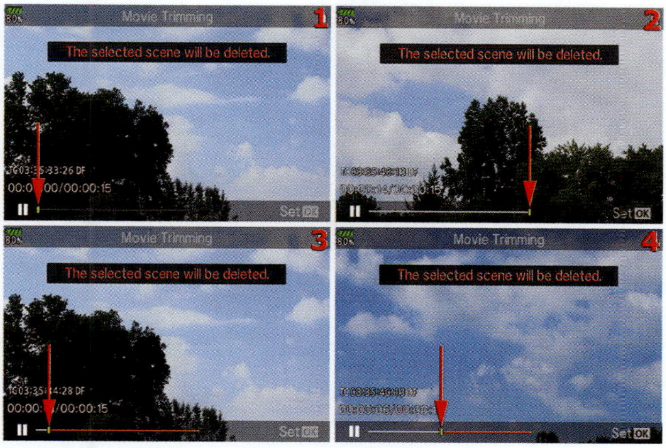

Figure 5.5D: Deleting selected frames from the end of the video

10. Figure 5.5D begins where figure 5.5B ends, and replaces the first three screens in figure 5.5C. This set of screens describes how to delete images from the end of the video, whereas figure 5.5C showed how to delete frames from the beginning of the video. Note that the yellow indicator is again at the beginning of the video (figure 5.5C, image 1, red arrow).
11. Press right on the Arrow Pad and the yellow indicator will jump to the end of the video, with no frames selected in red to the left of the indicator (figure 5.5C, image 2, red arrow).
12. Press the OK button and the yellow indicator will jump almost to the beginning of the video (figure 5.5D, image 3, red arrow). Note also that the red area has reappeared. Any frames covered by the red area to the right of the indicator will soon be deleted from the end of the video.
13. Scroll to the right with the Arrow Pad, watching as frames flow by on the monitor (figure 5.5D, image 3). When you have reached the position in the video where you want to delete all following frames, stop scrolling and press the OK button. You will again see the last three screens shown in figure 5.5C (images 4 to 6). Highlight No to cancel and return to the previous screen, or Yes to delete the selected frames. Press the OK button to finalize the deletion.

Share Order

If you want to share certain videos with your smartphone or tablet, you can create a Share Order. When you then open the Olympus OI.Share software and connect via Wi-Fi, the videos will present themselves for upload to your smart device. Let's examine how to create a Share Order.

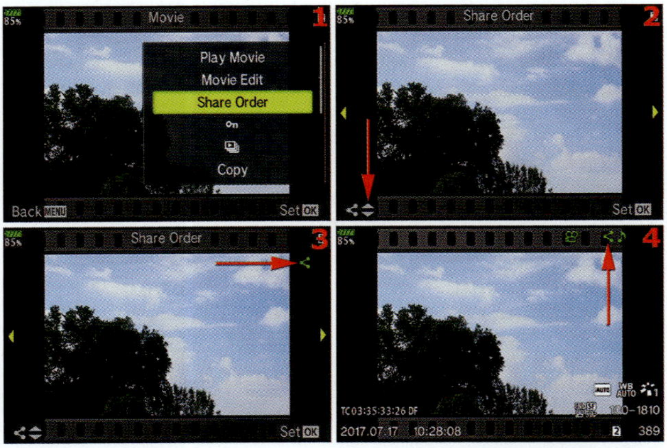

Figure 5.5E: Creating a Share Order for uploading to a smart device

Use the following steps to create a Share Order for uploading videos to Olympus OI.Share software:

1. Scroll through the pictures and videos on the camera's monitor until you locate the video you want to share. Press the OK button to open the Movie Playback Menu (figure 5.5E, image 1). Highlight Share Order and press the OK button again.
2. On the left and right sides of the screen shown in figure 5.5E, image 2, you will see yellow arrow tips informing you that you can scroll left or right to select a different video, or additional videos, to share. In the lower-left corner of the monitor you will see a share symbol along with up and down arrow tips (figure 5.5E, image 2, red arrow). You can toggle the Share Order symbol on and off by pressing up or down on the Arrow Pad.
3. Figure 5.5E, image 3, shows the green share symbol. This video is marked for sharing. You can scroll left or right to select additional videos for sharing. Press the OK button to finish creating a Share Order.
4. Any shared videos will have the share symbol displayed in the upper-right corner of the screen (figure 5.5E, image 4, red arrow). Press the Wi-Fi button displayed on the camera's monitor (not shown), and then connect the Olympus OI.Share App to the camera's Wi-Fi. The OI.Share App will report: *There is an image marked by Share Order in the camera. Import/Cancel*. Select Import, and the video(s) will appear on your smart device after a few minutes of uploading.

[Protect]

The [Protect] function allows you to protect certain videos from accidental deletion when you select *Setup menu > Card Setup > All Erase,* press the Delete button, or select Erase from the Movie Playback Menu.

Note: Protecting a video will not prevent its deletion during a card format operation (*Setup menu > Card Setup > Format*).

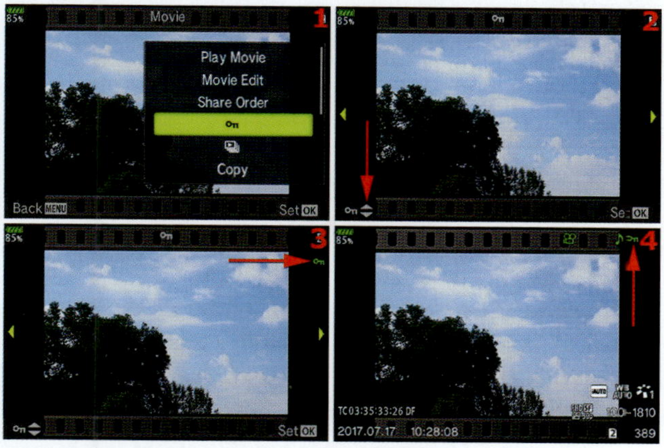

Figure 5.5F: Protecting videos from accidental deletion

Use the following steps to protect videos from accidental deletion:

1. Scroll through the pictures and videos on the camera's monitor until you locate the video you want to protect. Press the OK button to open the Movie Playback Menu (figure 5.5F, image 1). Highlight the [Protect] key symbol and press the OK button again.
2. On the left and right sides of the screen shown in figure 5.5F, image 2, you will see yellow arrow tips informing you that can may scroll left or right to select a different video, or additional videos, to protect. In the lower-left corner of the monitor you will see a [Protect] key symbol along with up and down arrow tips (figure 5.5F, image 2, red arrow). You can toggle the [Protect] symbol on and off by pressing up or down on the Arrow Pad.
3. Figure 5.5F, image 3, shows the green [Protect] symbol in the upper-right corner of the screen (red arrow). This video is marked as protected. You can scroll left or right to select additional videos to protect. Press the OK button when you are finished marking the videos that you would like to protect from deletion. Any protected videos will have the [Protect] key symbol displayed in the upper-right corner of the screen (figure 5.5F, image 4).

[Slide Show] Behavior

When you are presenting a slide show on the monitor of the images on the camera's memory card, you can also play part or all of the videos found on the card. Let's examine how to set the length of time a video plays for during a slide show.

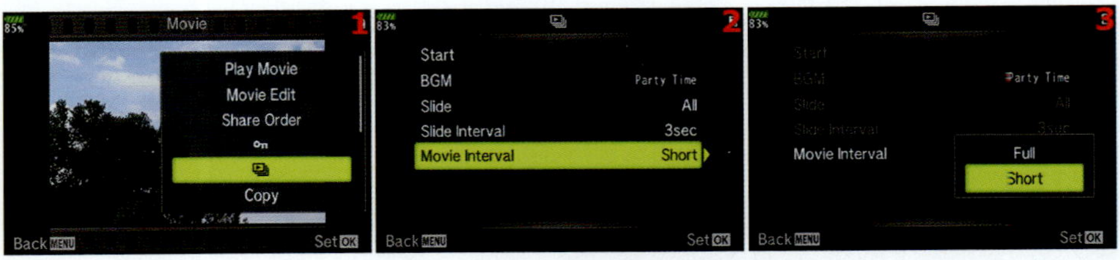

Figure 5.5G: Setting the Movie Interval for video playing length in slide shows

Use the following steps to choose a Movie Interval for when you are displaying an image-and-video slide show on your camera's monitor:

1. Scroll through the pictures and videos on the camera's monitor until you locate any video. Press the OK button to open the Movie Playback Menu (figure 5.5G, image 1). Highlight the [Slide Show] symbol and press the OK button again.
2. The screen that is now displayed (figure 5.5G, image 2) is a duplicate of the screen found under *Playback Menu > [Slide Show]*. Choose the Movie Interval setting and scroll to the right.
3. A menu will pop up with the following choices: Full and Short (figure 5.5G, image 3). If you choose Full, the camera will play the entire length of any videos it finds during a slide show. If you choose Short, the camera will play only a few seconds of each video. Press the OK button to lock in your choice.

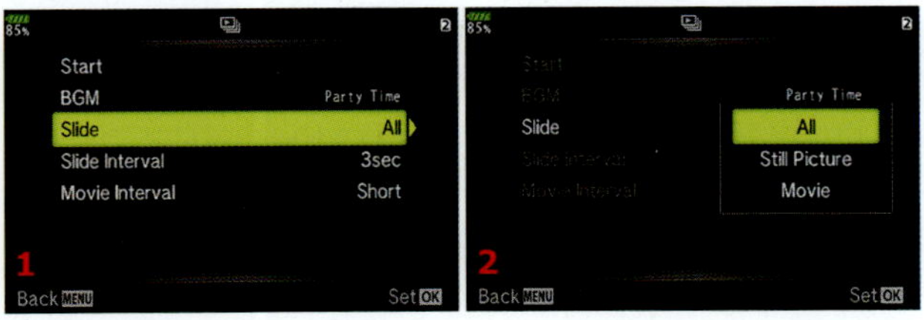

Figure 5.5H: Selecting the slide show type

You can set the camera so that during a slide show it displays only images, plays only videos, or presents both images and videos. Use the following steps:

1. Select Slide from the [Slide Show] menu and scroll to the right (figure 5.5H, image 1).
2. Choose Still Picture to include only images in your slide show, Movie to play only videos, or All to include both images and videos (figure 5.5H, image 2). Press the OK button to lock in your choice.

We will not go deeper into this menu in this chapter. Again, this is a duplicate of the screen found under *Playback Menu > [Slide Show]*, which we will consider in much greater detail in the **Playback Menu** chapter, under the **[Slide Show]** heading (page 359).

Copy

If you want to make a backup copy of a video on the secondary memory card (not the one currently assigned to accept video), you may do so with the Copy function (page 279). Let's see how.

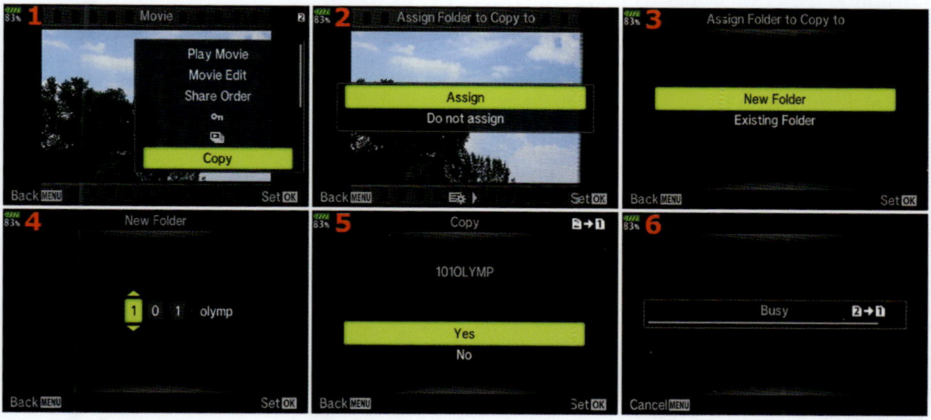

Figure 5.5l: Making a copy of a video

Use the following steps to create a copy of a video on the secondary memory card:

1. Scroll through the pictures and videos on the camera's monitor until you locate the video you want to duplicate. Press the OK button to open the Movie Playback Menu (figure 5.5l, image 1). Highlight Copy and press the OK button again.
2. The following screen (figure 5.5l, image 2) allows you to choose whether you want to store the copy of your video in a specific folder on the secondary memory card (Assign), or in the default folder (Do not assign). For this example we will use Assign. If you have previously used this function and made a copy folder assignment, you will see a folder name (e.g., 101OLYMP) instead of the word Assign. You may continue using that folder, or you may choose a different folder by selecting New Folder on the following screen. (***Note:*** If you do not care which folder the camera chooses to use for the copied video, select Do not assign and the camera will use the default folder on the secondary card.)
3. The next screen will offer you two choices: New Folder or Existing Folder (figure 5.5l, image 3). If you have not previously created a new folder in which to place a copied video, or you want to use a different folder, you should select New Folder and press the OK button. In this example, we will use New Folder to create a brand-new folder for the copied video. Select New Folder and press the OK button. (***Note:*** If you choose

Existing Folder, the camera will present you with a list of folders to choose from [see figure 5.5J].)

4. Use the up/down menus to enter three numerals for the beginning of the folder name (figure 5.5I, image 4). You can choose from 100 to 999. The partial word olymp will be appended to the number you choose (e.g., 101OLYMP), forming a new folder name. Once you have input your new folder number, press the OK button to accept the new folder name and create the new folder.
5. The next screen allows you to make a final choice before copying the file (figure 5.5I, image 5). Choose Yes to copy the video, or No to cancel. In the top-right corner of image 5, you can see the copy direction symbol, which tells you that I have been saving my videos to memory card slot 2, and the camera is copying my video into memory card slot 1 (2→1).
6. The final screen is a *Busy* screen with a progress indicator (figure 5.5I, image 6). When the video file has been successfully copied, the screen will revert to the original video on the monitor.

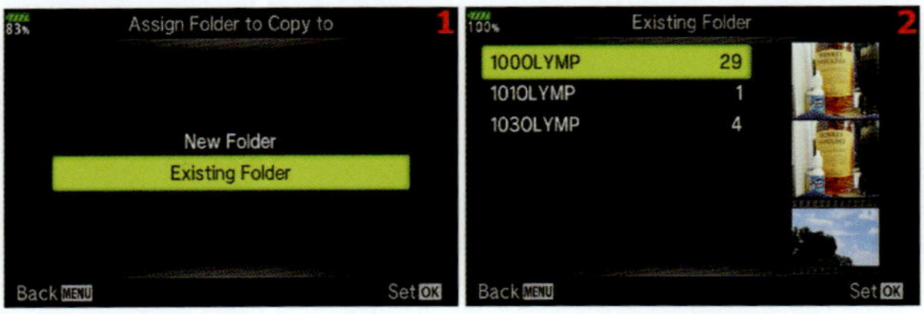

Figure 5.5J: Choosing an Existing Folder for video copying

Erase

If you are running out of space on your memory cards and you are about to shoot a critical video, you may want to delete a less important video to make room. The Erase function gives you that ability. Let's see how it works.

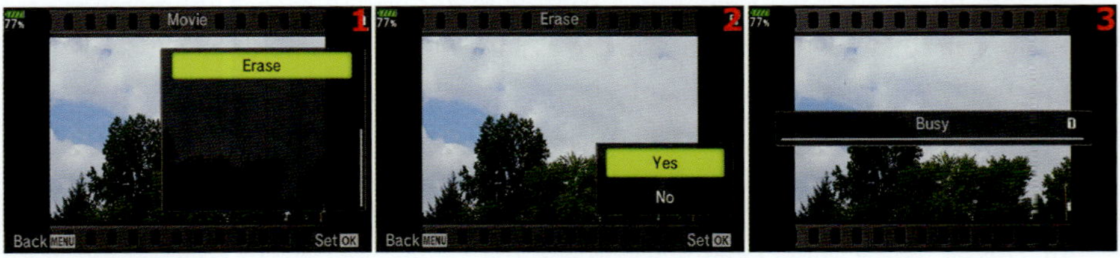

Figure 5.5K: Erasing a video

Use the following steps to erase a video:

1. Scroll through the pictures and videos on the camera's monitor until you locate the video you want to erase. Press the OK button to open the Movie Playback Menu (figure 5.5K, image 1). Highlight Erase, which is located at the very bottom of the menu, and press the OK button again.

2. You will be presented with two choices: Yes and No (figure 5.5K, image 2). Choose No to cancel, or choose Yes and press the OK button to delete the currently selected video.
3. A *Busy* screen with a progress indicator will be displayed (figure 5.5K, image 3). When the E-M1II is finished deleting the video, it will return to the Playback screen with a previous file displayed (not shown).

Note: When you erase a video that has automatically been split into multiple 4 GB sections, the camera will offer you a menu with the following items:

- ***Delete Entire [Movie]:*** Deletes all segments of a split movie.
- ***Erase:*** Deletes only the currently selected segment of a split movie.

PART 2: Video Menu

The Video Menu in the E-M1II camera is designed to put all the most important video functions in one place, making it easier to find the ones you need. In previous EM cameras, the video functions were attached to other camera menus.

If you enjoy shooting video with the E-M1II, why not take some time now—with your camera in hand—to consider each of these video functions at least once? Later, you will have greater control of the camera's flexible movie system.

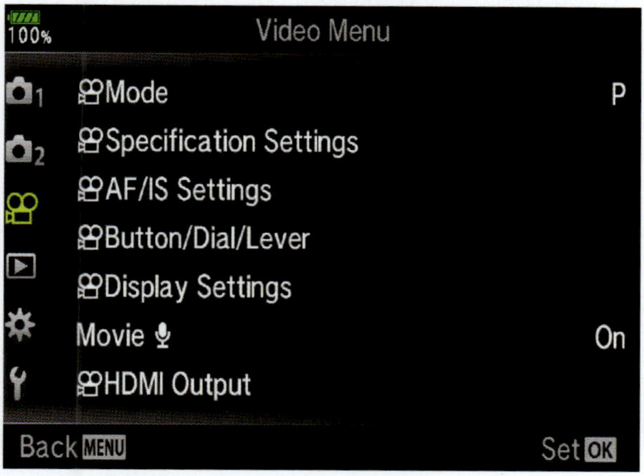

Figure 5.6: Video Menu

As you can see on the left side of the screen in figure 5.6, the Video Menu is the third menu item from the top. Look for the yellow camera symbol. We will use the word [Movie] in brackets to refer to the video camera symbol shown in menus.

Now let's examine each of the Video Menu functions in detail, starting at the top and proceeding downward through the entire menu.

[Movie] Mode

The [Movie] Mode setting allows you to select one of the four primary exposure modes for video recording: Programmed auto (P), Aperture priority (A), Shutter priority (S), and Manual (M). Here is a description of the four modes:

- **P:** Programmed auto (P) mode allows the camera to select the optimal aperture according to how bright the subject is.
- **A:** Aperture priority (A) mode is used to control the depth of field in your video. This value must be set *before* you start the video recording. You cannot adjust the aperture while the camera is making a movie. Use the Rear Dial to adjust the aperture before the recording begins. During a video recording, the camera will use the aperture you selected and will automatically select whatever shutter speed and ISO sensitivity are required to get a usable video.
- **S:** Shutter priority (S) mode is used to control motion blur. Generally, the shutter speed should be set to double the frame rate of the movie. For example, if you are using 1080p at 30 fps, the best shutter speed will be 1/60 second. However, you can adjust the shutter speed from as low as 1/24 second to as high as 1/8000 second for special effects. You cannot change the shutter speed during video recording, so be sure to choose the setting you want before you start making your movie. Use the Rear Dial to adjust the shutter speed before the recording begins. During a video recording, the camera will use the shutter speed you selected and will automatically select whatever aperture and ISO sensitivity are required to get a usable video.
- **M:** Manual (M) mode allows you to select both the shutter speed and the aperture for motion blur and depth of field control. You cannot adjust the aperture or shutter speed during the creation of a video. You must set the aperture and shutter speed you want to use before starting the recording. You will control the aperture with the Front Dial and the shutter speed with the Rear Dial. Shutter speed can be set between 1/3 second and 1/8000 second. During a video recording, the camera will use the aperture and shutter speed you selected, and you can also select an ISO range between 200 and 6400 before you start the video. Auto ISO is not used during video recordings in M mode; you have to adjust the camera for the correct lighting conditions before you start the video. To prevent over- or underexposure, you must be careful not to move into areas where the light varies drastically.

Note: Manual exposure compensation is not available in any video recording mode. In P, A, and S modes, the camera will automatically compensate for light variation. In M mode there is no way to compensate for light variance, unless you are using a lens with an integrated manual aperture ring that lets you open and close the aperture to allow for light changes.

Now let's examine how to prepare the camera to record a video.

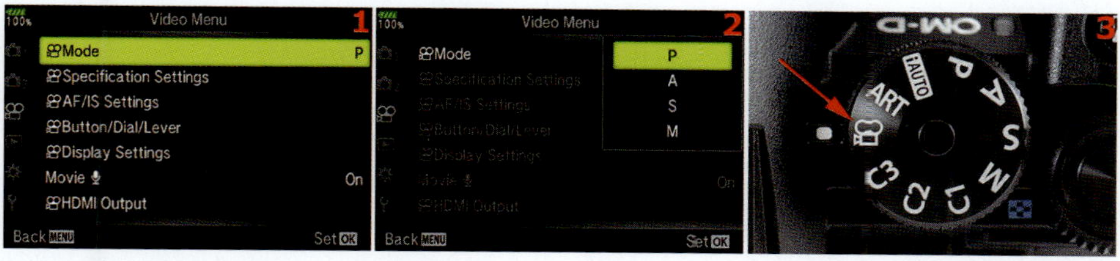

Figure 5.7: Using various exposure modes when recording video

Use these steps to select an exposure mode before you record a video:

1. Select the [Movie] Mode function from the Video Menu and scroll to the right (figure 5.7, image 1).
2. A small exposure mode menu will appear with four exposure modes: P, A, S, and M (figure 5.7, image 2). Refer to the previous list for a description of each mode. Choose one of the exposure modes and press the OK button to lock it in.
3. Set the Mode Dial to the movie camera symbol (figure 5.7, image 3, red arrow). When you record the video, the E-M1II will use the exposure mode you selected in step 2. Before you start the video recording, configure the shutter speed, aperture, or ISO, depending on which exposure mode you selected (see previous list). The camera will record your video when you press the Movie Button.

Note: Using the [Movie] Mode function is the equivalent of manually setting the Mode Dial to one of the four exposure modes (P, A, S, M). Some videographers set the exposure mode manually with the Mode Dial before they shoot a movie, instead of using this [Movie] Mode function. This [Movie] Mode function has no effect unless you set the Mode Dial to the Movie Mode (movie camera symbol; figure 5.7, image 3) Manually setting P, A, S, or M on the Mode Dial overrides this [Movie] Mode menu item.

Settings Recommendation: If you are using a lens with an aperture ring (which will allow you to control the depth of field and the amount of light entering the camera), I suggest using the Manual (M) exposure mode. If you don't have such a lens, and therefore have no way to control the camera when the light level changes drastically, it may be best to use P, A, or S mode when you record a video. That way the camera can use Auto ISO sensitivity to control the exposure when the light varies greatly.

[Movie] Specification Settings

The [Movie] Specification Settings function allows you to control the quality of your video recordings. You will adjust the following settings, which vary according to the mode you have selected:

- ***Size:*** The Movie Resolution (Size) controls the pixel ratio of the video recording (e.g., 3840×2160). See the Movie Resolution (Size) and Pixel Ratio/Frame Rate (fps) columns in table 5.2.

- ***Bit Rate:*** The Bit Rate affects the quality of a video. Basically, the higher the Bit Rate, the better the clarity of the video. See the Bit Rate column in table 5.2.
- ***fps:*** The fps, or Frame Rate, affects how motion is recorded in a video. Slow frame rates allow fast moving objects to blur in the video, while faster Frame Rates tend to stop motion better. See the Pixel Ratio at Frame Rate (fps) column in table 5.2.
- ***Clip Recording Time [Clips]:*** The Clip Recording Time allows you to create short movie clips, from one to eight seconds long, for individual use or for including in a My Clips Movie (page 339).
- ***Slow or Fast Motion (Slow/Fast):*** This setting allows you to create slow motion or faster-than-normal motion videos.

Please refer to table 5.2, which includes information on the various video settings.

Movie Resolution (Size), or [Record Mode]	Pixel Ratio at Frame Rate (fps)	Bit Rate for: ALL-Intra (A-I), SuperFine (SF), Fine (F), and Normal (N) Compression Rates
C4K (Cinematic 4K)	4096×2160 at 24p	237 Mbps
4K (Ultra HD)	3840×2160 at 24p, 25p, 30p	102 Mbps
FHD (Full HD)	1920×1080 at 24p, 25p, 30p	202, 52, 30, 18 Mbps
HD	1280×720 at 24p, 25p, 30p, 50p, 60p	102, 26, 24, 10 Mbps
M-JPEG (Motion JPEG)	1280×720 at 30p	Info not available

Table 5.2: Adjustable video subsetting values

Internal Video Capture

The E-M1II offers a series of video modes that allow you to make movies up to 29 minutes long or 4 GB in size, per segment. If a video segment exceeds 4 GB in size, the camera will continue recording a new segment without pausing the video. However, when you are finished recording, you will need to assemble the segments with your computer into one big video.

The camera has five Movie Resolution (Size) modes: Cinematic 4K, Ultra HD, Full HD, HD, and Motion JPEG. For in-camera recording to a memory card, the E-M1II uses one of two selectable compressed-video formats: H.264 MPEG-4 AVC or Motion JPEG.

For most of the Movie Resolution (Size) modes, there are variable frame and bit rates. Frame rates can vary from 24 to 60 frames per second using the progressive (p) recording method (24p to 60p).

The bit rate varies according to the compression level you select. Using FHD as an example (see table 5.2), the bit rates are as follows for each compression level: A-I=202 Mbps, SF=52 Mbps, F=30 Mbps, and N=18 Mbps. A-I or ALL-Intra means the camera is using no inter-frame compression. This compression level is great for editing, but since it provides little compression, it will result in much larger video file sizes. Olympus does not provide information on the bit rate for Motion JPEG.

The standard 16:9 aspect ratio is used by the Ultra HD (4K), Full HD, HD, and Motion JPEG recording formats. This matches today's computer monitors, some smart devices, and most HDTVs. Cinematic 4K (C4K) uses the 17:9 aspect ratio, which matches the widescreen aspect ratio used in digital cinema cameras and projectors per an industry standards agreement between major movie producers.

External Video Capture

For maximum quality in video recordings you may choose to record live video to an external video recorder, such as the Ninja Inferno recorder/monitor made by Atomos, Inc. **(https://www.atomos.com)**. You can send a clean (no camera information overlays), 4:2:2 subsampled, 8-bit video stream through the camera's HDMI port to the external video recorder. When you record to an external recorder, the recording time and file size of the video are limited only by the storage size of the external recorder.

Choosing and Adjusting [Movie] Specification Settings

Now let's consider how to select and adjust the individual settings. There are seven video settings available and we will look into each one so that you can master how they work.

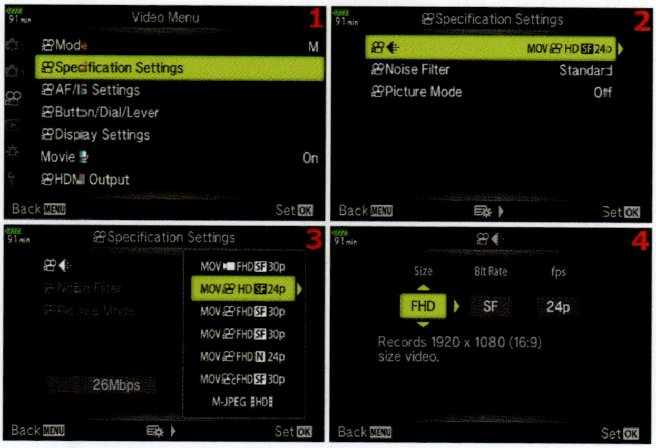

Figure 5.8A: Choosing and changing [Movie] Specification Settings overview

Use the following steps to choose and adjust a video specification setting:

1. Choose [Movie] Specification Settings from the Video Menu and scroll to the right (figure 5.8A, image 1).
2. Highlight [Movie][Record Mode] and scroll to the right (figure 5.8A, image 2).
3. Choose one of the seven video settings and scroll to the right (figure 5.8A, image 3). We will consider each of the settings shortly.

4. Scroll left or right with the Arrow Pad to highlight an individual subsetting (e.g., Size), and then scroll up or down to change the selected subsetting. Refer to table 5.2 for information about each subsetting.

Now let's examine the individual video settings and see how the subsettings work.

Clips Video Setting

The Clips video setting allows you to create short, one- to eight-second video clips. These clips can be used for uploading to social media sites, or can be included in the My Clips feature, which allows you to create movies up to 15 minutes long that contain short video clips and images. When you shoot a video Clip, the camera defaults to adding it to the current My Clips movie. You should not use this video setting for general video recording.

We will discuss the My Clips feature in full detail in **Part 3: My Clips Movie Creation** of this chapter (page 339).

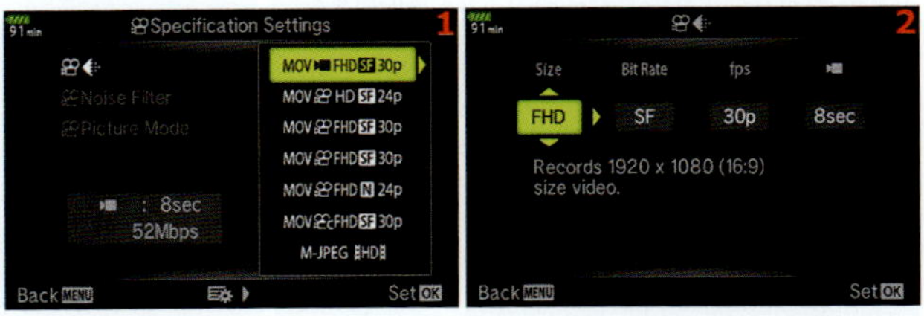

Figure 5.8B: The Clips video setting

Use the following steps to choose and adjust the Clips video setting:

1. Figure 5.8B begins where figure 5.8A, image 3, leaves off. To capture a one- to eight-second (1sec to 8sec) video Clip, choose the top video setting from the [Movie][Record Mode] menu. Scroll to the right to open the subsetting adjustment screen.
2. You will now adjust the Size (Movie Resolution), Bit Rate (Compression/Bit Rate), fps (Frame Rate), and [Clip Length] of this video Clip (figure 5.8B, image 2). Scroll left or right with the Arrow Pad to choose one of the four subsettings. Scroll up or down to change the subsetting to a new value. Refer to table 5.2 (page 284) for information about the available values. As previously mentioned, the [Clip Length] can vary from 1sec to 8sec. When you are done, press the OK button to lock in this setting.

Standard Video Settings

The camera provides four standard video recording types that are exactly the same in functionality so that you can configure each of them for different types of video capture. Each provides a Size, Bit Rate, and fps setting that you can vary according to your needs. This is convenient for those videographers who capture different types of video at different times. For example, you may have one video recording setting configured to 4K at 24 fps, another set to FHD with SF compression at 30 fps, and another set to FHD Fine compression at 60 fps, with one to spare.

You cannot shoot Clips or slow- and fast-motion videos with these four standard video settings. Three of the five Movie Resolutions (4K, FHD, and HD) are available in these settings. C4K is available under the custom video setting, and M-JPEG has its own setting, too. (We will discuss C4K and M-JPEG in the next two subsections.)

Let's see how to use the four standard video settings.

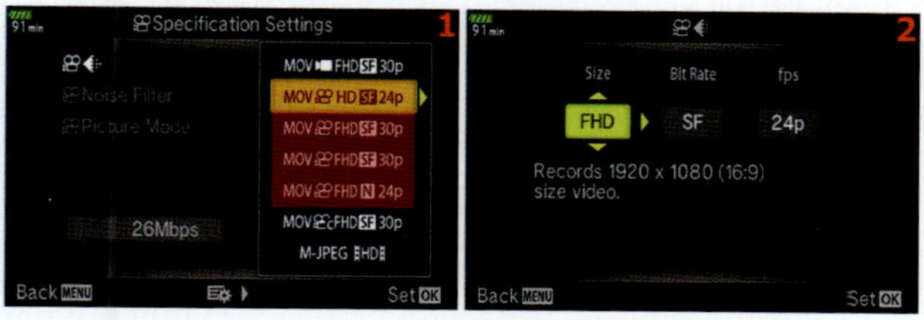

Figure 5.8C: The four standard video settings (highlighted in red)

Use the following steps to configure each of the four standard video settings:

1. Figure 5.8C begins where figure 5.8A, image 3, leaves off. Choose any of the four standard video settings and scroll to the right (figure 5.8C, image 1). [***Note:*** All four of the settings highlighted in red in image 1 are identical and have three internal subsettings (Size, Bit Rate, and fps).]
2. Scroll left or right with the Arrow Pad to choose one of the three subsettings (Size, Bit Rate, or fps) for adjustment, and then scroll up or down to change the subsetting values (figure 5.8C, image 2). Refer to table 5.2 (page 284) for information about the available values. After making your adjustments, press the OK button to lock in setting.

Custom Video Setting

The single custom video setting places all five of the available video subsettings (Size, Bit Rate, fps, [Clip Length], and Slow/Fast) in one place. This is a one-size-fits-all video setting. It can take the place of the Clips and standard video settings, and is the only setting that provides C4K (17:9 cinematic 4K widescreen aspect ratio) recording. Let's examine the best way to use the custom video setting.

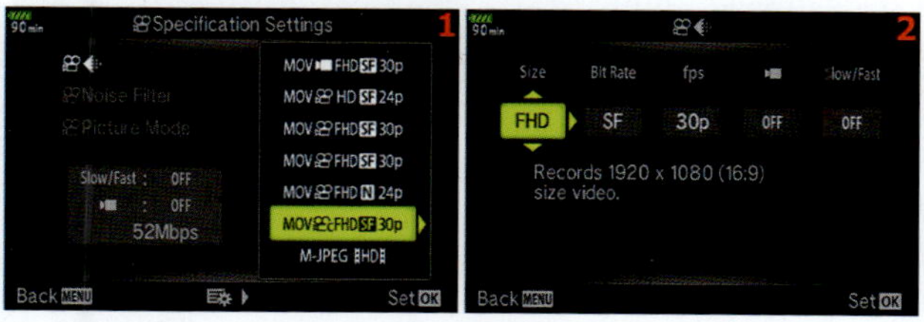

Figure 5.8D: The custom video setting with all five video subsettings

Use the following steps to configure a custom video recording session:

1. Figure 5.8D begins where figure 5.8A, image 3, leaves off. Choose the next to last video function on the [Movie] Specification Settings menu and scroll to the right (figure 5.8D, image 1).
2. This custom video setting presents you with all five of the video subsettings for configuring the style of video you need to capture (figure 5.D, image 2). Choose from Size, Bit Rate, fps, [Clip Length], and Slow/Fast by scrolling left or right with the Arrow Pad, and then scroll up or down to adjust the values for each subsetting. Refer to table 5.2 (page 284) for the available values for the first three subsettings (Size, Bit Rate, and fps). The [Clips Length] subsetting (tiny movie camera icon) offers you choices ranging from one second (1sec) to eight seconds (8sec). This subsetting controls the length of each video clip you record. Each clip will automatically be placed at the end of the current My Clips Movie. You may leave the clip there or use each clip individually. The Slow/Fast setting allows you to shoot slow-motion video. Its options vary according to the frame rate (fps) you have selected. For instance, if you have Size at FHD, Bit Rate at SF, and fps at 24p you will have the following slow motion and fast motion choices: Slow motion – x0.4, x0.48, x0.8, and x0.96; Fast Motion – x1.6, x2, x3, x4, and x8. Configure all your settings and then press the OK button to lock them in.

Note: One thing to be aware of when shooting Slow/Fast motion videos is that the playing time does not match the time the camera will be recording the video. For instance, to generate one second of video play time when you are using x8, you need to record for 8 seconds. Therefore, a 10-second Fast motion video will require 80 seconds of recording time. It is the opposite for Slow motion video. If you want to create a 10-second Slow motion video at a speed of x0.48, the actual recording time will be 4.8 seconds.

Any value below Off in the Slow/Fast menu is a Slow motion value. Any value above Off is a Fast motion value. Also, any value that starts with x0 is Slow motion value. Any value that does not start with x0 is a Fast motion value.

Motion JPEG Setting

Motion JPEG, or M-JPEG, is an HD (720p) only video format. It runs at approximately 30 fps (varies if you use some Art Filters). Each individual frame of an M-JPEG movie is a small, compressed JPEG image, using normal JPEG compression. A video captured with M-JPEG is easy to post-process (grade) for the same reason that it is easy to post-process a JPEG still image. This format has excellent quality, but creates rather large file sizes. The E-M1II limits the file size to 2 GB instead of the normal 4 GB allowed for a MOV-type movie.

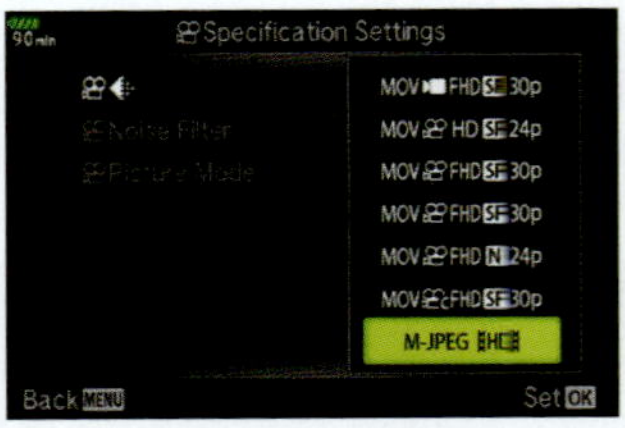

Figure 5.8E: Motion JPEG (M-JPEG) video setting

Use the following step to choose a Motion JPEG (M-JPEG) recording session:

1. Figure 5.8E begins where figure 5.8A, image 3, leaves off. Choose M-JPEG [HD] from the [Movie] Specification Settings menu and press the OK button to lock in the setting.

Note: A Share Order cannot contain a Motion JPEG video; the Olympus OI.Share app will not allow you to transfer an M-JPEG movie to your smart device. Also, you cannot use Time Codes when capturing in M-JPEG.

[Movie] Noise Filter

The Noise Filter function is designed to remove high-ISO noise from your videos by blurring the image slightly. The blurring action tends to blend the grainy noise detail into the darker background, lessening the degrading effect of noise. Of course, noise reduction also tends to make the video slightly less sharp, especially when you use the High setting.

It will be hard to see how the noise reduction system affects the image on the small camera monitor; therefore, I suggest you test important video by examining the movie on a larger computer monitor or HDTV.

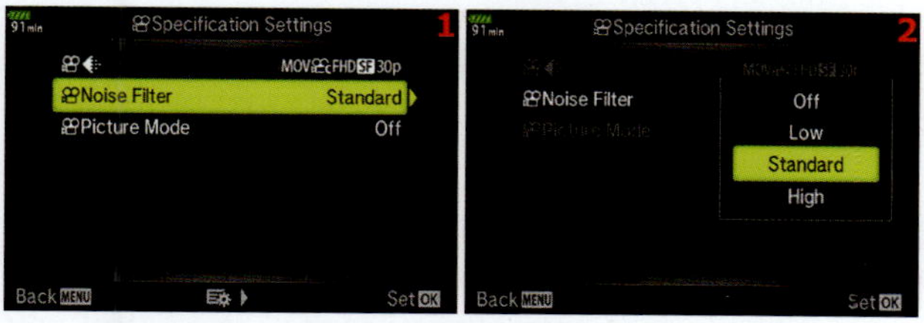

Figure 5.8F: Noise reduction with the Noise Filter

Use the following steps to configure the Noise Filter:

1. Figure 5.8F begins where figure 5.8A, image 2, leaves off. Highlight [Movie] Noise Filter on the [Movie] Specification Settings menu and scroll to the right (figure 5.8F, image 1).
2. There are four settings: Off, Low, Standard, and High (figure 5.8F, image 2). The camera defaults to Standard. Choose the setting you want to use and press the OK button to lock it in. The higher the setting (from Low to High), the more the camera blurs the video, making noise less apparent and removing image detail.

[Movie] Picture Mode

The [Movie] Picture Mode setting is for those who choose to grade (post-process) their videos after recording. The majority of photographers will not use this mode; instead, they will set a certain Picture Mode (e.g., Natural, Vivid, or Portrait), according to the style of video they are shooting. That way the video is ready to use as soon as it is captured and it can be shown without any post-processing.

However, a commercial videographer will want to grade a video, changing the color saturation level and other items. When you enable the [Movie] Picture Mode, it overrides the normal Picture Mode selection in the Super Control Panels and Live Control, and places the camera into Flat Picture Mode, where colors are less saturated and contrast is lower overall. The pale look this mode provides may not be acceptable to a casual video shooter. However, it allows an experienced videographer to better control how the video looks later by manipulating it in the computer.

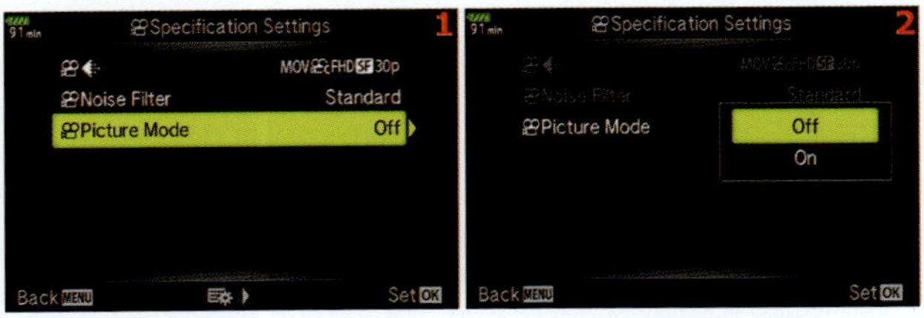

Figure 5.8G: Special [Movie] Picture Mode for video grading

Use the following steps to use the [Movie] Picture Mode:

1. Figure 5.8C begins where figure 5.8A, image 2, leaves off. Highlight [Movie] Picture Mode on the [Movie] Specification Settings menu and scroll to the right (figure 5.8G, image 1).
2. A small popup menu will open with two choices: Off and On (figure 5.8G, image 2). Choose Off to cancel, or On to select the less-saturated, low-contrast Flat [Movie] Picture Mode. (If you check on the two Super Control Panels or the Live Control, you will see that the Flat Picture Control is in use while [Movie] Picture Mode selected. Normally the Flat Picture Mode does not appear on the Picture Mode menu. This is how you enable it.) Press the OK button to lock in your selection.

Note: When the Flat [Movie] Picture Mode is enabled, you cannot choose a different Picture Mode for video capture from the Super Control Panels or the Live Control. Flat mode works only when you have the camera set to Movie Mode (movie camera icon) on the Mode Dial. Flat Picture Mode is not functional when the camera is not in Movie Mode on the Mode Dial, even if you selected it using the screens shown in figure 5.8G.

As we head to press, Olympus has released firmware update 2.0 for the E-M1II. With this update, an LUT file is released for movies recorded in the Flat Picture Mode. This file converts recorded videos to BT.709 in DaVinci Resolve from Blackmagic Design Pty. Ltd. for color grading.

[Movie] AF/IS Settings

[Movie] AF Mode allows you to choose the type of focus your camera will use when you capture videos. [Movie] Image Stabilizer (IS) lets you select a type of image stabilization for video capture. Let's consider each of these modes (AF/IS) separately.

[Movie] AF Mode Settings

There are six focus settings available in [Movie] AF Mode:

- ***S-AF:*** (1) Before you start the video recording, the camera will behave as follows: When you press the Shutter button halfway down, the camera focuses on the subject and locks the focus. The green AF Area Pointer will be displayed, and a small green dot (AF confirmation mark) will appear in the top-right corner of the monitor when focus is confirmed. This type of focus is best for subjects that are not moving or are moving very slowly. The camera *does not update the focus* unless you release the Shutter button and reapply pressure. (2) When you are recording video, the camera will behave as follows: When you press the Shutter button halfway down, no beep or focus indicators will sound or display on the monitor during autofocus. You will *not* be able to move the focus point around the screen with the Arrow Pad. However, you will be able to focus on any part of your subject, anywhere on the monitor, by using the touch focus method—simply touch the the monitor on the exact point where you want the best focus.
- ***C-AF:*** (1) Before you start the video recording, the camera will behave as follows: The camera will continuously update the focus as long as you or the subject are moving. If you force a refocus by pressing the Shutter button halfway down, the green AF confirmation mark (dot) will appear in the top-right corner of the monitor upon accurate focus. If you or the subject start moving, the camera will notice the movement and attempt to update the focus. The difference between S-AF and C-AF is that S-AF does not update focus, whereas C-AF will continuously update the focus. (2) When you are recording video, the camera will behave as follows: The autofocus system will attempt to keep the focus updated for your subject, using the central area of the monitor as the focus point. No beep or focus indicators will sound or display on the monitor. You will *not* be able to move the focus point around the screen with the Arrow Pad. You can force an update of focus by pressing halfway down on the Shutter button at any time. If you want to focus on a specific area of the subject that is not in the central area of the monitor, you can use the touch focus method—simply touch the monitor on the exact point where you want the best focus.
- ***MF:*** You must use the focus ring on the lens to focus manually when this mode is enabled. Autofocus is disabled and you are responsible for focusing. This mode is often used by people who shoot macro (closeup) videos to increase the reliability of focusing, and by those who love using the pull-focus method to draw attention to the subject. No focus indicators are displayed on the screen. Many videographers use Focus Peaking (page 294) [and Magnify (page 294) before starting the recording] when capturing video using manual focus.
- ***S-AF+MF:*** This mode works exactly the same as the S-AF mode The only difference is that S-AF does not let you fine-tune autofocus with the manual focus ring, whereas S-AF+MF does. You can let the camera autofocus, and then manually adjust the focus yourself with the focus ring on the lens. If you have Focus Peaking enabled *(Custom*

Menu > A3. AF/MF > MF Assist > Peaking), a red outline will be displayed on the edges of your image to help you fine-tune the focus.

- ***C-AF+TR:*** This mode gives the camera the ability to track a moving subject while maintaining accurate autofocus. There are several ways to start the tracking process: (1) Before you start the video, select the subject by pressing the Shutter button halfway until focus locks on the subject. (2) Simply start the video recording with the central area of the screen pointing at a higher-contrast area of your subject, and the camera will automatically begin tracking. (3) The easiest way to select a point on your subject for tracking, either before or after the video is started, is to use touch focus. Touch the monitor on the area of your subject you want to track. If you need to change areas, just touch the monitor again at the new area. While tracking the subject, the AF Area Pointer will use a green square with a line sticking out of each side (figure 5.9B, image 2). As the subject moves, the camera will maintain focus and track it across the viewfinder or monitor. As long as the AF Area Pointer remains green, the camera is tracking. If it turns red, the camera has lost the subject and you should reacquire it by refocusing (touching the monitor again is easiest) until the focus locks on the subject and tracks it again. The C-AF Lock function (page 410) controls how well the camera can track a moving subject when other objects intervene.
- ***Preset MF:*** This mode allows you to preset a particular focus distance and a unit of measurement (meters or feet). As soon as you select Preset MF from one of the Super Control Panels or Live Control, the camera will immediately jump to that preset focus distance. You can set the distance in two ways: (1) Select the PreMF setting from one of the Super Control Panels or Live Control, press the info button, and then press halfway down on the Shutter button to focus on the exact distance you want to use; or, (2) Set the distance manually (meters or feet) via *Custom Menu > A3. AF/MF > Preset MF distance*. We will discuss both shortly.

Let's first consider how to choose a [Movie] AF Mode setting, and then we will examine how to use each of them.

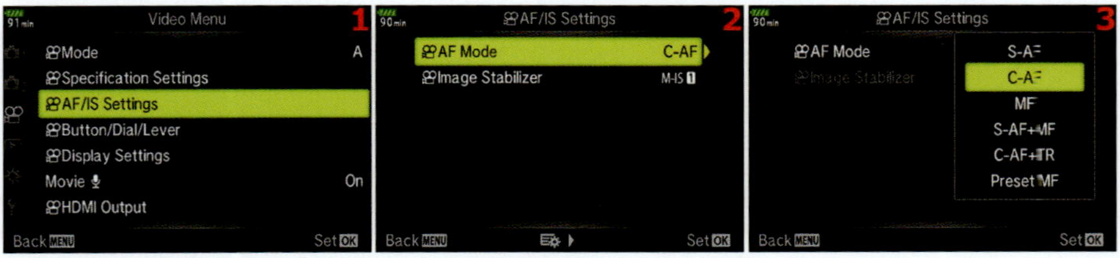

Figure 5.9A: Selecting a [Movie] AF Mode setting

Use the following steps to choose a [Movie] AF Mode setting:

1. Highlight [Movie] AF/IS Settings on the Video Menu and scroll to the right (figure 5.9A, image 1).

2. Choose [Movie] AF Mode from the [Movie] AF/IS Settings menu and scroll to the right (figure 5.9A, image 2).
3. A popup menu will appear with all six [Movie] AF Mode choices. After referring to the previous descriptive list, select the mode you want to use and press the OK button to lock it in.

Next let's consider the types of AF Area Pointers you may see while recording a video.

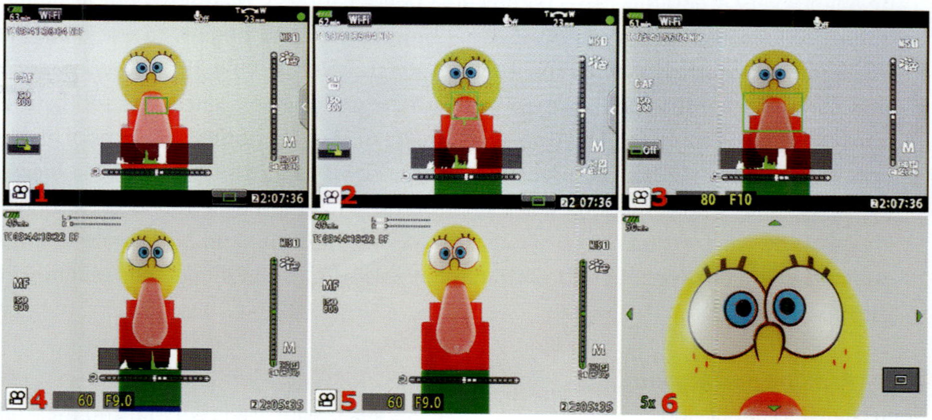

Figure 5.9B: AF Area Pointers and focus methods

Following is a description of each of the autofocus AF Area Pointers you may see when using the video system:

- *Figure 5.9B, image 1,* displays the normal AF Area Pointer associated with S-AF, C-AF, and S-AF+MF (see figure 5.9A, image 3). You will see this small, green AF Area Pointer rectangle only when you are not recording a video, and briefly during initial autofocus.
- *Figure 5.9B, image 2,* shows the tracking AF Area Pointer you'll see on the screen before and during a video recording. This odd-shaped AF point will attempt to stay with the selected area of your subject. You may touch a different area of the monitor to refocus the tracking system on a different subject, and the AF pointer will move to where you touched the screen.
- *Figure 5.9B, image 3,* displays the touch focus AF Area Pointer. When you touch the screen, this larger green rectangle will appear and stay on the screen. As long as the rectangle is over an appropriate area of your subject, the camera will maintain focus or not (according to the AF Mode you have selected). Experiment with this touch system; it is very flexible.
- *Figure 5.9B, image 4,* shows how the screen looks when you are using manual focus (MF) mode. No AF Area Pointer appears when you are manually focusing.
- *Figure 5.9B, image 5,* displays focus Peaking. The camera has been set to manual focus (MF) and Peaking has been enabled in *Custom Menu > A3. AF/MF > MF Assist > Peaking*.

It is a little hard to see in book graphics, but there is a red outline showing excellent focus around the eyes of the pink-tongued book mascot. As you change the focus manually by rotating the focus ring on the lens, you will see a red outline surrounding the edges where focus is best. Focus Peaking works either before or during a video recording. We will discuss how to enable focus Peaking in the next subsection.

- *Figure 5.9, image 6,* shows the 5x Magnify capability, which allows you to zoom in on your subject and focus manually. If you combine Magnify with focus Peaking, you will be able to very accurately focus on any area of your subject. Magnify is not available during a video recording; you must use it before recording begins. To use Magnify, touch the screen to display the touch AF Area rectangle shown in figure 5.9, image 3. Now simply rotate the focus ring on your camera and the area encompassed by the touch AF Area rectangle will be displayed (image 6). You will notice a 5x symbol in the bottom-left corner of the monitor. This means the current display is the area inside the AF Area rectangle, magnified five times larger than normal. If you look closely at image 6, you will see that my camera has focus Peaking turned on, too—note the red outline around the eyes of our book mascot. We will discuss how to enable Magnify in the next subsection.

Focus Peaking and Magnify

Focus Peaking and Magnify allow you to obtain very accurate focus when using manual focus (MF). Peaking surrounds the in-focus area with a red border. Magnify zooms in on the subject by five times (5x), enabling you to see fine details.

We will discuss both Peaking and Magnify in much greater detail in the **Custom Menu** chapter. For now, let's see how to select either or both of the features to help with your manual focus.

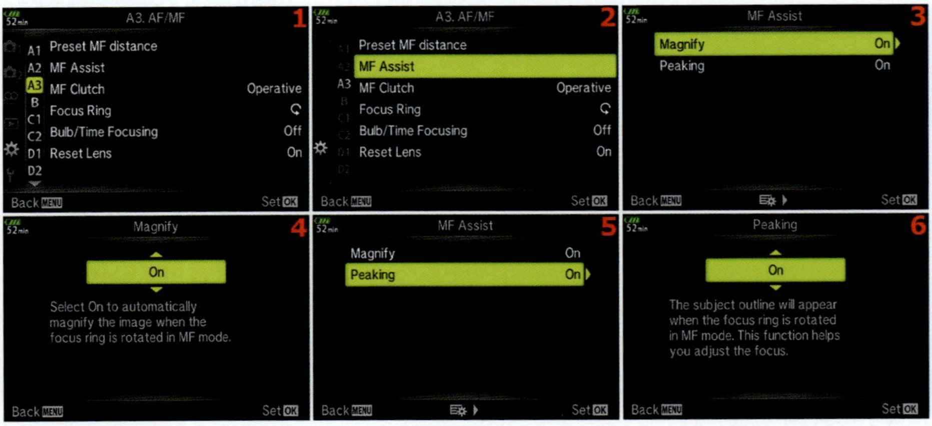

Figure 5.9C: Enabling focus Peaking and/or Magnify

Use the following steps to enable focus Magnify and/or Peaking:

1. Highlight A3 on the Custom Menu (gear icon) and scroll to the right (figure 5.9C, image 1).
2. Highlight MF Assist on the A3. AF/MF menu and scroll to the right (figure 5.9C, image 2).
3. Choose Magnify from the MF Assist menu and scroll to the right (figure 5.9C, image 3).
4. Choose On or Off from the up/down menu to enable or disable Magnify (figure 5.9C, image 4). Press the OK button to lock in your choice.
5. The camera will return to the screen shown in figure 5.9C, image 5. Highlight Peaking and scroll to the right.
6. Choose On or Off from the up/down menu to enable or disable Peaking (figure 5.9C, image 6). Press the OK button to lock in your choice.

Next let's consider how to use the [Movie] Image Stabilizer (M-IS) function for shooting videos.

Image Stabilizer (IS) Settings

I have heard the E-M1 II's M-IS system for movies described as one of the best ever for shooting video. The camera can definitely be held more steadily than most other cameras you've used to shoot video. It is almost as good as having a video frame with a stabilizer that you bolt the camera into. If you are standing fairly still or walking slowly, you will be amazed by how steady the video looks. Here is a description of the three available modes for video stabilization:

1. ***M-IS 1:*** The camera uses normal 5-axis, sensor-shift stabilization along with additional digital stabilization (pixel shifting on the sensor).
2. ***M-IS 2:*** The camera uses 5-axis, sensor-shift stabilization, but does not use extra digital stabilization (pixel shifting).
3. ***M-IS Off:*** The camera provides no video stabilization.

Let's examine how to select the movie stabilizer mode you will likely use most often.

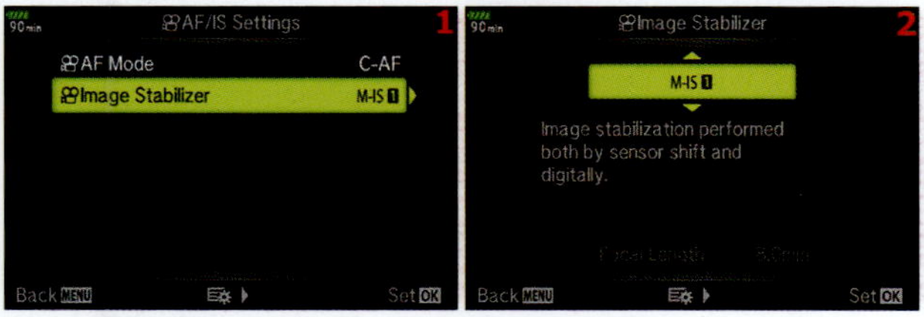

Figure 5.9D: Selecting Image Stabilization for video

Use the following steps to choose a movie stabilization level:

1. Highlight [Movie] Image Stabilizer from the [Movie] AF/IS Settings menu and scroll to the right (figure 5.9D, image 1).
2. Select one of the three stabilization levels (M-IS 1, M-IS 2, or M-IS Off) from the up/down menu (figure 5.9D, image 2). Refer to the previous list to make the best choice. Once your choice is highlighted in the up/down menu, press the OK button to lock it in.

Next we will examine the Button, Dial, and Lever function that you can use while recording videos.

[Movie] Button/Dial/Lever

The Olympus OM-D E-M1 Mark II camera has quite a few buttons, dials, and levers. Interestingly, the programmable camera controls can be programmed separately for still images and videos. That means you can program, let's say, the Fn1 button for still images with a certain Button Task, and then program the Fn1 button for video capture with a completely different Button Task. The camera will know when you are shooting pictures or capturing videos and will respond to an Fn1 button press with the correct assigned task.

I have created two downloadable documents that list all of the available Button Tasks for making still images and videos: **Appendix A: Still Image Button Task Reference** and **Appendix B: Video Capture Button Task Reference**. These documents can be found on the downloadable resources website:

www.rockynook.com/olympusem1markii

Some of the functionality in the Button Tasks overlap between the two appendices; however, some of the usage information is quite different.

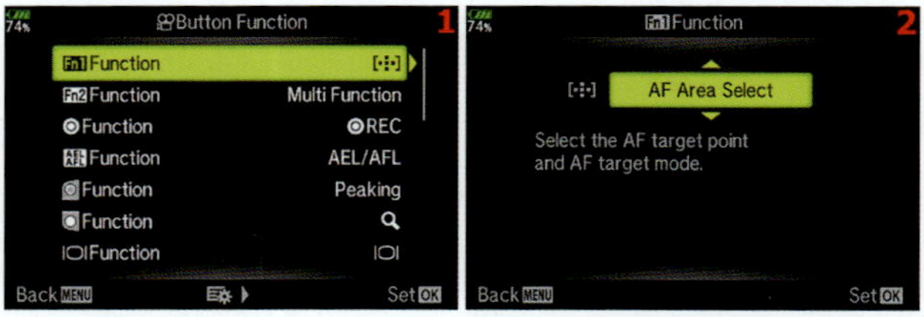

Figure 5.10A: Button/Dial/Lever Functions and Button/Dial/Lever Tasks

To understand this chapter section better, keep these facts in mind (figure 5.10A):

- Olympus calls each button, dial, and lever by a special name when referring to its programmable functionality. Each is referred to by the name of the control followed by the word "Function" (figure 5.10A, image 1). In this book, I will refer to each control by its Olympus name. For instance, when referring to its programmability, I will call the Fn1 button the "Fn1 Function." The Fn2 button is referred to as the "Fn2 Function." Each "Function" can have one of multiple tasks assigned to it.

- Each Button Function (e.g., Fn1 Function) for video capture can have one of several tasks assigned to it (figure 5.10A, image 2). This book will call each of the options that can be assigned to the buttons, dials, and levers by the name "Tasks." Therefore, the Fn1 Function can have one of several "Button Tasks" (e.g., AF Area Select, Peaking, Magnify; figure 5.10A, image) assigned to it.

Now let's examine how to choose any one of the Button/Dial/Lever Functions and select a Button Task for that function.

Fn1 Function

The Fn1 button (figure 5.10B) can accept the assignment of most tasks in the **Button Tasks List** in **Appendix B: Video Capture Button Task Reference**, found on the downloadable resources website (see page 10). The default assignment for the Fn1 Function is [•••] AF Area Select.

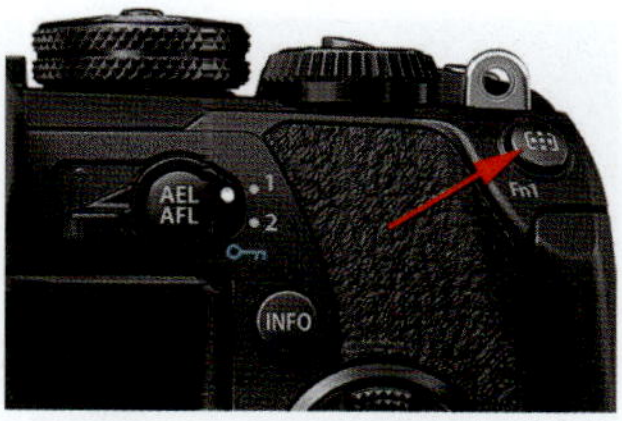

Figure 5.10B: The Fn1 button

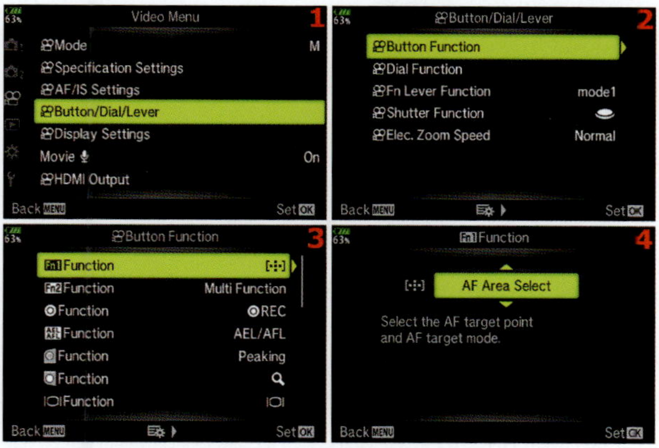

Figure 5.10C: Assigning a Button Task to the Fn1 Button Function

Use the following steps to assign one of the Button Tasks to the Fn1 Function:

1. Highlight [Movie] Button/Dial/Lever on the Video Menu and scroll to the right (figure 5.10C, image 1).
2. Choose [Movie] Button Function from the [Movie] Button/Dial/Lever menu and scroll to the right (figure 5.10C, image 2).
3. Select the Fn1 Function from the [Movie] Button Function menu and scroll to the right (figure 5.10C, image 3).
4. Choose one of the available Button Tasks from the up/down menu (figure 5.10C, image 4). Use the **Button Tasks List** found in **Appendix B: Video Capture Button Task Reference** to decide which task you will assign to the Fn1 button.
5. Press the OK button to Set the task for the Fn1 button.

Fn2 Function

The Fn2 button (figure 5.10D) can accept most task assignments shown in the **Button Tasks List** in **Appendix B: Video Capture Button Task Reference**, found on the downloadable resources website (see page 10). The default assignment for the Fn2 Function is the Button Task named Multi Function.

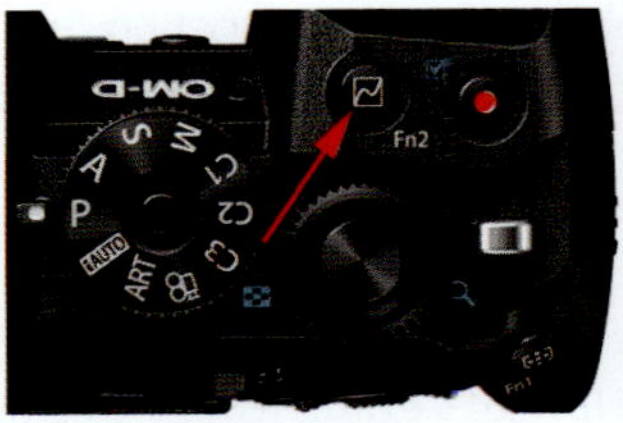

Figure 5.10D: The Fn2 button

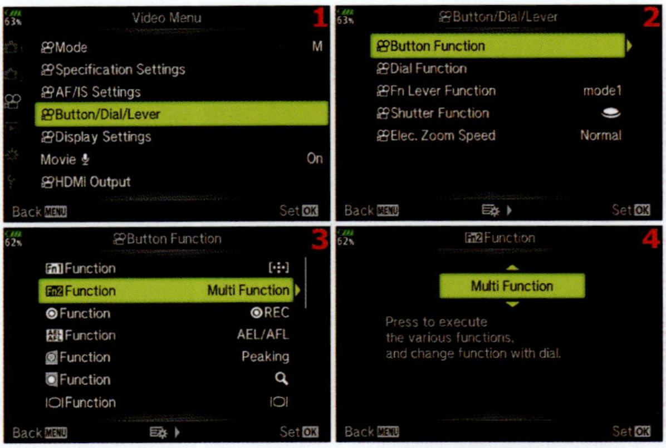

Figure 5.10E: Assigning a Button Task to the Fn2 Button Function

Use the following steps to assign one of the Button Tasks to the Fn2 Function:

1. Highlight [Movie] Button/Dial/Lever on the Video Menu and scroll to the right (figure 5.10E, image 1).
2. Choose [Movie] Button Function from the [Movie] Button/Dial/Lever menu and scroll to the right (figure 5.10E, image 2).
3. Select the Fn2 Function from the [Movie] Button Function menu and scroll to the right (figure 5.10E, image 3).
4. Choose one of the available Button Tasks from the up/down menu (figure 5.10E, image 4). Use the **Button Tasks List** in **Appendix B: Video Capture Button Task Reference** to decide which task you will assign to the Fn2 button.
5. Press the OK button to Set the task for the Fn2 button.

[Movie Button] Function

The Movie button (figure 5.10F) can accept the assignment of most tasks in the **Button Tasks List** in **Appendix B: Video Capture Button Task Reference**, found on the downloadable resources website (see page 10). The default assignment for the [Movie Button] Function is REC, which you use to record movies.

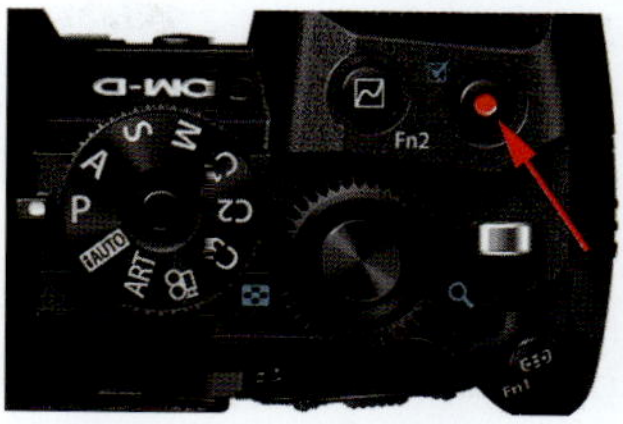

Figure 5.10F: The Movie button

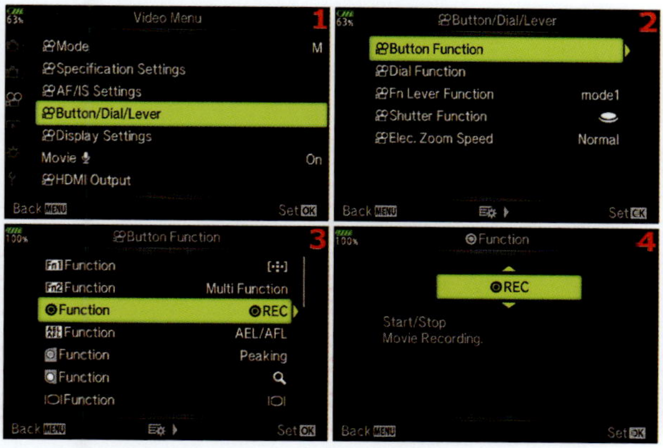

Figure 5.10G: Assigning a Button Task to the [Movie] Function

Use the following steps to assign one of the Button Tasks to the [Movie Button] Function:

1. Highlight [Movie] Button/Dial/Lever on the Video Menu and scroll to the right (figure 5.10G, image 1).
2. Choose [Movie] Button Function from the [Movie] Button/Dial/Lever menu and scroll to the right (figure 5.10G, image 2).
3. Select the [Movie Button] Function from the [Movie] Button Function menu and scroll to the right (figure 5.10G, image 3).
4. Choose one of the available Button Tasks from the up/down menu (figure 5.10G, image 4). Use the **Button Tasks List** in **Appendix B: Video Capture Button Task Reference** to decide which task you will assign to the Movie button.
5. Press the OK button to Set the task for the Movie button.

AEL/AFL Function

The AEL/AFL button (figure 5.10H) can accept the assignment of most tasks in the **Button Tasks List** in **Appendix B: Video Capture Button Task Reference**, found on the downloadable resources website (see page 10). The default assignment for the AEL/AFL Function is the Button Task named AEL/AFL.

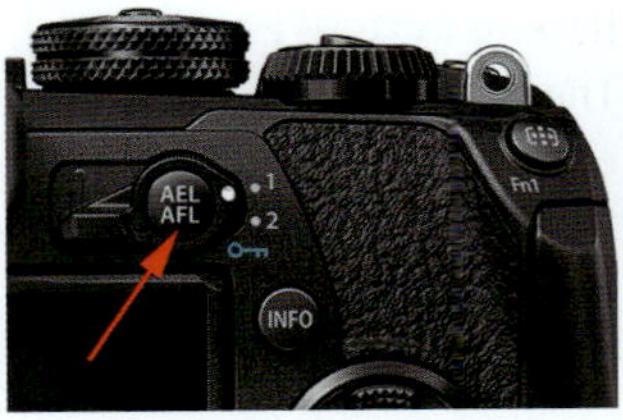

Figure 5.10H: The AEL/AFL Button

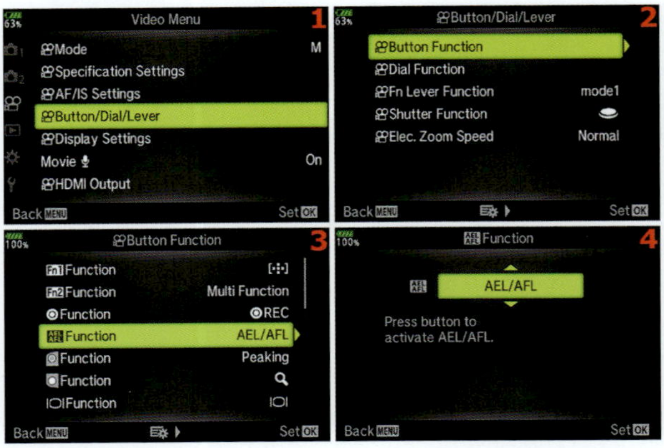

Figure 5.10I: Assigning a Button Task to the AEL/AFL Button Function

Use the following steps to assign one of the Button Tasks to the AEL/AFL Function:

1. Highlight [Movie] Button/Dial/Lever on the Video Menu and scroll to the right (figure 5.10I, image 1).
2. Choose [Movie] Button Function from the [Movie] Button/Dial/Lever menu and scroll to the right (figure 5.10I, image 2).
3. Select the AEL/AFL Function from the [Movie] Button Function menu and scroll to the right (figure 5.10I, image 3).
4. Choose one of the available Button Tasks from the up/down menu (figure 5.10I, image 4). Use the **Button Tasks List** in **Appendix B: Video Capture Button Task Reference** to decide which task you will assign to the AEL/AFL button.
5. Press the OK button to Set the task for the AEL/AFL button.

[One Touch WB] Function

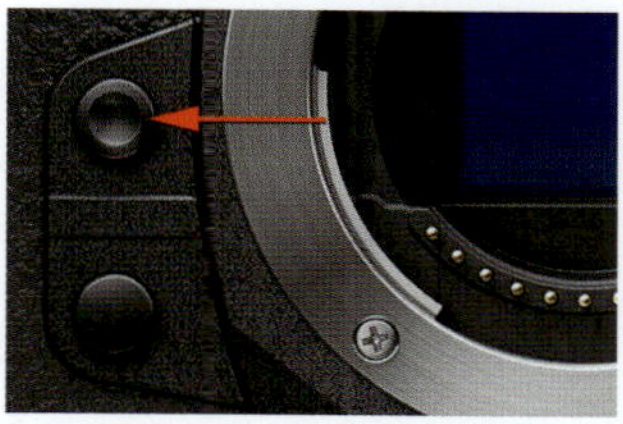

Figure 5.10J: The One-Touch WB button

The One-Touch WB button (figure 5.10J) can accept the assignment of most tasks in the **Button Tasks List** in **Appendix B: Video Capture Button Task Reference**, found on the downloadable resources website (see page 10). The default assignment for the [One-Touch WB] Function when you are capturing video is Peaking.

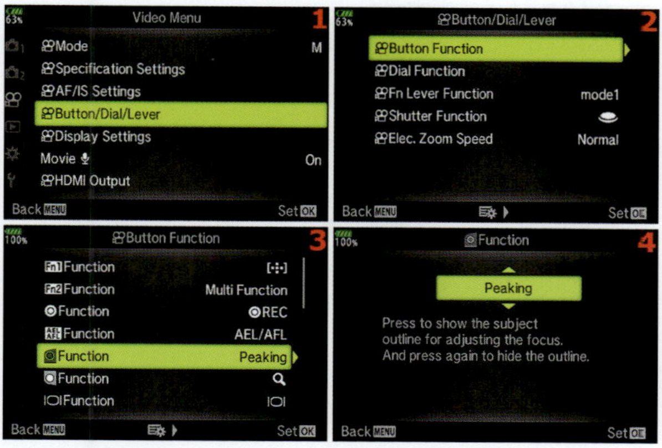

Figure 5.10K: Assigning a Button Task to the [One-Touch WB] Button Function

Use the following steps to assign one of the Button Tasks to the [One-Touch WB] Function:

1. Highlight [Movie] Button/Dial/Lever on the Video Menu and scroll to the right (figure 5.10K, image 1).
2. Choose [Movie] Button Function from the [Movie] Button/Dial/Lever menu and scroll to the right (figure 5.10K, image 2).
3. Select the [One-Touch WB] Function from the [Movie] Button Function menu and scroll to the right (figure 5.10K, image 3).
4. Choose one of the available Button Tasks from the up/down menu (figure 5.10K, image 4). Use the **Button Tasks List** in **Appendix B: Video Capture Button Task Reference** to decide which task you will assign to the [One-Touch WB] button.
5. Press the OK button to Set the task for the [One-Touch WB] button.

[Preview] Function

The Preview button (figure 5.10L) can accept the assignment of most tasks in the **Button Tasks List** in **Appendix B: Video Capture Button Task Reference**, found on the downloadable resources website (see page 10). The default assignment for the [Preview] Function when you are capture video is Magnify.

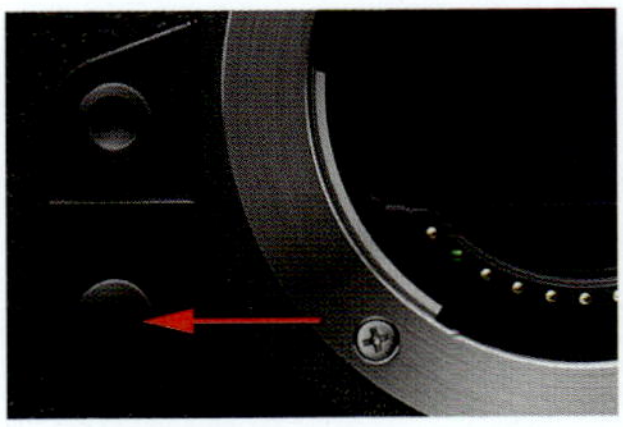

Figure 5.10L: The Preview button

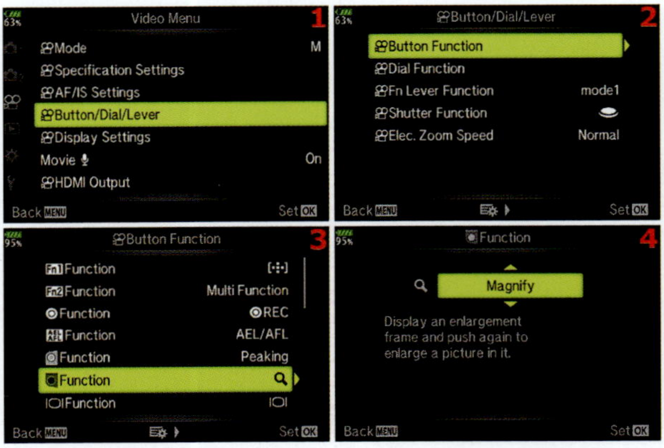

Figure 5.10M: Assigning a Button Task to the [Preview] Button Function

Use the following steps to assign one of the Button Tasks to the [Preview] Function:

1. Highlight [Movie] Button/Dial/Lever on the Video Menu and scroll to the right (figure 5.10M, image 1).
2. Choose [Movie] Button Function from the [Movie] Button/Dial/Lever menu and scroll to the right (figure 5.10M, image 2).
3. Select the [Preview] Function from the [Movie] Button Function menu and scroll to the right (figure 5.10M, image 3).
4. Choose one of the available Button Tasks from the up/down menu (figure 5.10M, image 4). Use the **Button Tasks List** in **Appendix B: Video Capture Button Task Reference** to decide which task you will assign to the Preview button.
5. Press the OK button to Set the task for the Preview button.

[LV Button] Function

The LV button (figure 5.10N) can accept the assignment of most tasks in the **Button Tasks List** in **Appendix B: Video Capture Button Task Reference**, found on the downloadable resources website (see page 10).The default assignment for the [LV Button] Function when you are capturing video is View Selection.

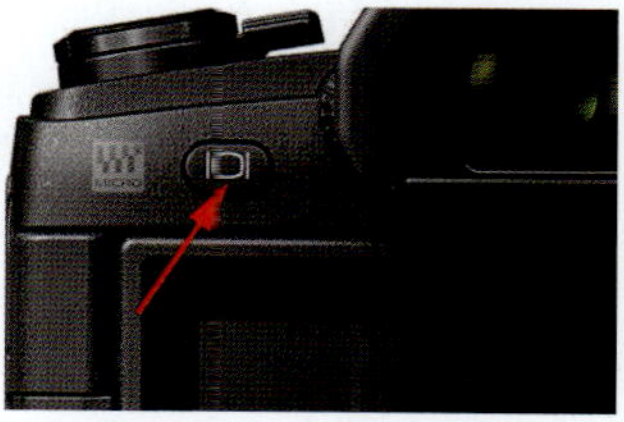

Figure 5.10N: The LV button

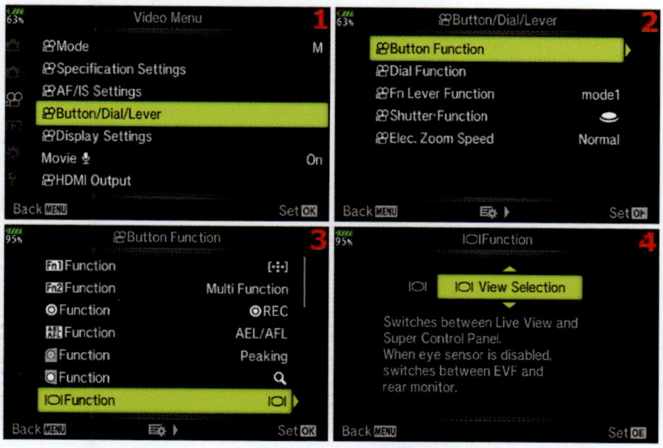

Figure 5.10O: Assigning a Button Task to the [LV Button] Function

Use the following steps to assign one of the Button Tasks to the [LV Button] Function:

1. Highlight [Movie] Button/Dial/Lever on the Video Menu and scroll to the right (figure 5.10O, image 1).
2. Choose [Movie] Button Function from the [Movie] Button/Dial/Lever menu and scroll to the right (figure 5.10O, image 2).
3. Select the [LV Button] Function from the [Movie] Button Function menu and scroll to the right (figure 5.10O, image 3).
4. Choose one of the available Button Tasks from the up/down menu (figure 5.10O, image 4). Use the **Button Tasks List** in **Appendix B: Video Capture Button Task Reference** to decide which task you will assign to the LV button.
5. Press the OK button to Set the task for the LV button.

[Arrow Pad ◄▼▲►] Function

The [Arrow Pad ◄▼▲►] Function can accept one of three Button Tasks: Off, AF Area Select, or Direct Function. The default task is Direct Function when capturing video, as described in the **Button Tasks List** in **Appendix B: Video Capture Button Task Reference**, found on the downloadable resources website (see page 10).

Using the Direct Function Button Task allows you to free up some other buttons on the camera by letting you assign one of six different Button Tasks to the right press and down press keys of the Arrow Pad (figure 5.10P). Assigning AF Area Select or Off, instead of Direct Function, will cancel the task assignments of the two Button Functions covered in the next two subsections: the **[Arrow Pad ▶] Function** (page 305) and the **[Arrow Pad ▼] Function** (page 306). When Off or the AF Area Select Button Task is chosen, the [Arrow Pad ▶] Function and the [Arrow Pad ▼] Function will be grayed out on the [Movie] Button Function menu. If you want to use the ▶ and ▼ buttons for one of the six Button Tasks they each support, you must set the [Arrow Pad ◀▼▲▶] Function to Direct Function.

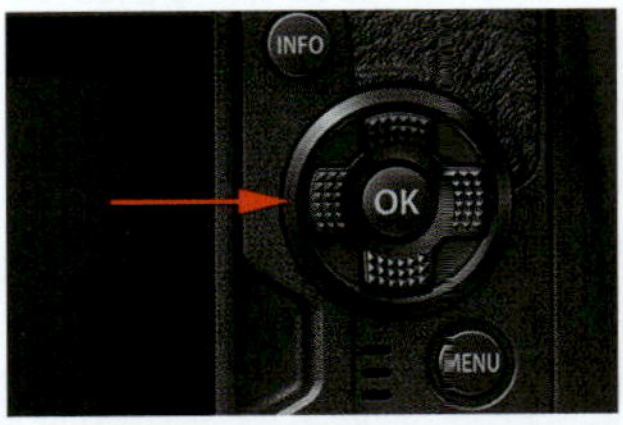

Figure 5.10P: The Arrow Pad

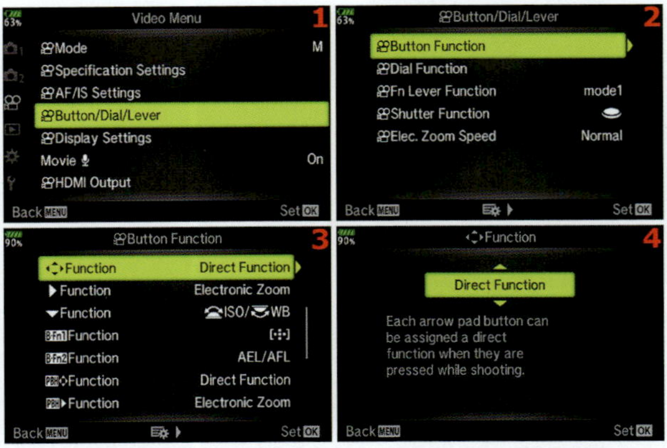

Figure 5.10Q: Assigning a Button Task to the [Arrow Pad ◀▼▲▶] Function

Use the following steps to configure the [Arrow Pad ◀▼▲▶] Function:

1. Highlight [Movie] Button/Dial/Lever on the Video Menu and scroll to the right (figure 5.10Q, image 1).
2. Choose [Movie] Button Function from the [Movie] Button/Dial/Lever menu and scroll to the right (figure 5.10Q, image 2).
3. Select the [Arrow Pad ◀▼▲▶] Function from the [Movie] Button Function menu and scroll to the right (figure 5.10Q, image 3).
4. Choose one of the available Button Tasks from the up/down menu (figure 5.10Q, image 4). Use the **Button Tasks List** in **Appendix B: Video Capture Button Task Reference** to decide which task you will assign to the Arrow Pad.
5. Press the OK button to Set the task for the Arrow Pad.

[Arrow Pad ▶] Function

The Arrow Pad ▶ key (figure 5.10R) can accept only six tasks from the **Button Tasks List** in **Appendix B: Video Capture Button Task Reference**, found on the downloadable resources website (see page 10). The default assignment for the [Arrow Pad ▶] Function when you are capturing video is the Button Task called Electronic Zoom Selection.

The [Arrow Pad ▶] Function will be grayed out and unavailable unless you have the [Arrow Pad ◀▼▲▶] Function (previous subsection) set to the Direct Function Button Task.

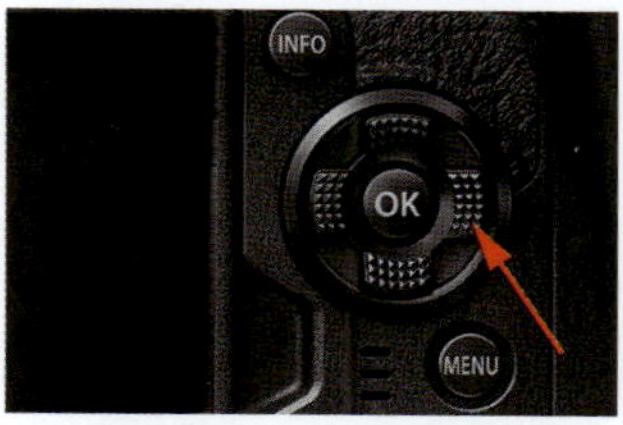

Figure 5.10R: The Arrow Pad ▶ key

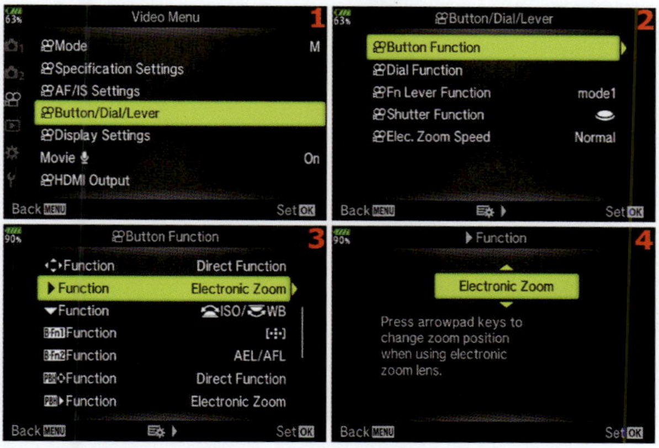

Figure 5.10S: Assigning a Button Task to the [Arrow Pad ▶] Button Function

Use the following steps to assign one of the Button Tasks to the [Arrow Pad ▶] Function:

1. Highlight [Movie] Button/Dial/Lever on the Video Menu and scroll to the right (figure 5.10S, image 1).
2. Choose [Movie] Button Function from the [Movie] Button/Dial/Lever menu and scroll to the right (figure 5.10S, image 2).
3. Select the [Arrow Pad ▶] Function from the [Movie] Button Function menu and scroll to the right (figure 5.10S, image 3).
4. Choose one of the available Button Tasks from the up/down menu (figure 5.10S, image 4). Use the **Button Tasks List** in **Appendix B: Video Capture Button Task Reference** to decide which task you will assign to the Arrow Pad ▶ key.
5. Press the OK button to Set the task for the Arrow Pad ▶ key.

[Arrow Pad ▼] Function

The Arrow Pad ▼ key (figure 5.10T) can accept only six tasks from the **Button Tasks List** in **Appendix B: Video Capture Button Task Reference**, found on the downloadable resources website (see page 10). The default assignment for the [Arrow Pad ▼] Function when you are capturing video is [Front Dial] ISO/[Rear Dial] WB.

The [Arrow Pad ▼] Function will be grayed out and unavailable unless you have the [Arrow Pad ◀▼▲▶] Function (page 303) set to the Direct Function Button Task.

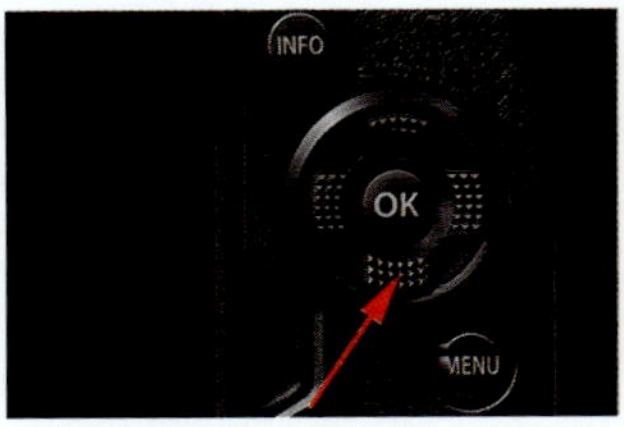

Figure 5.10T: The Arrow Pad ▼ key

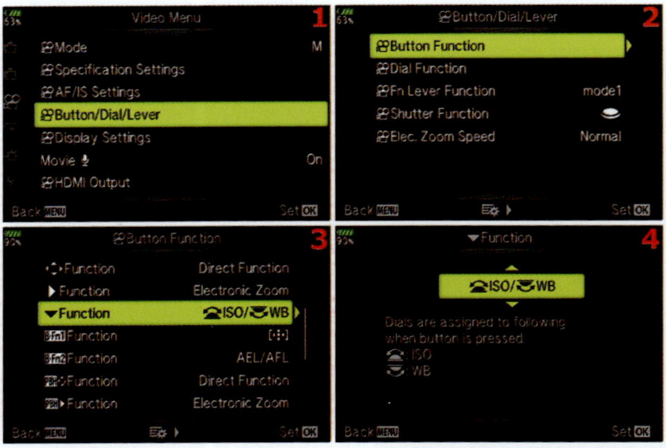

Figure 5.10U: Assigning a Button Task to the [Arrow Pad ▼] Button Function

Use the following steps to assign one of the Button Tasks to the [Arrow Pad ▼] Function:

1. Highlight [Movie] Button/Dial/Lever on the Video Menu and scroll to the right (figure 5.10U, image 1).
2. Choose [Movie] Button Function from the [Movie] Button/Dial/Lever menu and scroll to the right (figure 5.10U, image 2).
3. Select the [Arrow Pad ▼] Function from the [Movie] Button Function menu and scroll to the right (figure 5.10U, image 3).
4. Choose one of the available Button Tasks from the up/down menu (figure 5.10U image 4). Use the **Button Tasks List** in **Appendix B: Video Capture Button Task Reference** to decide which task you will assign to the Arrow Pad ▼ key.
5. Press the OK button to Set the task for the Arrow Pad ▼ key.

B-Fn1 Function

The B-Fn1 button (figure 5.10V) is found on the optional HLD-9 Power Battery Holder (PBH). You can use this function only if you have an HLD-9 mounted on your camera.

The B-Fn1 button can accept the assignment of most tasks in the **Button Tasks List** in **Appendix B: Video Capture Button Task Reference**, found on the downloadable resources website (see page 10). The default assignment for the B-Fn1 Function is AF Area Select.

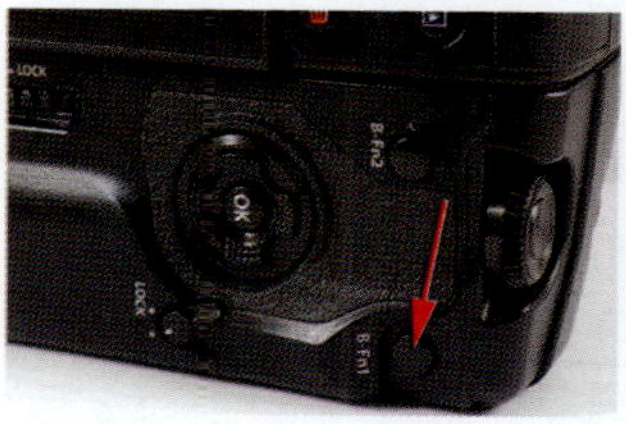

Figure 5.10V: The B-Fn1 button on the HLD-9 Power Battery Holder

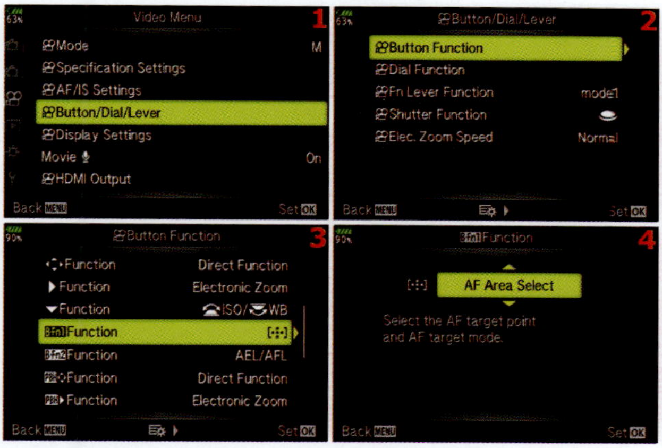

Figure 5.10W: Assigning a Button Task to the B-Fn1 Button Function

Use the following steps to assign one of the Button Tasks to the B-Fn1 Function:

1. Highlight [Movie] Button/Dial/Lever on the Video Menu and scroll to the right (figure 5.10W, image 1).
2. Choose [Movie] Button Function from the [Movie] Button/Dial/Lever menu and scroll to the right (figure 5.10W, image 2).
3. Select the B-Fn1 Function from the [Movie] Button Function menu and scroll to the right (figure 5.10W, image 3).
4. Choose one of the available Button Tasks from the up/down menu (figure 5.10W, image 4). Use the **Button Tasks List** in **Appendix B: Video Capture Button Task Reference** to decide which task you will assign to the B-Fn1 button.
5. Press the OK button to Set the task for the B-Fn1 button.

B-Fn2 Function

The B-Fn2 button (figure 5.10X) is found only on the optional HLD-9 Power Battery Holder (PBH). You can use this function only if you have an HLD-9 mounted on your camera.

The B-Fn2 button can accept the assignment of most tasks in the **Button Tasks List** in **Appendix B: Video Capture Button Task Reference**, found on the downloadable resources website (see page 10). The default assignment for the B-Fn2 Function is AEL/AFL.

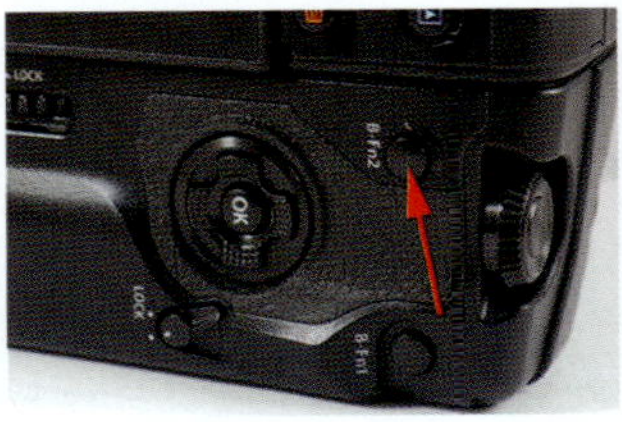

Figure 5.10X: The B-Fn2 button on the HLD-9 Power Battery Holder

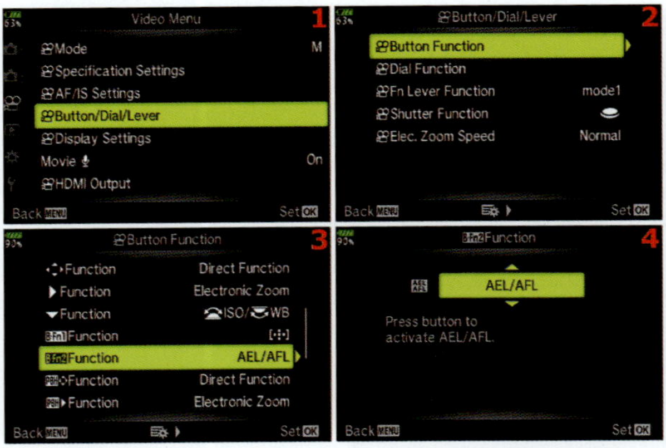

Figure 5.10Y: Assigning a Button Task to the B-Fn2 Button Function

Use the following steps to assign one of the Button Tasks to the B-Fn2 Function:

1. Highlight [Movie] Button/Dial/Lever on the Video Menu and scroll to the right (figure 5.10Y, image 1).
2. Choose [Movie] Button Function from the [Movie] Button/Dial/Lever menu and scroll to the right (figure 5.10Y, image 2).
3. Select the B-Fn2 Function from the [Movie] Button Function menu and scroll to the right (figure 5.10Y, image 3).
4. Choose one of the available Button Tasks from the up/down menu (figure 5.10Y, image 4). Use the **Button Tasks List** in **Appendix B: Video Capture Button Task Reference** to decide which task you will assign to the B-Fn2 button.
5. Press the OK button to Set the task for the B-Fn2 button.

PBH [Arrow Pad ◄▲▼►] Function

The PBH Arrow Pad (figure 5.10Z) is found on the optional HLD-9 Power Battery Holder. You can use this function only if you have an HLD-9 mounted on your camera.

The PBH [Arrow Pad ◄▼▲►] Function can accept one of three Button Tasks: Off, AF Area Select, or Direct Function. The default task is Direct Function when capturing video, as described in the **Button Tasks List** in **Appendix B: Video Capture Button Task Reference**, found on the downloadable resources website (see page 10).

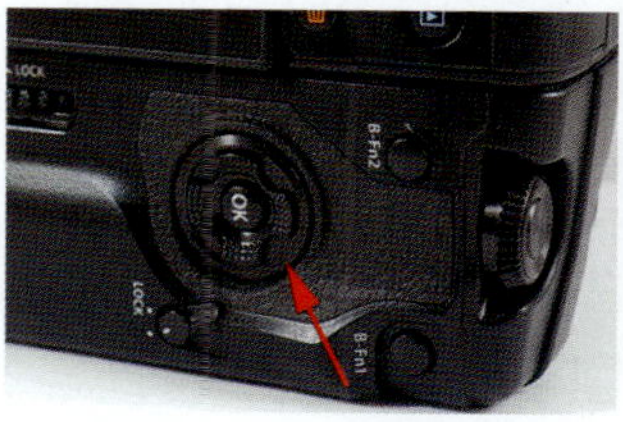

Figure 5.10Z: The HLD-9 PBH Arrow Pad

Using the Direct Function Button Task allows you to free up some other buttons on the camera by letting you assign one of six different Button Tasks to the right press and down press keys of the PBH Arrow Pad. Assigning AF Area Select or Off, instead of Direct Function, will cancel the task assignments of the two Button Functions covered in the next two subsections: the **PBH [Arrow Pad ►] Function** (page 310) and the **PBH [Arrow Pad ▼] Function** (page 311). When Off or the AF Area Select Button Task is chosen, the PBH [Arrow Pad ►] Function and the PBH [Arrow Pad ▼] Function will be grayed out on the [Movie] Button Function menu. If you want to use the ► and ▼ buttons for one of the six Button Tasks they each support, you must set the PBH [Arrow Pad ◄▼▲►] Function to the Button Task named Direct Function.

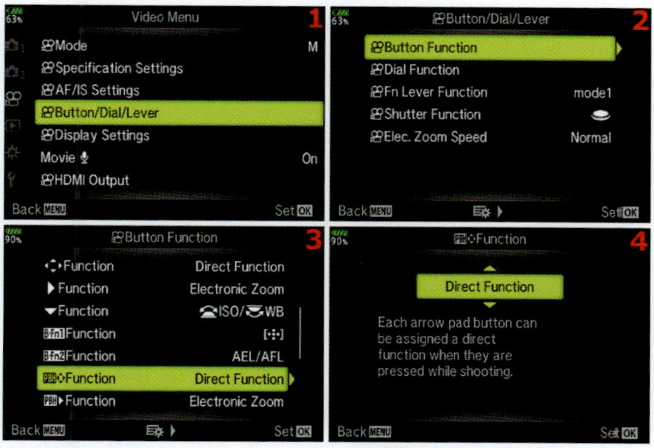

Figure 5.10Z1: Assigning a Button Task to the PBH [Arrow Pad ◄▼▲►] Function

Use the following steps to configure the PBH [Arrow Pad ◄▼▲►] Function:

1. Highlight [Movie] Button/Dial/Lever on the Video Menu and scroll to the right (figure 5.10Z1, image 1).

2. Choose [Movie] Button Function from the [Movie] Button/Dial/Lever menu and scroll to the right (figure 5.10Z1, image 2).
3. Select the PBH [Arrow Pad ◄▼▲►] Function from the [Movie] Button Function menu and scroll to the right (figure 5.10Z1, image 3).
4. Choose one of the available Button Tasks from the up/down menu (figure 5.10Z1, image 4). Use the **Button Tasks List** in **Appendix B: Video Capture Button Task Reference** to decide which task you will assign to the PBH Arrow Pad.
5. Press the OK button to Set the task for the PBH Arrow Pad.

PBH [Arrow Pad ►] Function

The PBH Arrow Pad ► key (figure 5.10Z2) is found on the optional HLD-9 Power Battery Holder. You can use this function only if you have an HLD-9 mounted on your camera.

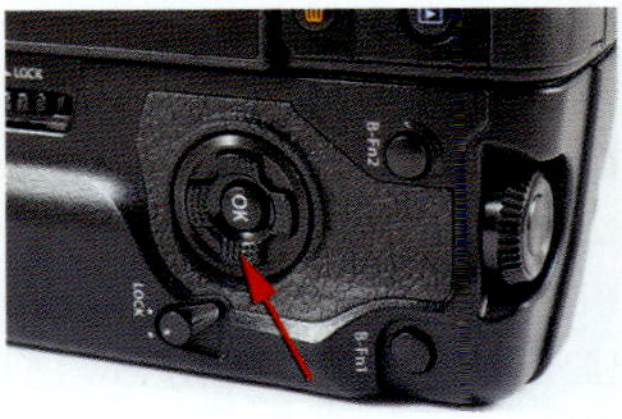

Figure 5.10Z2: The HLD-9 PBH Arrow Pad ► key

The PBH [Arrow Pad ►] Function can accept only six tasks from the **Button Tasks List** in **Appendix B: Video Capture Button Task Reference**, found on the downloadable resources website (see page 10). The default assignment for the PBH [Arrow Pad ►] Function when capturing video is Electronic Zoom.

The PBH [Arrow Pad ►] Function will be grayed out and unavailable unless you have the PBH [Arrow Pad ◄▼▲►] Function (previous subsection) set to the Direct Function Button Task.

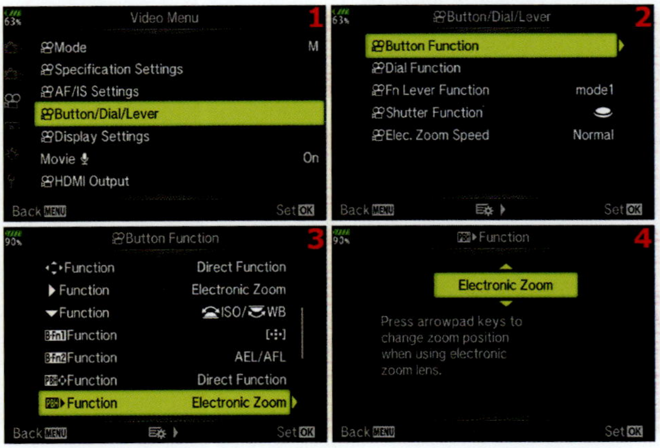

Figure 5.10Z3: Assigning a Button Task to the PBH [Arrow Pad ►] Function

Use the following steps to assign one of the Button Tasks to the PBH [Arrow Pad ►] Function:

1. Highlight [Movie] Button/Dial/Lever on the Video Menu and scroll to the right (figure 5.10Z3, image 1).

2. Choose [Movie] Button Function from the [Movie] Button/Dial/Lever menu and scroll to the right (figure 5.10Z7, image 2).
3. Select the L-Fn Function from the [Movie] Button Function menu and scroll to the right (figure 5.10Z7, image 3).
4. Choose one of the available Button Tasks from the up/down menu (figure 5.10Z7, image 4). Use the **Button Tasks List** in **Appendix B: Video Capture Button Task Reference** to decide which task you will assign to the L-Fn button.
5. Press the OK button to Set the task for the L-Fn button.

[Movie] Dial Function

The E-M1II has two dials on top of the camera: the Front Dial and the Rear Dial. These two dials are used to control various camera settings, and similar to the programmable camera buttons, they can be configured to do something different than the default settings.

The Front and Rear Dials have a relationship with the selected [Movie] Mode (P, A, S, M), the position of the Fn Lever (1, 2), and the [Movie] Fn Lever Function mode (mode1, mode2). Each position of the Fn Lever (1, 2) changes what the Front and Rear Dials do, according to which [Movie] Mode you have selected (P, A, S, M) and which [Movie] Fn Lever Function mode is active (mode1, mode2).

Let's examine each of the six available Dial Tasks that can be assigned to the Front and Rear Dials, based on each of the Movie Modes and Fn Lever positions.

Available Dial Tasks List

- ***+/–:*** Manually adjust the exposure on the camera (exposure compensation), allowing more (+) or less (–) exposure, by turning one of the camera's dials.
- ***WB:*** Manually choose one of the camera's white balance (WB) settings (e.g., AUTO, Sunny, Cloudy) by turning one of the camera's dials.
- ***CWB Kelvin:*** Manually choose a CWB Kelvin temperature setting for the white balance (e.g., 5000K, 5400K, 8000K) by turning one of the camera's dials.
- ***[Mic] VOL:*** Manually adjust the microphone input volume on a scale from –10 to +10 by turning one of the camera's dials.
- ***[Headphone] VOL:*** Manually adjust the headphone listening volume on a scale from –10 to +10 by turning one of the camera's dials.
- ***Off:*** Disable a particular dial for when you are capturing video.

Programming the Dials

Programming the two camera dials seems like a fairly simple process at first glance. You simply go to *Video Menu > [Movie] Button/Dial/Lever > [Movie] Dial Function* and select one of the exposure modes (P, A, S, M) displayed there. Then you choose what you want each dial to do when you are using that exposure mode by selecting from the six items in the *Available Dial Tasks List*.

However, in addition to the exposure mode, there are two more items that must be taken into consideration. These items each affect the way the Front and Rear Dials work once they are programmed. To make things simple, let's use a series of steps to program the two dials and see how it is best done.

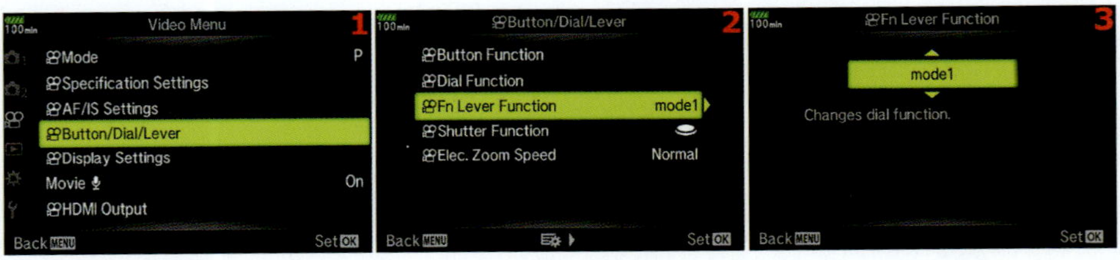

Figure 5.10Z8: Setting the [Movie] Fn Lever Function mode first

Use the following steps to program the camera's Front and Rear Dials:

1. To begin the programming process we need to set the [Movie] Fn Lever Function to mode1. When using mode1, you can flip the Fn Lever between 1 and 2, giving you two separate ways to use the dials for each exposure mode. Highlight [Movie] Button/Dial/Lever on the Video Menu and scroll to the right (figure 5.10Z8, image 1).
2. Choose [Movie] Fn Lever Function from the [Movie] Button/Dial/Lever menu and scroll to the right (figure 5.10Z8, image 2).
3. Select mode1 from the up/down menu and press the OK button to lock in the setting (figure 5.10Z8, image 3). The camera will now return to the previous [Movie] Button/Dial/Lever menu screen.

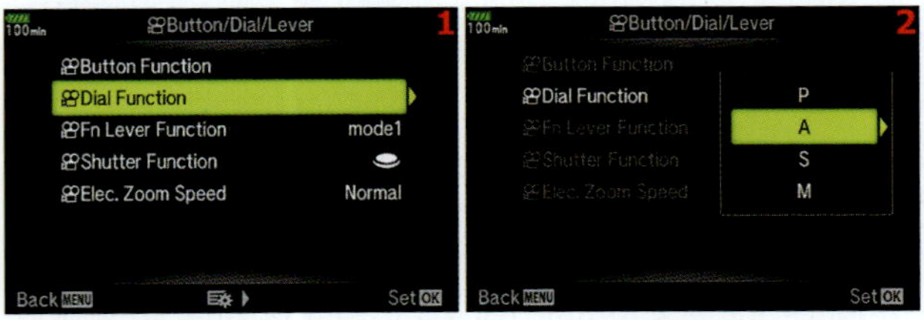

Figure 5.10Z9: Choosing an exposure mode for Front and Rear Dial programming

4. Choose [Movie] Dial Function from the [Movie] Button/Dial/Lever menu and scroll to the right (figure 5.10Z9, image 1).
5. You will be presented with a popup menu with four exposure mode choices: P, A, S, and M (figure 5.10Z9, image 2). The Front and Rear Dials can work differently for each exposure mode. In other words the Front and Rear Dials can be programmed with certain Dial Tasks for A mode, and a completely different set of Dial Tasks for S mode (see previous list). (***Note:*** You can repeat the steps starting from here for each of the four

exposure modes, if you'd like.) Select the exposure mode you want to configure and scroll to the right (figure 5.10Z9, image 2). The Dial Task selection screen will now open for that particular exposure mode.

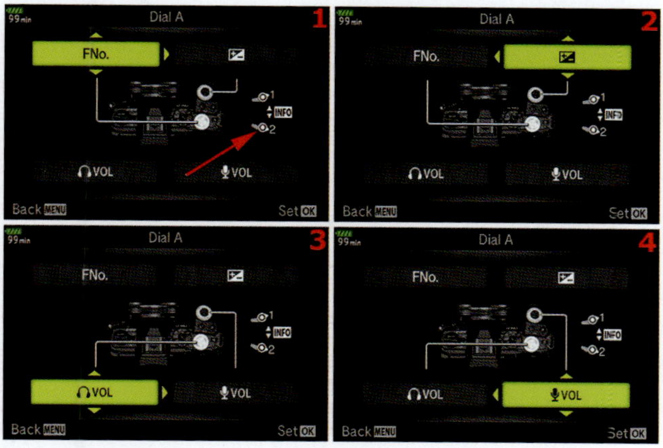

Figure 5.10Z10: Choosing Dial Tasks for the Front and Rear Dials

6. The Dial Task selection screen for exposure mode A (Dial A) is shown in figure 5.10Z10, images 1–4. You will note that there are two configurations available, one on the top and one on the bottom of each screen. The top dial configuration is available when the Fn Lever is set to position 1, and the bottom dial configuration is available when the Fn Lever is set to position 2 (figure 5.10Z10, image 1, red arrow). Notice how the lines on the top part of the screen in images 1 and 2 are pointing to the Front and Rear Dials—these settings will be used when the Fn Lever is in position 1. The bottom lines in images 3 and 4 are pointing to the same Front and Rear Dials—these settings will be used when the Fn Lever is in position 2. In summary, you have the ability to set a separate set of dial tasks for each exposure mode, and even within a particular mode you can use separate configurations for the same two dials, according to how the Fn Lever is set. Talk about flexibility! Choose a Dial Task for each of the four positions in figure 5.10Z10, images 1–4. Use the previous *Available Dial Tasks List* as a reference. You can either scroll to the right after setting each Dial Task, or you can press the info button to toggle between the top and bottom settings. Next we need to select an exposure mode to use while capturing the video.

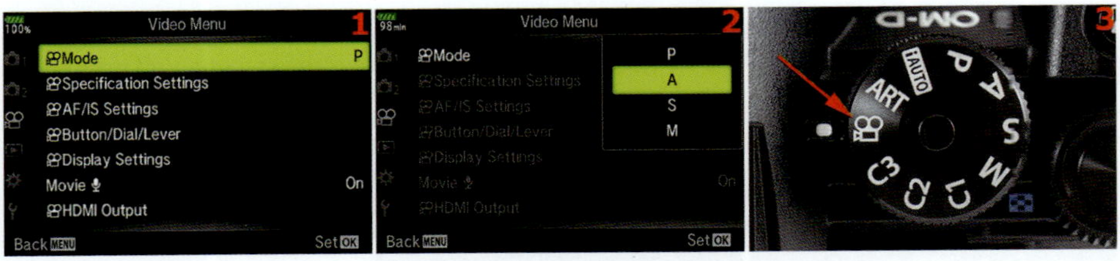

Figure 5.10Z11: Choosing an exposure mode for video capture

7. To choose an exposure mode, select the [Movie] Mode function from the Video Menu and scroll to the right (figure 5.10Z11, image 1).
8. A small exposure mode menu will appear with four exposure modes: P, A, S, and M (figure 5. 10Z11, image 2). Choose one of the exposure modes and press the OK button to lock it in. (***Note:*** You can also use the Live Control, instead of the Video Menu, to select the exposure mode.) We were configuring Dial Tasks for A mode in step 6, so we'll select A mode in this step to use those assigned tasks.
9. Set the Mode Dial to the movie camera symbol (figure 5.10Z11, image 3). When you record the video, the E-M1II will use the exposure mode you selected in step 8, and you will have control of the Dial Tasks you previously selected in step 6 for that exposure mode. To finish up, let's locate the Fn Lever and Front and Rear Dials.

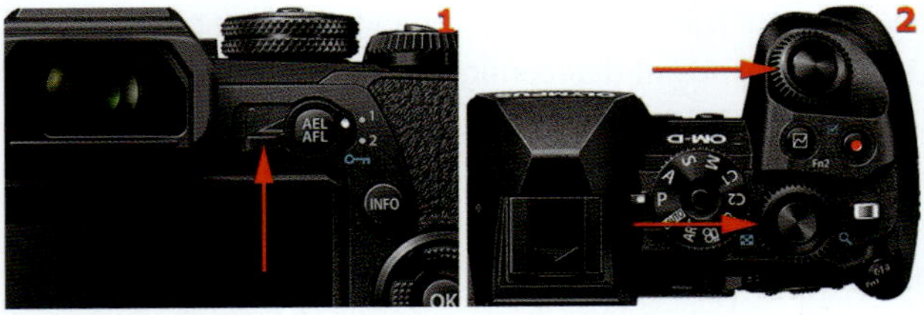

Figure 5.10Z12: Fn Lever and Front and Rear Dials

10. To use your new configuration while recording a movie, flip the Fn Lever to position 1 or 2, according to which set of Dial Tasks you prefer to use (figure 5.10Z11, image 1).
11. Then turn the Front Dial (figure 5.10Z11, image 2, top arrow) or Rear Dial (bottom arrow) while watching the camera monitor for Dial Task adjustment displays.

[Movie] Fn Lever Function

You can use the Fn Lever to quickly change how the Front and Rear Dials work (see previous subsection), or to select various autofocus modes. There are three Lever Tasks that can be assigned to the Fn Lever, to be used when you are recording videos.

Lever Task List

- ***mode1:*** This mode allows you to select how the Front and Rear Dials function. Each position of the level (1 or 2) allows you to use separate Dial Tasks for the Front and Rear Dials.
- ***mode2:*** This mode allows you to select a separate AF Mode, AF Target Setting, and AF Area Mode for each position of the Fn Lever (1 or 2).
- ***Off:*** The Fn Lever provides no functionality while recording videos.

Mode1

Mode1 allows the camera to use the Front and Rear Dial configurations created in the previous subsection **[Movie] Dial Function** (page 313). When you flip the Fn Lever between positions 1 and 2, the camera changes what the Front and Rear Dials do, as described in the subsection **Programming the Dials,** starting on page 313. Please refer to the previous subsection to see the results of what happens when you use mode1.

Let's see how to choose mode1 from the Video Menu.

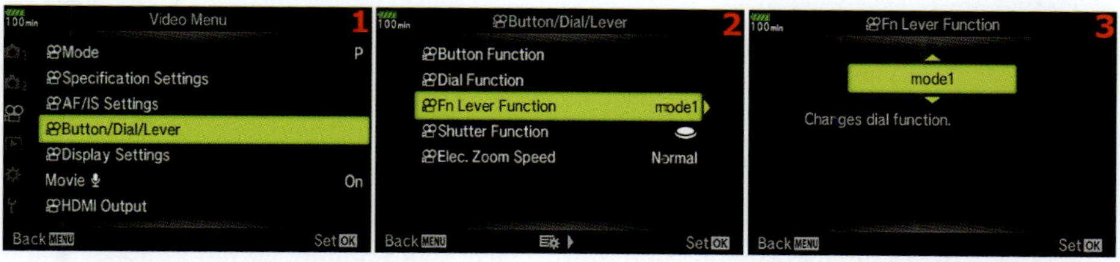

Figure 5.10Z13: Configuring the Fn Lever Function with the mode1 Lever Task

Use the following steps to choose the mode1 task for the Fn Lever Function:

1. Highlight [Movie] Button/Dial/Lever on the Video Menu and scroll to the right (figure 5.10Z13, image 1).
2. Choose [Movie] Fn Lever Function from the [Movie] Button/Dial/Lever menu and scroll to the right (figure 5.10Z13, image 2).
3. Select mode1 from the up/down menu and press the OK button to lock in the setting (figure 5.10Z13, image 3).

Again, please refer to the **Programming the Dials** subsection on page 313 for details on using mode1.

Mode2

Mode2 gives you the ability to assign different choices of AF Mode, AF Target Setting, and AF Area Mode for each position of the Fn Lever (1 or 2). You can also disable any one of the three AF choices so that it is not affected by the Fn Lever. Let's examine how mode2 works.

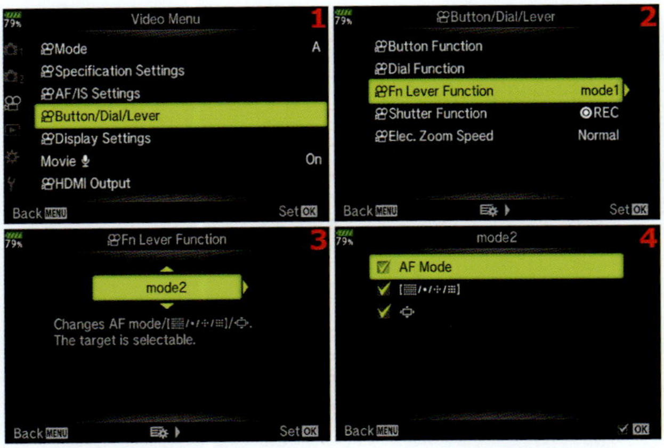

Figure 5.10Z14: Configuring the Fn Lever Function with the mode2 Lever Task

Use the following steps to choose the mode2 task for the Fn Lever Function:

1. Highlight [Movie] Button/Dial/Lever on the Video Menu and scroll to the right (figure 5.10Z14, image 1).
2. Choose [Movie] Fn Lever Function from the [Movie] Button/Dial/Lever menu and scroll to the right (figure 5.10Z14, image 2).
3. Select mode2 from the up/down menu and press the OK button to lock it in (figure 5.10Z14, image 3). At this point, you have two separate configurations for the AF Mode (page 291), AF Target Mode (page 415), and AF Area Mode (pages 38, 317). For instance, you might set the AF Mode to S-AF for Fn Lever position 1, and C-AF for Fn Lever position 2. And, you might set the AF Target/AF Area Modes to 5-Target Group for Fn Lever position 1, while you have AF Target/AF Area set to 9-Target Group for position 2. If you want to enable or disable one of the three available AF settings under mode2, scroll to the right.
4. The camera will present you with a list of three AF settings: AF Mode, [AF Target Mode], and [AF Area Mode] (figure 5.10Z14, image 4). You will note that there are check marks before each of these items by default. If you would like to prevent one of the three items from changing when the Fn Lever is flipped from one position to the other, simply uncheck the one you want to stay the same. To uncheck an item, highlight it and press the OK button. The OK button toggles the check mark on and off. Press the Menu button when you are done.

[Movie] Shutter Function

If you are a serious videographer, you may configure the Shutter button so that it starts and stops a video recording—instead of the Movie button.

If you choose to change the Shutter button into a video recording button, you will be unable to take still photographs *while in Movie Mode*. When the Mode Dial is *not* set to Movie Mode (camera icon), you may use the Shutter button to do still photography. It is only when you place the camera in Movie Mode that this assignment will be active, if selected.

Also, the normal Movie button cannot be used for recording video when the Shutter button is assigned to record video. In this case, you may reassign the Movie button to some other Button Task.

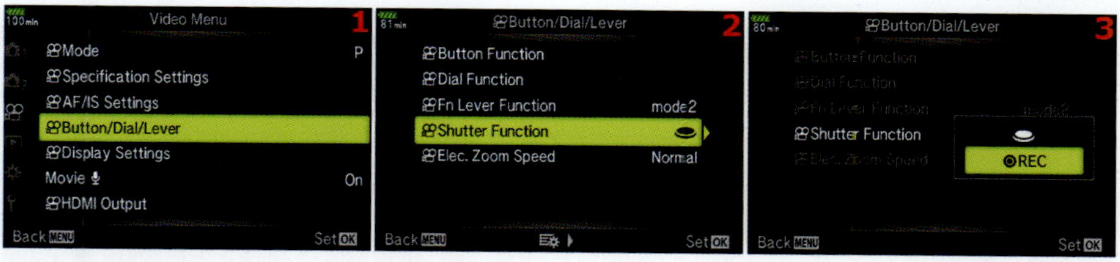

Figure 5.10Z15: Assigning the Shutter button for use in Movie Mode

Use these steps to assign the Shutter button for use while in Movie Mode on the Mode Dial:

1. Highlight [Movie] Button/Dial/Lever from the Video Menu and scroll to the right (figure 5.10Z15, image 1).
2. Select [Movie] Shutter Function from the [Movie] Button/Dial/Lever menu and scroll to the right (figure 5.10Z15, image 2).
3. As shown in figure 5.10Z15, image 3, use the up/down menu to select [Shutter Button] (top menu item) for normal still photography needs, or [Movie Button] REC (second menu item) for recording videos. If you select [Movie Button] REC, the Shutter button will start and stop video recordings when pressed. The normal Movie button—the one with the red dot, next to Fn2—will not start or stop a movie, but it can be reassigned to some other Button Task (page 432). It will be set to Off in the Video Menu unless you reassign it. Make your choice and press the OK button to lock it in.

[Movie] Elec. Zoom Speed

Olympus makes a few power zoom lenses that allow you to zoom in and out by turning a ring or pressing camera buttons. My favorite power zoom lens is the M.Zuiko ED 14–42mm f/3.5–5.6 EZ lens. When I am out with my family, having a good time like a tourist, I often use that sharp little pancake lens to cut down on weight and bulk.

The E-M1II allows you to select three speeds for how fast the camera zooms in and out. When I am shooting still pictures, I don't want to wait for the lens to zoom. I want it to zoom as quickly as possible so I won't miss my shot.

However, when I am shooting video, I want the lens to zoom in and out more slowly because that is less jarring and looks better in a video. The slow zoom speed allows me to smoothly pull focus for those cool focus point changes that used to be available only on video cameras that cost thousands of dollars.

Let's see how to adjust the zoom speed of your power zoom lenses for shooting both still images and videos.

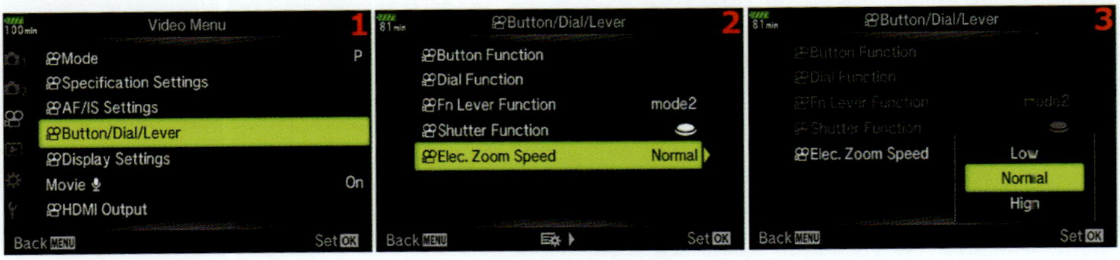

Figure 5.10Z16: Assigning a zoom speed for electronic zoom lenses

Use these steps to change the power zoom speed of your lens:

1. Highlight [Movie] Button/Dial/Lever from the Video Menu and scroll to the right (figure 5.10Z16, image 1).
2. Select [Movie] Elec. Zoom Speed from the [Movie] Button/Dial/Lever menu and scroll to the right (figure 5.10Z16, image 2).
3. Choose Low, Normal, or High from the menu and press the OK button to lock in the speed setting (figure 5.10Z16, image 3). Low gives you a slow zoom, which is good for pulling or pushing focus; Normal gives you a medium setting; and High speeds up the zoom significantly. Experiment with these three settings to see which one works best for you.

[Movie] Display Settings

The [Movie] Display Settings function is designed to let you control certain features of the camera's monitor display for when you are capturing video. There are four separate display settings that we will discuss in the following subsections.

[Movie] Control Settings

The [Movie] Control Settings function allows you to choose whether the camera provides both the Live Control and LV Super Control Panel (Live SCP) when you are recording video. If one is your favorite control, you can disable the other, or you can turn them both on or off.

This setting does not affect your use of the Live Control or LV Super Control Panel when you are taking still pictures.

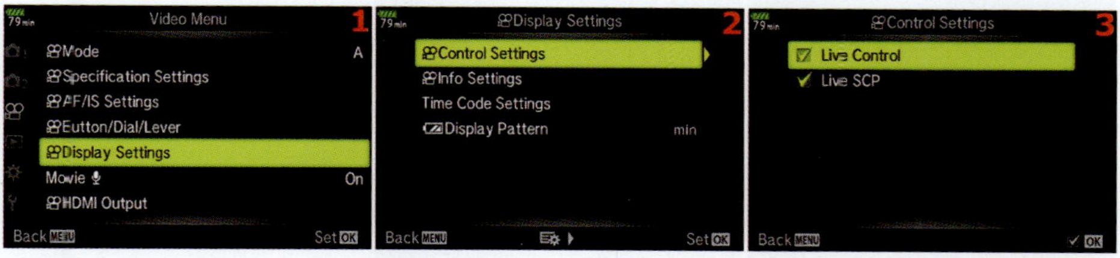

Figure 5.11A: Enabling or disabling the Live Control and Live SCP for movie recording

Use the following steps to enable or disable the Live Control and/or LV Super Control Panel for recording videos:

1. Highlight [Movie] Display Settings on the Video Menu and scroll to the right (figure 5.11A, image 1).
2. Choose [Movie] Control Settings from the [Movie] Display Settings menu and scroll to the right (figure 5.11A, image 2).
3. You will now see your two display control choices: Live Control and Live SCP (figure 5.11A, image 3). Placing a check mark in either position makes that control available during video capture. You can add or remove a check mark by highlighting the control name and pressing the OK button. When you have placed or removed the check marks, press the Menu button to lock in your choices. The camera will return to the previous screen (figure 5.11A, image 2).

[Movie] Info Settings

The [Movie] Info Settings function lets you control the video information details on the movie recording screen (figure 5.1D on page 253). There are 13 video information details available (e.g., Live Histogram, Level Gauge, Picture Mode, WB), which you can add to or remove from the movie recording screen.

You also have two custom configurations available—Custom1 and Custom2—for the video information details on the movie recording screen. You can switch between the two custom configurations by pressing the info button. Let's see how it works.

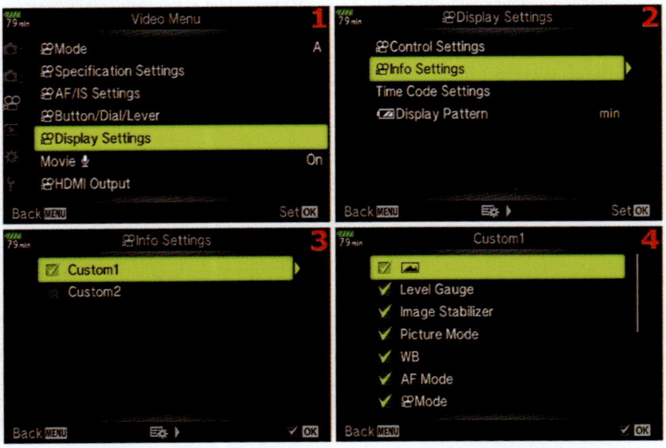

Figure 5.11B: Determining what video information to include on the monitor during video recording

Use these steps to customize the display of information during video recording:

1. Highlight [Movie] Display Settings on the Video Menu and scroll to the right (figure 5.11B, image 1).
2. Choose [Movie] Info Settings from the [Movie] Display Settings menu and scroll to the right (figure 5.11B, image 2).
3. You will now be presented with a choice of two custom settings: Custom1 and Custom2 (figure 5.11B, image 3). The camera default is for Custom2 to be unchecked. If you leave Custom2 unchecked, the camera will offer you only one configurable view of the movie recording screen. If you put a check mark next to both Custom1 and Custom2, you will have two configurable video recording screens available, and you can switch between them with the info button. To enable the Custom2 setting, highlight it and press the OK button to add a check mark. Now highlight whichever custom setting you want to configure first and scroll to the right.
4. You will now see a screen with 13 items (figure 5.11B, image 4). You must scroll up or down to see all of the available items. Custom1 has all items enabled (checked) by default, as indicated by the check marks. Custom2 has all items enabled except Movie Effect (near the bottom of the list of items, not shown) by default. To disable an option,

select it and press the OK button to remove the check mark. Put the check mark back to reenable it. When you have configured one of the custom settings, press the Menu button to return to the previous screen (figure 5.11B, image 3), select the other custom setting, and repeat this step.

5. Press the Menu button to lock in the configuration when you are finished.

Time Code Settings

The Time Code Settings function allows your camera to synchronize with other devices, such as sound recorders and other video recorders. The Olympus Time Code system in the E-M1II is based on Society of Motion Picture and Television Engineers (SMPTE) time code standards. The time code is recorded along with each frame of a movie. The format is Hour:Minute:Second:Frame, with Frame being the integer frame number within a particular second. For technical information on the time code and other video standards, please refer to this website (plus there are several videos on YouTube):

http://en.wikiaudio.org/SMPTE_time_code

If your video efforts are limited to documenting the kids during their early years, you may find that you can ignore this section. But if you edit your movies or want to merge several segments, you will likely want to use either a recording-time clock or an elapsed-time clock.

When you have several different videographers working in concert and giving different views of a scene, it is often desirable to be able to slice-and-dice segments from different cameras to develop a single, seamless end product. This requires each camera to be set to the same time, down to the number of the frame within the referenced hour:minute:second.

Other video projects shot with a single camera will require only that the recording time across the segments be captured. These are the needs that the Time Code Settings address.

Time Code Mode

There are two Time Code Modes and they address how the camera will handle timing when a frame is dropped while recording. Here is a description of the two modes:

- ***Drop Frame:*** Records the time code *with corrections* for dropped frames (errors) while recording. Use when extreme accuracy is required!
- ***Non-DF*** (no drop frame): Records the time code *with no corrections* for dropped frames while recording.

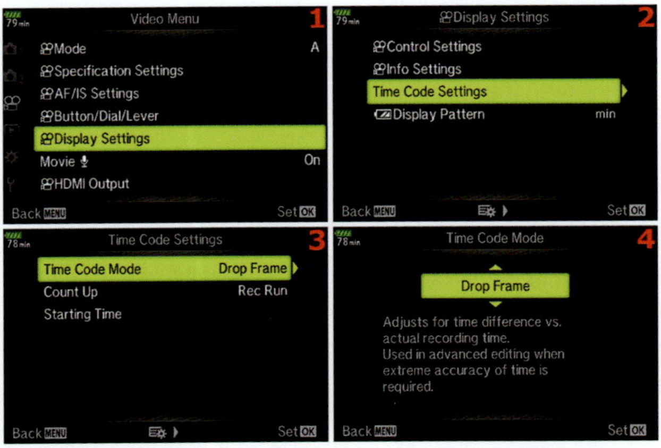

Figure 5.11C: Setting the Time Code Mode

Use these steps to select a Time Code Mode:

1. Highlight [Movie] Display Settings on the Video Menu and scroll to the right (figure 5.11C, image 1).
2. Select Time Code Settings from the [Movie] Display Settings menu and scroll to the right (figure 5.11C, image 2).
3. Choose Time Code Mode from the Time Code Settings menu and scroll to the right (figure 5.11C, image 3).
4. Use the up/down menu and select Drop Frame to enable corrected time codes, or select Non-DF to disable it (figure 5.11C, image 4).
5. Press the OK button to Set your choice.

Count Up

The Count Up function lets you decide when to run the Time Code count. There are two settings available. Let's examine each one.

- ***Rec Run:*** The Time Code will run only while you are actually recording a video.
- ***Free Run:*** The Time Code will start running as soon as you enable Free Run and will continue running, even if you turn the camera off.

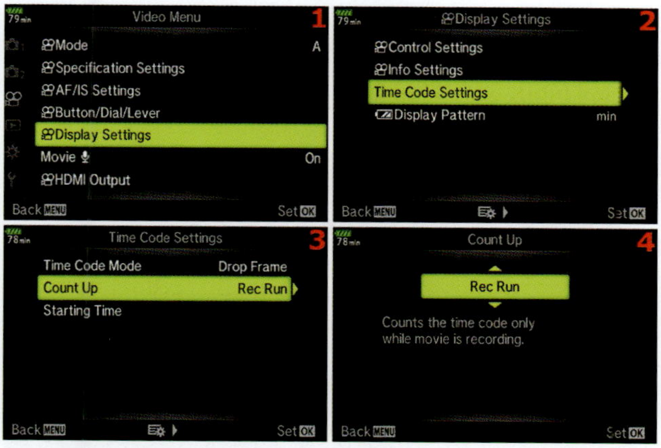

Figure 5.11D: Setting the Count Up value

Use these steps to choose one of the Count Up settings:

1. Highlight [Movie] Display Settings on the Video Menu and scroll to the right (figure 5.11D, image 1).
2. Select Time Code Settings from the [Movie] Display Settings menu and scroll to the right (figure 5.11D, image 2).
3. Select Count Up from the Time Code Settings menu and scroll to the right (figure 5.11D, image 3).
4. Use the up/down menu and select Rec Run to run the Time Code only while the camera is recording video, or select Free Run to have the camera count time as a single continuous time, regardless of whether the camera is actually recording a movie or is even powered on (figure 5.11D, image 4).
5. Press the OK button to Set your choice.

Starting Time

As mentioned previously, the Time Code is recorded along with each frame of a movie in the following format: *Hour:Minute:Second:Frame,* with Frame being the integer frame number within a particular second. There are three subsettings within the Starting Time setting, as follows:

- ***Reset:*** The Reset option forces each of the four Time Code segments to return to 00, indicating no elapsed time. When Rec Run is set in Count Up (previous subsection) and you are recording a brand-new video, a Time Code of 00:00:00:00 is usually used as a starting time.

- ***Manual Input:*** You can set all four of the segments (00:00:00:00) yourself with Manual Input. If you're using Rec Run, but are not working with the first portion of a video project, you will probably use Manual Input to tell the camera what Start Time to use for the portion you're getting ready to shoot.
- ***Current Time:*** This setting uses the camera's time-of-day clock as the Starting Time (HH:MM:SS:00), with the last segment (Frame) starting at 00. Many videographers using Free Run in Count Up (previous subsection) will opt for Current Time.

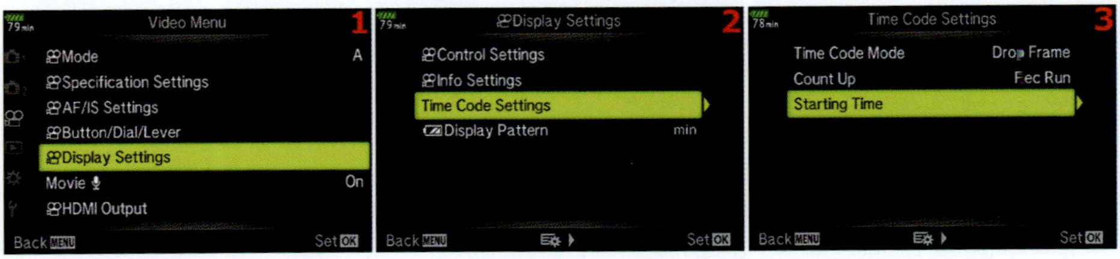

Figure 5.11E: Establishing movie-recording starting time

Use these steps to set the Starting Time for movie recording:

1. Highlight [Movie] Display Settings on the Video Menu and scroll to the right (figure 5.11E, image 1).
2. Select Time Code Settings from the [Movie] Display Settings menu and scroll to the right (figure 5.11E, image 2).
3. Select Starting Time from the Time Code Settings menu and scroll to the right (figure 5.11E, image 3). The following steps will describe how to configure each of the items from the previous list (Reset, Manual Input, or Current Time).

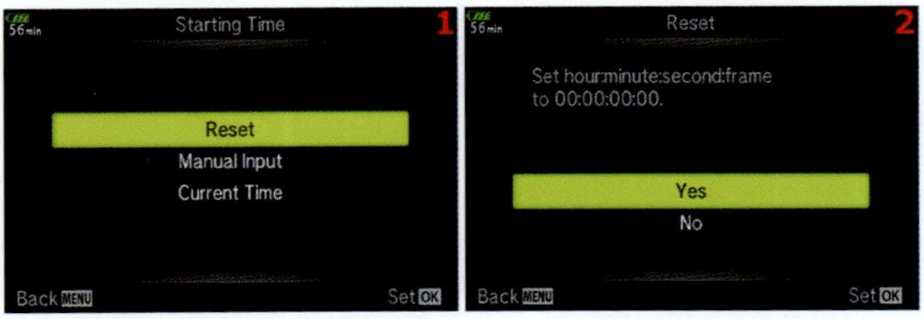

Figure 5.11F: Resetting the Time Code to 00:00:00:00

4. If you do not wish to use Reset, skip steps 4 and 5. Figure 5.11F begins with the screen that comes after figure 5.11E, image 3. Choose Reset from the Starting Time menu and press the OK button (figure 5.11F, image 1).
5. Select Yes from the Reset menu to set the Time Code to 00:00:00:00, or choose No to cancel (figure 5.11F, image 2). Press the OK button to lock in your choice.

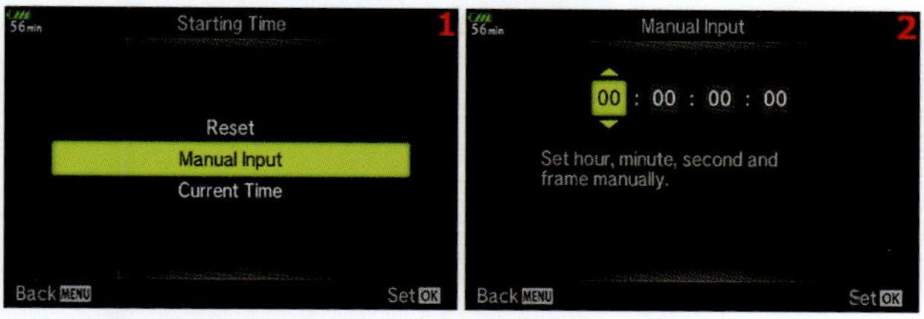

Figure 5.11G: Input a Time Code manually

6. If you do not wish to use Manual Input, skip steps 6 and 7. Figure 5.11G begins with the screen that comes after figure 5.11E, image 3. Choose Manual Input from the Starting Time menu and press the OK button (figure 5.11G, image 1).
7. You will now see four up/down menus—one two-digit segment for each of the hour, minute, second, and frame number settings (figure 5.11G, image 2). The *hour* segment (first position, starting from the left) allows you to select from 0 to 23; the *minute* (second position) and *second* segments (third position) each allow you to select from 00 to 59; and the *frame* segment (fourth position) allows you select from 00 to 29 (according to the frame rate you chose under the [Movie] Record Mode setting [page 254]). Input your manual values for each segment and press the OK button to Set your choice.

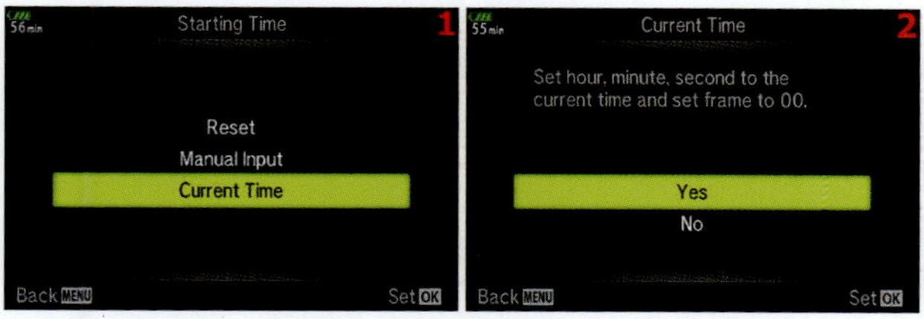

Figure 5.11H: Using the camera's current time for the Time Code

8. Figure 5.11H begins with the screen that comes after figure 5.11E, image 3. Choose Current Time from the Starting Time menu and press the OK button (figure 5.11H, image 1).
9. Select Yes from the menu and press the OK button to set the starting time to the camera's time-of-day clock (HH:MM:SS:00), with the frame number set to zero (last segment). Select No to cancel. Press the OK button to lock in your (figure 5.11H, image 2).

[Battery] Display Pattern

The [Battery] Display Pattern setting allows you to choose whether the battery status displayed in the upper-left corner of the movie recording screen is given in minutes or a percentage.

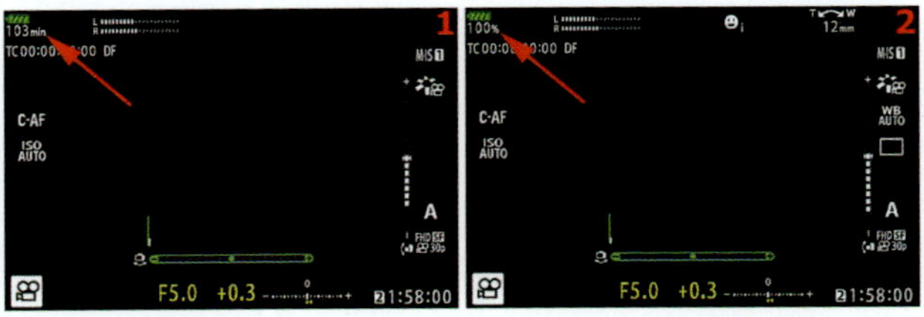

Figure 5.11I: Minute (min) or percentage (%) battery display type

Figure 5.11I, image 1, shows the minutes pattern (103 min) for an E-M1II with a full battery, and image 2 shows the percentage pattern (100 %).

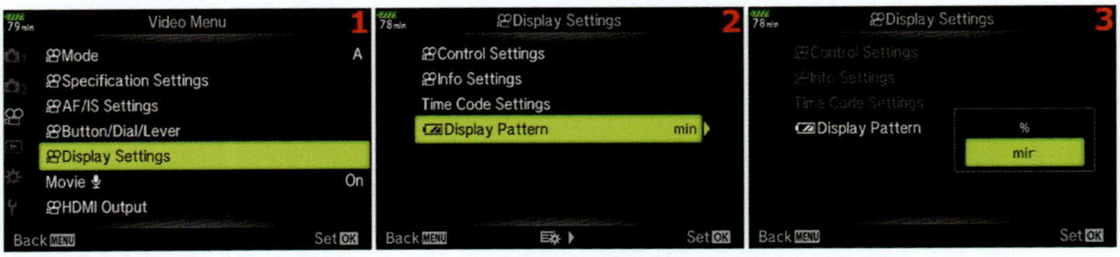

Figure 5.11J: Choosing a [Battery] Display Pattern

Use these steps to set the [Battery] Display Pattern for the movie recording screen:

1. Highlight [Movie] Display Settings on the Video Menu and scroll to the right (figure 5.11J, image 1).
2. Choose [Battery] Display Pattern from the [Movie] Display Settings menu and scroll to the right (figure 5.11J, image 2).
3. Choose either the minutes (min) setting or the percentage (%) setting from the small popup (figure 5.11J, image 3). Press the OK button to Set your choice.

Next let's consider how to configure the built-in, stereo sound-recording system on your camera.

Movie [Sound]

You can control the camera's built-in microphone very effectively with the Movie [Sound] function. You can also use this function to control an external microphone. The Movie [Sound] function has six settings—with several subsettings—allowing you to adjust various aspects of recording sound.

Let's examine how to open the Movie [Sound] function and adjust each of its internal settings.

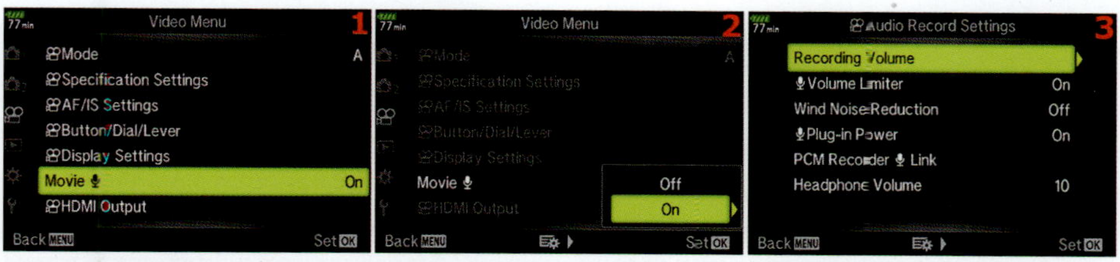

Figure 5.12A: Enabling or disabling the camera's mic input and adjusting its subsettings

Use these steps to enable (or disable) the camera's microphone for video capture, and then proceed to the following six subsections to configure the microphone's six settings (listed in figure 5.12A, image 3):

1. Select the Movie [Sound] function from the Video Menu and scroll to the right (figure 5.12A, image 1).
2. A small menu will appear with Off and On selections for the mic input (figure 5.12A, image 2). If you select Off, the camera will not record any sound when you record a video. If you leave this set to On (default), the built-in mic or an external mic plugged in to the mic port will record sound.
3. Press the OK button to Set the microphone to On (or Off). If you are interested in configuring any or all of the six available sound recording settings, select On and scroll to the right.
4. You will now see the [Movie] Audio Record Settings menu (figure 5.12A, image 3). This menu provides six settings that allow you to fine-tune the use of the internal or an external microphone. Each of the settings will be considered in the following subsections.

Settings Recommendation: I leave my mic set to On because I often record family videos with the camera's built-in mic. Sometimes I even use an external mic mounted in the hot shoe and plugged into the external mic port. If you use the camera for commercial video and use an external digital recorder to capture high-quality sound, you may want to set this function to Off.

Recording Volume

With the Recording Volume function you can adjust the microphone sensitivity (gain). There are separate controls for the built-in stereo mic, an external stereo mic plugged in to the mic port, and an external stereo device that produces sound (e.g., music from an iPhone) through the line-in feature of the mic port.

You can record sound to your video from any of these devices (one at a time), and the camera allows you to control the sound input types individually. Let's see how.

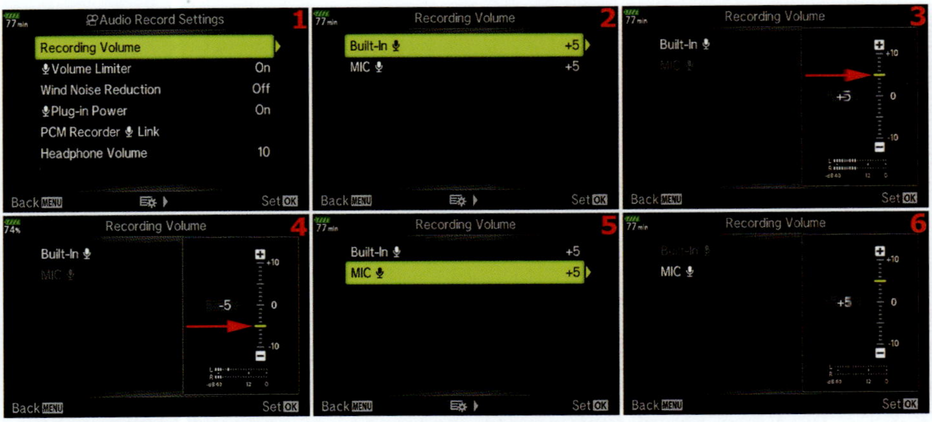

Figure 5.12B: Setting the Recording Volume level for the sound recording system

Use the following steps to set the Recording Volume or turn it off:

1. Figure 5.12B, image 1, begins where figure 5.12A, image 3, left off. Select Recording Volume from the [Movie] Audio Record Settings menu and scroll to the right (figure 5.12B, image 1).
2. Choose Built-in to adjust the camera's built-in stereo mic, or MIC to adjust an external microphone or smart device, and scroll to the right (figure 5.12B, image 2). Use the following steps for either of the two input types to get similar results.
3. Figure 5.12B, image 3, shows the control you will use to adjust the sensitivity of either microphone type (or smart device). There is a sliding indicator scale with a yellow bar (red arrow) that you move up or down by rotating the Rear Dial or pressing the up and down keys on the Arrow Pad. You can adjust the mic sensitivity over a 20-level range from +10 to –10, and the sensitivity value will appear in the gray box that contains a +5 in image 3. The camera is set to +5 built-in mic sensitivity in figure 5.12B, image 3, and –5 sensitivity in image 4 (red arrow). The best way to do the adjustment is to watch the sound level bars on the L (left) and R (right) scale just below the sliding indicator. The L and R scales show the sound input level for each channel. As you watch the average sound level with the L and R channel sound-level bars, you may decide to increase or decrease the sound input by moving the yellow sliding indicator bar up or down until the sound stays in a range you feel is usable.
4. Figure 5.12 B, images 5 and 6, show that the MIC input—for external devices—works the same as the Built-in mic setting. Move the yellow bar toward +10 or –10 while watching the L and R sound-level bars, until the sound is being recorded within a usable range.
5. After adjusting the sensitivity for the input type you are using, press the OK button to Set the sensitivity level.

Settings Recommendation: This is a powerful function that allows you to set different sensitivities for the built-in mic, an external mic, or an external sound device, such as an iPhone, iPod, or iPad (or other smart device) that is playing music. The camera does a pretty good job of managing the sound level for both mic types, so I rarely use this function. However, when I feed music from my iPhone into the camera—with a wire that has a 3.5mm stereo plug on both ends—I find that I have to turn the volume down very low on the iPhone and carefully watch the L and R sound-level scales to make sure I don't overpower the line-in (Mic) port. With a little experimentation and adjustment, you can play your favorite music directly into your camera for videos that need no other type of sound. I bet none of your friends' cameras can do that. Make them jealous!

[Microphone] Volume Limiter

When you capture sound of any type while you record a video, the sound may suddenly become overpoweringly loud. Maybe you are recording a basketball game and the player SCORES! The crowd erupts with fist-shaking screams of delight and generates a sudden explosion of noise that sets off car alarms outside the auditorium. Do you want the energetic yelling and foot stomping to be recorded as distorted crackling in the sound of your video? No? Simply leave the [Sound] Volume Limiter function set to its default of On. The camera will sense the sudden blast of loud sound and limit the input to the camera, hopefully saving your video from requiring extensive sound editing later.

Let's see how to enable or disable the [Microphone] Volume Limiter.

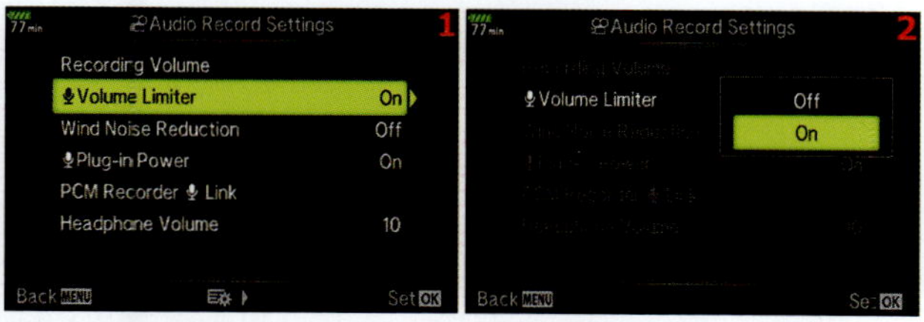

Figure 5.12C: Limit the maximum recording volume for loud sounds

Use the following steps to enable or disable the [Microphone] Volume Limiter for video recording:

1. Figure 5.12C, image 1, begins where figure 5.12A, image 3, left off. Select the [Microphone] Volume Limiter function from the [Movie] Audio Record Settings menu and scroll to the right (figure 5.12C, image 1).
2. A small menu will appear with On and Off choices (figure 5.12C, image 2). Select Off to disable the [Microphone] Volume Limiter function or On (default) to enable it.
3. Press the OK button to Set your choice.

Settings Recommendation: It's a good idea to leave this function enabled at all times. Although you can control sound most of the time, sometimes sudden noises can happen too fast to manually compensate for them. To preserve the sound quality in your video, it may be a good idea to let the camera automatically react to overpowering sound.

Wind Noise Reduction

When you are recording a video with the built-in mic or an external mic, sometimes the wind blowing on the mic will make a low-frequency rumbling noise that is quite objectionable. It is usually not possible to completely eliminate strong wind noise, especially with an unprotected mic, but the objectionable sound can be reduced with a low-cut filter. The camera has one built into the mic circuitry, and it can be set to various levels, including off.

Let's examine how to configure the low-cut Wind Noise Reduction filter in your E-M1II.

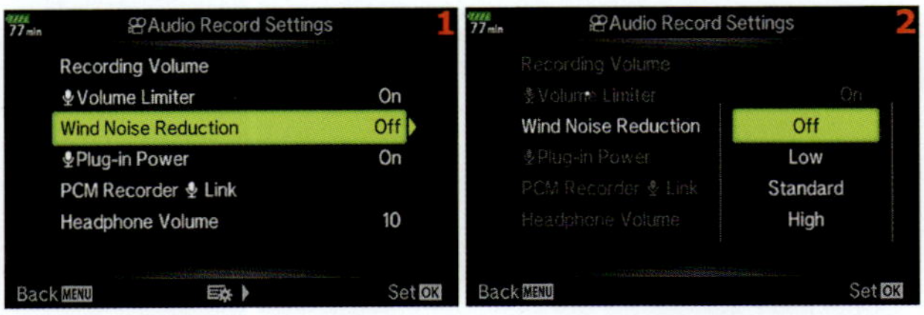

Figure 5.12D: Enabling or disabling the camera's Wind Noise Reduction filter

Use the following steps to set the Wind Noise Reduction level for video recording, or turn it off:

1. Figure 5.12D, image 1, begins where figure 5.12A, image 3, left off. Select the Wind Noise Reduction function from the [Movie] Audio Record Settings menu and scroll to the right (figure 5.12D, image 1).
2. A small menu will appear with Off, Low, Standard, and High options (figure 5.12D, image 2). Select Off to disable the Wind Noise Reduction filter, or choose Low, Standard, or High to select various levels of wind noise reduction. The camera defaults to Off.
3. Press the OK button to Set your choice.

Settings Recommendation: This is an especially useful function if you mostly use the camera's built-in mic. However, most people who are serious about video use a better external mic with special foam shielding around the sensitive mic head to prevent wind noise. I do not generally leave this setting enabled because a low-cut filter of this type tends to reduce some normal low-frequency sounds. However, if you are recording in a windy environment with the built-in mic, or if you are using an unprotected external mic, by all means use this filter. Even a small amount of wind blowing across the face of the camera can make a rumbling noise on the video soundtrack. You will need to experiment with the three levels of Wind Noise Reduction to see which level you prefer.

[Microphone] Plug-In Power

This feature is set to provide power to an external microphone connected to the microphone input terminal on the left side of the camera. You do not need this feature if you only use the camera's built-in microphone.

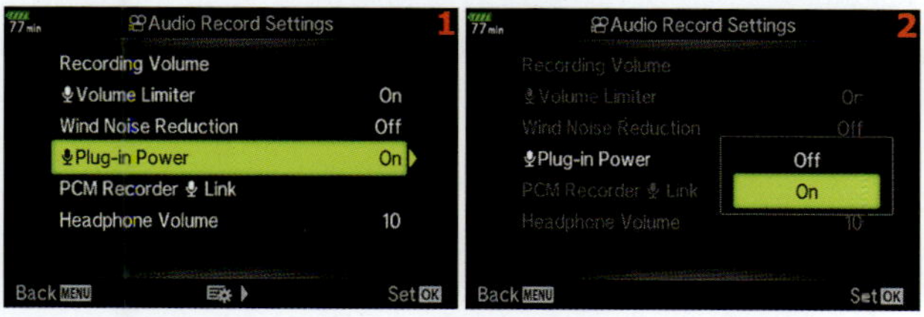

Figure 5.12E: Enabling the [Microphone] Plug-in Power feature

Use these steps to enable or disable the [Microphone] Plug-in Power capability:

1. Figure 5.12E, image 1, begins where figure 5.12A, image 3, left off. Select the [Microphone] Plug-in Power function from the [Movie] Audio Record Settings menu and scroll to the right (figure 5.12E, image 1).
2. Choose On to enable [Microphone] Plug-in Power, or select Off to disable it (figure 5.12E, image 2).
3. Press the OK button to Set your choice.

Settings Recommendation: This function works to power external microphones, such as the Olympus SEMA-1 or Olympus ME-52W mic. I have tested a Nikon ME-1 mic with my E-M1II and it works great. Plug in your external mic and test this function to make sure it works to power your favorite mic.

PCM Recorder [Microphone] Link

There is a class of digital sound recorders, known as PCM recorders, that can be used with the camera when recording movies. With a low-resistance cable between the PCM recorder and the USB port on the camera, you need only to enable the PCM Recorder [Microphone] Link to make the system operational.

You can also use an IC recorder connected to the camera's microphone jack for sound recording (see the upcoming sidebar **Audio Recorder Types** on page 335 for information on audio recorder types).

There are three settings within this function, each of which allows you to control the sound recording process. Let's consider how to adjust the settings.

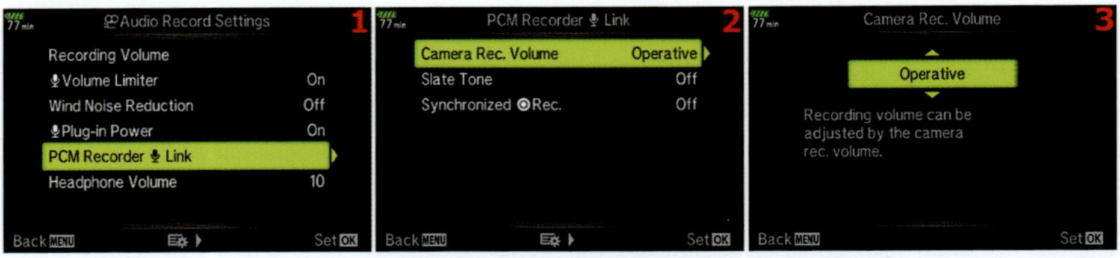

Figure 5.12F: Enabling the PCM Recorder [Microphone] Link

Use these steps to enable and configure the PCM Recorder [Microphone] Link:

1. Figure 5.12F, image 1, begins where figure 5.12A, image 3, left off. Select the PCM Recorder [Microphone] Link function from the [Movie] Audio Record Settings menu and scroll to the right (figure 5.12F, image 1).
2. First we will configure the Camera Rec. Volume setting. Choose Camera Rec. Volume from the PCM Recorder [Microphone] Link menu and scroll to the right (figure 5.12F, image 2).
3. The Camera Rec. Volume up/down menu provides you with two choices: Operative and Inoperative. If you choose Operative, the camera will control the sound recording volume. The Inoperative setting allows the external PCM recorder to control the sound recording volume. Make your selection and press the OK button to lock it in.

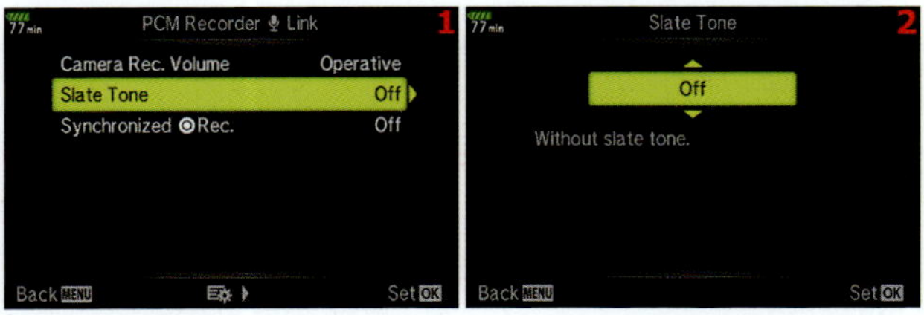

Figure 5.12G: Enabling a Slate Tone

4. Next we will configure the Slate Tone. Select Slate Tone from the PCM Recorder [Microphone] Link menu and scroll to the right (figure 5.12G, image 1).
5. The Slate Tone menu will offer you two choices: On or Off. If you select Off, no slate tone will be generated. However, if you select On, a USB-connected PCM recorder (e.g., Olympus LS-100) will generate a slate tone when you hold down the OK button during a video recording. Make your selection and press the OK button to lock it in.

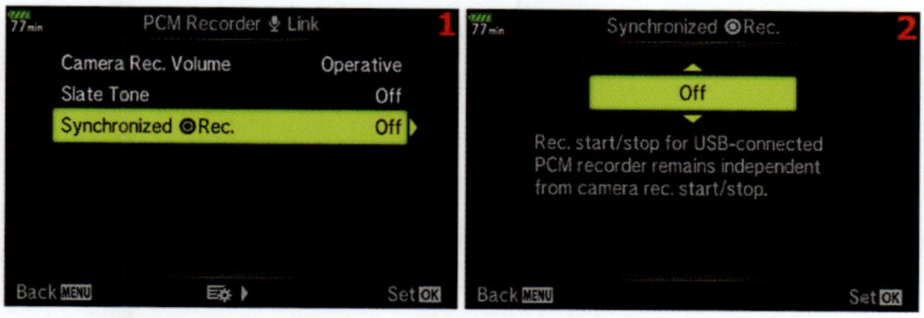

Figure 5.12H: Enabling Synchronized [Movie Button] Rec.

6. Now we will examine Synchronized [Movie Button] Rec. Choose Synchronized [Movie Button] Rec. from the PCM Recorder [Microphone] Link menu and scroll to the right (figure 5.12H, image 1).
7. The Synchronized [Movie Button] Rec. up/down menu offers you two choices: On and Off. Select On to allow a USB-connected PCM recorder (e.g., Olympus LS-100) to automatically start and stop sound recording when you start and stop the video recording with the Movie button. If you choose Off, the camera will not synchronize the video recording's on/off state with the PCM recorder, letting the PCM recorder continue recording even if video is not being recording. Press the OK button to Set your choice.

Settings Recommendation: If you would rather control the sound recording with a PCM or IC recorder instead of a mic, you can use this function to prepare the camera. There are all sorts of PCM recorders available on the market, such as the Olympus LS-100 PCM Recorder. You could also choose from a wide array of IC recorders, such as the Olympus VN-7200 IC Recorder. IC recorders are generally much less costly than PCM recorders.

Audio Recorder Types (PCM versus IC)

Linear PCM recorders (which connect to the USB port) use the audio data format from normal audio CDs. The word "linear" refers to a lack of data compression in the audio signal. The recorder's analog audio signal is directly converted to a virtually noncompressed digital format. Unfortunately, due to the lack of compression, a linear audio recorder generates a very large amount of sound data, so you will need to balance best sound quality with storage capacity. A PCM recorder may be the best choice for hard-core videographers who must have the best in both video and audio quality, and who have the necessary storage to deal with the large file sizes.

On the other hand, an IC recorder (which connects to the microphone jack) creates a compressed MP3 file with much smaller storage requirements, even though there is little degradation in sound quality and a significant reduction in sound data size. An IC recorder, with its MP3 format, may be the best choice for advanced noncommercial videos and some longer commercial videos.

Headphone Volume

The E-M1II camera gives you the ability to attach headphones for monitoring the sound during video recording. As some headphones are more efficient than others, you will need to be able to adjust the volume level, and this function allows you to do just that.

Caution: I tend to treat an unknown set of headphones cautiously, and start the volume level at about 5, turning it up gradually while listening to the sound. I value my hearing too much to start off with a potentially damaging volume level.

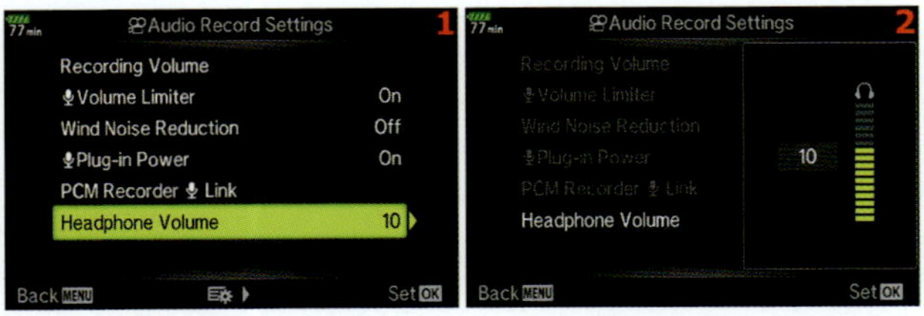

Figure 5.12I: Adjusting the Headphone Volume

Use these steps to adjust the Headphone Volume:

1. Figure 5.12I, image 1, begins where figure 5.12A, image 3, left off (page 329). Select the Headphone Volume function from the [Movie] Audio Record Settings menu and scroll to the right (figure 5.12I, image 1).
2. Use the up/down buttons on the Arrow Pad or turn the Rear Dial to select a value between 1 (lowest volume) and 16 (highest volume) (figure 5.12I, image 2). Press the OK button to Set your choice.

Settings Recommendation: There are all sorts of headphones available these days, from low-end ear buds to excellent Sony or Shure studio headphones. Choose the type of headphones that suit you best. If you are just now experimenting with using headphones with your camera, just use the set of ear buds that came with your smartphone. You can upgrade to a studio-quality headphone set later if you need to. Watch that volume and don't damage your ears!

[Movie] HDMI Output

For hard-core videographers and advanced video enthusiasts, the HDMI port on the E-M1II allows the use of external recording devices, such as the Atomos Ninja Flame (**https://www.atomos.com/ninja-flame**).

The [Movie] HDMI Output function's Record Mode setting allows you to control the HDMI port for live video capture. You can send a clean (no camera info overlays), virtually uncompressed (4:2:2) video signal from the camera's HDMI port to an external recorder, with no limitations on video recording time, and get very high-quality video.

Additionally, the camera's Monitor Mode setting lets you send a video stream, along with camera shooting information overlays, to an external monitor.

Note: If you simultaneously record video to an internal video card and an external video recorder, the HDMI output will be limited to a 4:2:0 video stream, upsampled to 4:2:2. For best quality external video recording, at 4:2:2 color subsampling, do not record to the internal cards at the same time as the external recorder.

Let's examine how to use the [Movie] HDMI Output function.

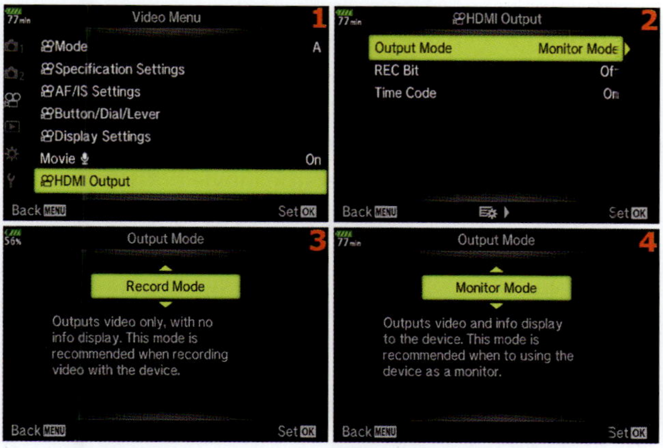

Figure 5.13A: Setting the Output Mode

Use the following steps to configure the [Movie] HDMI Output function:

1. Highlight [Movie] HDMI Output on the Video Menu and scroll to the right (figure 5.13A, image 1).
2. Choose Output Mode from the [Movie] HDMI Output menu and scroll to the right (figure 5.13A, image 2).
3. Figure 5.13A, images 3 and 4, show the two choices on the Output Mode up/down menu: Record Mode and Monitor Mode. You should choose Record Mode when you want to send a clean (no camera information overlays), 4:2:2 video stream to an external recorder (e.g., Atomos Ninja Flame). This allows you to record video with no time constraints; you are limited only by the capacity of the storage on your external recorder. Monitor Mode is for when you want to use the HDMI output with an external video monitor and need all of the information displays normally seen on the movie recording screen (page 257). Monitor Mode is not suitable for recording video unless you want a video with all of the camera information overlays included. Choose the Output Mode you want to use and press the OK button to lock it in and return to the previous screen. Next we will configure the REC Bit.

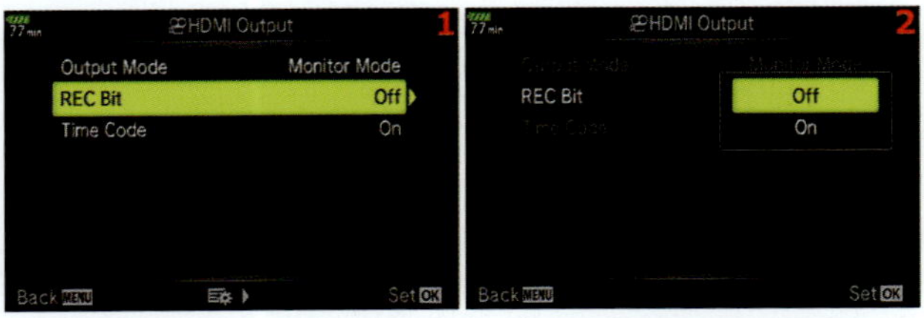

Figure 5.13B: Setting the REC Bit (sending an HDMI REC trigger)

4. Choose REC Bit from the [Movie] HDMI Output menu and scroll to the right (figure 5.13B, image 1).
5. A small menu will open offering you two choices: On and Off (figure 5.13B, image 2). If you choose On, the camera sets the REC Bit (flag), which sends an HDMI REC trigger signal to the external video recorder, letting it know when the Movie button has been pressed on the camera. This will trigger the external recorder to start and stop recording at the camera's command. Choosing Off prevents the camera from sending a REC trigger signal. Choose On or Off and press the OK button to lock in your choice. Now let's configure the Time Code.

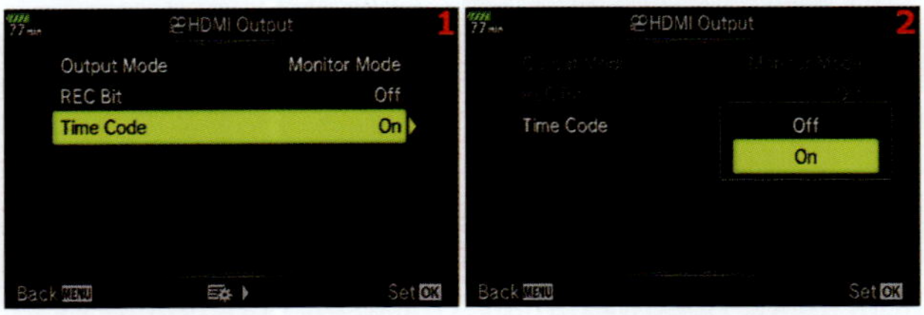

Figure 5.13C: Setting the Time Code (sending an HDMI rolling time code REC trigger)

6. Highlight Time Code on the [Movie] HDMI Output menu and scroll to the right (figure 5.13C, image 1).
7. A small menu will appear with two choices: On and Off (figure 5.13C, image 2). Choose On to send an *HDMI rolling time code REC trigger* to an external recorder that requires a rolling time code to start and stop recording when you press the camera's Movie button. In other words, some external recorders will start and stop recording when they receive (or do not receive) a Time Code. Select Off if you do not want to send a Time Code. Press the OK button to lock in your choice.

Now let's move on into **Part 3** of this chapter and consider how to use the camera's **My Clips Movie Creation** function.

PART 3: My Clips Movie Creation

My Clips allows you to combine multiple video clips (1 to 8 seconds each) and still images in-camera into a movie up to 15 minutes in length. You can apply a visual transition (i.e., fade) between movie clips and images, as well as a few Art Filter effects and canned music.

The My Clips video system allows you to create up to 99 My Clips folders, each of which will be numbered (from 1 to 99). Each My Clips folder can contain up to 99 video clips and still images before combining them into a movie.

Each transition between a video clip and another video clip, or between a video clip and a still picture, is called a "cut" in moviemaking terms. Therefore, you can have up to 99 cuts per My Clips movie.

Creating a My Clips movie is a great way to make a short movie without having to use a computer. You can visually assemble the movie right on the camera's monitor by using a concept somewhat similar to a "timeline" in computer software (e.g., iMovie, Adobe Premier Elements or Pro, and Final Cut Pro X).

Within the My Clips timeline for the current My Clips folder, you can do the following:

- control the order of video clips and still pictures (cuts)
- choose from six visual Art Filter effects (e.g., Old Movie, Pin Hole)
- add a transition effect (Fade)
- include downloadable Olympus music (BGM, see page 353)
- change the output volume of the final movie
- create a new My Clips folder and timeline

Let's get started by learning how to access and use the My Clips system, which is not entirely intuitive.

How to Open the My Clips Movie System

Opening the My Clips movie system can seem a little daunting the first time you try it. There are several different ways to open My Clips folders, which we will discuss in the following subsections.

No Existing My Clips Movie Folders

If you have never used the My Clips system on your camera, and there are no existing My Clips folders that contain video clips and images, you can open the My Clips system to make a movie by using one of the following methods:

- Create your first new video clip as described in the upcoming **Creating Your First Video Clip** subsection (page 340). Once the clip has finished recording, the new My Clips movie folder will be created by the camera, the My Clips screen will show, and your new video clip will be the first item in the movie.

- Find an existing RAW or JPEG image you would like to include in a future My Clips movie by pressing the Playback button and displaying it on the monitor. Press the OK button to open the image edit menu and select *Add to My Clips* from the menu. The My Clips system will open with your image in the new timeline.

My Clips Movie Folders Do Exist

If you have used the My Clips system before, and one or more My Clips folders already exist, you can use the following methods to access the My Clips system:

- Press the Playback button so that any image or video displays on the monitor, and then rotate the Rear Dial clockwise (only) by two or three clicks. The My Clips movie system will open if any My Clips folders exist.
- Press the Playback button and find any video clip or still picture marked with a clapperboard symbol and press the OK button. A menu will open with a menu item named *See all My Clips*. Select the menu item and press the OK button.
- Create a new 1- to 8-second video clip.

Creating Your First Video Clip

To start your first My Clip movie you must make at least one new 1- to 8-second video clip (a new cut). Once that clip has been created, the My Clips system will open with the just-created clip showing in a My Clips window. From that point, you may add new clips and images until you are finished.

Let's walk through a clip creation.

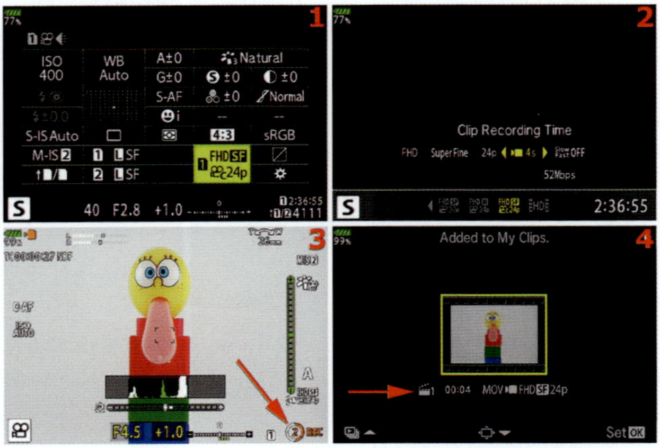

Figure 5.14A: Creating a My Clips video

Use the following steps to create your first My Clips movie clip:

1. Use the Super Control Panel or Live Control to select the [Movie][Record Mode] setting. Figure 5.14A, image 1, shows this setting selected on the LV Super Control Panel. Now you must set a Clip Recording time.
2. Choose either the first or sixth [Movie][Record Mode] setting (figure 5.14A, image 2). You can choose from seven different [Movie][Record Modes] for normal video recording; however, modes one and six are the only two [Movie][Record Modes] that offer a Clip Recording Time subsetting, and only those two modes can be used to record a clip for inclusion in a My Clips movie. [Movie][Record Mode] number six is highlighted in figure 5.14A, image 2, as can be seen along the bottom of the screen (HD to the right is number seven).
3. Once [Movie][Record Mode] one or six is selected, quickly press the nfo button to open the subsetting for configuration. Scroll over to the Clip Recording Time subsetting, as seen in image 2 (4s). Scroll up or down to select a Clip Recording Time in seconds (from 1s to 8s). ***Note:*** It is critical that ***all*** the clips you record are exactly the same type. Any variance in the [Movie][Record Mode] subsetting in any clip will prevent that clip from being used in the current My Clip movie. Now it's time to record a clip.
4. Place the camera in Movie Mode on the Mode Dial (video camera icon), set up the camera controls (aperture, shutter, etc.) and press the Movie button to start recording the clip. Figure 5.14A, image 3, shows the movie recording screen halfway through the first clip recording of four seconds (4s). The countdown timer for the clip (image 3, red arrow) records the number of seconds (1s to 8s) you previously selected in step 2.
5. When the clip has finished recording, the camera will present the Added to My Clips screen with your new clip showing (figure 5.14, image 4). You can record more video clips or add images. Notice how there is movie information right below the clip seen in image 4 (red arrow). The first symbol—a clapperboard followed by a 1—signifies that this is My Clips folder number 1 (up to 99). Following that is information on the length of the movie, which is currently 4 seconds (00:04). Next is the type of movie—a MOV container, Full HD (FHD), SuperFine (SF), 24p movie.

Adding Another Clip and a Still Image

Once your first video clip is created, you can create more clips and add still images. Let's see how.

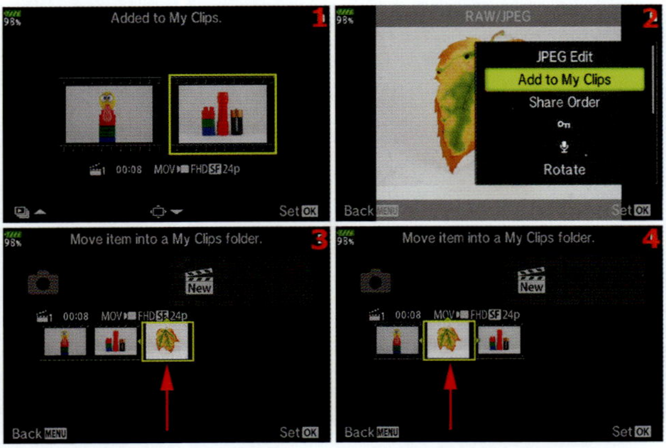

Figure 5.14B: Adding and positioning a still image

Use the following steps to create more video clips and add previously created still images:

1. In figure 5.14B, image 1, another four-second video clip has been recorded, and it appeared just after the previous clip. The movie is now 8 seconds long (00:08). You could keep creating movie clips, and each of them would appear after the previous clip. Remember, all the clips for this movie must have exactly the same settings to remain in this My Clips folder (1).
2. To add a still picture to the movie, you must leave the My Clips system briefly and find a nice picture (figure 5.14B, image 2). Once you've found a picture you want to include in the movie, press the OK button to open the picture edit menu, select Add to My Clips from the menu, and press the OK button again.
3. The still picture will now appear at the end of the current series of movie clips (figure 5.14B, image 3). You can scroll left or right to reposition the image between movie clips (figure 5.14B, image 4). Once you have the image positioned where you would like it in the timeline, press the OK button to secure its position.

Rearranging Clips and Pictures

It is possible to rearrange video clips and still images in the movie timeline. Let's examine how to move either type of movie element to a new location.

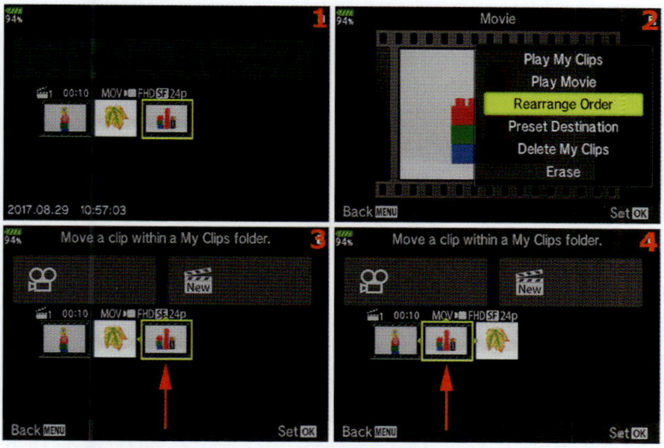

Figure 5.14C: Rearranging video clips and still images in the timeline

Use the following steps to rearrange clips or images in the current timeline:

1. The selected video clip (surrounded by a yellow frame) shown in figure 5.14C, image 1, is the last video clip that was recorded and added to the timeline (My Clips folder). To move the clip to a different location in the timeline, press the OK button.
2. A Movie or Still Picture menu will open, according to what was selected when the OK button was pressed. In the example shown in figure 5.14C, image 2, the Movie menu has opened because a video clip was selected. Highlight Rearrange Order on the Movie menu and press the OK button.
3. Notice how the selection frame has now changed (figure 5.14C, image 3). There are pointers on the top and left side of the yellow selection frame, signifying that pressing up or left with the Arrow Pad will do something. In the example in image 3, we want to move the video clip one place to the left so that it will play before the image of the leaf is played, instead of after. Press the left Arrow Pad key once to move the clip over one space to the left (figure 5.14C, image 4).

The video clip that was *after* the leaf image is now *before* it. This moved video clip will now be played before the leaf image is shown.

Now let's examine how to remove a video clip or image from a My Clips folder.

Remove from My Clips

After you have added an image or clip (item), you may decide that you don't like it and want to remove it from the current My Clips folder.

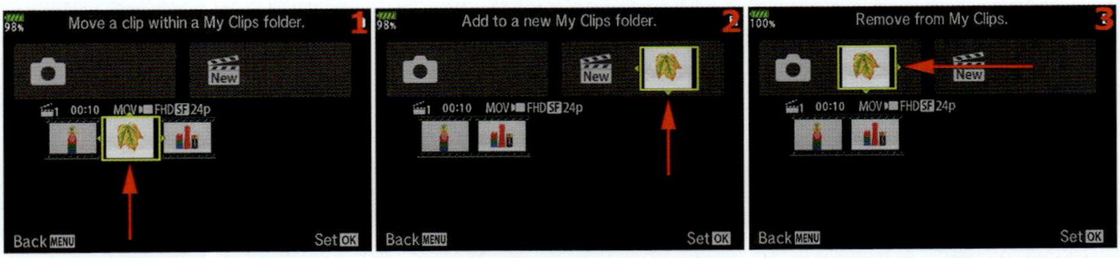

Figure 5.14D: Removing an item from a My Clips folder

Use the following steps to remove an item from a My Clips folder (timeline):

1. At the top of the screens shown in figure 5.14D, images 1–3, there are two gray rectangles. The rectangle on the left has a camera symbol, and the one on the right has a clapperboard symbol with the word New on it. These rectangles appear any time you add an image to the movie or highlight one of the movie items, press the OK button, and select Rearrange Order from the menu (like we did in the previous subsection). To delete an item you no longer need, select it (as seen in figure 5.14D, image 1) and press up on the Arrow Pad.
2. The movie item will move into the New folder, as seen in figure 5.14D, image 2. We need to move it one more time to finally delete it. Press left on the Arrow Pad to move the item into the gray rectangle with the camera symbol.
3. In figure 5.14D, image 3, you can see that Remove from My Clips is now shown above the gray rectangles. Once the item you want to remove has been moved into the rectangle with the gray camera symbol (red arrow), press the OK button to delete it. Be careful, the camera offers no deletion confirmation screen; instead, it immediately deletes the item from the My Clips folder (timeline). No worries though, the item is not deleted from the camera's memory card; it is just removed from the current My Clips folder.

What if you don't want to remove an item, but you want to use it in a completely different My Clips movie? Let's see how to do that.

Creating a New My Clips Folder (Timeline)

So far, we have been working with only one My Clips movie timeline. The camera can have up to 99 My Clips folders at any one time. The folders are not physical folders on the camera's memory card. Upon examination of the cards in my E-M1II, there are no special folders created for each My Clips folder. Evidently, the camera marks the video clips and still images in some way so that the items can be sorted by the camera into separate in-camera-memory folder representations.

In the last subsection, we discussed how to delete an item from a folder. We first moved the item into the gray rectangle with a clapperboard labeled New. Let's start from there, and instead of deleting the item, let's use it as the base for a brand new My Clips movie folder (timeline).

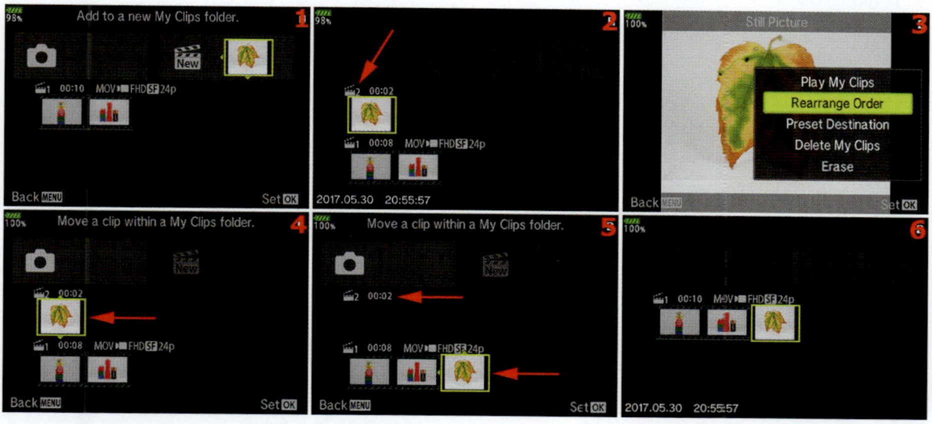

Figure 5.14E: Creating a New My Clips folder (timeline)

1. In the previous subsection (**Remove from My Clips**) we removed an item from a My Clips folder by moving it first to the [Clapperboard] New rectangle, and then into the deletion rectangle labeled Remove from My Clips (with a camera symbol). In figure 5.14E, image 1, the movie item has been moved from the My Clips timeline labeled [Clapperboard] 1 into the [Clapperboard] New rectangle.
2. Press the OK button while the item is in the [Clapperboard] New rectangle, and the camera will immediately create a brand-new My Clips movie timeline (folder) with the name [Clapperboard] 2 (figure 5.14E, image 2, red arrow). [***Note:*** You can move still images between any My Clips movie timeline (folder). You can move movie clips in the same way as long as the clip has exactly the same recording settings (e.g., FHD, SF, 24p) as the other clips in the destination timeline. If the recording settings are different, you cannot move the video clip into an alternate My Clips folder.]
3. Now let's move the still image back into its original My Clips folder. As seen in figure 5.14E, image 2, select the item and then press the OK button.
4. Since we are moving a still image, the Still Image menu will open (figure 5.14E, image 3). Select Rearrange Order from the menu and press the OK button.
5. The Move a Clip within a My Clips folder window will now open (figure 5.14E, image 4). Notice that the yellow selection rectangle has a down pointer on it (image 4, red arrow). Press down on the Arrow Pad.

6. In figure 5.14E, image 5, you can see that the item has now been moved back into its original My Clips movie timeline (folder) and is awaiting confirmation of the move. Also, please notice that the previous [Clapperboard] 2 My Clips folder is now empty (image 5, top red arrow). Press the OK button to let the camera know you approve of the current location for the item.
7. Figure 5.14E, image 6, displays the [Clapperboard] 1 timeline with the item back in place. The deletion and new rectangles and the [Clapperboard] 2 folder are gone. The camera is awaiting a new image or video clip.

Preset Destination

If you are using multiple My Clips folders (timelines), you may want to choose a particular folder in which to place the next video clip. Preset Destination allows you to choose a particular My Clips folder for the next recording of a video clip. In other words, the camera will add the next video clip to the end of whichever timeline you select. Let's see how to do it.

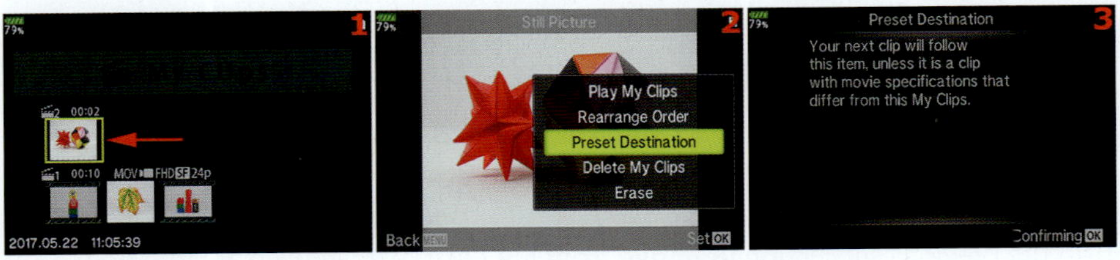

Figure 5.14F: Choosing a Preset Destination for the next video clip recording

Use the following steps to choose a Preset Destination for the next video clip:

1. Select an item in the destination folder (the timeline to which you want to add your next recording) and press the OK button (figure 5.14F, image 1).
2. Choose Preset Destination from the menu and press the OK button (figure 5.14F, image 2).
3. Now you must confirm the initial location that you selected in step 1. The Preset Destination confirmation screen will inform you: *Your next clip will follow this item, unless it is a clip with movie specifications that differ from this My Clips*. As we have previously discussed, all video clips in a particular timeline (folder) must have exactly the same movie specifications (e.g., FHD, SF, 24p). Press the OK button to confirm the destination for the next video clip.

Erase

Erasing an item is different from removing a video clip or still image from a My Clips movie (which we discussed earlier in the **Remove from My Clips** subsection on page 344). *Removing* an item does not delete it from the memory card, it just removes it from the current My Clips folder (timeline). *Erasing* an item (this function) removes it from the current My Clips folder and ***deletes it from the camera's memory card, too***. Use this item very carefully, especially with carefully crafted video clips!

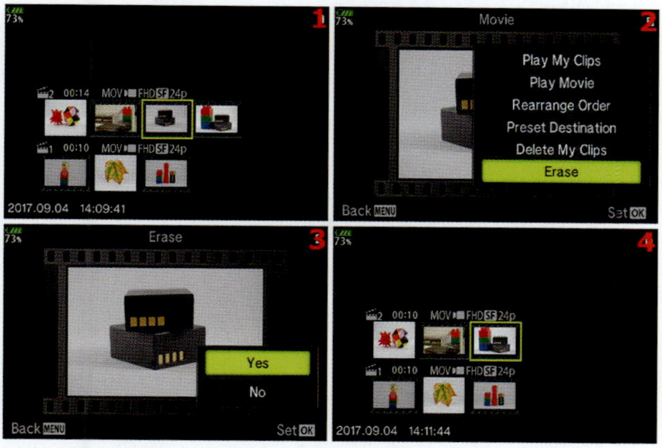

Figure 5.14G: Erasing (permanently deleting) an item from a My Clips folder

Use the following steps to remove an item from a My Clips folder and erase it permanently from the camera's memory card (be careful with this function!):

1. Figure 5.14G, image 1, shows that the sample contains two My Clips folders [Clapperboard] 1 and [Clapperboard] 2, with a separate timeline for each. The third item, a video clip in folder [Clapperboard] 2 is no longer needed and we will delete it. Highlight the item you want to delete and press the OK button.
2. A menu will open with an Erase selection. Choose Erase and press the OK button (figure 5.14G, image 2).
3. The camera will present a popup confirmation menu with Yes and No choices (figure 5.14G, image 3). Choose Yes to remove the item from the folder (timeline) and also ***permanently erase it from the camera's memory card!*** Make sure you want to delete this item, and then press the OK button to destroy it. Select No and press the OK button to cancel.
4. A *Busy* screen will appear with a progress indicator during the Erase process (not shown), and the camera will return to the My Clips screen with the item deleted from the folder and memory card (figure 5.14G, image 4).

Play My Clips

Once you have prepared a My Clips timeline, you can watch a preview of the final movie without any of the music, special effects, or fade transitions applied.

Later, you can export the movie (page 350)—applying the music, effects, and transitions—and the movie will be a standalone MOV file ready to be transferred to your computer or smart device and played for your audience or uploaded to social media.

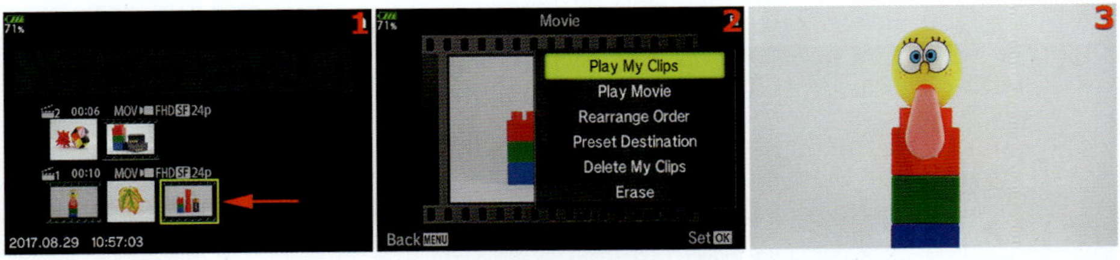

Figure 5.14H: Play a bare preview of the movie with no effects applied

Use the following steps to play a bare preview of your carefully crafted movie:

1. Choose any item in a My Clips folder (timeline) to play the entire timeline as a bare movie with no effects applied (figure 5.14H, image 1). Press the OK button to start the playing process.
2. A menu will open with a Play My Clips selection (figure 5.14H, image 2). Choose Play My Clips and press the OK button, and your movie will play in its entirety. No music, effects, or transitions will be applied to this bare movie preview (figure 5.14H, image 3).

Note: In figure 5.14H, image 2, you will see a menu selection Play Movie, just below the Play My Clips selection we discussed in this subsection. The Play Movie selection is for when you want to play just one movie item in the entire timeline, not the entire timeline. There is no selection for playing still images because, well, I reckon you could just look at an image on the monitor ☺. To use Play Movie, choose a video clip in a timeline, press the OK button, and select Play Movie from the menu (figure 5.14H, image 2). When you press the OK button again, the individual video clip will play.

Delete My Clips

If you have created a My Clips folder with many items in it and have viewed a bare preview of it (as described in the previous subsection), you may feel the movie is not up to par and decide you want to delete the entire timeline all at once. This is what the Delete My Clips function allows you to do. Just be careful, this could be a rather dangerous function for your data if used incorrectly or accidentally!

The Delete My Clips function will delete the entire timeline, including all movies and still images from the current My Clips folder, and it will permanently erase them from the camera's memory card! Please read that last sentence again carefully. You could have spent many hours or even days creating the individual components of a movie and then lose it all, just by using this function accidentally.

Why does this function even exist? Well, I suppose some people may not want to keep the individual components of a My Clips movie *after* they have exported the movie to its final form. If that describes you, this function will serve you well.

However, for most of us, this function is so ***dangerous*** that it might be a good idea to use Wite-Out on your camera's monitor to hide the Delete My Clips menu item (I'm just kidding, don't use Wite-Out on your camera).

If you want an easy way to ***destroy*** days of carefully crafted work, or delete a My Clips folder (timeline) you no longer want, let's learn to use this function.

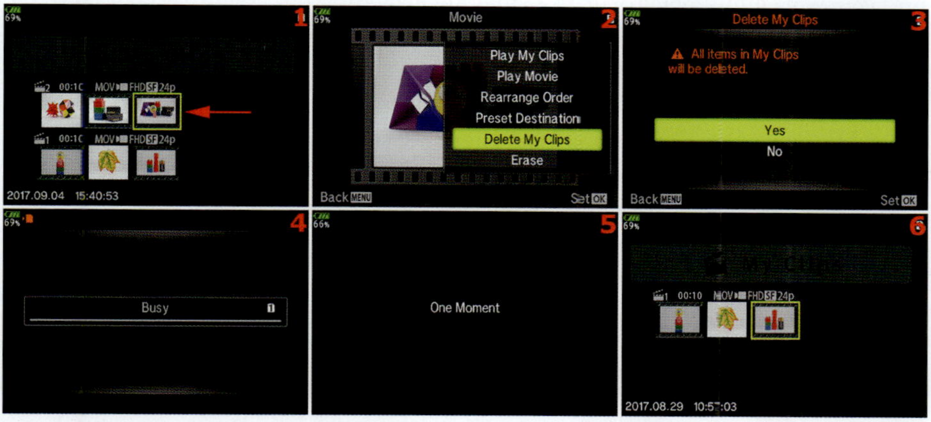

Figure 5.14l: Deleting an entire My Clips folder (entire timeline of items) at once

Use the following steps to delete an entire timeline (folder full of items) in one operation:

1. To begin the process of deleting a My Clips folder (an entire timeline of up to 99 video clips and still images) you no longer need, choose any item in the timeline and press the OK button (figure 5.14l, image 1).
2. A menu will appear with a selection called Delete My Clips. Choose that selection and press the OK button (figure 5.14l, image 2).
3. You will see the message: *All items in My Clips will be deleted* (figure 5.14l, image 3). Notice how the screen's heading and primary text is all in red? Olympus is reminding you of the destructive power of this function. Make sure you understand that you are about to delete an entire timeline of items from the memory card, ***permanently!*** Choose Yes to erase the timeline or No to cancel. Press the OK button once you've made your choice.
4. As the timeline (folder) is being deleted, a screen will appear with the word *Busy* and a progress indicator bar (figure 5.14l, image 4). This could take several seconds if you have a lot of items (up to 99 items).

5. The final deletion screen will now appear (figure 5.14I, image 5). This sparse, black (dare I say ominous) screen—with the words *One Moment*—gives you a brief moment to experience one of the following feelings: 1) a *satisfying* feeling of having removed a large number of items you no longer need, or 2) the *horrifying* realization that you just deleted several days of hard work.
6. The camera will now return to the My Clips main screen with whatever My Clips folders still exist (figure 5.14I, image 6). Have you made good backups of all your data today?

Exporting a Movie

Now that you have compiled a timeline of many video clips and still images, it's time to export your work into a movie of up to 15 minutes in length. The camera will take a selected timeline (My Clips folder) and allow you to apply a special appearance effect, a transition effect, and background music.

Once the new movie has been created, it will appear on the monitor, ready to play. Each individual video clip and still image item will still be on the memory card after the export is complete, in case you want to create a new movie with the same items.

Let's examine how to begin the export process, and then we will examine each step until the movie is created.

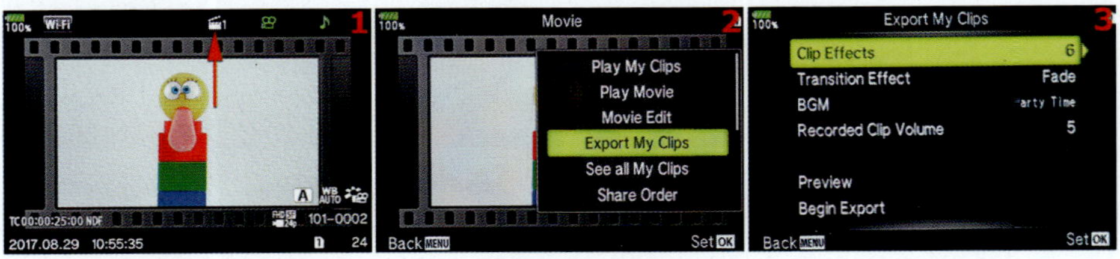

Figure 5.15A: Starting the movie export process (six steps)

Use the following steps to begin the My Clips movie export process:

1. Press the Playback button and look for any video clip or still image that you previously included in a My Clips movie folder (timeline). Each item will be marked with a numbered clapperboard symbol (figure 5.15A, image 1, red arrow). The example image is from the My Clips folder named [Clapperboard] 1.
2. Once you have located any item in the series on the camera monitor, press the OK button to open the menu (figure 5.15A, image 2). Select Export My Clips from the menu and press the OK button to open the Export My Clips configuration screen.
3. The Export My Clips screen offers you six selections (figure 5.15A, image 3). Four of the selections allow you to modify the movie, one allows you to preview the movie after you have added the effects, and the last item begins the actual export process, applying all effects and finalizing the movie. [***Note:*** The Export My Clips menu also has a menu selection called See all My Clips, just below the Export My Clips selection

(figure 5.15A, image 2). See all My Clips shows you a screen with the movie timeline, allowing you to examine the items in your movie timeline one more time.]

Now let's examine each Export My Clips menu item and see how to best apply it.

Clip Effects

The E-M1II provides six Clip Effects that can be applied to your movie during export. Following is a numbered list that describes each of the effects, using the same numbers that the camera uses:

1. ***Pop Art:*** This mode is like the Vivid Picture Mode on steroids. All colors are quite saturated, and contrast is raised to an even higher level than in Vivid Mode. This mode is best when you are in a playful mood and want to create an exciting movie. The intense colors will not be close to reality, but who needs reality when you are having fun?
2. ***Light Tone:*** This mode lowers contrast and desaturates colors. The colors have a less-saturated, brighter look. Light Tone makes the movie look like the effect you see when an overdone high dynamic range (HDR) image has too few shadows. It is not overly strong, but it is noticeable.
3. ***Pin Hole:*** This mode has a relatively saturated look, but it adds a heavy vignette effect to the corners of the image, as if the light rapidly diminishes. It's as though you were using a pinhole camera to make the image, except the video is still sharp. Primarily, Pin Hole provides a vignette effect.
4. ***Cross Process:*** This mode imitates the look you would get from an old method of developing film in chemicals that were designed for different types of film. Videos shot with Cross Process have a slight green cast and somewhat higher contrast.
5. ***Sepia:*** This mode converts all colors to monochrome and adds a warm, brownish effect that resembles less-saturated sepia toning. It could be used with old-fashioned clothing to imitate an old movie, or you could shoot a nature video with this mode and make it look like a bygone era.
6. ***Old Film:*** This mode combines a pulsating vignette effect along with random long scratches, so it looks like you are watching a scratched-up, old movie that has been played too many times. Colors appear normal (not overly saturated).

Now let's see how to choose one of the six effects for the movie.

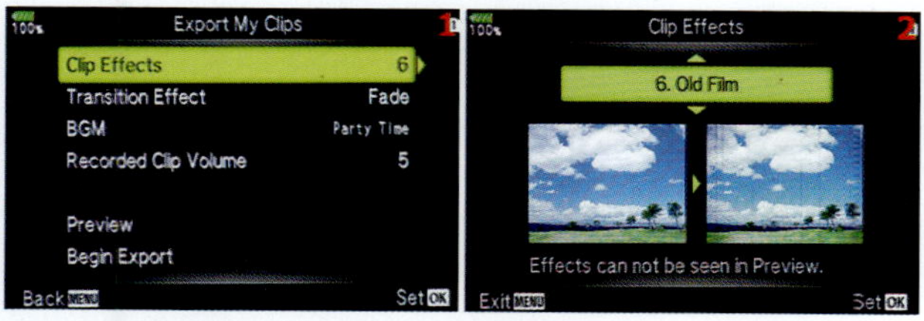

Figure 5.15B: Choosing one of the Clip Effects for your movie

Use the following steps to choose one of the six effects for your movie:

1. Figure 5.15B, image 1, begins where figure 5.15A, image 3, left off. Highlight Clip Effects and scroll to the right.
2. From the up/down menu, choose one of the six available Clip Effects, or Off, using the previous list as a reference (figure 5.15B, image 2). Notice the two small pictures in image 2. The picture on the left is how your video will appear with no effect applied. The picture on the right shows how the effect will look when your video is played. If you decide to preview the video with the Preview selection on the Export My Clips menu (image 1), you will not see the effect on the preview video. The effect is applied only as the video is being exported.

Next let's examine how to select the one available transition effect (Fade), for use between video clips and images (cuts).

Transition Effect

A transition effect provides a very short buffer between major changes (cuts) in your movie, such as between video clips and still images. Unfortunately, with firmware versions 1.0 and 1.1, the camera provides only one transition effect, Fade. This effect lasts only about ¼ second between cuts, but does provide a better look than a simple hard transition between cuts. One movie item fades out while the other fades in, slightly overlapping, for each cut. Let's examine how to select the Transition Effect.

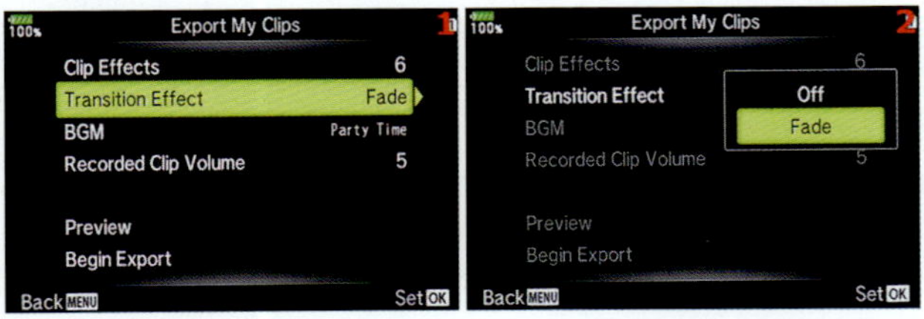

Figure 5.15C: Adding the Fade Transition Effect to your movie

Use the following steps to add the Fade Transition Effect to your movie:

1. Figure 5.15C, image 1, begins where figure 5.15A, image 3, left off. Highlight Transition Effect and scroll to the right.
2. From the Transition Effect menu, choose Off to use no transition effect, or Fade to add a ¼-second fade effect for each cut (figure 5.15C, image 2). Press the OK button to lock in the Fade effect.

Next let's see how to add some background music (BGM) to your movie.

BGM (Background Music)

Each My Clips movie can be composed of both video clips and still images. Each video clip will have its own sound recording that will play as the video plays. You can also add background music (BGM) to spice things up a bit.

The camera initially comes with only one BGM song available, called Party Time. If you want more background music to select from, you must download it from Olympus, and then choose a new song for your movie.

First, we will examine how to use existing BGM songs, and then we will discuss how to download new BGM songs directly from Olympus.

Choosing Existing Background Music (BGM)

This subsection will describe how to use the built-in BGM song called Party Time (or other BGM songs) as background music in your movie. If you have already downloaded other BGM songs, we will examine how to choose a different song from the 14 downloadable songs available from Olympus.

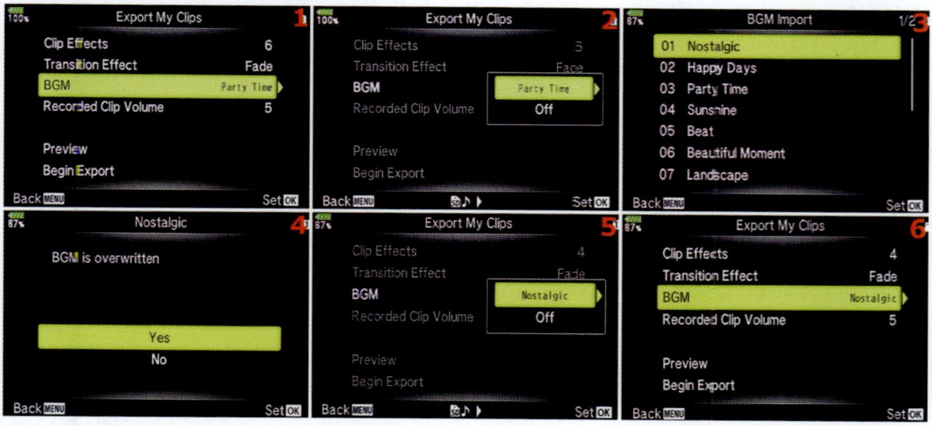

Figure 5.15D: Adding background music (BGM) to your movie

Use the following steps to add background music (BMG) to your movie:

1. Figure 5.15D, image 1, begins where figure 5.15A, image 3, left off. Highlight BGM and scroll to the right.
2. A menu will open with two selections: Party Time and Off (figure 5.15D, image 2). Choose Party Time (the default BGM song) and press the OK button to use that song, and the camera will return to the Export My Clips screen. If you previously downloaded other BGM songs and saved them to your memory card, you can highlight Party Time and scroll to the right to select another BGM song. [***Note:*** If you see the screen shown in figure 5.15E, there are no additional BGM songs available on your memory card. A total of 14 downloadable songs are available from Olympus (at the time of writing, 2017). See the next subsection—**Downloading New Background Music (BGM)**—for downloading instructions.]

3. If you have already downloaded additional BGM songs, you will be presented with a list of songs (figure 5.15D, image 3). Select one of the songs, such as the song Nostalgic, and press the OK button.
4. The next screen gives you a choice of overwriting the default song (e.g., Party Time) with your new song (figure 5.15D, image 4). Choose Yes and press the OK button to overwrite the old song (Party Time) with the new song (Nostalgic). Select No to cancel.
5. The camera now reverts back to the BGM menu, with the new song (Nostalgic) available instead of the default Party Time (figure 5.15D, image 5). Press the OK button to choose Nostalgic as the background music for your video, or select Off to cancel.
6. Once you have chosen a BGM song (or Off), the camera will return to the Export My Clips screen for additional configuration before exporting the movie (figure 5.15D, image 6).

Now let's see how to download some new BGM songs.

Downloading New Background Music (BGM)

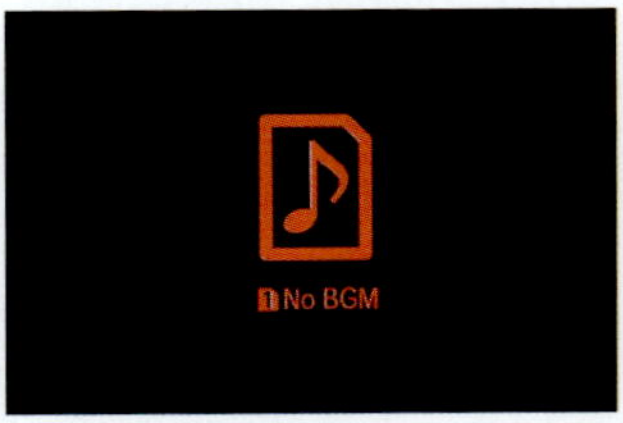

Figure 5.15E: No BGM other than Party Time is available

If you decided to use different background music than the default Party Time (see previous subsection), only to see the screen shown in figure 5.15E, all is not lost. You can download up to 14 new BGM songs (at the time this book was being written, 2017) from the Olympus website.

If you download new BGM songs, you cannot simply install them all and select one from a list, as you might expect. When you install a new song, it overwrites the current song (Party Time). You can install only one song at a time.

Unless you don't want to ever use Party Time again, be sure to download it from the Olympus website along with the other songs because it will be overwritten when you replace it, and you will have to reinstall it if you want to use it later. This will give you 14 songs you can install in your camera.

You can listen to the songs on the Olympus website to see if you like them, and then you can download one song or all of them. Each song is 6 MB and is in a nonstandard WAV format. I tried to play them on my computer but they would not play in iTunes, and I could not use a WAV file I created either.

To use the songs, create a folder on your memory card named BGM. Copy all of the songs into the BGM folder. When you reinsert the memory card into the camera and select a song, a list of songs will replace the No BGM screen (figure 5.15E).

Use these steps to download BGM songs from the Olympus website and copy them to a memory card:

1. Insert an SD card into your computer's SD card slot, or into a card reader on your computer.
2. Create a new folder on the SD card and name it BGM.

3. Download the BGM songs to your computer from the 14 available songs (WAV format) you will find at: **http://support.olympus-imaging.com/bgmdownload/**
4. Copy the downloaded music files to the BGM folder on your camera.
5. Insert the SD card into your E-M1II, and follow the instructions in the previous subsection, **Choosing Existing Background Music (BGM),** on page 353.

Next let's examine how to set the volume level of the sound recorded in the video while BGM music is playing, or how to enable/disable the recorded sound altogether.

Recorded Clip Volume or Sound

This is an export function that changes its name and function according to whether you have a background music (BGM) song selected (page 353).

Let's consider how to use this chameleon-like function to control how the recorded sound is handled during movie export.

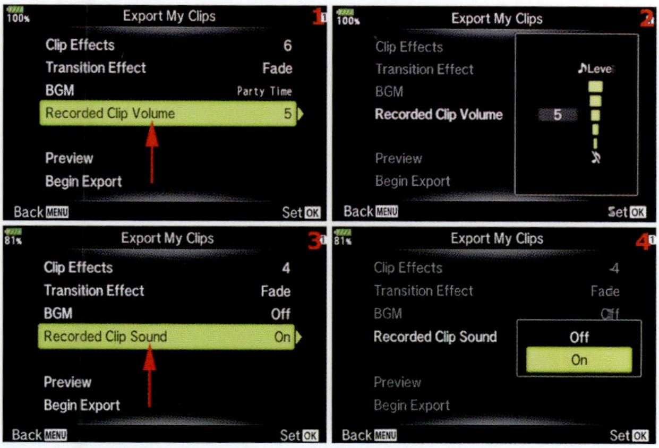

Figure 5.15F: Using the Recorded Clip "Volume" or "Sound" feature

Use the following steps to control the *Volume* or *Sound* in your My Clips movie:

1. Figure 5.15F, image 1, begins where figure 5.15A, image 3, left off. Highlight Recorded Clip Volume (red arrow) if BGM ***is not*** set to Off (i.e., a BGM song, such as Party Time, ***is selected,*** as seen in figure 5.15F, image 1), and then scroll to the right. However, if BGM ***is*** set to Off (i.e., a BGM song ***is not selected,*** as seen in figure 5.15F, image 3), you will select Recorded Clip Sound (red arrow) instead. Recorded Clip Volume allows you to control the volume of the recorded sound in the video clip, so that the background (BGM) does not overpower the sound. BGM does not replace the recorded sound; it only supplements it. Choose a sound volume Level from 1 to 5 (or off at the bottom of the scale) and press the OK button to lock it in (figure 5.15F, image 2). On the other hand, Recorded Clip Sound allows you to enable or disable the recorded sound in the video clip, so that no sound will play at all when the My Clips movie plays. Choose

Recorded Clip Sound and scroll to the right. Choose On or Off from the popup menu to enable or disable the sound in your exported movie (figure 5.15F, image 4). Press the OK button to lock in your choice.

Next let's examine how to watch a preview of your My Clips movie before finishing the export process.

Preview

The Preview function lets you see a rough draft of your movie, with no effects applied. Preview will play all the video clips and display the still images in the order laid out in the My Clips timeline (folder).

Once you have viewed the Preview, you may want to rearrange some video clips or still images. When you're happy with what you see, you are ready to export the movie to its final form.

Let's see how to preview your movie.

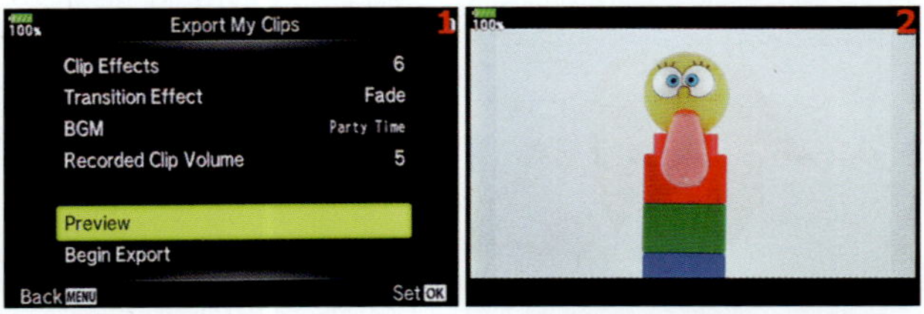

Figure 5.15G: Previewing your movie before export

Use the following steps to preview your movie:

1. Figure 5.15G, image 1, begins where figure 5.15A, image 3, left off. Highlight Preview and press the OK button to start the preview.
2. The camera will immediately display the rough-draft preview of your movie (figure 5.15G, image 2).

Finally, it's time to export your My Clips movie for you and others to enjoy.

Begin Export

The actual exporting process is automated and easy. Once you have chosen your clip effects, transition effect, and background music, set the volume, and previewed your My Clips movie, you are ready to export it to its final form with everything applied. Let's see how.

Use the following steps to export your movie with all effects and background music applied:

1. Figure 5.15H, image 1, begins where figure 5.15A, image 3, left off. Highlight Begin Export and press the OK button to start the final, fully configured export.

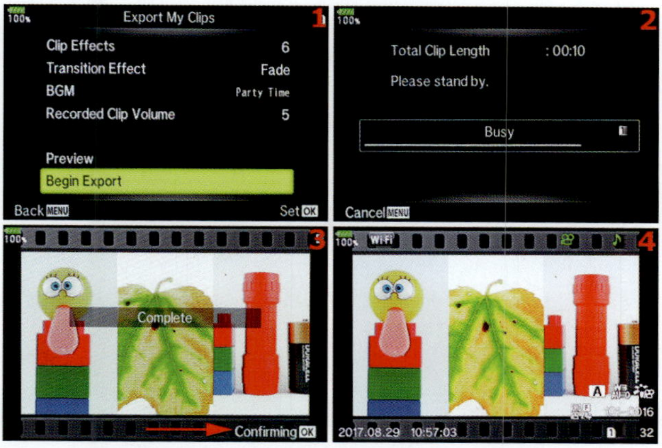

Figure 5.15H: Exporting to the final version of your movie

2. The camera will immediately begin exporting your movie (figure 5.15H, image 2). You will be informed of the Total Clip Length in minutes and seconds (00:10), with up to 15 minutes maximum (15:00). While you are standing by watching the export process, which takes some time (especially if you have many video clips and still images in the timeline), you will see a Busy progress bar. When it gets to the end, the movie is ready to be confirmed.
3. The following screen tells you the export process is Complete and lets you know the final version now requires Confirming (figure 5.15H, image 3, red arrow). Press the OK button to confirm the movie.
4. The finished movie will now be presented to you on the monitor (figure 5.15H, image 4). Thumbnail images of the first three items in the My Clips folder (timeline) are combined into a picture representing the movie, and it is shown on the monitor with the film sprocket edges you are accustomed to for videos. To play your new movie, press the OK button and select Play Movie from the menu that appears (not shown).

Author's Conclusion

Whew! There is a lot of information on the E-M1II's video system! The camera gives you deep control of the video recording process, whether for a basic family movie recorded to the camera's memory card, a commercial movie recorded on an external video recorder, a slow or fast motion video, or even a My Clips movie.

Have a good time trying out all of the various video recording features in this powerful camera. Learn it well and make some great movies!

Next, let's move deeper into configuration of the E-M1II for still photography by considering the seven major functions of the Playback Menu.

06 Playback Menu

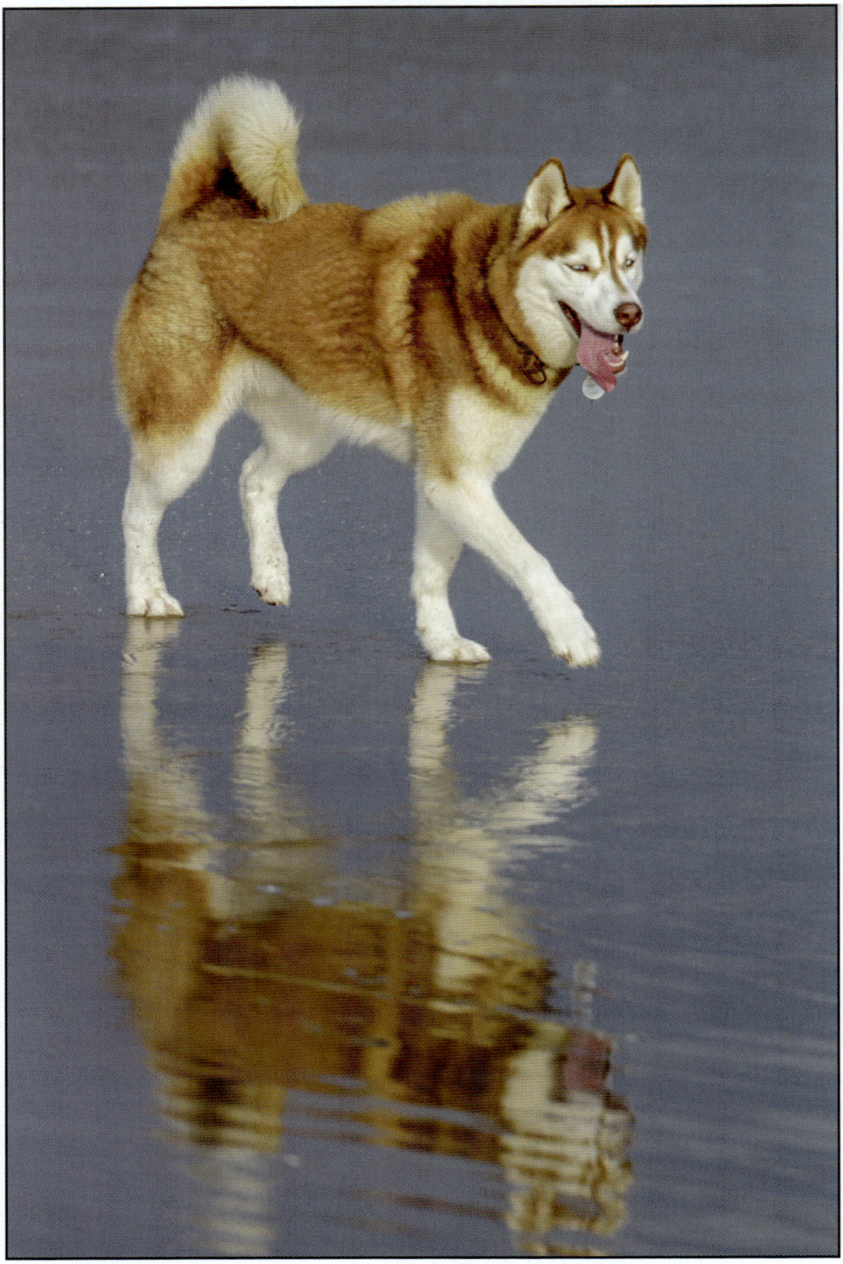

Image © Alan Hess

The Playback Menu is the fourth system menu in this camera, and it is primarily used for working with images you've already taken. In this chapter, we will discuss all of the options in the Playback Menu, including viewing and printing images and transferring them to devices via Wi-Fi.

Let's consider each of the seven functions in full detail (figure 6.1).

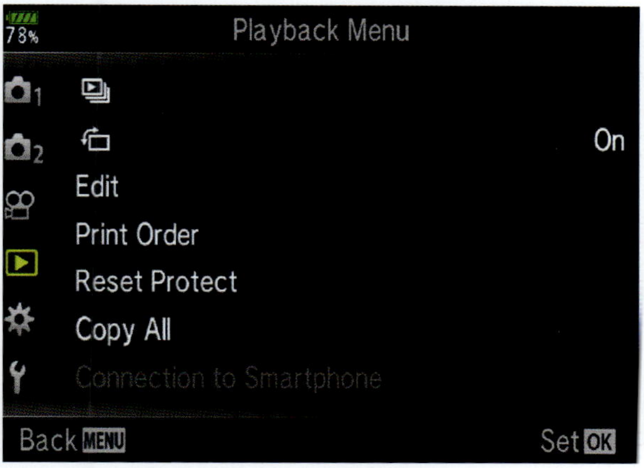

Figure 6.1: The Playback Menu

[Slideshow]

When you have a card full of great pictures, you may want to share a slideshow with friends and family. The camera makes it easy and allows you to display timed still images or movies with background music, if you choose.

There are basically three ways to view a slideshow: on the camera monitor (but not in the viewfinder) or on an HDTV or other HDMI-compatible device.

Viewing a slideshow on the camera monitor is very easy, and we will discuss the steps in the upcoming subsection called **Configuring and Displaying a Slideshow**. But first let's briefly consider how you might use the camera to display your slideshow on an HDTV.

Output to HDTV via HDMI Port

The E-M1II has a micro HDMI port on its left side, which you can use to display your images and movies on a large HDTV screen for much greater viewing pleasure.

You can adjust the camera's output for C4K (2160p at 17:9 ratio), 4K UHD (2160p at 16:9 ratio), 1080p, 720p, or 480p/576p video output with the *Custom Menu > D4. Disp/[Sound]/PC > HDMI > Output Size* setting. You can even use a compatible HDTV remote to control the camera directly if you set the *Custom Menu > D4. Disp/[Sound]/PC > HDMI > HDMI Control* to On.

To connect to an HDTV that has a standard HDMI port, you will need a cable with an HDMI type A connector for the HDTV and a micro-HDMI type D connector for the camera's HDMI port. This cable is readily available online and at stores.

We will discuss connecting the camera to an HDTV in more detail in the chapter titled **Custom Menu** and the subsection called **HDMI** on page 497.

Configuring and Displaying a Slideshow

There are five selections within the [Slideshow] menu, four of which are configurable. Most of the time you will not need to change the configurable settings, but you can if you want to. Here are descriptions of each setting:

- **Start:** Start begins the slideshow immediately, using the values found in the next four configurable settings.
- **BGM:** This acronym stands for background music. The camera comes with one song called Party Time. You can download several other songs from the Olympus website to replace Party Time.
- **Slide:** This setting controls the type of slideshow the camera will display. You can display still pictures only, movies only, or both within one slideshow.
- **Slide Interval:** This setting controls the interval of time between each image or movie in the slideshow. You can choose from 2 to 10 seconds.
- **Movie Interval:** This setting controls what happens when the slideshow displays a movie. You can show each movie in its entirety or only a few seconds at the beginning of each movie before you continue to the next movie.

First we'll examine how to start a slideshow with the default settings. Then we'll see how to configure a slideshow and take advantage of all the options.

Starting a Slideshow with Default Settings

If you want to display a slideshow right away, with no fuss or configuration, you can simply start it. The slideshow will use whatever settings are already configured, which will be either the factory default settings or settings you used for the previous slideshow.

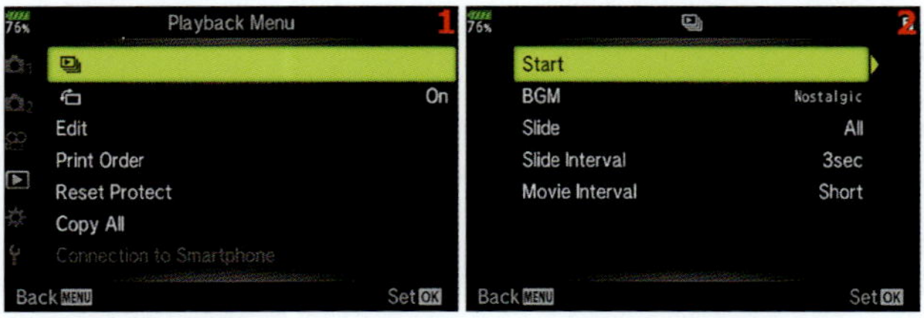

Figure 6.2A: Starting a slideshow with default options

Use the following steps to start a slideshow:

1. On the camera monitor, view the image or movie that you want to use as the first item in the slideshow.
2. Select the [Slideshow] symbol from the Playback Menu and scroll to the right (figure 6.2A, image 1).
3. Choose Start from the menu then scroll to the right. The slideshow will begin immediately with the default settings (figure 6.2A, image 2).
4. Press the OK button or Menu button to stop the slideshow. It will repeat until you stop it. If you want to restart the slideshow where it left off, repeat steps 1 and 2.

Note: The camera starts the slideshow on the most recently displayed image. If you want the slideshow to start with the first image on the memory card, you must view that image immediately before you start the slideshow. If you take a new picture just before you start a new slideshow, the camera will start the slideshow on that picture because it was the last picture displayed. Even removing the card and reinserting it does not cause the camera to start at the beginning of the memory card.

Modifying the Default Settings for Slideshows

You may want your slideshow to include still images only, videos only, or both. You might not want the camera to play background music during the show, or you might want each image in the show to be displayed for longer than the default time of 3 seconds.

You can configure these settings before you start a new slideshow. Let's see how.

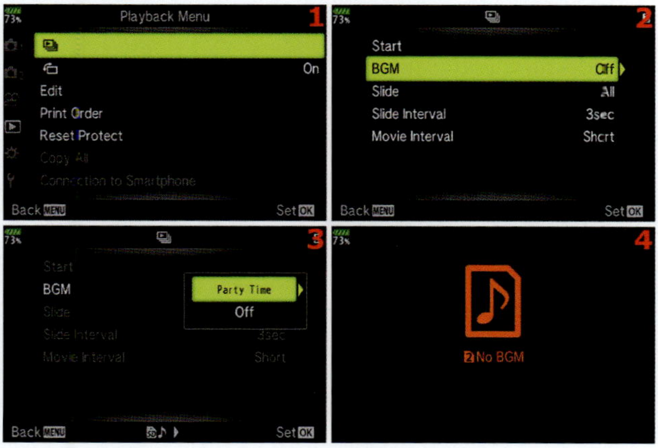

Figure 6.2B: Configuring settings before starting a slideshow

Use the following steps to configure and then start a slideshow:

1. Select the [Slideshow] symbol from the Playback Menu and scroll to the right (figure 6.2B, image 1).

2. Select BGM (background music) then scroll to the right (figure 6.2B, image 2).
3. In figure 6.2B, image 3, you can see that the song Party Time is available as the factory default. The song will play as soon as this screen appears so you can decide if you want to use it as background music.
4. An arrow tip appears beside the song name, so it looks like you can scroll to the right and select another song. If you do, and you have not downloaded any new BGM songs, you will see a big red musical note in an SD card-shaped frame and *No BGM* (figure 6.2B, image 4). We will discuss how to download new BGM songs in an upcoming subsection. Party Time is the only song included with the camera. If you want to use it, press the OK button with Party Time highlighted, and then move to the next step. You can adjust the volume of the background music during the slideshow by pressing up or down on the Arrow Pad keys. You can also adjust the balance of the background music with the recorded sound in a video by pressing left or right on the Arrow Pad. If you do not want to use background music, highlight Off and press the OK button.

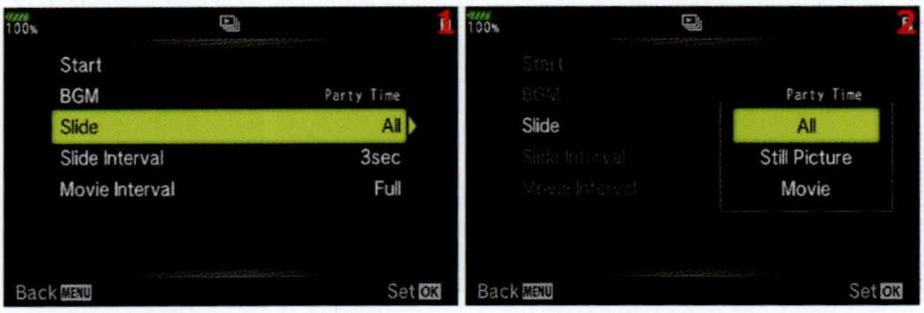

Figure 6.2C: Choosing what displays in a slideshow

5. Next you must decide whether you want to display images only (Still Picture), videos only (Movie), or both (All). Choose Slide and scroll to the right (figure 6.2C, image 1), and then choose the type of slideshow you want to display from the popup menu (figure 6.2C, image 2). After you have highlighted your selection, press the OK button to lock it in.

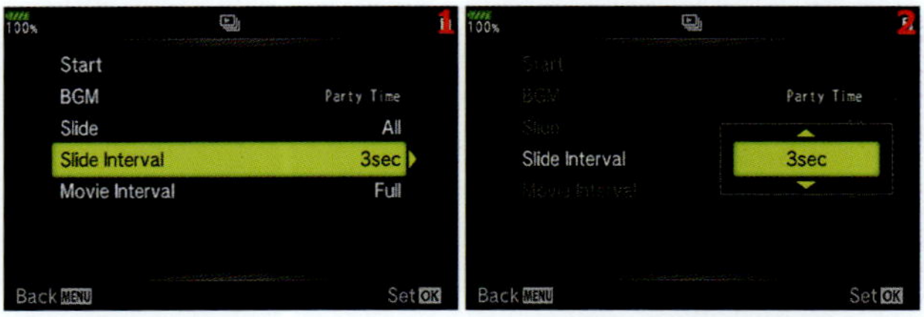

Figure 6.2D: Choosing a delay between items in a slideshow

6. Now you can choose a delay between each image or video. The default is 3 seconds (3sec), but you can choose an interval from 2 seconds to 10 seconds (2sec to 10sec). Select Slide Interval from the menu and scroll to the right (figure 6.2D, image 1). A small up/down menu will appear. Scroll up or down and choose from 2sec to 10sec (figure 6.2D, image 2). Press the OK button to lock in your time delay.

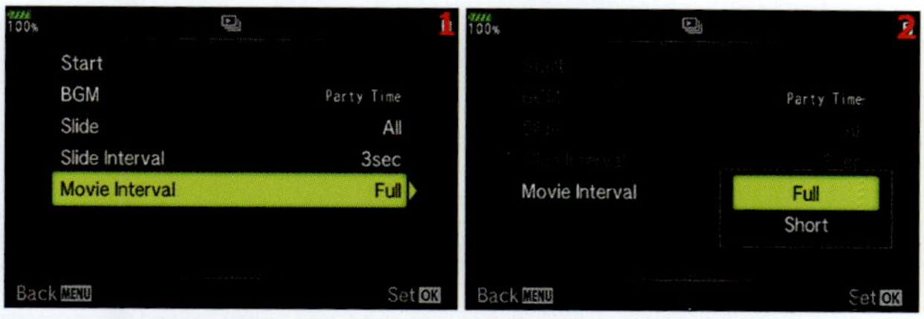

Figure 6.2E: Choosing entire (Full) or partial (Short) videos

7. You can choose whether your movies play all the way through or partially before the slideshow moves to the next movie or image. If you chose Still Picture in step 5, ignore this step. But if you chose Movie or All in step 5, you can decide how much of each movie will play. Select Movie Interval from the menu and scroll to the right (figure 6.2E, image 1). Choose Full or Short from the menu and press the OK button to lock in your choice (figure 6.2E, image 2).
8. Now that you have configured all the settings for a slideshow, select Start from the menu and scroll to the right to start it (figure 6.2A, mage 2).

Downloading Alternate Slideshow Songs from Olympus

If you want to play a different song than "Party Time" with your slideshow, you can download more songs from Olympus at this website:

http://support.olympus-imaging.com/bgmdownload/

As of late 2017, there were 14 available song choices, as follows:

- Nostalgic
- Happy Days
- Party Time
- Sunshine
- Beat
- Beautiful Music
- Landscape
- Cool
- Joy
- Love
- Melancholy
- My Life
- Precious Memory
- The Drums

If you download these songs, you cannot simply install them and select one from a list, as you might expect. When you install a new song, it replaces "Party Time." You can install only one song at a time, and it overwrites the current song. Unless you don't want to ever use "Party Time," be sure to download it from the Olympus website because it will be overwritten when you replace it, and you will have to reinstall it if you want to use it later.

You can listen to the songs on the Olympus website to see if you like them, and then you can download one song or all of them. Each song is about 6.1 MB in size.

To use the downloaded Olympus songs, create a folder on your camera's memory card named BGM. Copy all the songs into the BGM folder. When you reinsert the memory card into the camera and select a BGM song, a list of songs will replace the *No BGM* error (figure 6.2B, image 4).

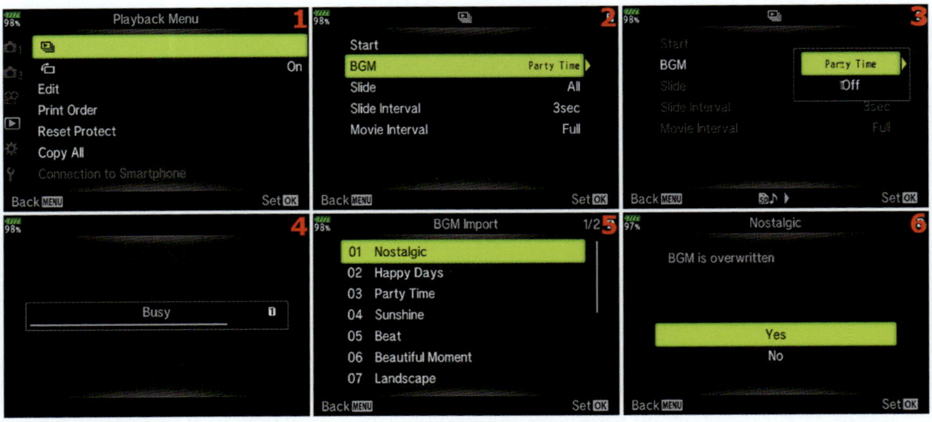

Figure 6.2F: Installing a song

Use these steps to install a song other than Party Time from the BGM folder on your memory card:

1. Select the [Slideshow] symbol from the Playback Menu and scroll to the right (figure 6.2F, image 1).
2. Highlight BGM and scroll to the right (figure 6.2F, image 2).
3. Highlight the current BGM song (e.g., Party Time), which you will hear playing, and scroll to the right (figure 6.2F, image 3).
4. A *Busy* screen will appear while the camera identifies the songs in the BGM folder on the SD card (figure 6.2F, image 4). When the progress bar reaches the right side of the screen, the camera will switch to the list of available BGM songs.
5. Select a song from the BGM Import menu (figure 6.2F, image 5). Press the OK button to choose the song (e.g., Nostalgic), which starts playing immediately for verification.
6. A screen with the words *BGM is overwritten* will appear (figure 6.2F, image 6). Select Yes from the menu, or No to cancel, and then press the OK button. When you start the next slideshow, your new song will play instead of Party Time.

Settings Recommendation: I configured my slideshow settings before I displayed my first slideshow, and I rarely change things. I might want to change the background music from time to time, but that's about all. I normally turn off movie replay during a slideshow because I want to see just still images. If I want to watch a movie, or a series of movies, I find it more convenient to simply choose one from the monitor when I am ready to view it.

When you choose to display movies in a slideshow, they cleverly blend with still images. However, the music keeps playing through the movie, which I find distracting most of the time. Unless your movies are lovely nature videos, it may be better to leave music turned off in a slideshow that includes both movies and still images. You can adjust the balance of the recorded sound and the background music by pressing left and right on the Arrow Pad while the movie is playing.

[Image Rotation]

[Image Rotation] allows you to choose if an image taken in portrait (vertical) orientation is displayed upright or rotated onto its side on the camera monitor.

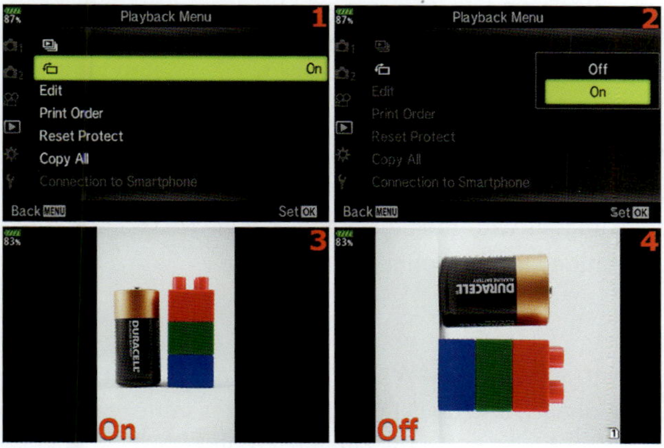

Figure 6.3: Choose how a vertical image will display on the camera monitor

Use these steps to choose how a vertical image will display:

1. Select the [Image Rotation] symbol from the Playback Menu and scroll to the right (figure 6.3, image 1).
2. A small menu with On and Off choices will open (figure 6.3, image 2). If you want a vertical image to display as shown in figure 6.3, image 3, choose On. If you want it to be rotated onto its side, as shown in figure 6.3, image 4, choose Off. Press the OK button to lock in your choice.

Settings Recommendation: I leave this function set to On so the image on the monitor will be easier to review as I scroll through all my images. The E-M1II displays an image on the monitor for only about one-half second, unless you change the default image review timeout setting in *Setup Menu > Rec View* (page 598). I leave Rec View set to one-half second (0.5sec) so it won't delay my ability to take the next picture.

If you change the Rec View default to a longer time, you may want to leave [Image Rotation] Off so you can review your image on the monitor in the same direction you were holding the camera when you took the picture.

Edit

If you don't like working with images on the computer, or if you are on a tour in the wilds and don't have a computer available, you can still do basic in-camera image processing. You can take an original RAW or JPEG image, modify it in various ways, then save it as a new JPEG image.

Sel. Image

Sel. Image (Select Image) is the first of the two image editing tools. We will consider the second—Image Overlay—later in this chapter.

There are four ways to modify images with the Sel. Image tool: RAW Data Edit, JPEG Edit, Movie Edit, and [Voice Annotation]. Let's examine each of these.

RAW Data Edit

RAW Data Edit allows you to convert a file from RAW to JPEG in-camera. If you prefer to shoot in RAW for maximum image quality, and quickly need a JPEG for some reason, you can create one without using a computer. Here are the conversion types:

- **Current:** You will choose a RAW image on the monitor and the camera will create a JPEG image using whatever camera settings are currently set on the camera.
- **Custom1 and Custom2:** These two functions allow you to select individual changes to image exposure settings. The camera will then convert a RAW image into a JPEG image with the settings you choose. You can save the Custom1 or Custom2 settings and use them later.
- **ART BKT:** You can choose a RAW file, apply one of the camera's Art Modes to it, then save it as a JPEG. This is a good way to apply an Art Mode to an image after the fact.
- **No:** Cancel image editing with Sel. Image.

The RAW Data Edit function works only with RAW files. There is a separate JPEG Edit function for JPEG files, which we will discuss in the upcoming **JPEG Edit** subsection. If there are only JPEG images on the memory card, the RAW Data Edit choice will be grayed out and unavailable.

There are 11 conversion factors to consider when you convert a file from RAW to JPEG. When you use the Current and Custom RAW Data Edit functions, you will notice that each has a different way to configure the 11 settings.

RAW to JPEG conversion factors

- JPEG quality setting (e.g., LSF, LF, MN)
- Picture Mode (e.g., Vivid, Natural, Muted)
- White Balance (e.g., Sunny, Cloudy, Incandescent)
- Exposure Compensation (±3.0 EV)
- Shadow Area Adjust (Sh; ±7 steps)

- Midtone Area Adjust (Mid; ±7 steps)
- Brighten Area Adjust (Hi; ±7 steps)
- Image Aspect Ratio (e.g., 4:3, 16:9, 3:2)
- Noise Filter (i.e., Low, Std, High)
- Color Space (i.e., sRGB, Adobe RGB)
- Keystone Compensation (swing and tilt correction)

Let's examine each of the RAW to JPEG conversion types: Current, Custom1 and Custom2, and ART BKT.

Current

This form of RAW (ORF) to JPEG conversion uses the camera's current settings as a guide to conversion. These 11 settings are listed in the previous ***RAW to JPEG conversion factors*** list. Before you start the RAW Data Edit in Current mode, you must configure your camera settings for converting a file to JPEG.

After you have adjusted each of these items, you will execute the following steps to convert the image from RAW to JPEG.

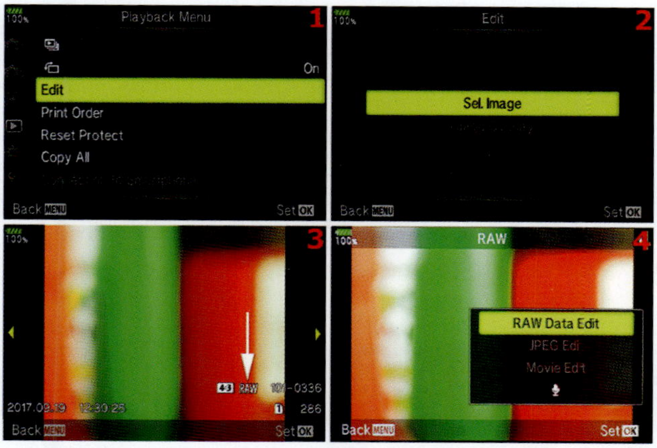

Figure 6.4A: Converting RAW to JPEG with Current camera settings (steps 1–4)

Use these steps to convert a RAW file on the memory card into a new JPEG file, which will have a new file number and show up as the last image on the memory card:

1. Choose Edit from the Playback Menu and scroll to the right (figure 6.4A, image 1).
2. Choose Sel. Image from the Edit menu and press the OK button (figure 6.4A, image 2).
3. The camera will display the images on the memory card, along with the format of each image (figure 6.4A, image 3, white arrow). Scroll through the images with the Arrow Pad until you find the RAW file you want to convert. Press the OK button to select the image.

4. Choose RAW Data Edit from the menu and press the OK button (figure 6.4A, image 4). [***Note:*** The camera will display a menu with both RAW Data Edit and JPEG Edit if an image has been taken in a RAW + JPEG format (e.g., LF+RAW).]

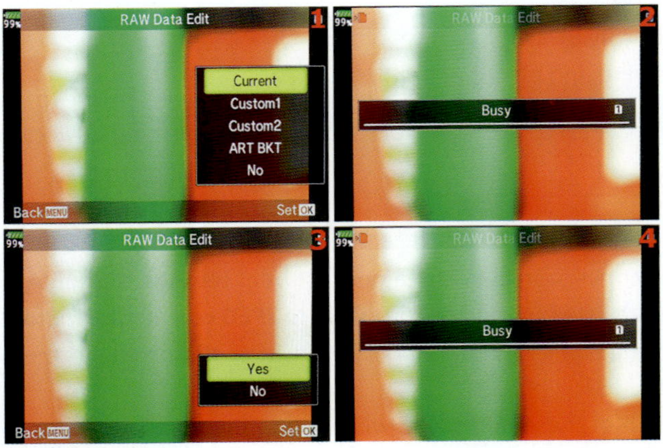

Figure 6.4B: Converting RAW to JPEG with Current camera settings (steps 5 and 6)

5. Figure 6.4B begins where figure 6.4A ends. Select Current from the menu (figure 6.4B, image 1). This tells the camera to use its current settings (see the ***RAW to JPEG conversion factors*** on page 366 to convert the file from RAW to JPEG. Press the OK button to continue, and you will briefly see a *Busy* screen (figure 6.4B, image 2).
6. Next you decide whether the image looks okay on the camera monitor with the current settings applied (figure 6.4B, image 3). If you think it looks fine, select Yes and press the OK button, which will make a new JPEG file while a *Busy* screen is displayed (figure 6.4B, image 4). If you want to adjust the image further, select No and start over with new camera settings.

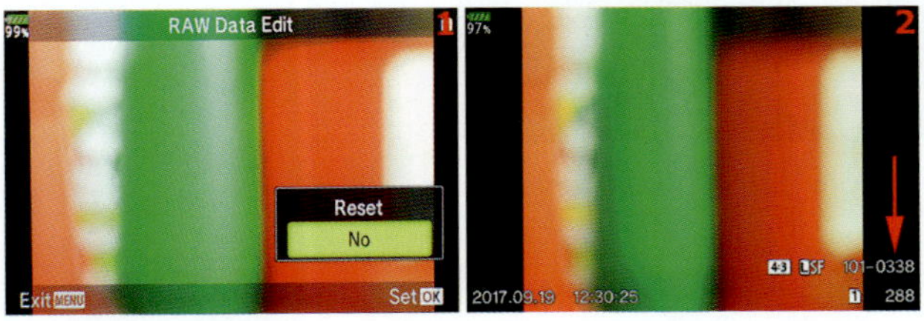

Figure 6.4C: Converting RAW to JPEG with Current camera settings (step 7)

7. Figure 6.4C begins where figure 6.4B ends. The camera gives you a preview of the conversion, which hasn't yet been saved to the memory card. A menu with Reset and No choices will appear (figure 6.4C, image 1). If you select Reset, the camera will abandon the current conversion and jump back to the screen shown in figure 6.4B, image 1, so you can start over at step 5. If you select No—which, ironically, means you do want to save the newly converted JPEG image—the camera will save the JPEG to a new file name as the last image on the memory card. The new JPEG image will appear on the monitor with the new file name displayed (figure 6.4C, image 2, red arrow).

Custom1 and Custom2

The two Custom RAW Data Edit modes let you choose 11 factors for conversion. Unlike the Current RAW Data Edit mode discussed in the previous subsection, which used current camera settings for the conversion, the Custom functions allow you to adjust individual settings before you convert your image from RAW to JPEG.

The 11 settings you can adjust are shown in the ***RAW to JPEG conversion factors*** list (page 366). These are the same 11 functions used by the Current method. The difference between the Current and Custom RAW Data Edit settings is that the camera automatically saves the Custom settings so you can use them later. If you use the Custom function again without changing the settings, the camera will use your previous settings.

There are two Custom settings: Custom1 and Custom2. Configuring them works exactly the same way, so we will use only Custom1 as an example. Remember that Custom1 and Custom2 can be configured with different settings and you can reuse them later. Maybe you will use one Custom setting to convert RAW images to high-quality JPEGs and the other to convert RAW images to smaller JPEGs for online use.

Note: Pressing the Movie button at any time while you configure any of the 11 conversion factor settings will give you a Preview Update of what the image will look like after conversion. The Movie button is on top of the camera—just behind the Shutter button, next to the Fn2 button—and has a red dot. Preview Update will apply the current conversion settings, without saving the file, so you can see what the conversion looks like up to that point. You can test the conversion with each change if you want to. Each screen has a reminder that you can see a Preview Update (figure 6.4E, image 2, bottom red arrow).

Now, let's see how to use the Custom RAW Data Edit function.

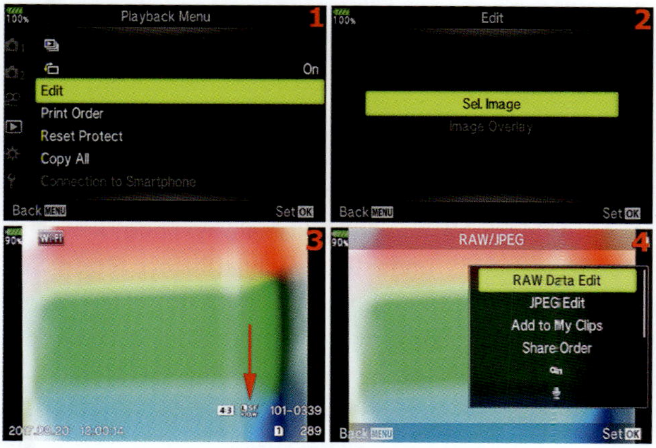

Figure 6.4D: Converting RAW to JPEG with Custom camera settings

Use the following steps to convert from RAW to JPEG with Custom RAW Data Edit's 11 settings:

1. Choose Edit from the Playback Menu and scroll to the right (figure 6.4D, image 1).
2. Choose Sel. Image from the Edit menu and press the OK button (figure 6.4D, image 2).

3. The camera will now display the images on the memory card. Scroll through the images with the Arrow Pad until you find the RAW file you want to convert. The format of the image will be displayed on the monitor (figure 6.4D, image 3, red arrow). The picture in our example is stored in both RAW and JPEG formats (LSF+RAW) on the memory card. Press the OK button.
4. The camera will display a menu with two choices: RAW Data Edit and JPEG Edit (figure 6.4D, image 4). Since the picture in image 4 has both RAW and JPEG versions available (JPEG+RAW), both choices are available on the menu. Choose RAW Data Edit and press the OK button.

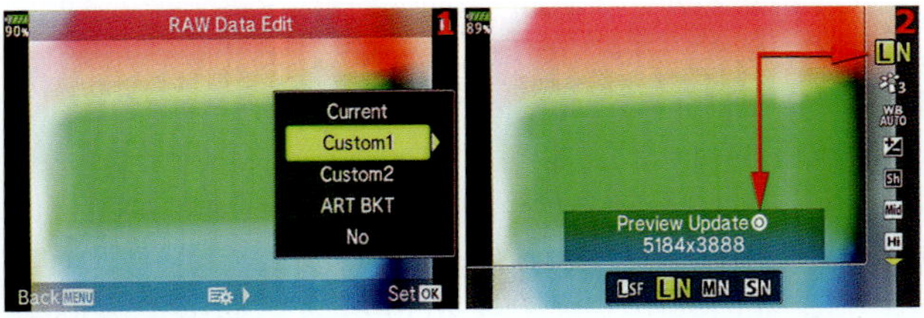

Figure 6.4E: Choosing a Record Mode (image size and quality) for the converted JPEG

5. Figure 6.4E begins where figure 6.4D ends. You will see a menu with the two Custom settings. Select Custom1 or Custom2 and scroll to the right (figure 6.4E, image 1).
6. Figure 6.4E, image 2, shows the first of 11 screens we will use to configure the RAW to JPEG conversion settings, shown in the ***RAW to JPEG conversion factors*** list (page 366). The first setting is Record Mode (image size and quality). The items along the right side of the screen are headings, and their adjustments are shown at the bottom of the screen. Scroll up or down on the right side of the screen with the Arrow Pad to select a conversion setting, and scroll left or right on the bottom of the screen to make adjustments to that conversion setting. The Record Mode heading on the right (LN) has the following choices at the bottom of the screen: LSF, LN, MN, and SN (figure 6.4E, image 2). Your new camera may display LF, LN, MN, and SN instead. (You can adjust the image size and quality by changing *Custom Menu > G. [Record Mode]/ WB/Color > [Record Mode] Set*. I use LSF, LF, MF, and SF so I can always shoot JPEG Fine images instead of JPEG Normal. See page 532, under the heading **[Record Mode] Set,** for more information about image size and quality settings.) Choose one of the Record Modes, such as LF (Large Fine JPEG) or LN (Large Normal JPEG), by scrolling left or right (LSF is available only when configured in the Custom Menu under [Record Mode] Set). Press the Movie button for a Preview Update to see how the conversion will look so far. *Do not press the OK button until you have completed all the changes you want to make.* After you have chosen a Record Mode, scroll down one space on the right side of the screen to select a Picture Mode.

7. You can choose a Picture Mode to give a certain look to your new JPEG image (figure 6.4F). There are nine Picture Modes available on the bottom of the screen. The Natural Picture Mode is selected in figure 6.4F. (See page 151, under the heading **Picture Mode,** for more information about Picture Modes.) Choose the Picture Mode you want to use for this conversion by scrolling left or right with the Arrow Pad. Press the Movie button for a Preview Update to see how the image conversion will look so far. *Do not press the OK button unless you have completed all the changes you want to make.* (***Note:*** You can also use Art Picture Mode filters while converting from RAW to JPEG by using the ART BKT selection discussed on page 202). Scroll down to the next setting, White Balance (WB).

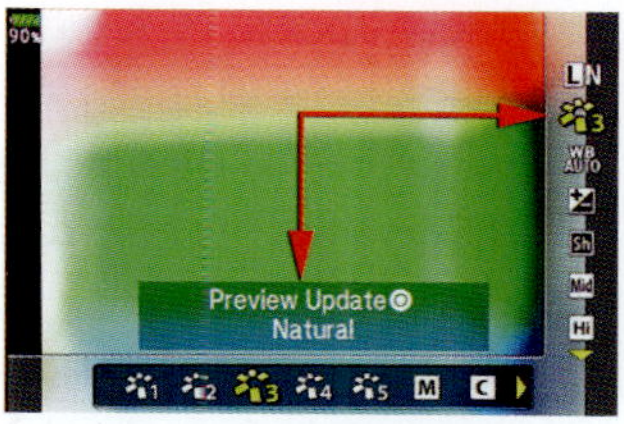

Figure 6.4F: Choosing a Picture Mode for the converted JPEG

8. The White Balance (WB) setting (figure 6.4G) lets you choose from 13 WB types, including eight standard settings (e.g., Auto, Sunny, Cloudy), four custom WB settings captured previously with a gray card, and a kelvin setting (2000K to 14000K). (See the chapter titled **Custom Menu** on page 536, under the **White Balance (WB)** heading, for more information about WB settings.) Choose the WB you want to use for this conversion by scrolling left or right with the Arrow Pad. I chose the WB Auto setting in figure 6.4G. For WB settings that allow changes (e.g., CWB), press the INFO button and scroll with the Arrow Pad to make changes. Press the Movie button for a Preview Update to see how the image conversion will look so far. *Do not press the OK button unless you have completed all the changes you want to make.* Scroll down to the next setting, Exposure compensation (+/–).

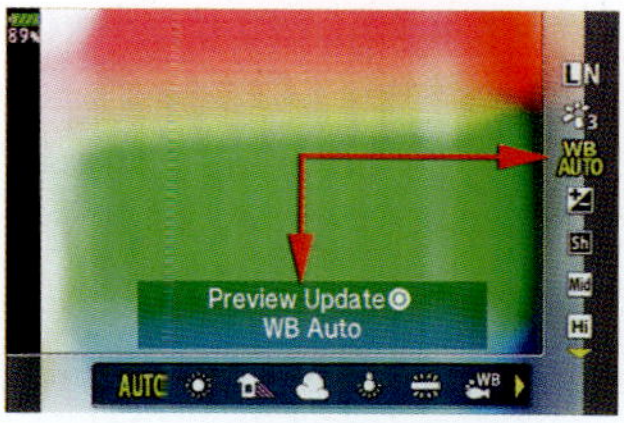

Figure 6.4G: Choosing a White Balance setting for the converted JPEG

9. The Exposure compensation (+/–) setting lets you add or subtract light from the converted image in 1/3 EV steps, with maximum increments from –3.0 to +3.0 EV steps (figure 6.4H). Choose an Exposure compensation value for this conversion by scrolling left or right with the Arrow Pad. You will see the number next to the +/– symbol change in 1/3 EV step increments. Press the Movie button for a

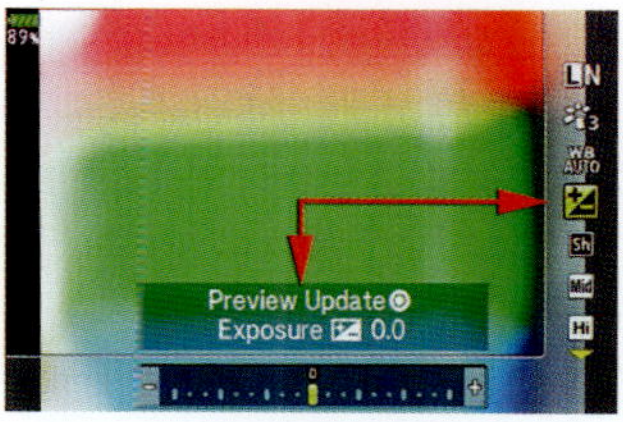

Figure 6.4H: Using Exposure compensation on the converted JPEG

Preview Update to see how the image conversion will look so far. *Do not press the OK button unless you have completed all the changes you want to make.* Scroll down to the next setting, Shadow Area Adjust (Sh).

10. The Shadow Area Adjust (Sh) setting lets you add or subtract light from the darker areas of the image in +/–7 steps (e.g., +1, +2, –1, –2) (figure 6.4I). Choose a Shadow Area Adjust (Sh) value for this conversion by scrolling left or right with the Arrow Pad. You will see the number next to Shadow Area Adjust change one step at a time. Press the Movie button for a Preview Update to see how the image conversion will look so far. *Do not press the OK button unless you have completed all the changes you want to make.* Scroll down to the next setting, Midtone Area Adjust (Mid).

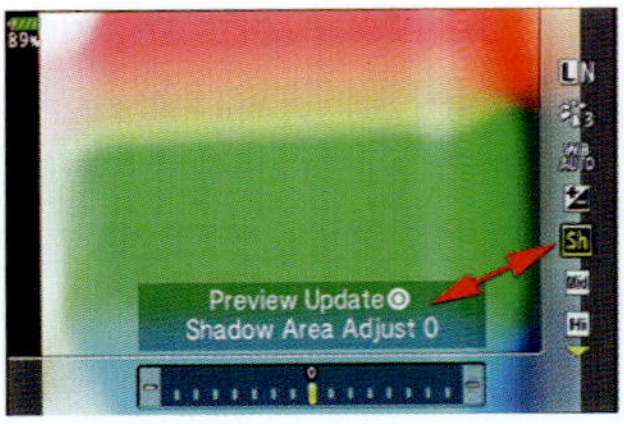

Figure 6.4I: Choosing a Shadow Area Adjust value for the converted JPEG

11. The Midtone Area Adjust (Mid) setting lets you add or subtract light from the middle tones of the image in +/–7 steps (e.g., +1, +2, –1, –2) (figure 6.4J). Choose a Midtone Area Adjust (Mid) value for this conversion by scrolling left or right with the Arrow Pad. You will see the number next to Midtone Area Adjust change one step at a time. Press the Movie button for a Preview Update to see how the image conversion will look so far. *Do not press the OK button unless you have completed all the changes you want to make.* Scroll down to the next setting, Brighten Area Adjust (Hi).

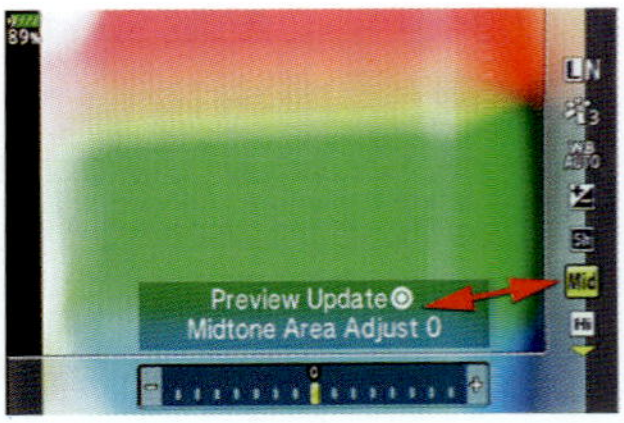

Figure 6.4J: Choosing a Midtone Area Adjust value for the converted JPEG

12. The Brighten Area Adjust (Hi) setting lets you add or subtract light from the highlights of the image in +/–7 steps (e.g., +1, +2, –1, –2) (figure 6.4K). Choose a Brighten Area Adjust (Hi) value for this conversion by scrolling left or right with the Arrow Pad. You will see the number next to Brighten Area Adjust change one step at a time. Press the Movie button for a Preview Update to see how the image conversion will look so far. *Do not press the OK button unless you have completed all the changes you want to make.* Scroll down to the next setting, image Aspect Ratio (e.g., 4:3).

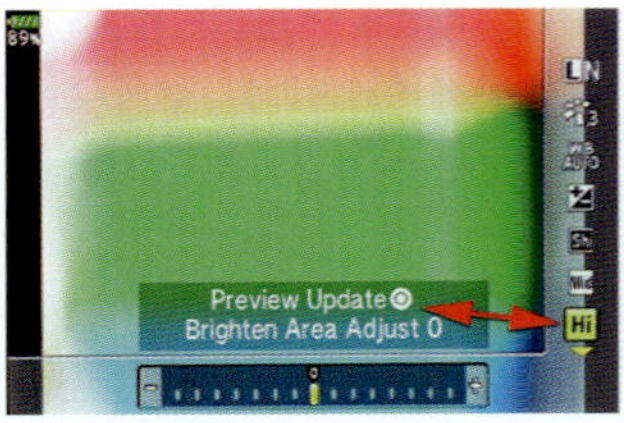

Figure 6.4K: Choosing a Brighten Area Adjust value for the converted JPEG

13. The image Aspect Ratio setting (e.g., 4:3) lets you change the shape of the image (figure 6.4L). You can change it from the normal Micro Four Thirds setting (4:3) to a different Aspect Ratio, such as a long and narrow HD view (16:9); the shape of most non-Micro Four Thirds digital images (3:2); square (1:1); or vertical Micro Four Thirds portrait mode (3:4). Choose one of the Aspect Ratio values for the conversion by scrolling left or right with the Arrow Pad. You will notice that the camera displays the pixel ratio for each Aspect Ratio (e.g., 5184 × 3888). To see how the change affects the image, press the Movie button for a Preview Update. *Do not press the OK button unless you have completed all the changes you want to make.* Scroll down to the next setting, Noise Filter (NF).

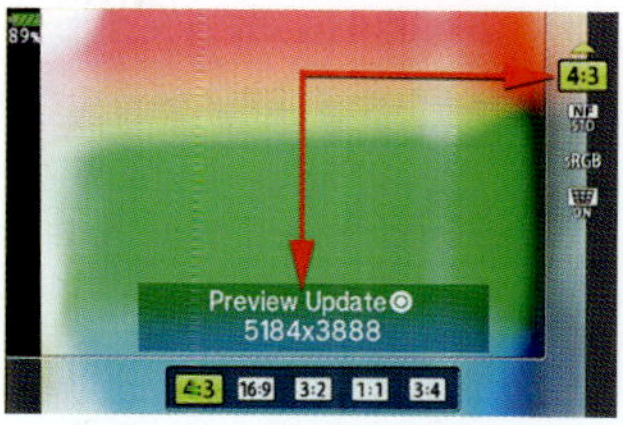

Figure 6.4L: Choosing an image Aspect Ratio for the converted JPEG

14. The Noise Filter (NF) setting lets you select the strength of noise reduction for those higher-ISO images (figure 6.4M). You can select from OFF, LOW, STD, and HIGH. It will be hard to see how the noise reduction system affects the image on the small camera monitor. You may want to experiment with noise reduction in advance so you can make a better choice during the conversion process. Most people leave Noise Filter (NF) set to Standard (STD). Press the Movie button for a Preview Update to see how the image conversion will look so far. *Do not press the OK button unless you have completed all the changes you want to make.* Scroll down to the next setting, Color Space (sRGB).

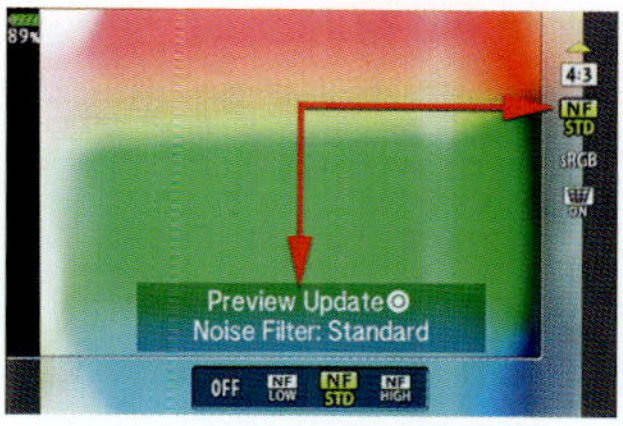

Figure 6.4M: Choosing noise reduction for the converted JPEG

15. The Color Space (sRGB) setting lets you choose whether to use the generally noncommercial sRGB color space or the commercial Adobe RGB color space (figure 6.4N). Most noncommercial photographers will leave Color Space set to sRGB because that works best for home, online, and superstore printing, and for display on social media sites and websites. If you are a stock photographer who submits images to a stock agency or are involved in other purely commercial photography endeavors where the images will be printed on an offset press,

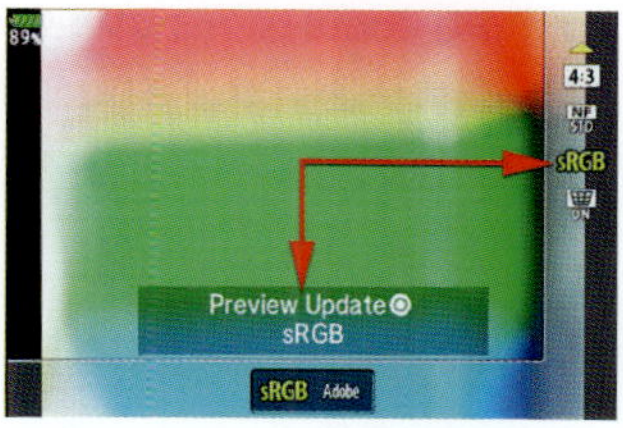

Figure 6.4N: Choosing a Color Space for the converted JPEG

you will usually need to shoot with the Adobe RGB color space because it matches commercial CMYK color printing more closely. (See page 546 under the heading **Color Space** for more information.) Press the Movie button for a Preview Update to see how the image conversion will look so far. *Do not press the OK button unless you have completed all the changes you want to make.* Next, let's discuss how to use Keystone Compensation during your RAW to JPEG conversion.

16. Keystone Compensation allows you to add corrections to images that have perspective distortion, such as when you take a picture of a building with a wide-angle lens and the building looks like it's falling over backward. Keystone Compensation gives you swing and tilt controls, like you'll find on an old-fashioned, film view camera. Swing allows you to move the left or right edge of a picture toward and away from you, and tilt allows you to tilt the top or bottom of the image toward or away from you. To use this function, press the INFO button when the screen shown in figure 6.40 is on the monitor. Then use the Front Dial to swing the left or right edges of the image toward or away from you, and the Rear Dial to tilt the top or bottom of the image. (***Note:*** See **Keystone Comp.** on page 226 for more information on how this function works.) Now it's time to finish the RAW to JPEG conversion with all of the custom settings applied. The camera saves your settings so you can make more conversions using the settings you just prepared. Press the OK button to start the final conversion process.

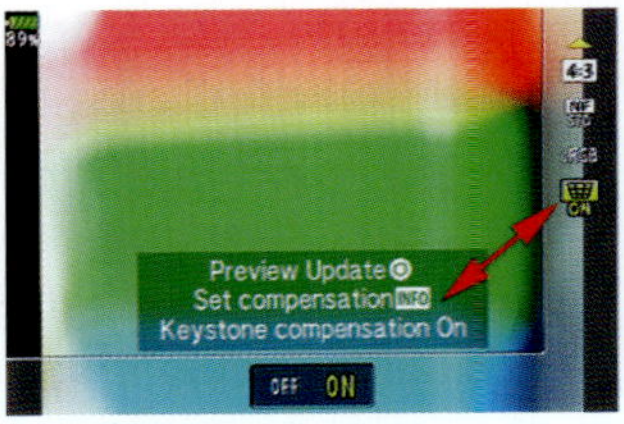

Figure 6.40: Using Keystone Compensation

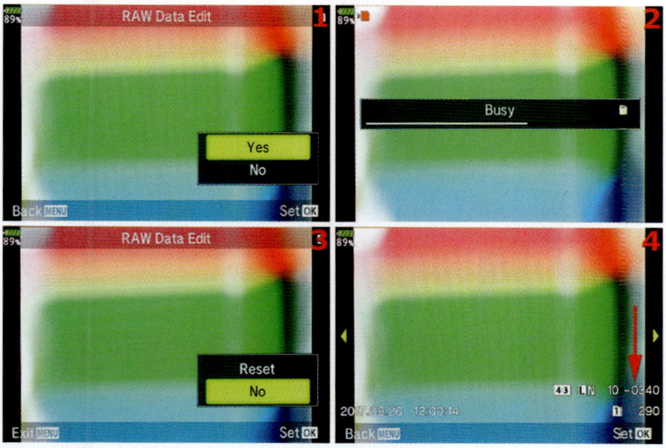

Figure 6.4P: Viewing a final Preview Update and then converting the image

17. The camera will display a final Preview Update of the image, with all your carefully crafted settings in place. You will also see a small menu with Yes and No choices (figure 6.4P, image 1). If you choose No the camera will revert to the image selection screen and you will have to start over. If you choose Yes the camera will execute the final conversion from RAW to JPEG.
18. During the conversion, a *Busy* screen with a progress bar will display (figure 6.4P, image 2). When the progress bar is complete, you will have one final decision to make before the image is saved to the memory card.
19. Before you save the new JPEG image to the memory card, the camera opens a menu with Reset and No options (figure 6.4P, image 3). If you select Reset, the camera will not save the new image. Instead, it will jump back to the beginning of the conversion. If you select No, the camera will save the new JPEG image under a new file name as the last JPEG image on the memory card. The final converted image will be displayed on the camera monitor with a new file name (101–0340; figure 6.4P, image 4, red arrow).

Now, let's consider how to use the third type of RAW to JPEG conversion: converting to JPEG with an Art Mode.

ART BKT

The ART BKT function allows you to choose a single RAW image and create up to 37 JPEG images from it. Each image will automatically have a different Picture Mode or Art Mode applied to it, which is why the function has the letters BKT (bracket) in its name. In effect, you will be creating more than one JPEG image from a single RAW file, an Art Mode Bracketing (ART BKT) series.

The camera allows you to select all Picture Modes and Art Modes in the ART BKT function, not just the Art Modes, as the function name implies. (We discussed each of the Picture and Art Modes in the chapter titled **Shooting Menu 1,** under the subheading

Picture Mode (page 151). For more information on each mode, see the corresponding subsection.)

If you are unsure which Picture Modes—Basic, Creative, or Art—you want to use, and if you would like to make a test image with each one, you can do it with ART BKT. Or if you want to make a single JPEG image with only one of the special Art Mode looks applied (e.g., Pop Art, Grainy Film, Gentle Sepia), you can do that, too.

Now, let's examine how to create a RAW to JPEG conversion with multiple JPEG files, each with a specific Picture Mode or Art Mode effect applied.

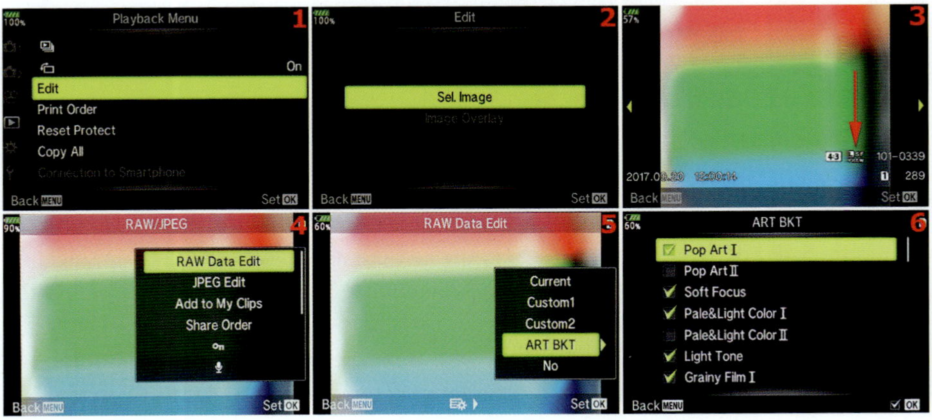

Figure 6.4Q: Creating a RAW to JPEG ART BKT conversion (steps 1–6)

Use the following steps to make a RAW to JPEG conversion using one or more of the camera's available Picture or Art Modes:

1. Select Edit from the Playback Menu and scroll to the right (figure 6.4Q, image 1).
2. Choose Sel. Image from the Edit menu and press the OK button (figure 6.4Q, image 2).
3. The camera will display the images on the memory card. Scroll through the images with the Arrow Pad until you find the RAW file you want to convert. The format of the image will be displayed on the monitor (figure 6.4Q, image 3, red arrow). The picture in our example is stored in both JPEG and RAW formats on the memory card. Press the OK button to select the image.
4. The camera will display a menu with multiple choices (since the picture has both RAW and JPEG versions available): RAW Data Edit and JPEG Edit (figure 6.4Q, image 4). Choose RAW Data Edit and press the OK button.
5. You will now see the RAW Data Edit menu and a choice of conversion types (figure 6.4Q, image 5). Highlight ART BKT and scroll to the right.
6. The ART BKT list of available modes will now appear, with the Art Modes (e.g., Pop Art, Soft Focus) at the top (figure 6.4Q, image 6). When this screen first appears, quite a few modes will already be checked. Only 7 of the 37 available modes are visible on the

screen in image 6—you must scroll down to see the rest. If you do the ART BKT conversion with more than one Picture or Art Mode checked, the camera will create a JPEG image for each of the checked items. To check or uncheck a mode simply highlight it and press the OK button, and you will see the check mark appear or disappear. Check whichever modes you want to use, and then scroll to the left with the Arrow Pad or press the Menu button once to get back to the previous screen (figure 6.4R, image 1) where you will execute the ART BKT conversion.

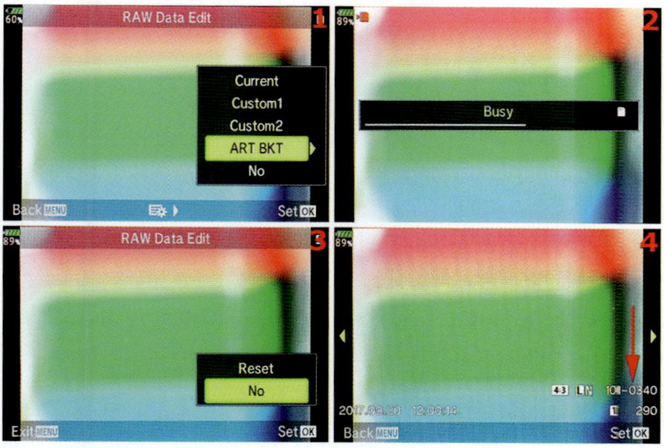

Figure 6.4R: Creating a RAW to JPEG ART BKT conversion (final steps)

7. Now you will execute the conversions and create a new JPEG file for each Picture and Art Mode you selected in step 6. Make sure ART BKT is still highlighted and press the OK button to start the conversions (figure 6.4R, image 1).
8. You will see a *Busy* screen with a progress indicator while the camera creates the new JPEG images (figure 6.4R, image 2). The more images you are converting, the longer the *Busy* screen will be displayed. At the right end of the progress indicator, you can see the symbol for the memory card to which the files are being written (1 or 2). Allow some time if you checked a lot of Picture or Art Modes in step 6.
9. When the conversion is complete, the camera will display one of the images from the conversion, along with a menu that has two choices: Reset and No (figure 6.4R, image 3). If you select Reset at this point, the camera will return to the screen shown in figure 6.4R, image 1, which stops the conversion and lets you select a different Picture Mode from the ART BKT list. If you choose No, the camera will save the new JPEG image(s) to the memory card and display the last image in the series—or a single image if you chose only one Picture or Art Mode—on the monitor (figure 6.4R, image 4). If there are multiple JPEGs in the conversion, you can scroll to the left with the Arrow Pad to see each of the images with the Picture or Art Mode applied.

Now, let's examine the next type of image editing, JPEG edit.

JPEG Edit

The JPEG Edit function lets you make in-camera changes to your existing JPEG image files and then save them as new files. It works only with JPEG files. There is a separate RAW Data Edit function for RAW files, which we discussed in the previous **RAW Data Edit** subsection (pages 368, 369, 376).

When you select and modify a JPEG file, the original file is not changed. A new modified JPEG file is created and stored with a new file name as the last image on the memory card. If you don't like using computers to modify files, or if you immediately need a modified JPEG, the JPEG Edit function is quick and easy to use.

There are nine adjustments for JPEG images:

- ***Shadow Adj:*** This setting automatically adjusts the shadows of an image to reveal more image data. Use it to brighten mildly underexposed images or to open the shadows on well-exposed images.
- ***Redeye Fix:*** The camera attempts to remove red eye when the subject has that strange-looking, red-eye reflection caused by flash.
- ***[Crop]:*** You can crop the image up to four ways: both horizontal and both vertical sides.
- ***Aspect:*** This setting changes the aspect ratio from the standard Micro Four Thirds 4:3 ratio to 3:2, 16:9, 1:1, or 3:4.
- ***Black & White:*** You can convert an image to a retro-looking, grayscale, black-and-white image.
- ***Sepia:*** The camera will give your image an old-fashioned sepia, brown-toned look.
- ***Saturation:*** This setting allows you to increase or decrease the color saturation by using a sliding +/- indicator.
- ***[File Size]:*** You can choose from three smaller file sizes: 1280×960 (1.2 MP), 640×480 (0.3 MP), and 320×240 (0.075 MP).
- ***e-Portrait:*** This setting makes skin tones smoother and adds translucense for an anti-aging effect.

Adjusting a JPEG image is different from cumulatively setting the conversion factors on a RAW file, as we did in the previous subsection. You can apply a new adjustment to a previously adjusted image, but be careful because making repeated changes to one JPEG file results in data losses due to recompression of the image. To maintain maximum quality, think of these adjustments as effects that you can apply to different images, not as cumulative steps that you'll apply to one JPEG image.

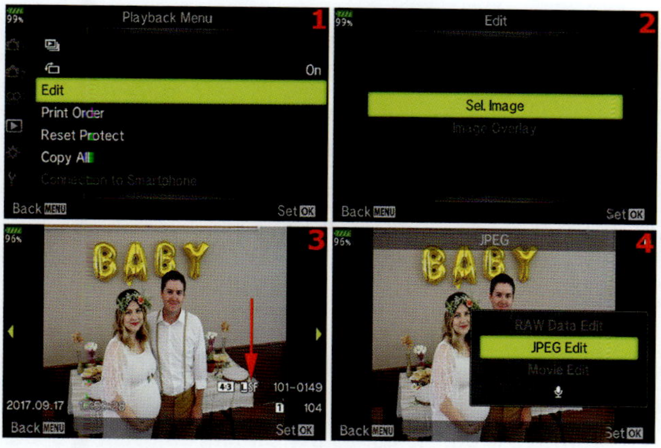

Figure 6.5A: Choosing a JPEG image and starting the JPEG Edit steps

Use the following steps to choose an image for modification and to make some or all of the available changes:

1. Select Edit from the Playback Menu and scroll to the right (figure 6.5A, image 1).
2. Choose Sel. Image from the Edit menu and press the OK button (figure 6.5A, image 2).
3. The camera will display the images on the memory card. Scroll through the images with the Arrow Pad until you find the JPEG file you want to convert. The format of the image will be displayed on the monitor (figure 6.5A, image 3, red arrow). Press the OK button to select the image.
4. You will see a menu with four choices: RAW Data Edit, JPEG Edit, Movie Edit, and the [Voice Annotation] microphone symbol (figure 6.5A, image 4). You can tell that this image is not a RAW file because it is labeled LSF in image 3, and in image 4, the RAW Data Edit choice is grayed out and unavailable. If this image had been shot in a JPEG+RAW format, the memory card would have both files and you could edit either the RAW file or the JPEG file. Choose JPEG Edit and press the OK button.

The images in figure 6.5A are the first four screens for the next nine subsections (figures 6.5B to 6.5J). Each of the upcoming adjustments will begin where figure 6.5A leaves off.

Shadow Adj (Opening the Shadows)

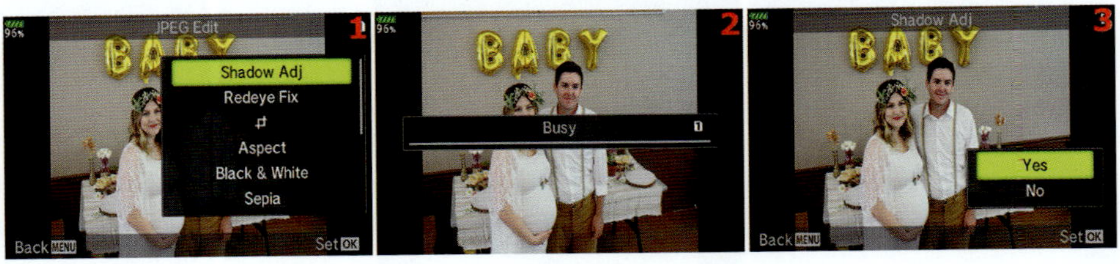

Figure 6.5B: Opening the shadows

1. Figure 6.5B begins where figure 6.5A ends. Choose Shadow Adj from the JPEG Edit menu and press the OK button (figure 6.5B, image 1).
2. You will briefly see a *Busy* screen with a progress bar as the camera adjusts the shadows (figure 6.5B, image 2).
3. When it is done, you will see the adjusted image with a menu that has Yes and No choices (figure 6.5B, image 3). To make the Shadow Adj modification permanent, select Yes. The camera will apply the adjustment and save the new JPEG image with a new file name. To cancel and start over, select No.

Redeye Fix (Removing Red Eye)

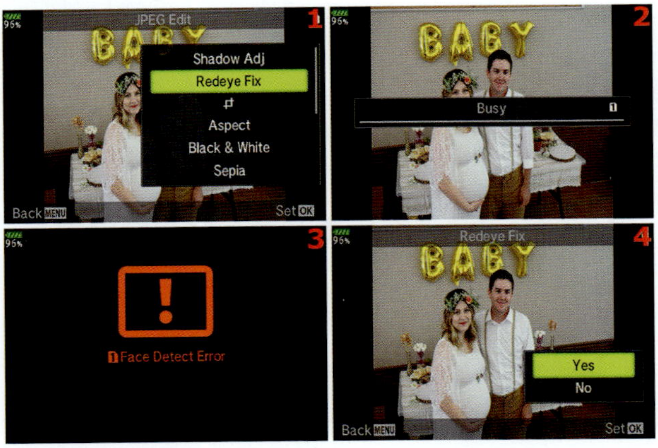

Figure 6.5C: Removing red eye

1. Figure 6.5C begins where figure 6.5A ends. The Redeye Fix adjustment removes glowing red eyes that occur when the subject's retinas reflect flash light back into the lens. Choose Redeye Fix from the JPEG Edit menu and scroll to the right (figure 6.5C, image 1).
2. The camera will now find and remove red eye from the image. A *Busy* screen and progress bar will stay on the monitor for a few moments while face detection and red-eye removal takes place (figure 6.5C, image 2). The camera will attempt to remove red eye even from images in which there is no red eye.

3. If the camera does not detect a human face, it will display an error message (figure 6.5C, image 3). Either the picture has no people in it, their faces are too small, or their faces are at a bad angle. If you see this screen, the camera cannot work with the image. If the camera does detect a human face, you will see the screen shown in image 4.
4. Since the camera can detect a human face in the example picture, you will see a menu with Yes and No choices (figure 6.5C, image 4). Choose Yes to save the new JPEG image with red eye removed, or No to cancel and start over.

[Crop] (In-Camera Image Cropping)

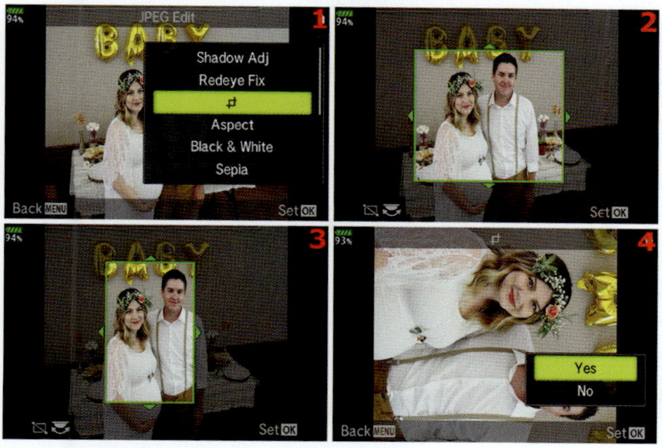

Figure 6.5D: Cropping the image

1. Figure 6.5D begins where figure 6.5A ends. You can crop an image to remove unwanted surroundings and show only the most important part of the picture. Select [Crop] from the JPEG Edit menu and press the OK button (figure 6.5D, image 1).
2. Rotate the Rear Dial to see a series of preset image crop sizes. Figure 6.5D, image 2, shows the largest horizontal crop, and image 3 shows the largest vertical crop. There are also two smaller crop sizes that you can see when you rotate the Rear Dial. Select one of the crop sizes, use the Arrow Pad to move the green crop rectangle to the desired location, and press the OK button to execute the crop. I have not found a way to resize these crops.
3. You will see an unsaved preview of the cropped image on the monitor (figure 6.5D, image 4). The screen will have a menu with Yes and No choices. Select Yes to save the new image, or No to cancel and start over.

Aspect (Changing Image Proportions)

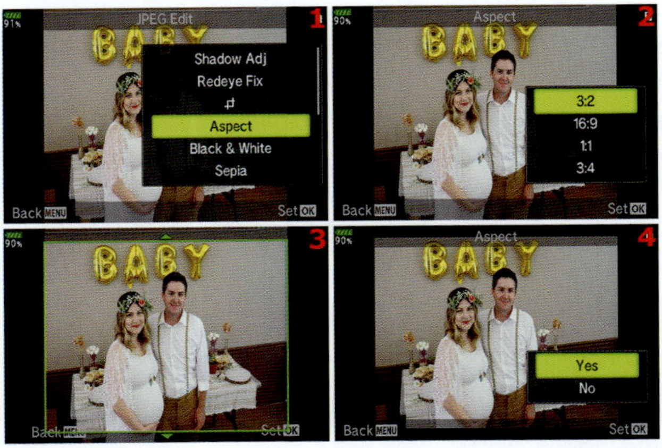

Figure 6.5E: Adjusting the Aspect ratio

1. Figure 6.5E begins where figure 6.5A ends. The aspect ratio is the relationship of the picture's horizontal sides to its vertical sides. The Aspect ratio setting allows you to choose from several preset image sizes. The basic Micro Four Thirds (4:3) ratio can be cropped to one of four additional ratios. Choose Aspect from the JPEG Edit menu and press the OK button (figure 6.5E, image 1).
2. A menu will open with several aspect ratio choices: 3:2, 16:9, 1:1, and 3:4 (figure 6.5E, image 2). Choose the aspect ratio that best fits the subject matter and press the OK button.
3. A green aspect ratio frame will surround the subject (figure 6.5E, image 3). Use the Arrow Pad buttons to move the green aspect ratio frame to the desired position, then press the OK button to execute the aspect ratio change. I selected the 3:2 aspect ratio. This converts the image into the slightly longer and narrower 3:2 format used by many DSLR cameras (e.g., Nikon). If you do not like the aspect ratio you chose, simply press the Menu button and the camera will return to the screen shown in figure 6.5E, image 2, and you can choose a different one. After you have chosen a ratio, positioned the frame, and are ready to execute the change, press the OK button.
4. You will see an unsaved preview of the new image on the monitor (figure 6.5E, image 4). The screen will have a menu with Yes and No choices. Select Yes to save the new image, or No to cancel and start over.

Black & White (Converting to Grayscale)

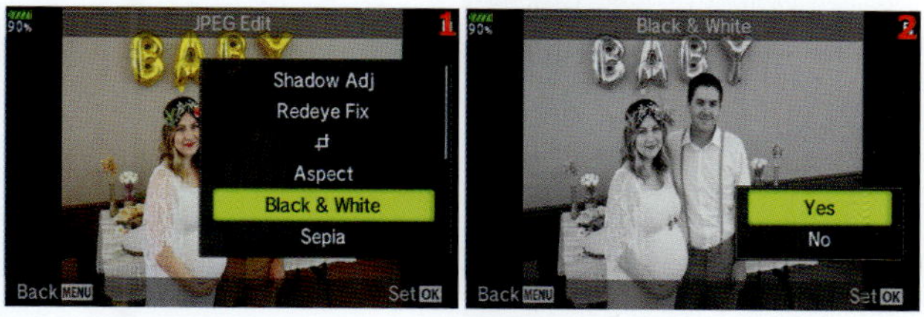

Figure 6.5F: Converting an image to Black & White

1. Figure 6.5F begins where figure 6.5A ends. Black & White conversion lets you change a color image into a grayscale (monochrome) picture. Choose Black & White from the JPEG Edit menu and press the OK button (figure 6.5F, image 1).
2. You will see an unsaved preview of the new image on the monitor (figure 6.5F, image 2). The screen will have a menu with Yes and No choices. Select Yes to save the new image, or No to cancel and start over.

Sepia (Converting to Antique Brown Tones)

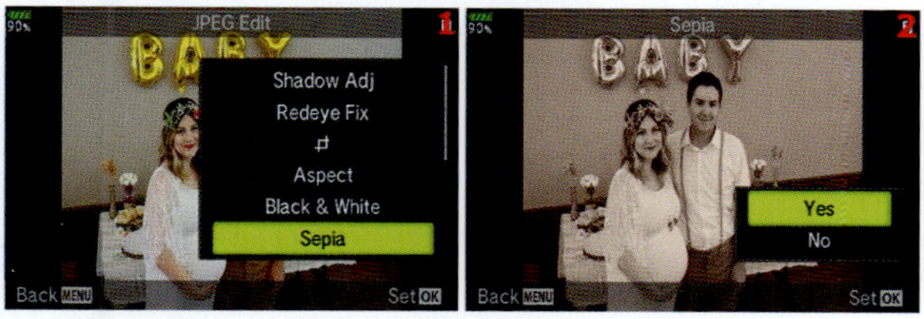

Figure 6.5G: Converting an image to Sepia

1. Figure 6.5G begins where figure 6.5A ends. Sepia conversion lets you change a color image to a monochrome image with brown tones instead of gray tones. Choose Sepia from the JPEG Edit menu and press the OK button (figure 6.5G, image 1).
2. You will see an unsaved preview of the new image on the monitor (figure 6.5G, image 2). The screen will have a menu with Yes and No choices. Select Yes to save the new image, or No to cancel and start over.

Saturation (Changing Image Color Strength)

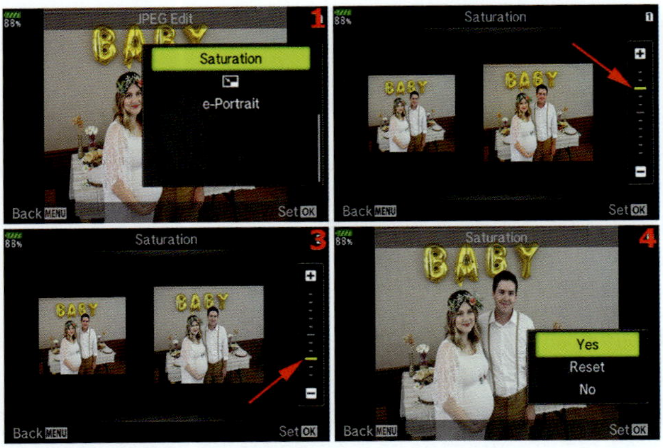

Figure 6.5H: Changing the color saturation

1. Figure 6.5H begins where figure 6.5A ends. The Saturation setting lets you change the strength of the colors in the image. Choose Saturation from the JPEG Edit menu and press the OK button (figure 6.5H, image 1).
2. You will see small before (left) and after (right) versions of the selected image (figure 6.5H, image 2). There will be a sliding scale with a green dash that indicates the current Saturation position. You can make the colors stronger (more saturated) by moving the slider up, or weaker (less saturated) by moving the slider down, on a scale of 10 steps. I moved the slider three steps toward increased Saturation (figure 6.5H, image 2, red arrow). Use the up and down buttons on the Arrow Pad to change the Saturation level. I then reduced the Saturation level (figure 6.5H, image 3, red arrow). You can see the differences in Saturation on the right sides of images 2 and 3. When you are happy with the Saturation level, press the OK button.
3. You will see an unsaved preview of the new image on the monitor (figure 6.5H, image 4). The screen will have a menu with Yes, Reset, and No choices. Select Yes to save the new image. Select Reset to move the slider back to the middle of the scale so you can make new adjustments. Select No to cancel and start over. When you are done, press the OK button to create and save the new JPEG image.

[File Size] (Downsizing an Image)

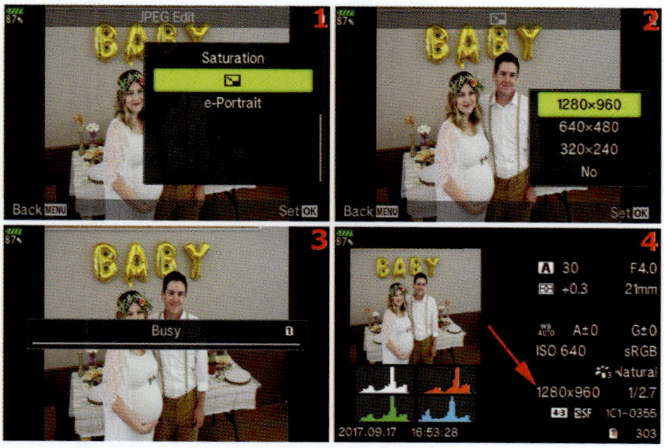

Figure 6.5I: Downsizing an image

1. Figure 6.5I begins where figure 6.5A ends. Normal 4:3 images from your E-M1II have 5184×3888 megapixels. That is equivalent to a 20 MP image, which is much too big to display on social media sites and usually too large to e-mail. You can quickly make a smaller JPEG by using the [File Size] function. Select the [File Size] symbol from the JPEG Edit menu and press the OK button (figure 6.5I, image 1).
2. You will see a menu of file sizes: 1280×960 (1.2 MP), 640×480 (0.3 MP), and 320×240 (0.075 MP). There is also a No option, which cancels the operation. Any of these smaller file sizes can be e-mailed or used on social media sites. Select the file size you want to use and press the OK button, or select No to cancel (figure 6.5I, image 2).
3. A *Busy* screen with a progress indicator will display on the camera monitor while the image is converted to the smaller size (figure 6.5I, image 3). Then the camera will display the new, smaller JPEG image, which is saved as the last image on the memory card. To validate that the camera reduced the size of the new image to 1280×960, I pressed the INFO button to switch to the image detail/histogram screen. Instead of 5184×3888, the image shows a size of 1280×960 (figure 6.5I, image 4, red arrow).

e-Portrait (Smoothing Skin Tones)

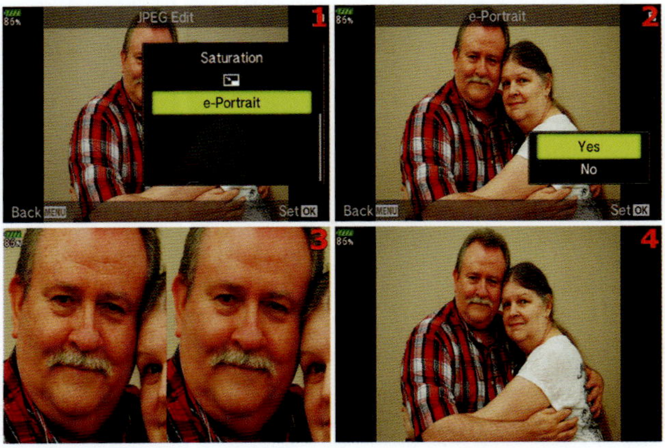

Figure 6.5J: Smoothing skin tones

1. Figure 6.5J begins where figure 6.5A ends. The e-Portrait function converts a normal JPEG portrait into a new portrait with smoother skin tones. Choose e-Portrait from the JPEG Edit menu and press the OK button (figure 6.5J, image 1).
2. You will see a small menu with Yes and No selections. Choose Yes to start the conversion process, or No to cancel and start over (figure 6.5J, image 2).
3. A *Busy* screen with a progress indicator will display during the conversion process (not shown). When the conversion is done, a before-and-after screen will appear (figure 6.5J, image 3). This screen stays on the monitor for a few seconds, then the camera displays the new image that has been saved to the memory card (figure 6.5J, image 4).

We have now worked our way through all of the options in the JPEG Edit menu.

Movie Edit

The Movie Edit function allows you to trim a movie from the front or back end. You will thereby shorten the movie, keeping only the desired frames in the middle of the movie.

This function is a duplicate of the function we covered in chapter 5 on Movie Editing after a video recording. It takes several pages to describe; therefore, instead of duplicating material here, please refer to the **Movie Edit** heading and description on page 273.

Now let's examine the final form of image editing, [Voice Annotation].

[Voice Annotation]

The [Voice Annotation] setting lets you add a voice message to an image file while you view it on the camera monitor. This is a powerful tool found only in professional-level cameras, such as the E-M1II.

How can voice annotation be useful for a professional, or an enthusiast, for that matter? Let's say you are shooting a beautiful landscape on the Blue Ridge Parkway and you add a voice annotation to the first image in the series with important information from a sign so you can later create an accurate caption. Or maybe you are photographing the bride's grandmother, Myrtle May, at a wedding and you want to remember her name later when you are preparing the wedding album. Voice annotation is an easy way to take notes about an image, without carrying anything extra.

The voice file is a standard WAV format that can be played by your computer, tablet, smartphone, or camera. That makes sense because you want to store the sound file with the image file so you can reference it years later, long after your camera is obsolete and we are using holographic imaging like on *Star Trek*.

If you use Olympus Viewer 3 software to transfer your images from your camera to your computer, you can listen to the voice sound files from within the software. Open the image in Viewer 3 and use the following menu selections to play the sound file: *File Menu > Linked Sound > Play*.

If you transfer images to your computer another way, do not overlook copying your sound files along with the image files. The sound files will have the same names as the image files, except the three-character extension is different. For instance, if you record a sound file for an image with a filename of P4000250.JPG, the linked sound file will have the filename of P4000250.WAV.

Let's see how to make a voice recording for any image on the memory card.

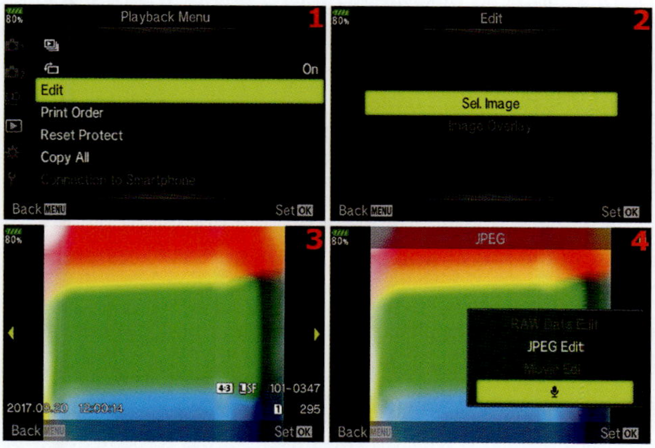

Figure 6.6A: Making a [Voice Annotation] for an individual image

Use these steps to make a [Voice Annotation] for any image you can view on your camera monitor:

1. Select Edit from the Playback Menu and scroll to the right (figure 6.6A, image 1).
2. Choose Sel. Image from the Edit menu and press the OK button (figure 6.6A, image 2).

3. Images will be displayed on the camera monitor. Use the Arrow Pad buttons to scroll back and forth until you find an image to which you want to add a voice annotation (figure 6.6A, image 3). After you have found the image, press the OK button.
4. I chose a JPEG image, and the camera displayed a menu with a microphone symbol, the [Voice Annotation] setting (figure 6.6A, image 4). Highlight it and press the OK button.

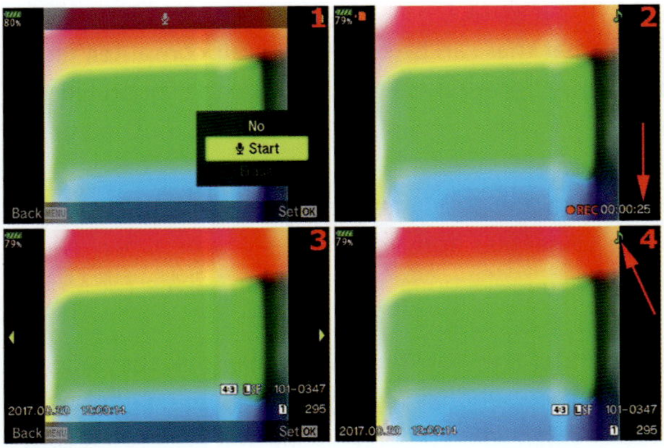

Figure 6.6B: Making the voice recording

5. Figure 6.6B starts where figure 6.6A ends. Now you will record the actual voice annotation. Before you record your voice, you need to know the location of the Stereo microphone pickups on your camera so you can talk directly into them for the best reception. Look at the Olympus logo on the viewfinder bump on the *front* of your camera. On either side of the bump you will see a small hole. One of them is located just above the E-M1II logo. Each of the holes is a Stereo microphone pickup (left channel and right channel). The best recording will be made if you talk with your mouth near the top of the camera. Just act as if the Hot shoe is a microphone, and your voice will be picked up. In figure 6.6B, image 1, you can see the recording menu that appeared when you completed step 4. Select Start from the menu, and press the OK button to start recording the voice annotation.
6. Figure 6.6B, image 2, shows the screen that will be visible while you are recording a voice annotation. A red REC symbol will appear at the bottom of the screen along with a timer (red arrow). The red card access symbol will blink in the top-left corner of the screen while you make the recording. Even though the timer seems to indicate that you could record for a long time, you are limited to 30 seconds. When you are done recording, press the OK button to stop. If you keep talking longer than 30 seconds, the camera will cut you off.
7. Nothing obvious appears on the screen when you are done making a voice recording. The camera continues to display the image for which you were making the voice annotation (figure 6.6B, image 3). If you want to hear the recording, press the Playback button just below the Menu button and the annotation will play back through the

Speaker to the left of the Menu button on the back of the camera. ***Note:*** You can record new voice annotations for different images by pressing the OK button on a new image, selecting the microphone symbol (similar to figure 6.6A, image 4), then starting again at step 5.

8. A green musical note symbol will appear on the camera monitor for any image that has a voice annotation (figure 6.6B, image 4, red arrow). As soon as the camera displays an image with a musical note symbol on the monitor, the recording will play. You can adjust the volume with the Arrow Pad buttons: up increases the volume, and down decreases it. A volume indicator scale will appear on the right side of the monitor when you adjust the volume (not shown).

Settings Recommendation: Recording a voice annotation through the Edit menu is really the long way around. You can record a voice recording any time you see an image on the camera monitor by pressing the OK button and selecting the [Voice Annotation] microphone symbol (review steps 5–8).

Image Overlay

Image Overlay allows you to take two or three images, vary their transparency, and overlay them into one image. This is an easy way to do something like add a picture of the moon to a nighttime landscape image.

This works differently than Multiple Exposures because there is no Auto Gain function to keep the backgrounds from overwhelming multiple subjects in different parts of the image. Instead you use a transparency adjustment to vary the transparency of each image in the overlay.

The effectiveness of this method will vary greatly depending on how complex the images are. Let's examine how it works and see how you might use it to combine two or three images.

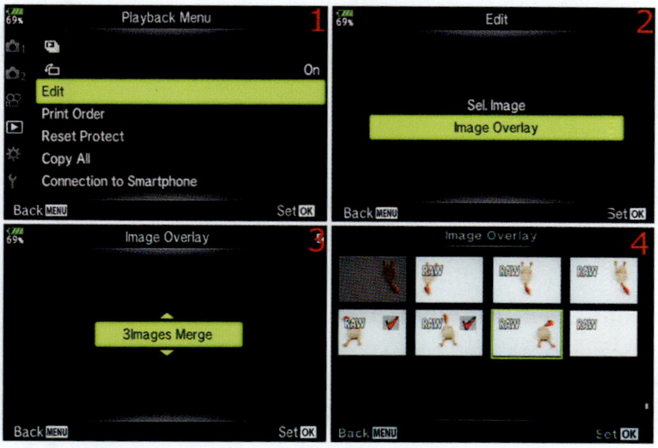

Figure 6.7A: Creating a three-image overlay (steps 1–4)

Use the following steps to start combining images:

1. Choose Edit from the Playback Menu and scroll to the right (figure 6.7A, image 1).
2. Select Image Overlay from the Edit menu and press the OK button (figure 6.7A, image 2).
3. Choose 2Images Merge or 3Images Merge from the Image Overlay up/down menu, depending on whether you want to combine two or three images (figure 6.7A, image 3). I chose 3Images Merge.
4. The screen will display images from the memory card (figure 6.7A, image 4). Although it shows both JPEG and RAW images, only RAW images can be selected for overlaying. The word RAW will appear in the top-left corner of each available image. JPEG images are dimmed and cannot be selected. Choose each image you want to use with the green selection frame and press the OK button, which will place a red check mark in the top-right corner of the image. On the bottom row of the rubber chicken images you can see that I have selected two images because they have red check marks. The third image I want to use in the overlay is surrounded by the green selection frame. As soon as you select the final image, the camera will start creating the overlay. You won't see the check mark for the final image. When the overlay process begins, a *Busy* screen appears with a progress bar. When the overlay is done, the screen shown in figure 6.7B, image 1, appears.

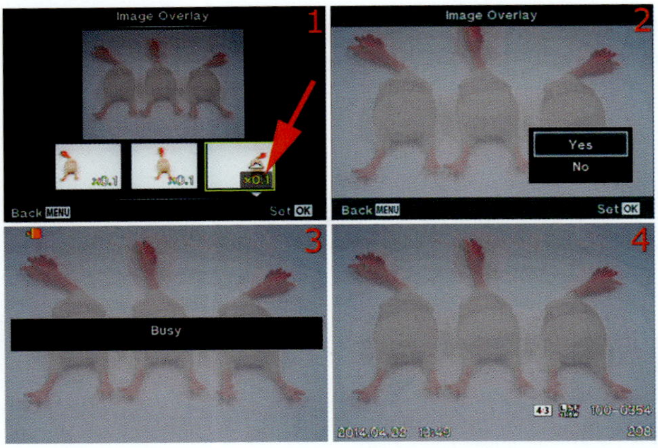

Figure 6.7B: Creating a three-image overlay (steps 5–7)

5. You will see before and after images on the screen. The after image is the larger one on top, and the before images are on the bottom (figure 6.7B, image 1). The red arrow points to an up/down menu with a range from x0.1 to x2.0. You adjust the transparency of each image with the up and down buttons of the Arrow Pad. Each before image has this up/down menu that ranges from x0.1 to x2.0 and controls the transparency of the corresponding image. You can see that I set each image to the lowest setting of x0.1 so the combined backgrounds do not obscure the chicken. At first I was confused

because my after image was pure white, and I couldn't see any rubber chickens. That's because each image contains both a chicken and a white background. Each chicken is positioned differently, but in the overlay the backgrounds of the other two images completely hid them. After I lowered the transparency of all the images, the three chickens appeared. Although you see three chickens in the after image, you also see the backgrounds of each one, with the transparency lowered to let the other pictures show through. When you change the transparency level, allow a little time after each change for the camera to respond. After you have the transparency adjusted the way you want it on each picture, press the OK button.

6. The camera will display the overlaid image and a menu with Yes and No choices (figure 6.7B, image 2). Choose Yes to finish creating the new JPEG image or No to cancel and start over. Press the OK button.
7. A *Busy* screen will appear with a progress bar (figure 6.7B, image 3). When it is done, the finished JPEG image will appear, which is saved with a new file name as the last image on the memory card (figure 6.7B, image 4).

Settings Recommendation: The final picture in figure 6.7B, image 4, is not very colorful or useful. You may be able to come up with a better example of how to overlay two or three images than my rubber chicken and white background; however, if you are really into overlaying images, you might want to consider Multiple Exposure for better-looking images.

Print Order

When you create a Print Order on your memory card, you can insert the card into a Digital Print Order Format (DPOF) printing device, such as a photo kiosk at a superstore or a DPOF-compatible inkjet printer. The kiosk or printer will then print the order without your camera. If you don't like to post-process images or work with computers, you can print images without doing much more than inserting a memory card into a compatible printing device. It's convenient even if you do like computers.

There are three things you need to know about the Print Order function:

- How to print copies of a few selected images on the memory card
- How to print one copy of each image on the memory card
- How to clear a Print Order from the memory card

There can be only one Print Order at a time on a memory card. If you are the curious sort, you will find the Print Order in a folder named MISC on the memory card. The camera creates that folder and saves the Print Order inside it. The Print Order is held in a small file named AUTPRINT.MRK, which can be read by all DPOF-compatible printing devices.

Now, let's examine each of the Print Order methods.

Selected Image(s) Print Order

This Print Order method lets you scroll through the images on your memory card. As each image is displayed on the camera monitor, you can select the number of prints (up to 10) you want to make for that image. Let's see how it works.

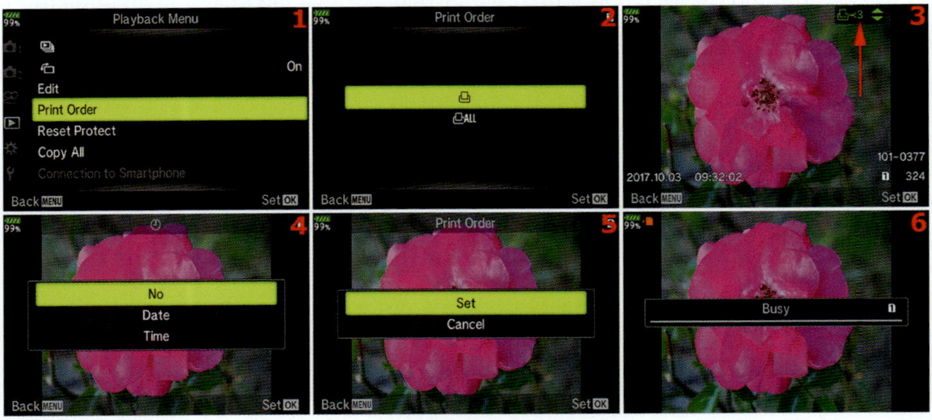

Figure 6.8A: Creating a Print Order for individual images

Use these steps to create a new Print Order for individual images. The upcoming steps assume there is no current Print Order on the memory card. If there is an existing Print Order, you will see an extra screen between images 2 and 3 in figure 6.8A, as we will discuss:

1. Choose Print Order from the Playback Menu and scroll to the right (figure 6.8A, image 1).
2. Select the printer symbol from the Print Order menu to choose how many prints you want for individual images. Press the OK button (figure 6.8A, image 2).
3. If there is an existing Print Order on the memory card, an additional screen will appear. Instead of figure 6.8A, image 3, you will see the screen shown in figure 6.8B, image 3, which allows you to Reset or Keep the current Print Order. If you Reset it, the camera will remove the current Print Order. If you Keep it, the camera will start displaying pictures, as seen in figure 6.8A, image 3, and it will leave any current Print Orders intact. In effect, you will update an existing Print Order.
4. Use the adjustable counter to select the number of copies you want of the current picture (figure 6.8A, image 3, red arrow). Scroll up and down with the Arrow Pad to select a number from 0 to 10. I selected 3 copies. Scroll left or right to choose other images and select the number of copies you want. Leave any images you do not want printed set to 0. When you have selected the number of copies for each of the images you want to print, press the OK button to lock in the numbers.
5. The camera will now display the Date and Time screen (figure 6.8A, image 4). This allows you to have either the shooting Date or Time written on the print. Select Date for the shooting date, Time for the shooting time, or No for neither. Press the OK button to lock in your choice.

6. The camera will switch to the final Print Order menu where you can Set the order or Cancel it (figure 6.8A, image 5). If you select Set, the camera will display the *Busy* screen (figure 6.8A, image 6). The progress indicator will advance, and the red card symbol will blink in the top-left corner of the monitor as the camera writes the Print Order to the memory card. If you select Cancel the selections you made will be ignored and the camera will return to the Playback Menu.

If you simply want to clear the Print Order from your memory card, it is a straightforward process, as we will discuss in the next subsection.

Clearing a Print Order

You may want to remove an old Print Order after you print your images. To do so, use the Print Order Reset function.

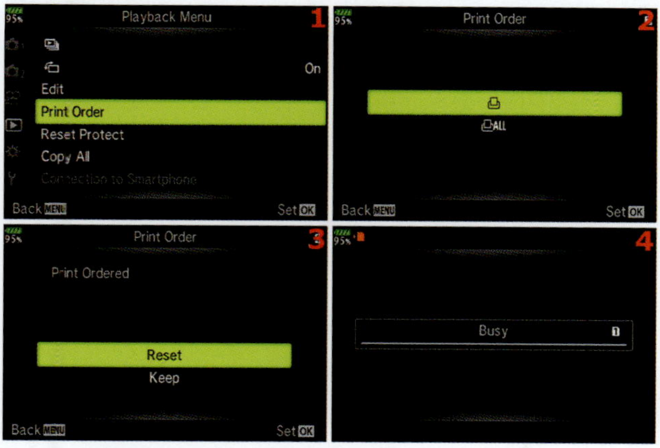

Figure 6.8B: Resetting a Print Order for individual images

Use these steps to clear an old Print Order from a memory card:

1. Choose Print Order from the Playback Menu and scroll to the right (figure 6.8B, image 1).
2. Select either of the two symbols from the Print Order menu. I chose the top symbol for individual images (figure 6.8B, image 2). The following instructions work the same way for the All selection, which we will discuss in the next subsection (**All Print Order**). Press the OK button with one of the Print Order items selected.
3. You will now have two choices: Reset and Keep (figure 6.8B, image 3). If you select Reset, the camera will immediately reset, or delete, the current Print Order. The *Busy* progress indicator will show the progress, and the red card activity symbol will flash in the top-left corner of the camera monitor (figure 6.8B, image 4). If you choose Keep, the camera will leave the existing Print Order on the memory card and return to the images in the existing Print Order, with the number of copies you selected, so you can make modifications.

Now, let's see how to select a Print Order in which every image on the card is set to print one copy.

All Print Order

All Print Order allows you to create a Print Order that will cause a DPOF printing device to make one copy of each image. After we explore how this works, we'll take a look at how you can have the camera print more than one copy of selected pictures and one copy of the rest of the pictures.

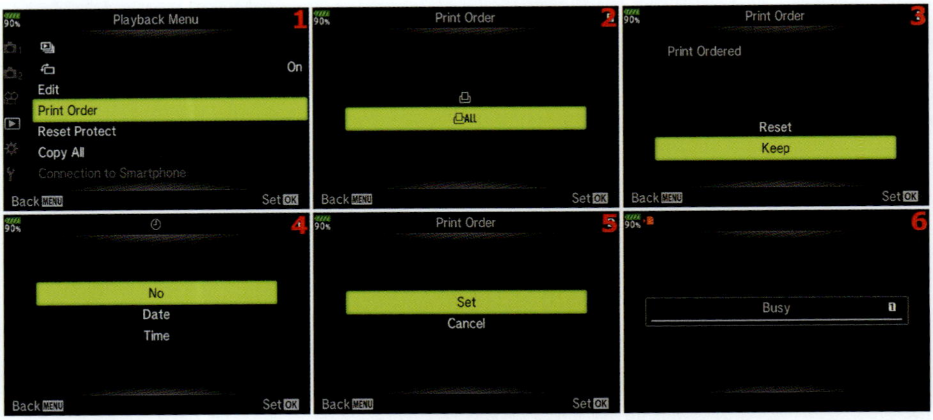

Figure 6.8C: Create or Reset a Print Order for all images

Use the following steps to create or reset a Print Order for all images on the current memory card:

1. Choose Print Order from the Playback Menu and scroll to the right (figure 6.8C, image 1).
2. Select the bottom symbol from the Print Order menu. It looks like a printer with the word All after it. This will cause one copy of each image on the memory card to be printed. Press the OK button (figure 6.8C, image 2).
3. The screen shown in figure 6.8C, image 3, *will not appear* if there are no existing Print Orders on the memory card. If you are like me, you will forget to remove the last Print Order you created. Carefully read and understand this step through step 5 if you want to Keep an existing Print Order. If there is an old Print Order on the memory card, the screen shown in image 3 will appear and you will need to choose either Reset or Keep. Choosing Reset will immediately delete the old Print Order. Choosing Keep will leave the old Print Order in place *only if you select Cancel in step 5* (figure 6.8C, image 5). Otherwise, it makes absolutely no difference whether you choose Reset or Keep; the old Print Order will be deleted anyway.

4. If you are creating a new Print Order you can choose whether a Date or Time stamp is applied to the printed image (figure 6.8C, image 4). If you selected Keep in the previous screen to prevent the deletion of the old Print Order, just select No and press the OK button to move forward—there is no point in selecting a Date or Time stamp because you must press Cancel in the next step to Keep an existing Print Order.
5. Pay careful attention here so you don't lose the old Print Order you want to Keep. If you select Set the camera will merrily overwrite the Print Order you told it to Keep in step 3. Selecting Set always recreates the Print Order with one copy selected for each image. Select Cancel if you are working with an *existing* Print Order that you want to Keep, or select Set if you want to create a *new* one. You will see a *Busy* screen and a progress bar if you create a new Print Order (figure 6.8C, image 6). The *Busy* screen will show the progress of the images being marked for printing. When the Print Order has been created the camera will return to the Playback Menu.

The circular logic of these last few steps is quite confusing. It is a rather weak screen-flow design, in my opinion. Instead of continuing when you selected Keep in figure 6.8C, image 3, the camera should simply exit the screens and go back to the images on the monitor, with the number of copies still in place, so you can make direct modifications to the Print Order you decided to Keep. That is the way it works for individual images as described in the **Selected Image(s) Print Order** subsection.

Increasing the Number of Copies on a Few Images in an All Print Order

As you know, an All Print Order sets the number of printed copies to 1 for each image on the memory card. But what if you want more than 1 printed copy of a few images and 1 printed copy of the rest? There is a way to increase the number of copies to more than 1 for selected images within the All Print Order. Here's how.

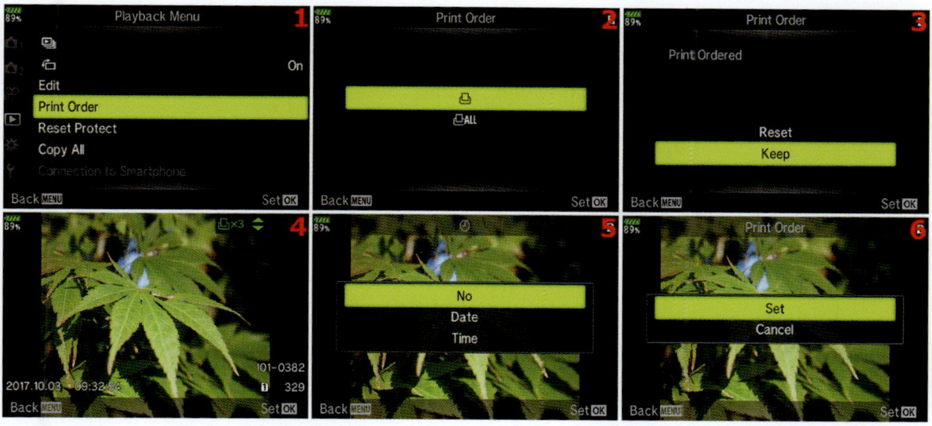

Figure 6.8D: Increasing the print count for a few images in an All Print Order

Use the following steps to increase the print count on selected images within the All Print Order:

1. First you must create a new All Print Order by using the steps accompanying figure 6.8C. The next few steps assume that a new All Print Order is on the card with 1 selected as the print count for each image on the memory card.
2. Choose Print Order from the Playback Menu and scroll to the right (figure 6.8D, image 1).
3. Select the top symbol from the Print Order menu, which allows you to select the number of copies for individual images (figure 6.8D, image 2). Press the OK button.
4. Select Keep from the Print Order menu (figure 6.8D, image 3). Press the OK button to continue. You have just told the camera that you want to keep the All Print Order you created in step 1. Now we will modify it!
5. The camera will display the images that are currently on the memory card, and each one will have the number of printed copies set to 1 because we are looking at the results of an All Print Order. Scroll back and forth with the Arrow Pad keys until you find an image for which you want to increase the number of printed copies. I chose a picture I took of my Japanese Maple tree. I want 3 copies of this image, so I increased the print count to 3 by scrolling up on the Arrow Pad (figure 6.8D, image 4). You can keep scrolling back and forth to find other images you want more prints of and increase the numbers. When you are done increasing the numbers, press the OK button to modify the All Print Order. Now you will get one copy of most of the images, and you'll get the number of copies you chose for the rest of the images.
6. On the Date and Time stamp screen, choose Date, Time, or No (neither) and press the OK button (figure 6.8D, image 5).
7. The final screen allows you to confirm the modification of the existing All Print Order. Select Set and press the OK button (figure 6.8D, image 6). The camera will show the *Busy* screen progress indicator with a flashing red card icon in the top-left corner (not shown). When it's done, the card is ready to insert into a DPOF-compatible device to print your custom All Print Order. Select Cancel and press the OK button to cancel the process.

Settings Recommendation: Print Orders can be quite useful in some circumstances. You may want to print a few images, so you create a Selected Image(s) Print Order and make your prints. Or you may have shot an event and would like to deliver the images to your client so they can have them printed right away. You could create an All Print Order (and modify it if necessary) and then give the memory card to your client. They can go straight to a DPOF printing device and plug in the memory card. The DPOF device will do the rest.

Reset Protect

If you have previously set an image protection lock on any of the images on a memory card, you can cancel the protection lock with the Reset Protect function.

Adding Image Protection

When you press the OK button while viewing an image on the camera monitor, you will see a menu for editing that image. The menu has a key symbol, which means you can add protection to an image. Select the key symbol and press the OK button to set protection on that image.

After you apply protection, the image will be displayed on the monitor with a green key (lock) symbol in the top-right corner, and it won't be deleted during an All Erase operation (*Setup Menu > Card Setup > [Card Slot] > All Erase*). We discussed image protection in the chapter titled **Screen Displays for Camera Control,** on page 120, under the subheading **Protecting Images**. For more information on adding protection, please review that subheading.

It's easy to remove image protection, as we'll see in the next subsection.

Removing Image Protection

To remove image protection, you simply choose Reset Protect from the Playback Menu and answer Yes to the query.

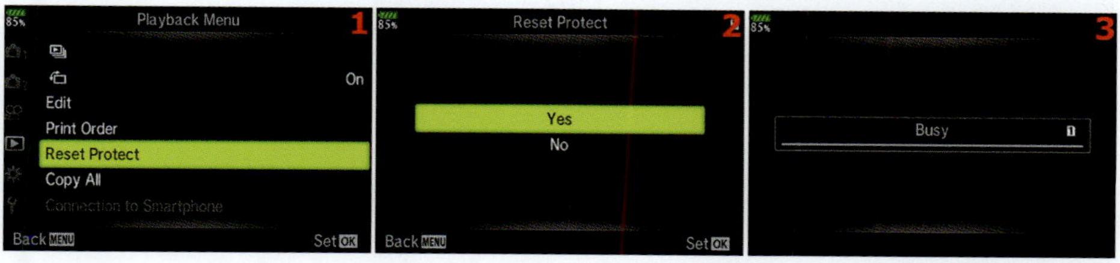

Figure 6.9: Removing image protection with Reset Protect

Use the following steps to remove image protection from all protected images on the memory card:

1. Select Reset Protect from the Playback Menu and scroll to the right (figure 6.9, image 1).
2. A menu with Yes and No choices will appear (figure 6.9, image 2). Choose Yes to reset the image protection or No to cancel.
3. Press the OK button to remove protection. A *Busy* screen with a progress bar will appear briefly (figure 6.9, image 3), and then the camera will return to the main screen of the Playback Menu.

Settings Recommendation: This function resets all protected images at the same time. If that is too drastic, you can remove protection from individual images by following these steps:

1. Display an image with the green key protection symbol on the monitor.
2. Press the OK button and select the key symbol from the menu.
3. Scroll up or down with the Arrow Pad until the green key symbol disappears.
4. Press the OK button to remove the protection.

This process is the opposite of adding protection. Adding protection is discussed in the chapter titled **Screen Displays for Camera Control,** on page 320.

Copy All

The Copy All function allows you to copy all of the images saved on one memory card (e.g., Slot 1) to the other memory card in the camera (e.g., Slot 2). It provides a quick way to backup important images. Let's see how to copy images from one card to the other.

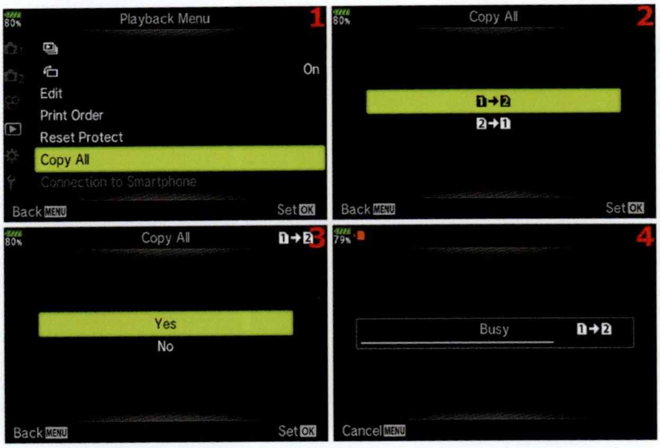

Figure 6.10: Copy all images from one card to the other

Use the following steps to copy all the images on one memory card to the other memory card in the camera:

1. Highlight Copy All on the Playback Menu and scroll to the right (figure 6.10, image 1).
2. Choose the source and destination memory cards (1→2 or 2→1), where the card slot on the left is the source and the card slot on the right is the destination (figure 6.10, image 2). Our example shows that we are copying all of the images on the memory card in slot 1 to the memory card in slot 2 (1→2). Press the OK button to make your selection.

3. Select Yes to copy all images from the chosen source card to the destination card, or select No to cancel (figure 6.10, image 3). Press the OK button to start copying the images.
4. Copying a large number of images from one card to the other may take considerable time, several minutes at the minimum. During the copy process a *Busy* screen with a progress indicator will be displayed (figure 6.10, image 4). The copy direction (1→2) is shown on the right end of the bar. When the progress bar reaches the right side of the screen, the operation is complete and the camera will return to the screen shown in figure 6.10, image 1.

Settings Recommendation: This is a very valuable function. You may use it copy critical images to additional memory cards. If you are a commercial shooter or an enthusiast, you will surely find reasons to use Copy All.

Connection to Smartphone (or Tablet)

The E-M1II has a powerful feature that relatively few cameras have—the ability to become a Wi-Fi wireless access point. That means the camera can wirelessly communicate with your smartphone or tablet, which I'll refer to collectively as a smart device.

You can use the screen of your smart device as a remote monitor and control the camera directly from the device. You can also transfer images wirelessly to your smart device for immediate use on social media sites, blogs, and websites.

There is a free Olympus app for both iOS (iPhone and iPad) and Android devices. Do a search for "Olympus Image Share" in your app store and download it to your smart device before you proceed with this section.

There are two parts to communicating with a smart device. First you must enable Wi-Fi on the camera, then you must create a relationship between the camera and the device. Let's examine the process.

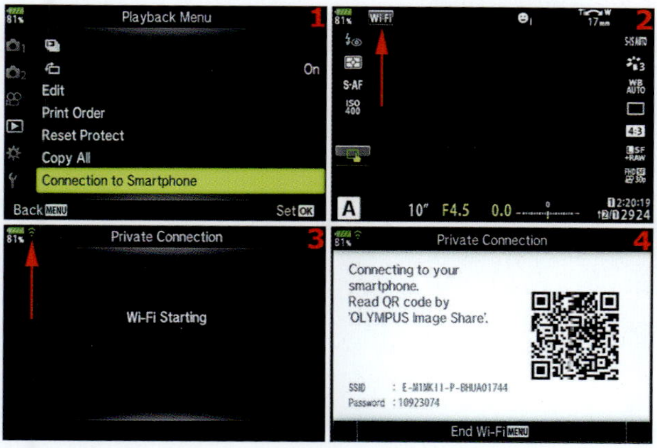

Figure 6.11A: Making a Wi-Fi connection to your smart device

Use the following steps to connect your camera to the Olympus Image Share (OI.Share) app:

1. Figure 6.11A, images 1 and 2, show two entry points to the Wi-Fi system. You will not see image 2 unless you are accessing the Wi-Fi system from the Live View screen instead of the Playback Menu. However, I wanted to show the alternate entry point (image 2, red arrow) so you can access it if you want to. You can touch the Wi-Fi icon on the touch screen, or you can select Connection to Smartphone on the Playback Menu and scroll to the right. Either one of these screens will take you to the screen in image 3.
2. Figure 6.11A, image 3, shows that Wi-Fi is in the process of activating. The green Wi-Fi broadcast symbol in the upper-left corner of image 3 (red arrow) will blink while Wi-Fi is starting up.
3. When Wi-Fi is active, you will see the screen shown in figure 6.11A, image 4. This screen contains all of the information you need to connect your camera and your smart device. It even includes a QR code that the Olympus Image Share app can scan and use to connect with your camera.

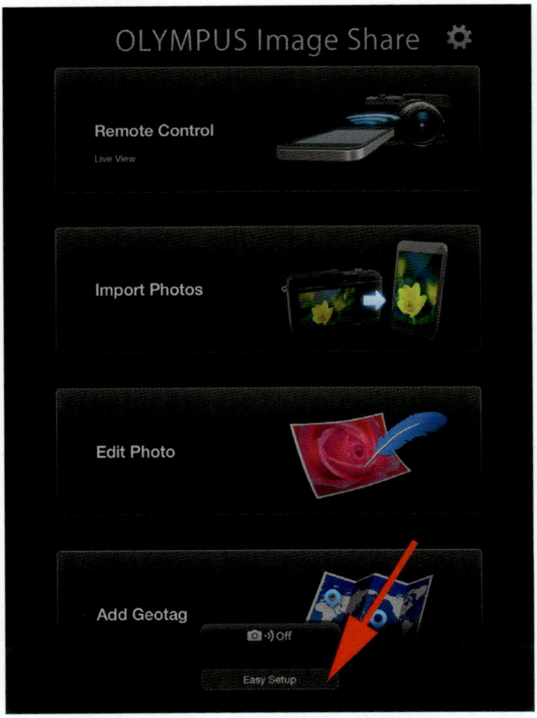

Figure 6.11B: Olympus Image Share setup

4. Figure 6.11B shows the main screen of the Olympus Image Share app on an iPad. Touch the bottom tab that has a camera symbol and Off, then touch the Easy Setup button (red arrow). The app will walk you through the process of scanning the QR code on the camera monitor, creating a profile on your smart device, and using the app.

Note: Within the camera's Setup Menu is another menu called Wi-Fi Settings (see the chapter **Setup Menu** under the heading **Wi-Fi Settings** on page 399). Within the Wi-Fi Settings menu you can change the connection type and password, reset the share order, and completely reset the camera's Wi-Fi settings.

Settings Recommendation: The Olympus Image Share app is great for controlling your camera. However, it is beyond the scope of this book to describe its many functions. That would take an extra chapter!

You can control many camera settings from within the app, including the shutter speed, aperture, exposure compensation, ISO, white balance, and shutter-release mode. Plus, you can import your photos, edit them on your smart device, and even add a geotag (GPS information) to the pictures. You can also take pictures remotely by using the larger screen on your smart device.

There are many YouTube videos that demonstrate how to make a connection between the camera and a smart device. Do a YouTube search on the words "Olympus Image Share" to find dozens of how-to videos. Most people don't have trouble making the connection because it is a fairly automated process. But if you do have problems, there are easily accessible resources.

Author's Conclusion

This chapter covered different ways you can view and use images from your Olympus E-M1II.

Our next chapter, **Custom Menu,** covers the dozens of functions you can customize on this camera. It is a primary reference chapter for many of the settings you will use when you configure buttons and dials on the camera. Although there are a lot of functions, you will be a master of your camera if you take time to carefully study the chapter.

Now, let's customize our cameras!

7 Custom Menu

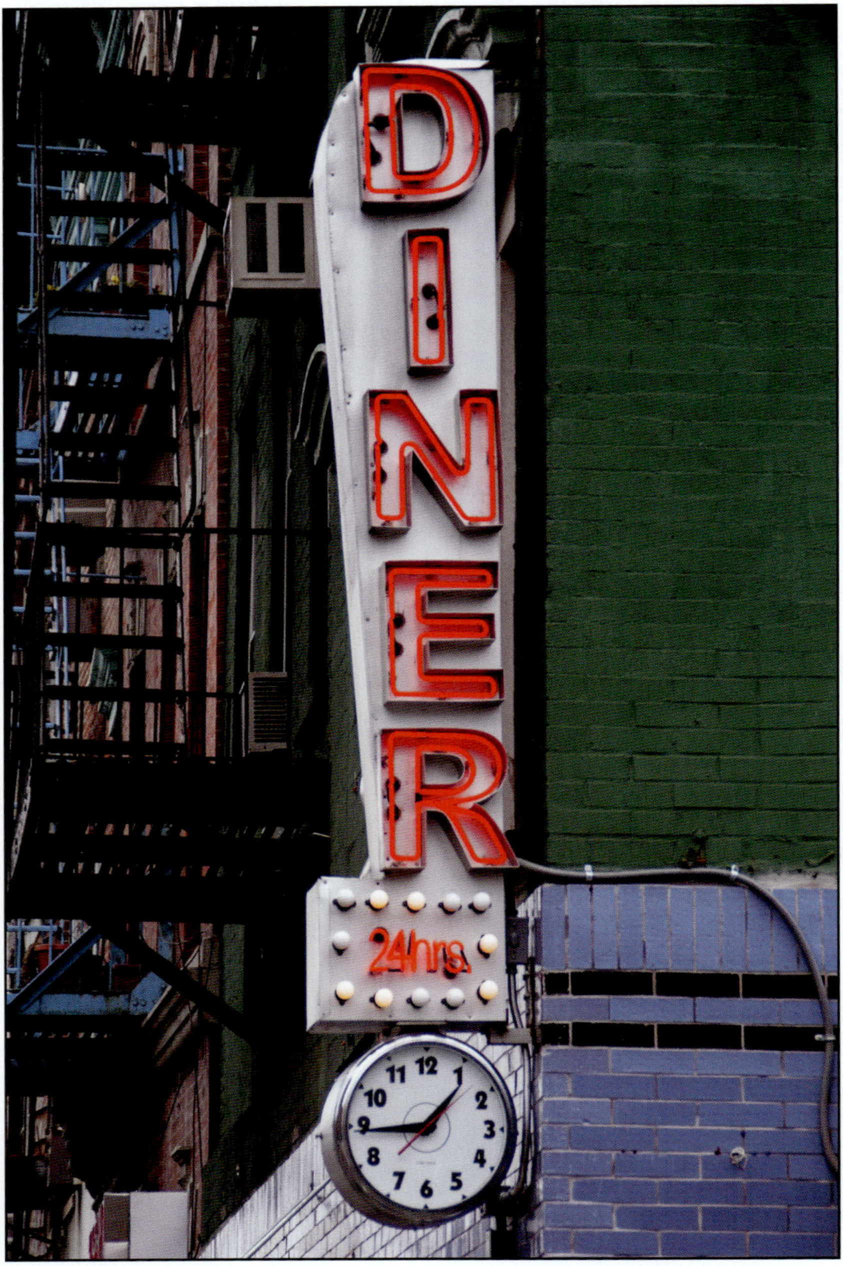

Image © Alan Hess

The Custom Menu is the heart of camera configuration for enthusiast and professional users. It allows you to make extensive customizations to the camera functions. There are 106 functions in the Custom Menu, and each one affects an aspect of camera performance. The sheer number of functions may seem overwhelming, but just take your time and configure each setting the way you want it to work. Many of these settings can be set once and then left alone.

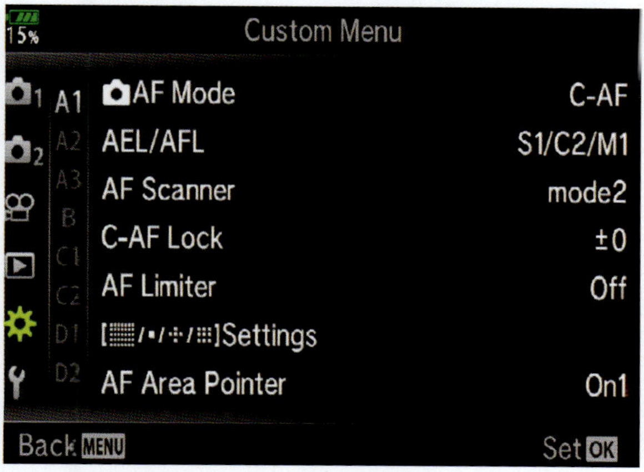

Figure 7.1: The Custom Menu

The Custom Menu is composed of 10 major sections (A–J), with numerous individual functions in each section. Many of the main sections are divided into subsections for ease of navigation. For example, there are three A sections: A1–A3.

Now let's see how each and every one of the functions in the Custom Menu works.

Custom Menu A1–A3. AF/MF

There are three separate AF/MF menus, A1–A3, which give you complete control over the autofocus and manual focus capabilities of your camera. These menus are shown in figure 7.2, images 1–3.

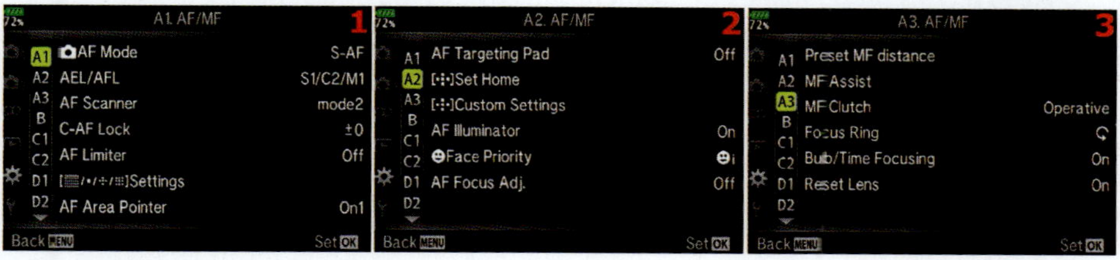

Figure 7.2: The Custom Menu – Menus A1–A3 AF/MF

[Photo] AF Mode (A1)

[Photo] AF Mode allows you to choose the type of focus when you take still pictures and shoot videos. There are six focus settings available in the [Photo] AF Mode menu

AF Mode focus settings

- **S-AF:** When you press the Shutter button halfway down, the camera focuses on the subject, locks the focus, and sounds a beep. The green AF Area Pointer will be displayed, and a small green dot (AF confirmation mark) will appear in the top-right corner of the monitor when focus is confirmed. This type of focus is best for subjects that are not moving or are moving very slowly. The camera *does not update the focus* unless you release the Shutter button and reapply pressure. When you shoot video, no beep or focus indicators will sound or display on the monitor.
- **C-AF:** As long as you continuously hold the Shutter button halfway down, the camera will continuously update the focus. When it can acquire focus, the camera will beep and the green AF confirmation mark (dot) will display without blinking. If you or the subject start moving, the camera will notice the movement and attempt to update the focus. It will beep each time it locks focus on the subject, up to twice, then it stops the beep so it doesn't become a nuisance in a quiet environment. This mode is best for moving subjects. The difference between S-AF and C-AF is that S-AF does not update focus, whereas C-AF causes the focus to continuously update. When you are shooting a video, no beep or focus indicators will sound or display on the monitor.
- **MF:** You must use the focus ring on the lens to focus manually when this mode is enabled. Autofocus is disabled and you are responsible for focusing. This mode is often used by people who shoot macro (closeup) still images and videos to increase the reliability of focusing.
- **S-AF+MF:** This mode works exactly the same as the S-AF mode. The only difference is that S-AF does not let you fine-tune autofocus with the manual focus ring, whereas S-AF+MF does. You can let the camera autofocus, and then manually adjust the focus yourself with the focus ring on the lens. If you have focus Peaking enabled *(A3. AF/MF > MF Assist > Peaking)*, a white outline will be displayed on the edges of your image to help you fine-tune the focus.
- **C-AF+TR:** This mode makes the camera sensitive to moving subjects. Select the subject by pressing the Shutter button halfway until focus locks on the subject. The AF Area Pointer will change from its normal small green rectangle to a much larger square with a line sticking out of each side. As the subject moves, the camera will maintain focus and track it across the viewfinder or monitor. As long as the AF Area Pointer remains green, the camera is tracking; if it turns red, the camera has lost the subject and you should reacquire it by refocusing until the focus locks and tracks again. The C-AF Lock function (considered later in this chapter section) controls how well the camera can track a moving subject when other objects intervene. When you shoot a video, the

camera will not beep, but it will display the tracking AF Area Pointer so you will know that it is tracking successfully.

- **Preset MF:** This mode ignores the subjects and just focuses the camera on a specific preset distance when you are shooting. You can set the distance by selecting *A3. AF/MF > Preset MF Distance*.

Now let's see how to select your favorite focus mode.

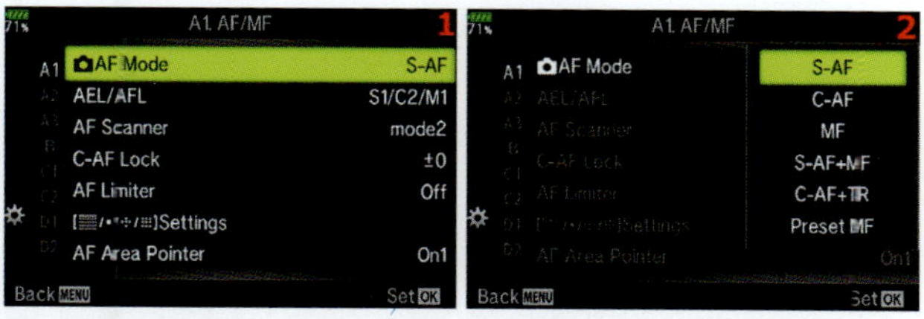

Figure 7.3: Selecting a focus mode for still pictures and movies

Use these steps to select a focus mode:

1. Select AF Mode from the A1. AF/MF menu and scroll to the right (figure 7.3, image 1).
2. A menu will appear with six focus mode choices (figure 7.3, image 2). Refer to the ***AF Mode focus settings*** list and select the mode you want to use.
3. Press the OK button to Set the mode. Now, take your pictures.

Settings Recommendation: For everyday shooting of still pictures, the S-AF mode works well. If the subject is moving erratically, it may be a good idea to use C-AF. I leave my camera set to S-AF+MF most of the time because, as a nature photographer, I find that it allows me the most flexibility. I can use autofocus and then fine-tune it for things like macro shots or portraits in nature.

When I am shooting video I often use C-AF, but I find myself helping a little from time to time by pressing the Shutter button halfway down to force an AF operation. Many serious videographers like to use MF so they can have full control of what is in focus.

When I shoot sports, action, or wildlife, I use C-AF and Sequential H modes so I can get good focus updating on my subjects, especially for creatures like flying birds.

AEL/AFL (A1)

The AEL/AFL button allows you to control autoexposure lock (AEL) and autofocus lock (AFL). The AEL/AFL button has a strong relationship with the Shutter button. The camera allows you to configure various combinations of the two buttons to accomplish different methods of locking exposure and autofocus, and taking a picture.

There are three focus modes that we must consider: single AF (S-AF), continuous AF (C-AF), and manual focus (MF). We will configure the AEL/AFL button and Shutter button for each focus mode.

First, select a focus mode (S-AF, C-AF, or MF) from the AF Mode function. Second, configure the AEL/AFL button and Shutter button relationship for the focus mode you just chose. (See the previous **AF Mode** subheading for AF Mode selection.)

There are three combination modes available for the AEL/AFL button and Shutter button when you use S-AF and MF: mode1, mode2, and mode3. When you use C-AF mode, a fourth mode, mode4, is also available.

Let's consider these button combination modes for each focus mode.

S-AF Mode

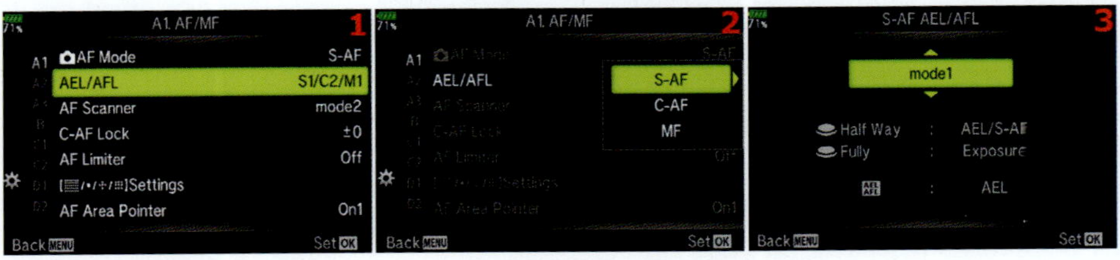

Figure 7.4: AEL/AFL button and Shutter button relationship in S-AF focus mode

Use the following steps to configure the relationship of the AEL/AFL and Shutter buttons when you select S-AF focus mode:

1. Select AEL/AFL from the A1. AF/MF menu and scroll to the right (figure 7.4, image 1).
2. A menu with three choices will appear: S-AF, C-AF, or MF (figure 7.4, image 2). Choose S-AF and scroll to the right.
3. An up/down menu will appear with the choices of mode1, mode2, or mode3 (figure 7.4, image 3). Below the up/down menu is a short description of what each mode does. Here are better descriptions of what the AEL/AFL and Shutter buttons do in each mode:
   a. *mode1*
      - **Shutter button:** Pressing the Shutter button Half Way provides autoexposure lock (AEL) and single AF (S-AF) autofocus. Pressing the Shutter button Fully takes the picture (Exposure).
      - **AEL/AFL button:** Pressing the AEL/AFL button toggles autoexposure lock (AEL).

   b. *mode2*
      - **Shutter button:** Pressing the Shutter button Half Way provides single AF (S-AF) autofocus. Pressing the Shutter button Fully provides autoexposure lock (AEL) and takes the picture (Exp).
      - **AEL/AFL button:** Pressing the AEL/AFL button toggles autoexposure lock (AEL).

   c. *mode3*
      - **Shutter button:** Pressing the Shutter button Half Way provides autoexposure lock (AEL). Pressing the Shutter button Fully takes the picture (Exposure).
      - **AEL/AFL button:** Pressing the AEL/AFL button provides single AF (S-AF) autofocus.

4. Scroll up or down with the Arrow Pad and select one of the modes. Press the OK button to Set it. Now whenever you choose S-AF or S-AF+MF from the AF Mode menu, your camera will use the relationship mode you chose.

C-AF Mode

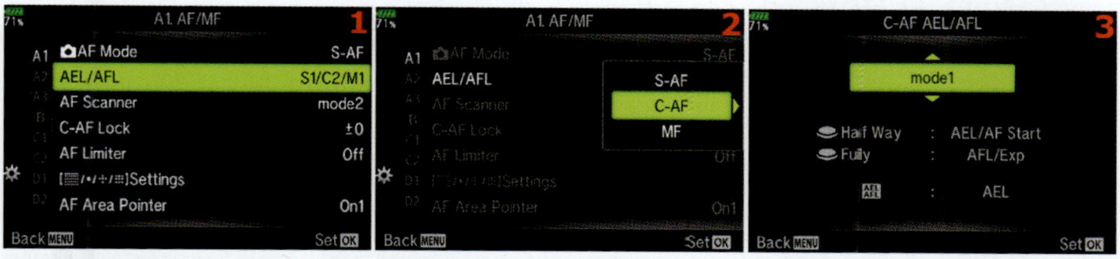

Figure 7.5: AEL/AFL button and Shutter button relationship in C-AF focus mode

Use the following steps to configure the relationship of the AEL/AFL and Shutter buttons when you select C-AF focus mode:

1. Select AEL/AFL from the A1. AF/MF menu and scroll to the right (figure 7.5, image 1).
2. A menu with three choices will appear: S-AF, C-AF, or MF (figure 7.5, image 2). Choose C-AF and scroll to the right.
3. An up/down menu will appear with the choices of mode1, mode2, mode3, or mode4 (figure 7.5, image 3). Below the up/down menu is a short description of what each mode does. Here are better descriptions of what the AEL/AFL and Shutter buttons do in each mode:
   a. *mode1*
      - **Shutter button:** Pressing the Shutter button Half Way provides autoexposure lock (AEL) and starts continuous autofocus (C-AF; AF Start). Pressing the Shutter button Fully locks autofocus (AFL) and takes the picture (Exp).
      - **AEL/AFL button:** Pressing the AEL/AFL button toggles autoexposure lock (AEL).

   b. *mode2*
      - **Shutter button:** Pressing the Shutter button Half Way starts continuous autofocus (C-AF; AF Start). Pressing the Shutter button Fully provides autoexposure lock (AEL), autofocus lock (AFL), and takes the picture (Exp).
      - **AEL/AFL button:** Pressing the AEL/AFL button toggles autoexposure lock (AEL).

   c. *mode3*
      - **Shutter button:** Pressing the Shutter button Half Way provides autoexposure lock (AEL). Pressing the Shutter button Fully provides autofocus lock (AFL) and takes the picture (Exp).
      - **AEL/AFL button:** Pressing the AEL/AFL button starts continuous autofocus (C-AF; AF Start).

d. *mode4*
   - **Shutter button:** Pressing the Shutter button Half Way does nothing. Pressing the Shutter button Fully provides autoexposure lock (AEL), autofocus lock (AFL), and takes the picture (Exp).
   - **AEL/AFL button:** Pressing the AEL/AFL button starts continuous autofocus (C-AF; AF Start).

4. Scroll up or down with the Arrow Pad and select one of the modes. Press the OK button to Set it. Now whenever you choose C-AF or C-AF+TR from the AF Mode menu, your camera will use the relationship you chose.

MF Mode

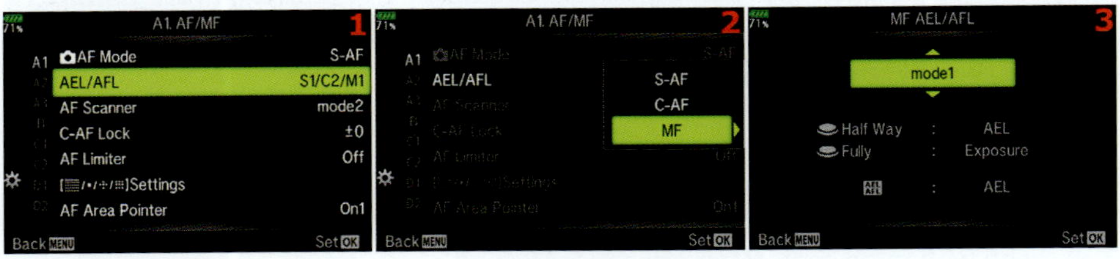

Figure 7.6: AEL/AFL button and Shutter button relationship in MF focus mode

Use the following steps to configure the relationship of the AEL/AFL and Shutter buttons when you select MF focus mode:

1. Select AEL/AFL from the A1. AF/MF menu and scroll to the right (figure 7.6, image 1).
2. A menu with three choices will appear: S-AF, C-AF, or MF (figure 7.6, image 2). Choose MF and scroll to the right.
3. An up/down menu will appear with the choices of mode1, mode2, or mode3 (figure 7.6, image 3). Below the up/down menu is a short description of what each mode does. Here are better descriptions of what the AEL/AFL and Shutter buttons do in each mode:

   a. *mode1*
      - **Shutter button:** Pressing the Shutter button Half Way provides autoexposure lock (AEL). You must manually focus the lens. Pressing the Shutter button Fully takes the picture (Exposure).
      - **AEL/AFL button:** Pressing the AEL/AFL button toggles autoexposure lock (AEL).

   b. *mode2*
      - **Shutter button:** Pressing the Shutter button Half Way does nothing, and you must manually focus the lens. Pressing the Shutter button Fully provides autoexposure lock (AEL) and takes the picture (Exp).
      - **AEL/AFL button:** Pressing the AEL/AFL button toggles autoexposure lock (AEL).

c. *mode3*
   - **Shutter button:** Pressing the Shutter button Half Way provides autoexposure lock (AEL), and you must manually focus the lens. Pressing the Shutter button Fully takes the picture (Exposure).
   - **AEL/AFL button:** Pressing the AEL/AFL button provides single AF (S-AF) autofocus.

4. Scroll up or down with the Arrow Pad and select one of the modes. Press the OK button to Set it. Now whenever you choose MF or S-AF–MF from the AF Mode menu, your camera will use the relationship mode you chose.

Back-Button Focus Using the AEL/AFL Button

The E-M1II can provide back-button focus for people who want to separate the autofocus and shutter-release actions that are normally assigned to the Shutter button. The configuration steps for S-AF, C-AF, and MF modes are as follows:

Single AF (S-AF) mode

1. Set *Custom Menu > A1. AF/MF > AF Mode* to S-AF.
2. Set *Custom Menu > A1. AF/MF > AEL/AFL > S-AF* to mode3.

Continuous AF (C-AF) mode

1. Set *Custom Menu > A1. AF/MF > AF Mode to* C-AF.
2. Set *Custom Menu > A1. AF/MF > AEL/AFL > C-AF* to mode4.

Manual focus (MF) mode

1. Set *Custom Menu > A1. AF/MF > AF Mode* to MF.
2. Set *Custom Menu > A1. AF/MF > AEL/AFL > C-AF* to mode3.

Note: The Shutter button will not initiate autofocus when you set the camera to manual focus (MF) mode. This allows you to use the manual focus ring on your lens for precise focusing. To enable back-button focus in manual focus (MF) mode, you can use single AF (S-AF) by pressing the AEL/AFL button. This gives you the best of both worlds: full manual focus and autofocus on demand.

For all three focus modes, the Shutter button will not start autofocus; instead, it will initiate AEL, AFL (or both), and/or shutter release only. The AEL/AFL button will provide autofocus in this manner: single AF for S-AF and MF focus modes, and continuous AF for C-AF focus mode.

Settings Recommendation: Because I am a nature photographer, I do not use back-button focus very often. When I am shooting nature, events, or portraits and use the Shutter button for focus, I configure my AEL/AFL settings as follows: S-AF mode: mode1; C-AF mode: mode2; and MF mode: mode3.

If you want to use back-button focus instead of Shutter button focus, use these settings: S-AF mode: mode3; C-AF mode: mode3 or mode4; and MF mode: mode3.

AF Scanner (A1)

The AF Scanner function tells the camera how long it should continue trying to achieve focus when it cannot focus using the selected focus point(s) or the contrast is not clear when you press the Shutter button halfway. There are three modes available. Let's take a look at what each mode does:

- **mode1:** AF Scanner is not activated. If focus is not achieved, the camera does not try to look for something to lock focus on.
- **mode2:** AF Scanner is activated once only. The camera will try once to achieve focus, and will then stop.
- **mode3:** AF Scanner is activated. The camera will continue trying to achieve focus until you remove pressure from the Shutter button.

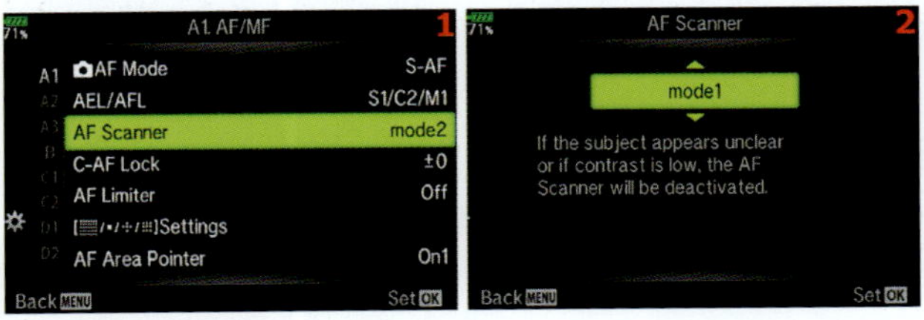

Figure 7.7: The AF Scanner menu

Use the following steps to set the AF Scanner mode:

1. Select AF Scanner from the A1. AF/MF menu and scroll to the right (figure 7.7, image 1).
2. An up/down menu with three choices will appear: mode1, mode2, or mode3 (figure 7.7, image 2). Select the mode you want to use and press the OK button to Set your choice.

Settings Recommendation: I set AF Scanner to mode2 because I want the camera to try to achieve focus, but I don't want it to keep trying if the scene is really tough. I would rather just remove my finger from the Shutter button and start over.

C-AF Lock (A1)

The C-AF Lock function controls the amount of time the camera waits after it has lost a subject it was tracking before the AF system moves onto another subject. The setting is based on a scale that ranges from +2 to −2. The higher numbers are labeled Loose and the lower numbers are labeled Tight. If you choose a Loose (high) number, the camera will switch to a new subject quickly after losing focus on the original subject. If you select a Tight (low) number, the camera will wait for a longer period of time before switching to a new subject. Let's see how to select a C-AF Lock mode.

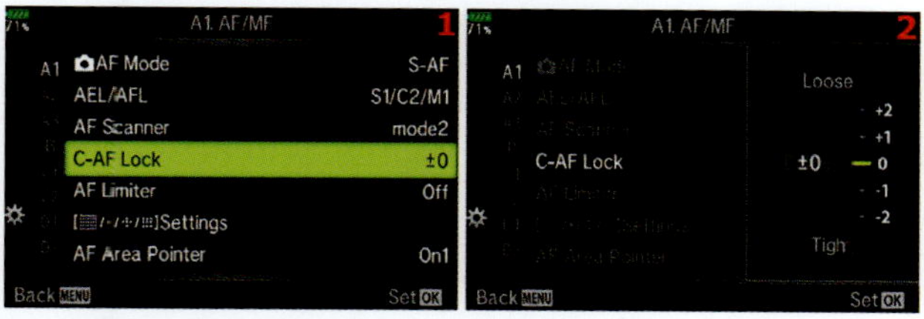

Figure 7.8: Using C-AF Lock

Use these steps to adjust the C-AF Lock function:

1. Choose C-AF Lock from the A1. AF/MF menu and scroll to the right (figure 7.8, image 1).
2. A menu will open with five choices: +2, +1, 0, –1, –2 (figure 7.8, image 2).
3. Press the OK button to Set your choice.

Settings Recommendation: I find the C-AF Lock function to be most useful when I am shooting sports or action and I want the camera to wait before switching to a new subject if something comes between me and the subject. In this case, I will set C-AF Lock to –2. For most people and subjects, 0 works just fine.

AF Limiter (A1)

Autofocusing works faster if you can limit the distance ranges that the camera needs to examine. The AF Limiter function allows you to define three different distance ranges for the autofocus system to examine, and it allows one (or none) of these ranges to be applied when shooting.

This function works with all lenses, even those without a focus limiter. You can set up the distance ranges depending on the type of photographs you are taking. For example, if you routinely shoot sports that take place a fair distance away, you can set the AF Limiter so that the camera will only try to focus from 20 feet to infinity. Or if you are shooting portraits, you can set a distance range that spans from 5 feet to 25 feet.

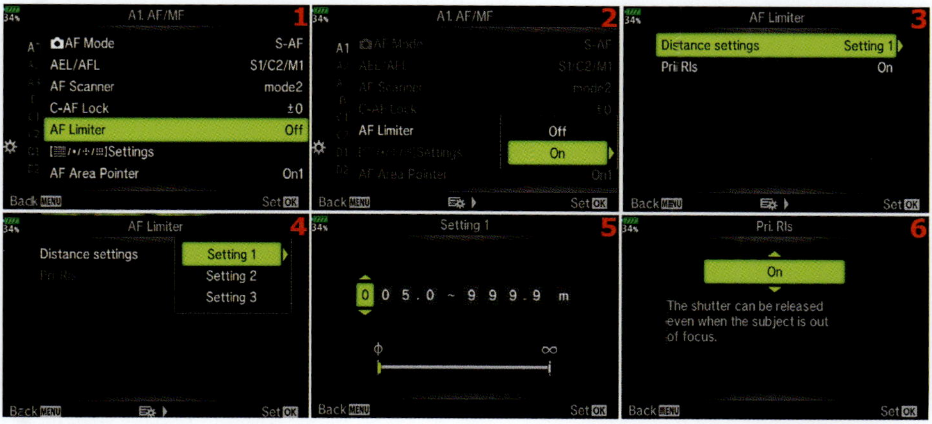

Figure 7.9: The AF Limiter menu

Use the following steps to set any of the three AF Limiter distance settings:

1. Choose AF Limiter from the A1. AF/MF menu and scroll to the right (figure 7.9, image 1).
2. A menu will open with On and Off options (figure 7.9, image 2). Select On and scroll to the right.
3. Select Distance Settings from the AF Limiter menu and scroll to the right (figure 7.9, image 3).
4. A menu will open with three options: Setting 1, Setting 2, and Settings 3 (figure 7.9, image 4). As I mentioned previously, you can set three different AF Limiter distance ranges, which can be selected later depending on the type of subject you are photographing. Choose one of the Setting options and scroll to the right to set the distance range for that Setting.
5. The next screen allows you to set the distance range for the Setting you selected (figure 7.9, image 5). Use the arrow keys to set the minimum and maximum distances for the range you want the autofocus system to examine. Use the left and right arrows to move between the boxes, and the up and down arrows to set the numbers for each box. Once you have entered the distances, press the OK button to Set your choice and return to the AF Limiter menu (image 3).
6. Select Pri. Rls from the AF Limiter menu and scroll to the right. This setting controls whether the shutter can be released if the subject is out of focus. If Pri. Rls is turned On, the shutter can be released even if the subject is out of focus. If it is turned Off, the shutter will not be released unless the subject is in focus. Select On or Off and press the OK button to Set your choice.

Settings Recommendation: The AF Limiter function is useful in specific situations where you know the subject is going to be a certain distance from the camera. However, it is important that you remember to turn this function off when you are done photographing in that situation, or else you will have issues when trying to focus on a subject outside of the set distance range.

[AF Target] Settings (A1)

The [AF Target] Settings function allows you to determine which AF patterns are available for selection when you are choosing an AF Target. You can hide the [Full Grid], [Cross], or [Square] patterns on the AF Target selection screen by unchecking the corresponding boxes in the [AF Target] Settings menu. You cannot hide the [Spot] selection.

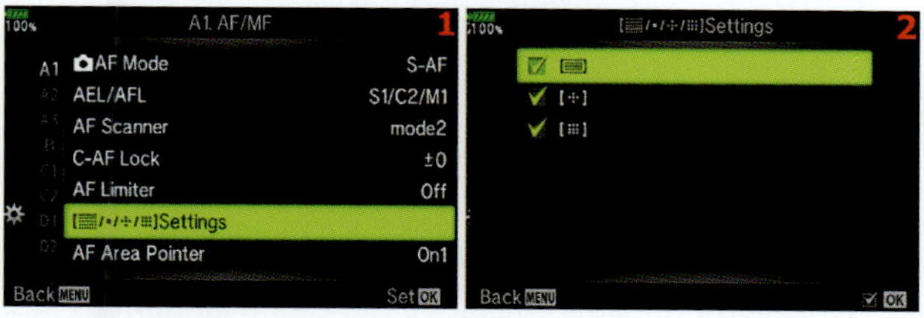

Figure 7.10: The [AF Target] Settings menu

Use the following steps to select which of the AF Target patterns is displayed on the AF Target selection screen:

1. Choose [AF Target] Settings from the A1. AF/MF menu and scroll to the right (figure 7.10, image 1).
2. A menu will open with three choices: [Full Grid], [Cross], and [Square] (figure 7.10, image 2). Use the Arrow Pad to select an AF Target pattern, and then press the OK button to check or uncheck the corresponding box. Any pattern that does not have a check mark next to it will not be displayed on the AF Target selection screen.
3. Press the Menu button to lock in your choices and return to the previous screen.

Settings Recommendation: I use all three of these AF Target patterns at various times, so I leave all of them turned on.

AF Area Pointer (A1)

The AF Area Pointer is green rectangles or squares, of various sizes, that signify when and where the camera has achieved autofocus. You can turn the AF Area Pointer On or Off with this function.

Notice that the current position of the AF Area Pointer has very faint black corner brackets where it will display the green AF Area Pointer when focus is locked. The green square with lines for focus-tracking mode (C-AF+TR) and the white face-tracking square for face detection (Face Priority) cannot be disabled.

Let's see how to enable or disable the standard green symbol for the AF Area Pointer.

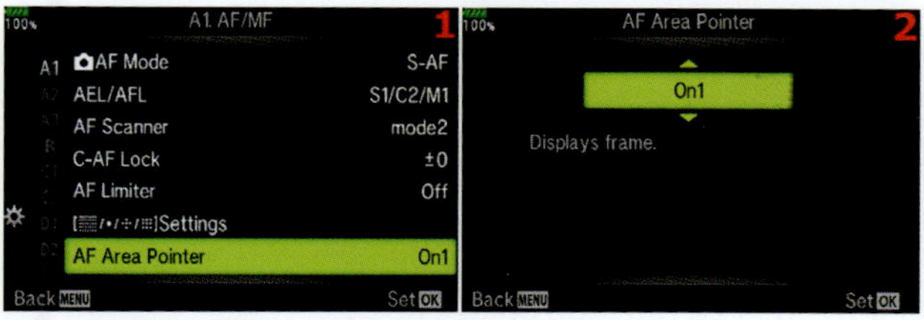

Figure 7.11: Enabling or disabling the AF Area Pointer

Use these steps to turn the AF Area Pointer On or Off:

1. Choose AF Area Pointer from the A1. AF/MF menu and scroll to the right (figure 7.11, image 1).
2. An up/down menu will open and allow you to scroll through three choices: On1, On2, and Off (figure 7.11, image 2). Choose On1 to allow the AF Area Pointer to flash green on the area that is in focus; choose On2 to allow the AF Area Pointer to appear as a non-blinking green rectangle on the area that is in focus, as long as the shutter button is pressed halfway; or choose Off to make the AF Area Pointer disappear. With no AF Area Pointer enabled, you will have to depend on the round green AF confirmation mark, in the top-right corner of the screen, or the focus beep to tell you when the subject is in focus.
3. Press the OK button to Set your choice.

Settings Recommendation: The AF Area Pointer is not a distraction to me at all. I use it to set the area I want to focus by moving it around within the 81 focus points on my camera screen. When I initiate autofocus, I like that it flashes green (setting On1) when the subject is in focus and that it's backed up by the AF confirmation mark (green dot) and beep.

With the AF Area Pointer, I know which area of the subject the camera is focusing on. I find it extremely useful. However, if you are simply using your camera as an expensive point-and-shoot, or if the AF Area Pointer interferes with viewing the subject in some way, such as in extreme macro shooting, by all means disable it. Most photographers leave it enabled.

AF Targeting Pad (A2)

With AF Targeting Pad enabled, you can tap on the monitor and slide your finger around to position the AF Target during viewfinder photography. When this function is set to On, you can enable or disable it by double tapping on the screen.

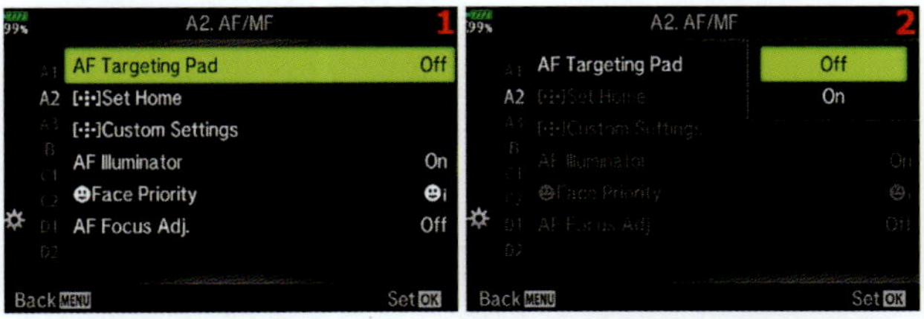

Figure 7.12: The AF Targeting Pad

Use these steps to turn the AF Targeting Pad function on or off:

1. Choose AF Targeting Pad from the A2. AF/MF menu and scroll to the right (figure 7.12, image 1).

2. You will be presented with an On/Off menu (figure 7.12, image 2). Choose On to enable this function or Off to disable it. Press the OK button to Set your choice.

Settings Recommendation: I find that trying to move the AF Target on the monitor with my finger while using the viewfinder to compose my images can be quite awkward. But it doesn't hurt to try this out and see if it works for you.

[•••] Set Home (A2)

The [•••] Set Home function works in conjunction with a Button Task called [•••] Home. This is where you can select which AF settings the camera will use when the [•••] Home function is applied. You can set the AF Mode (S-AF, C-AF, MF, S-AF+MF, C-AF+TR, and Preset MF), the AF Target mode ([Full Grid], [Spot], [Cross], and [Square]), and the AF Target position. Each of the three main choices can be easily turned on or off using the checkbox next to the selection.

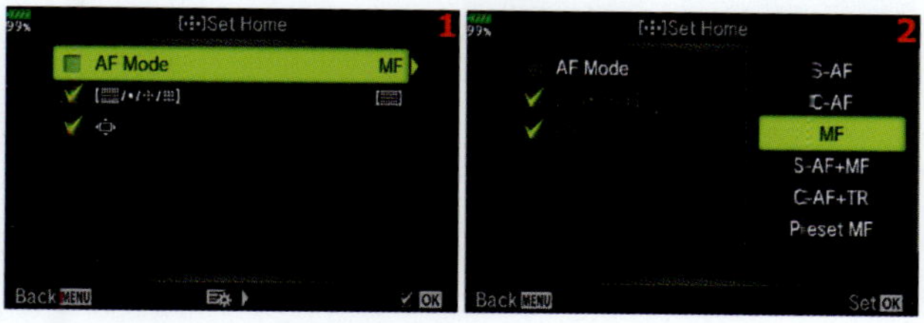

Figure 7.13: Choosing the AF Mode

Use the following steps to select the AF Mode to be used by the [•••] Home function:

1. Choose [•••] Set Home from the A2. AF/MF menu and scroll to the right. Then choose AF Mode and scroll to the right (figure 7.13, image 1).
2. A menu will open with the following AF Mode selections: S-AF, C-AF, MF, S-AF+MF, C-AF+TR, or Preset MF (figure 7.13, image 2). Choose an AF Mode and press the OK button to Set your choice and return to the previous screen.
3. You can now toggle the selected AF Mode on and off by pressing the OK button to place or remove a check mark in the AF Mode checkbox.

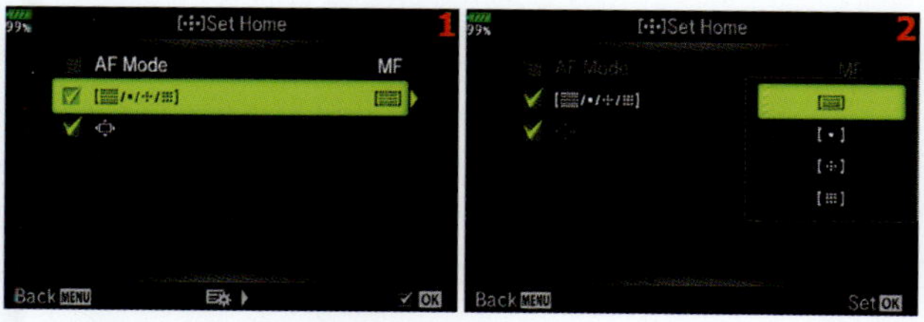

Figure 7.14: Choosing the AF Target mode

Use the following steps to select the AF Target mode to be used by the [•••] Home function:

1. Choose [•••] Set Home from the A2. AF/MF menu and scroll to the right. Then choose [AF Target] and scroll to the right (figure 7.14, image 1).
2. A menu will open with the following [AF Target] mode options: [Full Grid], [Spot], [Cross], and [Square] (figure 7.14, image 2). Choose an [AF Target] mode and press the OK button to Set your choice and return to the previous screen.
3. You can now toggle the selected [AF Target] mode on and off by pressing the OK button to place or remove a check mark in the [AF Target] mode checkbox.

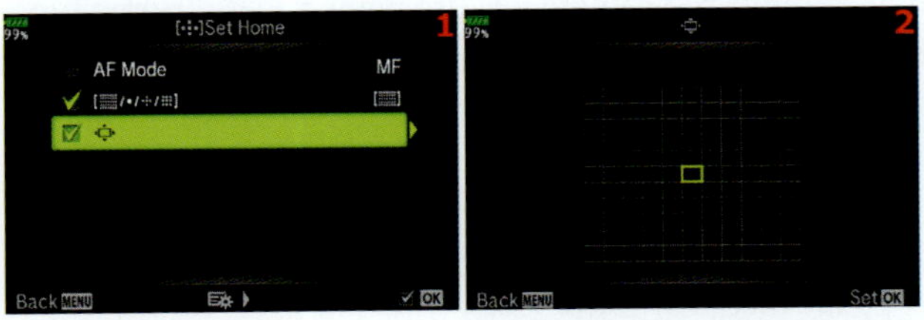

Figure 7.15: Choosing the AF Target position

Use the following steps to select the AF Target position to be used by the [•••] Home function:

1. Choose [•••] Set Home from the A2. AF/MF menu and scroll to the right. Then choose [AF Target position] and scroll to the right (figure 7.15, image 1).
2. A screen will open showing all of the selectable AF Target positions (figure 7.15, image 2). Use the Arrow Pad to move the AF Target to where you want the default position to be, and then press the OK button to Set your choice and return to the previous screen.
3. You can now toggle the selected AF Target position on and off by pressing the OK button to place or remove a check mark in the [AF Target position] checkbox.

Settings Recommendation: I normally leave my camera set to S-AF with the center AF point set to the home position, so that the AF Area Pointer will jump to the center of the screen when I press the button that has been assigned the [•••] Home function.

[•••] Custom Settings (A2)

This menu choice allows you to configure the AF Area interface, which is used to set the location and shape of the AF Target and the face detection preferences. You get to define which command dial or Arrow Pad buttons will be used to control the AF Target shape, and which will control Face Priority. You can save two separate configurations: Set 1 and Set 2.

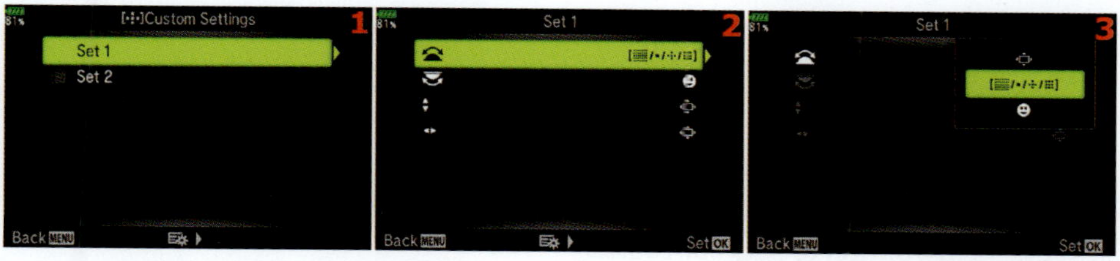

Figure 7.16: The [•••] Custom Settings menu

Use the following steps to configure the two [•••] Custom Settings interfaces:

1. Choose [•••] Custom Settings from the A2. AF/MF menu and scroll to the right.
2. Select Set 1 and scroll to the right (figure 7.16, image 1)
3. A menu will open with four control options: [Front Dial], [Rear Dial], [Arrow Pad Up/Down], [Arrow Pad Left/Right] (figure 7.16, image 2). Select the control you want to configure and scroll to the right.
4. A menu will open with three options: [AF Target position], [AF Target] mode, and ☺ (Face Priority) (figure 7.16, image 3). Select the function that you would like to be controlled by the previously selected dial or button (e.g., the Front Dial), and press the OK button to Set your choice.
5. Repeat steps 3 and 4 for any or all of the Set 1 options, and then press the OK button return to the [•••] Custom Settings menu (figure 7.16, image 1).
6. Repeat the process to configure Set 2.

Settings Recommendation: I find that the default settings work great and there really is no need to change them.

AF Illuminator (A2)

The AF Illuminator is the small light next to the OM-D label on the front of the camera. It shines red when you start autofocus in a dark area. The light assists the camera by shining on nearby objects.

The light may be distracting sometimes, so you can turn it Off with the AF Illuminator function.

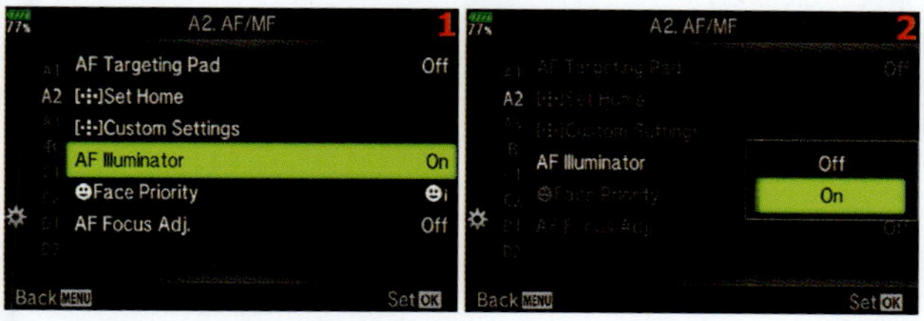

Figure 7.17: Enabling or disabling the AF Illuminator light

Use these steps to control whether the AF Illuminator light is On or Off:

1. Choose AF Illuminator from the A2. AF/MF menu and scroll to the right (figure 7.17, image 1).
2. A menu will open with two choices: On and Off (figure 7.17, image 2). Choose On to allow the light to assist with autofocus, or choose Off to disable the light.
3. Press the OK button to Set your choice.

Settings Recommendation: When I am shooting in an environment where people will not appreciate a shining light, such as at some very traditional weddings, or if I am trying to sneak some pictures and don't want to call attention to myself, I disable the light.

The camera senses when the light is low enough that the AF Illuminator is needed. The light doesn't shine when the ambient light is bright or when you use a flash unit that has a built-in assist light. Therefore, most of the time I leave AF Illuminator set to On.

☺ Face Priority

Face Priority is a very efficient and accurate human face detection system that is built into the camera. It tells the camera to watch for human faces and, if found, make them the priority for accurate autofocus.

When you are shooting nonhuman subjects the camera works normally and displays a regular green AF Area Pointer as it focuses. However, when the camera detects human faces, it switches all its attention to the faces and uses a much larger white AF square (figure 7.18).

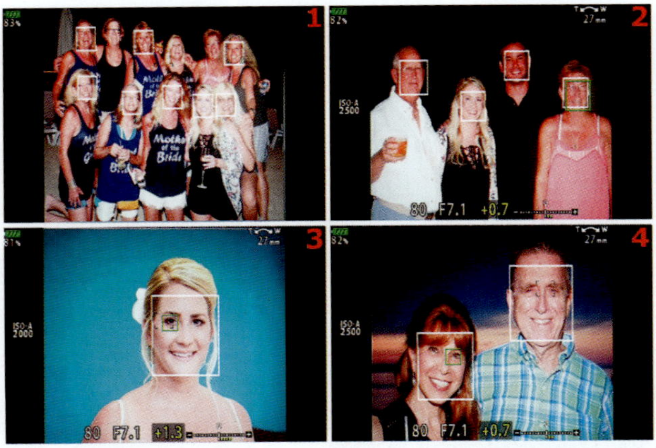

Figure 7.18: Using Face Priority

Notice how all the faces in figure 7.18 are surrounded by the white face-tracking square. The white squares tend to stay with detected faces as they move, so they'll jump a little as the camera keeps track of detected faces. The white squares are not really in-focus indicators; they merely show the location of a face in the subject area.

When focus initially locks on a face, a separate green focus-confirmation square—the same size as the white square—will appear briefly, along with a beep from the camera. You can see both the white and green AF squares in figure 7.18, image 2, surrounding the face on the right. The green focus-confirmation square is slightly offset from the white face-tracking square.

Figure 7.18, images 3 and 4, show a tiny green square surrounding an eye. This tiny green eye-focus confirmation square appears briefly when Eye Priority is enabled and focus has locked on an eye. Which eye it locks on is controlled by which Face Priority mode is enabled, as described in the upcoming ***Face Priority Types*** list.

Note that an AF confirmation mark (small green dot) appears in the top-right corner of the viewfinder or monitor when focus has locked on the subject

Here are the four Face Priority modes (plus Off) and descriptions of how they work:

Face Priority Types

- ☺ **(Face Priority On):** This setting causes the camera to seek human faces and give them autofocus priority. The camera will find and frame each face it detects and try to balance autofocus on the faces depending on which AF mode is selected (e.g., S-AF or C-AF).
- **☺iL (Face Priority and L. Eye Priority On):** This setting causes the camera to seek the pupil on the left side of the frame and give it autofocus priority. You will see the small green eye-focus confirmation square appear briefly. The camera uses the autofocus mode that is currently selected (e.g., S-AF or C-AF).
- **☺iR (Face Priority and R. Eye Priority On):** This setting causes the camera to seek the pupil on the right side of the frame and give it autofocus priority. You will see the small green eye-focus confirmation square appear briefly, and the camera will beep when focus has locked on an eye. The camera uses the autofocus mode that is currently selected (e.g., S-AF or C-AF).
- **☺i (Face Priority and Eye Priority On):** This setting causes the camera to seek a pupil in the eye of the closest human face and give that face autofocus priority. The camera uses the autofocus mode that is currently selected (e.g., S-AF or C-AF).
- **☺OFF (Face Priority Off):** This setting disables human face-detection autofocus priority and uses normal autofocus.

Let's see how to enable Face Priority. Most photographers leave it enabled all the time.

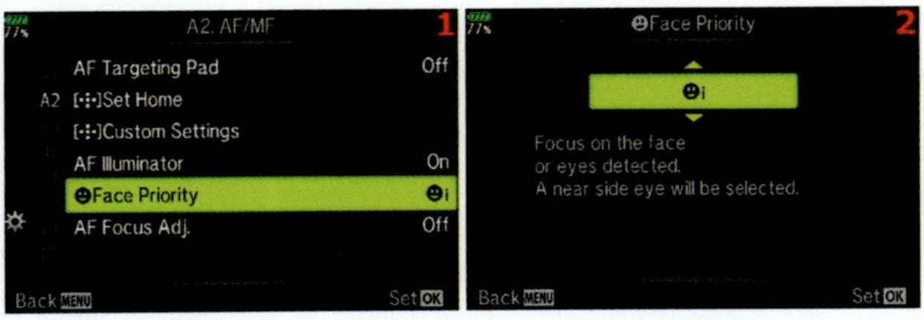

Figure 7.19: Enabling Face Priority face detection

1. Choose ☺ Face Priority from the A2. AF/MF menu and scroll to the right (figure 7.19, image 1).
2. An up/down menu will open with the five choices shown in the ***Face Priority Types*** list (figure 7.19, image 2). Choose one of the face detection methods or Off. I chose Face Priority and Eye Priority (☺i).
3. Press the OK button to Set the face detection type.

Note: When Face Priority is enabled and when no people are in the subject area, the camera will use its normal AF Area Pointers and switch to the larger Face Priority squares only if a human face is suddenly detected.

If you want your camera to ignore human faces so you can use the normal AF Area Pointers all the time, set Face Priority to Off.

Settings Recommendation: Face detection works very well in this camera. When I am using any form of face detection, autofocus still works just as well for normal autofocus without face detection when no people are present in the image. Therefore, I see no reason to turn it off for the type of photography I do (primarily nature). If a person is in the subject area, I want their face to take autofocus priority—that is, if I am interested in photographing the person.

There may be times when you want the camera to ignore faces, and then Face Priority would be an aggravation. If you are trying to photograph a nonhuman subject while humans happen to be in the frame, and if the camera is paying undue attention to the human faces, turn Face Priority Off. When this setting is On, the camera is very persistent about focusing on human faces.

The factory default is for Face Priority to be enabled because so many photographers love people photography.

AF Focus Adj. (A2)

Some lenses have a tendency to not focus exactly where they should. The lens may focus a little in front of or behind the point where you want the focus to be. A lens may focus well when mounted on one camera body and not so well on another. It is almost as if some lenses have a personality.

If you have a lens that acts like that, you may need to have it repaired. However, if the problem is minor, you can use the AF Focus Adj. function to fine-tune the focus of an individual lens, or even all lenses that you mount on your camera.

Let's examine how to work with the focus adjustment system.

Setting an AF Focus Adjustment for All Lenses

If you think your camera has a tendency to focus incorrectly with all lenses you mount on it, you may need to have your camera repaired. In the meantime, though, you may have to shoot some important pictures and want to fine-tune the camera so all lenses focus more accurately.

Experiment first and determine whether you need to push the focus away from the camera or pull it back in to increase sharpness. That is the purpose of the Default Data subfunction. Let's see how to use it.

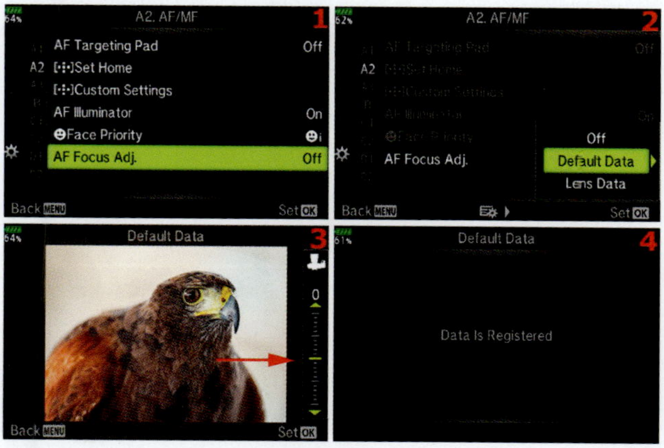

Figure 7.20: Adjusting the focus for all lenses you mount on your camera

Use these steps to adjust the focus for all lenses you mount on your camera:

1. Select AF Focus Adj. from the A2. AF/MF menu and scroll to the right (figure 7.20, image 1).
2. Highlight Default Data on the menu and scroll to the right (figure 7.20, image 2).
3. In figure 7.20, image 3 (red arrow), you can see the adjustment indicator. You can move this yellow bar up and down with the keys on the Arrow Pad over a range of 40 increments (+20 to −20). Moving this bar up moves the focus forward by up to 20 increments; moving it down moves the focus backward by up to 20 increments. The number at the top of the indicator is 0 in the figure, but it will change as you move the yellow bar to a plus or minus value. Choose the amount of focus adjustment you need to use.
4. Press the OK button to Set your choice, then a screen will appear that says *Data Is Registered* (figure 7.20, image 4). Test the focus and readjust as necessary by repeating steps 1–3.

Now let's examine how to adjust the focus for just one lens. All other lenses will focus normally.

Setting an AF Focus Adjustment for an Individual Lens

If you have a lens that is not focusing correctly and do not want to send it in for repair, you may be able to use the Lens Data subfunction to adjust the focus for only that lens and make it more accurate. You can maintain a custom focus adjustment for up to 20 separate lenses. Let's see how to adjust the focus for a single lens.

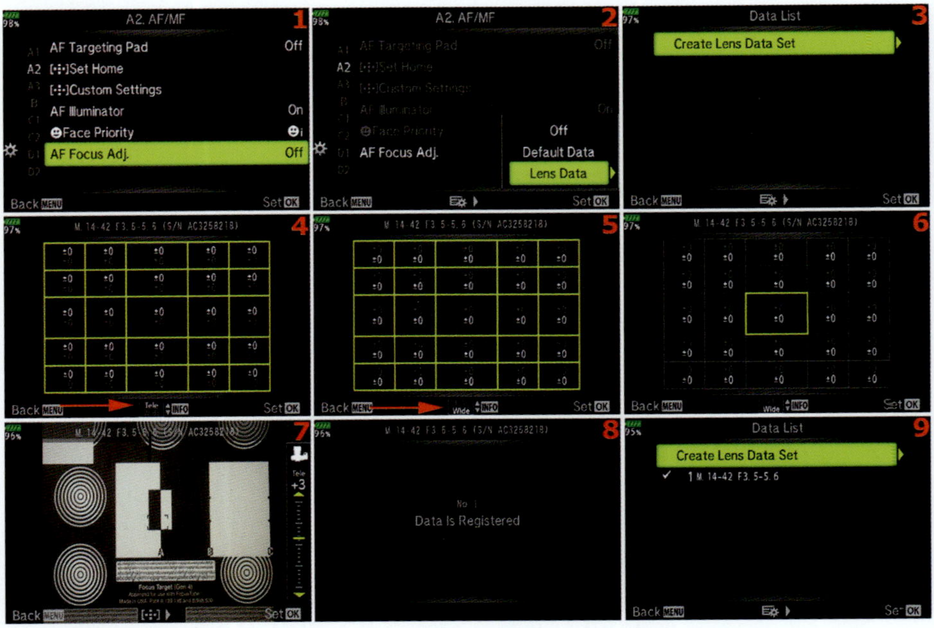

Figure 7.21: Adjusting the focus for a single lens

Use these steps to adjust the focus for a single lens that is mounted on the camera:

1. Select AF Focus Adj. from the A2. AF/MF menu and scroll to the right (figure 7.21, image 1).
2. Highlight Lens Data on the menu and scroll to the right (figure 7.21, image 2).
3. Notice in figure 7.21, image 3, that there is a single selection, Create Lens Data Set. Later, after you have adjusted at least one lens, the lens name will appear in a list on this screen. In our example there are no adjusted lenses to show, so scroll to the right.
4. As soon as you scroll to the right, you will see the screen in figure 7.21, image 4. This screen shows the 25 adjustable focus points in a highlighted grid. You can adjust all of the points at the same time for this lens, or you can adjust a single AF point. If you scroll to the left or right with the keys on the Arrow Pad, you will see that only one focus point

will be highlighted (figure 7.21, image 6); the other 24 points have been deselected. In figure 7.21, images 4 and 5 (red arrows), the words Tele and Wide are displayed. Press the Info button to move between Tele and Wide so you can adjust the lens for the corresponding ends of the zoom range. When you toggle between Tele and Wide you can see that the ±0 settings in each square of the grid change from the top to the bottom. This indicates that you can have separate adjustments for the Tele and Wide settings. To make the actual adjustment, you must choose one of the setting types, as shown in images 4–6. When the type of adjustment you want to make is displayed on the screen, press the OK button.

5. Now you will see the screen shown in figure 7.21, image 7. This screen allows you to adjust the focus forward or backward for the AF points you selected in images 4–6. You can adjust the focus forward up to 20 increments (0 to +20) by scrolling up with the Arrow Pad key. The yellow bar on the scale at the right side of the screen in image 7 will move up or down as you scroll. Move the yellow bar down with the Arrow Pad to pull the focus backward by up to 20 increments (0 to –20). Image 7 shows that I have moved the bar (and focus) by +3 increments in a forward position, which means the lens now has a small amount of front focus dialed in. Also notice that the word Tele is displayed just above the indicator, signifying that I am adjusting focus only for the telephoto end of the zoom lens. Adjust the indicator up or down to move the focus forward or backward. When you have moved the bar to where you want it for both the Tele and Wide positions, you are ready to test the adjustment. Press the OK button to lock in the new adjustment, and take a few pictures to test your settings. Use the information in the upcoming subsection if you want to change an existing adjustment for greater accuracy.
6. When you have saved the adjustment by pressing the OK button, a screen will appear that says *Data Is Registered,* along with a lens number assignment (*No. 1;* figure 7.21, image 8). The camera will switch back to the Data List menu and display your lens in the list. You can edit the lens number, as discussed in the next subsection.

Note: You will need to adjust each lens individually with this subfunction. If you want to fine-tune the focus on more than one lens, the camera will remember each lens separately. It will create a numbered list of up to 20 lenses that have been adjusted, and you can edit the adjustment for each lens.

Let's now consider how to edit the previous adjustment of a single lens.

Editing an Existing AF Focus Adjustment for a Single Lens

After you have created a lens adjustment for one or more lenses, the camera will allow you to edit the settings. You can change the amount of front or back focus adjustment, and then resave the Lens Data Set.

Let's examine how to edit one of your lens adjustments.

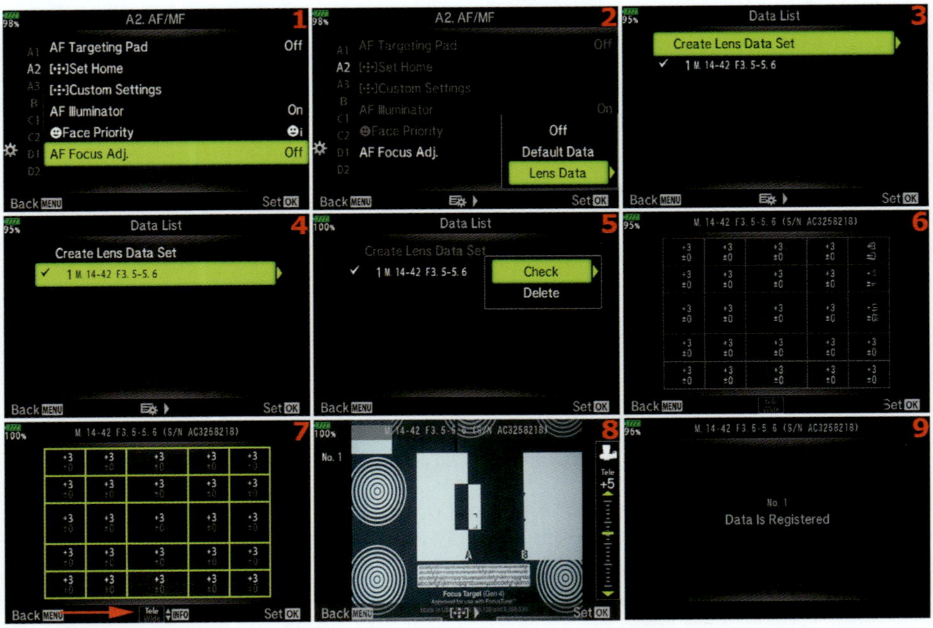

Figure 7.22: Editing an existing focus adjustment

Use these steps to edit an existing focus adjustment:

1. Select AF Focus Adj. from the A2. AF/MF menu and scroll to the right (figure 7.22, image 1).
2. Highlight Lens Data on the menu and scroll to the right (figure 7.22, image 2).
3. Notice on the screen shown in figure 7.22, image 3, that there is an existing adjustment for a lens. It is displayed as 1 M. 14–42 F3. 5–5.6 (1 indicates the lens number). Had I adjusted any other lenses, they would also appear in this list (up to 20 lens adjustments). Let's edit the current adjustment for my lens. Select the lens from the Data List and scroll to the right (figure 7.22, image 4).
4. The next screen lets you either Check or Delete a current lens adjustment. Choose Check and scroll to the right (figure 7.22, image 5).
5. As you can see in the boxes of figure 7.22, image 6, the lens is adjusted to +3 on the Tele end of the zoom range. The Tele end of the lens is indicated by the top number of each square (which represents AF points), and the Wide lens position is indicated by the bottom number in each square. After you have examined the current settings, scroll to the right.
6. Figure 7.22, image 7, is the screen that allows you to choose which part of the focus adjustment you want to change. At the point of the red arrow you can see that I was adjusting the Tele position, and the AF rectangles indicate that the current setting is +3 forward focus. If you scroll left or right, you can deselect all 37 of the AF points and

choose a single AF point to work with. If you press the Info button, you will toggle between Tele and Wide. When you have selected the AF points you want to change, press the OK button to move into the final adjustment screen.

7. As previously mentioned, the Tele position is set to +3 forward focus. Let's move that to +5 to add a little more forward focus (figure 7.22, image 8). I am now ready to save this new focus adjustment and retest my lens.
8. Press the OK button to save the new focus adjustment. A screen that says *Data Is Registered,* along with the lens number, will appear briefly (figure 7.22, image 9). The camera will switch back to the Data List menu and display your list of lenses in case you want to edit the adjustment for another lens.

Next let's consider how to get rid of a lens focus adjustment you no longer need.

Deleting an Existing AF Focus Adjustment for a Single Lens

If your lens has been repaired or if it miraculously starts focusing correctly, you will no longer need a focus adjustment. Let's see how to delete it.

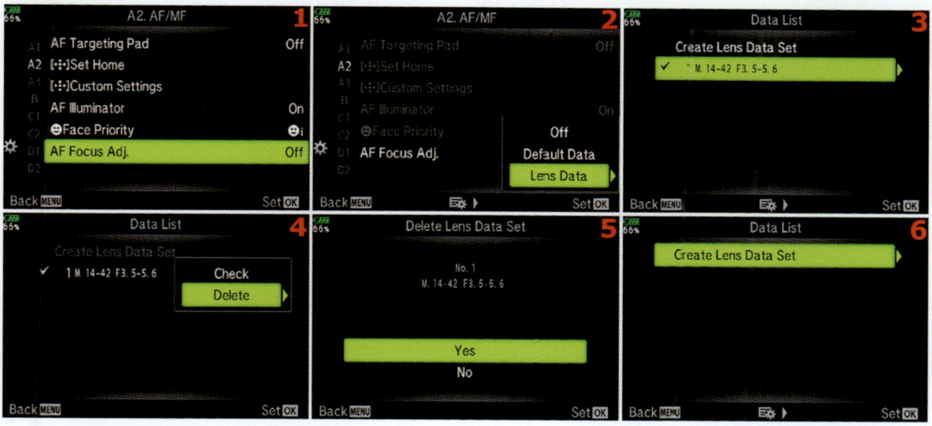

Figure 7.23: Deleting an unneeded lens focus adjustment

Use these steps to delete an existing lens focus adjustment:

1. Select AF Focus Adj. from the A2. AF/MF menu and scroll to the right (figure 7.23, image 1).
2. Highlight Lens Data on the menu and scroll to the right (figure 7.23, image 2).
3. Choose the Lens Data Set you want to Delete and scroll to the right (figure 7.23, image 3).
4. Choose Delete from the menu and scroll to the right (figure 7.23, image 4).
5. A Yes/No menu will appear, along with information on the Lens Data Set you are about to Delete. Select Yes and press the OK button to delete the lens adjustment (figure 7.23,

image 5). When you are done, the camera will switch back to the Data List screen, with the lens removed from the list (figure 7.23, image 6).

Settings Recommendation: This complex function allows you to control how all or a few of your lenses focus on your camera. Even if you don't want to use it now, why not experiment with AF Focus Adj. in case one of your lenses starts having focus problems in the future?

Preset MF Distance (A3)

The Preset MF distance function allows you to set the distance used for focusing when you switch to Preset MF mode. The default value is 999.9m (infinity), which makes sense, but you can set it to any distance you want.

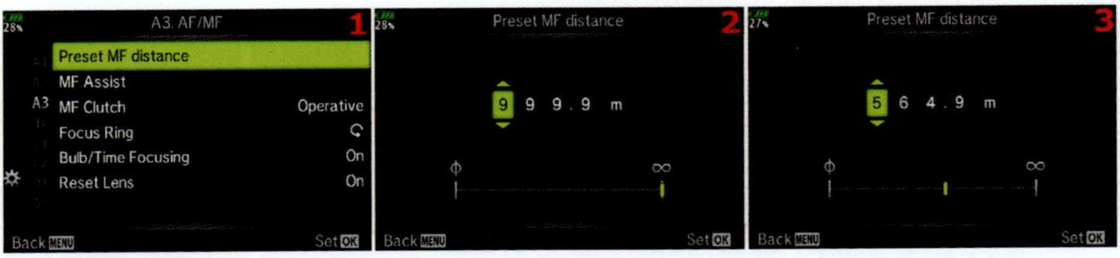

Figure 7.24: Setting the Preset MF distance

Use these steps to set the Preset MF distance:

1. Select Preset MF distance from the A3. AF/MF menu and scroll to the right (figure 7.24, image 1).
2. You can now use the Arrow Pad keys to input the Preset MF distance (figure 7.24, image 2). Scroll to the left or right to select an individual digit, and then scroll up or down to change that digit.
3. Once you've input the value you would like to use, press the OK button to Set the Preset MF distance (figure 7.24, image 3).

Settings Recommendation: I keep the Preset MF distance function set to infinity, which works well as a starting point. Unless you have a very specific reason to change this, I suggest leaving it set to infinity, as that makes it easy to adjust when needed.

MF Assist (A3)

MF Assist helps you accurately focus on a subject when you shoot in manual focus (MF) mode. There are two types of MF Assist: Magnify and Peaking.

In figure 7.25, image 1, the subject is red, green, and blue blocks. When the focus ring is turned with both Magnify and Peaking enabled, the camera displays what you see in figure 7.25, image 2. The camera zooms in by 10x so you can see fine detail and manually focus more easily.

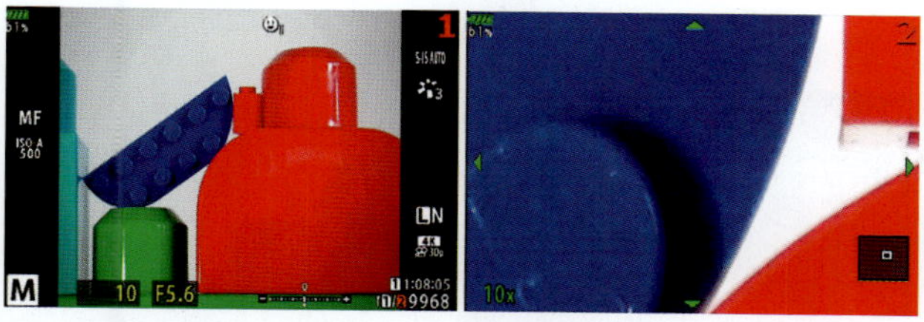

Figure 7.25: Using Magnify and Peaking to assist with manual focusing

Notice that Peaking is active, as shown by the white outline on the blue and red block borders and white dust specks. Peaking emphasizes the in-focus edges of the subject with a white, black, red, or yellow tone to help you see the exact point of focus. Peaking appears only briefly, while you turn the focus ring, as does the magnification. If you stop focusing for about a half second, both Magnify and Peaking turn off. As soon as you turn the focus ring again, they reappear.

The combination of these methods gives you very fine control over manual focus. Let's see how to enable and disable the two focus assistance aids.

Magnify

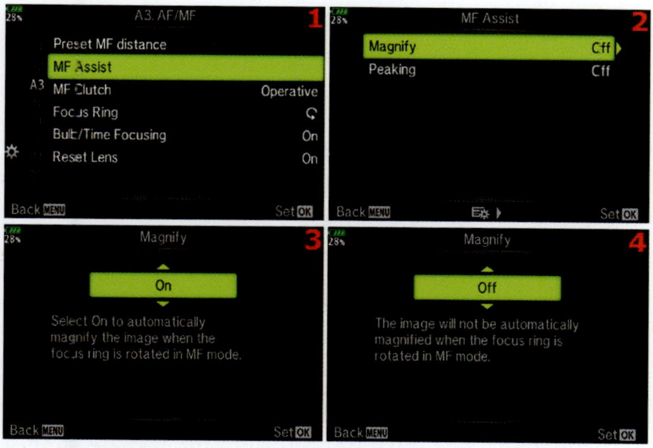

Figure 7.26: Enabling Magnify to assist with manual focusing

Use these steps to enable or disable Magnify for manual focus assistance:

1. Select MF Assist from the A3. AF/MF menu and scroll to the right (figure 7.26, image 1).
2. Choose Magnify and scroll to the right (figure 7.26, image 2).
3. From the up/down menu, choose On or Off (figure 7.26, images 3 and 4). On enables Magnify and Off disables it.
4. Press the OK button to Set your choice.

Peaking

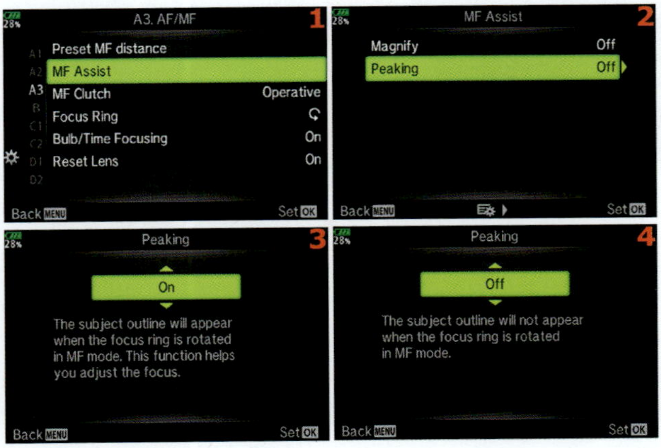

Figure 7.27: Enabling Peaking to assist with manual focusing

Use these steps to enable or disable Peaking for manual focus assistance:

1. Select MF Assist from the A3. AF/MF menu and scroll to the right (figure 7.27, image 1).
2. Choose Peaking and scroll to the right (figure 7.27, image 2).
3. From the up/down menu, choose On or Off (figure 7.27, images 3 and 4). On enables Peaking and Off disables it.
4. Press the OK button to Set your choice.

Settings Recommendation: I use both of these functions to assist with manual focus. I leave Peaking On all the time and Magnify On part of the time. Some subjects require both to get accurate focus, others do not. Experiment with both of these focus aids so you will have full control with no other focusing aids.

MF Clutch (A3)

The MF Clutch is a feature of the premium MZD Pro lenses. This function allows you to switch between autofocus and manual focus by pulling or pushing the lens focus ring. This is a fast and convenient way to switch between AF and MF. However, you may find that when the MF Clutch is enabled, it is easy to inadvertently switch between AF and MF. If you rarely use manual focus, you may want to disable the clutch to avoid accidentally switching focus.

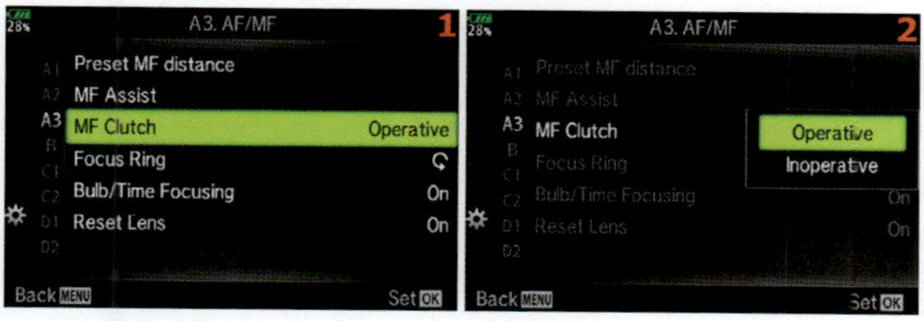

Figure 7.28: MF Clutch menu

Use these steps to enable or disable the MF Clutch:

1. Select MF Clutch from the A3. AF/MF menu and scroll to the right (figure 7.28, image 1).
2. Choose Operative to enable the MF Clutch, or Inoperative to disable it (figure 7.28, image 2).
3. Press the OK button to Set your choice.

Settings Recommendation: I set MF Clutch to Operative because I like being able to easily switch between autofocus and manual focus. If you don't often use manual focus, you may want to disable this feature.

Focus Ring (A3)

When you turn the focus ring toward infinity, you normally rotate it counterclockwise (from behind the camera). For focusing on items close to the lens, you rotate the focus ring clockwise. If you want to reverse the direction, you can change it with this setting.

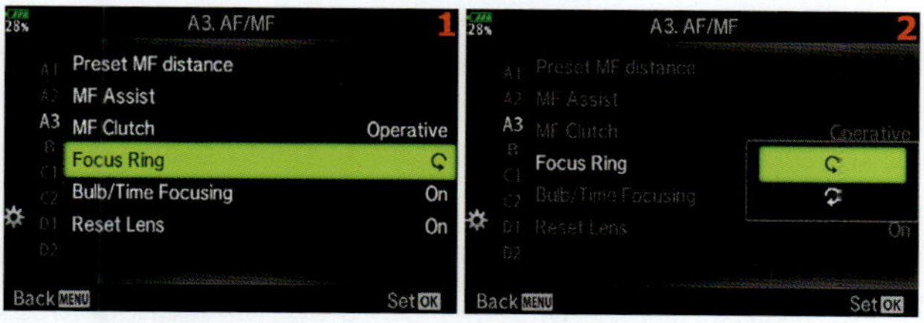

Figure 7.29: Reversing the directional effect of rotating the lens focus ring

Use the following steps to change the directional effect of rotating the lens focus ring:

1. Choose Focus Ring from the A3. AF/MF menu and scroll to the right (figure 7.29, image 1).
2. A small menu will appear with two circular arrows that represent rotation directions (figure 7.29, image 2). Choose clockwise or counterclockwise rotation to select the direction you want to turn the lens when you move from far to near.
3. Press the OK button to Set the choice.

Settings Recommendation: I changed the direction to the opposite of the factory default—clockwise for infinity—so the rotation direction matches my Nikkor lenses, which I sometimes mount with an adapter on my E-M1II. Why confuse myself by having things work backwards when I switch cameras?

If you do not use lenses from other camera brands that focus in the opposite direction, this function may have little interest to you. However, remember it is there in case you ever want to change it.

Bulb/Time Focusing (A3)

When you use Live Bulb or Live Time modes to see a short time-exposure image come up gradually on the monitor, or when you do light writing in an image, the camera normally locks focus during the long exposure when you use manual focus (MF) mode.

If you want to use the focus ring on your lens to update focus during the long exposure, you must set this function to On.

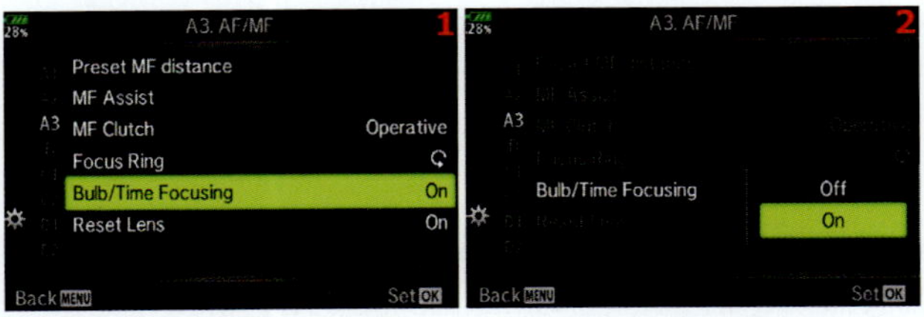

Figure 7.30: Enabling manual focus during Live Bulb and Live Time modes

Use the following steps to enable or disable manual focus during Live Bulb and Live Time operations:

1. Choose Bulb/Time Focusing from the A3. AF/MF menu and scroll to the right (figure 7.30, image 1).
2. A menu will appear with two choices: On and Off (figure 7.30, image 2). Choose On to enable manual focus with the lens focus ring, or select Off to disable manual focus during a long exposure.
3. Press the OK button to Set the choice.

Settings Recommendation: I leave Bulb/Time Focusing set to On. When I take a Live Bulb shot, I may want to change the focus slightly to focus on multiple people who are light writing. Why disable something you may need to use, even if only occasionally?

Reset Lens (A3)

Reset Lens is a simple function that resets the focus of your lens to infinity each time you turn the camera off. It works for both standard zoom and power zoom lenses.

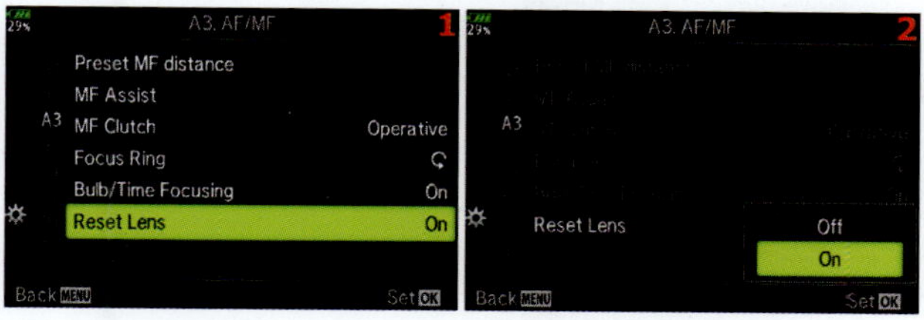

Figure 7.31: Set the lens to infinity when the camera powers off

Use the following steps to enable or disable Reset Lens:

1. Choose Reset Lens from the A3. AF/MF menu and scroll to the right (figure 7.31, image 1).
2. A menu will appear with two choices: On and Off (figure 7.31, image 2). Choose On to reset the lens to infinity when the camera powers off, or select Off to retain the focus position of the lens when the camera powers off. This function will have no effect on manual focus lenses.
3. Press the OK button to Set the choice.

Settings Recommendation: I leave this feature On. Why not focus the lens to infinity when the camera is turned off? This setting will not affect the zoom setting of the lens, just its focus position. Manual lenses are not controlled by the camera, so they will not be reset to infinity. If you don't want your lens to be set to infinity when the camera powers off, leave this setting Off.

Custom Menu B. Button/Dial/Lever

The B. Button/Dial/Lever menu (figure 7.32) allows you to assign Button Tasks to just about every button, dial, and lever on the camera. The E-M1II is one of the most configurable cameras I have ever seen, and this section is one of the primary reasons I say that.

First let's look at how to open the Button/Dial/Lever functions on the Custom Menu screen, and then we will consider how to assign tasks to the Button/Dial/Lever functions. Descriptions of the Button Tasks are provided in **Appendix A: Still Image Button Task Reference**, which can be found on the downloadable resources website:

www.rockynook.com/olympusem1markii

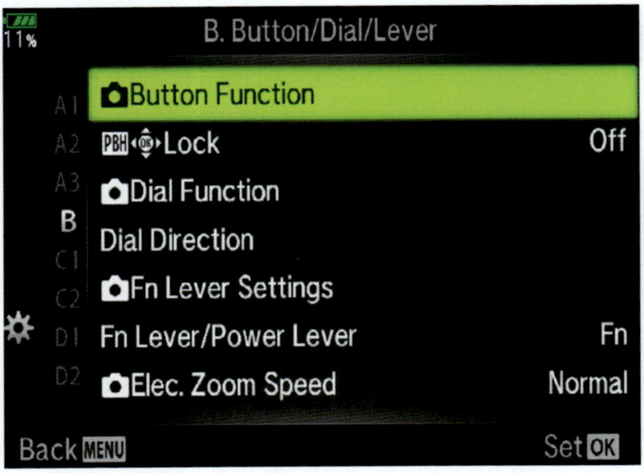

Figure 7.32: The B. Button/Dial/Lever menu

Important Naming Information

Olympus uses some unusual names for the buttons, dials, and levers on the OM-D E-M1II. For instance, you can see in the following menus that a button is not just called a button, it is called a Button Function (e.g., Fn1 Function, Fn2 Function). There are also Dial Functions (e.g., P, A, S, M) and Lever Functions (e.g., mode1, mode2).

You can assign certain actions to Button, Lever, and Dial Functions. To prevent confusion, I will call the assignable action items "tasks." Some examples of Button Function Tasks are HDR, ISO, BKT, and WB.

For example, the Fn1 Function can have the WB Task assigned to it. When you press the Fn1 button, the camera will allow you to adjust the White balance (WB). At the same time you could assign the Multi Function Task to the Fn2 Function.

Figure 7.32 displays the B. Button/Dial/Lever selection on the Custom Menu. All of the tasks you can assign to the Button, Dial, and Lever functions are available in this menu (see **Appendix A: Still Image Button Task Reference** on the downloadable resources website). To access them, choose B. Button/Dial/Lever and press the OK button, or scroll to the right with the Arrow Pad.

Button Function [Programmable Buttons] (B)

The Button Functions are a group of 16 programmable Button Functions (e.g., Fn1 Function, Fn2 Function). There are 28 available Button Tasks that can be assigned to the 16 Button Functions. Not all Button Functions can use all Button Tasks. You will find information for the 28 assignable Button Tasks in **Appendix A: Still Image Button Task** Reference, found on the downloadable resources website (www.rockynook.com/olympusem1markii). Let's examine each of the 16 Button Functions.

Fn1 Function

The Fn1 button can accept the assignment of most tasks in the **Button Tasks List** in **Appendix A: Still Image Button Task Reference**, found on the downloadable resources website (see page 10). The default factory assignment for the Fn1 Function is AF Area Select.

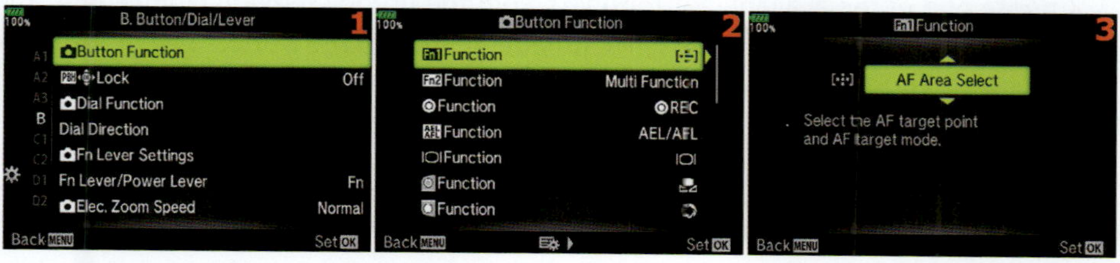

Figure 7.33: Assigning a Button Task to the Fn1 function

Use the following steps to assign one of the Button Tasks to the Fn1 Button Function:

1. Choose Button Function from the B. Button/Dial/Lever menu and scroll to the right (figure 7.33, image 1).
2. Select Fn1 Function from the Button Function menu and scroll to the right (figure 7.33, image 2).
3. Choose one of the available Button Tasks from the up/down menu (figure 7.33, image 3). Use the **Button Tasks List** found in **Appendix A: Still Image Button Task Reference** to decide which task you will assign to the Fn1 button.
4. Press the OK button to Set the tasks for the Fn1 button.

Settings Recommendation: I keep the Fn1 Function set to its default task, AF Area Select. This is a useful task for many photographers.

Fn2 Function

The Fn2 button can accept most task assignments shown in the **Button Tasks List** in **Appendix A: Still Image Button Task Reference**, found on the downloadable resources website (see page 10). The default factory assignment for the Fn2 Button Function is the Button Task named Multi Function.

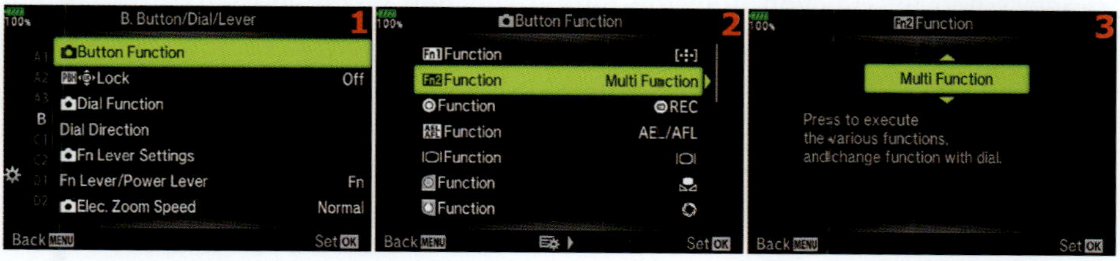

Figure 7.34: Assigning a Button Task to the Fn2 Button Function

Use the following steps to assign one of the Button Tasks to the Fn2 Button Function:

1. Choose Button Function from the B. Button/Dial/Lever menu and scroll to the right (figure 7.34, image 1).
2. Select Fn2 Function from the Button Function menu and scroll to the right (figure 7.34, image 2).
3. Choose one of the available Button Tasks from the up/down menu (Figure 7.34, image 3). Use the **Button Tasks List** in **Appendix A: Still Image Button Task Reference** to decide which task you will assign to the Fn2 button.
4. Press the OK button to Set the task for the Fn2 button.

Settings Recommendation: As mentioned previously, the default task assignment for the Fn2 Function is Multi Function. I have grown accustomed to using Fn2 for selecting one of the four functions on the Multi Function list. I sometimes use the Highlight&Shadow Control for visually fine-tuning an exposure, so I leave my camera set to the default.

[Movie] Function

The [Movie] button can accept the assignment of most tasks in the **Button Tasks List** in **Appendix A: Still image Button Task Reference**, found on the downloadable resources website (see page 10). The default factory assignment for the [Movie] Function is REC, which you use to start and stop movie recording.

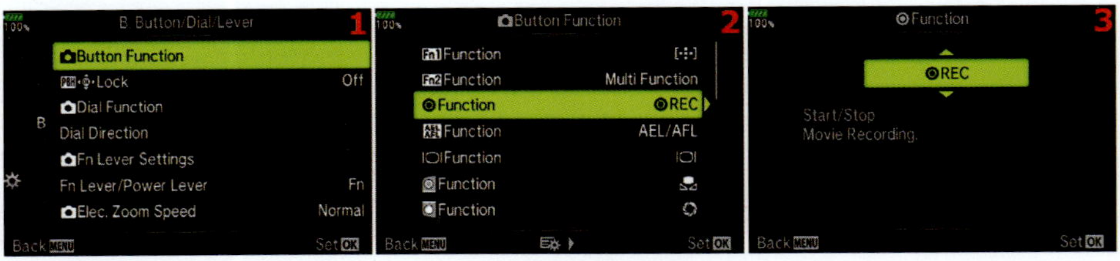

Figure 7.35: Assigning a Button Task to the [Movie] Function

Use the following steps to assign one of the Button Tasks to the [Movie] Button Function:

1. Choose Button Function from the B. Button/Dial/Lever menu and scroll to the right (figure 7.35, image 1).
2. Select [Movie] Function from the Button Function menu and scroll to the right (figure 7.35, image 2).
3. Choose one of the available Button Tasks from the up/down menu (figure 7.35, image 3). Use the **Button Tasks List** in **Appendix A: Still Image Button Task Reference** to decide which task you will assign to the [Movie] button.
4. Press the OK button to Set the task for the [Movie] button.

Settings Recommendation: If you shoot videos with your camera, leave this button set to the factory default of REC. Otherwise you will have no way to start and stop movie recording. REC cannot be assigned to any other button. However, if you do not shoot video, you can assign most of the other Button Tasks to the [Movie] button. It is conveniently located for quick access.

AEL/AFL Function

The AEL/AFL button can accept the assignment of most tasks in the **Button Tasks List** in **Appendix A: Still Image Button Task Reference**, found on the downloadable resources website (see page 10). The default factory assignment for the AEL/AFL Function is the Button Task named AEL/AFL.

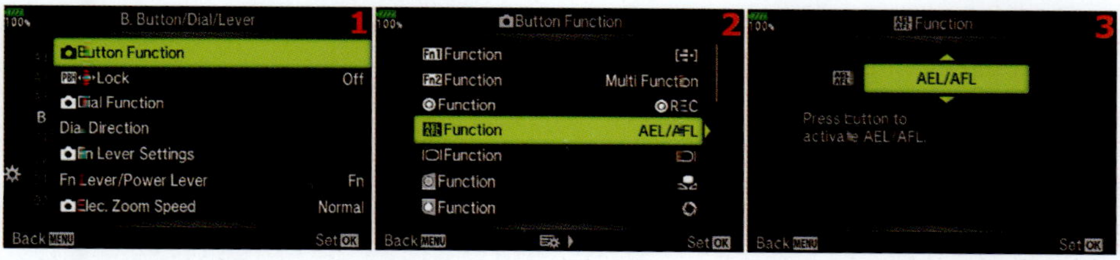

Figure 7.36A: Assigning a Button Task to the AEL/AFL Button Function

Use the following steps to assign one of the Button Tasks to the AEL/AFL Button Function:

1. Choose Button Function from the B. Button/Dial/Lever menu and scroll to the right (figure 7.36A, image 1).
2. Select AEL/AFL Function from the Button Function menu and scroll to the right (figure 7.36A, image 2).
3. Choose one of the available Button Tasks from the up/down menu (figure 7.36A, image 3). Use the **Button Tasks List** in **Appendix A: Still Image Button Task Reference** to decide which task you will assign to the AEL/AFL button.
4. Press the OK button to Set the task for the AEL/AFL button.

Settings Recommendation: The factory default for the AEL/AFL button is AEL/AFL (autoexposure lock and autofocus lock). However, many people enjoy using this button for back-button focus. You can set up back-button focus—where autofocus is initiated by pressing the AEL/AFL button instead of the Shutter button—by using the steps in the **Back-Button Focus Using the AEL/AFL Button** section (on page 409) earlier in this chapter.

[LV] Function

The [LV] button can accept the assignment of most tasks in the **Button Tasks List** in **Appendix A: Still Image Button Task Reference**, found on the downloadable resources website (see page 10). The default factory assignment for the [LV] Function is View Selection, which toggles between the Live View screen and the Super Control Panel on the rear monitor when the EVF Eye Sensor is on, or between the Live View screen and the EVF when the EVF Eye Sensor is off.

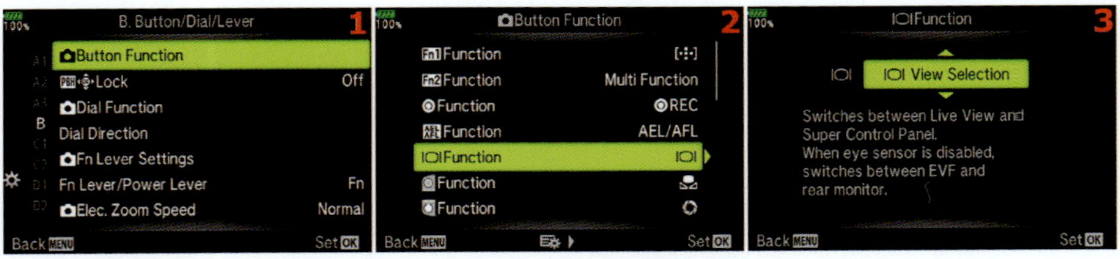

Figure 7.36B: Assigning a Button Task to the [LV] Button Function

Use the following steps to assign one of the Button Tasks to the [LV] Button Function:

1. Choose Button Function from the B. Button/Dial/Lever menu and scroll to the right (figure 7.36B, image 1).
2. Select [LV] Function from the Button Function menu and scroll to the right (figure 7.36B, image 2).
3. Choose one of the available Button Tasks from the up/down menu (figure 7.36B, image 3). Use the **Button Tasks List** in **Appendix A: Still Image Button Task Reference** to decide which task you will assign to the [LV] button.
4. Press the OK button to Set the task for the [LV] button.

Settings Recommendation: I leave this button set to its default because it is really useful to be able to switch between the monitor views easily.

[One-Touch WB] Function

The [One-touch WB] button can accept the assignment of most tasks in the **Button Tasks List** in **Appendix A: Still Image Button Task Reference**, found on the downloadable resources website (see page 10). The default factory assignment for the [One-touch WB] Function is the Button Task with a symbol of a flower (figure 7.37, image 3), which represents One-touch WB.

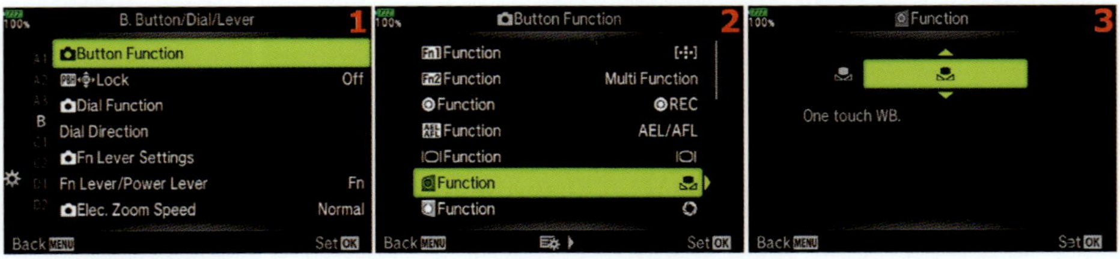

Figure 7.37: Assigning a Button Task to the [One-touch WB] Button Function

Use the following steps to assign one of the Button Tasks to the [One-touch WB] Button Function:

1. Choose Button Function from the B. Button/Dial/Lever menu and scroll to the right (figure 7.37, image 1).

2. Select [One-touch WB] Function from the Button Function menu and scroll to the right (figure 7.37, image 2).
3. Choose one of the available Button Tasks from the up/down menu (figure 7.37, image 3). Use the **Button Tasks List** in **Appendix A: Still Image Button Task Reference** to decide which task you will assign to the [One-touch WB] button.
4. Press the OK button to Set the task for the [One-touch WB] button.

Settings Recommendation: If you do regular white balance readings, the [One-touch WB] task makes it very simple to take a new WB reading from a white card and assign it to one of the four Capture WB memory locations on the WB menu.

On the other hand, if you usually use Auto WB and rarely take special WB readings, the [One-touch WB] Button Function can easily be assigned another Button Task of your choice, such as BKT (bracketing), Peaking, or Magnify (10x). Since I shoot mostly in RAW mode and seldom do specific WB readings, I often assign Magnify to the [One-touch WB] button.

[Preview] Function

The [Preview] button can accept the assignment of most tasks in the **Button Tasks List** in **Appendix A: Still Image Button Task Reference**, found on the downloadable resources website (see page 10). The default factory assignment for the [Preview] Button Function is the Preview task, which has a symbol of the shutter blades of a lens iris (figure 7.38, image 3), representing depth of field (DOF) Preview.

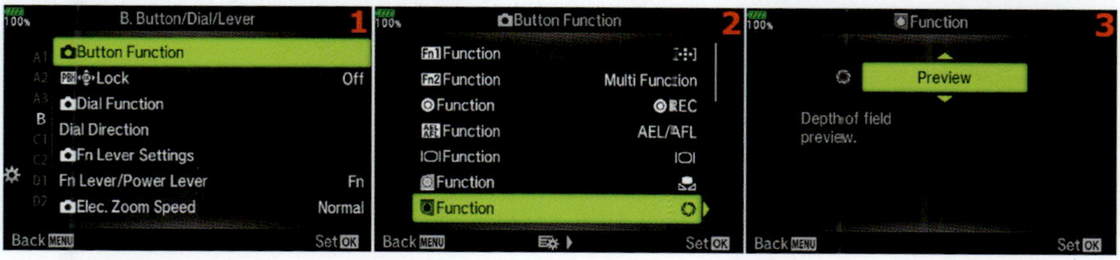

Figure 7.38: Assigning a Button Task to the [Preview] Button Function

Use the following steps to assign one of the Button Tasks to the [Preview] Button Function:

1. Choose Button Function from the B. Button/Dial/Lever menu and scroll to the right (figure 7.38, image 1).
2. Select [Preview] Function from the Button Function menu and scroll to the right (figure 7.38, image 2).
3. Choose one of the available Button Tasks from the up/down menu (figure 7.38, image 3). Use the **Button Tasks List** in **Appendix A: Still Image Button Task Reference** to decide which task you will assign to the [Preview] button.
4. Press the OK button to Set the task for the [Preview] button.

Settings Recommendation: Depth of field preview is a very important functionality. The muscle memory of many photographers is tuned to this location for a depth of field preview button because that's where it is on most cameras. I leave my Preview button set to the Preview task so I can determine how large the zone of sharp focus is for my subject. If you are not using depth of field preview or don't understand depth of field, please take time to learn about it. Depth of field is critical for most types of photography.

My book *Beyond Point-and-Shoot: Learning to Use a Digital SLR or Interchangeable-Lens Camera* covers depth of field quite well. You can review the book here:

http://www.pictureandpen.com/BeyondPS.asp.

◀▲▼▶ Function

The Arrow Pad's four buttons (◀▼▲▶) can have a single task from the **Button Tasks List** in **Appendix A: Still Image Button Task Reference** assigned to it, the [•••] AF Area Select task, or it can be turned off or set to Direct Function. Appendix A is located on the downloadable resources website (see page 10).

If you assign the [•••] AF Area Select task or set this to Off, it will cancel the task assignments of the next two Button Functions: the ▶ button and the ▼ button. When the normal factory default [•••] AF Area Select is chosen, the ▶ and ▼ Functions will be grayed out on the Button Function menu. If you want to use the ▶ and ▼ buttons for one of the eight Button Tasks they each support, you must set the ◀▼▲▶ Function to Direct Function.

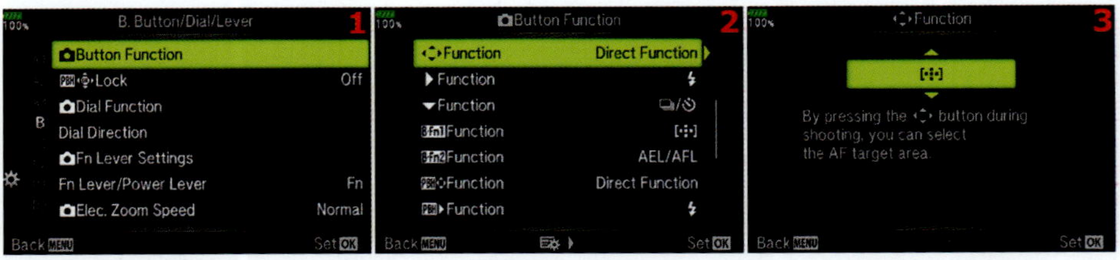

Figure 7.39: Assigning a Button Task to the ◀▼▲▶ Button Function

Use the following steps to configure the ◀▼▲▶ Function:

1. Choose Button Function from the B. Button/Dial/Lever menu and scroll to the right (figure 7.39, image 1).
2. Select ◀▼▲▶ Function from the Button Function menu and scroll to the right (figure 7.39, image 2).
3. Choose Off, [•••] AF Area Select, or Direct Function from the up/down menu (figure 7.39, image 3). When this function is set to Off, the Arrow Pad will still do normal things, such as scroll through pictures and move the AF Area Pointer around, but the individual buttons offer no extra functionality. If it is set to [•••] AF Area Select, the Arrow Pad displays the 121 point AF Area when you press any of the four arrow buttons, so you can move the AF Area Pointer to whichever AF point you want to use for autofocus. Either

of these two settings (Off or [•••] AF Area Select) disables the ▶ and ▼ Functions, and their menu choices become grayed out. If it is set to Direct Function, you can assign one of eight Button Tasks to each of the ▶ and ▼ buttons. Also, when Direct Function is active, the ▲ button opens ± Exposure compensation, and the ◀ button offers the 121 point AF Target screen.

4. Press the OK button to Set the value for the ◀▼▲▶ buttons.

Settings Recommendation: If you constantly move the AF Area Pointer around the screen and carefully choose which AF point to use for autofocus, you may want to set the ◀▼▲▶ Function to [•••] AF Area Select. This gives you the most direct control over which AF point is in use when you press any of the Arrow Pad buttons to open the AF screen with 121 points.

If you do not use AF points very often, you may want to set the ◀▼▲▶ Function to Direct Function and then experiment with the eight tasks you can assign to each of the right and down Arrow Pad keys.

▶ Function

The right button (▶) on the Arrow Pad can accept only eight tasks from the **Button Tasks List** in **Appendix A: Still Image Button Task Reference**, found on the downloadable resources website (see page 10). This Button Function will be grayed out and unavailable unless you have the ◀▲▼▶ Function set to the Direct Function task.

The default factory assignment for the ▶ Button Function is the Button Task called Flash Mode, represented by a lightning bolt symbol.

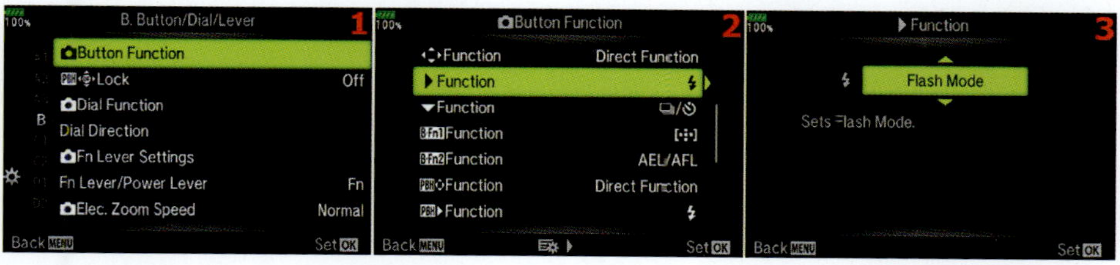

Figure 7.40: Assigning a Button Task to the ▶ Button Function

Use the following steps to assign one of the Button Tasks to the ▶ Button Function:

1. Choose Button Function from the B. Button/Dial/Lever menu and scroll to the right (figure 7.40, image 1).
2. Select ▶ Function from the Button Function menu and scroll to the right (figure 7.40, image 2).
3. Choose one of the available Button Tasks from the up/down menu (Figure 7.40, image 3). Use the **Button Tasks List** in **Appendix A: Still Image Button Task Reference** to decide which task you will assign to the ▶ button.
4. Press the OK button to Set the task for the ▶ button.

Settings Recommendation: I use this button to quickly access Flash Mode. This is faster than pressing the OK button when a subject is on the screen and finding the Flash Mode in the list of items. You can safely leave this function set to Flash Mode, or another mode, because it will work only when you are in shooting mode, which will not interfere with the normal use of the Arrow Pad buttons, such as scrolling through pictures.

▼ Function

The down Arrow Pad button (▼) can accept only eight tasks from the **Button Tasks List** in **Appendix A: Still Image Button Task Reference**, found on the downloadable resources website (see page 10). This Button Function will be grayed out and unavailable unless you have the ◀▲▼▶ Function set to the Direct Function task.

The default factory assignment for the ▼ Button Function is the Sequential Shooting/Self-Timer task, represented by the Sequential Shooting and Self-Timer symbols.

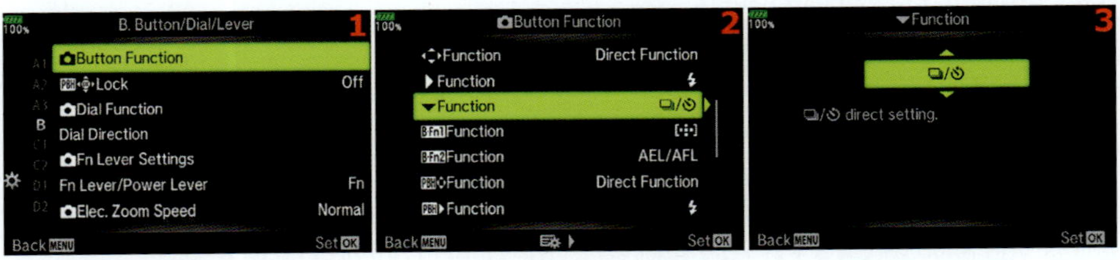

Figure 7.41: Assigning a Button Task to the ▼ Button Function

Use the following steps to assign one of the Button Tasks to the ▼ Button Function:

1. Choose Button Function from the B. Button/Dial/Lever menu and scroll to the right (figure 7.41, image 1).
2. Select ▼ Function from the Button Function menu and scroll to the right (figure 7.41, image 2).
3. Choose one of the available Button Tasks from the up/down menu (figure 7.41, image 3). Use the **Button Tasks List** in **Appendix A: Still Image Button Task Reference** to decide which task you will assign to the ▼ button.
4. Press the OK button to Set the task for the ▼ button.

Settings Recommendation: I use this button to quickly access the WB (white balance) settings. The camera already has a Sequential shooting/Self-timer/HDR button (on the top left of the camera, just above the On/Off button).

You can leave this function set to whatever mode you choose because it will work only when you are in shooting mode, which will not interfere with normal use of the Arrow Pad buttons, such as moving the AF Area Pointer around.

B-Fn1 Function

The B-Fn1 button is found on the optional HLD-9 battery holder. You can use this function only if you have an HLD-9 mounted on your camera. The B-Fn1 button can accept the assignment of most tasks in the **Button Tasks List** in **Appendix A: Still Image Button Task Reference**, found on the downloadable resources website (see page 10). The default factory assignment for the B-Fn1 Button Function is the Button Task named AF Area Select

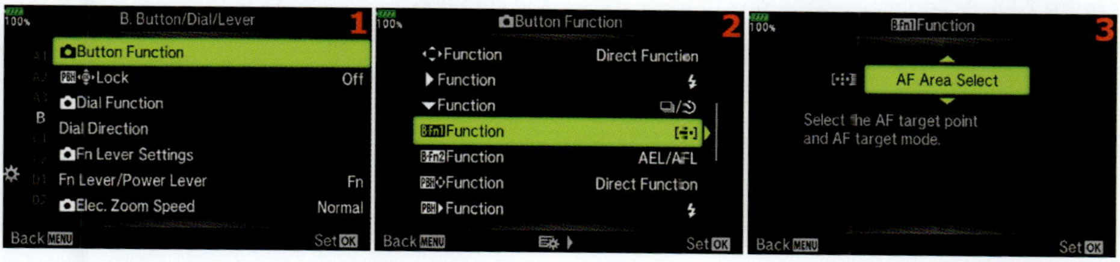

Figure 7.42: Assigning a Button Task to the B-Fn1 Button Function

Use the following steps to assign one of the Button Tasks to the B-Fn1 Button Function:

1. Choose Button Function from the B. Button/Dial/Lever menu and scroll to the right (figure 7.42, image 1).
2. Select B-Fn1 Function from the Button Function menu and scroll to the right (figure 7.42, image 2).
3. Choose one of the available Button Tasks from the up/down menu (figure 7.42, image 3). Use the **Button Tasks List** in **Appendix A: Still Image Button Task Reference** to decide which task you will assign to the B-Fn1 button.
4. Press the OK button to Set the task for the B-Fn1 button.

Settings Recommendation: I left this alone as it helps to have access to this function when holding the camera using the battery grip. Of course, there are so many tasks you can assign to the HLD-9 that this extra button adds functionality to the camera. The cost of an HLD-9 is very reasonable, and it adds a bigger grip and more mass for sharper handheld images.

B-Fn2 Function

The B-Fn2 button is found only on the optional HLD-9 battery holder. You can use this function only if you have an HLD-9 mounted on your camera. The B-Fn2 button can accept the assignment of most tasks in the **Button Tasks List** in **Appendix A: Still Image Button Task Reference**, found on the downloadable resources website (see page 10). The default factory assignment for the B-Fn2 Button Function is the Button Task named AEL/AFL.

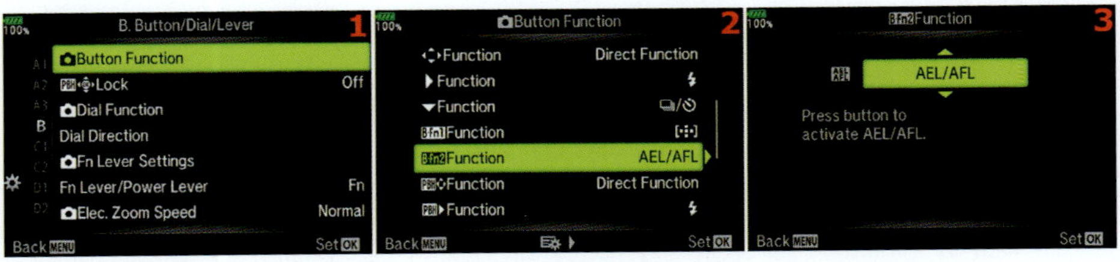

Figure 7.43: Assigning a Button Task to the B-Fn2 Button Function

Use the following steps to assign one of the Button Tasks to the B-Fn2 Button Function:

1. Choose Button Function from the B. Button/Dial/Lever menu and scroll to the right (figure 7.43, image 1).
2. Select B-Fn2 Function from the Button Function menu and scroll to the right (figure 7.43, image 2).
3. Choose one of the available Button Tasks from the up/down menu (figure 7.43, image 3). Use the **Button Tasks List** in **Appendix A: Still Image Button Task Reference** to decide which task you will assign to the B-Fn2 button.
4. Press the OK button to Set the task for the B-Fn2 button.

Settings Recommendation: I assigned the Preview task to the B-Fn2 button. When I rotate the camera for a vertical shot with the HLD-7's Shutter button, I often want to check the depth of field. However, when the camera is rotated my finger will not reach the normal Preview button, so I use the B-Fn2 button instead.

PBH◀▲▼▶ Function

The PBH Arrow Pad (◀▼▲▶) is found only on the optional HLD-9 power battery holder (PBH). It can have a single task from the **Button Tasks List** in **Appendix A: Still Image Button Task Reference** assigned to it, the [•••] AF Area Select task, or it can be turned off or set to Direct Function. Appendix A is located on the downloadable resources website (see page 10).

If you assign the [•••] AF Area Select task or set this to Off, it will cancel the task assignments of the next two Button Functions: the PBH▶ button and the PBH▼ button. When the normal factory default [•••] AF Area Select is chosen, the PBH▶ and PBH▼ Functions will be grayed out on the Button Function menu. If you want to use the PBH▶ and PBH▼ buttons for one of the eight Button Tasks they each support, you must set the PBH◀▼▲▶ Function to Direct Function.

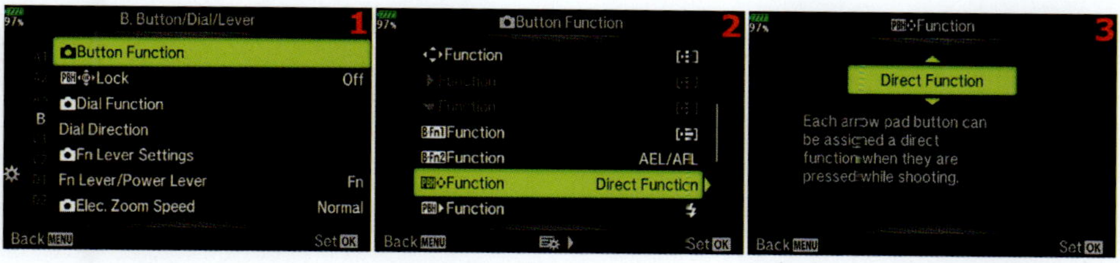

Figure 7.44: Assigning function to the PBH◀▼▲▶ Button Function

Use the following steps to configure the PBH ◀▼▲▶ Function:

1. Choose Button Function from the B. Button/Dial/Lever menu and scroll to the right (figure 7.44, image 1).
2. Select PBH◀▼▲▶ Function from the Button Function menu and scroll to the right (figure 7.44, image 2).
3. Choose Off, [•••] AF Area Select, or Direct Function (figure 7.44, image 3). When it is set to Off, the PBH Arrow Pad will still do normal things such as scroll through pictures and move the AF Area Pointer around, but the individual buttons offer no extra functionality. If it is set to [•••] AF Area Select, the PBH Arrow Pad displays the 121 point AF Area when you press any of the four arrow buttons, so you can move the AF Area Pointer to whichever AF point you want to use for autofocus. Either of these two settings (Off or [•••] AF Area Select) disables the PBH▶ and PBH▼ Functions, and their menu choices become grayed out. If it is set to Direct Function, you can assign one of eight Button Tasks to each of the PBH▶ and PBH▼ buttons. Also, when Direct Function is active, the PHB▲ button opens ± Exposure compensation, and the PBH◀ button offers the 121 point AF Target screen.
4. Press the OK button to Set the value for the PBH◀▼▲▶ buttons.

Settings Recommendation: I set these controls so that they match the Arrow Pad settings on the camera body. That way when I switch to a vertical grip, the controls are the same.

PBH▶ Function

The right Arrow Pad button (▶) on the optional HLD-9 power battery holder (PBH) can accept only eight tasks from the **Button Tasks List** in **Appendix A: Still Image Button Task Reference**, found on the downloadable resources website (see page 10). This Button Function will be grayed out and unavailable unless you have the PBH◀▲▼▶ Function set to the Direct Function task.

The default factory assignment for the PBH▶ Button Function is the Button Task called Flash Mode, represented by a lightning bolt symbol.

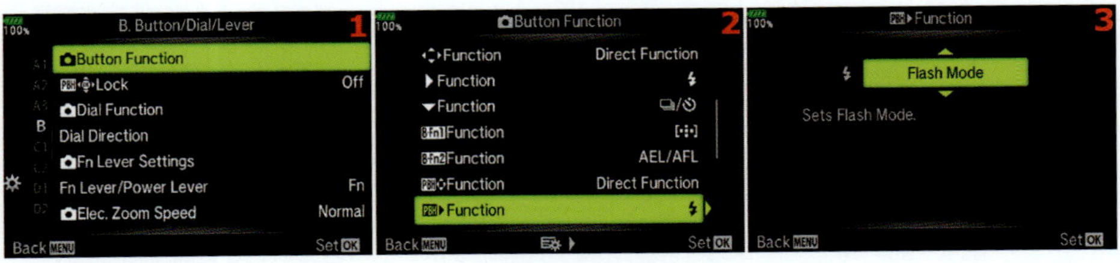

Figure 7.45: Assigning a Button Task to the PBH▶ Button Function

Use the following steps to assign one of the Button Tasks to the PBH▶ Button Function:

1. Choose Button Function from the B. Button/Dial/Lever menu and scroll to the right (figure 7.45, image 1).
2. Select PBH▶ Function from the Button Function menu and scroll to the right (figure 7.45, image 2).
3. Choose one of the available Button Tasks from the up/down menu (figure 7.45, image 3). Use the **Button Tasks List** in **Appendix A: Still Image Button Task Reference** to decide which task you will assign to the PBH▶ button.
4. Press the OK button to Set the task for the PBH▶ button.

Settings Recommendation: I set the Arrow Pad buttons on the optional HLD battery to match the Arrow Pad on the camera for ease of use when using the camera in a vertical orientation. I use this button to quickly access Flash Mode.

PBH▼ Function

The down Arrow Pad button (▼) on the optional HLD-9 power battery holder (PBH) can accept only eight tasks from the **Button Tasks List** in **Appendix A: Still Image Button Task Reference**, found on the downloadable resources website (see page 10). This Button Function will be grayed out and unavailable unless you have the PBH◀▲▼▶ Function set to the Direct Function task.

The default factory assignment for the PBH▼ Button Function is the Sequential Shooting/Self-Timer task, represented by the Sequential Shooting and Self-Timer symbols.

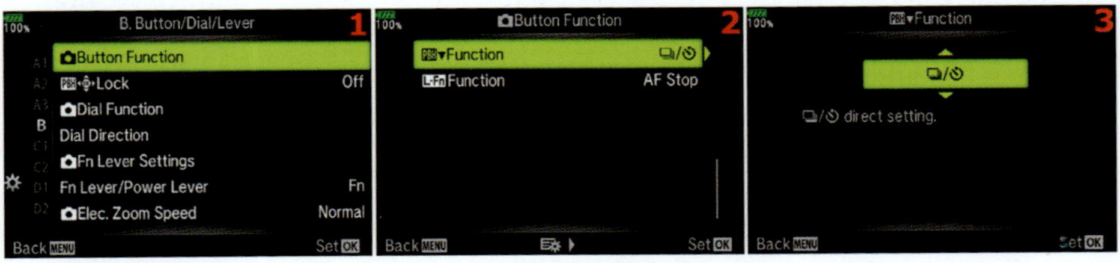

Figure 7.46: Assigning a Button Task to the PBH▼ Button Function

Use the following steps to assign one of the Button Tasks to the PBH▼ Button Function:

1. Choose Button Function from the B. Button/Dial/Lever menu and scroll to the right (figure 7.46, image 1).
2. Select PBH▼ Function from the Button Function menu and scroll to the right (figure 7.46, image 2).
3. Choose one of the available Button Tasks from the up/down menu (figure 7.46, image 3). Use the **Button Tasks List** in **Appendix A: Still Image Button Task Reference** to decide which task you will assign to the PBH▼ button.
4. Press the OK button to Set the Task for the PBH▼ button.

Settings Recommendation: I set the Arrow Pad buttons on the optional HLD battery to match the Arrow Pad on the camera for ease of use when using the camera in a vertical orientation. I use this button to quickly access the WB (white balance) settings.

L-Fn Function

The L-Fn button is found only on certain lenses. For instance, the professional M.Zuiko 12–40mm f/2.8 ED lens has one. You can use this Button Function only if the lens mounted on your camera has the L-Fn button. The L-Fn button can accept the assignment of most tasks in the **Button Tasks List** in **Appendix A: Still Image Button Task Reference**, found on the downloadable resources website (see page 10). The default factory assignment for the L-Fn Button Function is the Button Task named AF Stop, which cannot be assigned to any of the buttons on the camera body.

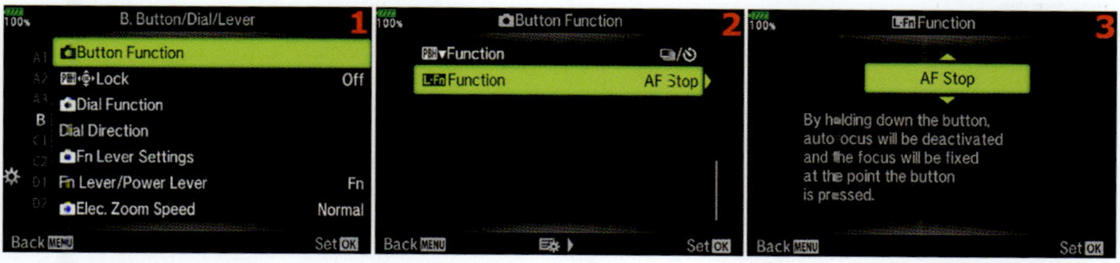

Figure 7.47: Assigning a Button Task to the L-Fn Button Function

Use the following steps to assign one of the Button Tasks to the L-Fn Button Function:

1. Choose Button Function from the B. Button/Dial/Lever menu and scroll to the right (figure 7.47, image 1).
2. Select L-Fn Function from the Button Function menu and scroll to the right (figure 7.47, image 2).
3. Choose one of the available Button Tasks from the up/down menu (figure 7.47, image 3). Use the **Button Tasks List** in **Appendix A: Still Image Button Task Reference** to decide which task you will assign to the L-Fn button.
4. Press the OK button to Set the task for the L-Fn button.

Settings Recommendation: I set the L-Fn button on my lens to [•••] AF Area Select because I often have the factory default button for [•••] AF Area Select (Fn1) assigned to ISO instead. It makes a lot of sense to have the [•••] AF Area Select function assigned to a button on the lens since the lens provides focus.

PBH ◄▼▲► LOCK (B)

The optional HLD-9 power battery holder (PBH) has a second Arrow Pad (◄▼▲►) that can be disabled with this menu choice.

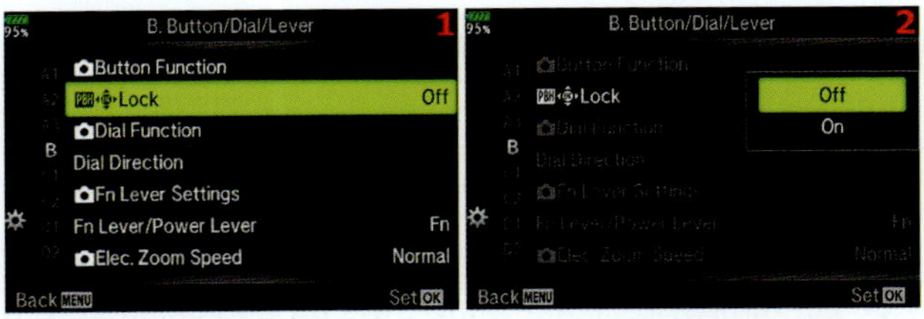

Figure 7.48: Disabling the optional HLD-9 PBH Arrow Pad (◄▼▲►)

Use the following steps disable the optional HLD-9 PBH Arrow Pad (◄▼▲►):

1. Choose PBH ◄▼▲► Lock from the B. Button/Dial/Lever menu and scroll to the right (figure 7.48, image 1).
2. Select On to lock the Arrow Pad on the HLD-9 PBH, or Off to enable it (figure 7.47, image 2).
3. Press the OK button to Set the your choice.

Settings Recommendation: I use the Arrow Pad on the battery grip when shooting in a vertical orientation. Since I like the control I get by using the optional Arrow Pad I do not lock it. Unless you find yourself inadvertently pressing the Arrow Pad on the battery grip when you don't mean to, I recommend keeping this option set to Off.

Dial Function (B)

The E-M1II has two dials on top of the camera: the Front Dial and the Rear Dial. These two dials are used to control various camera functions. Like the camera buttons, they can be configured to do something different than the factory default settings.

The Front and Rear Dials have a relationship with the Mode Dial, in that you can change what the Front and Rear Dials accomplish when you use the different modes (P, A, S, M) on the Mode Dial.

Additionally, the two dials have special functionalities when you use the camera menus or view pictures on the monitor.

Let's examine each of the functions that can be assigned to the Front and Rear Dials.

P Mode Functions

When you set the Mode Dial to P (Program) mode, the Front and Rear Dials offer the eight function combinations shown in table 7.1.

Rear Dial	Front Dial
Ps*	Exposure compensation +/–
Exposure compensation +/–	Exposure compensation +/–
Flash compensation +/–	Exposure compensation +/–
Ps	Flash compensation +/–
Exposure compensation +/–	Flash compensation +/–
Flash compensation +/–	Flash compensation +/–
Ps	Ps
Exposure compensation +/–	Ps

* Ps represents Program shift mode. In P mode the camera controls the shutter speed and aperture so you can simply take pictures. However, Ps allows you to override its choice of aperture for future pictures (until you return to P mode). Ps will be displayed on the camera screens while Program shift mode is active. When you rotate the dial until the camera returns to the original aperture, the camera switches back to P mode.

Table 7.1: P mode Front and Rear Dial function combinations

Now let's examine the screens and steps to choose one of the function combinations shown in table 7.1.

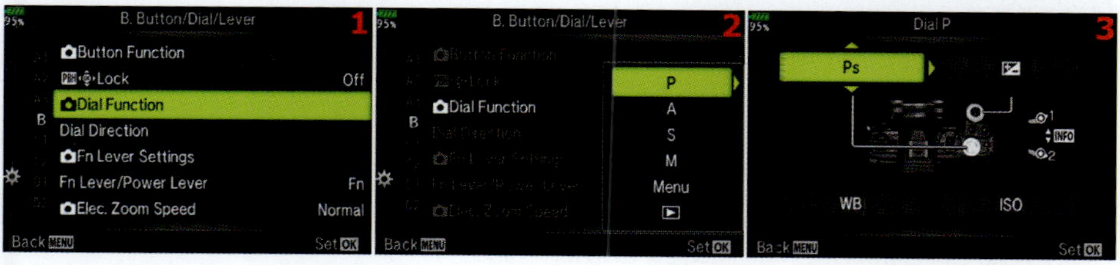

Figure 7.49: Configuring the Front and Rear Dials for P mode

1. Select Dial Function from the B. Button/Dial/Lever menu and scroll to the right (figure 7.49, image 1).
2. A small window will open with the following choices: P, A, S, M, Menu, and ▶. Choose P (Program mode) and scroll to the right (figure 7.49, image 2).
3. You will see a graphical representation of the two dials and their current function assignments (figure 7.49, image 3). The camera defaults to Ps for the Rear Dial and Exposure compensation (+/–) for the Front Dial. There is a small up/down menu. Press up or down to choose different combinations of functions for the two dials. Table 7.1 lists the sequential combinations for pressing down on the Arrow Pad.

4. When you have chosen your favorite dial function combination for P mode, press the OK button to Set the combination.

Settings Recommendation: I leave my camera set to the factory default of Ps/Exposure compensation +/– because I often override the aperture setting when I use P mode.

A Mode Functions

When you set the Mode Dial to A (Aperture-priority) mode, the Front and Rear Dials offer the five function combinations shown in table 7.2.

Rear Dial	Front Dial
FNo.*	Exposure compensation +/–
FNo.	Flash compensation +/–
FNo.	FNo.
Exposure compensation +/–	FNo.
Flash compensation +/–	FNo.

* FNo. stands for f/number or aperture number (e.g., f/2.8, f/5.6, f/8).

Table 7.2: A mode Front and Rear Dial function combinations

Now let's examine the screens and steps to choose one of the function combinations shown in table 7.2.

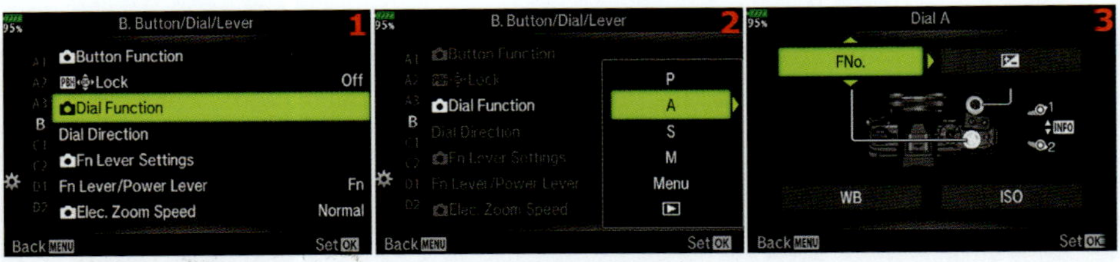

Figure 7.50: Configuring the Front and Rear Dials for A mode

1. Select Dial Function from the B. Button/Dial/Lever menu and scroll to the right (figure 7.50 image 1).
2. A small window will open with the following choices: P, A, S, M, Menu, and ▶. Choose A (Aperture-priority mode) and scroll to the right (figure 7.50, image 2).
3. You will see a graphical representation of the two dials and their current function assignments (figure 7.50, image 3). The camera defaults to FNo. for the Rear Dial and Exposure compensation (+/–) for the Front Dial. There is a small up/down menu. Press up or down to choose different combinations of functions for the two dials. Table 7.2 lists the sequential combinations for pressing down on the Arrow Pad.
4. When you have chosen your favorite dial function combination for A mode, press the OK button to Set the combination.

Settings Recommendation: I leave my camera set to the factory default of FNo./Exposure compensation +/– because it seems reasonable to have the aperture adjusted by the Rear Dial in Aperture-priority mode. However, if you are used to another camera brand, you may be accustomed to having the Front Dial adjust the aperture. Use whichever combination seems most natural to you.

S Mode Functions

When you set the Mode Dial to S (Shutter-priority) mode, the Front and Rear Dials offer the five function combinations shown in table 7.3.

Rear Dial	Front Dial
Shutter*	Exposure compensation +/–
Shutter	Flash compensation +/–
Shutter	Shutter
Exposure compensation +/–	Shutter
Flash compensation +/–	Shutter

* Shutter stands for shutter speed (e.g., 1/60, 1/125, 1/250).

Table 7.3: S mode Front and Rear Dial function combinations

Now let's examine the screens and steps to choose one of the function combinations shown in table 7.3.

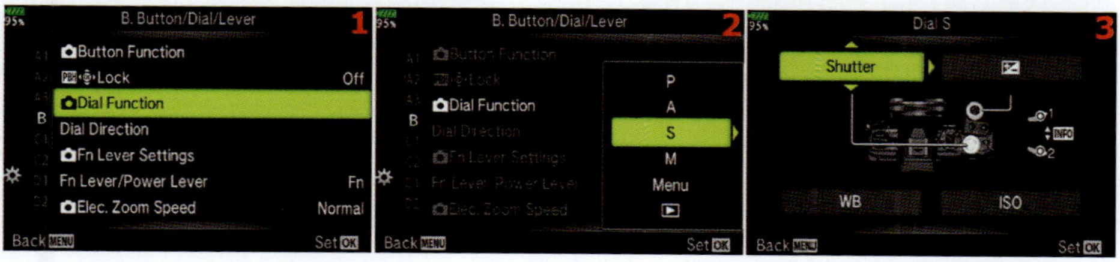

Figure 7.51: Configuring the Front and Rear Dials for S mode

1. Select Dial Function from the B. Button/Dial/Lever menu and scroll to the right (figure 7.51 image 1).
2. A small window will open with the following choices: P, A, S, M, Menu, and ▶. Choose S (Shutter-priority mode) and scroll to the right (figure 7.51, image 2).
3. You will see a graphical representation of the two dials and their current function assignments (figure 7.51, image 3). The camera defaults to Shutter for the Rear Dial and Exposure compensation (+/–) for the Front Dial. There is a small up/down menu. Press up or down to choose different combinations of functions for the two dials. Table 7.3 lists the sequential combinations for pressing down on the Arrow Pad.

4. When you have chosen your favorite dial function combination for S mode, press the OK button to Set the combination.

Settings Recommendation: I leave my camera set to the factory default of Shutter/Exposure compensation +/– because every camera I've used has the rear dial set to adjust the shutter speed in Shutter-priority mode. I don't want to make myself fight muscle memory when I take important pictures!

M Mode Functions

When you set the Mode Dial to M (Manual) mode, the Front and Rear Dials offer the two function combinations shown in table 7.4.

Rear Dial	Front Dial
Shutter*	FNo.*
FNo.	Shutter

* Shutter stands for shutter speed (e.g., 1/60, 1/125, 1/250), and FNo. stands for f/number or aperture number (e.g., f/2.8, f/5.6, f/8).

Table 7.4: M mode Front and Rear Dial function combinations

Now let's examine the screens and steps to choose one of the function combinations shown in table 7.4.

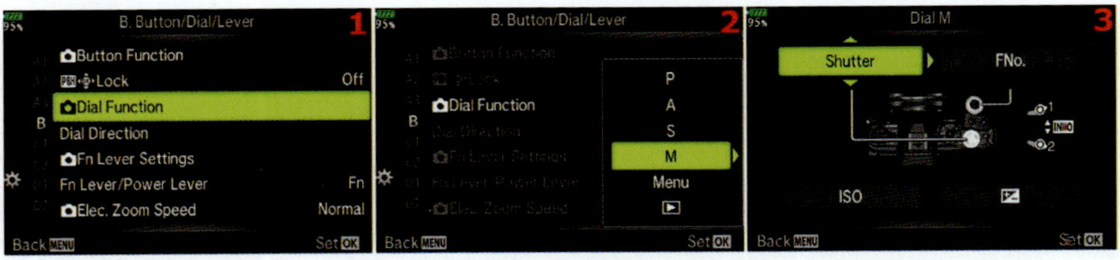

Figure 7.52: Configuring the Front and Rear Dials for M mode

1. Select Dial Function from the B. Button/Dial/Lever menu and scroll to the right (figure 7.52, image 1).
2. A small window will open with the following choices: P, A, S, M, Menu, and ▶. Choose M (Manual mode) and scroll to the right (figure 7.52, image 2).
3. You will see a graphical representation of the two dials and their current function assignments (figure 7.52, image 3). The camera defaults to Shutter for the Rear Dial and FNo. for the Front Dial. There is a small up/down menu. Press up or down to choose different combinations of functions for the two dials. Table 7.4 lists the sequential combinations for pressing down on the Arrow Pad.
4. When you have chosen your favorite dial function combination for M mode, press the OK button to Set the combination.

Settings Recommendation: I leave my camera set to the factory default of Shutter/FNo. because I'm accustomed to that combination. You may prefer a different combination.

Menu Functions

When you use the camera menus to make setting adjustments or when you simply navigate the Menu system, the Front and Rear Dials offer the two combinations shown in table 7.5.

Rear Dial	Front Dial
▲▼/Value	◀▶
◀▶	▲▼/Value

Table 7.5: Menu system navigation Front and Rear Dial function combinations

The arrows in table 7.5 indicate scrolling directions. The factory default is for Rear Dial to scroll up and down (▲ and ▼), and the Front Dial to scroll left and right (◀ and ▶) within the selected Value.

Now let's examine the screens and steps to choose one of the function combinations shown in table 7.5.

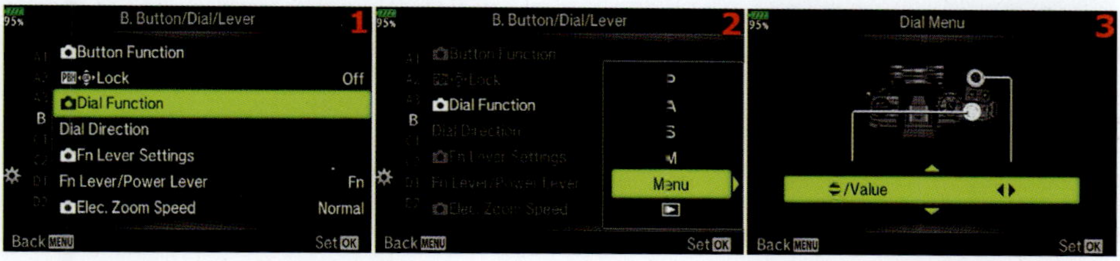

Figure 7.53: Configuring the Front and Rear Dials for moving around in the Menu system

1. Select Dial Function from the B. Button/Dial/Lever menu and scroll to the right (figure 7.53, image 1).
2. A small window will open with the following choices: P, A, S, M, Menu, and ▶. Choose Menu and scroll to the right (figure 7.53, image 2).
3. You will see a graphical representation of the two dials and their current function assignments (figure 7.53, image 3). The camera defaults to ▲▼/Value for the Rear Dial and ◀▶ for the Front Dial. There is a small up/down menu. Press up or down to choose different combinations of functions for the two dials. Table 7.5 lists the sequential combinations for pressing down on the Arrow Pad.
4. When you have chosen your favorite dial function combination for the Menu system, press the OK button to Set the combination.

Settings Recommendation: I leave my camera set to the factory default for using the dials within the Menu system. It seems most natural to me to scroll up and down with the

Rear Dial and left and right with the Front Dial. If you prefer the other direction, simply make the change.

Image Viewing Functions

When you review images on the camera monitor, the Front and Rear Dials offer the two function combinations shown in table 7.6.

Rear Dial	Front Dial
[Zoom in/out]*	Prev/Next
Prev/Next	[Zoom in/out]

* The [Zoom in/out] function uses a graphic that resembles a small checkerboard and a magnifying glass (Figure 7.54, image 3). You can zoom in and out on the picture and select the previous or next picture with the dials.

Table 7.6: Image review Front and Rear Dial function combinations

Now let's examine the screens and steps to choose one of the function combinations shown in table 7.6.

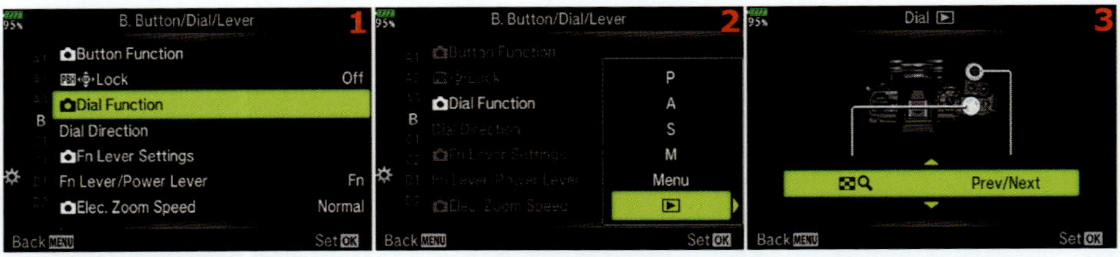

Figure 7.54: Configuring the Front and Rear Dials for Image review navigation (▶)

1. Select Dial Function from the B. Button/Dial/Lever menu and scroll to the right (figure 7.54, image 1).
2. A small window will open with the following choices: P, A, S, M, Menu, and ▶. Choose ▶ and scroll to the right (figure 7.54, image 2).
3. You will see a graphical representation of the two dials and their current function assignments (figure 7.54, image 3). The camera defaults to [Zoom in/out] for the Rear Dial and Prev/Next for the Front Dial. There is a small up/down menu. Press up or down to choose different combinations of functions for the two dials. Table 7.6 lists the sequential combinations for pressing down on the Arrow Pad.
4. When you have chosen your favorite dial function combination for Image review navigation (▶), press the OK button to Set the combination.

Settings Recommendation: I leave my camera set to the factory default of [Zoom in/out] on the Rear Dial and Prev/Next on the Front Dial. If you like the reverse order, you can change it.

Dial Direction (B)

Use Dial Direction to reverse the direction you turn a dial to open and close the aperture (A mode) or raise and lower the shutter speed (S mode). In other words, you can control the direction you turn the dial—clockwise or counterclockwise—to change the aperture or shutter speed.

Dial Direction also allows you to configure Program shift (Ps) mode so the direction you turn the dial either follows or turns in the opposite direction of the current A mode dial direction or S mode dial direction.

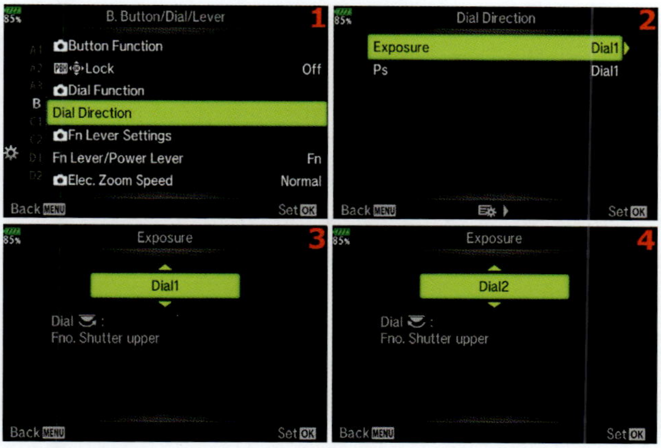

Figure 7.55: Changing the Dial Direction for the Exposure modes

To change the direction you turn the dial for exposure operations, use the following steps:

1. Select Dial Direction from the B. Button/Dial/Lever menu and scroll to the right (figure 7.55, image 1).
2. Choose the Exposure setting from the Dial Direction menu and scroll to the right (figure 7.55, image 2).
3. Select Dial1 from the Exposure up/down menu to leave the dial rotation direction that raises the f/number or aperture set to the factory default (figure 7.55, image 3), or select Dial2 to reverse the normal rotation direction (figure 7.55, image 4).
4. Press the OK button to Set the dial rotation direction.

Next you should consider if you want the direction you turn the dial in Ps mode to match the direction you turn the dial to change the shutter speed or aperture, or if you want it to turn in the opposite direction. Let's see how.

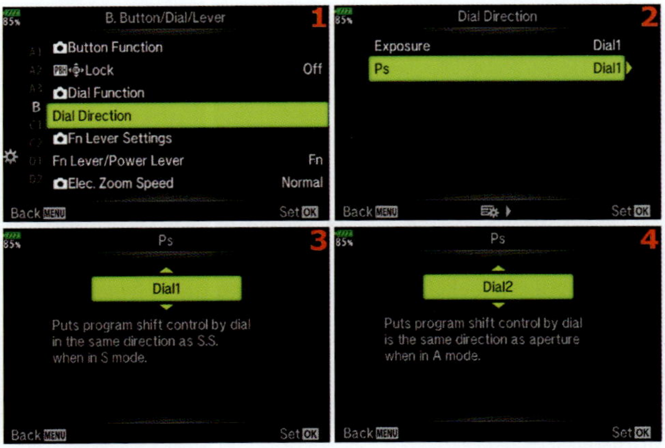

Figure 7.56: Changing the Dial Direction for Program shift (Ps) mode

To change the direction you turn the dial for Ps mode operations, use the following steps:

1. Select Dial Direction from the B. Button/Dial/Lever menu and scroll to the right (figure 7.56, image 1).
2. Choose Ps from the Dial Direction menu and scroll to the right (figure 7.56, image 2).
3. Select Dial1 from the up/down menu to cause the dial rotation to match the direction used when you have the camera set to Shutter-priority (S) mode (figure 7.56, image 3). Select Dial2 to cause the dial rotation to match the direction used when you have the camera set to Aperture-priority (A) mode (figure 7.56, image 4).
4. Press the OK button to Set the Ps mode's dial rotation direction.

Settings Recommendation: In addition to choosing which dial you use to change the shutter speed and aperture, you can use the Dial Direction setting to change the direction you rotate the dials to make exposure adjustments. This is nice for people who are accustomed to turning different dials or turning dials in a different direction.

Fn Lever Settings (B)

The Fn Lever Settings allow you to change how the Front and Rear Dials, Movie button, and Fn2 button work, as well as change the functions of the AF/HDR split button on the top left of the camera, depending on the position of the Fn lever.

Fn Lever Function

The Fn Lever Function allows you to program the Fn Lever so you can use it to quickly switch between two different function sets. In Figure 7.57 you can see that the lever has numbered upper (1) and lower (2) positions. Moving the lever between those two positions changes the basic camera functionality for a number of controls and settings.

First lets look at what the three different Fn Lever Function modes do:

- *mode1*
  e function of the Front and Rear Dials is reversed. You configure the actual dial movement and lever setting in the *B. Button/Dial/Lever > Dial Function* menu.

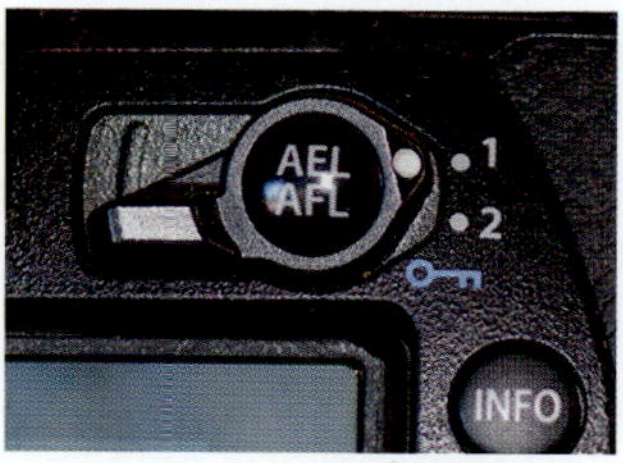

Figure 7.57: The Fn lever set to position I

- *mode2*
  This mode changes the AF mode. You can have one AF mode programmed for position 1 and a second programmed for position 2, allowing you to to easily switch between the two.
- *mode3*
  This allows you to easily switch between still and movie shooting modes, with position 1 being still photography and position 2 being movie recording.

Now let's examine how to choose one of the three modes for the Fn Lever Function.

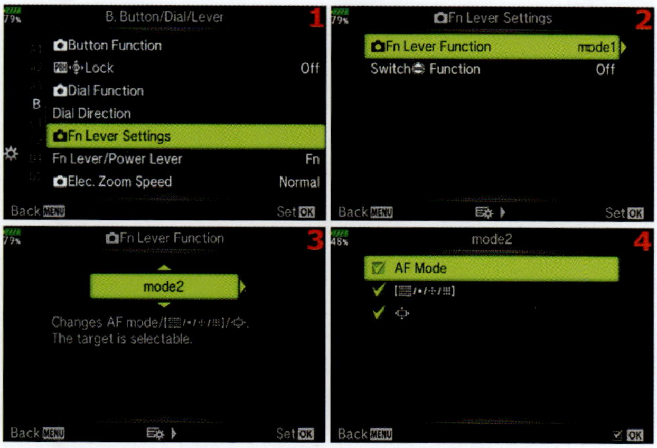

Figure 7.58: Changing modes for the Fn Lever Function

Use the following steps to assign a mode to the Fn Lever Function:

1. Choose Fn Lever Settings from the B. Button/Dial/Lever menu and scroll to the right (figure 7.58, image 1).
2. Choose Fn Lever Function and scroll to the right (figure 7.58, image 2).
3. From the up/down menu, choose one of the four Fn Lever Function modes (mode1, mode2, mode3) or Off (figure 7.58, image 3). When mode2 is selected, you can press the right arrow button and then set the AF modes available (figure 7.58, image 4)
4. Press the OK button to Set the mode for the Fn Lever Function.

Switch [AF/HDR] Function

The Switch [AF/HDR] Function allows you to change the functionality of the AF/HDR button when the Fn Lever is moved to position 2. When this is set to On, the front half of the split button (normally Sequential shooting/Self-timer/HDR) will change to BKT (bracketing) and the rear half of the split button (normally AF/Metering mode) will change to to Flash compensation when the Fn Lever is moved to position 2. It will maintain the normal functionality when the Fn Lever is in position 1.

When the Switch [AF/HDR] Function is set to Off, the AF/HDR button will maintain normal functionality in both Fn Lever positions.

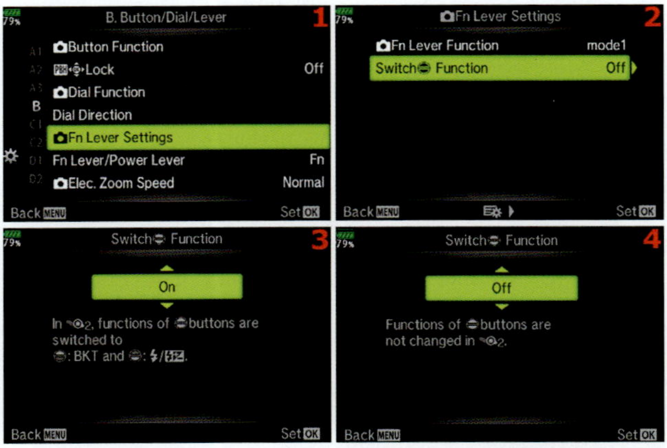

Figure 7.59: Changing the Switch [AF/HDR] Function

Use the following steps to change the functionality of the AF/HDR button with the Fn Lever is moved from position 1 to position 2:

1. Choose Fn Lever Settings from the B. Button/Dial/Lever menu and scroll to the right (figure 7.59, image 1).
2. Choose Switch [AF/HDR] Function and scroll to the right (figure 7.59, image 2).
3. From the up/down menu, choose On or Off (figure 7.58, images 3 and 4).
4. Press the OK button to Set your choice.

Settings Recommendation: This is a interesting way to customize the controls, but it can lead to unexpected behavior if you forget to switch it between modes. I find the mode2 setting in the Fn Lever Function to be very useful because I can set 2 different AF modes and easily switch between the two. For example, set the Fn Lever to the top position (1) and set the AF to C-AF, and then set the Fn Lever to the bottom position and set the AF to S-AF. Now you can switch between the two AF modes by simply moving the Fn Lever from position 1 to position 2. The camera remembers the AF size and the AF target position.

Fn Lever/Power Lever (B)

This setting allows you to use the Fn Lever as a power on/off switch, instead of using the On/Off lever on the top of the camera. When this is enabled, the settings in the Fn Lever Function are not used. There are three available settings:

- **Fn:** The Fn Lever functions according to the settings selected in the Fn Lever Settings menu.
- **Power 1:** The Fn Lever functions as a power on/off switch. Position 1 is On and position 2 is Off.
- **Power 2:** The Fn Lever functions as a power on/off switch. Position 1 is Off and position 2 is On.

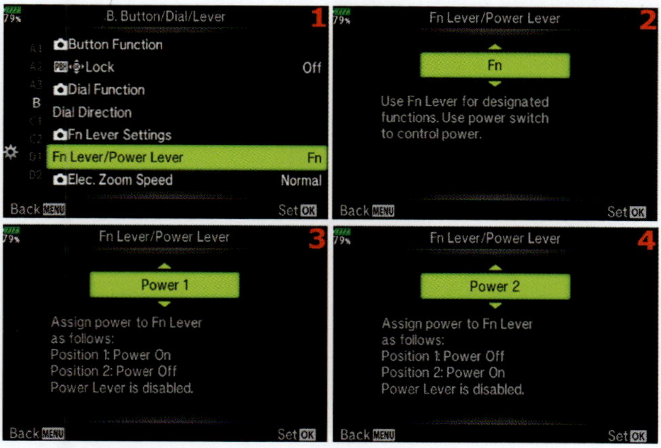

Figure 7.60: Changing the Fn Lever/Power Lever settings

Use the following steps to change the Fn Lever/Power Lever settings:

1. Choose Fn Lever/Power Lever from the B. Button/Dial/Lever menu and scroll to the right (figure 7.60, image 1).
2. Choose Fn, Power 1, or Power 2 from the menu (figure 7.58, image 2–4).
3. Press the OK button to Set your choice.

Settings Recommendation: This might be useful for some people who want to be able to access all of the controls with one hand, but it does reduce the number of functions you have access to.

Elec. Zoom Speed (B)

Olympus makes a few power zoom lenses that allow you to zoom in and out by turning a ring or pressing camera buttons. The Elec. Zoom Speed function allows you to adjust how fast the camera zooms in and out based on three speed levels: Low, Normal, and High. Let's see how to adjust the zoom speed of your power zoom lenses.

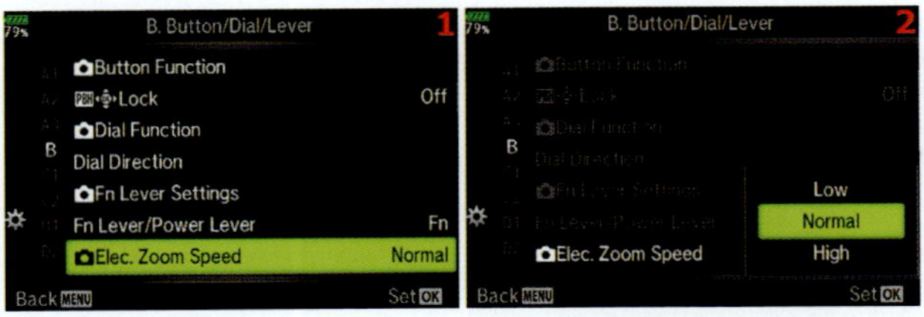

Figure 7.61: Changing the Electronic Zoom Speed

Use these steps to change the power zoom speed of your lens:

1. Select Elec. Zoom Speed from the B. Button/Dial/Lever menu and scroll to the right (figure 7.61, image 1).
2. Select Low, Normal, or High from the menu and press the OK button to Set the speed (figure 7.62, image 2).

Settings Recommendation: I like a fast power zoom when I am shooting pictures, so I set my speed to High. The default Normal power-zooming speed works fine for general use, so that may be sufficient for many photographers.

Custom Menu C1–C2. Release/[Sequential]/Image Stabilizer

The C. Release/[Sequential]/Image Stabilizer menu has two pages of menu options (C1 and C2) that deal with how the camera releases the shutter to take a picture and the built-in image stabilization (figure 7.62).

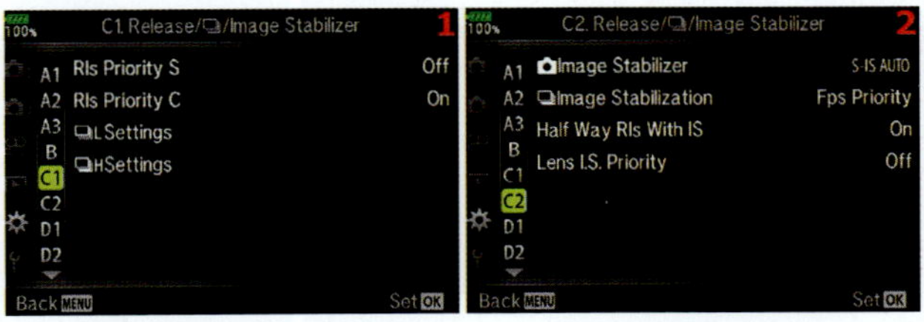

Figure 7.62: The C1-C2 Release/[Sequential]/Image Stabilizer menu

Let's examine each of the C. Release/[Sequential]/Image Stabilizer functions.

Rls Priority S (C1)

The Rls (release) Priority function tells the camera whether it is more important to release the shutter at all costs or to wait until autofocus has focused on the subject before allowing the shutter to release.

This is a major consideration for most types of photography. Who wants out-of-focus images? Rls Priority S is concerned with how release priority works when the camera is set to AF-S (single AF) release mode.

When you shoot one frame at a time, there is usually sufficient time to make sure the subject is in focus before you release the shutter. Therefore, for most types of single AF shooting (autofocus locks on the subject and does not automatically update) the best choice is to set Rls Priority S to Off (factory default).

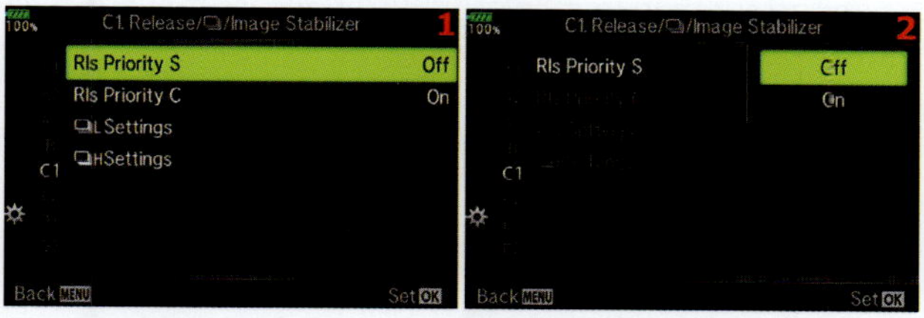

Figure 7.63: Setting release priority for single AF (AF-S) shooting

Use the following steps to enable or disable Rls Priority S:

1. Choose Rls Priority S from the C1. Release/[Sequential]/Image Stabilizer menu and scroll to the right (figure 7.63, image 1).
2. A small window will open with the choices of Off and On (figure 7.63, image 2). Choose Off if you want the camera to release the shutter only if something is in focus (hopefully the subject). Set it to On if you want the camera to release the shutter even if nothing is in focus.
3. Press the OK button to Set your choice.

Settings Recommendation: I am a nature shooter and usually have time to make sure the subject is in focus. I don't want the shutter to release unless the subject (or at least something) is in focus. Most photographers do not shoot moving subjects, action, or sports in AF-S release mode. Instead, they use AF-C for continuous AF. Therefore, for most of us, setting this function to On is the best choice.

Rls Priority C (C1)

When you are shooting in AF-C (continuous AF) mode, the camera never truly locks focus on the subject. It continually seeks the best focus, and you will notice the lens refocusing as the camera and subject move. Rls Priority C is concerned with how the camera releases the shutter in AF-C mode.

If you are photographing a car race, where the cars are passing parallel directly in front of you, your images are often fine with just an initial autofocus operation because the car, although it is moving very fast, does not change distance from you, which allows the depth of field to cover minor focus variations. The focus does not have to be updated often. You can get many shots of the car as it moves parallel to you. For this type of shooting, the camera could be set to release the shutter without concern about AF (Rls Priority C set to On). Shutter release has priority! There may be a few out-of-focus frames, but the majority of images will be in good focus as the camera tries to maintain AF on the subject.

On the other hand, if you are photographing a marathon and the participants are running toward you, autofocus is critical. In this situation it is probably best to set Rls Priority C to Off so the camera will not release the shutter unless the subject is in focus.

This is a highly subjective decision that is based on what type of photography you do. Simply ask yourself if AF is more important than immediate shutter release for your style of shooting.

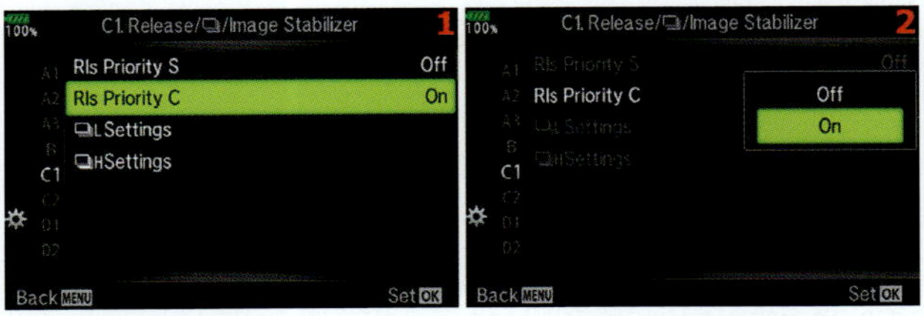

Figure 7.64: Setting release priority for continuous AF (AF-C) shooting

Use the following steps to enable or disable Rls Priority C:

1. Choose Rls Priority C from the C1. Release/[Sequential]/Image Stabilizer menu and scroll to the right (figure 7.64, image 1).
2. A small window will open with the choices of Off and On (figure 7.64, image 2). Choose Off if you want the camera to release the shutter only if something is in focus (hopefully the subject), or set it to On if you want the camera to release the shutter even if nothing is in focus.
3. Press the OK button to Set your choice.

Settings Recommendation: Being a nature photographer biases me toward making sure the subject is in focus for every shot. I don't often have to suffer the frustration of the subject moving at high rates of speed (other than some wildlife).

Again, whether releasing the shutter or obtaining the best focus has a higher priority is a subjective decision. For most photographers, Rls Priority C should be set to Off, because who wants a series of out-of-focus images mixed with in-focus images?

On the other hand, if you have a good understanding of depth of field and know how to use it to cover minor focus variations, releasing the shutter and getting the shot may be a bigger priority than how the camera focuses.

Experiment with Rls Priority C when you are using AF-C mode. If the camera performs well enough in AF-C to keep the subject in reasonable focus, you may want the shutter release to have priority over autofocus.

[Sequential] L Settings (C1)

The E-M1II can shoot in [Sequential] Low and [Sequential] High shooting modes, for low and high frames-per-second rates. The [Sequential] L Settings menu lets you define the Max fps and Frame Count Limiter for each of the following [Sequential] Low shooting modes: [Sequential]/[Steady Sequential], Silent [Sequential], and Pro Capture. The Max fps is the number of images taken per second when you press and hold the Shutter button, and the Frame Count Limiter is the total number of shots taken.

For the Pro Capture setting, you also set the number of Pre-shutter Frames you want the camera to capture. In Pro Capture mode, there are two parts to capturing a burst series of images. First, when you press and hold the Shutter button halfway down, the camera will capture a continuously replaced series of images; these are the Pre-shutter Frames. Second, when you then press the Shutter button all the way down the camera keeps the Pre-shutter Frames, and it continues capturing new images at the frame rate you selected until you release the Shutter button.

Let's walk through the steps to set the Max fps and Frame Count Limiter for each of the [Sequential] Low shooting modes. Then we'll walk through the settings for the Pro Capture Low shooting mode.

[Sequential] Low and [Steady Sequential] Low

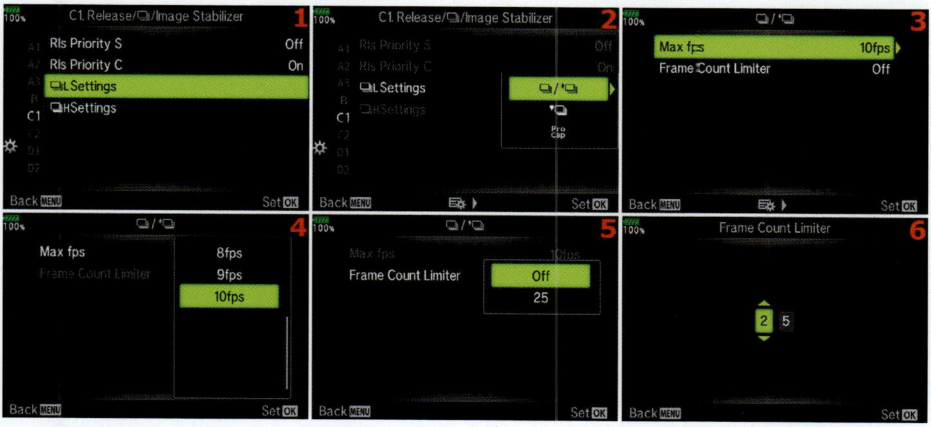

Figure 7.65: Setting the frame rate for the [Sequential] Low and [Steady Sequential] Low shooting modes

Use the following steps to set the frame rate for the [Sequential] Low and [Steady Sequential] Low drive modes:

1. Choose [Sequential] L Settings from the C1. Release/[Sequential]/Image Stabilizer menu and scroll to the right (figure 7.65, image 1).
2. A small window will open with three options: [Sequential]/[Steady Sequential], [Silent Sequential], and Pro Cap (figure 7.65, image 2). Choose [Sequential]/[Steady Sequential] and scroll to the right.
3. Select Max fps from the [Sequential]/[Steady Sequential] menu and scroll to the right (figure 7.65, image 3).
4. A small window will open with a list of frame rates from 1fps to 10fps (figure 7.65, image 4). Select a Max fps and press the OK button to Set your choice and return to the [Sequential]/[Steady Sequential] menu.
5. Use the Arrow Pad to scroll down to Frame Count Limiter, and then scroll to the right.
6. A small window will open with two options: Off and a two-digit number (figure 7.65, image 5). If you select the two-digit number and scroll to the right, you can enter any number from 02 to 99 (default is 25; figure 7.65, image 6). Select the total number of shots you want to take, or select Off to take an unlimited number of shots as long as the Shutter button is pressed.
7. Press the OK button to Set your choice.

[Silent Sequential] Low

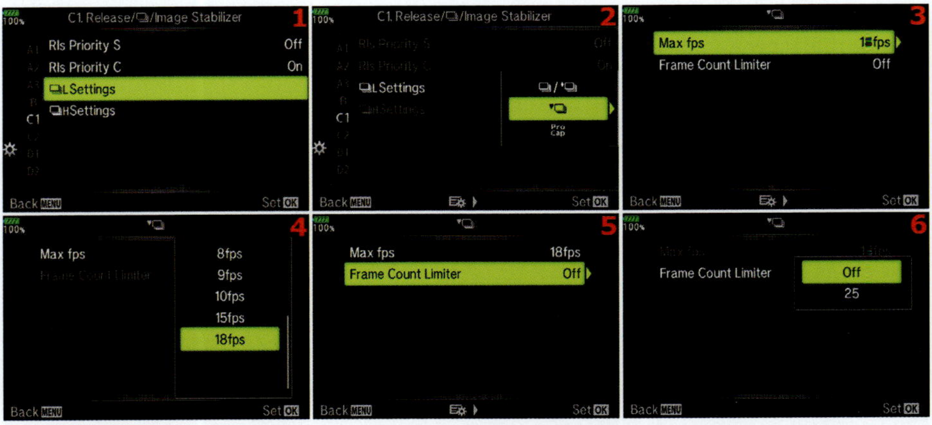

Figure 7.66: Setting the frame rate for the [Silent Sequential] Low shooting mode

Use the following steps to set the frame rate for the [Silent Sequential] shooting mode:

1. Choose [Sequential] L Settings from the C1. Release/[Sequential]/Image Stabilizer menu and scroll to the right (figure 7.66, image 1).

2. A small window will open with three options: [Sequential]/[Steady Sequential], [Silent Sequential], and Pro Cap (figure 7.66, image 2). Choose [Silent Sequential] and scroll to the right.
3. Select Max fps from the [Silent Sequential] menu and scroll to the right (figure 7.66, image 3).
4. A small window will open with a list of frame rates from 1fps to 10fps, 15fps, and 18fps (figure 7.66, image 4). Select a Max fps and press the OK button to Set your choice and return to the [Silent Sequential] menu.
5. Use the Arrow Pad to scroll down to Frame Count Limiter, and then scroll to the right (figure 7.66, image 5).
6. A small window will open with two options: Off and a two-digit number (figure 7.66, image 6). If you select the two-digit number and scroll to the right, you can enter any number from 02 to 99 (default is 25). Select the total number of shots you want to take, or select Off to take an unlimited number of shots as long as the Shutter button is pressed.
7. Press the OK button to Set your choice.

Pro Cap Low

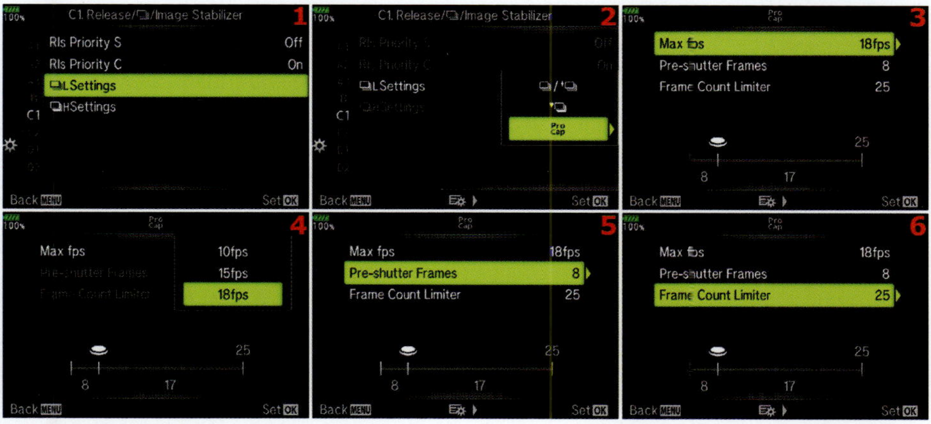

Figure 7.67: Setting the frame rate for the Pro Capture Low shooting mode

Use the following steps to set the frame rate and number of Pre-shutter Frames for the Pro Capture Low shooting mode:

1. Choose [Sequential] L Settings from the C1. Release/[Sequential]/Image Stabilizer menu and scroll to the right (figure 7.67, image 1).
2. A small window will open with three options: [Sequential]/[Steady Sequential], [Silent Sequential], and Pro Cap (figure 7.67, image 2). Choose Pro Cap and scroll to the right.
3. Select Max fps from the Pro Cap menu and scroll to the right (figure 7.67, image 3).

4. A small window will open with a list of three frame rates: 10fps, 15fps, and 18fps (figure 7.67, image 4). Select a Max fps and press the OK button to Set your choice and return to the Pro Cap menu.
5. Scroll down to Pre-shutter Frames and scroll to the right (figure 7.67, image 5). Select the number of frames you would like the camera to capture when you press the Shutter button halfway (before you press the Shutter button all the way down to capture your sequential images). You can choose from 1 to 35 images (default is 8). Press the OK button to Set your choice and return to the Pro Cap menu.
6. Scroll down to Frame Count Limiter and scroll to the right (figure 7.67, image 6). A small window will open with two options: Off and a two-digit number. If you select the two-digit number and scroll to the right, you can enter any number from 02 to 99 (default is 25). Select the total number of shots you want to take, or select Off to take an unlimited number of shots as long as the Shutter button is pressed.
7. Press the OK button to Set your choice.

Settings Recommendation: I leave this menu set to the factory defaults because I usually use the Sequential H shooting modes.

[Sequential] H Settings (C1)

The [Sequential] H Settings menu lets you define the Max fps and Frame Count Limiter for each of the following [Sequential] High shooting modes: [Sequential]/[Steady Sequential], Silent [Sequential], and Pro Capture. The Max fps is the number of images taken per second when you press and hold the Shutter button, and the Frame Count Limiter is the total number of shots taken.

For the Pro Capture setting, you also set the number of Pre-shutter Frames you want the camera to capture. In Pro Capture mode, there are two parts to capturing a burst series of images. First, when you press and hold the Shutter button halfway down, the camera will capture a continuously replaced series of images; these are the Pre-shutter Frames. Second, when you then press the Shutter button all the way down, the camera keeps the Pre-shutter Frames, and it continues capturing new images at the frame rate you selected until you release the Shutter button.

Let's walk through the steps to set the Max fps and Frame Count Limiter for each of the [Sequential] High shooting modes. Then we'll walk through the settings for the Pro Capture High shooting mode.

[Sequential] High and [Steady Sequential] High

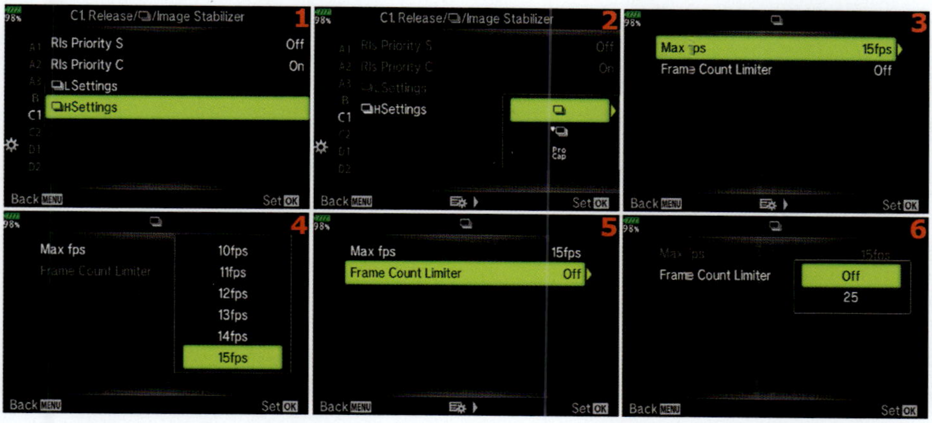

Figure 7.68: Setting the frame rate for the [Sequential] High and [Steady Sequential] High shooting modes

Use the following steps to set the frame rate for the [Sequential] High and [Steady Sequential] High shooting modes:

1. Choose [Sequential] H Settings from the C1. Release/[Sequential]/Image Stabilizer menu and scroll to the right (figure 7.68, image 1).
2. A small window will open with three options: [Sequential]/[Steady Sequential], [Silent Sequential], and Pro Cap (figure 7.68, image 2). Choose [Sequential]/[Steady Sequential] and scroll to the right.
3. Select Max fps from the [Sequential]/[Steady Sequential] menu and scroll to the right (figure 7.68, image 3).
4. A small window will open with a list of frame rates from 10fps to 15fps (figure 7.68, image 4). Select a Max fps and press the OK button to Set your choice and return to the [Sequential]/[Steady Sequential] menu.
5. Use the Arrow Pad to scroll down to Frame Count Limiter, and then scroll to the right (figure 7.68, image 5).
6. A small window will open with two options: Off and a two-digit number (figure 7.68, image 6). If you select the two-digit number and scroll to the right, you can enter any number from 02 to 99 (default is 25). Select the total number of shots you want to take, or select Off to take an unlimited number of shots as long as the Shutter button is pressed.
7. Press the OK button to Set your choice.

[Silent Sequential] High

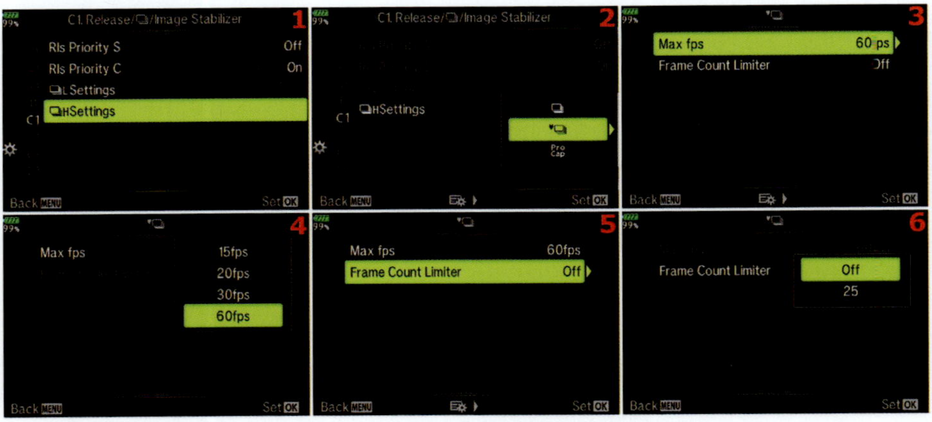

Figure 7.69: Setting the frame rate for [Silent Sequential] High shooting mode

Use the following steps to set the frame rate for the [Silent Sequential] High shooting mode:

1. Choose [Sequential] H Settings from the C1. Release/[Sequential]/Image Stabilizer menu and scroll to the right (figure 7.69, image 1).
2. A small window will open with three options: [Sequential]/[Steady Sequential], [Silent Sequential], and Pro Cap (figure 7.69, image 2). Choose [Silent Sequential] and scroll to the right.
3. Select Max fps from the [Sequential]/[Steady Sequential] menu and scroll to the right (figure 7.69, image 3).
4. A small window will open with a list of frame rates: 15fps, 20fps, 30fps, and 60fps (figure 7.69, image 4). Select a Max fps and press the OK button to Set your choice and return to the [Silent Sequential] menu.
5. Use the Arrow Pad to scroll down to Frame Count Limiter, and then scroll to the right (figure 7.69, image 5).
6. A small window will open with two options: Off and a two-digit number (figure 7.69, image 6). If you select the two-digit number and scroll to the right, you can enter any number from 02 to 99 (default is 25). Select the total number of shots you want to take, or select Off to take an unlimited number of shots as long as the Shutter button is pressed.
7. Press the OK button to Set your choice.

Pro Cap High

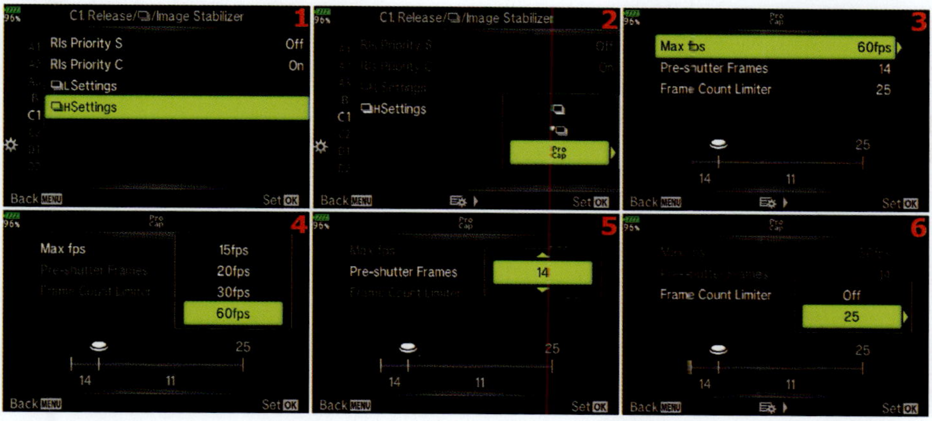

Figure 7.70A: Setting the frame rate for the Pro Capture High shooting mode

Use the following steps to set the frame rate for the Pro Capture High shooting mode:

1. Choose [Sequential] H Settings from the C1. Release/[Sequential]/Image Stabilizer menu and scroll to the right (figure 7.70A, image 1).
2. A small window will open with three options: [Sequential]/[Steady Sequential], [Silent Sequential], and Pro Cap (figure 7.70A, image 2). Choose Pro Cap and scroll to the right.
3. Select Max fps from the Pro Cap menu and scroll to the right (figure 7.70A, image 3).
4. A small window will open with a list of four frame rates: 15fps, 20fps, 30fps, and 60fps (figure 7.70A, image 4). Select a Max fps and press the OK button to Set your choice and return to the Pro Cap menu.
5. Scroll down to Pre-shutter Frames and scroll to the right (figure 7.70A, image 5). Select the number of frames you would like the camera to capture when you press the Shutter button halfway (before you press the Shutter button all the way down to capture your sequential images). You can choose from 1 to 35. Press the OK button to Set your choice and return to the Pro Cap menu.
6. Scroll down to Frame Count Limiter and scroll to the right (figure 7.70A, image 6). A small window will open with two options: Off and a two-digit number. If you select the two-digit number and scroll to the right, you can enter any number from 02 to 99 (default is 25). Select the total number of shots you want to take, or select Off to take an unlimited number of shots as long as the Shutter button is pressed.
7. Press the OK button to Set your choice.

Settings Recommendation: I leave the [Sequential] H settings at their factory defaults, which allows me to shoot at the highest possible frame rate when photographing action and sports.

[Photo] Image Stabilizer (C2)

The built-in image stabilizer on the E-M1II is very responsive and can help with getting a tack-sharp image at slower shutter speeds and when the camera isn't all that stable. However, there are times when you might not want the image stabilizer to work on all possible axes, such as when you are panning the camera to show motion. The Custom Menu's Image Stabilizer function allows you to set the following IS modes for still photography:

- **S-IS Off:** Image stabilizer is turned off.
- **S-IS Auto:** The camera detects the panning motion and applies the proper image stabilization.
- **S-IS 1:** The image stabilizer is on all the time and tries to compensate for all movement.
- **S-IS 2:** Image stabilization applies only to vertical movement.
- **S-IS 3:** Image stabilization applies only to horizontal movement.

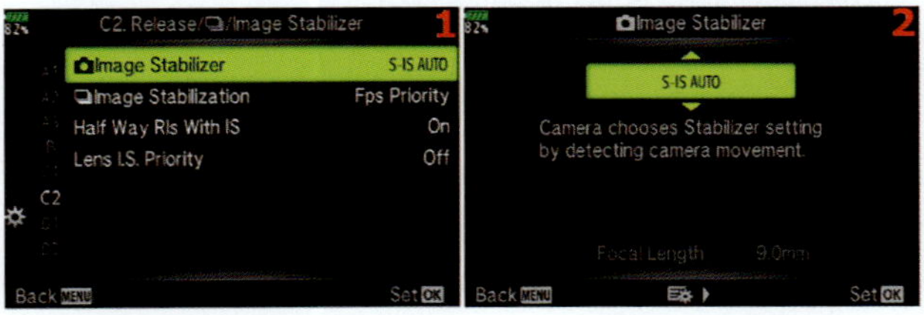

Figure 7.70B: Selecting an IS mode

Use the following steps to select an IS mode:

1. Choose [Photo] Image Stabilizer from the C2. Release/[Sequential]/Image Stabilizer menu and scroll to the right (figure 7.70B, image 1).
2. Refer to the previous list and select one of the IS modes from the up/down menu (figure 7.70B, image 2).
3. Press the OK button to Set your choice.

Settings Recommendation: The image stabilizer on the E-M1II works quite well, so I leave this set to S-IS Auto. Test it out to decide which setting works best for your photography.

Image Stabilization (C2)

The computer inside the E-M1II is very impressive, but even the best computers will slow down when performing multiple tasks. The Image Stabilization function lets you decide what is more important when you are shooting bursts of images: shooting speed (frame rate) or image stabilization.

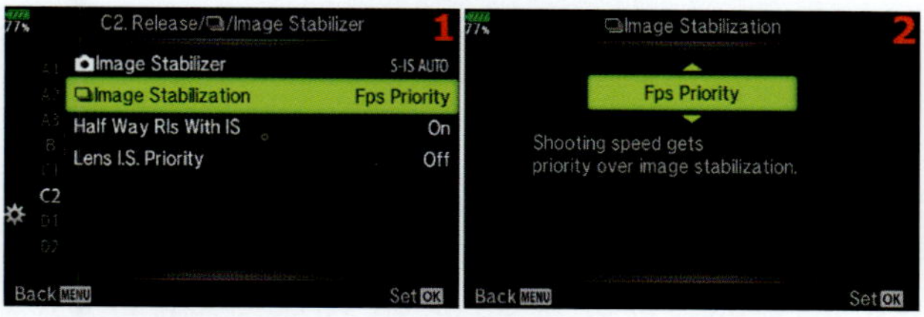

Figure 7.70C: Choosing an Image Stabilization setting

Use the following steps to select an Image Stabilization setting:

1. Choose Image Stabilization from the C2. Release/[Sequential]/Image Stabilizer menu and scroll to the right (figure 7.70C, image 1).
2. Choose Fps Priority or IS Priority from the up/down menu (figure 7.70C, image 2). Fps Priority gives priority to shooting speed (frame rate), and IS Priority gives priority to image stabilization.
3. Press the OK button to Set your choice.

Settings Recommendation: When I'm shooting action and sports with a high frame rate, it is more important to have a high frame rate than image stabilization, so I keep this set to Fps Priority.

Half Way Rls With IS (C2)

When you press the Shutter button halfway down with the Half Way Rls With IS function set to On, the 5-axis image stabilization (IS) system becomes active and stabilizes the image in the viewfinder or on the monitor.

Some people find the sudden cessation of small movements distracting, and others report that it makes them feel queasy. If you are bothered by seeing the IS system in action, you can disable it during subject viewing only. The camera still uses the IS system during the exposure, even if you turn it off for viewing the subject.

Let's examine how to turn IS on and off during subject viewing only (i.e., when you press the Shutter button halfway).

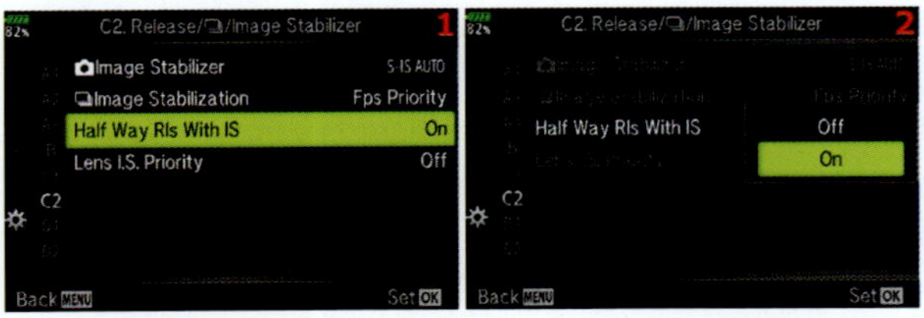

Figure 7.70D: Enabling or disabling the IS system during subject viewing only

Use the following steps to enable or disable the IS system during subject viewing in the viewfinder or on the monitor:

1. Choose Half Way Rls With IS from the C 2. Release/[Sequential]/Image Stabilizer menu and scroll to the right (figure 7.70D, image 1).
2. A small window will open with the choices of On or Off (figure 7.70D, image 2). If you choose On, the camera will use the IS system to stabilize the subject in the viewfinder or on the monitor. If it is set to Off, the camera stabilizes the image only during the actual exposure. The factory default is On.
3. Press the OK button to Set your choice.

Settings Recommendation: I leave this function set to On. I enjoy seeing my subject stabilized in the viewfinder when I hold the Shutter button halfway down. However, you may not like the way it makes you feel, so turn it off. Evidently, the camera will still use the IS system during the exposure. However, I think it is better to have the image stabilized before the exposure so it doesn't have to be done quickly at the moment of exposure. With fast shutter speeds it may not have time to stabilize. Test this for yourself and form your own opinion.

Lens I.S. Priority (C2)

Since the E-M1II is a Micro Four Thirds camera, within a sizable group of other Micro Four Thirds cameras, there are many non-Olympus lens choices. You may own or want to purchase another brand of Micro Four Thirds lens. If the lens has built-in image stabilization, it will work with the in-body stabilization of the E-M1II.

Lens I.S. Priority allows you to assign priority to a non-Olympus lens that has stabilization built in. Or you can make the E-M1II's IS system take priority. Let's see how it is done.

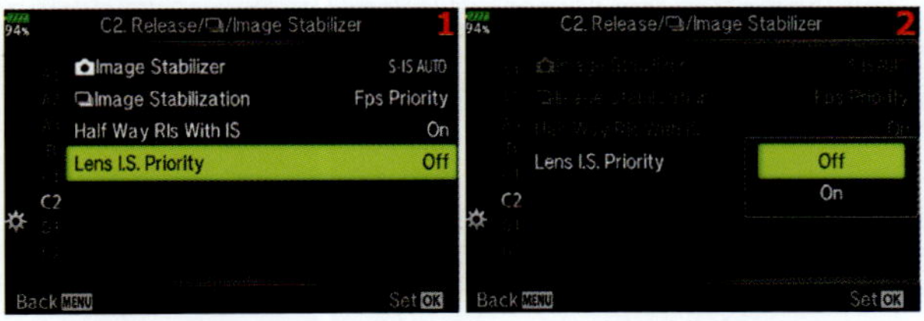

Figure 7.70E: Setting the priority for IS to lens or body

Use the following steps to enable Lens I.S. Priority or assign priority to the E-M1II's 5-axis in-body sensor stabilization:

1. Choose Lens I.S. Priority from the C2. Release/[Sequential]/Image Stabilizer menu and scroll to the right (figure 7.70E, image 1).
2. A small window will open with the choices of On or Off (figure 7.70E, image 2). If you choose On, the camera will use the I.S. system in the lens to stabilize the subject. If you choose Off, the camera's 5-axis IS system stabilizes the image instead. The factory default is Off. If you decide to use the in-camera stabilization with a lens that has built-in stabilization, set this function to Off to disable the stabilization in the lens.
3. Press the OK button to Set your choice.

Settings Recommendation: I enjoy M.Zuiko and Zuiko lenses (with my MMF-3 adapter). Therefore, I don't currently own other brands of Micro Four Thirds lenses, even though there are some mighty appealing lenses out there.

The 5-axis image stabilization in the E-M1II is so amazingly amazing that I am completely amazed! I doubt any other lens stabilization system could match it. Therefore, I prefer to use in-body stabilization and have this set to Off.

Custom Menu D1-D4. Disp/[Sound]/PC

Custom Menu D. Disp/[Sound]/PC contains 19 functions split over four menu pages (D1–D4) that pertain to the camera displays, sound system, and connectivity with a personal computer (PC).

Let's look at each of the four menu pages and what they contain, and then we will consider each of the 19 functions individually. The menu pages are displayed in figure 7.71, images 1–4.

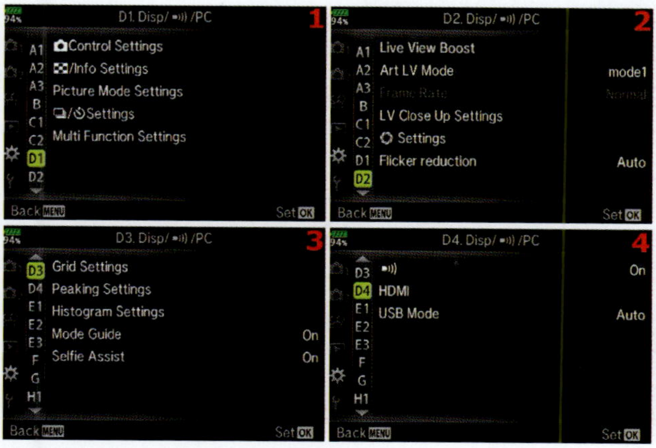

Figure 7.71: Custom Menu D1–D4. Disp/[Sound]/PC menu

[Shooting Mode] Control Settings (D1)

The E-M1II offers four control panel displays, as discussed further in the chapter **Screen Displays for Camera Control**. The [Shooting Mode] Control Settings function allows you to select which control panel screens are available when you use one of the modes on the Mode Dial: iAUTO, P/A/S/M, or ART.

The control panel displays are as follows (in alphabetical order):

- **ART menu (1):** Use to select one of 12 ART modes or ART BKT (bracketing).
- **Live Control (2):** Use to control image stabilization, picture mode, white balance, shutter release mode, image aspect, record mode, movie quality, flash mode, flash compensation, metering mode, autofocus mode, ISO, face & eye priority, and video sound.
- **Live Guide (3):** Use to change color saturation and warmth, brightness, background blur, motion effects, and shooting tips.
- **Super Control Panel (Live SCP) (4):** Use to control ISO, white balance, white balance fine-tuning, picture mode, image sharpness, image contrast, flash mode, AF area, AF mode, image saturation, image gradation, face priority, color space, flash intensity, sequential shooting/self-timer, metering mode, Fn1 button assignment, image stabilizer, record mode, and image aspect.

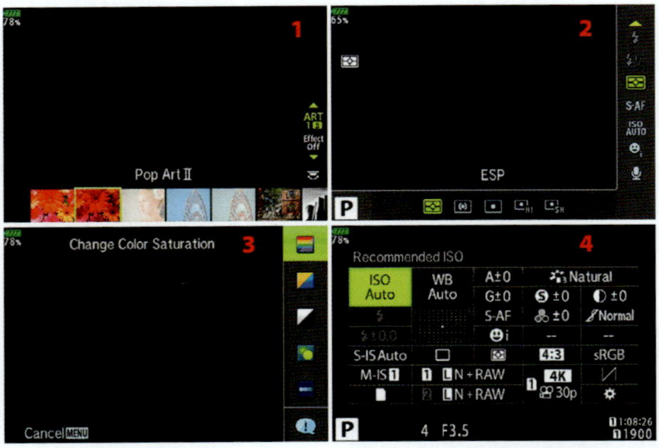

When you have a shooting mode selected on the Mode Dial and have pressed the OK button to open a control panel display, you can press the Info button to move among some of the displays. Table 7.9 shows which control panel displays can be used with which Mode Dial selections when you press the Info button.

	Art menu	Live control	Live guide	Live SCP
iAUTO		✓	✓	✓
P/A/S/M		✓		✓
ART	✓	✓		✓

Table 7.9: Control panel displays that can be used with Mode Dial selections

Now let's examine how to select which control panel displays cycle through with the Info button when you use each mode on the Mode Dial.

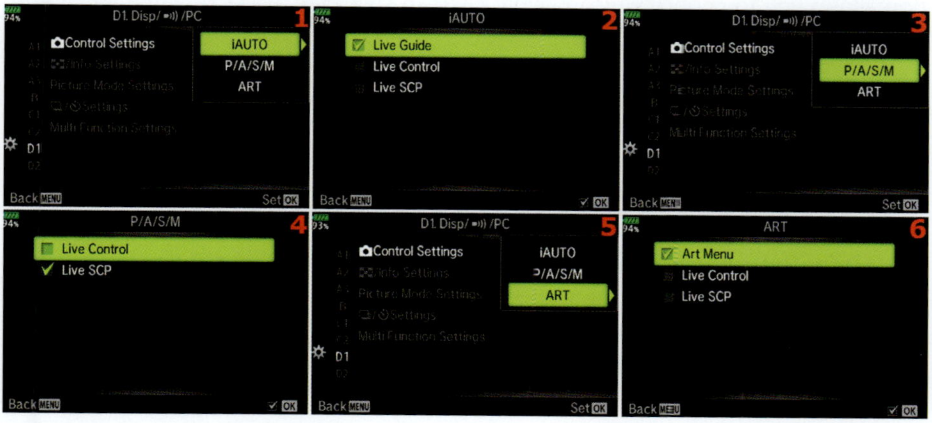

Figure 7.72: Choosing control panel displays for Mode Dial selections

Use the following steps to choose control panel displays for Mode Dial selections:

1. Select [Shooting Mode] Control Settings from the D1. Disp/[Sound]/PC menu and scroll to the right (figure 7.72, image 1).
2. Select one of the three shooting mode settings—iAUTO, P/A/S/M, or ART—from the [Shooting Mode] Control Settings up/down menu (figure 7.72, images 1, 3, and 5). Figure 7.72, images 2, 4, and 6, show the choices under each of the three shooting mode settings. Check each item you want to be available under that shooting mode by highlighting it and pressing the OK button to insert a check mark. Press the Info button to scroll through the selected screens for that shooting mode.
3. Press the OK button on each screen (figure 7.72, images 2, 4 and 6) to Set your choice for that shooting mode.

Settings Recommendation: I enjoy using Live control. It seems the most intuitive and easy to use, so I like it to be available on any shooting mode I use. The Super Control Panel (Live SCP) can also be useful in a similar way, although it is not as intuitive to me. However, I leave it as one of my choices in P/A/S/M and iAUTO modes.

I rarely use the ART mode as it seems to be useful only when I don't want to worry about camera settings. Therefore, I ignore the Live Control and Live SCP selections under the ART screen and place a check mark next to Art Menu only.

[Image Review]/Info Settings (D1)

The E-M1II can display several different picture information screens when you press the Info button. These screens vary depending on the current camera mode, and you can cycle through the available screens for each mode by continuing to press the Info button. The camera also provides five different Image Review screen styles.

The [Image Review]/Info Settings menu allows you to choose which information screens are available for each of the first three modes in the following list. The final option allows you to choose which playback screen styles are available when you are reviewing images.

- ► **Info:** This setting allows you to choose which information screens are available during image playback. The camera enters this mode when you press the image Playback button (►).
- **►[Magnify] Info:** This setting allows you to choose which information screens are available during magnified image playback.
- **LV-Info:** This setting allows you to choose which information screens are available when the camera is in shooting mode and you are viewing the subject on the monitor or in the viewfinder.
- **[Image Review] Settings:** This setting allows you to choose which of the following image viewing screens are available during image playback: Single-frame playback; 4, 9, 25, and 100 frame image index; My Clips; and Calendar display. After you press the ► Playback button, you can access these image viewing screens by rotating the Rear Dial clockwise. You do not use the Info button to access these screens.

Let's take a look at each of these modes.

► Info (Playback)

You can access the six Playback info screens by pressing the ► Playback button on the back bottom right of the camera, viewing an image on the screen, then pressing the Info button repeatedly.

The following list provides an overview of the six available screens you can use when you view images on the monitor. The Standard Image Review screen is always available and cannot be disabled.

- **Standard Image Review:** This basic screen displays the following: Date and time, image number, frame number, image aspect, and record mode. This screen cannot be disabled, and thus does not appear in the ► Info menu.
- **Image Only:** This is the most basic screen. It shows only a picture of the subject with no camera or shooting information. This is great for judging the quality of the image with no distractions.
- **Overall:** This more complex screen displays a number of informational items, along with a small picture of the subject. The following information is shown on the screen:
    - Exposure mode
    - Shutter speed
    - Aperture
    - Metering mode
    - ± compensation

    - Lens focal length
    - White balance mode
    - White balance adjustments
    - Image aspect
    - Record mode
    - Image number
    - Frame number
    - Date
    - Time
    - Luminance histogram
    - RGB channel histograms
    - Thumbnail image display with AF point shown
- **[Histogram]:** This shows the full image with the basic histogram overlaid, showing the distribution of the tones from black to white.
- **Highlight&Shadow:** This shows the full image with the areas that are blown out (pure white) as orange, and the areas that are totally underexposed (pure black) as blue. This allows you to easily and quickly see the areas that are pure white or pure black.
- **Light Box:** This feature allows you to compare two images side by side. With the first image displayed on the monitor, press the Info button until a split screen appears. The selected image is displayed on the left and the next image taken is displayed on the right. You can change the image displayed on the right by scrolling left or right with the Arrow Pad.

The factory default setting is for Image Only and Overall to be enabled, and for Histogram, Highlight&Shadow, and Light Box to be disabled. As previously mentioned, the Standard Image Review screen is always available.

Let's see how to select information screens for ▶ Info.

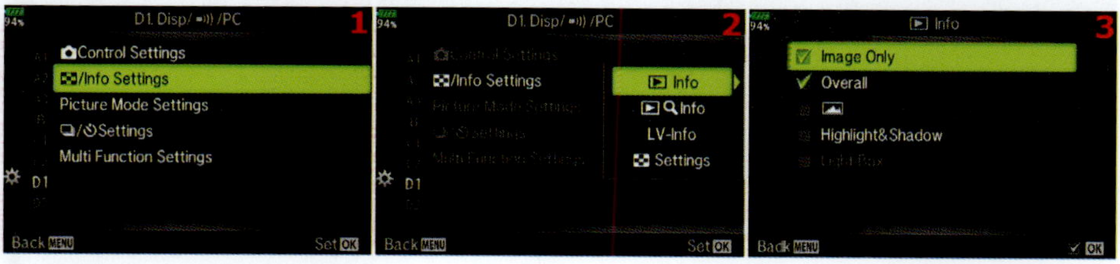

Figure 7.73: ▶ Info screen choices

Use the following steps to enable or disable information screens for ▶ Info:

1. Select [Image Review]/Info Settings from the D1. Disp/[Sound]/PC menu and scroll to the right (figure 7.73, image 1).
2. Select the ▶Info setting from the [Image Review]/Info Settings menu and scroll to the right (figure 7.73, image 2).

3. You will see five information screen choices (figure 7.73, image 3). Place a check mark to the left of each screen you want to use. To add or remove a check mark, simply highlight the choice and press the OK button.
4. When you insert a check mark, the camera automatically saves the choice. Press the Menu button to return to the previous screen.

Settings Recommendation: I set my camera to have all the ▶ Info screens available. They are all useful!

▶[Magnify] Info

When the camera is in Playback mode and you have set an Fn button to [Magnify] these are the screens that are available when you press the assigned Fn button or the Info button. There are three choices here:

- **Magnify Frame:** This shows the full frame with an outline of the area to be magnified. You can adjust the size of the area with the Rear Dial and you can move the frame by using your finger on the touch screen.
- **Magnify Scroll:** This magnifies a portion of the image. You can adjust the size of the magnified area with the Rear Dial and you can move to a different area of the image by using your finger on the touch screen.
- **Select Frame:** This magnifies a portion of the image displayed on the monitor, and stays in magnification mode as you scroll through the other images on the memory card.

Let's see how to select the information screens for ▶ [Magnify] Info.

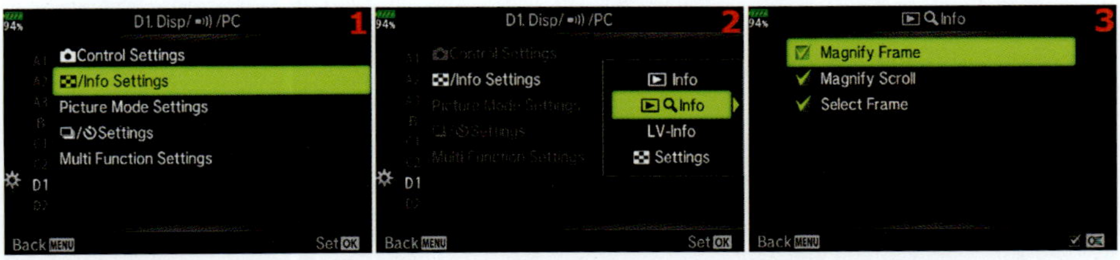

Figure 7.74: ▶[Magnify] Info screen choices

Use the following steps to enable or disable information screens for ▶[Magnify] Info:

1. Select [Image Review]/Info Settings from the D1. Disp/[Sound]/PC menu and scroll to the right (figure 7.74, image 1).
2. Select the ▶[Magnify] Info setting from the [Image Review]/Info Settings menu and scroll to the right (figure 7.74, image 2).
3. You will see three information screen choices (figure 7.74, image 3). Place a check mark to the left of each screen you want to use. To add or remove a check mark, simply highlight the choice and press the OK button.

4. When you insert a check mark, the camera automatically saves the choice. Press the Menu button to return to the previous screen.

Settings Recommendation: I keep all three options checked. This allows me to quickly and easily magnify the most important parts of the image.

LV (Live View) Info

The LV-Info screens have similar functionality to the ▶ Info screens, except they are live, based on the subject that is displayed on the monitor instead of an existing picture.

There are five Live View info screens, four which can be turned off or on in this menu. This menu is a little different from the other info menus because you decide which of the screens will be shown by adding or removing choices from two custom menu slots. Here are descriptions of the five screens and their functionalities.

- **Standard Live View:** This screen is always available and cannot be disabled; therefore, it does not appear as an option on the LV-Info menu. It provides basic shooting and exposure information, depending on which Mode Dial setting you are using. Some of the settings shown on the screen include the following: Face priority, sound setting, lens focal length, in-focus indicator, image stabilization mode, picture mode, white balance mode, ISO, point of focus (AF point), record mode, video mode, mode dial setting, shutter speed, aperture, ± compensation, exposure indicator scale, time, and frame number.
- **Image Only:** This is the most basic screen. It shows only what the lens currently sees, with no camera or shooting information. This is great for judging the potential quality of the image with no distractions.
- **[Histogram]:** The luminance histogram is a small bell curve graph in the lower part of the screen that shows the dynamic range (from light to shadow) in the image. The screen also contains a subset of the information found on the Standard Live View screen (previously discussed), with a few omissions.
- **Highlight&Shadow:** This screen is useful when you are shooting in very bright light or when the dynamic range of the scene exceeds the ability of the sensor to capture the full shadow-to-highlight range. The screen shows any blown-out highlight areas—where the image has become pure white with no detail—by continuously displaying orange where the highlight detail has disappeared. If the image is underexposed and some areas of the subject have gone to pure black (no dark detail), those areas will be blue. This screen also contains some basic exposure and camera settings.
- **Level Gauge:** This screen allows you to level your camera both horizontally and vertically. As you move the camera off level, you will see white squares appear in the two level indicators at the bottom of the screen, showing the degree and direction of level errors. The Level Gauge screen also contains basic exposure and camera settings.

Let's see how to select the information screens for LV-Info screens.

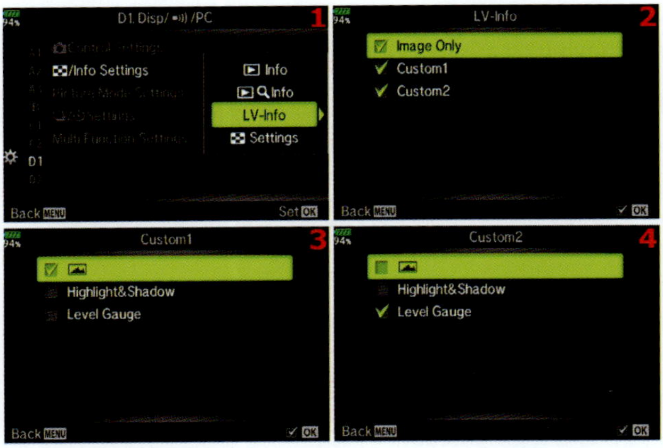

Figure 7.75: LV-Info screen choices

Use the following steps to enable or disable information screens for LV-Info:

1. Select [Image Review]/Info Settings from the D1. Disp/[Sound]/PC menu and scroll to the right.
2. Select the LV-Info setting from the [Image Review]/Info Settings menu and scroll to the right (figure 7.75, image 1).
3. You will see three information screen choices: Image Only, Custom1, and Custom2 (figure 7.75, image 2). To add or remove a check mark, simply highlight the choice and press the OK button. When you insert a check mark, the camera automatically saves the choice.
4. To set which screens are shown when Custom1 (or Custom2) is selected, select Custom1 (or Custom2) and scroll right.
5. You will see three information screen choices: [Histogram], Highlight&Shadow, and Level Gauge (figure 7.75, image 4). To add or remove a check mark, simply highlight the choice and press the OK button.
6. Press the Menu button to return to the previous screen.

Settings Recommendation: I set my camera to have all the LV-Info screens available As with the ▶ Info screens, they are all quite useful to me. I especially like using the Highlight&Shadow screen when I am shooting in difficult lighting environments. I check all the options in the Custom1 menu and make sure it is checked.

[Image Review] Settings

The Image Review screens provide different ways of viewing images on your memory card. After you press the ▶ Playback button, you can rotate the Rear Dial clockwise to select one of the following viewing options: Single-frame playback; image Index with 4, 9, 25, or 100 images per screen; My Clips; and Calendar display.

The My Clips setting shows any of the videos on the memory card, and the Calendar view allows you to scroll to a date and select images that were taken on that day. If there are no thumbnail images on a date, no pictures were taken that day.

Let's see how to select the Image Review screens.

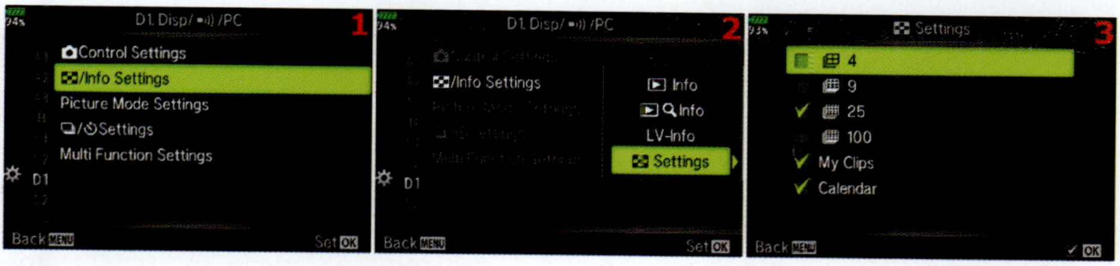

Figure 7.75: [Image Review] Settings choices

Use the following steps to enable or disable image view screens for [Image Review] Settings:

1. Select [Image Review]/Info Settings from the D1. Disp/[Sound]/PC menu and scroll to the right (figure 7.76, image 1).
2. Select [Image Review] Settings from the [Image Review]/Info Settings menu and scroll to the right (figure 7.76, image 2).
3. You will see the following choices: 4, 9, 25, 100, My Clips, and Calendar (figure 7.76, image 3). Place a check mark to the left of each image review screen type you want to use. To add or remove a check mark, simply highlight the choice and press the OK button.
4. When you insert a check mark, the camera automatically saves the choice. Press the Menu button to return to the previous screen.

Settings Recommendation: I set my camera to use the 4, 9, 25, My Clips, and Calendar image review screens. The 100 image view is a little small for my eyes. Experiment with these settings and see which are most useful to you.

Picture Mode Settings (D1)

The camera has a choice of 38 Picture Modes, as discussed in the **Shooting Menu 1** chapter. If you do not use some of the Picture Modes, you can use this function to hide them from the *Shooting Menu 1 > Picture Mode* menu and any of the camera screens that allow you to choose a Picture Mode.

Let's say you are not interested in using the Art Picture Modes. You could simply uncheck them from the Picture Mode Settings menu and they will disappear from any menu or screen that normally displays a choice of Picture Modes.

Let's examine how to enable and disable Picture Modes.

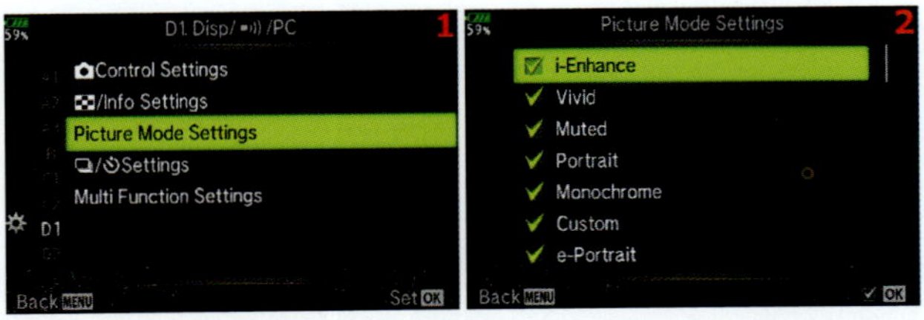

Figure 7.77: Enabling or disabling Picture Modes

Use the following steps to enable or disable Picture Modes from appearing on the camera menus and screens:

1. Select Picture Mode Settings from the D1. Disp/[Sound]/PC menu and scroll to the right (figure 7.77, image 1).
2. Scroll up or down with the Arrow Pad and highlight any Picture Modes you want to disable or enable (figure 7.77, image 2). Press the OK button to uncheck any modes that you do not want to use, or to check any modes you want to restore. The default is to have all Picture Modes available.
3. When you insert a check mark, the camera automatically saves the choice. Press the Menu button to return to the D1. Disp/[Sound]/PC screen.

Settings Recommendation: I leave all of the Picture Modes checked and available. Although I don't often use them, I play around with them sometimes. The E-M1II is a fun camera because it has many effects for JPEG pictures. If you are a RAW shooter, Picture Modes are not of much interest because you can apply effects after the fact.

[Sequential]/[Self-Timer] Settings (D1)

The E-M1II offers 19 different [Sequential]/[Self-timer] shooting modes that can be enabled or disabled on the camera's selection screens. It can be overwhelming and time-consuming to scroll through all of these options when you're trying to select a mode to use, and there may be modes that you never use. The [Sequential]/[Self-timer] menu allows you to select which of the following modes are displayed on the camera's selection screens:

- [Single] ♦ (Anti-Shock)
- [Single] ♥ (Silent)
- [Sequential] H (High)
- [Sequential] H ♥ (Silent)
- Pro Cap H (High)
- [Sequential] L (Low)
- [Sequential] L ♦ (Anti-Shock)
- [Sequential] L ♥ (Silent)

- Pro Cap L (Low)
- [Self-timer] 2s (2 sec)
- [Self-timer] 2s (2 sec) ♦ (Anti-Shock)
- [Self-timer] 2s (2 sec) ♥ (Silent)
- [Self-timer] 12s (12 sec)
- [Self-timer] 12s (12 sec) ♦ (Anti-Shock)
- [Self-timer] 12s (12 sec) ♥ (Silent)
- [Self-timer] C (Custom)
- [Self-timer] C (Custom) ♦ (Anti-Shock)
- [Self-timer] C (Custom) ♥ (Silent)
- High Resolution Shot

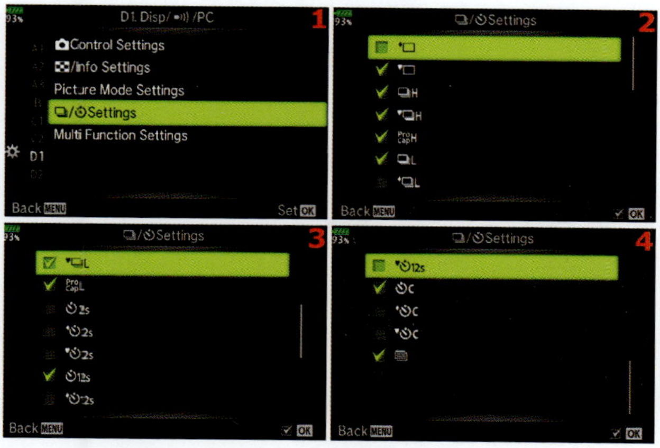

Figure 7.78: The [Sequential]/[Self-timer] Settings menu

Use these steps to decide which [Sequential]/[Self-timer] modes will be available on the camera's selection screens:

1. Select [Sequential]/[Self-timer] Settings from the D1. Disp/[Sound]/PC menu and scroll to the right (figure 7.78, image 1).
2. Scroll up or down with the Arrow Pad and highlight any [Sequential]/[Self-timer] modes you want to disable or enable (figure 7.78, images 2–4). Press the OK button to uncheck any modes that you do not want to use, or to check any modes you want to restore.
3. When you insert a check mark, the camera automatically saves the choice. Press the Menu button to return to the D1. Disp/[Sound]/PC screen.

Settings Recommendation: I find it time-consuming to scroll through all of these options if they are all enabled, so I only put check marks next to the modes I use regularly.

Multi Function Settings (D1)

The Multi Function Settings menu allows you to customize the controls that make up the Multi Function Button Task. By default, the Multi Function Button Task is assigned to the Fn2 button. To access each of its controls, you press and hold the Fn2 button (or alternate assigned button) while rotating the Rear Dial. This is a fast and easy way to access a lot of controls.

The following controls can be included as part of the Multi Function Button Task:

- Highlight&Shadow Control (you cannot turn this on or off)
- Color Creator
- ISO/WB (sets the ISO to the Front Dial and WB to the Rear Dial)
- WB/ISO (sets WB to the Front Dial and the ISO to the Rear Dial)
- Magnify
- Image Aspect
- S-OVF
- Peaking

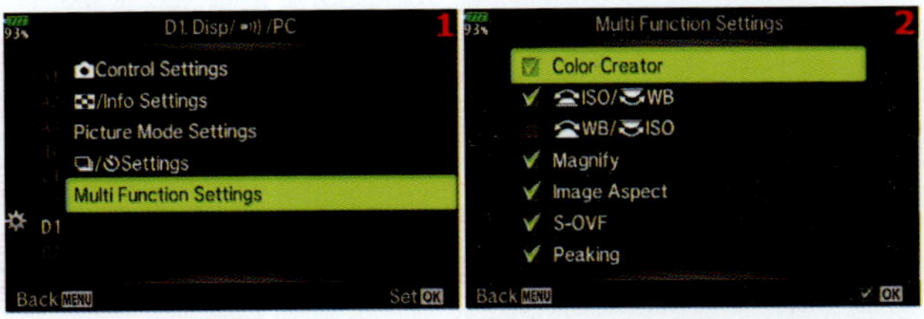

Figure 7.79: Enabling or disabling Multi Function controls

Use the following steps to select which controls are available when you use the button that has been assigned the Multi Function task:

1. Select Multi Function Settings from the D1. Disp/[Sound]/PC menu and scroll to the right (figure 7.79, image 1).
2. Scroll up or down with the Arrow Pad and highlight any Multi Function options you want to disable or enable (figure 7.79, image 2). Press the OK button to uncheck any options that you want to disable, or to check options that you want to restore.
3. When you insert a check mark, the camera automatically saves the choice. Press the Menu button to return to the D1. Disp/[Sound]/PC screen.

Settings Recommendation: I leave all of these checked because it allows me to keep all of the controls at my finger tips when shooting, and it doesn't take much time to scroll through them.

Live View Boost (D2)

Live View Boost makes the subject look bright on the monitor, regardless of how little ambient light there may be. It is amazingly capable of artificially opening up the shadows on the monitor and in the viewfinder. If the most important thing is to be able to see the subject in low light, you may want to enable this function. If carefully controlled exposures are more important, do not enable it.

Live View Boost does not affect the exposure of the picture; it affects only how the image appears on the monitor and in the viewfinder. Unfortunately, controls such as ± Exposure Compensation, although they still work normally to control exposure, will not display their effects on the screens when Live View Boost is enabled.

Live View Boost even prevents the Live Histogram display from updating correctly for Exposure Compensation changes. With Live View Boost enabled, the Live Histogram is limited to displaying the exposure the camera would provide without compensation. If you turn the dial for Exposure Compensation, the Histogram will not adjust and show the true exposure value, which could easily lead to under- or overexposure.

You can turn Live View Boost on or off for one (or more) of the following options: Manual Shooting, Bulb/Time, Live Composite, and Others. There are two separate On settings: On1 prioritizes the smoothness of the display, and On2 prioritizes image visibility in dark conditions by boosting the image brightness. Keep in mind that if you use On1 or On2, the view on the screen is not what the camera records.

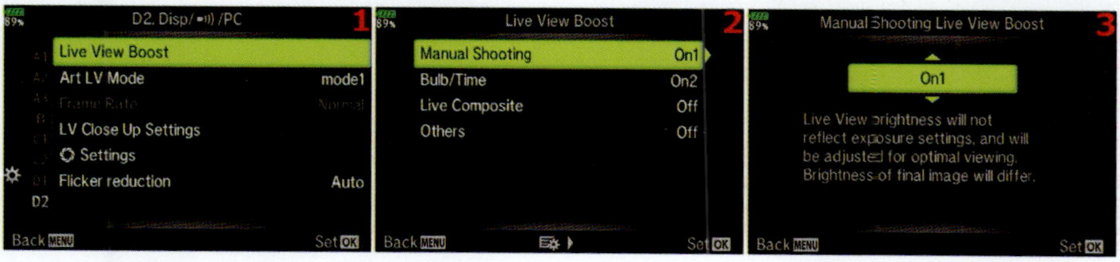

Figure 7.80: Enabling or disabling Live View Boost

Use these steps to turn Live View Boost on or off:

1. Select Live View Boost from the D2. Disp/[Sound]/PC menu and scroll to the right (figure 7.80, image 1).
2. Select the mode for which you wish to set Live View Boost: Manual Shooting, Bulb/Time, Live Composite, or Others (figure 7.80, image 2).
3. Select On1, On2, or Off from the up/down menu (figure 7.80, image 3).
4. Press the OK button to Set the value.

Settings Recommendation: When you turn the dial for Exposure Compensation, you expect to see the image brighten or darken until it looks just right. You will not see the brightening or darkening effect with Exposure Compensation when Live View Boost is enabled because the screen is doing its best to brighten the subject to the max. Also, the Live Histogram will not update correctly for compensation.

If you are in a dark room trying to shoot a subject by candlelight, Live View Boost can help you see the subject. However, I leave Live View Boost set to Off.

Art LV Mode (D2)

Using an Art filter places high demands on the camera microprocessor, which can lead to jerkiness in the electronic viewfinder (EVF) because it slows down the frame rate when you shoot quickly.

To counteract that demand, you can set the camera so it does not fully display the effect of the Art filter when you have the Shutter button pressed halfway down (mode2). In mode1 the camera displays the full Art filter effect and ignores the reduced EVF frame rate. That doesn't mean you won't see the effect of the Art filter on the monitor and in the viewfinder in mode2—it simply means the effect may not be as pronounced because the camera shoots images so quickly. This function does not affect the look of the pictures you take, just how they are displayed on the camera screens while you shoot.

The point of this function is to allow you to have a faster frame rate, even when you shoot with microprocessor-intensive Art filters.

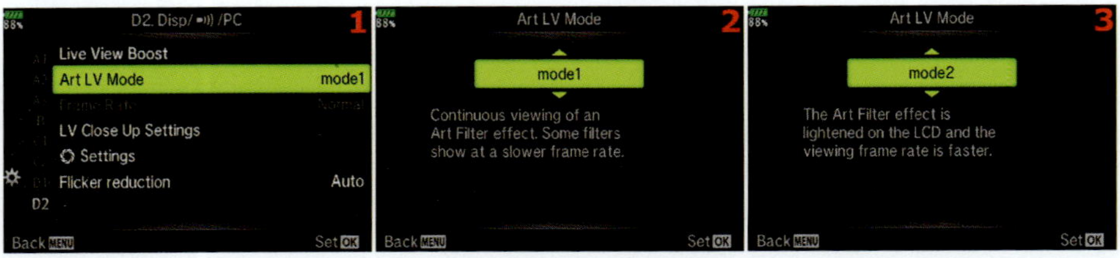

Figure 7.81: Selecting an Art LV Mode for the best frame refresh rate while using Art filters

Use the following steps to modify the Art LV Mode setting:

1. Select Art LV Mode from the D2. Disp/[Sound]/PC menu and scroll to the right (figure 7.81, image 1).
2. Select mode1 or mode2 from the up/down menu (figure 7.81, images 2 and 3). The factory default is mode1.
3. Press the OK button to Set the value.

Settings Recommendation: Since this function does not affect the pictures you take, only the display screens, you will need to decide if you really need the effect of an Art mode to display with its full effect while you shoot multiple pictures. Most people would rather not have their camera slow down while they shoot quickly, so my recommendation is to use mode2. Of course, if you rarely or never use the Art filters while shooting bursts of images, this function may not be useful to you. I leave mine set to mode2 for the best refresh rate in case I decide to blast off a bunch of Art Grainy Film black-and-white images. If I am shooting with an Art mode at several frames per second, I don't really need to examine each image as it flies by!

Frame Rate (D2)

This setting applies to the frame rate of the EVF. The higher the frame rate, the smoother the view looks in the EVF. However, the higher frame rate requires more processing power from the camera and can cause the camera to slow down, especially when using the high fps shooting modes. There are only two choices here, Normal and High.

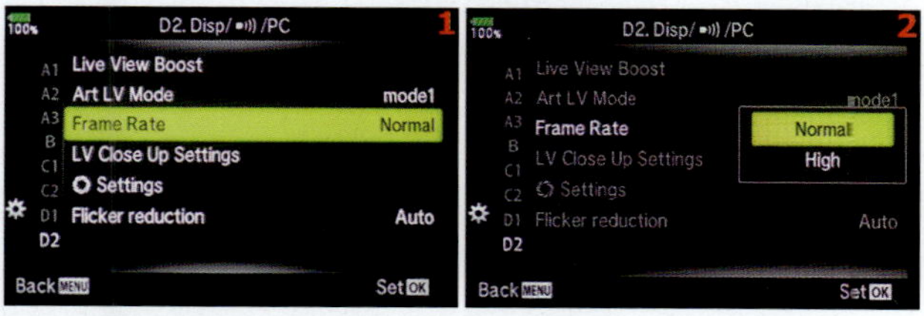

Figure 7.82: Choosing the EVF frame rate

Use the following steps to modify the Frame Rate setting:

1. Select Frame Rate from the D2. Disp/[Sound]/PC menu and scroll to the right (figure 7.82, image 1).
2. Select Normal or High from the up/down menu (figure 7.82, image 2).
3. Press the OK button to Set the value.

Settings Recommendation: I have not noticed any real performance impact by having this set to High, but I am not trying to get the absolute highest continuous frame rate very often. If you do notice any performance issues then set this back to Normal.

LV Close Up Settings (D2)

As discussed in the previous Button Functions section of this chapter and in **Appendix A: Still Image Button Task Reference**, you can assign the Magnify task to one of the Button Functions (e.g., Fn1, Fn2). The Magnify task will let one of the camera buttons zoom in to, or magnify, the subject and show an extreme closeup. This is a great focus aid because you can see a small portion of the subject up close while using autofocus.

The LV Close Up Settings menu includes two functions that allow you to determine how the camera will behave when you are using the magnified Live View: LV Close Up Mode and Live View Boost.

The camera defaults to mode2 of the LV Close Up Mode, which allows the autofocus system to work while the subject remains magnified on the enlarged Live View screen. If you select mode1, the magnification will go away before autofocus will work. The image will zoom back out to normal when you press the Shutter button to initiate autofocus, and it will force you to autofocus with no magnification. Manual focus can be used with full magnification in either mode1 or mode2.

When enabled, Live View Boost makes the subject appear brighter on the monitor during LV Close Up. This allows you to check for accurate focus when shooting in dark locations. If Live View Boost is turned off, the brightness is not adjusted during LV Close Up.

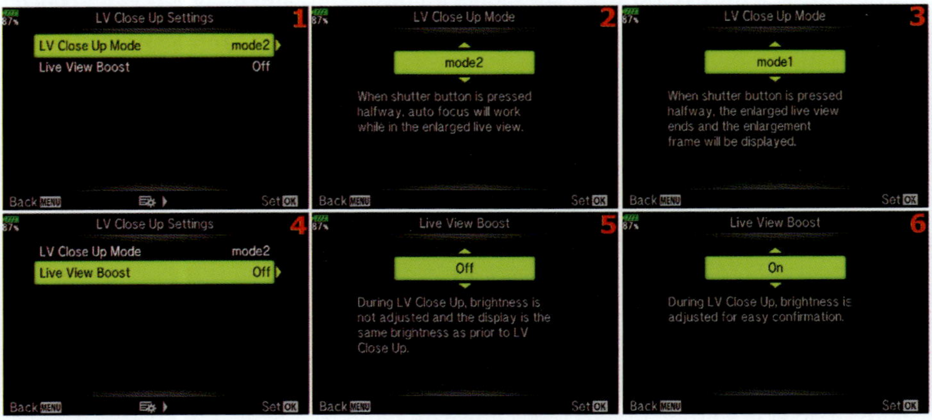

Figure 7.83: Choosing an LV Close Up Mode

Use the following steps to modify the LV Close Up Settings:

1. Select LV Close Up Settings from the D2. Disp/[Sound]/PC menu and scroll to the right.
2. Select LV Close Up Mode from the LV Close Up Settings menu and scroll to the right (figure 7.83, image 1).
3. Select mode1 or mode2 from the up/down menu (figure 7.83, images 2 and 3). The factory default is mode2, and AF works during magnification.
4. Press the OK button to Set the value and return to the previous screen.
5. Select Live View Boost and scroll to the right (figure 7.83, image 4).
6. Select Off or On from the up/down menu (figure 7.83, images 5 and 6), and then press the OK button to Set the value.

Settings Recommendation: One of the primary reasons I want to zoom in on or magnify the subject is to make sure autofocus is working well, so I leave LV Close Up Mode set to mode2.

▶ [Magnify] Default Setting (D2)

As we head to press, Olympus has released firmware update 2.0 for the E-M1II. With this update, you can use a 100% enlargement ratio during image playback, making it possible to review images at a 1/1 pixel ratio. You can set the magnification ratio with the ▶ [Magnify] Default Setting function.

[Aperture] Settings (D2)

The [Aperture] Settings menu deals with how the camera behaves when you use the Preview Button Task for depth of field preview. By default, this task is assigned to the Preview button on the front of the camera. When you press and hold the Preview button, it stops down (closes) the aperture so you can see the depth of field (zone of sharp focus) in your image before you take the photo.

Normally, the depth of field preview lasts only as long as the Preview button is depressed. However, when [Aperture] Lock is turned On, you can press the Preview button once to lock the aperture in its stopped-down position, allowing you to see the depth of field, then press it again to unlock the aperture and open it back up to maximum size.

The [Aperture] Settings menu also includes Live View Boost, which makes the subject appear brighter on the monitor during depth of field preview. This allows you to check for accurate focus when shooting in dark locations. If Live View Boost is turned off, the brightness is not adjusted during depth of field preview.

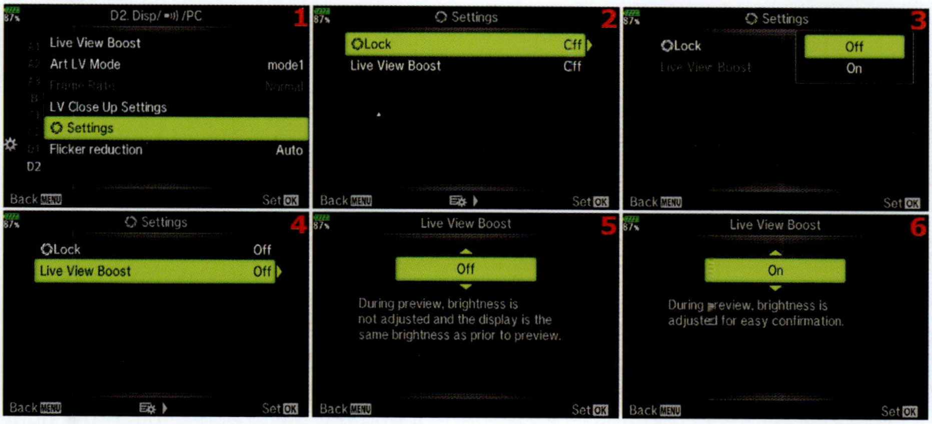

Figure 7.84: The [Aperture Preview] menu

Use the following steps to modify the [Aperture] Settings:

1. Select [Aperture] Settings from the D2. Disp/[Sound]/PC menu and scroll to the right (figure 7.84, image 1).
2. Select [Aperture] Lock from the [Aperture] Settings menu and scroll to the right (figure 7.84, image 2).
3. Select Off or On from the up/down menu (figure 7.84, image 3). The factory default is Off.
4. Press the OK button to Set the value and return to the previous screen.
5. Select Live View Boost and scroll to the right (figure 7.84, image 4).
6. Select Off or On from the up/down menu, and then press the OK button to Set the value (figure 7.84, images 5 and 6).

Settings Recommendation: Most of the time, I keep [Aperture] Lock turned off so that I don't have to press the Preview button multiple times. I would rather just press and hold the button while checking the depth of field. However, when I am working with macro shots and want to fine-tune where the depth of field falls within my image, I find it convenient to turn [Aperture] Lock on so I can view the depth of field preview while I use manual focus to move the depth of field back and forth until it is exactly where I want it to be.

Flicker Reduction (D2)

When you take pictures under certain types of lighting, such as fluorescent lamps, the camera monitor and viewfinder may tend to display dark bands moving through them. This flickering is caused by the normal fluctuations in the electrical flow of alternating current (the frequency of the current is measured in hertz, or Hz) moving through the lamps.

The camera has three modes for reducing flicker: Auto, 50Hz, and 60Hz. It defaults to Auto. Some areas of the world use 50Hz, and others use 60Hz. In Auto, the camera will try to determine which frequency is best for flicker reduction, or you can choose 50Hz or 60Hz and see which works best. You can also turn this function off.

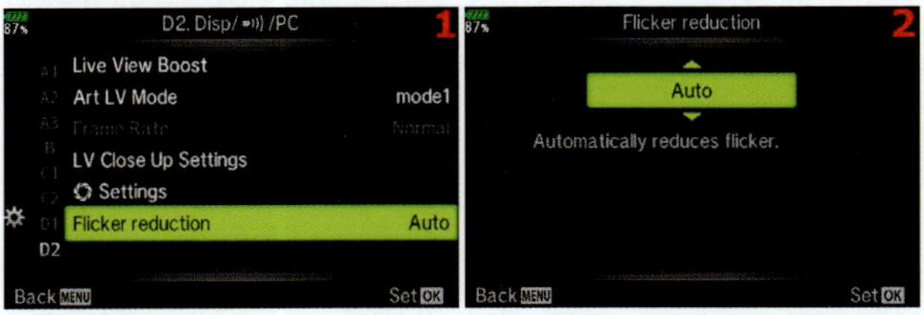

Figure 7.85: Choosing the best way to reduce flicker in the camera display screens

Use the following steps to modify the Flicker Reduction setting:

1. Select Flicker Reduction from the D2. Disp/[Sound]/PC menu and scroll to the right (figure 7.85, image 1).
2. Select Auto, 50Hz, 60Hz, or Off from the up/down menu (figure 7.85, image 2). The factory default is Auto.
3. Press the OK button to Set the value.

Settings Recommendation: A bane of digital photography with an electronic viewfinder or monitor is flickering under fluorescent lights. If you have problems with flickering, try out the three Flicker Reduction settings and see if they help.

Note: As we head to press, Olympus has released firmware update 2.0 for the OM-D E-M1II. Included in the update is the new [Photo] Flicker Scan function, which allows you to preview the scene and choose the proper shutter speed to avoid flickering when using the electronic shutter. This function is available for M and S modes only. It can be enabled in the E2. Exp/ISO/BULB/[Meter] menu.

Grid Settings (D3)

The grid is a very helpful set of fine lines superimposed on the monitor and in the EVF. This grid can help with composition and when you really need to make sure that the subject is in a certain spot.

The E-M1II offers six grid patterns as well as two color presets that allow you to customize the colors of the grid. You can set the camera so that the grid settings for the monitor also apply to the EVF. The following list describes the three Grid Settings submenus:

- **Display Color:** This menu allows you to create two custom grid colors and save them as presets. You can pick one of the two presets to be active. Preset 1 defaults to a dark grid with the following values: R38, G38, B39, and Alpha 75%. Preset 2 defaults to a lighter red with the following values: R180, G0, B0, and Alpha 75%.
- **Displayed Grid:** This menu allows you to choose which of the six grid patterns is active, or you can set it to Off. The default is to have the grid turned off.
- **Apply Settings to EVF:** This allows you to apply the monitor grid settings to the view in the EVF. The default for this setting is On, so the same settings used on the monitor are used in the EVF.

Let's take a look at how to modify the Grid Settings.

Display Color

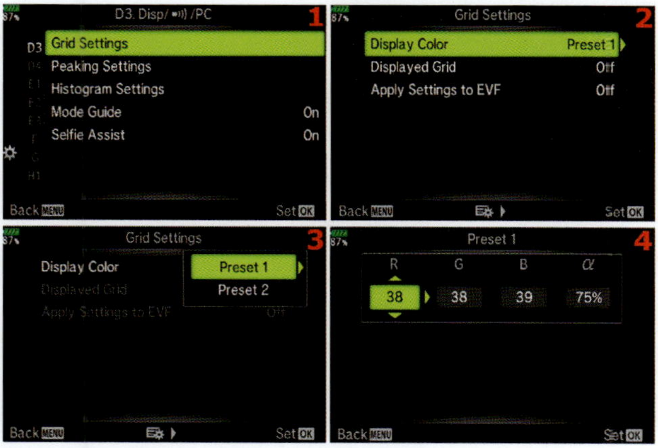

Figure 7.86: Selecting the grid Display Color

Use the following steps to modify the color of your grid:

1. Select Grid Settings from the D3. Disp/[Sound]/PC menu and scroll to the right (figure 7.86, image 1).

2. Select Display Color from the Grid Settings menu and scroll to the right (figure 7.86, image 2).
3. Select Preset 1 and scroll to the right (figure 7.86, figure 3).
4. A screen will open with value boxes for the R (red), G (green), and B (blue) color channels, as well as a box for α (alpha), which allows you to set the opacity of the grid lines (figure 7.86, image 4). Use the Arrow Pad to adjust the R, G, B, and α values (if wanted), and then press the OK button to Set the values and return to the previous menu.
5. Repeat the process for Preset 2 if wanted.
6. When you are finished adjusting the colors for each Preset, make sure the Preset you want to use is selected on the Grid Settings Menu.

Settings Recommendation: The default values for the two Display Color presets work well, especially against lighter backgrounds. If you are shooting against a darker background, you may want to set one of the presets to a lighter color. You can use the following values to get a pure bright white grid: R255, G255, B255, and α at 75% or 100%.

Displayed Grid

The next step is to choose a grid pattern. There are six patterns to choose from, or you can turn the grid off.

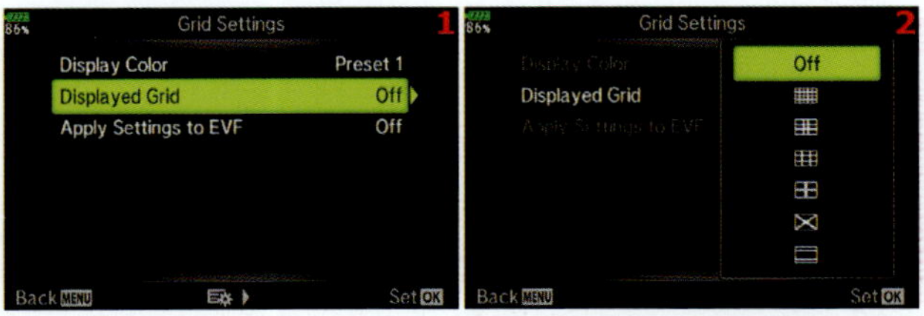

Figure 7.87: Choosing a grid pattern

Use the following steps to select a grid pattern:

1. Select Grid Settings from the D3. Disp/[Sound]/PC menu and scroll to the right.
2. Select Displayed Grid from the Grid Settings menu and scroll to the right (figure 7.87, image 1).
3. Select one of the six grid patterns, or Off, and press the OK button to Set the value and return to the previous menu (figure 7.87, image 2).

Settings Recommendation: Each of these grids can be useful, but for general shooting, I prefer the rule of thirds grid. The Displayed Grid does not show up in images or video, but it can be helpful to use one for composition, so pick the one that works best for you and your photography.

Apply Settings to EVF

The final step is to decide whether you want the same settings to be applied to the EVF.

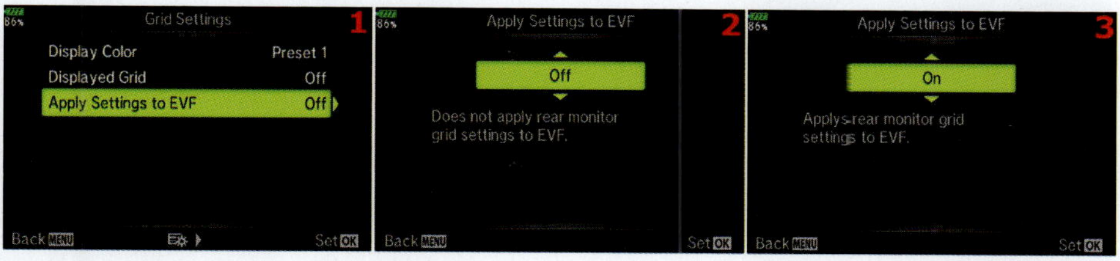

Figure 7.88: Applying grid settings to the EVF

Use the following steps to select whether the grid settings are applied to the EVF:

1. Select Grid Settings from the D3. Disp/[Sound]/PC menu and scroll to the right.
2. Select Apply Settings to EVF from the Grid Settings menu and scroll to the right (figure 7.88, image 1).
3. Select Off to eliminate the grid from the EVF, or On to apply the Display Color and Displayed Grid settings to the EVF (figure 7.88, images 2 and 3).
4. Press the OK button to Set the value and return to the previous menu.

Settings Recommendation: I like to use the same grid on the monitor and in the EVF, so I keep this set to On.

Peaking Settings (D3)

Peaking allows you to manually focus the subject by highlighting the in-focus areas with an outline. The default color of the outline is white, but you can change it to black, red, or yellow, and you can change its intensity. You can also adjust the brightness of the Live View image during Peaking to enhance the color of the outline.

- **Peaking Color:** This allows you to select the color of the outline. You can choose from White, Black, Red, and Yellow.
- **Highlight Intensity:** This controls the intensity of the highlighted areas. You can pick between High, Normal, and Low.
- **Image Brightness Adj.:** When this is turned on, the brightness of the Live View is automatically adjusted during Peaking so that the Peaking outline is easier to see.

Note: You can enable or disable Peaking with the *Custom Menu > A3. AF/MF > MF Assist > Peaking* function.

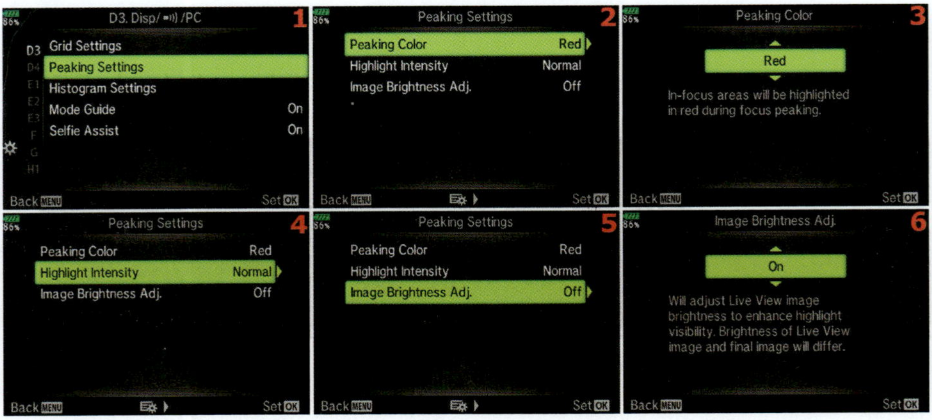

Figure 7.89: Modifying the Peaking Settings

Use the following steps to modify the Peaking Settings:

1. Select Peaking Settings from the D3. Disp/[Sound]/PC menu and scroll to the right (figure 7.89 image 1).
2. Select Peaking Color from the Peaking settings menu and scroll to the right (figure 7.89, image 2).
3. Select a color for the outline from the up/down menu (figure 7.89, image 3), and then press the OK button to Set the value and return to the previous screen.
4. Select Highlight Intensity from the Peaking Settings menu and scroll to the right (figure 7.89, image 4).
5. Select High, Normal, or Low from the up/down menu, then press the OK button to Set the value and return to the previous menu.
6. Select Image Brightness Adj. from the Peaking Settings menu and scroll to the right (figure 7.89, image 5).
7. Select On or Off from the up/down menu (figure 7.89, image 6), and then press the OK button to Set the value.

Settings Recommendation: I use this function in different ways depending on the subject and background I am photographing. When I shoot a subject in a natural environment, I find that White or Red is easier to see. When I shoot isolated images against a white background in my studio, I find that Black or Red works best. You may want to change this setting if you photograph different types of subjects.

Histogram Settings (D3)

The histogram display on the camera provides a window that shows the cutoff points for losing all detail in an image, which helps you determine how well the image is exposed. The left side of the histogram window represents shadows, and the right side represents highlights.

The range of light that the camera can capture is symbolized by a histogram scale that goes from 0 to 255, where 0 represents total black with no detail, and 255 represents pure white with no detail. Figure 7.90 shows a histogram in the shape of a bell curve. You can see the range of 0–255 along the horizontal axis.

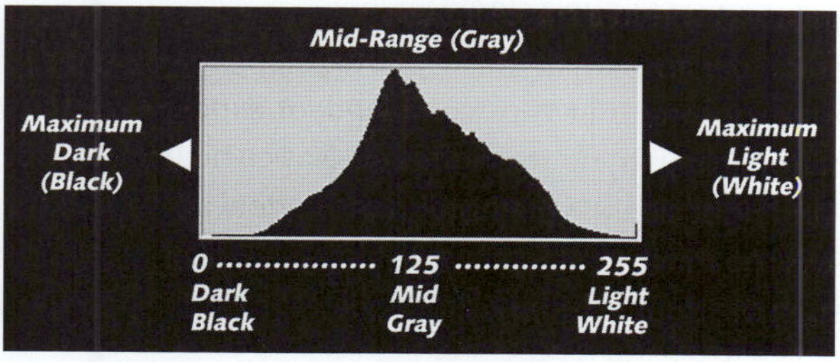

Figure 7.90: The Histogram scale represents total black (0) to pure white (255)

Using the Histogram

You can use the histogram to protect your images from over- and underexposure. Figure 7.91 shows how the histogram reacts to conditions ranging from underexposed to well exposed to overexposed.

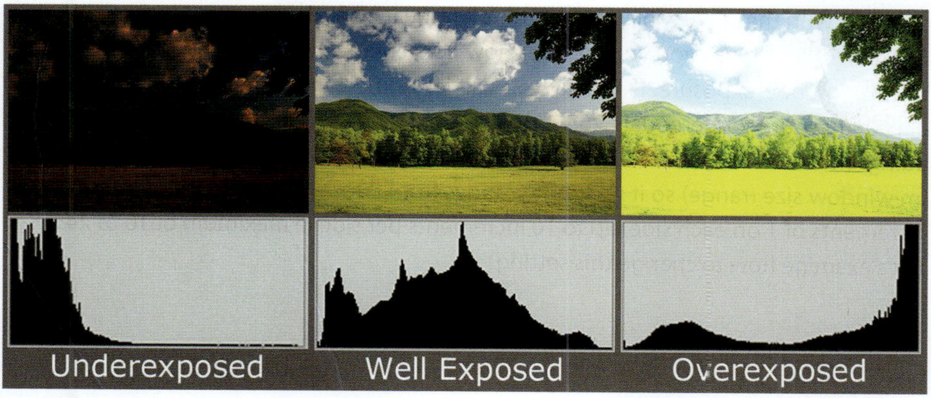

Figure 7.91: The Histogram scale can help you expose images properly

Notice how the bell curve graph is crammed to the left (clipped) for the underexposed image. It is cut off midpeak. The clipping indicates that some of the image is pure black (0), with no detail, and the overall image may be too dark.

In the well-exposed image in the middle, you can see that the graph is centered between the left (shadow) and right (highlight) sides.

The graph of the overexposed image is clipped off on the right, at the middle of the peak, and some of the image has become pure white.

Whenever you see the histogram graph clipped on the left, the image may be too dark; if it is clipped on the right, the image may be too light. If the histogram is clipped on both the shadow and highlight sides, there is too much light range (contrast) for the camera to capture all detail in the dark and light areas within a single image.

In that case, you must use either high dynamic range (HDR) photography, where multiple images are taken with different exposures and then combined, or expose for the highlights to prevent the histogram from clipping on the right side. Notice how the histogram graph just touches the left and right sides of the histogram window in the well-exposed image (figure 7.91). If there is too much contrast in the image, you may have to accept having the histogram just touch the right side (highlight) only, and allow clipping to occur on the left side. That is called exposing for the highlights.

When the histogram graph just touches the right side without clipping, but it is clipped on the left, there will be dark shadows in the image. That looks normal to our eyes. We expect shadows to be dark, but we do not expect to see a lack of highlight detail.

Use the normal exposure system—shutter speed, aperture, and ISO—to move the histogram to the left or right. You may need to use the ± Exposure Compensation system to fine-tune the position of the histogram graph for the best exposure. Fortunately, the camera gives you a Live Histogram display, which appears when you repeatedly press the Info button with the subject on the monitor or in the viewfinder.

The E-M1II also gives you control over how conservatively the histogram warns you of over- and underexposure. Normally you will leave the camera set so that pure black equals 0 and pure white equals 255. However, some photographers may want a little padding on either side of the histogram for extra protection. You can adjust the histogram window size (range) so it no longer ranges from 0 to 255. Instead it can be moved in increments of 1 on each side, up to 10 increments per side (a maximum of 10 to 245).

Let's examine how to change this setting

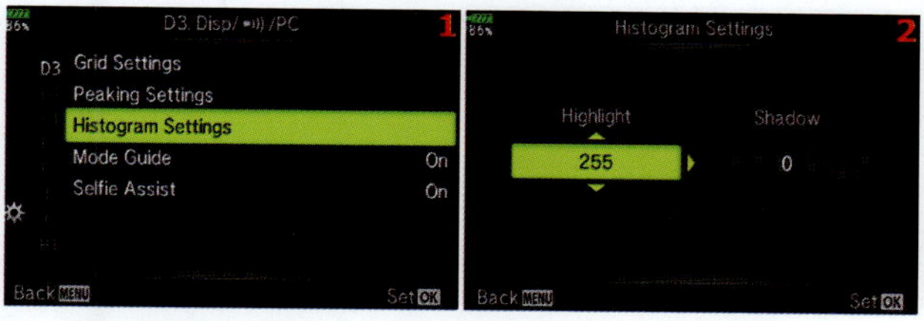

Figure 7.92: Making the histogram more or less conservative

Use these steps to change the range the histogram uses to warn you of exposure problems:

1. Select Histogram Settings from the D3. Disp/[Sound]/PC menu and scroll to the right (figure 7.92, image 1).
2. Select a value for Highlight from 245 to 255 and a value for Shadow from 0 to 10 from the up/down menus (figure 7.92, image 2).
3. Press the OK button to Set the new Histogram values.

Settings Recommendation: If you are ultraconservative in your exposures, you may want to adjust this setting. Otherwise, leave it at the industry standard of 0–255, which is what I use.

Mode Guide (D3)

The E-M1II is designed for all users, and the Mode Guide helps those who are new to photography. When this setting is turned on, the rear monitor briefly displays what the camera will do or what the photographer needs to do for each mode on the Mode Dial, excluding the three custom modes. The message appears when you select a mode by turning the Mode Dial. It lasts just a few seconds, and will disappear when the Shutter button is pressed. The message for each mode is as follows:

- **P:** Sets the Aperture and Shutter Speed Automatically
- **A:** Set the Aperture Manually
- **S:** Set the Shutter Speed Manually
- **M:** Set the Aperture and Shutter Speed Manually
- **Movie:** Start movie Rec
- **ART:** Apply Creative Effects
- **iAuto:** Auto selects the ideal mode, Live Guide menu is accessible

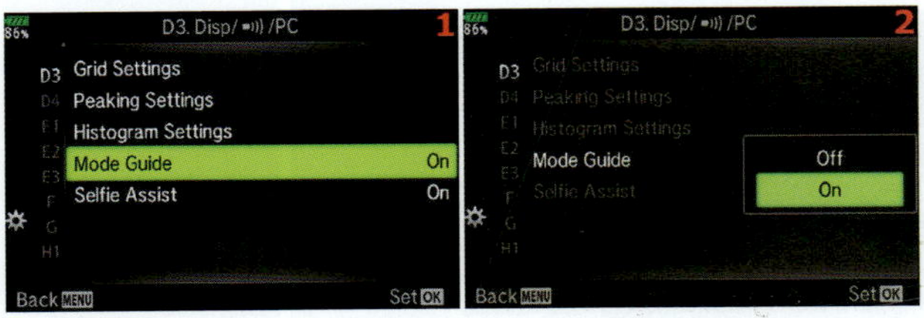

Figure 7.93: Enabling or disabling the Mode Guide system

Use the following steps to turn the Mode Guide system on or off:

1. Select Mode Guide from the D3. Disp/[Sound]/PC menu and scroll to the right (figure 7.93, image 1).
2. Select On or Off from the menu (figure 7.93, image 2).
3. Press the OK button to Set your choice.

Settings Recommendation: This can be a really great feature for those who are new to photography or just want a reminder of what each mode does. I keep this turned off because I find it distracting and I already know what each mode does.

Selfie Assist (D3)

Selfies are not just taken by smartphones anymore. With the E-M1II, you can flip the rear monitor out and use it to trigger the shutter release by tapping on the camera icon on the screen. When the Selfie Assist is turned on and the rear monitor is flipped out so that you can see the screen while pointing the lens toward you, the image on the screen is reversed, making it easier to compose the selfie.

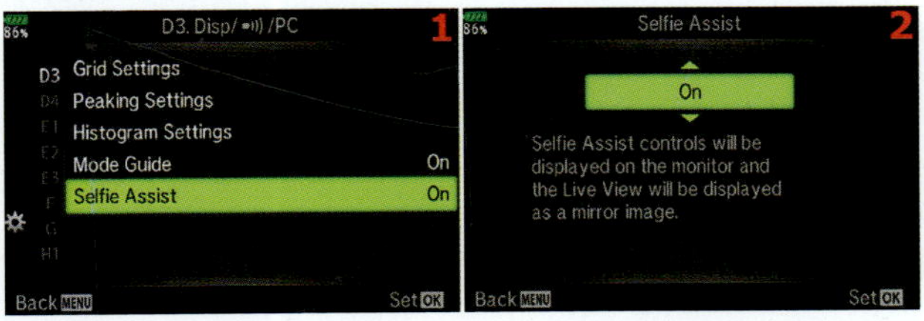

Figure 7.94: Setting the [Focus Beep] on or off

Use the following steps to turn Selfie Assist on or off:

1. Select Selfie Assist from the D3. Disp/[Sound]/PC menu and scroll to the right (figure 7.94, image 1).
2. Select On or Off from the menu (figure 7.94, image 2).
3. Press the OK button to Set your choice.

Settings Recommendation: I leave this turned on because it really does help with taking selfies, and there is no downside to having it on.

[Focus Beep] (D4)

The [Focus Beep] function controls the beep sound you hear when you are taking a picture and the camera successfully autofocuses.

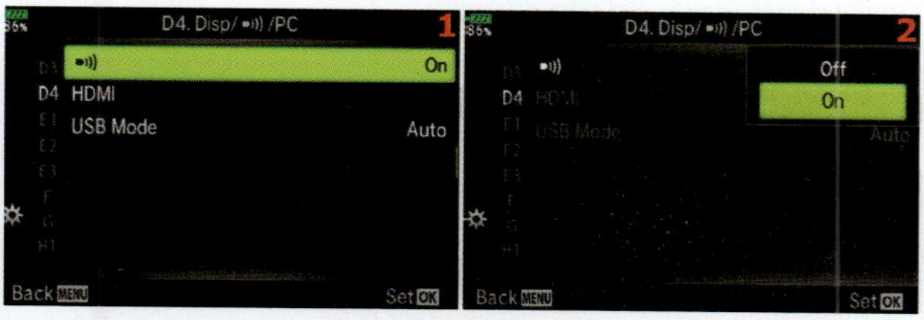

Figure 7.95: Enabling or disabling the [Focus Beep]

Use the following steps to enable or disable the [Focus Beep] sound:

1. Select [Focus Beep] from the D4. Disp/[Sound]/PC menu and scroll to the right (figure 7.95, image 1).
2. Select On or Off from the menu (figure 7.95, image 2).
3. Press the OK button to Set your choice.

Settings Recommendation: This can be really useful or really annoying depending on where and what you are photographing. If you're photographing a wedding or at an event where you need to be quiet, you will want to turn this off. If you like the camera to notify you with a beep when it has locked focus, then leave this setting turned on.

HDMI (D4)

High-definition multimedia interface (HDMI) lets your camera communicate with display devices for showing still pictures and videos. Like slideshows of the old film days, HDMI allows you to use a large screen to show off your work for family and friends (or clients).

The E-M1II has an HDMI type D cable connector under the lower rubber flap on the left side, just above the USB A/V Out port. HDMI is engraved in the rubber flap. You will need an HDMI type D to type A cable to plug your camera in to a high-definition television (HDTV) or other HDMI device. HDTVs use a type A connector, and the E-M1II uses a type D connector.

For your camera to interface with an HDTV or other display device, you will have to match the output frequency from your camera to the input frequency of the HDTV. The camera supports standard HDMI output frequencies, including C4K, 4K, 1080p, 720p, and

480p/576p. There are two ways to figure out which frequency to use when you plug your camera in to an HDTV:

- Look up the required frequency in your HDTV user's manual and set the camera to match.
- Plug the camera in to the HDTV and see if it displays pictures. If not, change the HDMI output frequencies until something shows up on the HDTV screen.

Let's examine how to change the HDMI frequency on the camera.

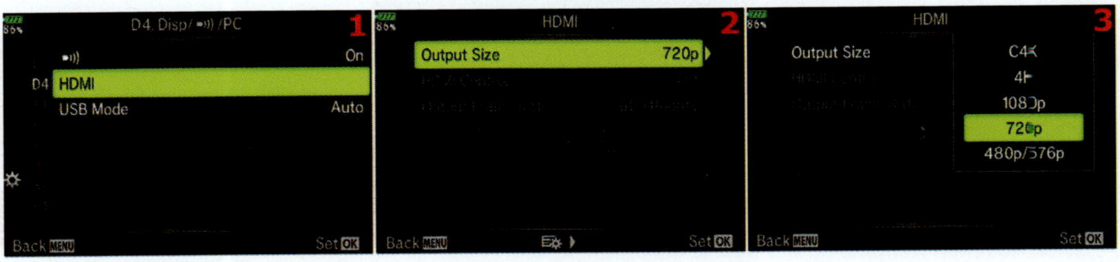

Figure 7.96: Changing the HDMI output frequency

Use the following steps to change the HDMI output frequency to match an HDMI display:

1. Select HDMI from the D4. Disp/[Sound]/PC menu and scroll to the right (figure 7.96, image 1).
2. Choose Output Size from the HDMI menu and scroll to the right (figure 7.96, image 2).
3. Select one of the listed HDMI output frequencies from the up/down menu (figure 7.96, image 3).
4. Press the OK button to Set the output frequency.

The E-M1II supports HDMI-CEC (Consumer Electronics Council) with its HDMI Control function, which allows you to control the camera with the HDTV's remote control. If your HDTV supports CEC, you can enable it in the camera menu and use the HDTV's remote control to direct the camera output.

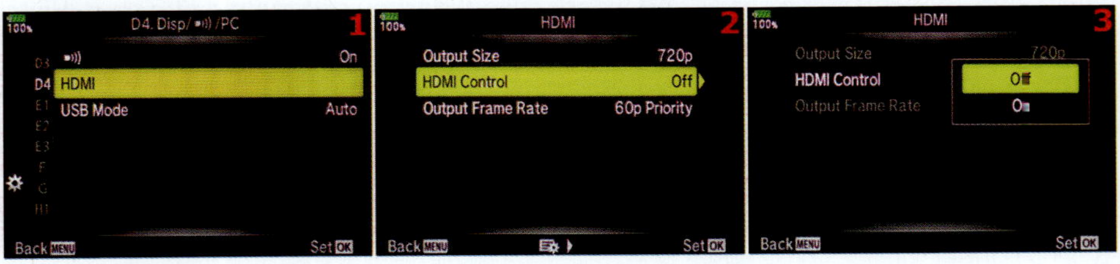

Figure 7.97: Using HDMI-CEC for camera remote control

Use the following steps to enable HDMI-CEC:

1. Select HDMI from the D4. Disp/[Sound]/PC menu and scroll to the right (figure 7.97, image 1).
2. Choose the HDMI Control setting from the HDMI menu and scroll to the right (figure 7.97, image 2).
3. Select Off or On from the HDMI up/down menu (figure 7.97, image 3). On enables HDMI-CEC, and Off disables it.
4. Press the OK button to Set your choice.

The final step is to set the Output Frame Rate. You have two options: 50p Priority and 60p Priority.

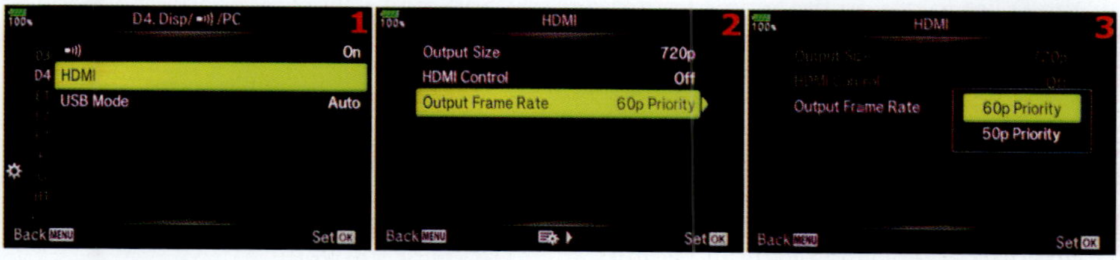

Figure 7.98: Setting the HDMI Output Frame Rate

Use the following steps to set the HDMI Output Frame Rate:

1. Select HDMI from the D4. Disp/[Sound]/PC menu and scroll to the right (figure 7.98, image 1).
2. Choose the Output Frame Rate setting from the HDMI menu and scroll to the right (figure 7.98, image 2).
3. Select 60p Priority or 50p Priority from the menu (figure 7.98, image 3).
4. Press the OK button to Set your choice.

Settings Recommendation: When I plug my camera into my Vizio flat screen HDTV using the 1080p setting, it works fine. I can even use HDMI-CEC to control the display of images with my HDTV remote control. This is way more fun than the old days of breaking out a slide projector and jumping through hoops to get everything working for a slideshow. I can display videos and still images on my 50-inch (127cm) HDTV.

USB Mode (D4)

The E-M1II offers several industry standard modes for connecting the camera to external devices through the factory-supplied USB cable. The camera has a USB connector under the bottom rubber flap to the left of the rear monitor. You can use the cable to transfer image and video files to your computer and to print pictures on a PictBridge-compatible printer.

Let's consider the protocols the camera supports for connection to external devices, plus its Auto detect mode:

- **Auto:** This mode lets the camera decide which type of connection to use, depending on the type of device you plug your camera in to. If you get no results with the Auto setting, test the other modes to see what works with the external device.
- **Storage:** This mode refers to the mass storage class (MSC) specification, which is an industry standard for connecting a device containing storage memory to a computer. The MSC protocol is used by your camera, external hard drives, and card readers. You can use the Storage mode to transfer image and video files to your computer through Olympus Viewer software or other software. When you use Storage mode the camera will show up in your computer's file browser as a local hard drive. You can then access the DCIM folder on the memory card directly, and manually copy images and videos to and from the camera. When you plug the camera in to a USB port on your computer using the factory-supplied USB cable, your computer should react by offering to load the Olympus Viewer software if you have installed it. Olympus Viewer will help you transfer images to your computer and allow you to enhance them (e.g., convert RAW files to JPEG). This is also the mode you must use when you are updating the firmware on your camera with Olympus Digital Camera Updater software.
- **MTP:** This mode refers to media transfer protocol (MTP), which was created by Microsoft as an extended set of tools for synchronizing pictures, videos, sound files, and songs from devices to a computer with Windows installed. It offers content management tools for creating playlists, autosyncing, and transferring DRM-protected (licensed) media.
- **Print:** This refers to PictBridge printing mode, which allows you to connect your camera directly to a PictBridge-compatible printer, without a computer, and print some or all of the images on the memory card.
- **[Olympus Capture]:** This mode allows you to use the Olympus Capture software to control the camera from a computer and transfer images from the camera to a computer. This mode works only when the Mode Dial is set to P, A, S, or M.
- **PCM Recorder:** This mode allows the camera to trigger and sync with an external Olympus PCM recorder.

Now let's consider how to select one of the USB modes.

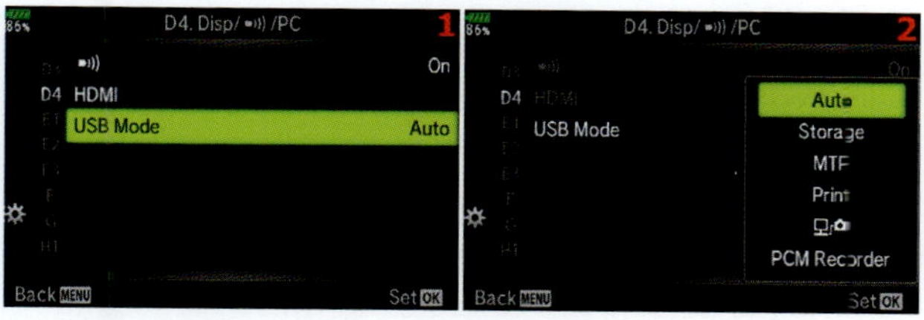

Figure 7.99: Selecting a USB mode for image or video transfer and still image direct printing

Use the following steps to select a USB Mode for image and video transfer and picture printing:

1. Select USB Mode from the D4. Disp/[Sound]/PC menu and scroll to the right (figure 7.99, image 1).
2. Select Auto, Storage, MTP, Print, [Olympus Capture], or PCM Recorder from the menu (figure 7.99, image 2).
3. Press the OK button to Set the value.

Settings Recommendation: I leave my camera set to Storage so I can transfer images and videos through my USB cable. I also update my camera's firmware whenever an update is available, which also requires the Storage mode. I rarely do any sort of PictBridge printing because I like to use a professional lab for my commercial work and a local lab for my snapshots.

Custom Menu E1–3. Exp/ISO/BULB/[Meter]

The E1–E3. Exp/ISO/BULB/[Meter] menu is primarily composed of functions that directly affect how the image is exposed. There are a total of fifteen different functions organized into three menus. We will start examining the functions by taking a look at the opening menu for the E1–E3. Exp/ISO/BULB/[Meter] functions in figure 7.100.

To enter the menu, you must select E1. (or E2. or E3.) Exp/ISO/BULB/[Meter] from the Custom Menu and scroll to the right. Lets look at each function in detail.

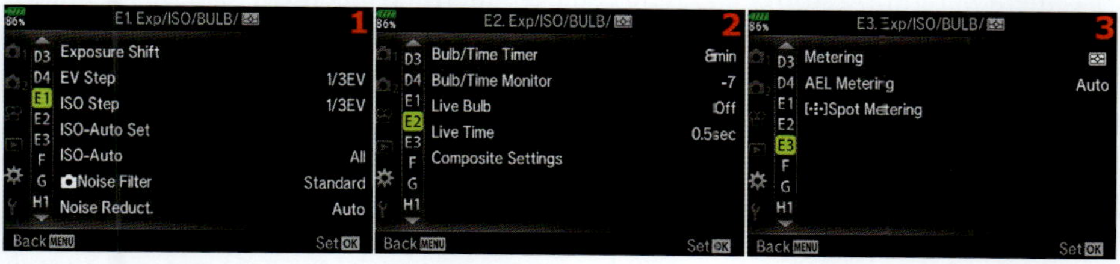

Figure 7.100: The E1–E3 Exp/ISO/BULB/[Meter] menu

Exposure Shift (E1)

If you think one of your camera light meters (Digital ESP, Center weighted, Spot) needs a little fine-tuning, you can use this function to set up a semipermanent exposure compensation for individual light meter types.

For instance, if you usually shoot with the Digital ESP meter and you want the meter to add a half stop of exposure beyond the default, you can set it up with this function.

The camera allows you to fine-tune each light meter type in 1/6 stop (1/6 EV step) increments, up to one full stop over- or underexposed.

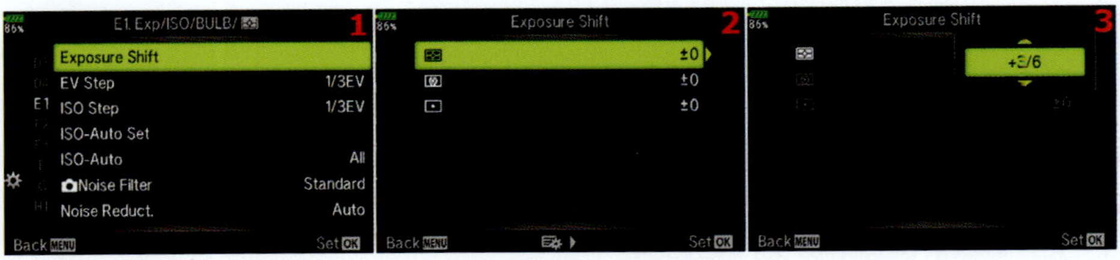

Figure 7.101: Fine-tuning the camera's exposure meters

Use these steps to set up a semipermanent Exposure Shift on any or all of the three light meter types:

1. Select Exposure Shift from the E1. Exp/ISO/BULB/[Meter] menu and scroll to the right (figure 7.101, image 1).
2. The top meter selection is the Digital ESP meter. The second meter type is the Center weighted meter, and the third meter type is the Spot meter (figure 7.101, image 2). Let's use the Digital ESP meter as an example of how to set up an Exposure Shift of 1/2 stop (+3/6). The process is the same for all meter types, so you can use these steps for whichever meter you want to fine-tune. Choose the meter you want to modify and scroll to the right.
3. In figure 7.101, image 3, the Digital ESP meter is selected and the Exposure Shift menu is open. Use the Arrow Pad keys to select from +1/6 to +1 stop of Exposure Shift in 1/6 stop increments. In image 3, you can see that I selected +3/6 EV steps (1/2 stop). The camera will add 1/2 stop of exposure compensation and mildly overexpose the image.
4. After you have selected how much you want to shift the exposure, press the OK button to lock in the Exposure Shift setting. Repeat these steps for any other meter type that you want to adjust.

Note: The Exposure Shift function is a form of exposure compensation. It is applied semipermanently; that is, it stays in place until you go back to the Exposure Shift function and remove the shift value. When you shift the exposure for any of the light meters, you may find that you do not have the normal range of exposure compensation after you adjust the meter.

Also, you will not see the effects of the Exposure Shift in the EVF or on the rear monitor, although you will be able to detect it in the image histogram.

Settings Recommendation: I have found that the exposure meters in the E-M1II are very accurate, and I am quite satisfied with their performance. However, you may be shooting a style of photography that easily fools your light meter. In that case, experiment with this function to see if it will help overcome the exposure problem. Don't forget that Exposure Shift is in place or you may find that your images are regularly over- or underexposed.

EV Step (E1)

Use this function to choose an exposure value (EV) increment when you select a shutter speed, aperture, exposure compensation, and bracketing exposure value. As photographers, we think of exposure in stops. A 1-stop increment doubles or halves the amount of light the camera can use for making a picture, depending on whether you are letting in more light (double) or less light (half). A single stop is equivalent to 1 EV step.

The camera allows you to use finer increments than 1 EV step when you make exposure adjustments. You can select from 1/3 EV step, 1/2 EV step, or 1 EV step. The following three EV step lists show a partial breakdown of EV steps that are available as you adjust an exposure:

1/3 EV step

- **Shutter:** 1/100, 1/125, 1/160, 1/200, 1/250, 1/320, etc.
- **Aperture:** f/5.6, f/6.3, f/7.1, f/8.0, f/9.0, f/10, etc.
- **Compensation/bracketing:** 0.0, 0.3, 0.7, 1.0, 1.3, 1.7, 2.0, 2.3, 2.7, 3.0, etc.

1/2 EV step

- **Shutter:** 1/90, 1/125, 1/180, 1/250, 1/350, 1/500, etc.
- **Aperture:** f/5.6, f/6.7, f/8.0, f/9.5, f/11, f/13, etc.
- **Compensation/bracketing:** 0.0, 0.5, 1.0, 1.5, 2.0, 2.5, 3.0, etc.

1 EV step (1 stop)

- **Shutter:** 1/60, 1/125, 1/250, 1/500, 1/1000, 1/2000, etc.
- **Aperture:** f/2.8, f/4.0, f/5.6, f/8.0, f/11, f/16, f/22, etc.
- **Compensation/bracketing:** 0.0, 1.0, 2.0, 3.0, 4.0, 5.0 (note that 5.0 is the maximum)

The fineness of your exposure control will vary depending on how you set this function; that is, which EV step increment you choose (1/3EV, 1/2EV, or 1EV step). Let's examine how to select one of the three EV increment values.

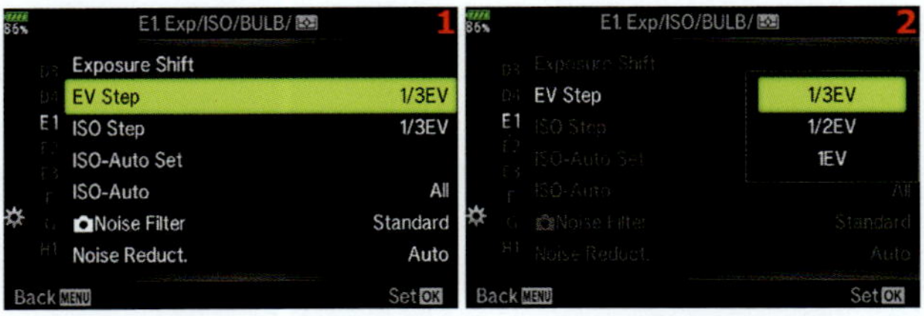

Figure 7.102: Choosing an EV step value for exposure control

Use the following steps to select an EV increment value for camera exposure settings:

1. Select EV Step from the E1. Exp/ISO/BULB/[Meter] menu and scroll to the right (figure 7.102, image 1).
2. Select 1/3EV, 1/2EV, or 1EV from the menu that appears (figure 7.102, image 2). Refer to the three previous EV step lists to help you decide which EV step is most appropriate for the type of pictures you are creating.
3. Press the OK button to Set the value.

Settings Recommendation: I leave my camera set to 1/3 EV step (1/3EV). Most photographers do the same. While using camera-supplied tools, such as the Live Histogram, it is best to have fine control over the exposure value. With 1/3 EV step you can adjust the exposure in fine increments. If you do not need such fine control, experiment with the other two selections.

ISO Step (E1)

All camera menus that allow you to change the ISO use the ISO Step function as the basis for the ISO increments on the camera displays. You can choose from either 1/3 EV step or 1 EV step.

Here is a partial list of ISO increments for both ISO Step values:

1/3 EV step: Auto, Low (100), 200, 250, 320, 400, 500, 640, 800, etc.

1 EV step: Auto, Low (100), 200, 400, 800, 1600, 3200, 6400, etc.

If you want to use smaller increments, leave this setting at the factory default of 1/3 EV. If you want to select ISO values in 1 EV step (1 stop) increments, you can change it here. Let's see how.

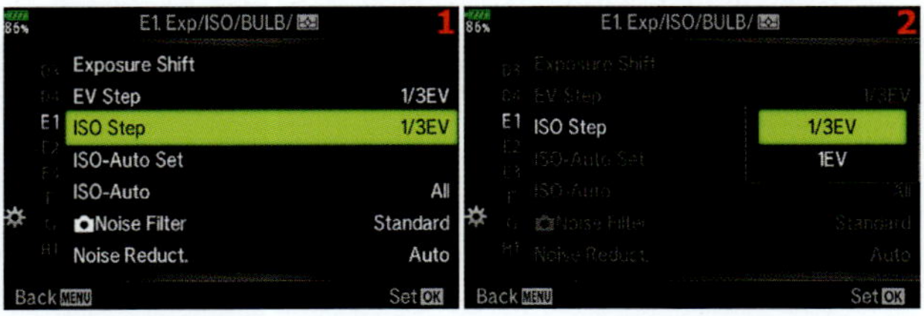

Figure 7.103: Choosing an ISO Step increment

Use the following steps to choose an ISO sensitivity setting:

1. Select ISO Step from the E1. Exp/ISO/BULB/[Meter] menu and scroll to the right (figure 7.103, image 1).
2. Select 1/3EV or 1EV from the menu that appears (figure 7.103, image 2).
3. Press the OK button to Set the value.

Settings Recommendation: I use the 1/3EV ISO Step value because I want fine increments of ISO values to choose from. If you prefer coarser 1-stop ISO sensitivity increments, choose 1EV instead.

ISO-Auto Set (E1)

When you set the ISO sensitivity to Auto, the camera will choose the best ISO to use for the current subject, without concern for image noise from high ISO values.

ISO-Auto Set is used to control the upper and lower range of your camera's ISO sensitivity when using Auto-ISO. In effect, you are telling the camera it can use any ISO value within a certain range, but it cannot exceed that range with higher or lower ISO values. The total available ISO range is from ISO 200 to ISO 6400.

You can also set the lowest shutter speed value that the camera will use when the ISO sensitivity is raised in P and A modes.

There are two submenus in the ISO-Auto Set function:

- **Upper Limit/Default:** The Upper Limit (a.k.a., High Limit) setting controls the maximum ISO value that you will allow the camera to use in difficult lighting conditions. The camera is free to use any ISO value up to the High Limit setting. The Default is the low ISO value at which the camera will start.
- **Lowest S/S Setting:** This is where you can set the lowest shutter speed that the camera will automatically use when you use the P or A modes. If you choose Auto, the camera will automatically set the shutter speed.

Look at the Default and High Limit as a floor and a ceiling. When you use Auto ISO the camera cannot drop the ISO below the Default floor or raise it above the High Limit ceiling. These values give you excellent control of the Auto ISO boundaries. The Lowest S/S Setting gives you another point of control when using Auto ISO in the P and A exposure modes.

Let's examine how to choose an ISO value for the High Limit and Default settings, as well as the Lowest S/S Setting.

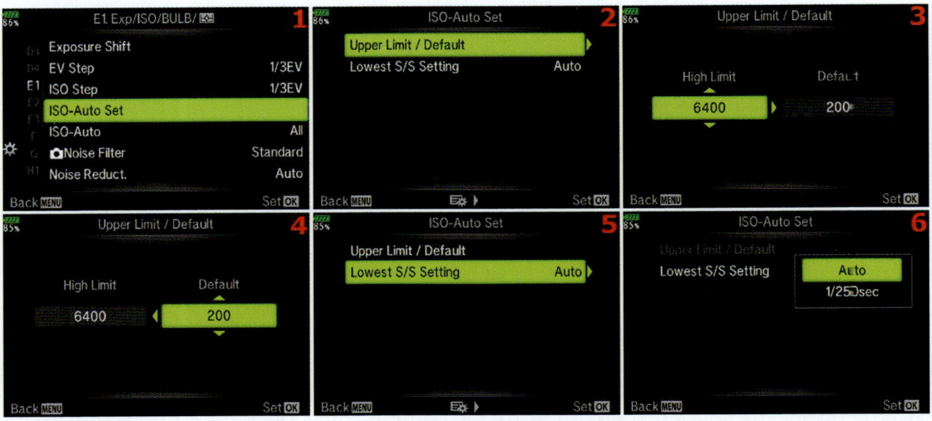

Figure 7.104: Choosing a High Limit and a Default value along with the lowest Shutter Speed for Auto ISO

Use the following steps to choose an ISO-Auto Set value for the High Limit and Default settings along with the lowest Shutter Speed:

1. Select ISO-Auto Set from the E1. Exp/ISO/BULB/[Meter] menu and scroll to the right (figure 7.104, image 1).
2. Select Upper Limit/Default and scroll to the right (figure 7.104, image 2).
3. Choose an ISO value from the High Limit up/down menu (figure 7.104, image 3). The available ISO values range from ISO 200 to ISO 6400.
4. Use the Arrow Pad to move to the right and choose an ISO value from the Default up/down menu (figure 7.104, image 4). The available ISO values range from ISO 200 to ISO 6400.
5. Press the OK button to Set the two values and return to the previous screen.
6. Scroll down to Lowest S/S Setting and scroll to the right (figure 7.104, image 5). Select Auto to allow the camera to automatically set the shutter speed, or choose the lowest shutter speed that you are comfortable with the camera using in P or A exposure mode (from 1/250 to 30 Seconds).
7. Press the OK button to Set the value.

Settings Recommendation: I use ISO 1600 as my High Limit. I don't like the noise that results with higher ISO values, especially if I don't nail the exposure. I use ISO 200 to ISO 400 as the lower Default value, depending on the ambient light and whether or not I am using flash. When I use flash indoors, I often use ISO 400 as Default and ISO 1600 as High Limit. I use the Auto Lowest S/S Setting.

ISO-Auto (E1)

Use the ISO-Auto function to control which modes on the Mode Dial allow the use of automatic ISO (called Auto on the ISO selection menus; I will use Auto ISO in this book). The factory default is for Auto ISO to be available only in Program (P), Aperture-priority (A), and Shutter-priority (S) modes. Normally Auto ISO is not available when you are using Manual (M) mode, so the selection is grayed out on the menu.

However, the camera allows you to use Auto ISO in Manual (M) mode. There are two settings in the ISO-Auto function:

- **P/A/S:** When this mode is selected the camera allows the Auto ISO function to be accessible on the menus only when you are using Program (P), Aperture-priority (A), and Shutter-priority (S) modes. Auto ISO will be grayed out and unavailable on all ISO selection menus when you are using Manual (M) mode.
- **All:** When you select this mode the camera will offer Auto ISO on all ISO selection menus when you use P, A, S, or M mode on the Mode Dial. Note that Manual (M) mode is included.

Let's see how to select a setting.

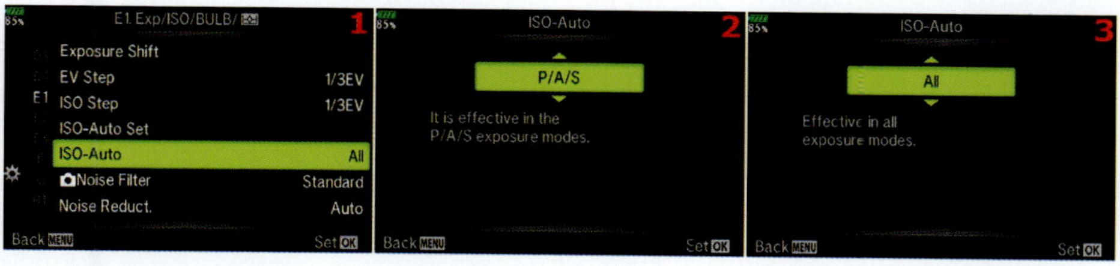

Figure 7.105A: Choosing which Mode Dial setting allows Auto ISO

Use the following steps to choose an ISO-Auto setting:

1. Select ISO-Auto from the E1. Exp/ISO/BULB/[Meter] menu and scroll to the right (figure 7.105A, image 1).
2. Select either P/A/S or All from the up/down menu (figure 7.105A, images 2 and 3).
3. Press the OK button to Set the value.

Settings Recommendation: The All setting makes sense for the types of photography I do (events and nature). I use Auto ISO only when I must get the shot at all costs or when I am shooting just for fun. However, if I wanted to shoot with Auto ISO in Manual (M) mode, I wouldn't want a limitation imposed upon me.

If you do not think you will use Auto ISO in M mode, simply leave this function set to the factory default of P/A/S.

Noise Filter (E1)

The Noise Filter function is designed to remove high-ISO noise from your images by blurring the image slightly. The blurring action tends to blend the grainy noise detail into the darker background, lessening the degrading effect of noise. The camera then resharpens the image to bring out more edge detail.

There are four settings: Off, Low, Standard, and High. The camera defaults to Standard. Each setting blurs the image more, making noise less apparent (and removing image detail), as you move from Low to High.

The camera does an excellent job of noise control for its small sensor.

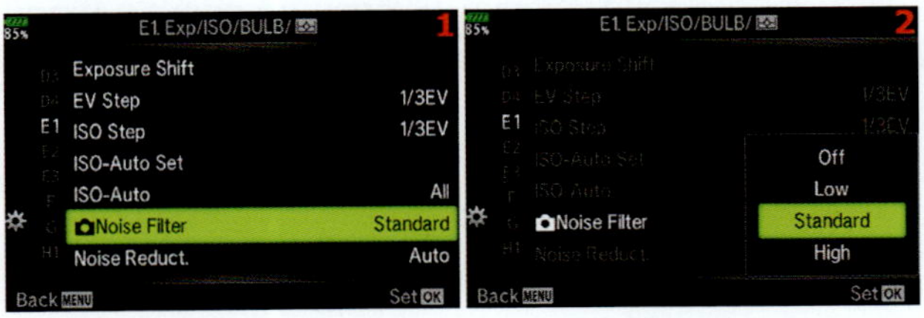

Figure 7.105B: Choosing a high-ISO Noise Filter setting

Use the following steps to select a high-ISO Noise Filter setting:

1. Select Noise Filter from the E1. Exp/ISO/BULB/[Meter] menu and scroll to the right (figure 7.105B, image 1).
2. Select Off, Low, Standard, or High from the menu that appears (figure 7.105B, image 2).
3. Press the OK button to Set the value.

Settings Recommendation: While I was shooting various indoor events (e.g., high school graduations, weddings, baptisms) with my E-M1II, I had to shoot in rather low light. I used ISO 1600 and got excellent results as long as I kept my Live Histogram pegged on the bright side (exposed for the highlights). I found that the Standard high-ISO Noise Filter, which is the default, worked well for me. It seems to balance noise removal blurring and resharpening.

With a smaller sensor, such as the E-M1II Micro Four Thirds sensor, it is critical that exposures are correct in low light. Brightening a high-ISO image will often lead to objectionable noise.

Judicious use of the high-ISO Noise Filter will help protect you from excessive noise in images where the light is not ideal.

Noise Reduct. (E1)

During a long exposure the sensor may exhibit more noise than is acceptable. The sensor gets warm after several seconds of use. This warming effect produces amp noise, which causes warmer sections of the sensor to have more noise than cooler sections.

This noise can resemble a foglike brightening around the edges of the frame. Also, there can be bright spots with various colors at numerous places in the image. This special type of long-exposure noise degrades the image in a different way than the noise from high-ISO sensitivity, which appears as grainy ugliness in darker areas of the image.

Using Noise Reduct.

When you enable Noise Reduct. (long-exposure noise reduction) and an exposure is longer than about 2.5 seconds, the camera will take two pictures with approximately the same exposure time. The first picture is normal. The second picture is a black-frame subtraction exposure, which is exposed for about the same duration as the first picture with the shutter closed.

The camera examines the noise in the black-frame subtraction exposure and subtracts it from the first image. Since long-exposure noise (bright spots in random places and fog at the edges) is different from high-ISO noise (grainy degradation in darker areas), the high-ISO Noise Filter function (next subsection) would not work well with long-exposure noise. Therefore, for those of us who shoot long exposures regularly, the Noise Reduct. function is very important.

The main drawback to long-exposure noise reduction is that the total exposure time is doubled—a 5-second exposure becomes a 10-second exposure—because two exposures are made. The black-frame subtraction exposure is not written to the memory card; therefore, when the noise reduction process is done you will have only one image with much less noise.

While the black-frame subtraction exposure is being processed, the orange memory card access symbol will blink in the top-left corner of any active displays. While the symbol is flashing, you cannot use the camera. If you turn the camera off during a long-exposure noise reduction session, the image will be lost.

There are three selections available within the Noise Reduct. function:

- **Auto:** The camera chooses whether or not to use long-exposure noise reduction. It will usually kick in at a shutter speed of about 2.5 seconds or with a small aperture that makes the shutter stay open that long.
- **On:** Long-exposure noise reduction is active on all pictures taken at all shutter speeds, not just long exposures.
- **Off:** No long-exposure noise reduction is performed on any image.

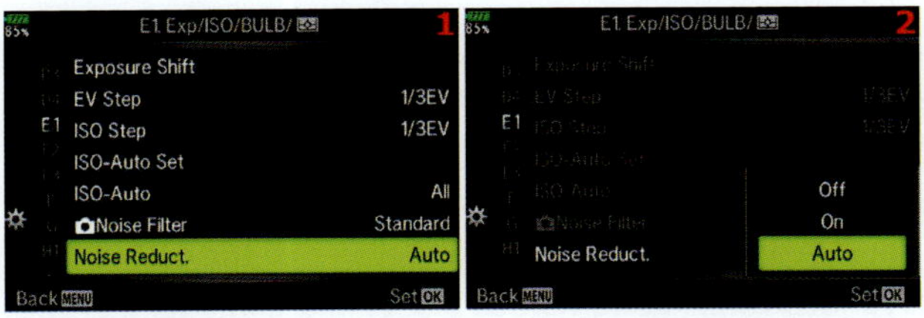

Figure 7.106A: Selecting a Noise Reduct. setting for long exposures

Use the following steps to select a long-exposure Noise Reduct. setting:

1. Select Noise Reduct. from the E1. Exp/ISO/BULB/[Meter] menu and scroll to the right (figure 7.106A, image 1).
2. Select Off, On, or Auto from the menu that appears (figure 7.106A, image 2).
3. Press the OK button to Set the value.

Note: Noise Reduct. may also kick in when ambient temperatures are high, such as on a hot summer day. The sensor can get quite warm when the camera is in the sun absorbing heat.

If you are shooting in [Sequential] H or [Sequential] L modes, firing off rapid bursts of images, the camera is smart enough to turn off Noise Reduct. for the image bursts. There is no need to slow the bursts down, even on a hot day.

Settings Recommendation: The factory default setting is Auto, and I've found that it works well for me. The camera consistently kicks in long-exposure noise reduction at a shutter speed of about 2.5 seconds and results in nicer-looking long exposures than without the setting enabled. When the picture is taken at a shutter speed faster than 2.5 seconds in Auto, the Noise Reduct. function is not used. Auto may be the best choice for most photographers because many exposures are shorter than 2.5 seconds, and Noise Reduct. will be used only when it is needed.

I don't need Noise Reduct. all the time, so I don't use the On setting, nor do I want to completely shut it Off. Make some long-exposure shots with and without Noise Reduct. enabled and see which works best for you.

Bulb/Time Timer (E2)

When you set your camera to Manual (M) mode on the Mode Dial and turn the shutter speed to its lowest setting with the Rear Dial, you will find specific shutter speed settings called BULB (or LIVE BULB) and LIVE TIME. (***Note:*** Do not confuse these camera shutter speed settings with the Live Bulb and Live Time function names in upcoming sections of this chapter.) The BULB, LIVE BULB, and LIVE TIME shutter speed settings allow you to make long exposures from 1 to 30 minutes in length.

The Bulb/Time Timer function allows you to control the maximum time for the long exposures. You can select from a range of 1min (1 minute) to 30min (30 minutes). When you use the BULB or LIVE BULB shutter speed setting you have to manually hold the shutter open by pressing the Shutter button or using a locking electronic shutter-release cable. We will discuss the BULB and LIVE BULB shutter speeds in more detail in upcoming subsections. When you use the LIVE TIME shutter speed setting, the camera holds the shutter open for you.

Let's examine how to select one of the Bulb/Time Timer settings.

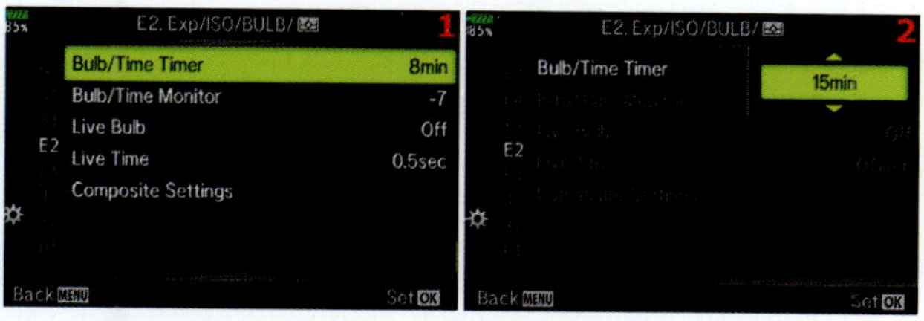

Figure 7.106B: Choosing a time-out setting for the BULB/TIME Timer function

Use the following steps to choose a time-out or maximum time to have the shutter open when you use the BULB, LIVE BULB, or LIVE TIME shutter speed settings for long exposures:

1. Select Bulb/Time Timer from the E2. Exp/ISO/BULB/[Meter] menu and scroll to the right (figure 7.106B, image 1).
2. Select one of the eight time-out values from the up/down menu. Your choices range from 1min to 30min (figure 7.106B, image 2).
3. Press the OK button to Set the value.

Note: If you are using the Noise Reduct. function (see the **Noise Reduct.** subsection), the camera will use long-exposure noise reduction for each of your BULB, LIVE BULB, or LIVE TIME exposures, effectively doubling the time of the exposure. Therefore, a 1-minute exposure will be doubled to 2 minutes, and an 8-minute exposure will be doubled to 16 minutes. This is due to the black-frame subtraction method the camera uses to reduce noise in long exposures. You can disable Noise Reduct. if you do not want the shutter to be open for double the exposure time, but your images may have fog and bright spots because of amp noise and hot pixels.

Settings Recommendation: You will have to decide how long your exposure needs to be for your purposes. For LIVE BULB and LIVE TIME shutter speed exposures, the camera will show you the light buildup of the actual exposure on the Live view display screen so you can see how the long exposure is progressing over time. The screen can update itself—showing you the progress of the exposure—up to 24 times during each exposure. The number of times the live exposure preview updates is governed by the sensitivity of the ISO setting. The amount of time between each screen update (from 0.5 to 60 seconds) is controlled by the upcoming Live Bulb and Live Time functions. For BULB shutter speed exposures, you will not see the light buildup on the Live view display screen. You will have to wait until you release the shutter and the Noise Reduct. function has finished removing long-exposure noise before the final image will appear on the screen.

Bulb/Time Monitor (E2)

You will normally use the BULB, LIVE BULB, and LIVE TIME shutter speeds to take long exposures in the dark. Therefore, you may want the monitor to be very dim to preserve your night vision.

On the other hand, you may be shooting a one- or two-minute daylight exposure with a neutral-density (ND) filter to hold back the brightness of the exposure and allow a long exposure in normal light. In that case you may want the monitor to be brighter than normal.

The camera allows you to change the brightness of the monitor when using the BULB, LIVE BULB, and LIVE TIME shutter speeds by using the Bulb/Time Monitor function. You can select from –7 to +7 levels of brightness. The factory default is –7 for a very dim monitor. You will see the monitor dim immediately when you select the BULB, LIVE BULB, or LIVE TIME shutter speeds.

Let's examine how to select the monitor brightness for long exposures.

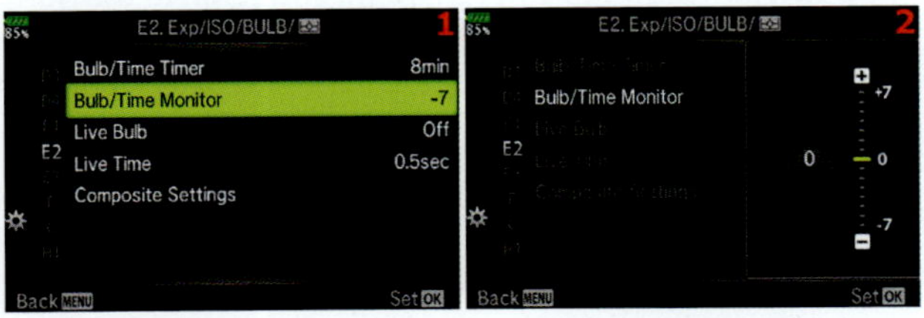

Figure 7.107: Choosing a monitor brightness level for BULB, LIVE BULB, and LIVE TIME

Use the following steps to choose a monitor brightness level when you use the BULB, LIVE BULB, or LIVE TIME shutter speeds for long exposures:

1. Select Bulb/Time Monitor from the E2. Exp/ISO/BULB/[Meter] menu and scroll to the right (figure 7.107, image 1).
2. Use the Arrow Pad up or down keys to choose one of the 15 brightness levels from –7 to +7 (figure 7.107, image 2). The factory default is –7 (very dim).
3. Press the OK button to Set the value.

Settings Recommendation: I do most of my long exposure shooting at night, so I leave this value set to –7. However, if you like to do daytime long exposures with a neutral-density filter, you will want your monitor to be bright. If you select the BULB, LIVE BULB, or LIVE TIME shutter speeds during the day, with this setting at –7, the monitor will be too dim to see in normal daylight. Therefore, set the value in advance.

Live Bulb (E2)

When you rotate the Rear Dial while using Manual (M) mode on the Mode Dial, you will find BULB, LIVE BULB, or LIVE TIME *shutter speeds* as the slowest shutter speed settings.

When you set the Live Bulb *function* to Off, the camera will use the BULB shutter speed to make exposures. If you select any other setting besides Off for the Live Bulb function, the camera will use the LIVE BULB shutter speed instead of the BULB shutter speed.

Note: To avoid confusion, please notice that this function is called Live Bulb. It controls a shutter speed setting named LIVE BULB. Notice the differences in uppercase and lowercase notations so you will not get Live Bulb (the Custom Menu function) and LIVE BULB (the shutter speed setting) confused as we discuss them. LIVE BULB and BULB work similarly when starting and ending the image exposure—notice which term is displayed on the camera screens during the exposure so you can tell the difference. Using the Live Bulb function with its LIVE BULB shutter speed allows you to see a buildup of the exposure on the camera's Live View monitor. If you use the BULB shutter speed setting, which is available only when the Live Bulb function is set to Off, you will not see a buildup of exposure on the monitor. Instead, you will see the results of the exposure when the camera has closed the shutter after the exposure is complete and any long-exposure noise reduction has been completed (see the *Custom Menu > E1. Exp/ISO/BULB/[Meter] > Noise Reduct.* function).

When you use the BULB or LIVE BULB shutter speed settings, the camera opens the shutter (starts the exposure) when you press and hold the Shutter button all the way down or when you manually hold the shutter open with a locking electronic cable release. The exposure ends when you release the Shutter button to close the shutter.

When Live Bulb (the function discussed in this section) is set to Off and you rotate the Rear Dial to the slowest shutter speed positions, BULB will be displayed instead of LIVE BULB as one of the last few shutter speed choices.

Let's consider each of the BULB-type shutter speed settings.

BULB Shutter Speed

When this setting is selected the word BULB will be displayed in the shutter speed position of the monitor or viewfinder (figure 7.108A, image 1).

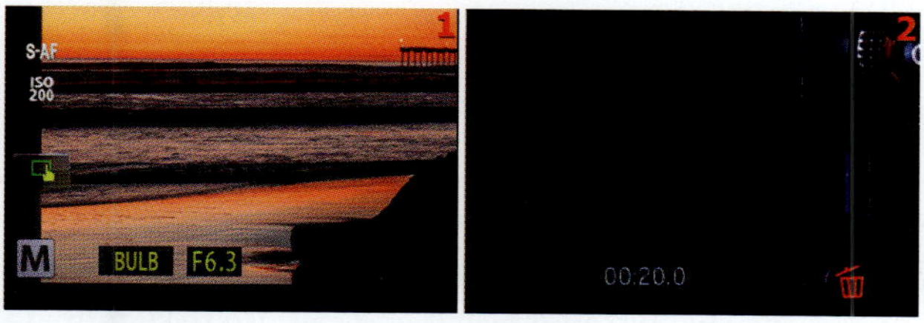

Figure 7.108A: Using the BULB shutter speed setting

When you press and hold the Shutter button and start exposing a picture using BULB, the monitor turns black. It displays a countdown timer at the bottom of the screen during the long exposure (figure 7.108A, image 2). The countdown timer shows how long you have held the shutter open when using the BULB shutter speed.

As soon as you release the Shutter button, the exposure ends. If the exposure was longer than about 2.5 seconds and if long exposure noise reduction is enabled (*Custom Menu > E1. Exp/[Meter]/ISO > Noise Reduct.*), the camera will execute a long-exposure noise reduction cycle, doubling the exposure time while removing long-exposure noise. You will see the orange card access symbol flashing in the upper-left corner of the screen during the noise reduction cycle. When it is done, the camera will display the new image on the monitor.

LIVE BULB Shutter Speed

When you use the LIVE BULB shutter speed setting, your camera makes an exposure over time and displays the live results on your camera's current display screen (viewfinder or monitor).

Press and hold the Shutter button to start the exposure, and the camera will start updating the live exposure on the current display screen. You can see the actual image being formed on the monitor during a LIVE BULB exposure in figure 7.108B, images 2–4

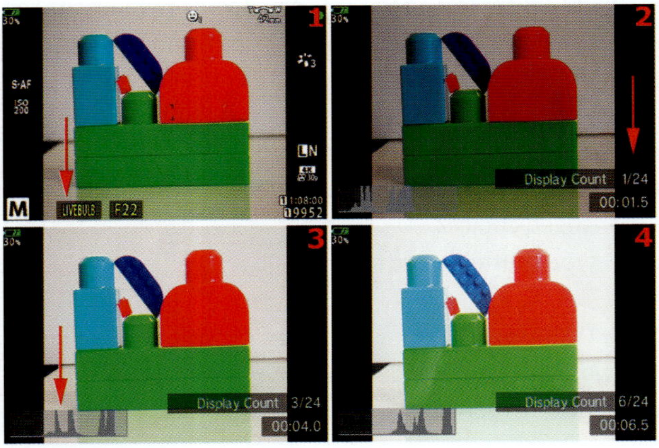

Figure 7.108B: Using the LIVE BULB shutter speed setting

When the Live Bulb function is set to any value besides Off, the LIVE BULB shutter speed selection displays on the bottom left of the screen (figure 7.108B, image 1, red arrow).

Figure 7.108B, image 2, shows the location of the Display Count (at the tip of the red arrow) so you can watch how many times the live exposure update has occurred (up to 24 times maximum). Image 3 shows the Live histogram that you can use to determine when the exposure is correct. If you want a good exposure, release the Shutter button when the histogram graph approaches or touches the right side of the histogram window.

The live exposure display will update in specific increments. You can select from 0.5sec (1/2 second) to 60sec (60 seconds) for the screen update increment. We will discuss how in a moment.

During an exposure using the LIVE BULB shutter speed, the camera will update the screen approximately 9 to 24 times (*how many times* is controlled by the ISO sensitivity). You can use the Live BULB function to choose *how often* the screen updates during the long exposure for each of the 9 to 24 times (Display Count).

In other words, if you select 4sec in Live BULB, the camera will update the live exposure display every four seconds up to 24 times during the actual live exposure process. You will see the image gradually appear on the screen.

The number of times (9 to 24) the live exposure display updates is controlled by the ISO sensitivity, as shown in the following Display Count list:

- **ISO LOW:** Approximately 24 times
- **ISO 400:** Approximately 19 times
- **ISO 800:** Approximately 14 times
- **ISO 1600:** Approximately 9 times

Now let's see how to choose a time increment for the Live Bulb function.

Setting a Time Increment for the Live BULB Function

Use the Live Bulb function to choose how frequently the monitor displays an updated live exposure view when you use the LIVE BULB shutter speed, or whether the camera shows no live exposure updates when you use BULB (with the Live Bulb function set to Off).

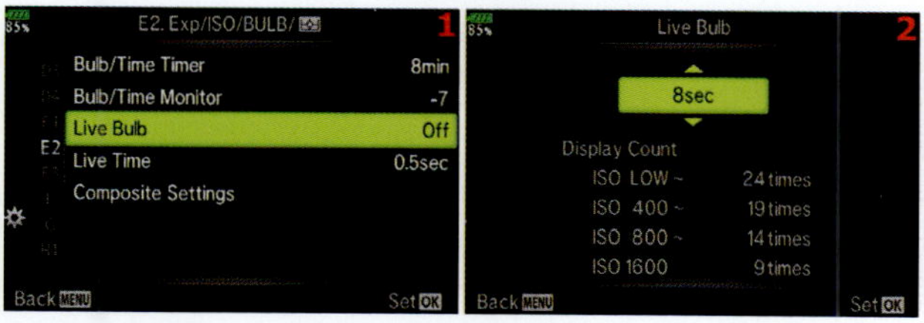

Figure 7.109: Choose how often the live exposure view updates for LIVE BULB time exposures

Use the following steps to choose an update increment for LIVE BULB during long exposures:

1. Select Live Bulb from the E2. Exp/ISO/BULB/[Meter] menu and scroll to the right (figure 7.109, image 1).
2. Choose one of the values from the up/down menu, ranging from 0.5sec to 60sec (figure 7.109, image 2). The factory default setting is Off for BULB mode (no live exposure updates). If you want to watch the LIVE BULB mode update the screen with a live exposure, you must select how often you want it to update (e.g., 4sec) from the up/

down menu. The approximate Display Count (9 times to 24 times) is shown below the up/down menu in image 2.
3. Press the OK button to Set the value.

Note: During the long exposure, if you have chosen to see the live exposure update—with Live Bulb set to anything other than Off—you will see the exposure forming on the screen. If you decide the exposure is correct for your subject, either by viewing it directly or by watching the Live histogram display on the screen, you can release the Shutter button and stop the exposure at that moment.

If you have the Noise Reduct. function enabled, the camera will do a noise reduction cycle equal in time to the original exposure. It will generally double the exposure time while using black-frame subtraction to reduce noise.

Settings Recommendation: I want my camera to show a live exposure update, so I set Live Bulb to something like 4sec, or maybe more for a very long exposure. The screen will be updated a maximum of 24 times, so you will need to do some math to calculate an update increment that matches the length of the planned exposure and the number of times the screen is updated.

I try to set the exposure frequency so the screen will update throughout the exposure. For instance, if I am doing a 1min exposure with the LIVE BULB shutter speed setting, at a lower ISO (24 steps) I set the Live Bulb function to 2sec so the camera will update each of the 24 steps every 2 seconds. That means I will see updates on my monitor every 2 seconds until the 24 update steps have completed.

There is a nearly identical function called Live Time (next subsection) that lets you control the updates of the screen when you use the LIVE TIME shutter speed.

Live Time (E2)

When you rotate the Rear Dial while using Manual (M) mode on the Mode Dial, you will find that LIVE TIME is one of the slowest shutter speed settings.

Note: To avoid confusion, please notice that the function we will discuss in this section is called Live Time. It controls the shutter speed setting named LIVE TIME. Notice the uppercase and lowercase differences so you will not get Live Time (the Custom Menu function) and LIVE TIME (the shutter speed setting) confused as we discuss them.

When you use the LIVE TIME shutter speed setting, the camera opens the shutter (starts the exposure) when you press the Shutter button all the way down. You do not need to hold the Shutter button down when you use LIVE TIME, as you do when you use LIVE BULB (or BULB), because the camera makes the exposure for you based on the time limit that was set in the previously discussed Bulb/Time Timer function *(Custom Menu > E2. Exp/ISO/BULB/[Meter] > Bulb/Time Timer)*.

The exposure ends when the Bulb/Time Timer function's exposure time has expired or when you press the Shutter button all the way down once more. You may manually stop the exposure when you think it looks right on the monitor (or on the Live histogram display) by pressing the Shutter button.

As the camera makes an exposure over time and displays the live results of that exposure on your camera's current display screen (viewfinder or monitor), you can see the actual image being formed.

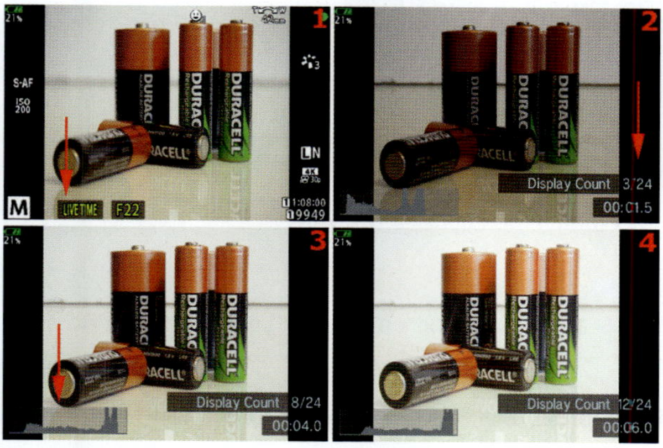

Figure 7.110: Using the LIVE TIME shutter speed setting

The LIVE TIME shutter speed selection is displayed on the bottom left of the screen (figure 7.110, image 1, red arrow). Press the Shutter button to start the exposure, and the camera will start updating the live exposure on the current display screen.

Figure 7.110, image 2, shows the location of the Display Count (at the tip of the red arrow) so you can watch how many times the live exposure update has occurred (up to 24 times). Image 3 shows the Live histogram that you can use to determine when the exposure is correct.

The live exposure display will update in specific increments. You can select from 0.5sec (1/2 second) to 60sec (60 seconds) for the screen update increment. We will discuss how in a moment. Figure 7.110, image 4, shows the final exposure.

After you have selected a value besides Off for this Live Time function, the camera will update the screen during a long exposure from approximately 9 to 24 times (*how many times* is controlled by the ISO sensitivity). You can use this Live Time function to choose *how often* the screen updates during the long exposure for each of the 9 to 24 times.

In other words, if you select 4sec in Live Time, the camera will update the live exposure display every 4 seconds up to 24 times maximum during the actual live exposure process. You will see the image gradually appear on the screen.

The number of times (9 to 24) the live exposure display updates is controlled by the ISO sensitivity, as shown in the following Display Count list:

- **ISO LOW:** Approximately 24 times
- **ISO 400:** Approximately 19 times
- **ISO 800:** Approximately 14 times
- **ISO 1600:** Approximately 9 times

Use the Live Time function to choose how frequently the monitor displays an updated live exposure view when you use the LIVE TIME shutter speed setting, or whether the camera shows no live exposure updates when you use LIVE TIME (with the Live Time function set to Off).

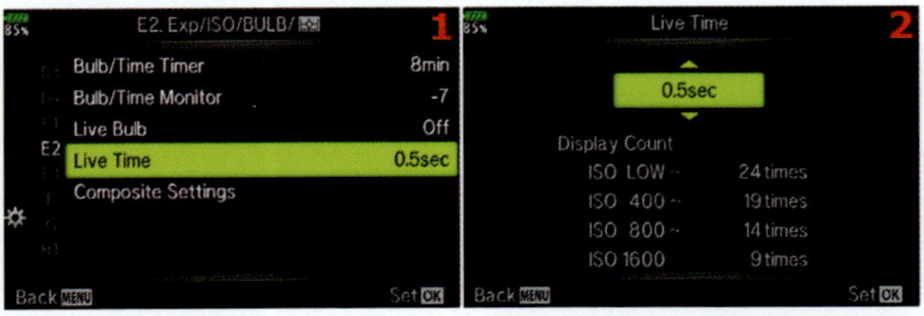

Figure 7.111: Choose how often the live exposure view updates for LIVE TIME long exposures

Use the following steps to choose an update increment for LIVE TIME during long exposures:

1. Select Live Time from the E2. Exp/ISO/BULB/[Meter] menu and scroll to the right (figure 7.111, image 1).
2. Choose one of the values from the up/down menu, ranging from 0.5sec to 60sec (figure 7.111, image 2). The factory default setting is 0.5sec (1/2 second live exposure updates). If you want to see up to 24 updates per ISO setting, you must select how often you want an update to display from the up/down menu (not Off). The approximate Display Count (9 times to 24 times) is shown below the up/down menu in image 2. During the exposure, you will see the Display Count and a timer on the lower-right side of the screen while a Live histogram appears on the lower-left side of the screen.
3. Press the OK button to Set the value.

Note: During the long exposure, if you have chosen to see the live exposure update—with the Live Time function set to anything other than Off—you will see the exposure forming on the screen. If you decide the exposure is correct for your subject, either by viewing it directly or by watching the Live histogram display on the screen, you can press the Shutter button again and stop the exposure at that moment.

If you have the Noise Reduct. function enabled, the camera will do a noise reduction cycle equal in time to the original exposure. It will generally double the exposure time while using black-frame subtraction to reduce noise.

Settings Recommendation: I want my camera to show a live exposure update, so I set Live TIME to a value, such as 2sec or 8sec, according to how long of an exposure is set in the Bulb/Time Timer function.

I try to set the exposure frequency so the screen will update all through the exposure. For instance, if I am doing an 8min exposure at a lower ISO (24 steps), I set the Live Time function to 15sec so the camera will update one of the 24 steps every 15 seconds. That means I will see the updates on my monitor every 15 seconds until the 24 update steps have completed.

Composite Settings (E2)

The Live Composite function allows you to create composite images of subjects like a fireworks display (figure 7.112). You can set up many multiple exposures on one frame, with each exposure acting independently.

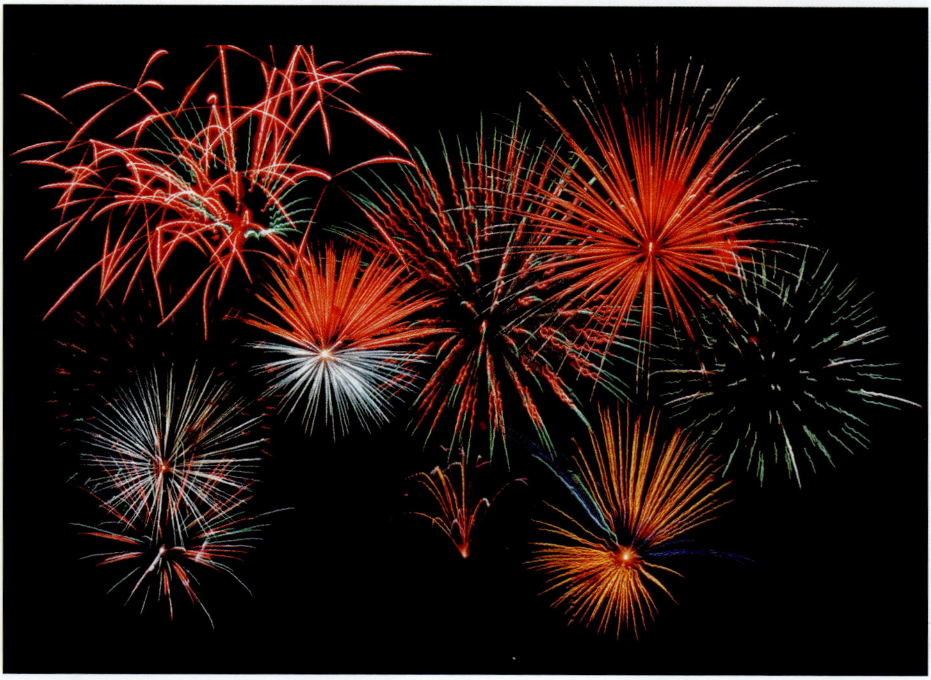

Figure 7.112: Sample composite fireworks image

The camera will automatically create a composite image as you watch the exposure timer count down. You can recompose the frame between exposures so you can capture multiple bright subjects with dark backgrounds. Figure 7.112 is a composite image that is made up of 10 separate exposures.

There are two ways to configure the Composite Settings. You can use the Custom Menu first to configure the exposure time and then enter the Live Composite system, or you can enter the Live Composite system first then set the exposure time just before you shoot the frames you want to combine. Let's consider both.

Setting the Composite Settings before Entering Live Composite

You can configure the exposure time for each frame before you enter the Live Composite system so your camera will be ready ahead of time. Here is how to preconfigure the composite exposure value (applies to each frame).

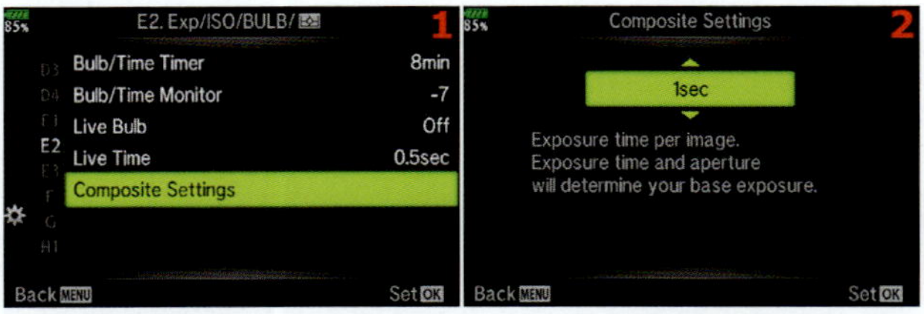

Figure 7.113: Configuring an exposure value before entering Live Composite mode

Use the following steps to preconfigure an exposure value that will be applied to each frame of the composite image:

1. Select Composite Settings from the E2. Exp/ISO/BULB/[Meter] menu and scroll to the right (figure 7.113, image 1).
2. Choose an Exposure time per image from the Composite Settings up/down menu (figure 7.113, image 2). Your choices in the up/down menu range from 1/2 second (1/2sec) to 60 seconds (60sec). Choose the time you want to use for each exposure in the composite series.
3. Press the OK button to Set your chosen value.

The camera is now ready to enter the Live Composite system and make your composite images.

Next, let's consider how to set the Exposure time per image when you are already in the Live Composite system.

Setting the Composite Settings after Entering Live Composite

Open the Live Composite system by selecting the LIVECOMP shutter speed setting, which is at the slow end of the shutter speed selections, along with BULB and LIVE TIME.

Let's see how to use the Live Composite system to create an image like the one shown in figure 7.114.

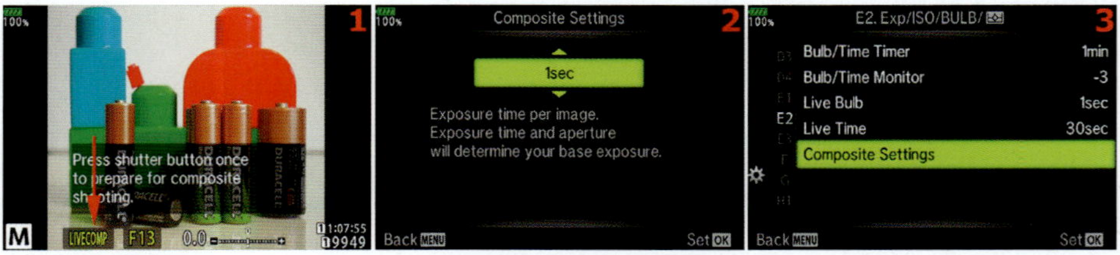

Figure 7.114: Selecting an exposure time while in Live Composite mode

Use these steps to set the Composite Settings after you activate the Live Composite system:

1. Set the camera to Manual (M) mode on the Mode Dial.
2. Using the Rear Dial, select LIVECOMP from the shutter speed settings. The LIVECOMP choice is the slowest available shutter speed; it is the last setting past BULB and LIVE TIME (figure 7.114, image 1, red arrow).
3. Press the Menu button to directly enter the Composite Settings screen (figure 7.114, image 2). Choose an Exposure time per image to be applied equally to each frame in the composite image. Your choices in the up/down menu range from 1/2 second (1/2sec) to 60 seconds (60sec).
4. Press the OK button to select the exposure time, and the camera will switch to the screen in figure 7.114, image 3. Nothing needs to be done on this screen, so press the Shutter button slightly to return to the first screen in the series (figure 7.114, image 1). The time value is selected and ready to use. The next few steps will take the pictures to be composited.

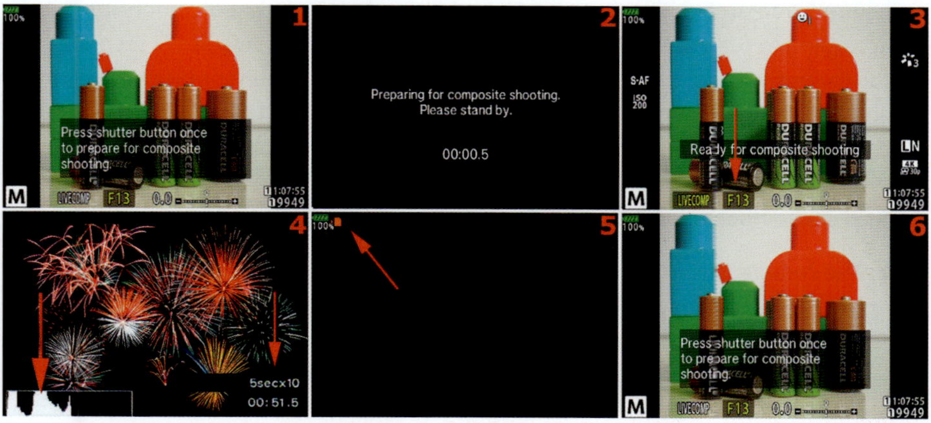

Figure 7.115: Taking pictures with the Live Composite system

5. The Live Composite screen (figure 7.115, image 1) will display this message: *Press shutter button once to prepare for composite shooting.*
6. Press the Shutter button all the way down once, and the camera will prepare to take the composite series. A dark screen will open for a few seconds that says, *Preparing for composite shooting. Please stand by* (figure 7.115, image 2).
7. The next screen says, *Ready for composite shooting*. It will use the settings and exposure value you selected. Before proceeding, use the Front Dial to set the aperture (figure 7.115, image 3, red arrow). Then focus the camera on the subject or on the area where the subject will appear. It may be a good idea to use manual focus for subjects that will appear later in the series, such as a fireworks show. After you have focused the camera, press the Shutter button completely down one time to start the exposures.

8. The camera will start taking a series of timed pictures until one of the following occurs: you stop Live Composite by pressing the Shutter button fully; three hours have passed; or the battery dies. Three hours is the maximum run time for the Live Composite system before it automatically shuts down. At the left red arrow in figure 7.115, image 4, you can see that the camera is building a live histogram as it takes the exposures. You can watch this histogram to prevent overexposure as additional images are taken over time. At the right red arrow in image 4, you can see the camera counting down the exposures and time. The image shows 5secx10, which means each exposure is 5 seconds long (5sec), and 10 exposures have been made so far (x10). Just beneath the exposure count is a timer that displays the actual time of the Live Composite session. The time is counted in 1/2 second increments up to three hours. During the series of exposures you can move the camera to position a bright subject somewhere else in the frame.
9. Stop the Live Composite session by completely pressing the Shutter button once. The monitor will go black except for the orange memory card access symbol in the upper-left corner, which will blink as the camera finishes combining the images (figure 7.115, image 5, red arrow). Finally, the camera will display the finished composite picture, according to the value you chose in *Setup Menu > Rec View* (default 1/2 second), then the camera will switch back to the main Live Composite screen so you can prepare for another session (figure 7.115, image 6).
10. If you would like to shoot another Live Composite series, simply repeat steps 3 through 9. If you are done shooting in Live Composite, select a different shutter speed to exit the Live Composite system.

Note: The camera will automatically adjust the brightness of the monitor during a Live Composite session. It may be best to use an HLD-7 battery pack so you will have two batteries available for long exposures if you shoot in Live Composite for hours at a time. Finally, if you want to see the number of composited shots in the final image, you can find it later in your computer with the included Olympus Viewer 3 software.

Metering (E3)

The E-M1II has five meter types, which gives you great flexibility in how you expose your images. Using the meter styles built in to the camera along with the Live Histogram will allow you to take some of the best-exposed images you've ever created.

Let's look more closely at the five types of light meters built in to the camera and discuss their differences:

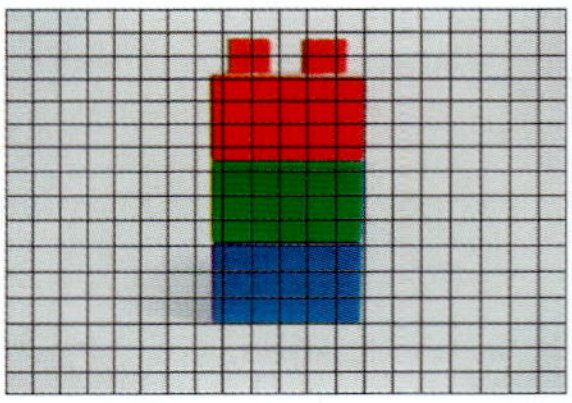

- **[Digital ESP Metering]:** ESP stands for electrosensitive pattern. The camera meters the image in a grid of 324 metered areas. It examines each of the 324 areas and uses complex mathematical computations to arrive at an excellent exposure most of the time. This metering mode works best for portraits when Face Priority is enabled.

- **[Center-Weighted Averaging Metering]:** The camera averages the light between the subject and the background. It places more emphasis on the center area of the screen (large fuzzy red circle in the accompanying image) with less emphasis on parts of the scene that are farther away from the center. This mode is provided for those of us who learned to use a center-weighted meter and prefer to use that metering method. You will see a medium-sized circle in the middle of the monitor. The circle does not represent the actual size of the averaging meter's most important metering area; it shows just the center.

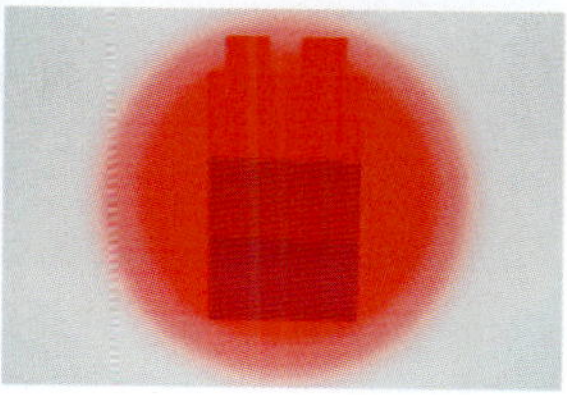

- **[Spot Metering]:** The camera uses a small circle in the center of the frame for metering. This circle is equivalent to 2 percent of the frame and is roughly represented by the red dot in the accompanying figure. All metering takes place in this 2 percent area. Therefore, you must place this nonmoveable spot on the area of the subject that you want to correctly meter by moving the camera, and then using autoexposure lock (AEL/AFL button) to lock the exposure while you recompose the image (see the next subsection, **AEL Metering**). Or you can take multiple readings of different areas of the scene, determine the total light range, and set the exposure manually.

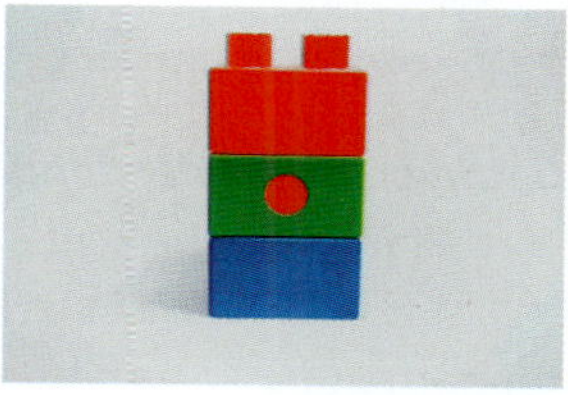

- **[Spot Metering—Highlight (HI)]:** This type of metering is similar to [Spot Metering] in that the camera uses a small circle in the center of the frame to meter. This circle is equivalent to 2 percent of the frame and is roughly represented by the red dot just above the White-Out logo in the accompanying figure. This metering mode is different because the camera tries to make white areas (highlights) stay white by increasing the exposure beyond a [Spot Metering] reading to give a bright, high-key look to the image.

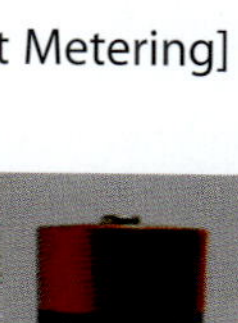

- **[Spot Metering—Shadow (SH)]:** This type of metering is similar to [Spot Metering] in that the camera uses a small circle in the center of the frame to meter. This circle is equivalent to 2 percent of the frame and is roughly represented by the red dot in the accompanying figure. This metering mode is different because the camera tries to make dark areas (shadows) stay dark by decreasing the exposure below a [Spot Metering] reading to give a low-key look to the image.

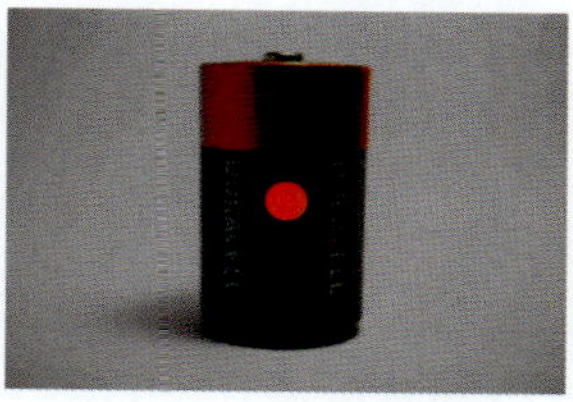

Now let's examine how to select one of the metering types.

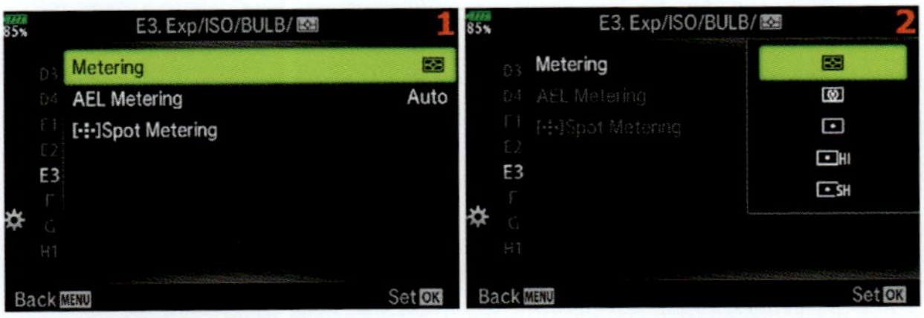

Figure 7.116: Choosing a light meter type

Use the following steps to choose a Metering type:

1. Select Metering from the E3. Exp/ISO/BULB/[Meter] menu and scroll to the right (figure 7.116, image 1).
2. Select one of the five meter types shown in the menu (figure 7.116, image 2).
3. Press the OK button to Set the value.

Settings Recommendation: I usually use [Digital ESP Metering]. I like the way it evaluates all areas of the screen and arrives at an excellent exposure. However, I have found that it is best to use Face Priority along with this meter type to have the best exposure for portraiture.

There is a meter type for each of us: the [Center-Weighted Averaging Meter] is good for old-timers who like this traditional meter style. The three types of [Spot Metering] allow extremely accurate metering of specific areas of a subject for those who understand how to use a spot meter. The highlight and shadow meters add icing to the cake.

I suggest experimenting with all these meter types until you are familiar with them.

AEL Metering (E3)

When you press the AEL/AFL button with the camera configured for autoexposure lock, the camera makes a meter reading then locks the exposure until you release the AEL/AFL button. Olympus has provided a means for you to choose which type of meter your camera will use to make the exposure reading that will be locked.

There are five AEL Metering modes:

- **Auto:** When you press the AEL/AFL button, the camera uses whichever metering mode you selected in the **Metering** subsection. This is the factory default setting, and it is apparently the only way to access [Digital ESP Metering] for autoexposure lock.
- **[Center-Weighted Averaging Metering]:** When you press the AEL/AFL button, the camera switches to [Center-Weighted Averaging Metering], as described in the **Metering** subsection.
- **[Spot Metering]:** When you press the AEL/AFL button, the camera switches to [Spot Metering], as described in the **Metering** subsection.
- **[Spot Metering—Highlight (HI)]:** When you press the AEL/AFL button, the camera switches to [Spot Metering—Highlight (HI)], as described in the **Metering** subsection.

- **[Spot Metering—Shadow (SH)]:** When you press the AEL/AFL button, the camera switches to [Spot Metering—Shadow (SH)], as described in the **Metering** subsection.

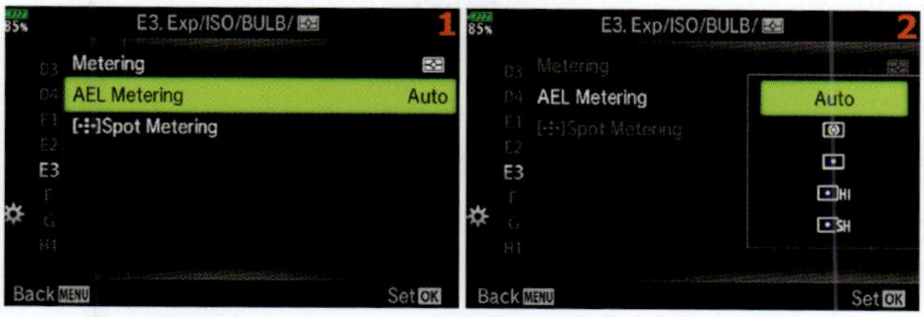

Figure 7.117: Choosing a metering mode for autoexposure lock

Use the following steps to choose a Metering type when you press the AEL/AFL button:

1. Select AEL Metering from the E3. Exp/ISO/BULB/[Meter] menu and scroll to the right (figure 7.117, image 1).
2. Select one of the five meter types shown in the menu (figure 7.117, image 2).
3. Press the OK button to Set the value.

Settings Recommendation: The Auto mode seems to be the most reasonable setting for me. I normally have the best light meter type already selected before I use autoexposure lock.

However, maybe you are metering a beautiful sunset and decide to use autoexposure lock to meter a bright orange cloud. You might want to use [Spot Metering]. If you already had the AEL Metering function set to [Spot Metering], you would be ready to shoot. You could meter the bright cloud, recompose, take the shot, then continue shooting with [Digital ESP Metering] for more images of other subjects. In cases like this it may be wise to separate the Metering types when you use normal metering and after pressing the AEL/AFL button.

[AF Target] Spot Metering

The E-M1II allows you to tie the spot metering (and spot highlight and spot shadow metering) to the currently selected AF Target area. This makes a lot of sense, as you would think the area of focus would also be the area where you want to measure the light.

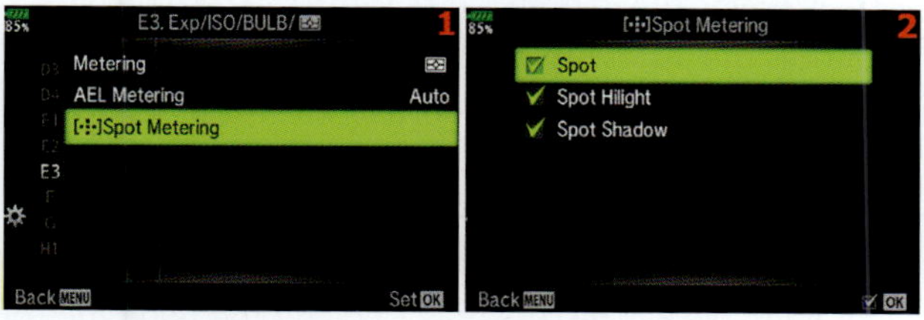

Figure 7.118: Metering the selected AF Target

Use the following steps to enable spot metering for the selected AF Target:

1. Select [AF Target] Spot Metering from the E3. Exp/ISO/BULB/[Meter] menu and scroll to the right (figure 7.118, image 1).
2. Place a check mark next to each spot metering type by highlighting it and pressing the OK button (figure 7.118, image 2).
3. Once you have made your selections, press the Menu button to return to the previous screen.

Settings Recommendation: I always tie the focus point to the spot metering so that the camera meters the most important area of the scene.

Custom Menu F. [Flash] Custom

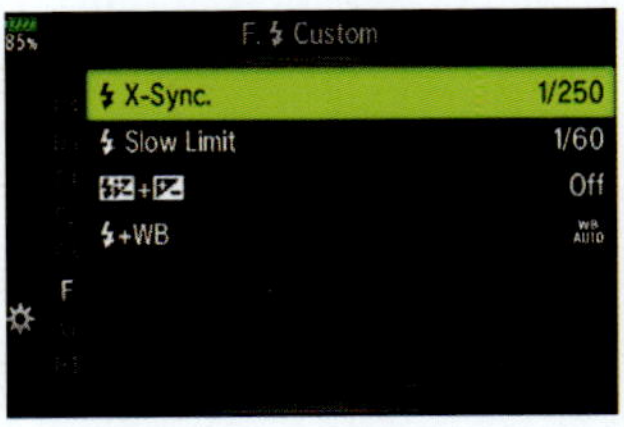

Figure 7.119: F. [Flash] Custom functions

The F. [Flash] Custom menu is composed of functions that directly affect how the flash system works. First we will take a look at the opening menu screen for the F. [Flash] Custom functions (figure 7.119).

To enter the menu, select F. [Flash] Custom from the Custom Menu and scroll to the right. There are four functions in the F. [Flash] Custom menu. Let's consider each of them in detail.

[Flash] X-Sync (F)

The [Flash] X-Sync function sets a maximum shutter speed for shooting with an electronic flash unit that is mounted in the hot shoe and turned on.

The X-Sync speed is necessary because the shutter blades in front of the sensor have to be out of the way before the flash can fire. If a shutter blade partially blocks the sensor, a dark shadow or band will appear in the image.

The X-Sync name comes from the old days when lenses had an actual X on them. You had to select the setting with a lever when you used flash. The old mechanical clockwork shutters had an electrical contact that closed the circuit and fired the flash when the shutter blades were completely out of the way. On the E-M1II, X-Sync is controlled by an electronic timing circuit instead of a mechanical contact.

The E-M1II allows you to select an X-Sync speed from 1/60 second to 1/250 second.

The [Flash] X-Sync function controls the fastest, or *maximum,* shutter speed you can use with flash (without banding). The next subsection will consider the [Flash] Slow Limit, which controls the slowest, or *minimum,* shutter speed you can use with flash in certain exposure modes. You can use the two functions—[Flash] X-Sync and [Flash] Slow Limit—to control the upper and lower limits of the shutter speed when you use flash to get a mixture of flash light and ambient light. We will discuss how to blend the two types of light in the next subsection, **[Flash] Slow Limit**.

The camera will use the maximum X-Sync value only when you are shooting in a very bright environment in direct flash (Fill In) mode to prevent the ambient light from overly influencing the exposure. Most of the time, in low ambient light, the camera will automatically select a somewhat slower shutter speed, such as 1/60 second, unless you have [Flash] Slow Limit (next subsection) set so it cannot use a speed that low.

Let's examine how to select an X-Sync value that matches your needs.

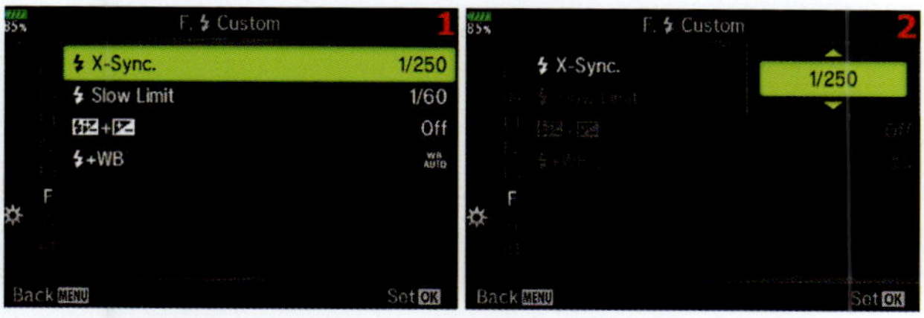

Figure 7.120: Selecting an X-Sync value

Use the following steps to choose a maximum shutter speed to use with flash:

1. Select [Flash] X-Sync from the F. [Flash] Custom menu and scroll to the right (figure 7.120, image 1).
2. Use the Arrow Pad up/down keys to choose one of the brightness levels, which range from 1/60 to 1/250 (figure 7.120, image 2). The factory default setting is 1/250 second.
3. Press the OK button to Set the value.

Settings Recommendation: I normally use 1/250 second for the X-Sync value when I am depending on the flash unit for lighting a subject. However, when I am trying to synchronize flash with evening light outdoors, I may use a combination of the [Flash] X-Sync speed and [Flash] Slow Limit to allow ambient light to influence the exposure for a more balanced look. The camera has a nice range of shutter speeds for slow flash use.

[Flash] Slow Limit (F)

The [Flash] Slow Limit function allows you to control the lower shutter speed limit when you use flash photography (slow flash). You may need this function when you want ambient light combined with light from a flash unit to illuminate the exposure. You may want ambient light to be the primary source of exposure, with the flash providing a little fill light. Or you may want the flash to provide the main illumination, with ambient light opening up the shadows in the background. You may even be using more than one flash in a wireless group of units that work with ambient light.

[Flash] Slow Limit works in partnership with the [Flash] X-Sync function (previous subsection) by allowing you to set the lower limit of the shutter speed when you shoot with flash. The shutter speed can be as slow as 30 seconds. The [Flash] X-Sync function controls the upper shutter speed limit, which cannot exceed 1/250 second and can be set as slow as 1/60 second.

When you have the camera set to Program (P) or Aperture-priority (A) mode on the Mode Dial, the camera controls the shutter speed and you control the aperture. Therefore, the lower shutter speed limit provided by the [Flash] Slow Limit function is important when you are using flash in P and A modes.

If you are using Shutter-priority (S) or Manual (M) mode on the Mode Dial, the [Flash] Slow Limit function has no effect because you can set the lower shutter speed to be as long (slow) as you would like.

Therefore, if you want to balance the illumination from the flash and the ambient light, you can either do it manually in S or M mode, or you can use P or A mode and depend on the [Flash] Slow Limit function to provide the minimum flash shutter speed.

To effectively balance the ambient light with the flash requires experimentation and experience and is beyond the scope of this book. You know that the camera cannot exceed 1/250 second for a maximum shutter speed ([Flash] X-Sync), and now you also know that the camera will allow you to set a minimum shutter speed ([Flash] Slow Limit). Therefore, you can use mostly ambient light by lengthening the shutter speed with a slower setting under [Flash] Slow Limit to let in more ambient light while the flash provides a burst of light for filling in some shadows.

Or you can use a shutter speed in [Flash] Slow Limit that is somewhat closer to the shutter speed in [Flash] X-Sync so the flash will provide the main light source while ambient light provides some background fill.

You will need to experiment with these two settings to find the appropriate balance for what you are trying to accomplish. Be sure to use a tripod if you use shutter speeds in [Flash] Slow Limit that are slow enough to allow camera shake or subject movement. Otherwise, ghosting will be apparent in the image where the flash-lit portion of the subject is sharp and the ambient-lit portion of the subject is blurred.

Let's examine how to set the [Flash] Slow Limit function for various shutter speeds.

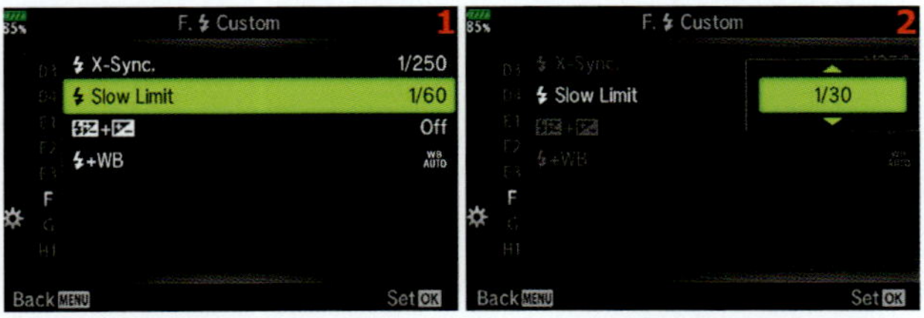

Figure 7.121: Setting a minimum shutter speed for flash photography

Use the following steps to choose a minimum shutter speed to use with flash:

1. Select [Flash] Slow Limit from the F. [Flash] Custom menu and scroll to the right (figure 7.121, image 1).

2. Use the Arrow Pad up/down keys to choose a minimum flash shutter speed, ranging from 30 seconds to 1/250 second (figure 7.121, image 2). The factory default setting is 1/60 second.
3. Press the OK button to Set the value.

Settings Recommendation: I raise the minimum flash shutter speed to 1/100 or 1/125 second when I am shooting with flash indoors. I find that often 1/60 second (the default) is too slow and may allow some ghosting to occur, especially at weddings where I am shooting people walking down the aisle when fairly bright ambient light influences the exposure. If the shutter is open for 1/60 second, the flash will make a nice sharp picture for a short segment of the exposure duration, and ambient light continues to illuminate the subject for the remainder of the exposure duration, resulting in a ghosted blur.

On the other hand, when I am shooting in bright ambient light outside, I may allow the shutter speed to remain slower and take advantage of some ambient light with flash fill. I use a smaller aperture to keep from overexposing the subject.

This type of thing is always an experiment and has to be balanced. You can take advantage of your camera's powerful tools to get the results you want.

[Flash Compensation] + [Exposure Compensation] (F)

This function allows you to combine exposure compensation and flash compensation, and you can control both at the same time with the Front Dial.

Normally, with this function set to Off, when you want to do exposure compensation for your image you simply turn the Front Dial (in P, A, and S modes) and dial in exposure compensation from –5.0 EV to +5.0 EV.

However, when you have a flash unit mounted on your camera, its output is not increased or decreased based on the exposure compensation. Instead, the camera simply opens or closes the aperture, or raises or lowers the shutter speed, to provide more or less exposure. The flash provides a constant output.

Sometimes increasing or decreasing the entire exposure is not sufficient. Maybe you would like to increase or decrease the power of the flash output to perform what Olympus calls "flash intensity control." By setting this function to On, whenever you turn the Front Dial to increase or decrease the camera exposure compensation, the compensation request also affects the flash unit. For example, if you raise the exposure compensation by 1.0 EV, the flash will also raise its power output by 1.0 EV. If you use negative exposure compensation to underexpose the image by 0.3 EV, the flash will also lower its power output by 0.3 EV.

This gives you the ability to control the *intensity* of the flash output very quickly, without having to use the flash unit's compensation controls. It allows you to raise or lower the brightness of the subject visually in case the flash is too strong or too weak.

Basically, Olympus gives you flash intensity control without having to use the camera menus or external flash unit menus. It is a quick way to control the intensity of the flash with the Front Dial when you need more or less light from the flash unit, and you'll still have time to make other adjustments.

Let's examine how to enable or disable [Flash Compensation] + [Exposure Compensation].

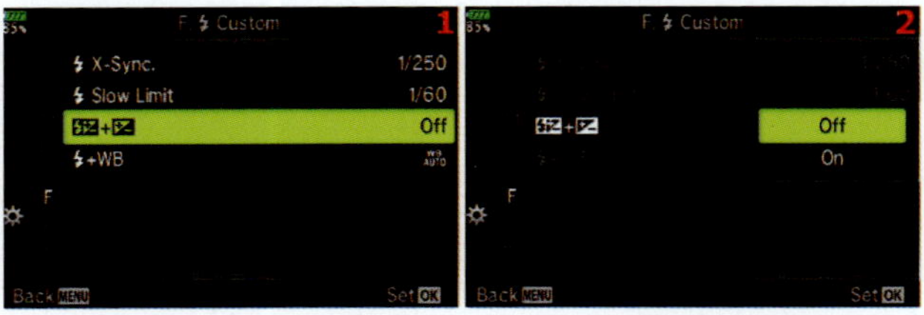

Figure 7.122: Combining flash compensation with exposure compensation

Use the following steps to connect or disconnect flash compensation with exposure compensation by using the Front Dial:

1. Select the dual symbols representing [Flash Compensation] + [Exposure Compensation] from the F. [Flash] Custom menu and scroll to the right (figure 7.122, image 1).
2. Choose On to combine flash and exposure compensation, or choose Off to disconnect the two (figure 7.122, image 2). The factory default setting is Off. This function takes effect only when a flash unit is mounted in the hot shoe.
3. Press the OK button to Set the value.

Settings Recommendation: I leave this function set to On because I love the way it lets me control the intensity of the flash when I turn the Front Dial on my camera in P, A, and S modes. Since it has no effect when a flash unit is not mounted, it is safe to leave it on all the time.

If you are an accomplished strobist who wants to completely separate the two forms of compensation to vary the exposures for the background and the subject, you may want to leave flash and exposure compensation separated and use the camera's and flash unit's manual exposure compensation controls.

For most people the power of this function is very useful.

[Flash] + WB (F)

This function allows you to choose various white balance (WB) types for when you use electronic flash. There are three settings for [Flash] + WB that determine what the camera will do when the flash is active:

- **Off:** The camera will use the current WB setting (e.g., Sunshine, Cloudy, Incandescent) without regard for the color temperature of the flash unit.
- **WB Auto:** The camera will attempt to balance itself to whatever light source is illuminating the subject.
- **WB [Flash]:** The camera will use the Flash WB setting, which is about 5500K.

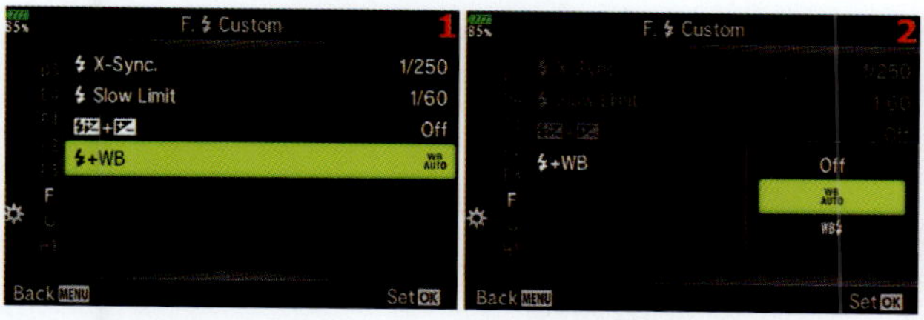

Figure 7.123: White balance choices for flash

Use the following steps to choose an appropriate WB setting for flash:

1. Select the [Flash] + WB function from the F. [Flash] Custom menu and scroll to the right (figure 7.123, image 1).
2. Choose one of the settings from the [Flash] + WB menu (refer to the previous list of choices) (figure 7.123, image 2).
3. Press the OK button to Set your choice.

Settings Recommendation: If you are shooting in JPEG mode, the WB needs to be exactly right. Be careful to select the WB Flash setting from the Live Control screen (press OK in Live View) or the WB [Flash] setting on this function's menu.

Alternatively, you can let the camera decide which WB is best by selecting WB Auto. It may not be the best idea to have a WB setting such as Cloudy or Fluorescent selected while shooting with flash because the color may be off.

For RAW shooters, this setting does not matter since the WB of a RAW file can be changed after the fact.

Custom Menu G. [Record Mode]/WB/Color

The G. [Record Mode]/WB/Color menu is primarily composed of functions that control JPEG image quality, image size, and color balance.

These functions do not affect a RAW file, other than providing initial settings when you view them on your computer, because each setting can be changed after the fact.

Think of these options as in-camera RAW to JPEG conversion functions (in-camera post-processing) that you would otherwise have to do on your computer after you shoot a RAW file and convert it to JPEG manually.

We will start examining the functions by taking a look at the opening menu screen for the G. [Record Mode]/WB/Color functions in figure 7.124.

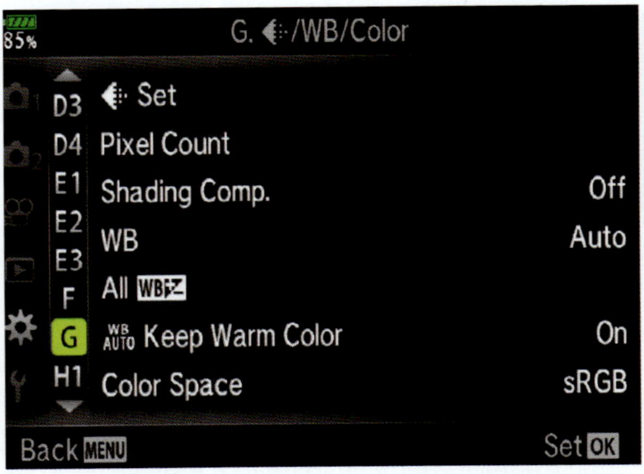

Figure 7.124: The G. [Record Mode]/WB/Color menu

To enter the menu, select G. [Record Mode]/WB/Color from the Custom Menu and scroll to the right. There are seven functions inside the G. [Record Mode]/WB/Color menu. Let's consider each of them in detail.

[Record Mode] Set (G)

Your E-M1II can create three JPEG image sizes: Large (L), Middle (M), and Small (S). All three sizes can use four levels of compression (quality) to reduce the file sizes: Super Fine (SF), Fine (F), Normal (N), and Basic (B). Each of these quality types have different lossy compression ratios, with Super Fine having the least amount of compression and Basic having the most (table 7.10).

You can combine JPEG types in the [Record Mode] Set function and they will appear on the [Record Mode] menus of the camera, where you select an image format (i.e., JPEG, RAW, JPEG+RAW).

Table 7.10 shows the available JPEG sizes and qualities, compression ratios, and Pixel Counts. The Pixel Count for the Middle and Fine JPEG sizes is controlled by the Pixel Count function (next subsection):

JPEG Type (size and quality)	Compression ratio	4:3 Pixel Count
Large Super Fine (LSF)	1/2.7	5184×3888
Large Fine (LF)	1/4	5184×3888
Large Normal (LN)	1/8	5184×3888
Large Basic (LB)	1/12	5184×3888
Middle Super Fine (MSF)	1/2.7	3200×2400
Middle Fine (MF)	1/4	3200×2400
Middle Normal (MN)	1/8	3200×2400
Middle Basic (MB)	1/12	3200×2400

JPEG Type (size and quality)	Compression ratio	4:3 Pixel Count
Small Super Fine (SSF)	1/2.7	1280×960
Small Fine (SF)	1/4	1280×960
Small Normal (SN)	1/8	1280×960
Small Basic (SB)	1/12	1280×960

Table 7.10: JPEG size and quality, compression ratio, and 4:3 Pixel Count

The lower the compression ratio, the higher the image quality and the larger its physical storage size on your computer hard drive. You can add any of these JPEG size and quality settings to the 1, 2, 3, and 4 positions of the screen shown in figure 7.125, image 2. Let's see how.

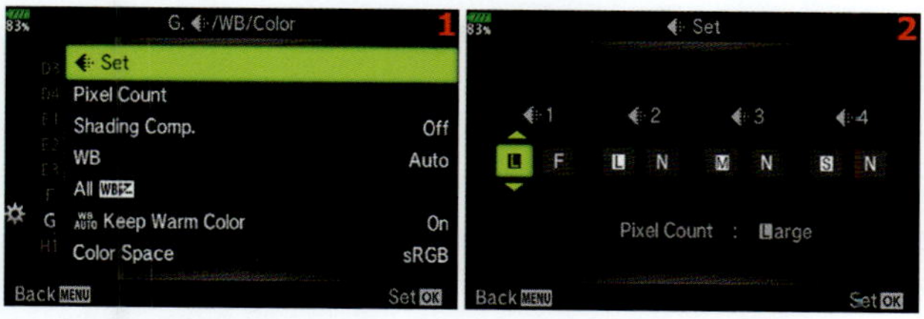

Figure 7.125: Using [Record Mode] Set to choose JPEG types for camera menus

Use the following steps to set various JPEG types in four available selection positions:

1. Select [Record Mode] Set from the G. [Record Mode]/WB/Color menu and scroll to the right (figure 7.125, image 1).
2. In figure 7.125, image 2, you will see four available JPEG type selection boxes, numbered 1, 2, 3, and 4. The factory default is LF, LN, MN, and SN. Using table 7.10 as a reference, choose any of the characters from the values in parentheses under the JPEG Type column and set them in these four positions. Whatever you put in the four positions will appear on any camera menus that allow you to select an image format type (JPEG, RAW, and JPEG+RAW).
3. Press the OK button to Set the value.

Settings Recommendation: I have no need for the smaller sizes, so I use LSF, LF, MF, and SF in my [Record Mode] Set function. I prefer to shoot in either RAW or JPEG Large Super Fine (LSF) most of the time.

However, if you need to put a lot of images on a small memory card, or if you are shooting images for use on a website, you could use any of the other size and quality settings. Anything you choose in [Record Mode] Set will appear on the Record Mode menus (image format selection screens).

Pixel Count (G)

The normal Pixel Count for a Micro Four Thirds (4:3) image on the E-M1II is 5184×3888. This is considered the Large Pixel Count size. The Pixel Count directly affects the megapixel size of the image. Simply multiply the Pixel Count to find the total megapixels. For instance, the large 4:3 Pixel Count results in an approximate size of 20 MP (5184×3888 = 20,155,392, or 20.1 million pixels).

The image does not use the full Pixel Count of the camera sensor because some pixels around the edges are used for color control. However, camera companies usually advertise the camera's megapixel rating based on the actual size of the sensor. That is the difference between the *actual* and *effective* Pixel Count; the effective count is what you actually get for a usable picture, and the actual count is the full sensor Pixel Count. Usually there is a megapixel or two difference between the actual pixel count (which is usually not provided by camera manufacturers) and the effective pixel count (the 5184×3888 image size).

Note: There are other Image Aspects (aspect ratios) and Large Pixel Counts available, such as 3:2, 1:1, and 16:9. When you select one of the alternate Image Aspect ratios, the Pixel Count for their Middle and Small sizes will vary a bit from those listed. The additional image sizes are controlled by the Image Aspect function in Shooting Menu 1 (*Shooting Menu 1 > Image Aspect*). Selecting one of the other aspect ratios will change the Pixel Count for Large, Middle, and Small JPEG images. None of the Large size Pixel Counts are variable, but the Middle and Small Pixel Counts are. The Middle and Small Pixel Count can change depending on your selections in this function.

Let's examine how to choose a different Pixel Count for when you need to shoot a Middle or Small image, such as for a website. First we will examine how to select one of the four available Middle Pixel Counts.

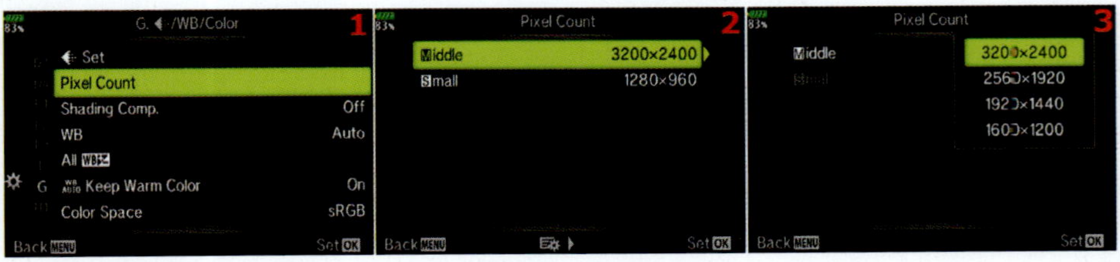

Figure 7.126: Choosing a Middle Pixel Count size

Use the following steps to choose a Middle Pixel Count size:

1. Select Pixel Count from the G. [Record Mode]/WB/Color menu and scroll to the right (figure 7.126, image 1).
2. Choose Middle from the Pixel Count menu and scroll to the right (figure 7.126, image 2).

3. The factory default Middle Pixel Count is 3200×2400 (figure 7.126, image 3). However, you can choose from three additional Pixel Counts: 2560×1920, 1920×1440, and 1600×1200.
4. Press the OK button to Set the new Middle Pixel Count value.

Next let's examine how to select one of the two available Small Pixel Counts.

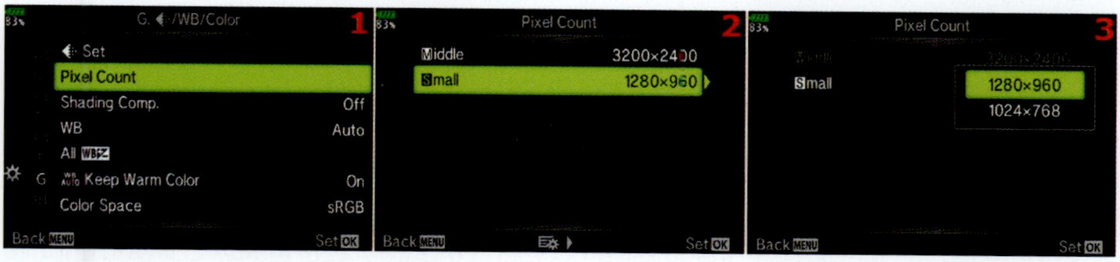

Figure 7.127: Selecting the Small Pixel Count size

Use the following steps to choose a Small Pixel Count size:

1. Select Pixel Count from the G. [Record Mode]/WB/Color menu and scroll to the right (figure 7.127, image 1).
2. Choose Small from the Pixel Count menu and scroll to the right (figure 7.127, image 2).
3. The factory default Small Pixel Count is 1280×960 (figure 7.127, image 3). However, you can choose a smaller Pixel Count: 1024×768.
4. Press the OK button to Set the new Small Pixel Count value.

Settings Recommendation: Since I rarely stray from Large Pixel Count because I want to use every available pixel for maximum image size, I don't often select Middle or Small Pixel Count sizes.

However, some sizes exactly fit, or are very close to, HDTV, computer monitor, tablet, and smartphone sizes. If you shoot specifically for these devices, other Pixel Count sizes may come in handy.

Shading Comp. (G)

With many lenses there can be some light falloff at the edges of the frame. Certain wide-angle lenses have this issue. In fact, most lenses have a little light falloff in the peripheral areas—that's just the laws of physics at work. Normally you can correct this problem during post-processing on a computer, especially for RAW files.

However, you may not have the time or inclination to post-process images, so the camera offers a solution. If you have lenses that are especially prone to light falloff, you can enable Shading Comp. and let the camera correct the peripheral dimness for you.

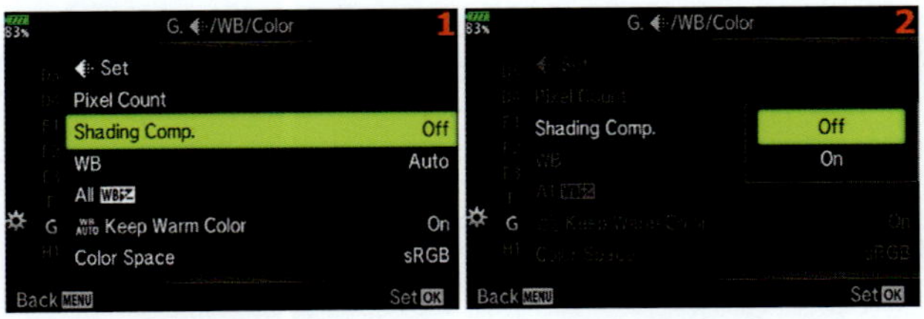

Figure 7.128: Changing the Shading Comp. setting

Use the following steps to enable or disable the Shading Comp. function:

1. Select Shading Comp. from the G. [Record Mode]/WB/Color menu and scroll to the right (figure 7.128, image 1).
2. Choose Off or On from the Shading Comp. menu (figure 7.128, image 2). If you choose On, the camera will correct for light falloff automatically, according to the type of lens you are using.
3. Press the OK button to Set the value.

Note: Brightening the edges of the image can lead to a little additional noise in those areas. Shading Comp. does not work for teleconverters and extension tubes.

Settings Recommendation: I have found that many Micro Four Thirds lenses are already corrected for light falloff problems, and I usually make any needed corrections when I post-process my RAW images in Photoshop. Therefore, I don't often use this function.

However, this is a useful function, especially for JPEG shooters. Try it for any lenses that may have light falloff issues and see if it helps.

WB (G)

Normally white balance (WB) is used to adjust the camera so that whites are truly white and other colors are accurate under any given light source. You can also use the WB controls to deliberately introduce color casts into your image for interesting special effects.

Camera WB color temperatures are backwards from the Kelvin scale we learned in school for star temperatures. Remember that a red giant star is cool, and a blue-white star is hot. The WB color temperatures are backwards because the WB system adds color to make up for a deficit of color.

For instance, fluorescent light lacks blue, which makes the subject appear greenish yellow. When blue is added, the image is balanced to a more normal appearance.

Another example is when you shoot on a cloudy, overcast day. The cool ambient light could cause the image to look bluish. The Auto WB control in your camera sees the cool color temperature and adds some red to warm up the colors a bit. The normal WB on a cloudy, overcast day might be about 6000K.

Remember that we use the Kelvin temperature range in reverse and that red colors are warm and blue colors are cool. Even though this is backwards from what we were taught in school, it fits our situation better. To photographers, blue seems cool and red seems warm! Just don't let your astronomer friends convince you otherwise.

White Balance Fundamentals

Understanding WB in a fundamental way is simply realizing that light has a range of colors that go from cool to warm. We can adjust our cameras to use the available light in an accurate and neutral, balanced way that compensates for the actual light source. Or we can allow a color cast to enter the image by unbalancing the settings. In this chapter we will discuss this from the standpoint of the E-M1II controls and how they deal with WB.

Using the WB Function

The E-M1II WB range varies from a very cool 2000K to a very warm 14,000K. What does that mean?

Figure 7.129 shows the same picture adjusted in Photoshop, with the use of photo filters, to three WB Kelvin (K) settings. Notice how the image in the center is about right, the image on the left is cooler (bluish cast), and the image on the right is warmer (reddish cast).

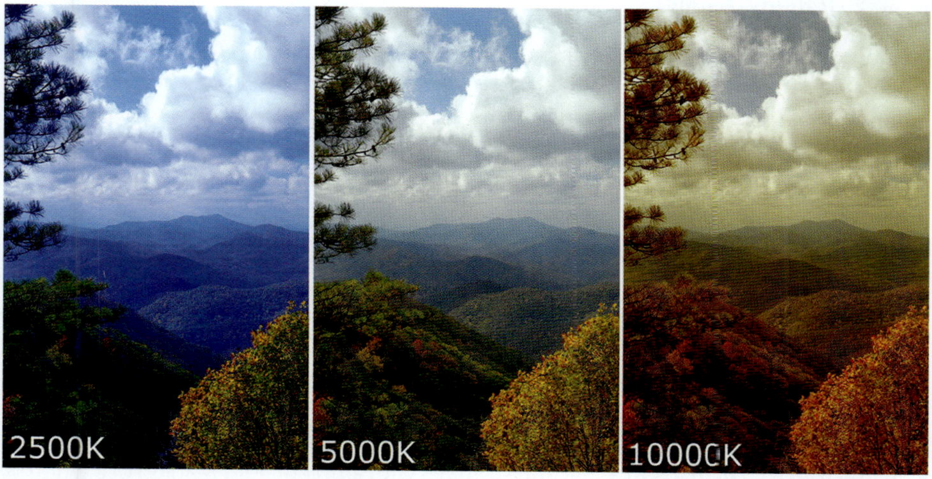

Figure 7.129: One image with three WB Color Temperature settings

The same adjustments we made in the good old days with film and filters can now be achieved with the WB settings built in to the E-M1II. To achieve the same effect as daylight film and a warming filter, simply select the Cloudy WB setting while shooting in normal daylight. This sets the E-M1II to balance at about 6000K, which makes nice warm-looking images. If you want to really warm up the image, choose the WB called Shade, which sets the camera to 7500K.

On the other hand, if you want to make the image appear cool or bluish, try using the Fluorescent (4000K) or Incandescent (3000K) settings in normal daylight.

Remember, the color temperature shifts from cool values to warm values. The E-M1II can record your images with any color temperature from 2000K (very cool or bluish) to 14,000K (very warm or reddish) and any major value in between. There is no need to carry different film emulsions or filters to deal with the range of color in light. The E-M1II has easy-to-use color temperature controls.

Normally you will set the WB from the Live Control screen by pressing the OK button while in Live View. However, you can also use this WB function to set the WB and even fine-tune it (add a color bias).

Here is a list of the 13 WB types you will find on the WB selection screen. Note that six of the WB symbols are followed by a number, such as 5300K. This is the color temperature value for that particular WB setting. We will also discuss how to do an ambient WB reading.

- **Auto:** Camera automatically chooses the best WB setting
- **[Sunlight] 5300K:** Direct sunlight pictures
- **[Shade] 7500K:** Shooting in the shade
- **[Cloudy] 6000K:** Taking pictures on an overcast day
- **[Incandescent] 3000K:** Shooting under an old-fashioned lightbulb
- **[Fluorescent] 4000K:** Making pictures under fluorescent light
- **[Underwater]:** Taking pictures with your E-M1II while underwater (in a waterproof underwater housing)
- **[Flash] 5500K:** Making images with an electronic flash unit providing the main light source
- **[One-Touch Capture WB] 1:** Set and store WB with ambient light reading of a white or gray card (must use the Live Control screen to do the reading)
- **[One-Touch Capture WB] 2:** Set and store WB with ambient light reading of a white or gray card (must use the Live Control screen to do the reading)
- **[One-Touch Capture WB] 3:** Set and store WB with ambient light reading of a white or gray card (must use the Live Control screen to do the reading)
- **[One-Touch Capture WB] 4:** Set and store WB with ambient light reading of a white or gray card (must use the Live Control screen to do the reading)
- **CWB (Custom White Balance):** Choose a WB color temperature manually, from a range of 2000K to 14,000K

First, let's consider how to do a One-Touch Capture WB reading.

One-Touch Capture WB Reading

For the most accurate WB, it is best to do an ambient light reading from a white or gray card under the same light source as your subject. This will adjust the camera to use the correct WB while you are under that light source. Be sure to set the WB back to Auto or do a new ambient light reading if the light source changes.

In the E-M1II user's manual, Olympus calls an ambient light WB reading both One-Touch WB and Capture WB. Therefore, I am combining the two and calling it a One-Touch Capture WB reading or simply a Capture WB reading. Your camera has four memory locations to store WB readings. If you shoot a lot under a certain light source, you can store a Capture WB reading in one location and use it again later.

Let's examine how to do a Capture WB reading. Use a white or gray card if you have one; otherwise, you can use a blank sheet of white printer paper.

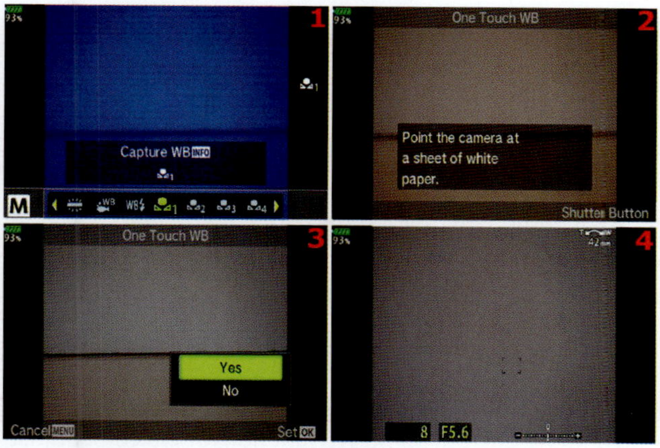

Figure 7.130: Making a One-Touch Capture WB reading from a white card

Use the following steps to do a One-Touch Capture WB reading from a white or gray card:

1. Press the OK button while in Live View to open the Live Control screen. Find the WB function on the right side by scrolling up or down with the Arrow Pad. After you have selected the WB function (figure 7.130, image 1), scroll to the left or right with the Arrow Pad until you highlight one of the Capture WB memory locations. In figure 7.130, image 1, I selected memory location 1 (looks like a flower with number 1 to the right of it). You have chosen where you are going to store the WB reading and are now ready to take the ambient light reading from the card.
2. Press the Info button to open the One Touch WB screen. You can tell that I am about to take a reading from an incandescent light source because of the warm orange look in figure 7.130, image 2. As instructed on the screen in image 2, place the card under the light source you want to measure, then press the Shutter button all the way down as

if you are taking a picture of it. The camera will fire the shutter and measure the color temperature of the light source that reflects from the card.

3. A WB reading is ready to be stored in the current Capture WB memory location; however, you must approve it first by scrolling up and selecting Yes from the menu then pressing the OK button (figure 7.130, image 3). If you do not like the reading, select No to cancel and repeat steps 1 and 2. If you approve of the WB reading it will be stored in the memory location for immediate use and later recall. You can select it on the Live Control screen or within the WB function (this function).
4. After you have approved the WB reading and pressed the OK button, the camera switches to the normal Live Control screen, with the new WB in place. You can tell by looking at the Live View screen in figure 7.130, image 4, that the camera successfully adjusted the WB under the ambient, incandescent light source so that whites look white and other colors look the same as in real life.

Note: In addition to doing a One-Touch Capture WB reading, you can select any of the 13 available White Balance choices from the Live Control screen (figure 7.130, image 1). Using the Live Control screen is much faster than scrolling down to the Custom Menu and selecting the WB function to choose a WB setting.

You must use the Live Control screen to do a One-Touch Capture WB reading, but you cannot adjust the amber–blue (A–B) and green–magenta (G–M) color balance of an individual WB setting. You must use the WB function to fine-tune the A–B and G–M color balance for an individual WB setting, but you cannot do a One-Touch Capture WB reading from the WB function.

Even though the 13 Live Control White Balance settings and the 13 Custom Menu White Balance settings are the same WB settings, you must use the Live Control WB to do a One-Touch Capture WB reading and the Custom Menu WB function for WB color adjustment. This is an unusual design, indeed. The only thing they have in common is the ability to select an individual WB setting for camera use and to choose a Custom WB (CWB).

Now let's see how to choose and fine-tune an existing WB setting from the Custom Menu WB function.

Choosing and Fine-Tuning a WB Setting from the Custom Menu

In addition to the Live Control screen we previously considered, you can select any of the 13 White Balance settings from the WB function. You can also adjust the amber–blue (A–B) and green–magenta (G–M) ratios for individual WB settings. Let's see how!

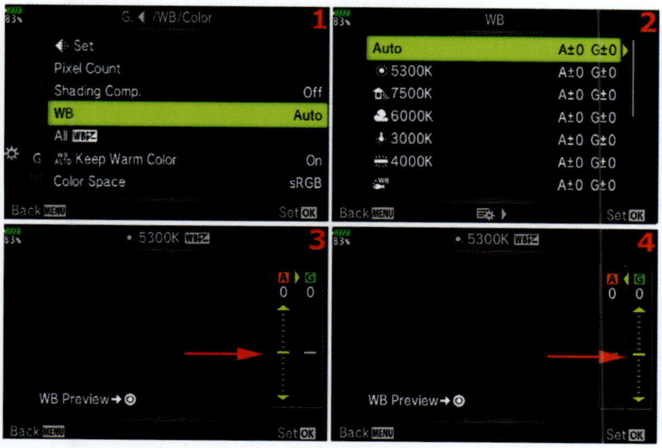

Figure 7.131: Choosing and adjusting an individual WB setting

Use the following steps to choose a WB value and modify the color of individual WB settings:

1. Select the WB function from the G. [Record Mode]/WB/Color menu and scroll to the right (figure 7.131, image 1).
2. Choose one of the individual WB settings, such as Auto, [Sunlight] 5300K, or [Shade] 7500K (figure 7.131, image 2). Refer to the previous list of 13 WB settings to determine what each WB setting does. If you don't need to adjust the color balance (A–B and G–M) of an individual WB setting, simply press the OK button to select a WB setting, and skip the next three steps.
3. If you want to fine-tune a certain WB setting you can do so by highlighting it and scrolling to the right. I scrolled to the right on the [Sunlight] 5300K WB setting, which led me to the screen in figure 7.131, image 3. I can now fine-tune the color balance of the [Sunlight] setting. You can see at the point of the arrow in image 3 that there is an adjustment available. You can slide the yellow bar up toward A (amber) to increase amber for this WB setting, or you can slide it down to reduce amber (add blue). You can see a WB Preview at any time by pressing the Movie button, which causes the camera to take a temporary picture of the subject, with the fine-tuned WB value applied, and display it on the monitor. If you need to fine-tune it some more, simply move the slider again and press the Movie button again to see the results. Do this as many times as you want to fine-tune the WB setting. When you are done, either press the OK button to Set the fine-tuned amber (A–B) ratio and skip the rest of these steps, or scroll to the right to move to the green (G–M) ratio adjustment.
4. After you have fine-tuned the amber (A–B) color balance, you can fine-tune the green (G–M) color balance by scrolling right and selecting the sliding adjustment shown in figure 7.131, image 4. You can add green to the WB setting by sliding the yellow bar up toward G (green), or you can scroll down to decrease green (add magenta). Press the

Movie button to take a temporary picture (WB Preview), examine the color balance, and make further adjustments if necessary. When you are satisfied with the G adjustment, press the OK button to Set the value.

5. Whenever you Set one of the color values in the previous steps by pressing the OK button, the camera will return to the WB function on the Custom Menu. You have modified this WB setting for all future pictures until you reset or modify it.
6. Repeat these steps for any other individual WB settings you want to fine-tune.

Choosing a Custom White Balance (CWB)

If you would like to experiment with entering direct Kelvin values into the camera, or if you have specific color temperature needs, you can use the CWB setting under the WB function to choose a custom WB from 2000K to 14,000K. Let's examine how!

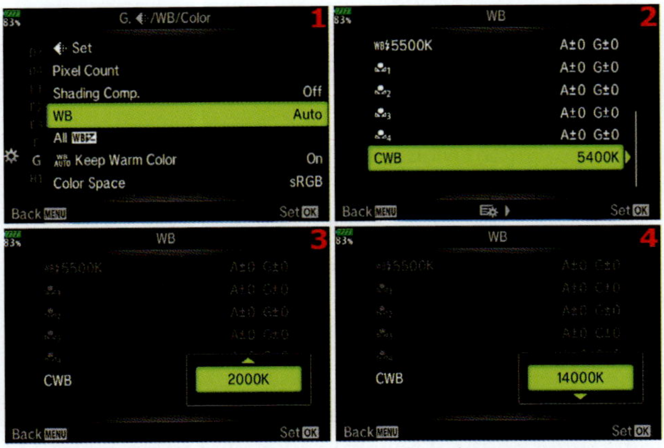

Figure 7.132: Manually choose a Kelvin WB value from 2000K to 14,000K

Use the following steps to choose a specific custom WB value:

1. Select the WB function from the G. [Record Mode]/WB/Color menu and scroll to the right (figure 7.132, image 1).
2. Choose the CWB setting (at the end of the list of 13 WB values) and scroll to the right (figure 7.132, image 2).
3. The CWB setting allows you to experiment with specific values from cool (2000K) to warm (14000K), as shown in figure 7.132, images 3 and 4. If you shoot in a studio and the light does not vary, you can manually find the best WB setting for your product images and portraits. The factory default is 5400K under CWB. Choose the best setting for your style of photography from the up/down menu.
4. Press the OK button to Set the custom WB value. In the future you can choose and use this CWB setting from the WB settings in the Live Control screen or here on the WB function menu.

Settings Recommendation: White balance is an art in itself, especially for JPEG shooters. For RAW shooters this setting does not matter because the WB of a RAW file can be changed after the fact.

You can let the camera choose the best WB by using Auto mode, which is what I often do because I shoot in RAW mode.

You must use an accurate WB if you shoot JPEGs because the WB value is a permanent part of a JPEG image. Although you can vary the color balance somewhat in a JPEG image, it never is quite right after it has been changed.

You can choose a preset WB value (e.g., Cloudy, Incandescent, Fluorescent), do a One-Touch Capture WB reading from a white or gray card, or enter a custom WB value under CWB. The E-M1II has a full range of WB controls that allow you to use whatever is most convenient.

All WB +/– (G)

In the previous section (**WB**) we discussed fine-tuning the colors of individual White Balance (WB) settings. You can change the amber–blue (A) ratio or the green–magenta (G) ratio for each WB setting individually; CWB cannot be modified.

The All WB +/– function is for people who dislike the color balance of all WB functions. All WB +/– allows you to adjust the amber and green ratios for *all WB settings at the same time* (not including CWB). When you use this function to set the amber–blue (A) ratio, and the green–magenta (G) ratio, it changes the color balance of every WB setting except CWB.

Let's examine how to make a global WB compensation (fine-tuning) adjustment.

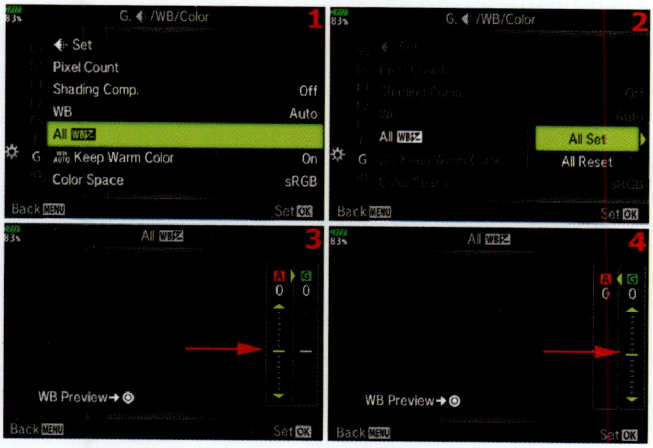

Figure 7.133: Adjusting the A and G color ratios for all WB settings at once (except CWB)

Use the following steps to modify the amber–blue ratio (A), and green–magenta ratio (G), for *all WB settings* at the same time (except CWB):

1. Select the All WB +/– function from the G. [Record Mode]/WB/Color menu and scroll to the right (figure 7.133, image 1).
2. Choose All Set from the All WB +/– menu and scroll to the right (figure 7.133, image 2).
3. You can see at the point of the arrow in figure 7.133, image 3, that there is an adjustment available. You can slide the yellow bar up toward A (amber) to increase the amber color for *all* WB settings, or slide it down to reduce amber (add blue). You can see a WB Preview of the current WB setting that the camera is using by pressing the Movie button, which causes the camera to take a temporary picture of the subject, with the fine-tuned WB value applied, and display it on the monitor. If you need to fine-tune it some more, simply move the slider again and press the Movie button again to see the results. Do this as many times as you want to fine-tune the WB settings. When you are done, you can either press the OK button to Set the fine-tuned (A–B) ratio and skip the rest of these steps, or you can scroll to the right to move into the (G–M) ratio adjustment.
4. After you have fine-tuned the amber (A–B) color balance ratio, you can fine-tune the green (G–M) color balance ratio by scrolling right and selecting the sliding adjustment shown in figure 7.133, image 4. You can add green to the WB setting by sliding the yellow bar up toward G (green), or you can slide it down to decrease green (add magenta). Press the Movie button to take a temporary picture (WB Preview), examine the color balance, and make further adjustments if necessary. When you are satisfied with the G adjustment, press the OK button to Set the value.
5. When you Set one of the color values in the previous steps by pressing the OK button, the camera will return to the WB function on the Custom Menu. You have modified all WB settings, other than CWB, for all future pictures the camera will take using any WB setting, until you reset or modify them with this function.

If you make this comprehensive WB setting modification and later want to change all the WB settings back to their factory default values, you can use the upcoming steps to do so.

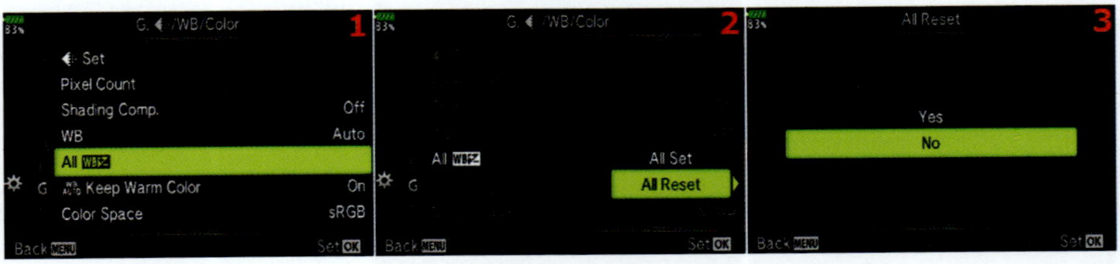

Figure 7.134: Resetting all modified WB settings

Use the following steps to reset 12 of the 13 WB settings (not CWB) back to factory specs:

1. Select the All WB +/– function from the G. [Record Mode]/WB/Color menu and scroll to the right (figure 7.134, image 1).

2. Choose All Reset from the All WB +/– menu and scroll to the right (figure 7.134, image 2).
3. Select Yes from the All Reset menu to reset all modified WB settings, or No to cancel (figure 7.134, image 3).
4. Press the OK button to Set your choice.

Settings Recommendation: I may modify one or two of the WB settings, but never all of them at the same time. However, this function is good for people who modify multiple WB settings and want to return them all to factory specs at the same time, instead of going into the menu settings for them one at a time.

WB Auto Keep Warm Color (G)

When you take pictures under incandescent light sources or warm light sources (reddish lighting), the camera will either allow the image to be a little warmer than normal (keep warm color), or it will not.

Many people love the look of warm colors. The human eye seems to be attracted to reddish colors more than bluish colors. Therefore, many people leave this setting On, which keeps the warm colors when the light source is warm. Selecting Off will cause the camera to balance the light toward neutral. The effect is noticeable.

Let's see how to choose one of the WB Auto Keep Warm Color settings.

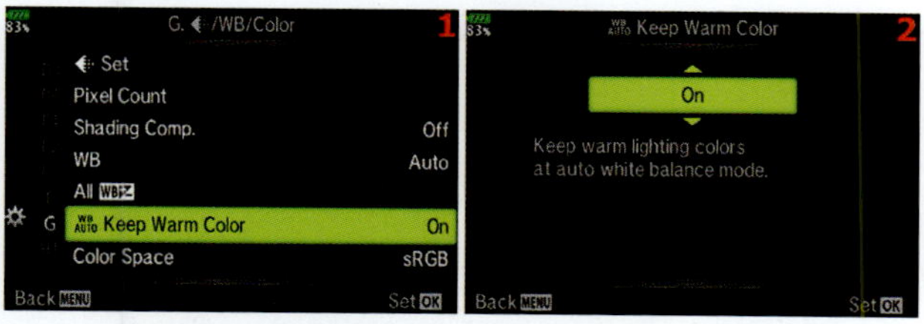

Figure 7.135: Choosing a color warmth setting

Use the following steps to choose color warmth over color neutrality when you shoot under warm light sources, such as incandescent:

1. Select the WB Auto Keep Warm Color function from the G. [Record Mode]/WB/Color menu and scroll to the right (figure 7.135, image 1).
2. Choose On from the WB Auto Keep Warm Color up/down menu to keep the warm colors, or choose Off to balance the light toward neutral (figure 7.135, image 2).
3. Press the OK button to Set your choice.

Settings Recommendation: After testing this function under various light sources, I noticed that warm light sources have a marked effect when this function is set to On. I like warmer colors, but at times the effect seems a little strong to me, especially when I am shooting JPEGs and cannot adjust them later.

I suggest testing this function under various warm light sources to see if the image looks too warm. You may love the warmer images. More neutral images will be best for people who shoot JPEGs, where color accuracy is a must.

If you shoot in RAW mode, it makes no real difference because you can simply change the WB after the fact.

Color Space (G)

Color space is an interesting and important part of digital photography. It helps your camera fit in to a much broader range of imaging devices. Software, printers, monitors, and other devices recognize which color space is attached to your image and use it, along with other color profiles, to help balance the image and produce the correct colors.

The two color spaces available on the E-M1II have different gamuts, or ranges of color. They are called sRGB and Adobe RGB. Let's discuss color space briefly so you can make an educated choice.

Which Color Space Should I Choose?

Adobe RGB uses colors from a broad selection of the total color range that approximates human vision (called CIELAB in the graphics industry), so it has a wider gamut than sRGB (figure 7.136). If you are taking images that might be printed commercially, Adobe RGB is often the best color space to use (see the sidebar called **Which Color Space Is Best, Technically?**).

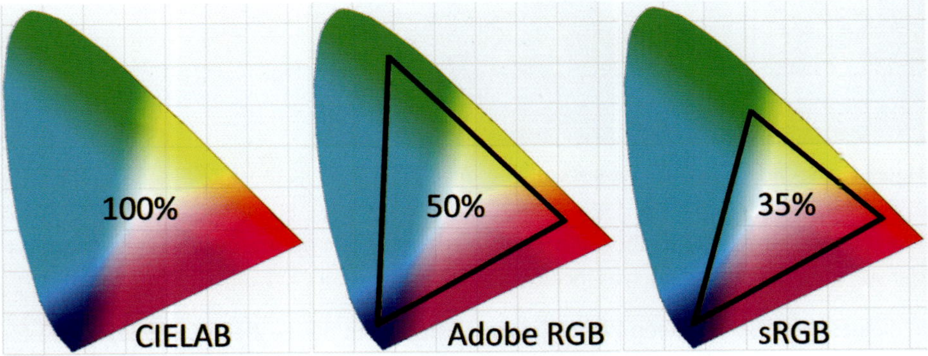

Figure 7.136: CIELAB, Adobe RGB, and sRGB color spaces

After a JPEG file is created, either in a camera or on a computer, both the Adobe RGB and sRGB color gamuts are compressed into the same number of color levels. A JPEG has only 256 levels for each of its red, green, and blue (RGB) channels. However, since the Adobe RGB color space takes its colors from a wider spectrum, you will have a better representation of reality when there are lots of colors in your image.

If you shoot in RAW format a lot, you may want to consider using Adobe RGB to store the maximum number of colors in your image files for later use, even though, for reasons we'll discuss in a moment, it really doesn't matter in RAW mode. However, it is still a good idea to leave your camera set to Adobe RGB.

An E-M1II lossless compressed 12-bit RAW (ORF) image file can contain 4,096 levels of color per RGB channel, instead of the limited 256 levels in an 8-bit JPEG. Using Adobe RGB makes a lot of sense when you shoot in RAW mode because of its capacity to contain more colors as a base storage medium.

There are some drawbacks to using Adobe RGB, though. The sRGB color space is widely used in printing and display devices. Many local labs print with sRGB because so many point-and-shoot cameras use that format. If you try to print directly to some inkjet printers that are configured for sRGB using the Adobe RGB color space, the colors may not be as brilliant as with sRGB. If you aren't going to modify your images in post-processing and plan to print them directly from your camera, you may want to use sRGB. If you shoot only JPEGs for computer display or Internet usage, it might be better to stay with sRGB for everyday shooting.

If you are a RAW shooter and regularly post-process your images, you should consider using Adobe RGB. You will have a wider gamut of colors to work with and can make your images the best they can be. Later, you can convert your images to another color space (e.g., sRGB, CMYK, CIELAB) so you can get great prints from inkjet printers and other printing devices. Here is a rough way to look at it:

- Many people who regularly shoot in JPEG format use sRGB.
- Many people who regularly shoot in RAW format use Adobe RGB.

These are not hard-and-fast rules, but many people follow them. I shoot RAW a lot, so I often use Adobe RGB.

In reality, though, *it makes no difference which color space you choose when you shoot in RAW* because the color space can be changed after the fact in your computer. However, many people are not in the habit of changing the color space during a RAW to JPEG conversion. Therefore, if you need the extra color range, why not leave the camera set to Adobe RGB for later convenience? Why add an extra step to your digital darkroom workflow? If you are shooting for money—such as for stock image agencies—most companies expect you to use Adobe RGB. It has a larger color range, so it's the quality standard for most commercial printing.

Now let's examine how to choose the color space you want to use.

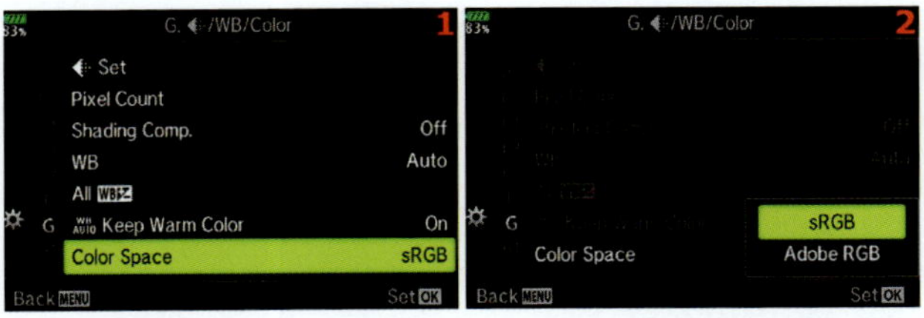

Figure 7.137: Choosing a Color Space for your images

Use the following steps to choose an appropriate Color Space for your type of photography:

1. Select the Color Space function from the G. [Record Mode]/WB/Color menu and scroll to the right (figure 7.137, image 1).
2. Choose one of the two Color Space settings (sRGB or Adobe RGB) from the Color Space menu after referring to the previous material in this chapter subsection (figure 7.137, image 2).
3. Press the OK button to Set your choice.

Settings Recommendation: I use Adobe RGB most of the time because I shoot a lot of nature pictures with a wide range of color. I want the most accurate color my camera can give me. Adobe RGB has a wider range of colors, so it can be more accurate when my subject has a lot of colors.

However, if you are taking JPEG snapshots, there's no need to worry about this. Leave the camera set to sRGB and have fun.

Which Color Space Is Best, Technically?

There is a large color space used by the graphics industry called CIELAB or CIE L*a*b* (figure 7.136). The CIELAB color space is designed to approximate human vision. Adobe RGB covers about 50 percent of the CIELAB color space, and sRGB covers only about 35 percent. In other words, Adobe RGB has a wider gamut. That means Adobe RGB gives your images access to significantly more colors, especially cyans (bluish tones) and greens. Another important consideration if you'll send your work to companies that use offset printing—such as book and magazine publishers—is that Adobe RGB maps very well to the four-color cyan, magenta, yellow, black (CMYK) printing process. If you are shooting commercial work, you may want to seriously consider Adobe RGB. Stock photo shooters are nearly always required to shoot in Adobe RGB.

Custom Menu H1–H2. Record/Erase

The H1–H2. Record/Erase menu is composed of functions that work with image file naming, photographer identity, copyright, and image deletion.

We will start examining the functions by taking a look at the opening menu for the H1–H2. Record/Erase functions in figure 7.138.

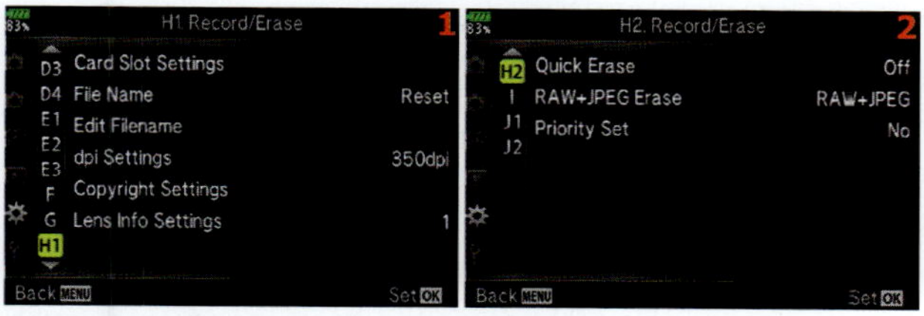

Figure 7.138: The H1 and H2 Record/Erase menu

To enter the menu, you must select H1. (or H2.) Record/Erase from the Custom Menu and scroll to the right. There are six functions inside the H1. Record/Erase menu and three functions in the H2. Record/Erase menu. Let's consider each of them in detail.

Card Slot Settings (H1)

The E-M1II has two memory card slots (figure 1.39). The Card Slot Settings function allows you to specify where your camera saves the images and videos you take. You can tell the camera which card to send still image files to, which card to send video files to, and how to deal with the files when a card is full.

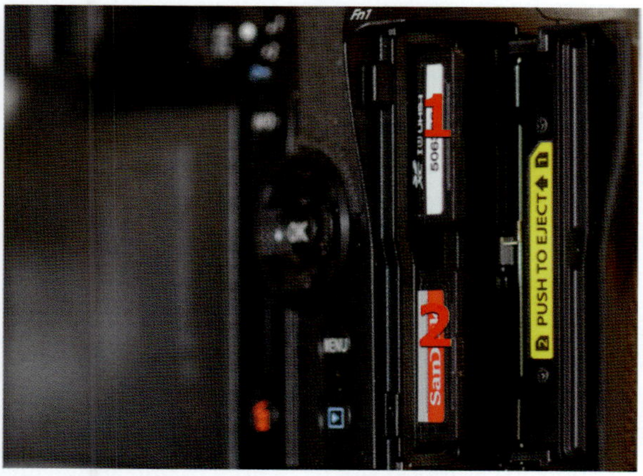

Figure 7.139: The two memory card slots on the E-M1II

Note: If there is only one memory card inserted in the camera, then the only available choice in the Card Slot Settings menu is Assign Save Folder. If there are no memory cards inserted in the camera, then the entire Card Slot Settings menu will be grayed out.

Let's take a look at all of the available settings.

- **[Photo] Save Settings:** This option allows you to choose which memory card combination the camera will use when it saves an image you just captured. The E-M1II defaults to saving all images in the top slot (Slot 1) and ignores the card in the bottom slot (Slot 2), but you can change this relationship if you wish. You have six choices:
  - **Standard:** If there is only one memory card in the camera, the camera will save all images to that card (of course). If there are two cards in the camera, the E-M1II will save all images to whichever card slot is specified in [Photo] Save Slot option (below [Photo] Save Settings in the Card Slot Settings menu). This mode provides for only one Image Quality format, such as Large Fine (LF) JPEG, or a combined format, such as LF+RAW, to be used at one time. When the selected memory card becomes full, you cannot save any more pictures or videos.
  - **Dual Same ↑:** This mode lets you choose a certain Image Quality format for both cards to receive at the same time. Whatever Image Quality you choose is written to both cards simultaneously. If either memory card becomes full, you may *continue taking pictures,* as long as the other memory card has available space.
  - **Dual Same ↓:** This mode works the same as Dual Same ↑ (previous list item) in that you can choose a certain Image Quality format for both cards to receive at the same time. However, If either memory card becomes full, you may *no longer take pictures.*
  - **Dual Independent ↑:** With this setting, the two cards are treated separately, and you can select a different Image Quality format for each memory card in Shooting Menu 1. For example, you can set Slot 1 to save a RAW file and Slot 2 to save Large Fine JPEG (LF). Then when you press the Shutter button, the camera will capture and save a RAW file to the card in Slot 1, and it will also save a Large Fine (LF) JPEG file to the card in Slot 2. If either card becomes full, *you may continue taking pictures*, as long as there is space available on the other memory card.
  - **Dual Independent ↓:** This mode works the same as Dual Independent ↑ (previous list item) in that you can choose a different Image Quality format for each memory card. However, if either card becomes full, you can *no longer take pictures*, even if there is space available on the other memory card.
  - **Auto Switch:** This mode is very similar to Standard mode. When the card you've chosen for [Photo] Save Slot is full, the camera will automatically switch to the other memory card, allowing you to continue taking images until both cards are full. You may use only one Image Quality format (or one combined format, such as LF+RAW) at a time. This setting does not apply to capturing video—it applies only to still image capture. The camera will not switch to the other memory card when it runs out of space for recording video. Instead, the video will merely stop recording when the

card becomes full. If you attempt to capture another video without changing to a memory card that has sufficient space, you will see an error message on the monitor telling you the card is full.

- **[Photo] Save Slot:** This option allows you to choose which card will record still image files. You can choose from Slot 1 or Slot 2. This option is only available when [Photo] Save Settings (the previous menu option) is set to Standard or Auto.
- **[Video] Save Slot:** This option allows you to choose which card will record video files.
- **[Playback] Slot:** When [Photo] Save Settings is set to any of the four Dual options, the camera will display the images from only one of the cards during image playback. This menu allows you to choose the card slot (1 or 2) from which you want to display images when you press the camera's Playback button. The images will look the same regardless of which card slot you choose. The only difference is that they may be in different image formats (e.g., RAW versus JPEG). However, one of the cards may have images on it that the other does not, so you may prefer to display images from one card over the other. You can switch the Playback image display between the two cards at any time with this setting.
- **Assign Save Folder:** This setting allows you to choose a specific folder on the memory card in which the camera will save your images. You can choose Do Not Assign, and the camera will simply create new folders as needed, or you can choose to save images to an existing folder or a new folder that you've created.

Now let's consider how to configure each of these options.

[Photo] Save Settings

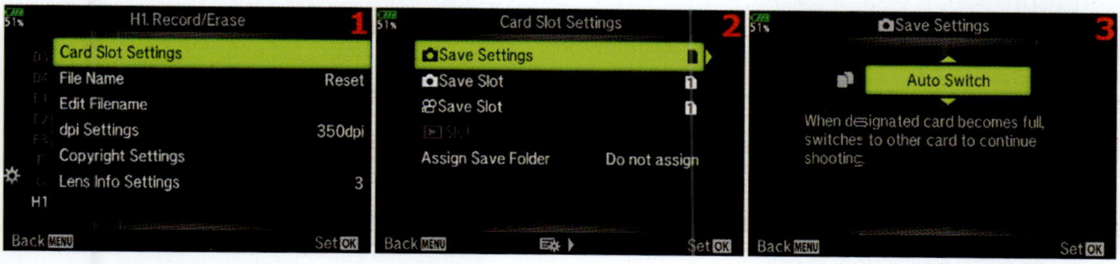

Figure 7.140: The [Photo] Save Settings menu

Use the following steps to choose a recording method for still images:

1. Select Card Slot Settings from the H1. Record/Erase menu and scroll to the right (figure 7.140, image 1).
2. Select [Photo] Save Settings from the Card Slot Settings menu and scroll to the right (figure 7.140, image 2).
3. Use the Arrow Pad to select an option from the up/down menu (figure 7.140, image 3). Refer to the previous list for an explanation of each option.
4. Press the OK button to Set your choice and return to the previous screen.

Settings Recommendation: This is a very useful menu for creating an in-camera backup and for recording two different file types at the same time. When I'm photographing events, I often need to turn over the JPEG images for editing, but I want to shoot RAW images for backup. I set this to Dual Independent ↓ so that if a single card fills up, the camera lets me know that I need to put in two new cards. This is the best protection because it ensures that there is enough space for both the RAW and JPEG files.

[Photo] Save Slot

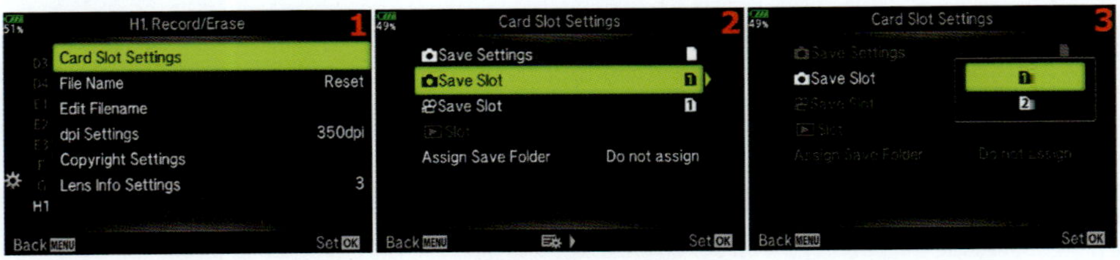

Figure 7.141: Selecting a card for still image files

This [Photo] Save Slot option is available when you set [Photo] Save Settings to either Standard or Auto Switch.

Use the following steps to choose which card will record your still image files:

1. Select Card Slot Settings from the H1. Record/Erase menu and scroll to the right (figure 7.141, image 1).
2. Select [Photo] Save Slot from the Card Slot Settings menu and scroll to the right (figure 7.141, image 2).
3. Select card slot 1 or card slot 2 from the up/down menu (figure 7.141, image 3).
4. Press the OK button to Set your choice.

Settings Recommendation: I always pick slot 1 because it supports the higher speed UHS-II type cards, whereas slot 2 supports the slower UHS-1 cards.

[Video] Save Slot

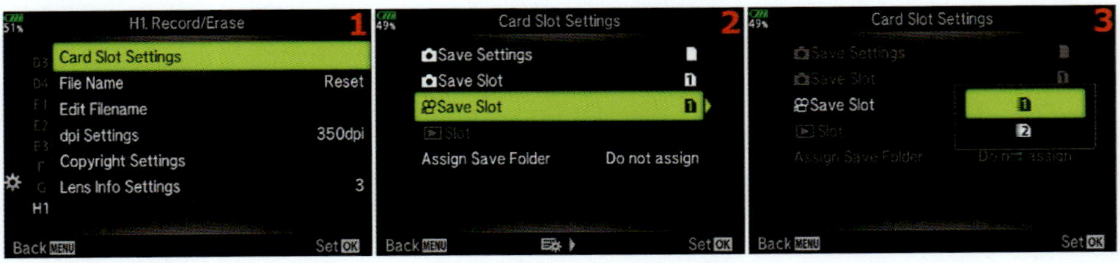

Figure 7.142: Selecting a card for video files

The [Video] Save Settings option is available regardless of how you configured [Photo] Save Settings.

Use the following steps to choose which card will record your video files:

1. Select Card Slot Settings from the H1. Record/Erase and scroll to the right (figure 7.142, image 1).
2. Select [Video] Save Slot from the Card Slot Settings menu and scroll to the right (figure 7.142, image 2).
3. Select card slot 1 or card slot 2 from the up/down menu (figure 7.142, image 3).
4. Press the OK button to Set your choice.

Settings Recommendation: As with the last menu, I usually pick slot 1 because it supports the higher speed UHS-II type cards, whereas slot 2 supports the slower UHS-1 cards. If I know I am going to be shooting a lot of video and a lot of still images, I will choose slot 2 for [Video] Save Slot and slot 1 for [Photo] Save Slot because it makes it easier to sort out my files later.

[Playback] Slot

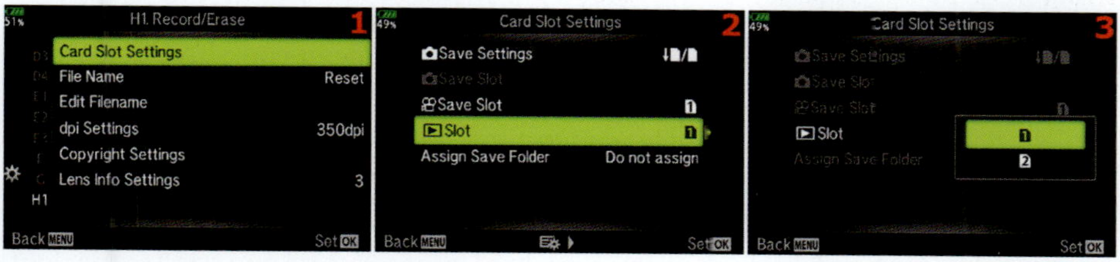

Figure 7.143: Setting the [Playback] Slot

This menu choice is available when you set [Photo] Save Settings to any of the Dual settings.

Use the following steps to choose the card from which you want to display images when you press the Playback button:

1. Select Card Slot Settings from the H1. Record/Erase menu and scroll to the right (figure 7.143, image 3).
2. Select [Playback] Slot from the Card Slot Settings Menu and scroll to the right (figure 7.143, image 2).
3. Select card slot 1 or card slot 2 from the up/down menu (figure 7.143, image 3).
4. Press the OK button to Set your choice.

Settings Recommendation: I choose whichever slot contains the card with JPEG images. I just want the camera to use the JPEG file for the preview.

Assign Save Folder

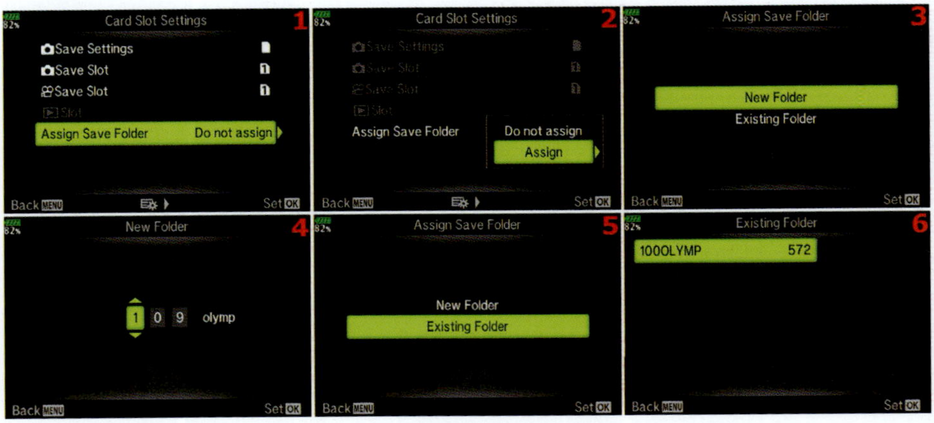

Figure 7.144: Assigning your images to a specific folder on the memory card

Use the following steps to assign your images to a specific folder on the memory card:

1. Select Card Slot Settings from the H1. Record/Erase menu and scroll to the right.
2. Select Assign Save Folder from the Card Slot Settings menu and scroll to the right (figure 7.144, image 1).
3. If you do not want to assign your images to a specific folder, and you want the camera to simply create new folders as needed, choose Do not assign and press the OK button to Set your choice (figure 7.144, image 2). If you want to assign your images to a specific new or existing folder on your memory card, choose Assign and scroll to the right.
4. To create a new folder on your memory card, choose New Folder and scroll to the right (figure 7.144, image 3). Use the Arrow Pad to enter a new three-digit folder number, and then press the OK button to Set your choice (figure 7.144, image 4). Your images will be saved to the folder that you created on your memory card.
5. To save your images to a folder that already exists on your memory card, choose Existing Folder and scroll to the right (figure 7.144, image 5). You will be presented with a list of folders on your memory card (figure 7.144, image 6). Choose the folder to which you want to your images and press the OK button to Set your choice. Your images will be saved to the folder that you selected.

Settings Recommendation: I leave my camera set to Do not assign, allowing the camera to create new folders as needed.

File Name (H1)

The camera can create a running sequence of image file numbers so you can maintain a series of image numbers over time, even when a freshly formatted memory card is inserted. Alternatively, the camera can start over with a new sequence of image numbers when you insert a blank, formatted card.

Here are the two available settings and an explanation of how they work:

- **Auto:** The last four digits of the image file name run in a continuous series, even if you insert a blank, formatted memory card. File numbers are remembered from the previous card, and the file number on the next new image will be one higher than the previous number. In other words, if the final image on the memory card you last used had a file name ending in 0135 (e.g., P1010135.JPG), the next image you make will use 0136 (e.g., P1010136.JPG). This numbering sequence will continue until you have taken 9,999 images, then the file number sequence for the last four digits will roll back over to 0001. (See the next subsection, **Edit Filename,** for a clever way to manage images after you have exceeded 10,000 images with the camera.)
- **Reset:** Similar to the Auto mode, the camera will use the next available image number for any series of existing pictures it finds on a memory card. However, if you insert a blank, formatted memory card into the camera, it will forget the previous memory card sequence and start fresh with image numbers beginning at 0001. In other words, when the camera detects a blank memory card, it resets the numbering sequence back to 0001.

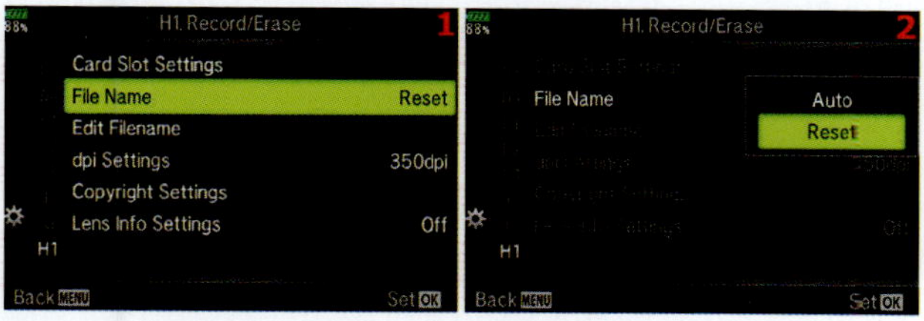

Figure 7.145: Choosing a file naming method (file number sequence)

Use the following steps to choose how you want the camera to handle file number sequences:

1. Select the File Name function from the H1. Record/Erase menu and scroll to the right (figure 7.145, image 1).
2. A small up/down menu will appear with two choices: Auto and Reset (figure 7.145, image 2). Make your selection (refer to the previous list for an explanation of how each selection works).
3. Press the OK button to Set your choice.

Special Image Number Sequence Information

If you are interested in maintaining a continuous file number sequence for all future images with the camera using Auto, there are three important facts you should take note of. If you are using Reset instead of Auto, none of the following bulleted items matter because the camera will reset the file number sequence whenever it sees a blank memory card. If you use Auto, read these three bullets carefully:

- **File folder management:** The camera creates a file folder to hold your individual images when you first format or use a blank memory card. The image folder will be in the DCIM folder on the memory card and will have a name like 100OLYMP. If you exceed 9,999 images in the existing 100OLYMP folder, the camera will create a new folder with one higher number (e.g., 101OLYMP). Additionally, if you insert a memory card that has a folder containing an image with a file number ending in 9999, the camera will create a new folder in preparation for the next 9,999 images, even if there aren't actually 9,999 images in the previous folder. Any time the camera sees the number 9999 on the end of an image, it will immediately create the next folder in the series and switch to the new folder.
- **Accidentally disrupting an existing file number sequence:** Since the camera remembers the last file number on the previous memory card that was inserted in the camera, if you insert a memory card with images that have a different sequence of file numbers, the camera will immediately remember the new sequence and disrupt your controlled sequence of file numbers. In other words, if the file number sequence you have been maintaining ends in 8995 and you insert a memory card with existing images that have a different number sequence (e.g., 3456), you will lose your controlled sequence. Therefore, if you want to keep a running sequence, never insert a memory card with foreign images on it. Always use an existing card in the image number series, or start with a blank, formatted card. If you accidentally insert a memory card that has a different sequence, you will need to reinsert a card that contains the old sequence and take a picture. If you cannot reinsert the old card, format a new card in the camera, copy the final image from the old sequence into the *DCIM > 100OLYMP* folder, then take a picture. That will reestablish the sequence.
- **Using a file number sequence on a new camera:** Be very careful to not insert any memory card with existing images from a different Olympus camera into a brand-new E-M1II. If you do, the camera will not start your number sequence at 0001 for the new camera. Instead, it may pick up the file number sequence from the other camera's images. Always start your new camera's file number sequence with a blank memory card, then follow the concepts in the previous bulleted item.

Settings Recommendation: I set my camera to Auto because I want to maintain a continuous file number sequence for my images. However, this means I have to be careful about using memory cards with foreign Olympus images on them. If you have no interest in maintaining a file number sequence, just set this File Name function to Reset and forget about it. The next subsection discusses how to start and maintain a file number sequence properly.

Edit Filename (H1)

File naming allows you to control the first four characters of the file name for each of your images shot with the sRGB color space, and three characters of the file name for images taken with the Adobe RGB color space. You can change the characters to any alphanumeric characters available on the camera.

The camera defaults to using the following file naming convention for your images:

- **sRGB color space:** P1011234
- **Adobe RGB color space:** _1011234

For the Adobe RGB color space, the camera adds an underscore to the beginning character position, instead of the default P, which allows you to use the next three characters for custom naming. For the sRGB color space, the camera does not add an underscore, so you can use all four character positions for custom naming.

I use this feature on my camera in a special way. Since the camera can count images in a file number sequence (see the previous **File Name** subsection) that continues from 0001 to 9999, I use the Edit Filename function to help me personalize my images. The camera cannot count images higher than 9,999. Instead, it rolls back to 0001 for the 10,000th image.

When I first got my camera, I changed the three default characters from P101 to DRY1 for the sRGB color space and DY1 for the Adobe RGB color space. The 1 tells me how many times my camera has passed 9,999 images, and DRY or DY are my initials, which helps me protect the copyright of my images in case they are ever stolen and misused.

Since the camera's file number sequence counter rolls back to 0001 when you exceed 9,999 images, you need a way to keep from accidentally overwriting images from the first set of 9,999 images. I use the following method:

sRGB color space

- **First 9,999 images:** DRY10001 through DRY19999
- **Second 9,999 images:** DRY20001 through DRY29999
- **Third 9,999 images:** DRY30001 through DRY39999
- **Fourth 9,999 images:** DRY40001 through DRY49999

Adobe RGB color space

- **First 9,999 images:** _DY10001 through _DY19999
- **Second 9,999 images:** _DY20001 through _DY29999
- **Third 9,999 images:** _DY30001 through _DY39999
- **Fourth 9,999 images:** _DY40001 through _DY49999

My system only works up to 89,991 images (9,999×9). If you start your camera at 0 (DRY09999 or _DY09999), you can count up to 99,990 images.

If my method doesn't work for your needs, you can use the three or four custom characters to classify your image names in all sorts of creative ways.

Let's see how to assign custom characters.

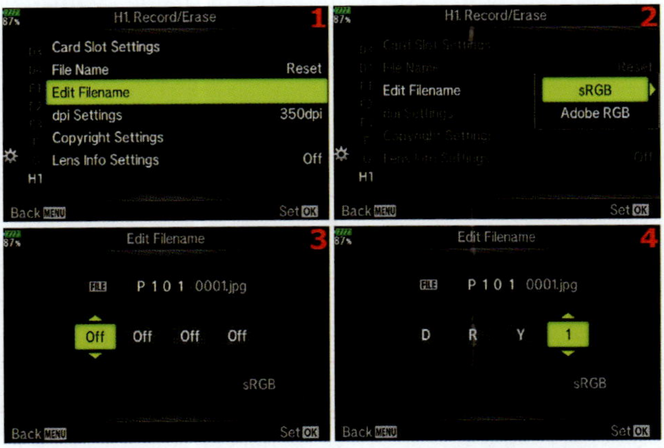

Figure 7.146: Selecting four beginning file name characters for sRGB image files

Use the following steps to choose four new initial characters for image files created with the sRGB color space:

1. Select the Edit Filename function from the H1. Record/Erase menu and scroll to the right (figure 7.146, image 1).
2. Choose sRGB from the up/down menu and scroll to the right (figure 7.146, image 2).
3. You will see the current file name for an sRGB file, which is shown as P101 0001.jpg in figure 7.146, image 3. Choose a number or alphabetical character for each of the up/down menus that have Off displayed. Those four boxes represent the first four characters of the file name, which you can customize. Scroll up or down to select a custom character for each box. After you have chosen a value for one of the boxes, scroll right or left to select other boxes and change them too. In figure 7.146, image 4, you can see that I have added my initials (DRY) to the first three custom positions and the number 1 to the fourth custom position. Now all my sRGB images will have a file name that begins with DRY1 (e.g., DRY10123.jpg).
4. Press the OK button to Set your choice.

Next, let's consider how to change the custom characters for Adobe RGB files.

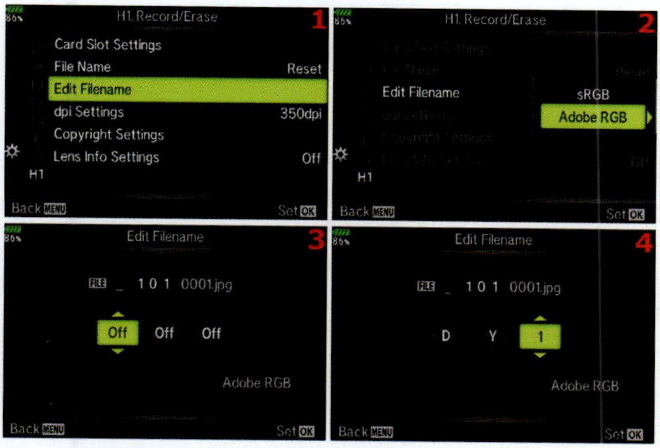

Figure 7.147: Selecting three beginning file name characters for Adobe RGB image files

Use the following steps to choose three new initial characters for image files created with the Adobe RGB color space:

1. Select the Edit Filename function from the H1. Record/Erase menu and scroll to the right (figure 7.147, image 1).
2. Choose Adobe RGB from the up/down menu and scroll to the right (figure 7.147, image 2).
3. You will see the current file name for an Adobe RGB file, which is shown as _101 0001.jpg in figure 7.147, image 3. Choose a number or alphabetical character for each of the small up/down menus that have Off displayed. The first character is not available to customize for Adobe RGB files, unlike sRGB files. The first character will always be an underscore. The three boxes with Off displayed represent the next three characters of the file name, which you can customize. Scroll up or down to select a custom character for each box. After you have chosen a value for one of the boxes, scroll right or left to select other boxes and change them, too. In figure 7.147, image 4, you can see that the default underscore is in the first position, I added my initials (DY) to the second and third character positions, and I added the number 1 to the fourth custom position. Now all my Adobe RGB images will have file names beginning with _DY1 (e.g., _DY10123.jpg). The alignment of the three Off boxes seems to indicate that you can change the underscore, but you can't. You can change only the second through fourth characters for the Adobe RGB color space.
4. Press the OK button to Set your choice.

Note: To change between the sRGB and Adobe RGB color spaces, see the function at *Custom Menu > G. [Record Mode]/WB/Color > Color Space*. Also, to prevent disrupting your carefully created file number sequence, review the subsection called **Special**

Image Number Sequence Information at the end of the previous **File Name** function on page 555.

Settings Recommendation: At the beginning of this section we discussed how I use these three or four custom characters. You may want to use your initials or some other numbers or letters. Some people leave these characters at their default values. I recommend at least using your initials so you can easily identify images as yours. With my family of photographers it sure makes it easier for me! If you use my method, be sure to watch for the images to roll over to 9999 so you can rename the numeric custom character for the next sequence of 9,999 images.

dpi Settings (H1)

With the dpi Settings function, you can select a default dpi (dots per inch) for your images. The dpi information is then embedded in the metadata of your images. This information is primarily for printers to control the dots per inch they use to make a print.

This value can be changed after the fact in computer software, such as Photoshop. You can therefore ignore this setting unless you want to print your images with a specific dpi setting. This is a useful setting for those who want to print directly from their camera or use DPOF (digital print order format) from a memory card.

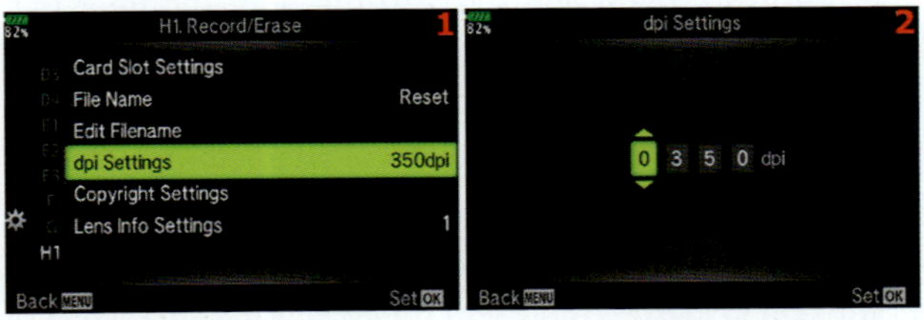

Figure 7.148: Choosing a dots per inch (dpi) setting for printing

Use the following steps to choose a default dpi value for your images:

1. Select the dpi Settings function from the H1. Record/Erase menu and scroll to the right (figure 7.148, image 1).
2. Select a dpi value from the up/down menus in figure 7.148, image 2. You can choose from a range of 0001 (1 dpi) to 9999 dpi. The dpi setting will affect the printing resolution of the image on an inkjet printer or other types of printers. Many printing devices have a much more limited range than 0001 to 9999 dpi. The most common dpi for commercial printing in books and magazines is 300 dpi. Since the tiny dots a printer creates to make up an image varies among printer types, you may have to experiment with different dpi settings to see which looks best on your printer.
3. Press the OK button to Set your choice.

Settings Recommendation: I set my camera to 300 dpi because most of my work is printed at that dpi setting. If you rarely print your work, or if you prefer changing the dpi later in the computer, you can ignore this function. The quality (resolution) of the image will not be affected, regardless of how this setting is configured.

In my opinion, it is better to set this value in the computer just before the image is printed; therefore, I look at this function as a convenience setting.

Copyright Settings (H1)

The Copyright Settings function allows you to embed Artist Name and Copyright Name into the metadata of each image. With image theft so rampant on the Internet today, it is a good practice to put your personal or business name inside each image so it can be read on a computer. The government has recently been considering legislation for how to handle images that are orphaned. It isn't a good idea to let your images be orphaned!

By adding your initials to the image file name with the Edit Filename function and adding artist and copyright names with this Copyright Settings function, you are invisibly marking your images internally so that, at the very least, you can prove that you own the copyright to the image. An unscrupulous person could strip out the image EXIF information; however, because your image contains the information in the first place, stripping the image is illegal and can indicate that the image was stolen. This gives you greater ammunition for proving copyright infringement. In addition to using these safeguards, you can register the copyright for your images at **www.copyright.gov**.

Now let's examine how to add your personal information to your images.

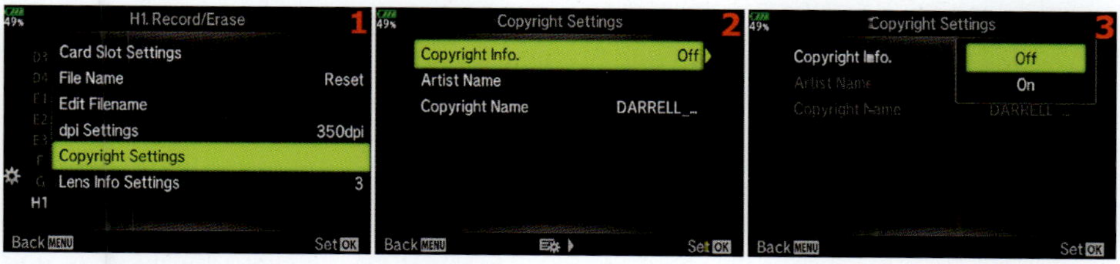

Figure 7.149: Enabling Copyright Settings

Use the following steps to enable or disable the Copyright Settings function:

1. Select the Copyright Settings function from the H1. Record/Erase menu and scroll to the right (figure 7.149, image 1).
2. Choose Copyright Info. and scroll to the right (figure 7.149, image 2).
3. A small up/down menu will appear and offer you these choices: Off to disable the inclusion of your Artist Name and Copyright Name inside your images, or On to include that very important information (figure 7.149, image 3).
4. Press the OK button to Set your choice.

Next let's create the Artist Name and Copyright Name so it will be in the image metadata.

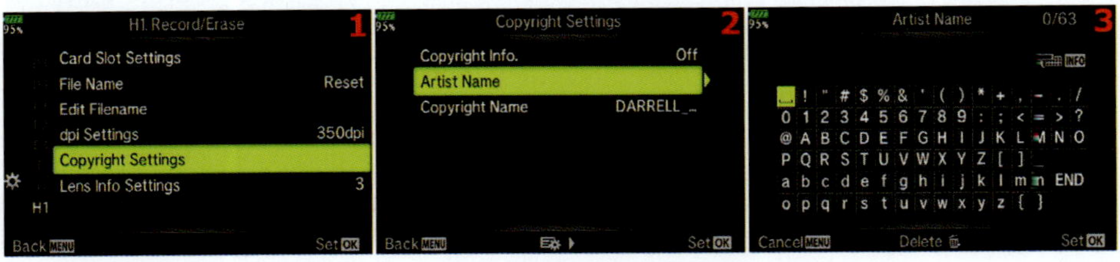

Figure 7.150: Including your Artist Name in the EXIF information of an image

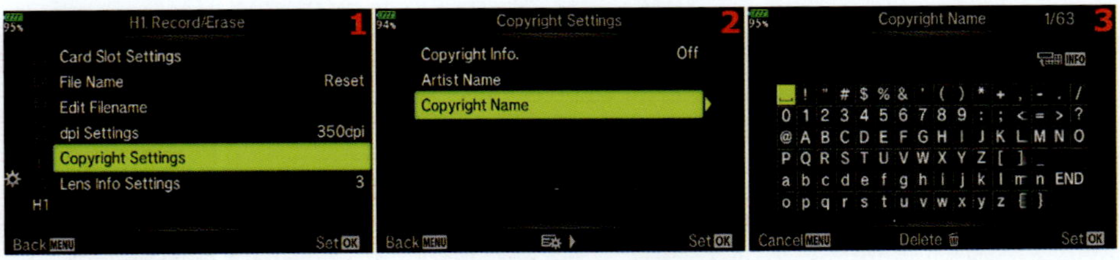

Figure 7.151: Including your Copyright Name in the EXIF information of an image

Use the following steps to add your Artist Name and Copyright Name to future images. Both names are inserted the same way, so the following steps will work for both:

1. Select the Copyright Settings function from the H1. Record/Erase menu and scroll to the right (figure 7.150 or 7.151, image 1).
2. Choose Artist Name or Copyright Name from the menu and scroll to the right (Figure 7.150 or 7.151, image 2).
3. You will now see a screen with a grid of characters you can use for the Artist Name or Copyright Name (Figure 7.150 or 7.151, image 3). There is a maximum of 63 characters available for each name. Now follow these steps to create the name:
   - **Inserting a character:** Use the Arrow Pad to move the yellow highlight square around the gray grid of characters. When the character you want to use is under the yellow highlight, press the OK button to add the character to the line at the top of the screen, where you can see my name, *Darrell Young,* in the figures. Note that there is a space character at the top-left corner of the character grid (yellow highlighted).
   - **Fixing a mistake:** If you make a mistake, simply press the Info button and the cursor will jump to the top where the already inserted characters are. Then you can scroll to the mistake and fix it. Position the cursor over the incorrect character and press the Delete button (red trash can). The incorrect character will disappear. Immediately press the Info button again and the cursor will jump back to the grid of characters so you can insert the correct character. When you select the correct character, the camera will insert it automatically and move the other characters to the right.
   - **Saving the name:** When you are done creating the Artist Name or Copyright Name, move the yellow highlight cursor down to the bottom right of the character grid to the END selection. Highlight END and press the OK button to save the name.

Settings Recommendation: One of the first settings I change on my camera is this one. I want my name and initials all over the internal metadata of my images. This is a form of protection. At the very least, the fact that you own the original image with correct metadata proves that you took the image and own the copyright. Above all else, if you are concerned about your images, especially for commercial reasons, gather up a few hundred of them, put them on a CD, and register them at **www.copyright.gov**.

Lens Info Settings (H1)

You can store the lens information (name, focal length, and aperture value) for up to 10 lenses that do not automatically supply their information to the camera. Information for each lens must be entered separately. Once a lens is entered, you can edit the information or delete the lens.

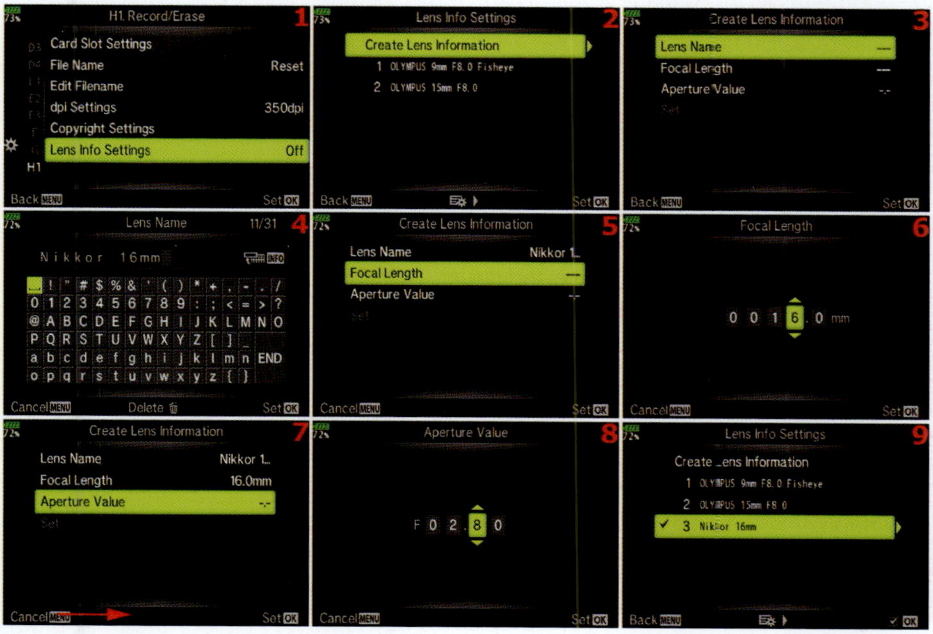

Figure 7.152: The Lens Info Setting in use

Use the following steps to add a lens to the built-in lens information database:

1. Select Lens Info Settings from the H1. Record/Erase menu and scroll to the right (figure 7.152, image 1).
2. Choose Create Lens Information from the menu and scroll to the right (figure 7.152, image 2).
3. You will now see a screen with Lens Name, Focal Length, and Aperture Value (figure 7.152, image 3). Highlight Lens Name and press the right arrow to open the screen in figure 7.152, image 4.

4. Now follow these steps to enter the lens name:
   - **Inserting a character:** Use the Arrow Pad to move the yellow highlight square around the gray grid of characters. When the character you want to use is under the yellow highlight, press the OK button to add the character to the line at the top of the screen, where you can see the lens name, *Nikkor 16mm,* in the figures. Note that there is a space character at the top-left corner of the character grid (yellow highlighted in figure 7.152, image 4).
   - **Fixing a mistake:** If you make a mistake, simply press the Info button and the cursor will jump to the top where the already inserted characters are. Then you can scroll to the mistake and fix it. Position the cursor over the incorrect character and press the Delete button (red trash can). The incorrect character will disappear. Immediately press the Info button again and the cursor will jump back to the grid of characters so you can insert the correct character. When you select the correct character, the camera will insert it automatically and move the other characters to the right.
   - **Saving the name:** When you are done creating the Lens Name, move the yellow highlight cursor down to the bottom right of the character grid to the END selection. Highlight END and press the OK button to save the name and return to the previous screen.
5. Now scroll down to Focal Length and press the right arrow key (figure 7.152, image 5).
6. Enter the focal length of the lens using the Arrow Pad up/down keys to select the numbers and the left/right keys to move between the fields (figure 7.152, image 6). Press the OK button to Set your choice and return to the previous screen.
7. Scroll down to Aperture Value and press the right arrow key (figure 7.152, image 7).
8. Enter the aperture value using the Arrow Pad up/down keys to select the numbers and the left/right keys to move between fields (figure 7.152, image 8). Press the OK button to Set your choice.
9. Return to the Lens Info Settings menu, and you will see that your lens is now included in the menu (figure 7.152, image 9). You can edit or delete the lens information at any time.

Quick Erase (H2)

The Quick Erase function gives you two ways to delete an unwanted image from the memory card: with explicit permission only, and immediately upon request. To erase an image you must display it on the camera monitor and press the Erase button on the back panel of the camera (looks like a red trash can).

At the time of deletion you can have the camera ask your permission first or you can simply delete the image as soon as you press the Erase button. If you use the latter method (immediate erase), make sure you have selected the correct image to delete because the camera will truly delete it immediately.

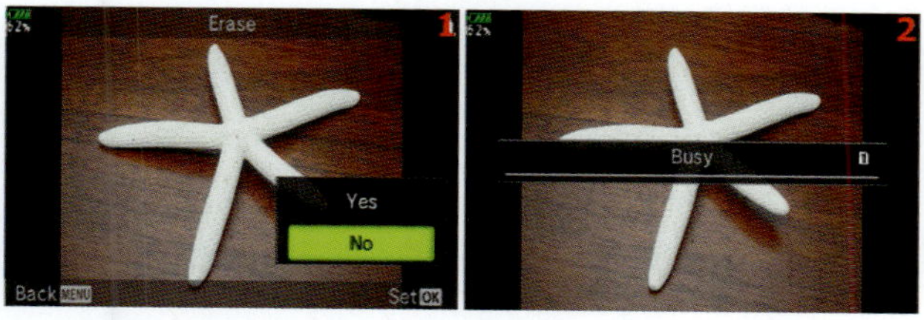

Figure 7.153: Two types of image deletion: with permission (image 1) and immediate (image 2)

Figure 7.153 shows the screens you will see depending on how you configure this function. Image 1 shows the screen that asks permission before erasing the image. Image 2 shows what happens when no permission is required; the image will be immediately deleted when you press the Erase button.

Whichever method you choose affects erasing only one image at a time, and the image to be erased must be displayed on the camera monitor. Let's consider how to choose an erase method for unwanted images.

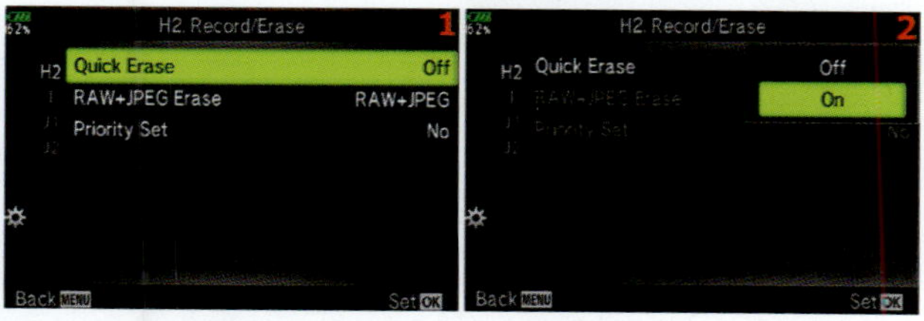

Figure 7.154: Choosing erase with permission only, or immediate deletion upon request

Use the following steps to choose the single-image deletion method you prefer:

1. Select the Quick Erase function from the H. Record/Erase menu and scroll to the right (figure 7.154, image 1).
2. From the Quick Erase menu (figure 7.154, image 2) choose Off if you want the camera to ask for your explicit permission before it deletes an image when you press the Erase button. Choose On if you want the camera to instantly delete a displayed image as soon as you press the Erase button, without confirmation. The factory default is Off.
3. Press the OK button to Set your choice.

Settings Recommendation: At first I set my camera to erase an image immediately (Quick Erase set to On), then I accidentally deleted a precious image of my pregnant daughter. I had to go through the trouble of using an image recovery program to save the deleted image. This made me rethink immediate deletion. Now I use the permission required method (Quick Erase set to Off) because it displays the image with a Yes/No choice, giving me a moment longer to think before deleting an image.

If you delete a lot of images after you take them, the immediate deletion method (On) will save you considerable time. Just make sure you are deleting the correct image!

RAW+JPEG Erase (H2)

When you set the Record Mode for still pictures to JPEG+RAW, the camera creates one identical image in each format for every picture you take.

That means two images are being stored for each picture, which uses up a lot of memory card capacity. Therefore, you will probably delete more images than normal to save space.

The RAW+JPEG Erase function lets you specify how to erase single image pairs. When you press the Erase button, do you want to erase both the RAW and JPEG file, just the RAW file, or just the JPEG file? You can choose. Let's see how!

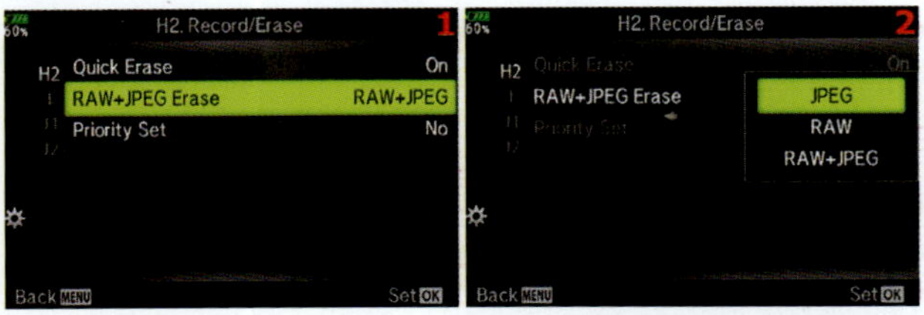

Figure 7.155: Choosing which image formats to erase with the Erase button

Use the following steps to choose how you want to erase RAW+JPEG image pairs:

1. Select RAW+JPEG Erase from the H2. Record/Erase menu and scroll to the right (figure 7.155, image 1).
2. From the RAW+JPEG Erase menu, choose RAW+JPEG if you want to delete both images in the set when you press the Erase button (figure 7.155, image 2). Choose RAW to delete only the RAW (ORF) file and leave the JPEG file on the memory card. Or choose JPEG to delete just the JPEG image and keep the RAW file. The factory default for this setting is RAW+JPEG.
3. Press the OK button to Set your choice.

Note: This function is effective only when you are using single-frame playback, where one image at a time is displayed on the monitor or in the viewfinder. Also, if you use All Erase or Format from the *Shooting Menu 1 > Card Setup* function, *all your images will be erased.* The RAW+JPEG Erase function is for erasing a single image that is displayed on the camera monitor or in the viewfinder.

Settings Recommendation: Generally I leave this function set to the factory default of RAW+JPEG. If I want to delete an image, I normally don't want to keep either of the formats.

However, if you are worried that the image may have some value later, or if you need to free up some memory card space while keeping at least one of the images, you can choose to delete just the RAW file or just the JPEG file when you press the Erase button.

Priority Set (H2)

When you decide to erase an image, as discussed in the previous Quick Erase function, you press the Erase button and are presented with a choice of Yes or No on a small menu.

The camera has *many* confirmation screens of this type, with Yes or No choices, and you can select which choice the camera defaults to when it asks for confirmation of various actions you want to perform.

Let's see how to select a default value for Yes/No confirmation screens.

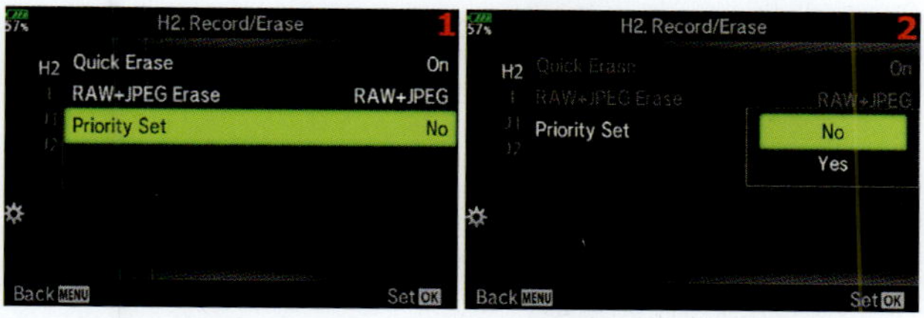

Figure 7.156: Default answer of Yes or No on confirmation screens

Use the following steps to choose a default value for when you request a change or deletion that requires a Yes or No answer:

1. Select the Priority Set function from the H2. Record/Erase menu and scroll to the right (figure 7.156, image 1).
2. Choose Yes if you want the camera to always have Yes selected when a Yes/No confirmation screen appears, or choose No if you prefer No to be selected. The camera defaults to No (figure 7.156, image 2).
3. Press the OK button to Set your choice.

Note: The choice of Yes or No in step 2 affects many confirmation screens throughout the camera's entire menu system. All screens with a Yes or No selection will obey the choice you make in step 2.

Settings Recommendation: I set my camera to Yes because I don't want to make an additional choice when a Yes/No confirmation screen appears. I would rather it just default to Yes, and I can select No if I change my mind.

Custom Menu I. EVF

The I. EVF menu is primarily composed of functions that manage the electronic viewfinder (EVF) behind the eyepiece of the camera. It provides settings for things like the style of the EVF, overlays that are displayed on the EVF, how the eye sensor works, and the brightness and color balance of the EVF.

We will start examining the functions by taking a look at the opening menu for the I. EVF functions in figure 7.157.

To enter the menu, select I. EVF from the Custom Menu and scroll to the right. There are seven functions inside the I. EVF menu. Let's consider each of them in detail.

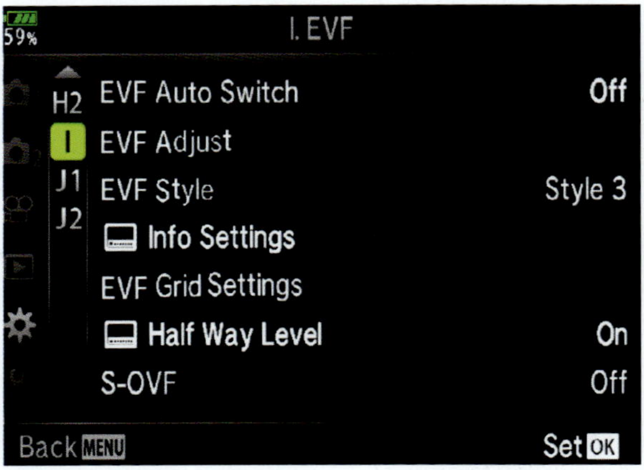

Figure 7.157: The I. EVF Menu

EVF Auto Switch (I)

The camera has a small eye detector built in to the right side of the viewfinder, which is why the rubber viewfinder attachment has such an odd shape. If you look closely you will see two tiny lenses at the bottom right of the viewfinder. These lenses detect when anything gets close to the viewfinder, then it closes the EVF Auto Switch and enables the internal EVF, which turns the rear monitor off.

If you prefer to use the rear monitor for all your pictures, you can disable the EVF Auto Switch. Then the camera will ignore your eye or anything else that gets close to the viewfinder and leave the rear monitor active for shooting pictures.

Let's see how to enable or disable the EVF Auto Switch (eye sensor).

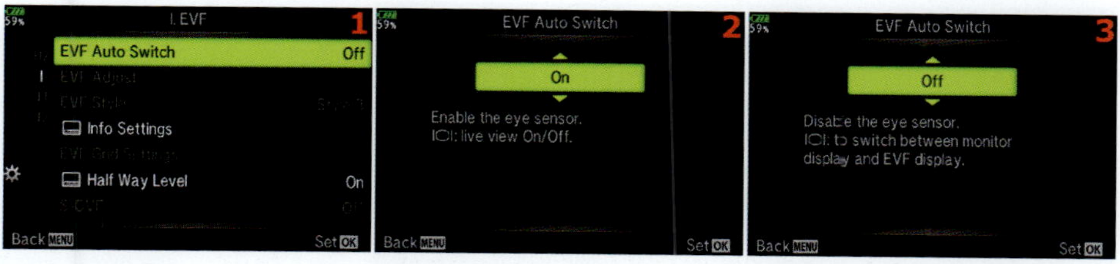

Figure 7.158: Enabling or disabling the EVF eye sensor

Use these steps to enable or disable the viewfinder eye detector:

1. Select EVF Auto Switch from the I. EVF menu and scroll to the right (figure 7.158, image 1).
2. Use the up/down menu to select either On or Off for the eye sensor (figure 7.158, images 2 and 3). The On setting enables the Live View monitor until the camera senses something close to the viewfinder eyepiece, then it enables the EVF and disables the monitor. The Off setting uses the Live View monitor only and turns off the eye sensor. If this function is set to Off, you can manually switch to the EVF by pressing the LV button at the left of the viewfinder, which will toggle the camera between the EVF and the rear monitor.
3. Press the OK button to Set your choice.

Note: If you hold down the LV button to the left of the viewfinder eyepiece for about two seconds, the camera will open the EVF Auto Switch menu directly, and then you can select On or Off to enable or disable the eye sensor very quickly.

Settings Recommendation: I prefer to use the EVF for most of my photography. However, I do find the Live View monitor to be quite handy for casual photography and for macro shooting. Therefore, I usually leave EVF Auto Switch set to On so the camera will sense my eye approaching the viewfinder and automatically turn on the EVF and turn off the monitor.

However, I shoot macros with the Live View monitor, and I sometimes get my hand too close to the viewfinder and the monitor goes off, causing me to lose sight of my subject. When that happens, I may temporarily disable EVF Auto Switch (set it to Off) so I can keep the Live View monitor active at all times.

EVF Adjust (I)

The E-M1II automatically controls the brightness and color balance (hue) of the EVF, depending on the ambient light conditions. If you want to control the brightness and color balance of the EVF yourself, you can use this function to do so. Let's see how.

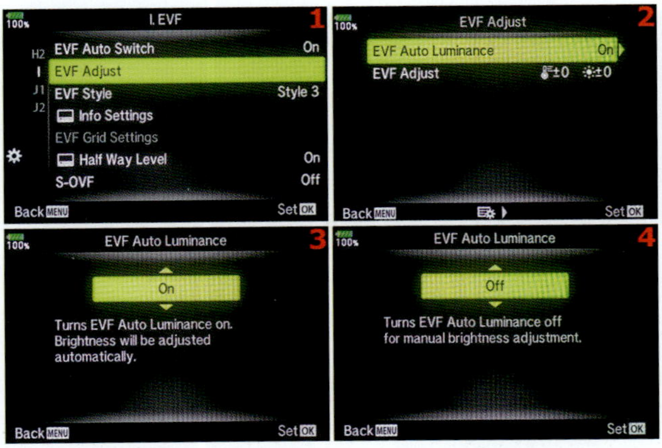

Figure 7.159: Enabling or disabling EVF Auto Luminance

Use these steps to enable or disable EVF Auto Luminance:

1. Select EVF Adjust from the I. EVF menu and scroll to the right (figure 7.159, image 1).
2. Choose EVF Auto Luminance from the EVF Adjust screen and scroll to the right (figure 7.159, image 2).
3. Use the up/down menu to select either On or Off (figure 7.159, images 3 and 4). If you select On (default), the camera will adjust the EVF brightness and hue automatically. If you choose Off, you can use the EVF Adjust setting (second menu item in image 2) to control the EVF brightness and hue manually.
4. Press the OK button to Set your choice.

Next let's see how to adjust the EVF brightness and hue manually instead of letting the camera control it automatically.

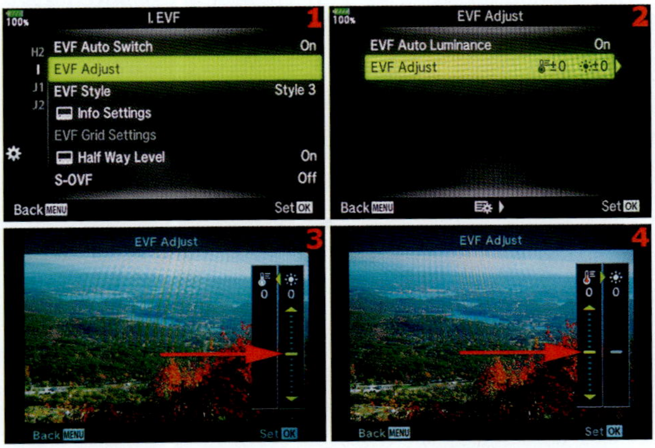

Figure 7.160: Setting the EVF brightness and color balance

Use these steps to manually control the brightness and hue of the EVF screen. While you make these adjustments, remember that they apply to the EVF, not the Live View monitor. To make the adjustments shown in figure 7.160, images 3 and 4, you must be looking into the viewfinder to see the screens:

1. Select EVF Adjust from the I. EVF menu and scroll to the right (figure 7.160, image 1).
2. Choose EVF Adjust from the EVF Adjust screen and scroll to the right (figure 7.160, image 2).
3. You will now see a screen in the EVF that displays the last picture you took or the last picture you viewed from the memory card. The picture is overlaid with two adjustment sliders on the right: one for brightness and one for hue or color temperature. The adjustment for brightness is on the far right side of the EVF screen. You can use the keys of the Arrow Pad to scroll up or down to adjust the brightness of the EVF over a range of 15 levels. You can move the yellow bar at the point of the red arrow up seven levels (+7) or down seven levels (–7), which brightens or darkens the backlight of the EVF screen.
4. When you are done, scroll to the left with the left key of the Arrow Pad to adjust the hue (color temperature) of the EVF (figure 7.160, image 4). Notice at the point of the arrow that the hue setting is 0. You can adjust the hue up seven levels (+7) or down seven levels (–7). An upward adjustment makes the hue shift toward blue (cooler), and a downward adjustment makes the hue shift toward red (warmer). Adjust the EVF color temperature until it seems right to you.
5. Press the OK button to Set your EVF brightness and hue choices.

Note: The EVF brightness and hue settings are for comfort only and do not affect the brightness or hue of the images you create. The brightness and color temperature of your pictures are controlled by the exposure and white balance settings.

Settings Recommendation: I normally leave EVF Auto Luminance set to On. This lets the camera control the brightness and hue of the monitor, similar to how my iPhone adjusts when the ambient light changes. I have found the camera's choices to be satisfactory, and the automatic control is quite convenient.

However, if you are shooting in a controlled studio environment with careful color matching, you may want to adjust the EVF until it looks best for your light source.

EVF Style (I)

The camera offers three EVF Styles, as shown in Figure 7.161. Style 1 and Style 2 have a retro film camera look. Style 3 is the factory default, which looks more modern. Style 3 imitates the layout of the rear monitor, so many people prefer this Style.

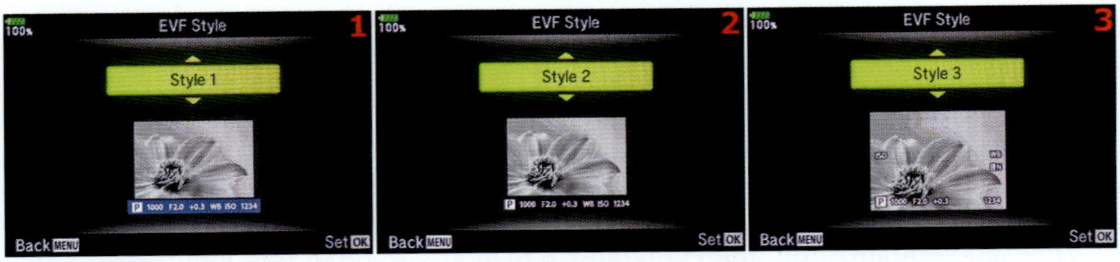

Figure 7.161: EVF Styles 1, 2, and 3

Styles 1 and 2 provide shooting information in a band at the bottom of the EVF. Style 1 has a blue band with yellow and white characters. Style 2 has a dark gray (almost black) band with yellow and white characters. Style 3 is the default. It has bright white characters with exposure information in yellow. Notice in the figure that Style 3 provides a little more magnification of the subject, making it somewhat easier to see.

Let's examine how to select one of the Styles.

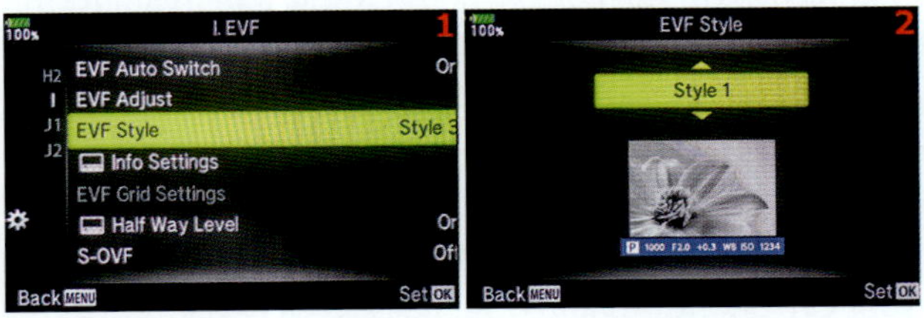

Figure 7.162: Choosing an EVF Style

Use these steps to select one of the EVF Styles:

1. Select EVF Style from the I. EVF menu and scroll to the right (figure 7.162, image 1).
2. Use the up/down menu to select one of the three Styles (figure 7.162, image 2). Refer to figure 7.161 to choose your favorite.
3. Press the OK button to Set your choice.

Settings Recommendation: I generally leave my camera set to the factory default of Style 3. I like the larger view of the subject in the viewfinder and having the monitor and viewfinder look the same. However, before you make a final decision about which EVF Style you will use, examine the rest of the functions in the I. EVF menu. Some of the upcoming functions work differently when you use Styles 1 and 2.

[EVF] Info Settings (I)

Depending on which Style you chose for the EVF Style, you can have the EVF display things that are traditionally seen only on the rear monitor. The EVF can display a Live Histogram, show a Highlight&Shadow screen, present a Level Gauge, or allow a sparse Basic Information screen.

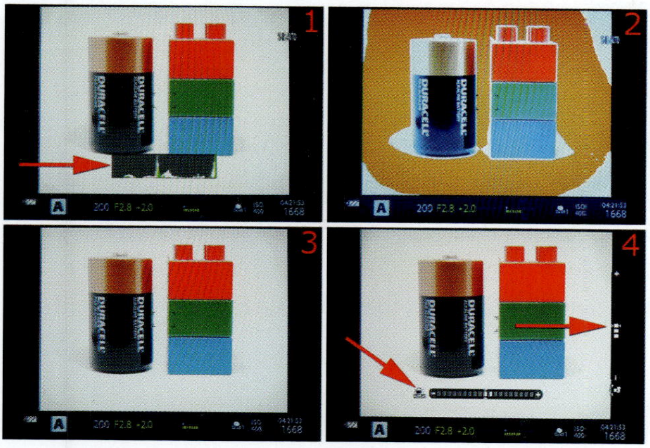

Figure 7.163: The four [EVF] Info Settings types: Live Histogram (image 1), Highlight&Shadow (image 2), Basic Information (image 3), and Level Gauge (image 4)

While choosing [EVF] Info Settings, remember that the Info overlays apply to the EVF, not the Live View monitor. To see all the selected [EVF] Info Settings, you must look into the viewfinder while pressing the Info button repeatedly.

Let's examine what each of the three EVF Styles display, using the screen overlays in figure 7.163, images 1–4, as examples:

- **Style 1:** This Style offers a blue band at the bottom with exposure information displayed similarly to a retro film camera. You can select several overlays by pressing the Info button repeatedly. The camera offers Live Histogram (image 1), Highlight&Shadow (overexposed areas turn orange, image 2), Basic Information (image 3), and Level Gauge (image 4).
- **Style 2:** This Style is virtually identical to Style 1, except it uses a black band at the bottom of the EVF instead of a blue band. See Style 1 in the previous bullet for details about the displays.
- **Style 3:** This Style makes the EVF perform like a smaller version of the monitor on the back of the camera. The EVF and monitor will generally look identical. Style 3 offers all the features of Styles 1 and 2 with the exception of the Highlight&Shadow (orange overexposure) mode in figure 7.163, image 2.

Now let's examine how to select which Info Settings you want to use in the EVF.

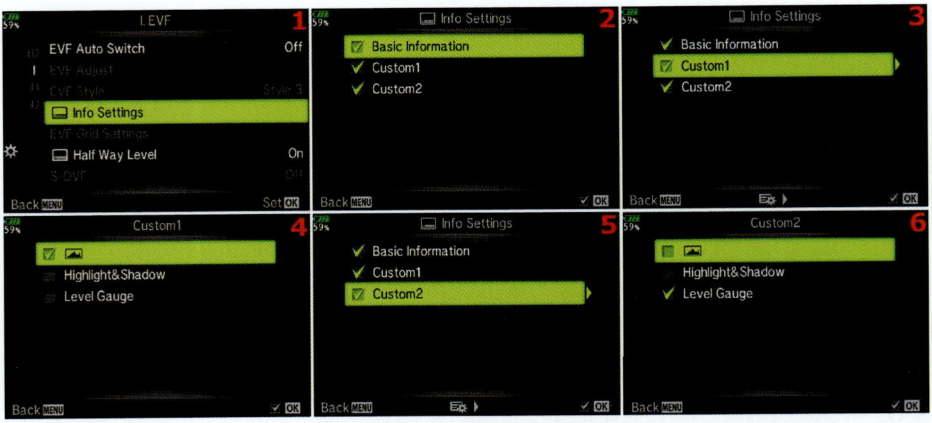

Figure 7.164: Choosing an [EVF] Info Settings type

Use these steps to select the Info Settings you want to use on the EVF:

1. Select [EVF] Info Settings from the I. EVF menu and scroll to the right (figure 7.164, image 1).
2. There are three options on the Info Settings screen: Basic Information, Custom 1, and Custom 2 (figure 7.164, image 2). When you highlight Custom 1 or Custom 2 and scroll to the right, you can access the following settings: [Live Histogram], Highlight&Shadow, and Level Gauge (figure 7.164, images 3–6). Remember that if you are using Style 3, Highlight&Shadow is of no use. However, if you are using either Style 1 or 2, you may want to check the Highlight&Shadow setting so it will show blown-out (overexposed) areas in the EVF. To check or uncheck an item, highlight it and press the OK button. When an item is checked, each Info Setting will appear on the EVF when you press the Info button repeatedly.
3. Press the Menu button to return to the main menu when you are done.

Settings Recommendation: I check all the available [EVF] Info Settings in case I decide to use an EVF Style that works with that setting. I don't see a problem with checking all of them, so why not?

EVF Grid Settings (I)

The camera can display a series of six grid types, in two custom colors, as overlays in the EVF, as seen in figure 7.165.

The six grid types will help you align your image correctly for various types of photography. The grid overlays are available only when you use EVF Styles 1 or 2 (not Style 3). If this menu choice is grayed out, it means that you have selected EVF Style 3, or that *Custom Menu > D3. Disp/[Sound]/PC > Grid Settings > Apply Settings to EVF* is turned on (which means that that monitor grid settings have been applied to the EVF).

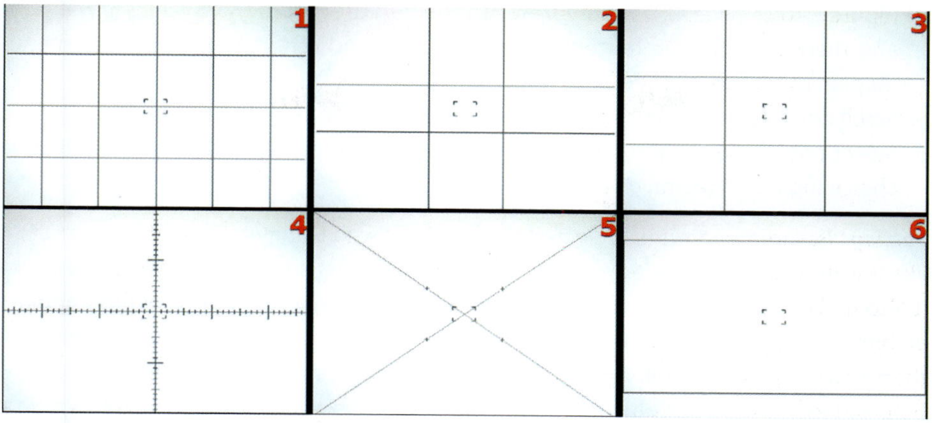

Figure 7.165: The default EVF screen and six grid types

When you choose a grid type, remember that the grids apply to the EVF, not the Live View monitor. To see the grid, you must be looking into the viewfinder.

Let's examine how to select a grid color and type for EVF Styles 1 and 2.

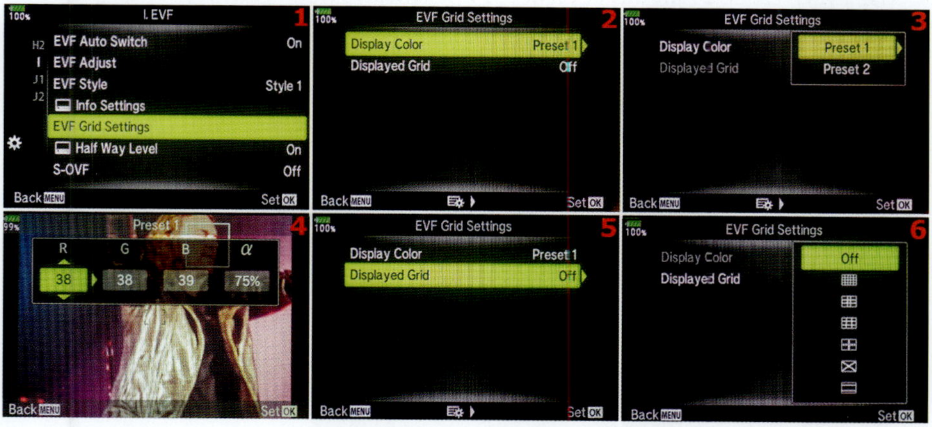

Figure 7.166: Choosing a Display Color and Displayed Grid type for EVF Styles 1 and 2 (only)

Use these steps to select a Display Color and Displayed Grid type when you are using EVF Styles 1 and 2:

1. Select EVF Grid Settings from the I. EVF menu and scroll to the right (figure 7.166, image 1).
2. Select Display Color and scroll to the right (figure 7.166, image 2).
3. Select Preset 1 and scroll to the right (figure 7.166, image 3).
4. A screen will open with value boxes for the R (red), G (green), and B (blue) color channels, as well as a box for α (alpha), which allows you to set the opacity of the grid lines

(figure 7.166, image 4). Use the Arrow Pad to adjust the R, G, B, and α values (if wanted), and then press the OK button to Set the values and return to the previous menu. (Repeat this process for Preset 2, if you would like.)

5. Scroll down to Displayed Grid and scroll to the right (figure 7.166, image 5).
6. Select one of the six grid patterns, or Off, and then press the OK button to Set your choice (figure 7.166, image 6).

Settings Recommendation: I selected the first Displayed Grid type (directly under Off). I like this grid because it helps me align the horizon when I am shooting landscapes, and it also makes it easier to shoot buildings when I'm walking around town photographing architecture. There is a grid type to suit most photo needs, so experiment with each of them to see which you prefer, if any. Using a color for the grid that is easy to see can really help, so I set the Display Color to something that will stand out in light and dark shooting scenarios, like a solid red (R 100, G 0, B 0, and Alpha 100%).

[EVF] Half Way Level (I)

If you are using EVF Styles 1 and 2, the camera displays a small Half Way Level at the bottom of the EVF. The Half Way Level is not available with EVF Style 3.

The level is called a Half Way Level because it activates when you press the Shutter button halfway down. When the level appears, it replaces the –/+ exposure indicator at the bottom of the EVF screen.

When the camera is off level horizontally, a series of white bars will extend to the left or right of the center of the scale in the opposite direction of the camera body rotation. If you rotate the camera more than a few degrees horizontally, the scale will run out of white bars, and an orange arrow will appear above the scale to indicate the camera cannot register any more degrees of rotation.

When the camera is exactly level horizontally, the center bar and the two up/down arrows above the center bar will turn green.

Let's examine how to enable or disable the Half Way Level.

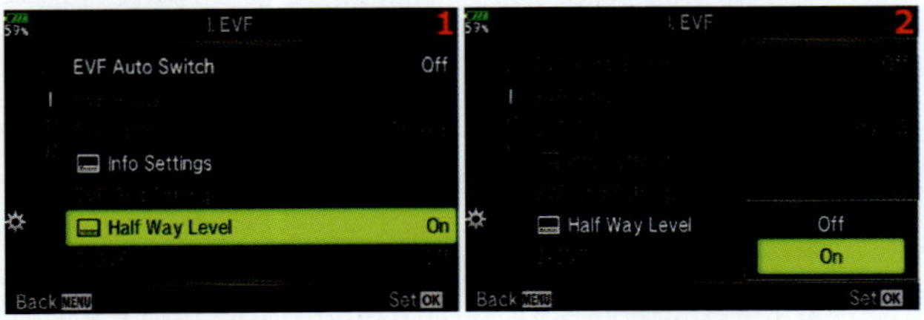

Figure 7.167: Enabling or disabling the Half Way Level

Use these steps to enable or disable the Half Way Level:

1. Select [EVF] Half Way Level from the I. EVF menu and scroll to the right (figure 7.167, image 1).

2. Use the menu to select On or Off to enable or disable the Half Way Level (figure 7.167, image 2).
3. Press the OK button to Set your choice.

Settings Recommendation: I leave this level enabled in case I decide to use a different EVF Style than my normal Style 3. However, if I want to use a real level, I simply use the camera's main Virtual level. It is available when you press the Info button until the level appears on the monitor or in the EVF. The Virtual level shows left and right rotation along with forward and backward rotation.

S-OVF (I)

This setting allows the EVF to act like a traditional optical viewfinder. If this setting is turned off, the EVF will show the effects of the current camera settings on the scene, allowing you to see the effects of your exposure choices through the viewfinder before you actually take the photo.

This is a simple on/off menu choice, but the effects it can have as you are trying to properly capture an image are huge. Seeing the effects of your exposure choices in real time allows for better decision making, but this can take some time to get used to.

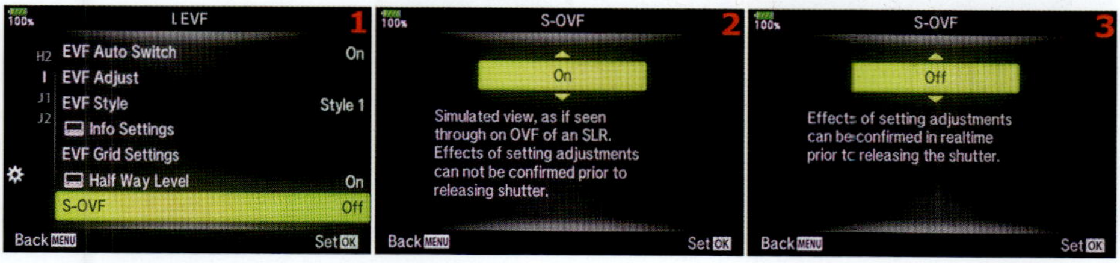

Figure 7.168: Enabling or disabling the S-OVF

Use these steps to enable or disable the S-OVF:

1. Select S-OVF from the I. EVF menu and scroll to the right (figure 7.168, image 1).
2. Select On to make the EVF function like a traditional optical viewfinder, or Off to see the effects of the current camera settings on the scene (figure 7.168, images 2 and 3).
3. Press the OK button to Set your choice.

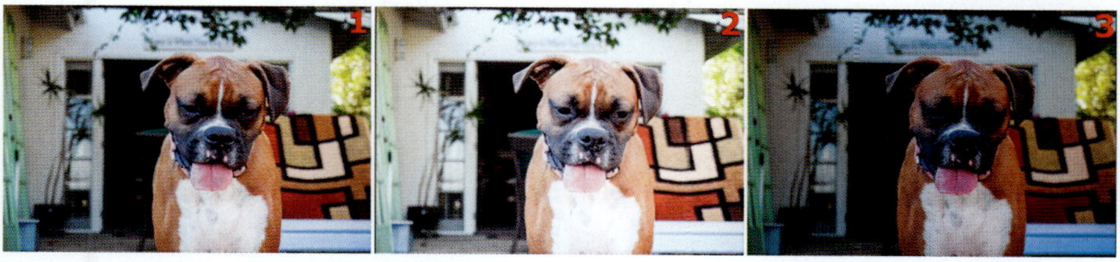

Figure 7.169: simulated difference when using S-OVF turn on or off

Figure 7.169, image 1, shows a scene as it would appear through the viewfinder with S-OVF turned on (the viewfinder does not reflect the effects of the current exposure settings). Images 2 and 3 show what you would see through the viewfinder with S-OVF turned off, and with exposure settings that overexpose (image 2) and underexpose (image 3) the scene by a full stop.

Settings Recommendation: The benefit of an EVF is that it provides instant feedback on your exposure settings. However, if you're used to an optical viewfinder, this may take some getting used to. It's nice to have the option to make the EVF function like an optical viewfinder if you find that you prefer it. Try it out both ways and see what you like best.

Custom Menu J1–J2. Utility

The J1–J2. Utility menu is composed of eleven functions that don't readily fit into one of the other Custom Menus. We will start examining the functions by taking a look at the opening menu for the J1–J2. Utility menu in figure 7.170. This is the last menu system in the group of Custom Menus.

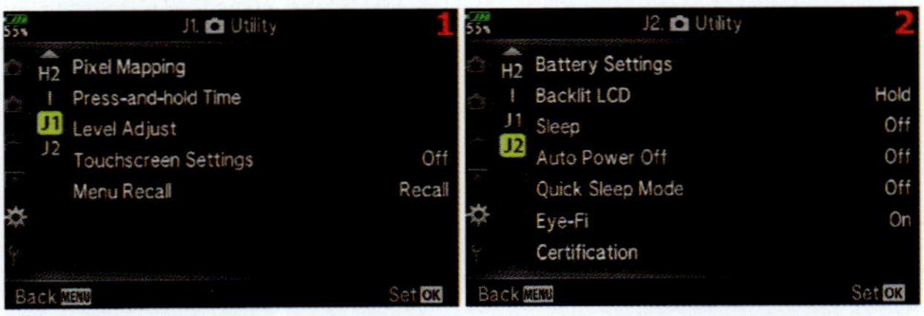

Figure 7.170: The J1–J2. Utility menu

To enter the menu, select J1. (or J2.) Utility from the Custom Menu and scroll to the right. There are five functions inside the J1. Utility menu and six functions in J2. Utility. Let's consider each of them in detail.

Pixel Mapping (J1)

The E-M1II allows you to run a self-check on the camera sensor and image processing functions. When your camera was first manufactured, one of the final steps before the camera was released was the Pixel Mapping process. Why?

All digital cameras suffer from two maladies, both initially and over time:

- **Dead pixels:** A dead pixel is a photosite on the sensor that has become unresponsive. It will appear as a tiny black spot in the same place on every image unless it is mapped out.
- **Stuck pixels:** A stuck pixel is a photosite that reports full exposure regardless of the actual exposure. This means the pixel will always appear as one color, usually red or white, at the same place in every image. It should be mapped out.

Because the E-M1II is an advanced camera, you can run a similar Pixel Mapping function as the one used by Olympus technicians. You don't want black, white, or colored spots in all your images, so you should run the Pixel Mapping function as needed to remap the dead and stuck pixels on your camera sensor.

Olympus recommends that you run the Pixel Mapping function at least once a year. However, if you detect dead or stuck pixels in your images when they are viewed at 100 percent on your computer monitor, you can run the Pixel Mapping function and map the bad photosites out of future images. The camera will interpolate data from surrounding pixels to fill in what should be captured at the mapped-out pixel, preventing image degradation that would otherwise be caused by using the Pixel Mapping function.

Mapping the bad pixels takes about 20 seconds, and you will hear the camera make some odd clicking noises as it tests and maps the entire sensor and image processing system.

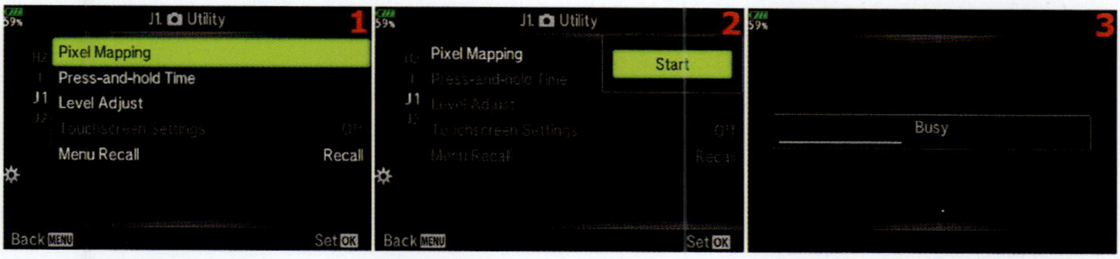

Figure 7.171: Remapping the sensor pixels

Use these steps to run the Pixel Mapping function to tune up your sensor and image processing system:

1. Select Pixel Mapping from the J1. Utility menu and scroll to the right (figure 7.171, image 1).
2. Choose Start from the menu and press the OK button to begin mapping the pixels (figure 7.171, image 2).
3. During the Pixel Mapping process, you will hear various clicks from the camera over a period of about 20 seconds. While the camera is working you will see a *Busy* indicator on the screen (figure 7.171, image 3). When Pixel Mapping is complete, the camera will return to the main menu.

Note: In addition to dead and stuck pixels, you may have heard of hot pixels. A hot pixel is not a dead or stuck pixel, and the Pixel Mapping function is not designed to deal with them specifically. Hot pixels are photosites on the sensor that have become overheated due to long exposures. They will appear in images as various incorrect colors. As the camera cools, the hot pixels will cool off and return to normal. Use the *Custom Menu > E1. Exp/ISO/BULB/[Meter] > Noise Reduct.* function to deal with hot pixels. The camera should not map out hot pixels because they move around on the sensor.

It is not a good idea to run the Pixel Mapping function after you take a lot of exposures or a long exposure, especially when you are shooting in a warm environment. You don't want the camera to map out pixels that are useful in normal exposures. Therefore, it is best to run Pixel Mapping before you start shooting images for the day. At the very minimum, allow the camera to cool down for at least one minute after you take pictures, and significantly longer if the camera is warm to the touch.

Settings Recommendation: This is a powerful and useful function for photographers who cannot afford to have spots on their pictures. I do not indiscriminately run this function. I run it at least once per year or more often if I see dead or stuck pixels. All digital cameras will lose a few pixels over time, although not enough to affect the image, even after many years of use. However, aren't you glad that Olympus gave you a Pixel Mapping function so you can take care of the problem yourself instead of having to send your camera in for service?

Press-and-hold Time (J1)

The E-M1II has 16 functions for which you must press and hold a button for a certain length of time before the camera actually responds. The Press-and-hold Time function allows you to set a specific hold time for each button. The default hold time for all buttons is 0.7 seconds, but you can change it to as quick as 0.5 seconds all the way to 3 seconds.

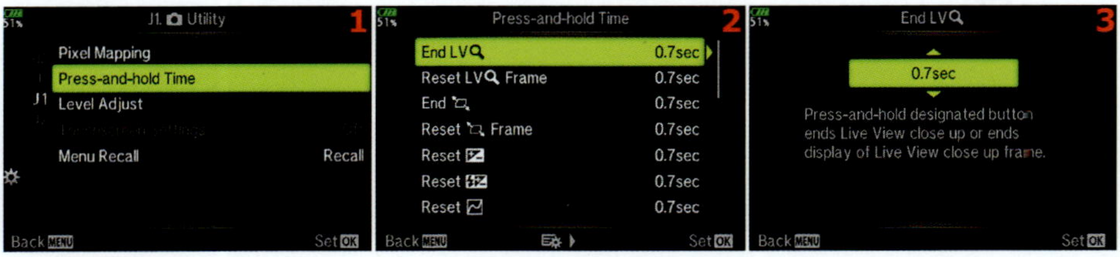

Figure 7.172: Here is the Press-and-hold time menu

Use these steps to change the Press-and-hold Time:

1. Select Press-and-hold Time from the J1. Utility menu and scroll to the right (figure 7.172, image 1).
2. Scroll through the list of buttons until you find the one you want to change, and then scroll to the right (figure 7.172, image 2).
3. Use the Arrow Pad keys to adjust the time from 0.05 – 3 seconds (figure 7.172, image 3).
4. Press the OK Button to Set the time and return to the list of buttons.

Settings Recommendation: I am not sure why you would want to change these times and slow the camera down. I leave all buttons set to the default 0.07 seconds, which seems to work just great.

Level Adjust (J1)

Normally, the camera's leveling system tells you when your E-M1II is level for roll and pitch. However, if you need the camera to indicate that it is level at an unusual angle, you can adjust the level indicator.

Maybe you are shooting an unusual, off-level still life and you want the camera to line up with the still life's angles instead of really being level. You can set the camera's leveling system to match your special camera-angle requirements.

Let's see how to make the camera report that it is level when it really isn't—and yet it matches your special angle needs.

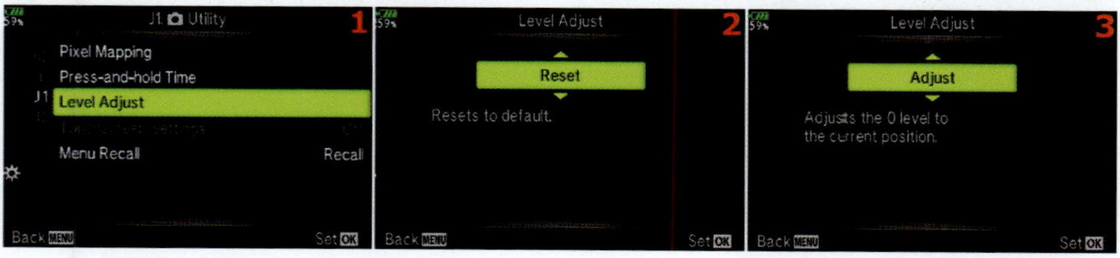

Figure 7.173: Adjusting the leveling system to give a false-level reading for special uses

Use these steps to adjust the angle the camera uses to indicate that it is level:

1. Select Level Adjust from the J1. Utility menu and scroll to the right (figure 7.173, image 1).
2. Position the camera so it is at the exact angle you want it to consider level, then select Adjust from the up/down menu and press the OK button (figure 7.173, image 2). The camera will consider the new angle to be level. The level indicators will zero out and turn green when you place the camera at the new false-level angle.
3. When you are done shooting at the false-level setting, reset the camera so it will use the true level again. Select Reset from the up/down menu and press the OK button (figure 7.173, image 3).

Settings Recommendation: This is certainly an unusual setting. I have found no use for it yet since I shoot a lot of nature images. However, I can imagine that some photographers will use this feature for specialized angle shooting, especially in the studio and maybe for some types of architectural photography. If you have a need for this setting, I'm sure you will immediately recognize it.

Touch Screen Settings (J1)

The E-M1II has a great touch screen built in to the Live View monitor on the back of the camera. You can activate various functions by simply tapping an icon or button on the screen.

However, you may not like using the touch screen and would rather just use the menu system to control the camera features. Or maybe you accidentally keep touching the screen and things happen that you did not intend. In that case you can disable the touch screen. Let's see how.

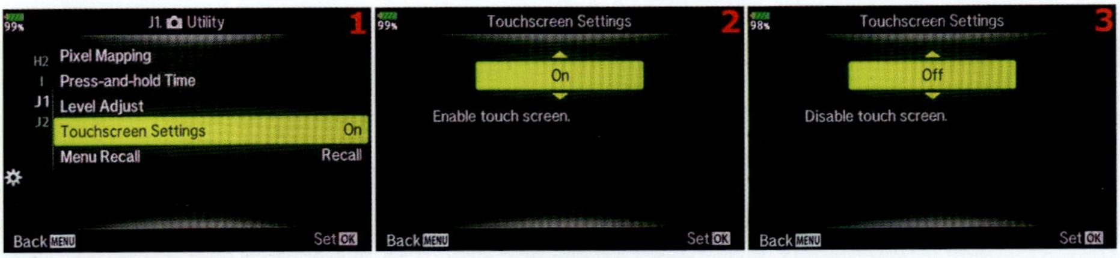

Figure 7.174: Enabling or disabling the touch screen capability

Use these steps to enable or disable the touch screen capability:

1. Select Touch Screen Settings from the J1. Utility menu and scroll to the right (figure 7.174, image 1).
2. Use the up/down menu to select On to enable the Touch Screen, or select Off to disable it (figure 7.174, images 2 and 3).
3. Press the OK button to Set your choice.

Settings Recommendation: I leave the touch screen enabled on my camera. When I first used a camera with touch screen capabilities I was not all that interested in using it, but then I started discovering various functions that are easier to manipulate by simply touching the screen instead of scrolling through menus. I suggest leaving the touch screen active on your camera unless you are having trouble with touching it at the wrong time.

Menu Recall (J1)

This function controls where your cursor appears when you press the Menu button. You can choose Recall or Reset. Recall will display the cursor at the last position of operation when you press the Menu button. The cursor will stay in the last position of operation even if you turn the camera off. Reset will cause the cursor to be displayed back at the beginning of the menu each time you press the Menu button. Given that the E-M1II has a very complicated menu system, it's helpful to have this function set to Recall.

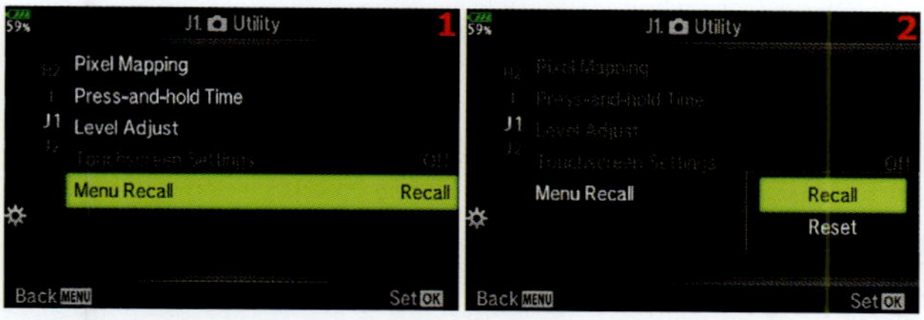

Figure 7.175: Enabling or disabling the Menu Recall feature

Use these steps to enable or disable the Menu Recall feature:

1. Select Menu Recall from the J1. Utility menu and scroll to the right (figure 7.175, image 1).
2. Use the up/down menu to select Recall or Reset (figure 7.175, image 2).
3. Press the OK button to Set your choice.

Settings Recommendation: I leave this set to Recall so that when I press the Menu button I go back to the previous menu and not back to the beginning each time.

Fisheye Compensation (J1)

As we head to press, Olympus has released firmware update 2.0 for the E-M1II. Fisheye Compensation is a new function in version 2.0 that allows you to use the M.Zuiko Digital ED 8mm F1.8 Fisheye PRO as a wide-angle lens without the fisheye effect. Select On to modify the angle of view. You can view the effects of this function on the Live View monitor before shooting. Fisheye Compensation can be applied to JPEG images; however, RAW files will retain the original fisheye effect.

Battery Settings (J2)

When you are using the optional Olympus Power Battery Holder on your E-M1II, the camera has two batteries at its disposal: the PBH battery and the Body Battery. This Battery Settings function gives you a choice of which battery to use first and it shows you the stats of each battery.

Most people choose to have the camera use the battery inside the PBH first so the camera can continue to operate on the Body Battery if the PBH is removed. If the Body Battery is used before the battery in the PBH and you remove the PBH, the camera will not operate due to the lack of power.

Use these steps to set which battery is used first when the optional PBH is attached and a battery is inserted:

1. Select Battery Settings from the J2. Utility menu and scroll to the right (figure 7.176, image 1).
2. Select Battery Priority and scroll to the right (figure 7.176, image 2).

3. Use the up/down menu to select either PBH Battery or Body Battery (figure 7.176, images 3 and 4).
4. Press the OK button to Set your choice.
5. You can also see the status of each battery by selecting Battery Status from the Battery Settings menu and scrolling to the right (figure 7.176, images 5 and 6).

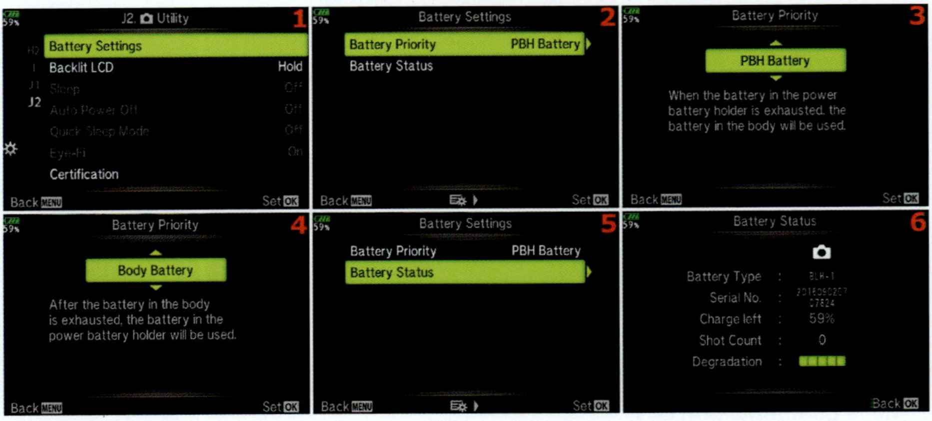

Figure 7.176: The Battery Settings Menu

Settings Recommendation: I always have this set to use the battery in the optional grip (PBH) before the battery in the camera as it is a lot easier to change the battery in the grip than it is to change the battery in the camera with the grip attached.

Backlit LCD (J2)

The LCD monitor on the rear of the camera uses a lot of battery power. In fact, powering this monitor drains more energy from the battery than any other part of the camera. The Backlit LCD function allows you to set a time limit for the LCD monitor to stay at full brightness. When the time-out expires the monitor will dim significantly and reduce the power drain. It does not go off completely—it just gets very dim. You can choose from 8 seconds (8sec), 30 seconds (30sec), 1 minute (1min), and Hold. The Hold setting effectively cancels the dimming process and retains the brightness all the time.

This function affects only the shooting mode when the subject is displayed on the monitor and the camera is ready to take a picture. If you venture into the camera menus with the Menu button or start viewing images with the Playback button, the time-out period does not apply. Also, the time-out period does not affect the electronic viewfinder (EVF) display, only the rear LCD monitor.

The camera also has a function called Sleep, which we will consider in the next subsection. The Sleep function completely turns off the camera monitor after one minute. If you have the Backlit LCD time-out set to 1min and Sleep set to 1min, you will not see the backlit display dim. Instead, the Sleep function will override the Backlit LCD function and turn off the monitor.

While the monitor is dimmed, you can return it to full brightness by slightly pressing the Shutter button. In fact, using any camera control will do the same. Let's see how to choose a time-out period for dimming the Backlit LCD monitor.

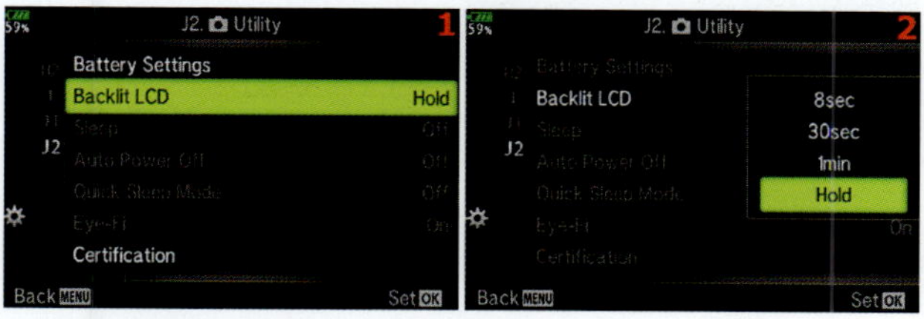

Figure 7.177: Choosing a Backlit LCD time-out period for dimming the monitor

Use the following steps to modify the Backlit LCD function:

1. Select Backlit LCD from the J2. Utility menu and scroll to the right (figure 7.177, image 1).
2. Select 8sec, 30sec, 1min, or Hold from the up/down menu (figure 7.177, image 2). The factory default is Hold, which never dims the screen.
3. Press the OK button to Set the value.

Settings Recommendation: I set my camera's Backlit LCD time-out to 8sec so I can save battery life. It is hard to make it through a full day of shooting with the EVF and monitor drawing so much power, so I am glad to have a dim function. I can undim the LCD by merely pressing the Shutter button halfway. If 8 seconds (8sec) is not enough time for you to compose and shoot with the LCD monitor, try 30sec or 1min. If you choose 1min, be aware that the Sleep function (next subsection) will likely prevent the monitor from dimming.

Sleep (J2)

The Sleep function could just as easily be called energy-saving mode. It puts the camera to sleep after a time-out period. Backlit LCD, discussed in the previous subsection, causes the monitor to dim significantly after a set period. The Sleep function takes it a step further by turning the monitor and electronic viewfinder (EVF) off until you use a camera control.

You can choose to have the display screens go to sleep after 1, 3, or 5 minutes (1min, 3min, or 5min), or you can turn the Sleep function off all together (Off). After the camera has gone to sleep it will not wake back up until you press a button or turn a dial. When you do press a button—while the camera is in energy-saving Sleep mode—the camera ignores the normal function of that button and simply wakes up.

If you accidentally forget to turn the camera off and leave it in Sleep mode, it will turn itself off after a set period of time, which you can control with the Auto Power Off function (discussed in the next subsection).

Let's consider how to choose a Sleep mode time-out.

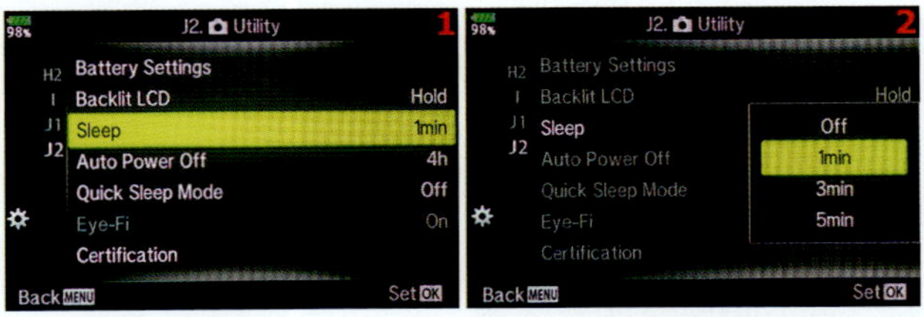

Figure 7.178: Choosing a Sleep time delay

Use the following steps to modify the Sleep function:

1. Select Sleep from the J2. Utility menu and scroll to the right (figure 7.178, image 1).
2. Select 1min, 3min, or 5min from the up/down menu (figure 7.178, image 2). You can also choose Off to disable the Sleep function. The factory default is 1min.
3. Press the OK button to Set the value.

Settings Recommendation: I leave my camera set to 1min. The battery draw is so high for the bright screens that I want my camera to go to sleep quickly when I'm not using it.

I have found that the camera will go to sleep even when I am carrying it on a strap around my neck. At first I thought the sensor on the viewfinder eyepiece, which tells the camera to switch to the EVF, might sense my clothing and not let the camera go to sleep, but that's not the case. If you do not use a physical camera control within the time-out period you chose in the Sleep function, the camera will shut down the display screens and go into energy-saving mode.

When the camera is in Sleep mode, it starts the countdown to Auto Power Off, which will shut down the camera completely. We will consider Auto Power Off next.

Auto Power Off (J2)

Auto Power Off shuts down your camera if you do not use it for a certain period of time. You can set the camera to automatically shut off after 5 minutes (5min), 30 minutes (30min), 1 hour (1h), or 4 hours (4h). You can also choose to disable this function so that the camera never turns off automatically.

The camera shuts down after the time-out period you select, even though the On/Off switch is set to On. If the camera has shut down with the On/Off switch set to On, you can to turn the switch Off and back On again to power up the camera. It will not come back on when you use any other camera control, unlike the Backlit LCD and Sleep functions.

Let's examine how to choose an Auto Power Off time-out period.

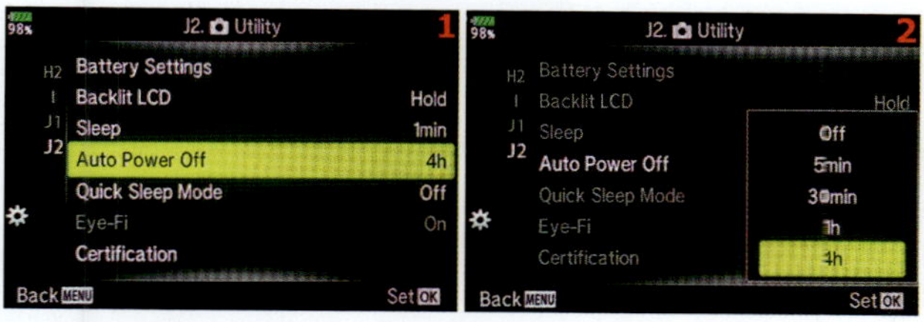

Figure 7.179: Choosing an Auto Power Off time delay

Use the following steps to modify the Auto Power Off function:

1. Select Auto Power Off from the J2. Utility menu and scroll to the right (figure 7.179, image 1).
2. Select Off, 5min, 30min, 1h, or 4h from the up/down menu (figure 7.179, image 2). The factory default is 4h.
3. Press the OK button to Set the value.

Settings Recommendation: The 1h setting seems about right to me. If I haven't used my camera in an hour, I probably won't use it for a while, and I can easily switch it off and back on when I need to take more pictures. The 4h setting will work, too; however, that seems like a long time to have the camera partially active. Even though the display screens are asleep while the camera is in energy-saving mode—if the Sleep function is configured correctly—the other parts of the camera are still using more power than when the camera is off.

Quick Sleep Mode (J2)

The Quick Sleep Mode conserves power by powering down the monitor when it is not in use. When this is set to On, the camera will go into a power-saving mode during shooting when the monitor is closed or when the camera is not in Live View mode. You can continue taking pictures with the monitor off.

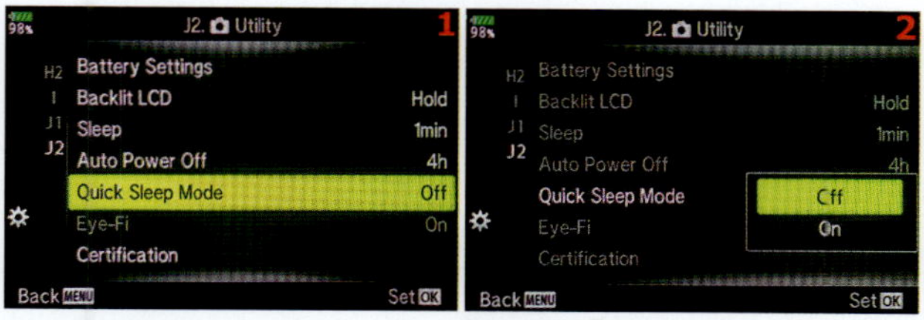

Figure 7.180: Setting the Quick Sleep Mode

Use the following steps to turn Quick Sleep Mode on or off:

1. Select Quick Sleep Mode from the J2. Utility menu and scroll to the right (figure 7.180, image 1).

2. Select On or Off from the up/down menu (figure 7.180, image 2).
3. Press the OK button to Set the value.

Settings Recommendation: I keep this turned on because it can really save some power. I can continue shooting pictures without having to worry about running out of power.

Eye-Fi (J2)

Although the E-M1II has a built-in, full-featured Wi-Fi system that allows you to control the camera remotely and lets you transfer pictures, you can also use an Eye-Fi card to transfer images directly to your computer over a local wireless network, to a remote computer through the Internet, or directly to a smart device (tablet or smartphone).

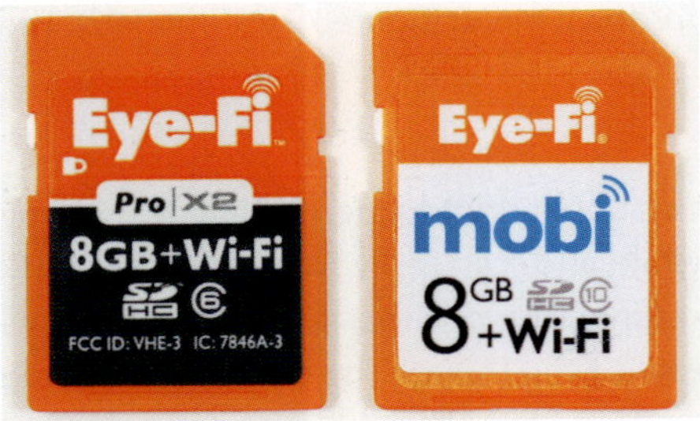

Figure 7.181: Pro X2 and mobi Eye-Fi cards

Eye-Fi cards come in two basic versions: Pro X2 and mobi. Pro X2 cards can create a direct ad hoc connection to your Wi-Fi enabled computer for automatic, in-the-field image transfer from as far as 90 feet away. The mobi version is designed specifically for use with smart devices, such as tablets or smartphones.

You will find an Eye-Fi app at all the major app stores. For more information on Eye-Fi products, go to **http://www.eyefi.com/**.

I've been using Eye-Fi cards for many years, and although the E-M1II has built-in Wi-Fi, the Eye-Fi cards have some unique properties that make them worth looking into. Let's see how to enable or disable the Eye-Fi capability.

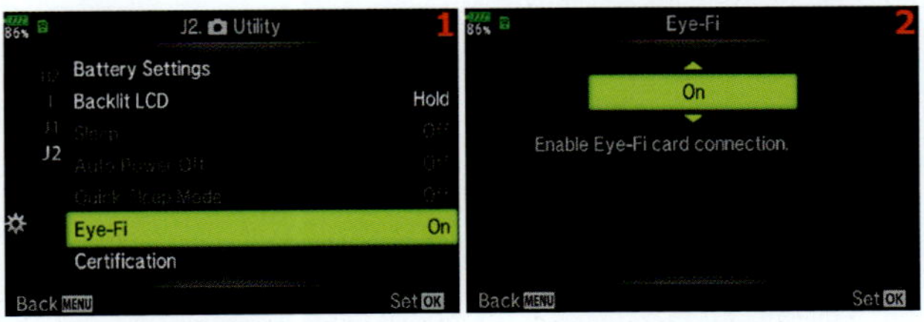

Figure 7.182: Enabling or disabling Eye-Fi capability

Use these steps to enable or disable the camera's Eye-Fi capability:

1. Select Eye-Fi from the J2. Utility menu and scroll to the right (figure 7.182, image 1).
2. Use the up/down menu and select On to enable Eye-Fi capability, or select Off to disable it (figure 7.182, image 2). You will see the green Eye-Fi symbol (red arrow) at the top-left corner of the menu when an Eye-Fi card is set to On. The symbol will also appear in the top-left corner of the Live View screen, just to the left of the Wi-Fi symbol. When the card is first enabled, the Eye-Fi card symbol will blink for a few seconds while the camera sets up initial communication with the card, and it will stop blinking when the card is ready to use.
3. Press the OK button to Set your choice.

Note: The Eye-Fi selection on the Custom Menu will be grayed out and not selectable unless an Eye-Fi card is inserted into the camera.

Settings Recommendation: The Eye-Fi card can do some things the camera's Wi-Fi system cannot do, such as send images across the Internet to a remote computer and use a local area network (Wi-Fi) to transfer images. Otherwise, the Eye-Fi functions are similar to the camera's built-in Wi-Fi system, with less functionality for remote camera control.

Certification (J2)

This is the last option in the J2. Utility menu. While it is selectable, there is nothing here for you to do. This is where Olympus puts the CAN ICES-3(B)/NMB-3(B) information (figure 7.183).

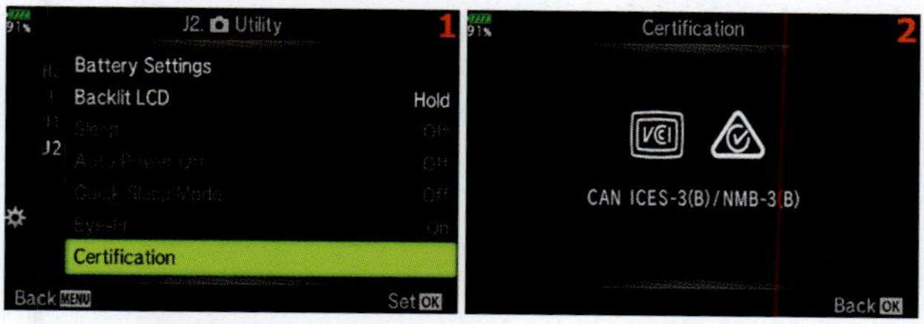

Figure 7.183: Certification

Author's Conclusions

Have you ever seen so many functions in one camera? I have never seen a camera with so many configuration possibilities. The advantage is that all these functions let you make your camera do almost any type of photography you can think of. And all this power is packed into such a diminutive camera.

The next chapter, **Setup Menu**, will cover the final functions in the camera—the initial setup functions you will probably configure only a few times while you own the camera.

08 Setup Menu

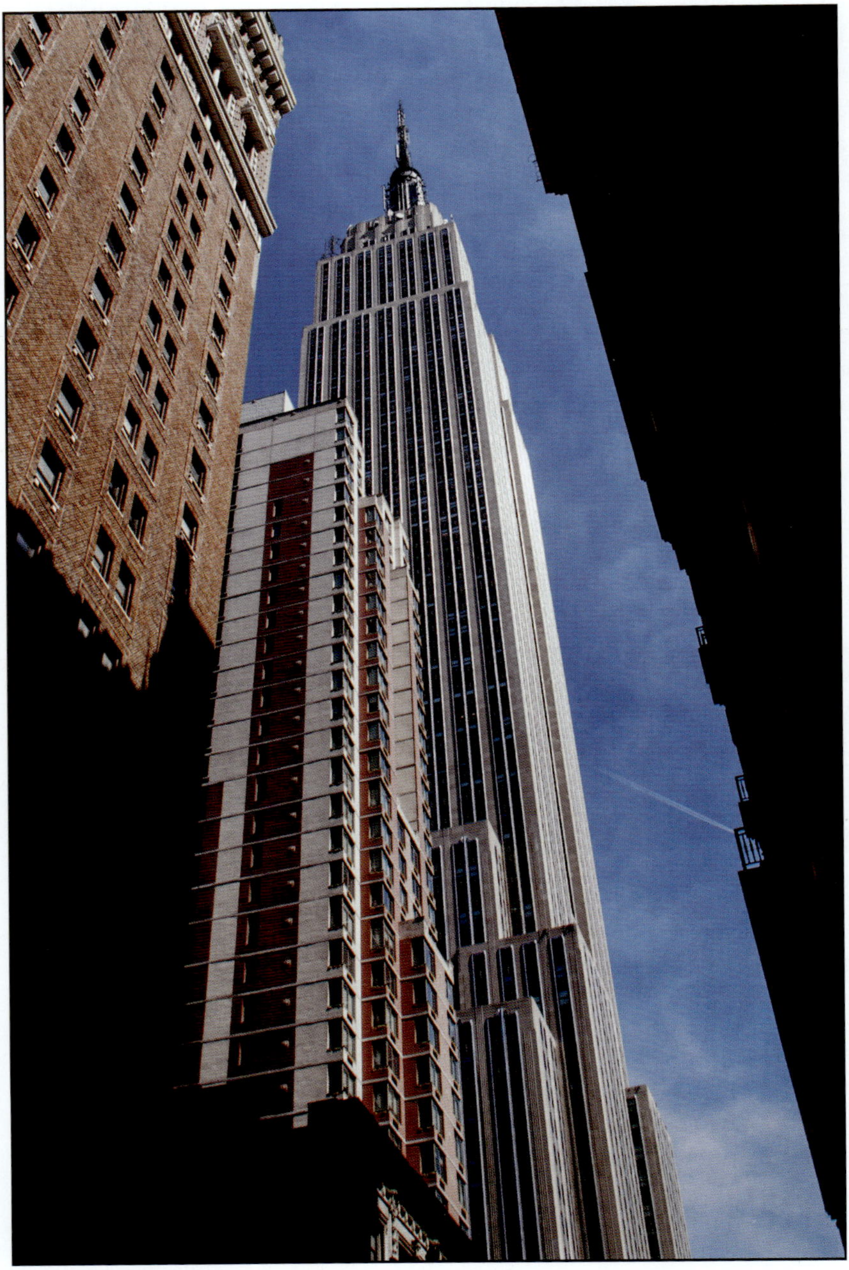

Image © Alan Hess

The Setup Menu is the final menu in the E-M1II. It gives you control over some functions that do not directly influence how an image is made. These are basic utility functions that you'll need primarily when you set up your camera.

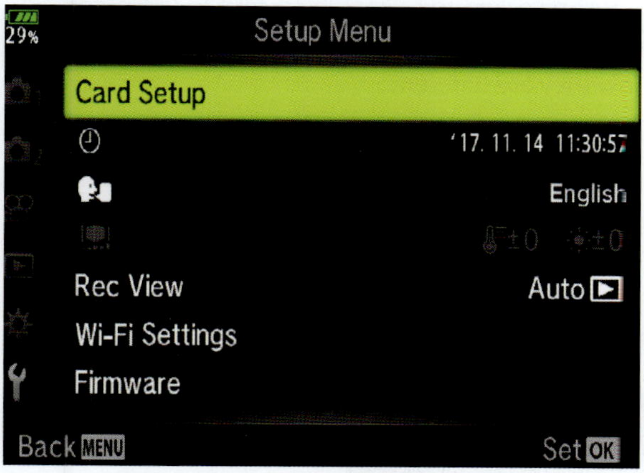

Figure 8.1: The Setup Menu for the E-M1II

There are seven items on the Setup Menu:

- **[Card Setup]:** This option allows you to either erase all nonprotected images or format the memory card (which will erase all images, including any protected images).
- **[Date and Time]:** This option allows you to set the camera's date, time (in 24-hour format), and date format (month, day, and year).
- **[Language]:** Select your language from a list of 34 languages.
- **[Monitor Adjustments]:** You can adjust the hue (color temperature), brightness level, and color saturation of the camera monitor.
- **Rec View:** Choose how long a picture is displayed on the camera monitor and in the electronic viewfinder immediately after you take it.
- **Wi-Fi Settings:** Connect your E-M1II to your smartphone or tablet and remotely control the camera, transfer pictures, and geotag your images. Olympus provides free apps for the iOS (iPhone and iPad) and Android platforms. The Wi-Fi Settings control how the Wi-Fi system works when it is enabled in the Playback Menu.
- **Firmware:** This function displays the camera and lens firmware versions.

Now let's discover what each item in the Setup Menu does.

Card Setup

Card Setup allows you to prepare a memory card for use in your camera. This menu item is available only when there are memory cards in one or both of the camera's card slots. If there are cards in both slots, you will be asked to select which card to use before you are given the menu options. There are two parts to Card Setup: All Erase and Format. Let's take a look at each option to see how they are different.

All Erase

All Erase allows you to remove all images that are not protected on the memory card. This is an easy way to get rid of images you do not want to keep. When an image is protected, the camera will ignore it when you execute the All Erase function. (See page 120 for more information about protecting an image.)

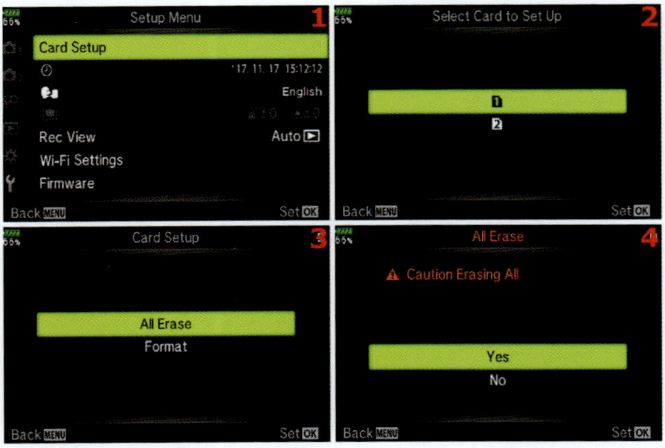

Figure 8.2A: Executing the All Erase function

Use the following steps to execute the All Erase function:

1. Select Card Setup from the Setup Menu and scroll to the right (figure 8.2A, image 1).
2. If there are two memory cards inserted in the camera, choose the card on which you want to erase images, 1 or 2, and scroll to the right (figure 8.2A, image 2).
3. Choose All Erase from the Card Setup menu and scroll to the right (figure 8.2A, image 3).
4. The camera will warn you, *Caution Erasing All* (figure 8.2A, image 4). Select Yes and press the OK button to erase all nonprotected images. Protected images will not be removed.

Format

The Format function deletes all images from the memory card, including protected images. Use this function when you get a new memory card or when you use a memory card that has been formatted in a different camera or in a computer. Formatting a card in the camera tends to cut down on long-term memory card problems.

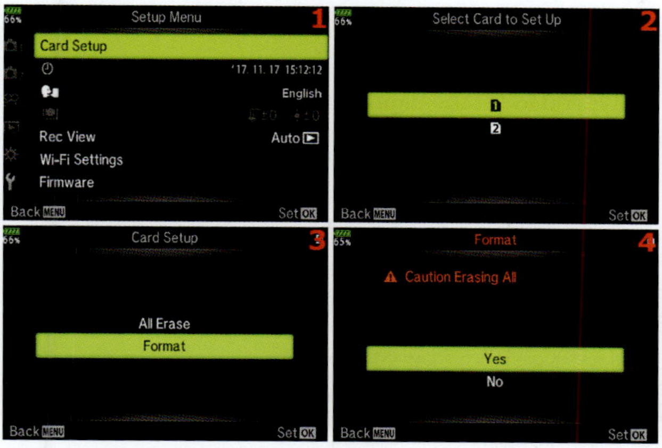

Figure 8.2B: Executing the Format function

Use the following steps to execute the Format function:

1. Select Card Setup from the Setup Menu and scroll to the right (figure 8.2B, image 1).
2. If there are two memory cards inserted in the camera, choose the card you want to format, 1 or 2, and scroll to the right (figure 8.2B, image 2).
3. Choose Format from the Card Setup menu and scroll to the right (figure 8.2B, image 3).
4. The camera will warn you, *Caution Erasing All* (figure 8.2B, image 4). Select Yes and press the OK button to erase *all* images on the memory card, even the protected ones.

Note: Formatting a memory card doesn't actually remove images from the card. Instead, it removes their entries from the memory card's file allocation table (FAT) so the images can no longer be seen or found by the camera. However, you can use card recovery software to rescue the images if you do not write any new pictures to the card after you format it. This is a good thing to remember, in case you accidentally format a card that contains images you wanted to keep.

Settings Recommendation: I always format a new memory card with the E-M1II's Format function before I use it. There is no way to know if the current format on the card is in good shape. Also, many other camera brands create their own folder structure when a card is formatted. It is wise to remove all traces of any other brand's folder structure by formatting a used card in your E-M1II. Why take chances with your valuable images?

I don't use the image protect system much, so the All Erase function is not that useful to me. However, you may want to protect your best images as you make them, and at the end of the day you can use All Erase to remove nonprotected images. Just be sure you haven't missed any images you wanted to keep. This approach seems a bit dangerous to me!

[Date and Time]

The [Date and Time] function allows you to set the date, time, and date format. These are, most likely, some of the first items you will adjust when you get your new camera. Let's see how to adjust each item.

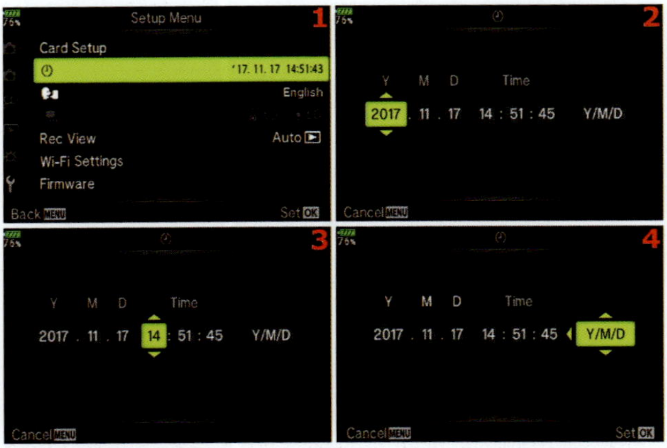

Figure 8.3: Setting the date, time, and date format

Use the following steps to adjust the date and time:

1. Select the clock symbol, which represents [Date and Time], from the Setup Menu and scroll to the right (figure 8.3, image 1).
2. The [Date and Time] screen has seven up/down menus. We will use those menus to adjust the year (Y), month (M), day (D), Time, and date format. In figure 8.3, image 2, you can see that the year (Y) is selected. Press the up or down buttons on the Arrow Pad to select from a range of years, starting at 2000 and ending at 2099. I chose 2017. Next, scroll to the right until month (M) is highlighted and press the buttons on the Arrow Pad to select a month (1–12). Finally, scroll to the right until day (D) is highlighted and press the buttons on the Arrow Pad until the day you want is selected (1–31). The camera knows how many days are in each month, even if it's a leap year, and will offer only that number of days for the month. My camera is set to November 17, 2017.
3. Now let's set the time. Scroll to the right until the first up/down menu under Time is highlighted (figure 8.3, image 3). That is the hour field, with the minute field

immediately to its right. Choose an hour, from 00–23. The camera uses a 24-hour clock, so 00 is midnight. Use the **12- to 24-Hour Time Conversion Chart** at the end of this section to choose the correct hour conversion if you use a 12-hour day. Press the buttons on the Arrow Pad until the hour you want is selected, then scroll to the minute field. You can choose from 00–59 in the minute field. Select the minute you want, and then do the same for the seconds field. My camera is set to 14:51:45 (2:51 p.m.).

4. Now let's set the date format. Scroll to the last up/down menu on the right, which is the date format selection (figure 8.3, image 4). You have three choices:
   - **Y/M/D:** Year/Month/Day (e.g., 2017/12/31)
   - **M/D/Y:** Month/Day/Year (e.g., 12/31/2017)
   - **D/M/Y:** Day/Month/Year (e.g., 31/12/2017)

   Refer to the list of date formats and select the one you prefer to use. My camera is set to year, month, day (Y/M/D). Camera owners in the United States will probably use the second setting (M/D/Y).
5. Review each of the fields and make sure that all the values are correct. When you are happy with your settings, make sure the date format field is selected and press the OK button to save the settings. If any field other than date format is selected when you press the OK button, the camera will jump to the next field in the series.

Settings Recommendation: The factory default date format is Y/M/D, which I did not change on my camera before I photographed the camera screens. I changed my camera to M/D/Y because I live in the United States. Be sure to use the **12- to 24-Hour Time Conversion Chart** to make sure you set the time correctly.

12- to 24-Hour Time Conversion Chart	
Settings for a.m.	Settings for p.m.
12:00 a.m. = 00:00 (midnight)	**12:00 p.m. = 12:00 (noon)**
01:00 a.m. = 01:00	01:00 p.m. = 13:00
02:00 a.m. = 02:00	02:00 p.m. = 14:00
03:00 a.m. = 03:00	03:00 p.m. = 15:00
04:00 a.m. = 04:00	04:00 p.m. = 16:00
05:00 a.m. = 05:00	05:00 p.m. = 17:00
06:00 a.m. = 06:00	06:00 p.m. = 18:00
07:00 a.m. = 07:00	07:00 p.m. = 19:00
08:00 a.m. = 08:00	08:00 p.m. = 20:00
09:00 a.m. = 09:00	09:00 p.m. = 21:00
10:00 a.m. = 10:00	10:00 p.m. = 22:00
11:00 a.m. = 11:00	11:00 p.m. = 23:00

Note: There is no 24:00; 23:59 is followed by 00:00.

[Language]

The E-M1II is multilingual. It can use one of 34 languages for on-screen displays and error messages. Most likely, your camera will come from the factory with the correct language already chosen for your area. However, if you prefer another language, simply scroll through the list and select your choice.

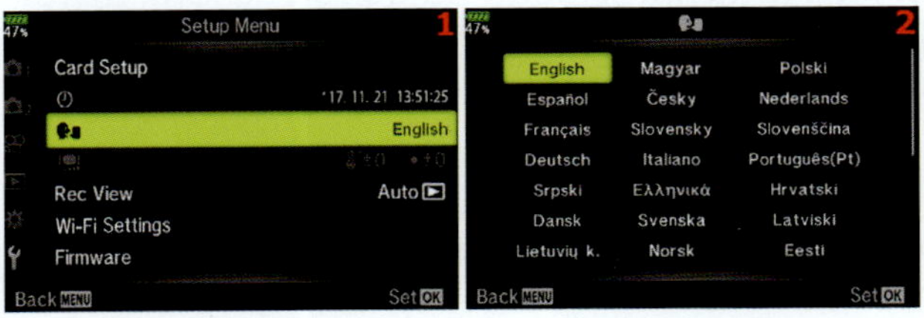

Figure 8.4: Choosing one of 34 languages for your camera

Use the following steps to select a language for your camera:

1. Choose the [Language] symbol from the Setup Menu (figure 8.4, image 1). The symbol looks like a face with a speech bubble. Scroll to the right.
2. As seen in figure 8.4, image 2, a screen will appear with a list of 34 languages (use the Arrow Pad to scroll down and see all the languages). Highlight the language you want to use—if you are changing it from English—and press the OK button to Set the language.

Settings Recommendation: Most readers of this book will leave the camera set to the default of English, as I did in figure 8.4, image 2. If you are not a native English speaker, you may be more comfortable with a different language. You should be able to find your language by examining the list.

[Monitor Adjustments]

The [Monitor Adjustments] setting lets you set the hue (color temperature) and brightness level of your camera monitor display. Each setting has an adjustment slider. You can also set the amount of monitor color saturation with two settings: Natural and Vivid. Let's see how.

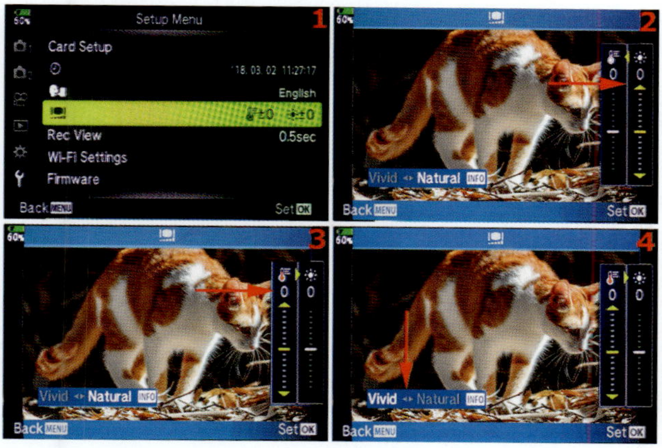

Figure 8.5: Changing the monitor hue, brightness, and color saturation

Use the following steps to change the monitor hue, brightness, and saturation. You can adjust one of the settings or all three:

1. Select the [Monitor Adjustments] symbol from the Setup Menu (figure 8.5, image 1). It looks like a small screen with an adjustment slider beneath it. Scroll to the right.
2. The next screen has two adjustable sliders. The brightness slider is on the right and has a sun symbol on top; it is automatically selected (figure 8.5, image 2). There are 14 steps of brightness change—seven steps (+1 to +7) to increase brightness and seven steps (–1 to –7) to decrease brightness. Choose a brightness level by scrolling up or down with the Arrow Pad. The monitor will immediately reflect the brightness change. If you don't want to change the hue setting, press the OK button, which Sets the brightness level. If you do want to change the hue, don't press the OK button; instead, scroll to the left with the Arrow Pad to select the hue slider.
3. The hue slider has a thermometer symbol at the top to indicate color temperature (figure 8.5, image 3). To adjust it, scroll up or down with the Arrow Pad. There are 14 steps of hue change—seven steps (+1 to +7) to cool down the image (add blue) and seven steps (–1 to –7) to warm up the image (add red). The monitor will immediately reflect the change in hue. Press the OK button to Set all changes, or move on to the color saturation setting.
4. The camera has a special feature for those who want a more color-saturated monitor view. You can see the Vivid and Natural selections in figure 8.5, image 4, at the red arrow. If you select Vivid, the monitor will display a more saturated image than the actual scene. Natural reflects the scene as it actually appears. This setting affects only the camera monitor and does not change the saturation of the photograph, which is controlled by other settings, such as the Picture Mode (e.g., Portrait, Muted, Natural, and Vivid). Choose a monitor saturation setting by pressing the Info button. You will see the selection change at the red arrow in figure 8.5, image 4. After you make your selection, press the OK button to Set your choices.

Note: The [Monitor Adjustments] setting affects only the monitor on the back of the camera. The electronic viewfinder (EVF) is not affected by the changes you make to the [Monitor Adjustments] setting.

Settings Recommendation: The brightness setting is useful when you want to manually control the brightness level of the monitor. The hue and saturation settings are rather subtle. Unless you want to make the camera monitor more closely match the appearance of a profiled computer monitor, the hue and saturation settings may not be useful to you.

Rec View

The unusually named Rec View sets the amount of time a picture is displayed on the camera monitor, or in the viewfinder, after you take it.

Here's how to adjust the Rec View time.

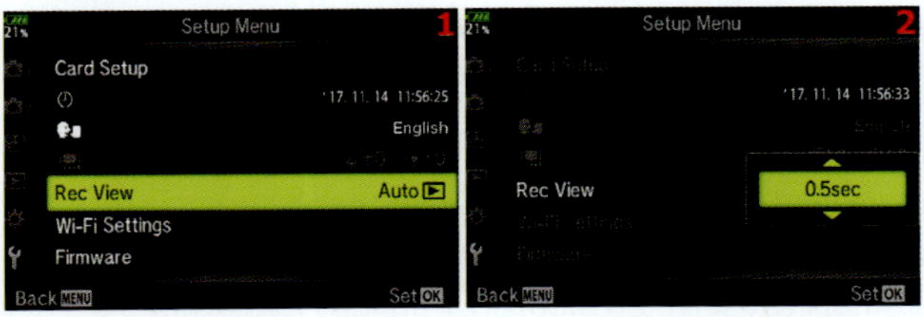

Figure 8.6: Setting a Rec View time for image display on the viewfinder or in the monitor

Use the following steps to choose how long your camera displays a picture after you take it:

1. Choose Rec View from the Setup Menu and scroll to the right (figure 8.6, image 1).
2. Use the up/down menu that appears to select a time from 0.3 to 20 seconds (0.3sec to 20sec), or choose Auto to let the camera decide. Press the OK button to Set the Rec View time. In figure 8.6, image 2, I chose one-half second (0.5sec). You can also set this to Off, which means that no preview is displayed after you take the photo.
3. After you take your pictures, the camera will display the image either in the viewfinder or on the monitor (mutually exclusive) for the Rec View display time you selected.

Settings Recommendation: If you have previously used a camera with an optical viewfinder (OVF), you may have to adjust your thinking when you use the E-M1II and its electronic viewfinder (EVF). With an OVF, it doesn't matter how long an image appears on the monitor because the OVF is not used to view images after you take them. With an EVF, it can be surprising to see the picture you just took appear in the viewfinder because it briefly obscures your view of the subject, which seems to freeze in the viewfinder.

When I set Rec View to more than a half second so I could see my picture on the monitor longer, I was shocked when my subject seemed to freeze in the viewfinder while the EVF displayed the new photo during the Rec View time period. It seemed to disconnect me from the subject. I quickly set the Rec View time back to 0.5 second, which seems about right. You will briefly see your picture and then you can take more. But what if you are shooting action shots and don't want anything to obscure your viewfinder and cause you to lose tracking on your subject?

One option, of course, is to set Rec View to Off. But I discovered another option for when you do have a Rec View time set: if you never fully release the Shutter button, and instead hold it halfway down while you shoot, the camera does not display the image in the viewfinder. When you release the Shutter button, the camera will display the last image you took until the Rec View time ends. Try it!

It's a good idea to set the Rec View period to a short value and press the Playback button to see your image on the monitor or in the viewfinder.

Wi-Fi Settings

The Wi-Fi Settings function has several parts that allow you to access the images on your memory card and transfer them to your smartphone or tablet (I'll call these smart devices). Olympus provides a free app called Olympus Image Share (OI.Share) for iOS (iPad, iPhone, iPod Touch) and Android devices.

The camera and app combo allows you transfer pictures to your smart device or to a friend's device. If you want to allow only certain people to access your memory card, you can mark images with the Share Order system. We'll talk more about Share Orders momentarily.

First, though, let's examine how to configure the settings for Wi-Fi and the ways you can connect to your camera with a smart device. After you start Wi-Fi, you can touch the Wi-Fi icon on the camera monitor, or select Connection to Smartphone from the Playback Menu, and the Wi-Fi system will function the way you want it to.

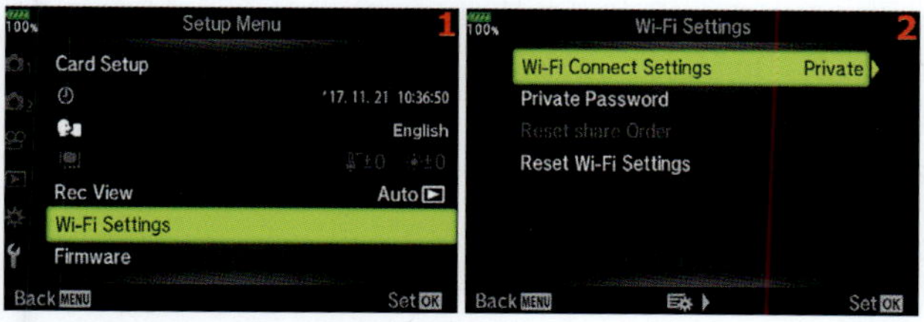

Figure 8.7A: Wi-Fi Settings configuration

Use the following steps to configure the Wi-Fi system:

1. Select Wi-Fi Settings from the Setup Menu and scroll to the right (figure 8.7A, image 1). There are four menu items on the Wi-Fi Settings menu: Wi-Fi Connect Settings, Private Password, Reset share Order, and Reset Wi-Fi Settings (figure 8.7A, image 2). The following steps and figures describe each one.
2. The first item on the Wi-Fi Settings menu is Wi-Fi Connect Settings. Choose it from the menu and scroll to the right.

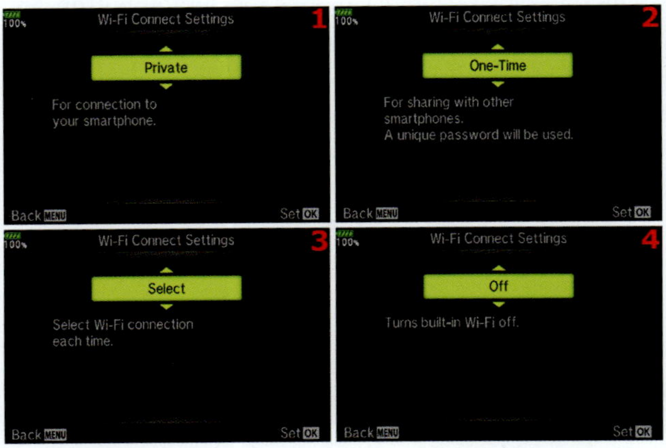

Figure 8.7B: Preparing the Wi-Fi connection type

3. You will now see an up/down menu with the following choices (figure 8.7B, images 1–4):
   - **Private** (image 1): You will connect to the camera with your smart device by using the same camera-supplied password each time, as shown on the camera's active Wi-Fi screen with the QR code. This password will not change unless you manually change it, as described in the next step.
   - **One-Time** (image 2): You will connect to the camera with your smart device with a new camera-supplied password each time.
   - **Select** (image 3): This very convenient feature offers you the choice of Private or One-Time connection in a menu that pops up when you start the camera's Wi-Fi.
   - **Off** (image 4): Wi-Fi is disabled when you select Off.

   Make your selection from the up/down menu, press the OK button, and your changes will be Set.

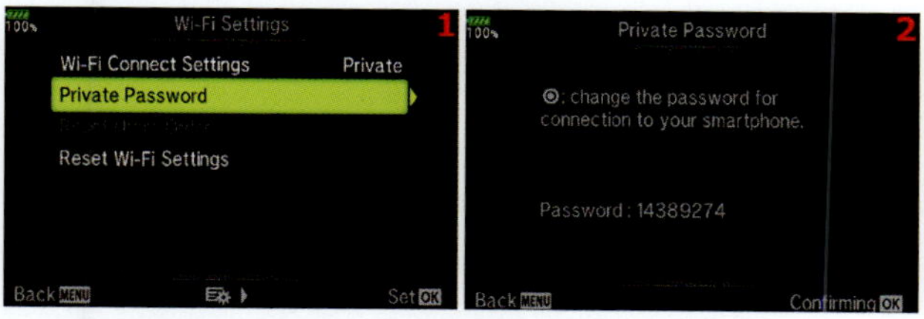

Figure 8.7C: Changing the Private Password for Wi-Fi sessions

4. You can change your camera's current Wi-Fi Private Password. Select Private Password from the Wi-Fi Settings menu and scroll to the right (figure 8.7C, image 1).
5. The Private Password change screen will display the current Password. Press the Movie button on top of the camera (with red dot in the middle), and the camera will generate a new Password and display it on the monitor (figure 8.7C, image 2). Each time you press the Movie button a new Password will appear.
6. When the Private Password has been changed, press the OK button to confirm the change.

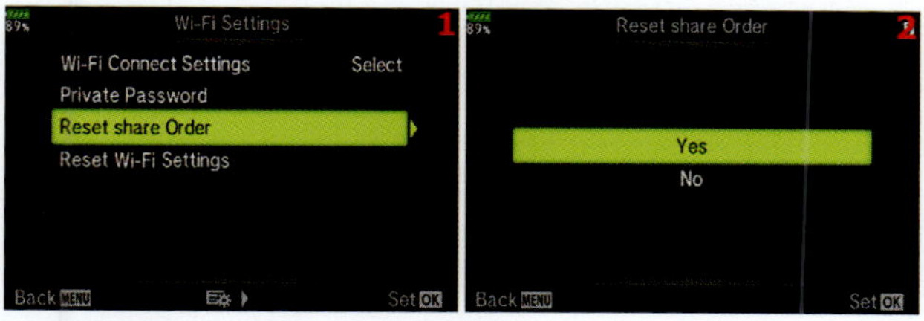

Figure 8.7D: Resetting a Share Order

7. The camera allows you to create a Share Order that lets you mark individual images as shareable. When you allow someone to connect to your camera with their smart device (they need to install the OI.Share app), you can prevent them from seeing anything except the marked images. For example, you could take images at a party, mark the ones you want to share, and have a friend connect to your camera and download the marked images. (See the chapter called **Screen Displays for Camera Control,** on page 112, under the subheading **Creating a Share Order,** for instructions on how to create a Share Order.) If you have marked images in a Share Order and no longer want people to access them, you can reset the Share Order by selecting Reset share Order from the Wi-Fi Settings menu and scrolling to the right (figure 8.7D, image 1). This option is grayed out if there are no images marked to share.
8. You will now see a menu with Yes and No choices (figure 8.7D, image 2). Select Yes to reset the Share Order or No to cancel and leave the Share Order intact. Press the OK button to execute your choice.

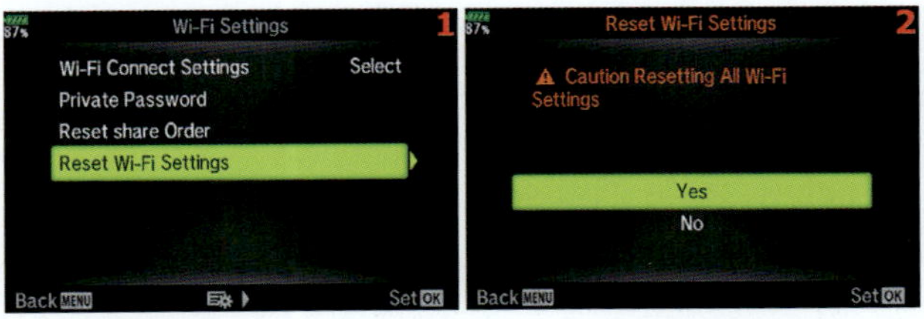

Figure 8.7E: Resetting the Wi-Fi system to factory defaults

9. To reset the Wi-Fi system to the factory defaults, select Reset Wi-Fi Settings and scroll to the right (figure 8.7E, image 1).
10. You will see a menu with Yes and No choices (figure 8.7E, image 2). You will also see a warning that says *Caution Resetting All Wi-Fi Settings*. Select Yes to reset the Wi-Fi system to the factory default, or select No to cancel and leave the current settings intact. Press the OK button to execute your choice.

Settings Recommendation: These Wi-Fi settings give you some flexibility in how your Wi-Fi system works. I leave my camera's Wi-Fi Connect Settings set to Select so my camera will offer me a Private Wi-Fi session or a One-Time Wi-Fi session if I want to give images to someone. All they need is a smart device and the free Olympus Image Share app, and I can create a Share Order to wirelessly give them selected images from my camera. It's the neatest thing I've seen since zoom lenses were invented.

Firmware

The Firmware setting displays the current camera, lens, and flash firmware versions. You cannot do anything with this setting except see the version number and decide if you need to update the firmware in your camera, lens, or flash.

At the time of this writing, firmware version 1.3 had been released and is installed on the camera. I had an Olympus 14–42mm f/3.5–5.6 lens mounted on the camera when I captured the screenshot shown in figure 8.8. Its current firmware version is 1.2. The attached flash is using firmware version 1.0.

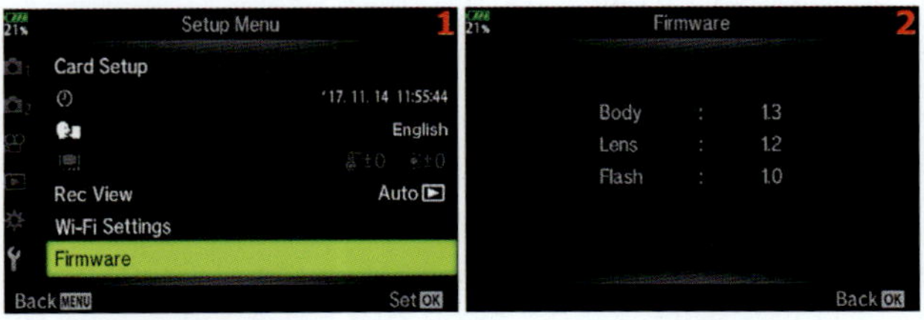

Figure 8.8: Viewing the firmware version

Use these steps to view the firmware version of your camera and mounted lens:

1. Select Firmware from the Setup Menu and scroll to the right (figure 8.8, image 1).
2. You will see three Firmware fields if you have a lens and flash mounted on your camera (figure 8.8, image 2). If no lens or flash is mounted, you'll see only one field. Body is the current firmware version for the camera body (version 1.3 in my E-M1II); Lens is the current firmware for the lens mounted on the camera (version 1.2); and Flash is the current firmware for the flash mounted on the camera (version 1.0).

Settings Recommendation: You can update the firmware in your camera and lenses by using the Olympus Digital Camera Updater software, which you can download from the following website:

http://www.olympusamerica.com/cpg_section/cpg_downloads_updater.asp

Download the software to your computer and use the included USB cable to keep your camera and lens firmware up to date.

Author's Conclusions

We've come a long way together, from taking a fresh camera out of the box with its myriad configuration abilities, to having a fully configured Olympus OM-D E-M1II ready to take on nearly any photographic task.

Thank you for sticking with me until the end of this technical book. I hope it has been useful to you and has helped you master your incredibly powerful and complex E-M1II, one of the best mirrorless cameras on the market today.

Please write a short review of this book on the website of the retailer where you purchased it. Your good review can really help the book succeed.

I hope to stay in touch with you to answer questions and give you a place to report any major typos or logic errors you might find in this book. I created a special, nonpublic Facebook group called **Master Your Olympus** (MYO), at the following web address:

https://www.facebook.com/groups/MasterYourOlympus/

Please request membership on the Facebook site so we can discuss Olympus cameras, lenses, and photography as a community of enthusiasts who help one another.

Again, thank you for buying my book (and reviewing it, if you will). Until we meet again,

Keep on capturing time…

Index

Symbols & Numbers

A

D

E

I

J

K

L

M

N

O

P

Q

R

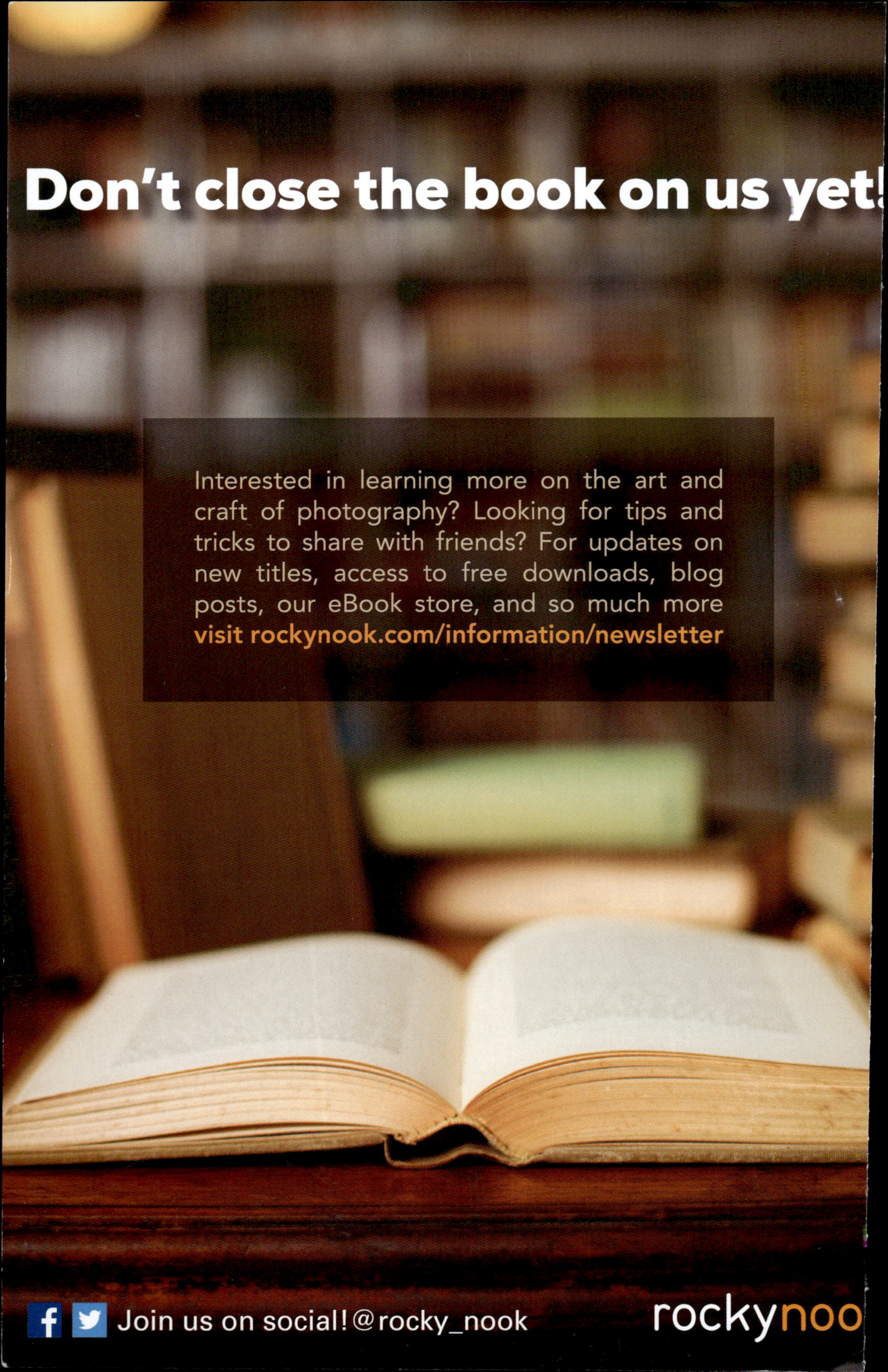
Don't close the book on us yet!
Interested in learning more on the art and craft of photography? Looking for tips and tricks to share with friends? For updates on new titles, access to free downloads, blog posts, our eBook store, and so much more visit rockynook.com/information/newsletter
Join us on social! @rocky_nook